Fourth Edition

Understanding Child Abuse and Neglect

Cynthia Crosson-Tower
Fitchburg State College

Allyn and Bacon
Boston • London • Toronto • Sydney • Tokyo • Singapore

To my students,
who have taught me so much over the years

Series Editor, Social Work and Family Therapy: Judy Fifer
Editor in Chief, Social Sciences: Karen Hanson
Editorial Assistant: Jennifer Muroff
Marketing Manager: Susan E. Brown
Editorial Production Service: Chestnut Hill Enterprises, Inc.
Manufacturing Buyer: Megan Cochran
Cover Administrator: Linda Knowles

Internet: www.abacon.com
America Online: keyword: College Online

Between the time Website information is gathered and published, it is not unusual for some sites to have closed. Also, the transcription of URLs can result in typographical errors. The publisher would appreciate notification where these occur so that they may be corrected. Thank you.

Library of Congress Cataloging-in-Publication Data

Tower, Cynthia Crosson.
    Understanding child abuse and neglect / Cynthia Crosson-Tower.—
4th ed.
      p. cm.
    Includes bibliographical references and index.
    ISBN 0-205-28780-8 (pbk.)
    1. Child abuse—United States.   2. Abused children—Services for–
–United States.   3. Social work with children—United States.
I. Title.
HV6626.52.T69   1998
362.7'0973–dc21   98–14648
                                               CIP

Printed in the United States of America

10 9 8 7 6 5 4 3 2 1   RRD-VA   03 02 01 00 99 98

Photo Credits: p. 4: Courtesy of the Library of Congress; p. 31: Will Faller; p. 72: Courtesy of the Library of Congress; p. 128: Robert Thomas; p. 210: Robert Thomas; p. 219: Robert Thomas; p. 331: Robert Harbison; p. 402: Robert Harbison.

CONTENTS

Preface   ix

1   The Maltreatment of Children from a Historical Perspective   1
Children as Property   1
Child Labor   4
Sexual Values, Attitudes, and Exploitation   5
The Incest Taboo   8
Recent History of Helping the Abused and Neglected Child   10
Child Protection Today   13
    Summary   16
    Exploration Questions   18
    Activities for Applied Learning   18
    Suggested Readings   18
    References   19

2   The Family: Roles, Responsibilities, and Rights   21
The Definition and Function of the Family   21
The Family as a System   23
Rituals   25
Minority Family Systems   26
Family Problems and Dysfunction   33
The Family and Child Maltreatment   35
    Summary   38
    Exploration Questions   39
    Activities for Applied Learning   39
    Suggested Readings   39
    References   40

3   Maltreatment and the Developing Child   42
Developmental Stages   43
Developmental Differences   57
    Summary   59
    Exploration Questions   59

Activities for Applied Learning   *60*
Suggested Readings   *60*
References   *61*

4 The Neglect of Children   63
Neglect Defined   *63*
Causes of Neglect   *68*
Problems in Intervention   *70*
Neglected Children   *70*
Neglectful Parents   *74*
    Summary   *85*
    Exploration Questions   *86*
    Activities for Applied Learning   *86*
    Suggested Readings   *86*
    References   *87*

5 The Physical Abuse of Children   89
Causes of Physical Abuse   *90*
Psychopathological Categories   *91*
The Abused Child   *97*
Abusive Parents   *105*
Domestic Violence and Other Abuse Within the Family   *110*
    Summary   *112*
    Exploration Questions   *112*
    Activities for Applied Learning   *113*
    Suggested Readings   *113*
    References   *113*

6 The Sexual Abuse of Children   116
Two Groups' Approaches to Child Sexual Abuse   *116*
Definition of Child Sexual Abuse   *118*
Types of Sexual Abuse   *119*
The Progression of Sexual Abuse   *120*
Incidence of Sexual Abuse   *123*
Profile of the Abused Child   *125*
Degree of Trauma   *128*
Profile of the Perpetrator   *129*
    Summary   *138*
    Exploration Questions   *139*
    Activities for Applied Learning   *139*
    Suggested Readings   *140*
    References   *140*

7 Incest: Familial Abuse   143

Incest as a Problem Today   143
Who Is to Blame?   144
Father-Daughter Incest   145
Father-Son Incest   155
Mother-Daughter Incest   157
Mother-Son Incest   159
Brother-Sister Incest   162
Homosexual Sibling Incest   165
Incest with Uncles, Grandfathers, and Cousins   166
Why Incest Stops   169
   Summary   170
   Exploration Questions   170
   Activities for Applied Learning   171
   Suggested Readings   171
   References   171

8 Extrafamilial Sexual Abuse, Misuse, and Exploitation   174

Sexual Abuse Outside the Family   174
Sexual Misuse and Exploitation   182
   Summary   200
   Exploration Questions   201
   Activities for Applied Learning   202
   Suggested Readings   202
   References   202

9 The Emotional and Psychological Maltreatment of Children   205

Emotional and Psychological Maltreatment Defined   205
   Summary   212
   Exploration Questions   213
   Activities for Applied Learning   213
   Suggested Readings   213
   References   214

10 Intervention: Reporting and Investigation   215

Culturally Sensitive Intervention   215
The Intervention Process   216
Assessing Aspects of Risk   223
   Summary   239
   Exploration Questions   239
   Activities for Applied Learning   240
   Suggested Readings   240
   References   240

11   Intervention: Case Management and Roles of Other Professionals   242

Case Management Considerations   242

Other Professional Involved in the Intervention Process   246

   Summary   257

   Exploration Questions   258

   Activities for Applied Learning   258

   Suggested Readings   258

   References   259

12   The Legal Response to Child Abuse and Neglect   261

The Legal Rights of Parents and Children   262

Types of Court Intervention   263

Juvenile Court   264

Advantages and Disadvantages of Juvenile Court   272

Criminal Court   273

The Media and the Court   277

   Summary   277

   Exploration Questions   278

   Activities for Applied Learning   278

   Suggested Readings   278

   References   279

13   Treatment: Physical Abuse and Neglect   281

Preparing to Provide Treatment   281

Providing Treatment   282

Treatment of Physically Abusive Families   287

Family-Centered Services   289

Treatment of the Child   291

Treatment of the Parents   296

Other Family Treatment   300

Treatment of the Siblings   301

Treatment of Neglectful Families   301

   Summary   306

   Exploration Questions   307

   Activities for Applied Learning   307

   Suggested Readings   307

   References   308

14   Treatment: Sexual Abuse   310

Issues Surrounding Treatment   310

Assumptions About Treatment of the Sexually Abusive Family   311

Treatment Models   312

Treatment Methods   313

Treatment of Specific Family Members   *316*
    Summary   *333*
    Exploration Questions   *334*
    Activities for Applied Learning   *334*
    Suggested Readings   *334*
    References   *335*

15 Foster Care as a Therapeutic Tool   337
Problems with Foster Care   *337*
Alternatives to Foster Care   *337*
Therapeutic Potential in Foster Care   *338*
The Role and Importance of the Natural Parents   *340*
The Role of Foster Parents   *341*
Other Placement for Abused or Neglected Children   *342*
    Summary   *344*
    Exploration Questions   *344*
    Activities for Applied Learning   *345*
    Suggested Readings   *345*
    References   *345*

16 The Social Worker and the System   347
A Day in the Life of a Protective Worker   *347*
The Role of a Protective Social Worker   *350*
Does the System Work?   *357*
Looking Toward the Future   *359*
    Summary   *361*
    Exploration Questions   *362*
    Activities for Applied Learning   *362*
    Suggested Readings   *362*
    References   *363*

17 Adults Abused as Children   364
Society's Misconceptions   *364*
Reasons for Adults' Disclosure   *365*
Residual Effects of Child Abuse and Neglect   *368*
Effects from the Neglecting Family   *369*
Effects from the Physically Abusing Family   *373*
Long-Term Effects of Domestic Violence   *375*
Effects from a Sexually Abusing Family   *376*
Effects from Extrafamilial Abuse   *386*
Treatment of Adults Who Were Abused as Children   *388*
    Summary   *394*
    Exploration Questions   *394*

Activities for Applied Learning   395
Suggested Readings   395
References   396

18 Prevention   398
Prevention Efforts in Schools   398
Prevention Efforts with Families   404
Prevention Efforts by Professionals   409
Prevention Efforts Within the Community   410
Summary   411
Exploration Questions   411
Activities for Applied Learning   412
References   412

19 Toward a Better Tomorrow   414
Changes in the Helping System   414
Changes in Society   419
Facing a New Era?   423
Research Needs   423
Summary   424
Exploration Questions   424
Activities for Applied Learning   425
Suggested Readings   425
References   425

Index   427

PREFACE

Today, we live in one of the most affluent countries in the world. With this knowledge comes the expectation that each citizen of such a culture will experience a sense of well-being and comfort. And yet, many of our number—our children—are being beaten, neglected, and molested in greater numbers than ever before. Every ten seconds a child is being abused or neglected. Granted, child abuse and neglect have existed for centuries. So, why now has the problem become so monumental? The answer may lie in several areas. It has been said that we live in a more violent society than ever before. Crime statistics would attest to this. The intensity and seriousness of the abuse perpetrated against children would as well. Does the answer also lie in the fact that the child protection system, set up to safeguard the lives of the children at risk for maltreatment, is not achieving its goal? As a former protective services worker, I recognize that individual professionals within protective services are often dedicated and well-meaning, but the system as a whole is not adequately protecting children.

Thus the questions arise: What can be done to reverse the upward trend in maltreatment? And how can society, and more specifically the child welfare system, better protect the children at risk?

These questions can be addressed from several vantage points. We must look not only to raising societal awareness and increasing research into causes of abuse and neglect, but we must also change social policy, triage the child welfare system and provide better training for protective workers, not only in the skills important to do their job but in culturally sensitive ways to approach a variety of people from many different backgrounds.

After over 20 years of teaching courses on child abuse and neglect, many years in the child protection system, and over 30 years in the field of social services, I have written this text, now in the fourth edition, to prepare future and even current professionals to better intervene and treat the children and families at risk. This book draws on my years of practice to present an all-encompassing view of maltreatment, in its various guises, from symptoms of abuse and neglect to motivations of those who abuse and neglect children as well as how the social services system intervenes. The questions asked of me by students, social service workers, and trainees have helped to shape the direction of the text. My experiences, not only as a protective social worker, but later as a therapist treating victims, families, and perpetrators, have helped to provide ideas for the illustrations and examples.

Plan for the Text

Chapter 1 lays a framework for the discussion of abuse and neglect by tracing the history of child maltreatment from biblical times to the present. Chapter 2 considers the responsibilities of families and what rights society accords families and children. Maltreatment and the developing child is the focus of Chapter 3, which examines the effects of abusive and neglectful behavior on children's progress, or lack of progress, through developmental stages. Chapters 4 through 9 outline the symptoms of neglect, physical abuse, sexual abuse, and emotional/psychological abuse, and examine the needs and motivations of abusive and neglectful parents. Chapter 7 looks more closely at the incidence of incest or sexual abuse within the family setting. Since sexual abuse can also be perpetrated by strangers, Chapter 8 considers abuse outside the family, including a discussion of child pornography, prostitution, and sex rings.

The next three chapters focus on how to combat the problem of abuse. Chapters 10 and 11 follow the intervention process—from the report through the investigation—and highlight such important elements of protective work as home visiting, investigative interviewing, case management issues, and the roles of other professionals. The court system and how it might be called upon to address abuse, neglect, and sexual abuse is considered in Chapter 12, distinguishing between intervention through the juvenile court process and prosecution through the criminal court system.

Chapters 13 and 14 outline the models of treatment available for abused and neglected children and their families. Therapy approaches for each type of maltreatment are considered separately. Chapter 15 discusses foster care as a therapeutic tool.

A typical day of a protective social worker is described in Chapter 16. The chapter suggests the skills needed for protective work and the frustrations that may be encountered. Protective workers also discuss their impressions of the effectiveness of the social service system and their feelings about their work.

Following this examination of intervention, Chapter 17 provides a view of the experiences of adults who, as children, never reported abuse. The treatment available for these survivors is discussed.

Chapter 18 looks at the prevention efforts under way and at possible further steps. The book concludes with a consideration of the changes necessary to reduce the incidence of child maltreatment—changes within the helping system and changes required of society.

In the second edition, more attention was given to the need for cultural sensitivity when understanding and working with abusive and neglectful families. The third edition included consideration of such topics as: abuse by cults, abuse by clergy, false allegations and false memories, and substance abuse as well as an expansion of emotional abuse.

The fourth edition provides more information in areas requested by students and reviewers as well. There is an added emphasis on cultural sensitivity as a vital ingredient to working in the field of protective services. More attention is given to the impact of violence within the family and its effect on children and overall family functioning. New research and findings in the field strengthen the underpinning of the knowledge already available to help us understand maltreatment. I have tried to pay special attention to what is working and not working in the child welfare system today.

Each chapter features Exploration Questions to enable students to test their own learning, and Activities for Applied Learning to invite readers to search within themselves or their communities for similarities or demonstrations of chapter material. Suggested Readings provide an opportunity for deeper investigation of the subject.

Understanding Child Abuse and Neglect can be used as a text for undergraduate or graduate courses in social work, human services, psychology, and sociology or in counseling and education programs.

Acknowledgments

Many people have contributed directly or indirectly to the writing of this book. My thanks go first to my family, especially to my sons, Chay, Jamie, and Andrew, who found numerous activities to keep themselves busy so Mom could write. They continue to give me emotional support and encouragement. And to my mother who was there when I couldn't be. My gratitude and love to Jim who provided so much emotional support and encouragement.

I have also learned a great deal from my students, whose interest, enthusiasm, and inquiries have done much to stimulate this endeavor. As graduates, they have continued their support. My special thanks go to Kate Martin, Richard Craig, Rhonda Rogers, and Kim McClure.

My thanks to the following reviewers for their helpful comments: Maureen Braun Scalera, Rutgers University; Morley D. Glicken, California State University–San Bernardino; Beatrice R. Beasley, Texas Southern University; George W. Caulton, Western New England College; Pamela Higgins Saulsberry, Northeast Louisiana University; Karen Hopkins, Syracuse University; Sherry L. Russell, University of North Florida; and Rosalie Ambrosino, University of Texas, Austin.

My colleagues at Fitchburg State College—especially Mary Ann Hanley and Richard Spencer—have provided ideas and help for which I am grateful. Muriel Crosson, whose editing and encouragement proved invaluable, earns particular appreciation.

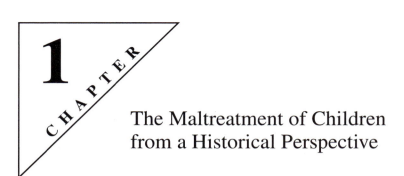

The Maltreatment of Children from a Historical Perspective

Maltreatment of children is deeply entwined with historical values and perspectives. The concept of child maltreatment has been defined and redefined throughout history. Society is slowly evolving from viewing children as property, subject to the whims of the family and society, to at least recognizing that children may have rights of their own. Each period in history—as well as each culture—has a concept of how children should be treated.

Children as Property

Early in history, children were seen as the property of their families—usually headed and ruled by fathers. Children looked to their fathers for their very existence. They had the right not only to determine the manner in which their child was cared for but if the child were to live or die.

Issues of Life and Death

Infanticide, or the killing of infants and young children, has occurred since early times. The Bible cites Abraham's intention to sacrifice his son, Isaac, to God. In early Rome, the father was given complete power to kill, abandon, or even sell his child (Thomas, 1972). In Greek legend, Oedipus was doomed to death until he was rescued by a family retainer. In Hawaii, China, and Japan, many female or disabled children were killed to maintain a strong race without overpopulation.

Infanticide was practiced for many reasons. Like the Hawaiians, Chinese, and Japanese, some cultures saw the practice of infanticide as a means of controlling and regulating the population so that society's resources could be expended on the strongest and most valued. As in the case of Abraham, babies were offered to appease gods, and infanticide was in some ways associated with religious beliefs. Attempts to limit family size or ensure financial security were also used as rationales for killing children.

In early England, as in many other cultures, infanticide was an unwed mother's solution to her act of shame. A well-known ballad tells of Mary Hamilton, lady-in-waiting to the Queen, who had the misfortune to become pregnant by the "highest Stewart of all," ostensibly the Queen's consort. As she bemoans her disgrace, the balladeer sings:

She tyed it in her apron
And she's thrown it in the sea;

1

Says, "Sink ye, swim ye, bonny wee babe
You'll ne'er get m'air o' me." (Friedman, 1956)

In Germany, newborns were sometimes plunged into frigid water to test their ability to survive. A similar ritual was practiced by some tribes of Native Americans. The child was fit to live only if he or she surfaced and cried (Kempe and Helfer, 1980). Records in England in the 1620s attest to the burial of infants murdered by drowning, burning, and scalding.

Issues of Dependence

Children were dependent on their families not only for their early existence but also for their later survival. The feudal system in Europe established a concept of ownership and articulated a hierarchy of rights and privileges. Children were at the bottom, and the children of poor families fared the worst. If parents were unable to support themselves and their children, the fate of the family was often the poorhouse. Poorhouses offered a meager subsistence, which often ended in death for the weaker members of the family.

In 1601, the Elizabethan Poor Law sought to give some help to families and children by dictating that relief must be offered to the destitute. The poor were separated into three categories:

1. The able-bodied poor—those who were considered capable and were, therefore, forced to work
2. The impotent poor—those who were old, disabled, or mothers, who were excused from work and for whom aid was provided by the state
3. Dependent children—those who were orphaned or abandoned and for whom aid was provided

The fate of children still depended largely on their family constellation. Able-bodied people were sent to work. In some cases, mothers and their children were provided for at home by contributions of food and clothing but never money. Education was not viewed as a right or privilege of such families (Popple and Leighninger, 1990).

For those who were not poor, children fared as their families saw fit. Still seen as property, some children were slaves to their guardians, performing whatever tasks were expected of them. Certainly the family life of a farming culture required that each member take part. For most children, this arrangement was satisfactory, but some children were assigned jobs far beyond their abilities or were beaten or neglected.

The early United States saw the arrival of immigrants other than Europeans. African slaves contributed greatly to the economic development of the new country, not only in the South but also in New England. The children of southern plantation slaves owed their allegiance to their parents as well as the masters who owned them. They were thought of as property and had little control over whether they worked, were sold (often without parents or siblings), or were used sexually by those more powerful. In the North, black children were not exempt from almshouses until, in 1822, the Quakers in Philadelphia established the first orphanage for such children (Billingsley and Giovannoni, 1972; Popple and Leighninger, 1990).

Asian and Pacific Island immigrants came to the United States with their own values about dependent children. The strong family-community orientation, based on the value that "the family is considered the one consistent institution for caring for the individual from birth to death" (Mass and Yap, 1992), meant that dependent children were often absorbed into the ethnic community. Native American children were also generally regarded as the responsibility of the community. In addition, Hispanic children relied on extended family members or friends to supplement or substitute for parental nurturance.

Issues of Discipline

The subject of discipline has always been controversial. Many methods used in early Western culture would certainly be open to censure today. The philosophies of our forebears, however, differ from those of most modern-day societies. Not only in the home but in the classroom, corporal punishment was a means to mold children into moral, God-fearing, respectful human beings. Parents were expected to raise religious, dedicated, morally sound, and industrious contributors to the community. Obedience was the primary virtue to develop in children. Disobedience often carried significant fines; even older children were subject to such rules. An 1854 Massachusetts law stated:

> If any children above sixteen years old and of sufficient understanding shall curse or smite their natural father or mother, they shall be put to death, unless it can be sufficiently testified that the parents have been unchristianly negligent in the education of such children or so provoked them by extreme and cruel correction that they have been forced thereunto to preserve themselves from death or maiming. (Bremner, 1970, p. 68)

The schoolmaster or mistress was accorded the same right to use corporal punishment:

> School masters in colonial Boston were conscious of the need to maintain the great English tradition of "education through pain" and, if anything added refinements to the flagellant tools they had inherited from the old country. One Bostonian invented an instrument called a "flapper"—a heavy piece of leather six inches in diameter with a hole in the middle which was fixed to a wooden handle. Every stroke on a bare bit of flesh raised an instant blister. (Inglis, 1978, p. 29)

Theologian John Calvin was of no help to children in the treatment accorded them by their elders. Calvin spoke of breaking a child's will in the hope of saving the spirit from evil. Discipline was severe in the hope that children could be transformed into God-fearing individuals.

For a short period during the eighteenth century, the treatment of children improved. Philosopher Jean Jacques Rousseau spoke of children as inherently good and encouraged educational methods that would enhance their positive development, not break their spirit (Lenoir-Degoumois, 1983).

Other cultures had their own interpretations about discipline. Many (e.g., Asian/Pacific, Hispanic) stressed the dominance of elders or males who had the right to determine how to deal with children. The strong kinship relationships of African Americans and the community responsibility inherent in Native American cultures indicated that the care and discipline of children were shared by parent figures.

Child Labor

One of the earliest forms of child labor was indenture—a system in which parents apprenticed their children to masters who taught them a trade but who were free to use them as virtual slaves in exchange for room and board. Indenture began at a very young age and continued until 14 or 16 years of age for boys and 21 years for girls. Writings by historians, novelists, and social reformers show that apprentice masters could be cruel—concerned more for the work they could extract than for the development or abilities of their juvenile charges. Charles Dickens wrote of Oliver Twist's days as an apprentice to an undertaker. Exposed to death in its basic forms, fed very little, and chided and belittled by his master's older apprentice, Oliver thought he had little recourse. In fact, English society assumed he had inherited a good lot and one for which he should be most thankful.

Indenture and child labor were also issues in early United States. As the Industrial Revolution progressed, the practice of prematurely bringing children into the labor market began to be a concern. Children were brought to the colonies to work until they were 24 years old. Child labor was seen as an inexpensive boon to the labor market, since a child could be hired for less wages than an adult. Some jobs, such as chimney sweeping or mining, were suited to children's small bodies (Kempe and Helfer, 1980; Stadium, 1995).

As the 1800s dawned in the United States, the role of children remained little changed. They continued to be the property of their parents who could choose to beat them, neglect them, or send them out to work. As the population increased and society became more impersonal, assaults on children were more easily hidden. In the late 1880s, the settlement house movement evolved. It contributed much to the future of children and their families and had a substantial impact on the reduction of child labor. The settlement houses became

known through the establishment of Toynbee Hall as a result of the influence of Arnold Toynbee in London. Inspired by the dedication of such an act, Jane Addams established Hull House in the Chicago slums. Hull House not only bridged the gap between new and more established immigrants but was the impetus for later reforms of benefit to children. One of Addams's special concerns was child labor:

> Our very first Christmas at Hull House, when we as yet knew nothing of child labor, a number of little girls refused the candy which was offered them as part of the Christmas good cheer, saying simply that they "worked in a candy factory and could not bear the sight of it." We discovered that for six weeks they had worked from seven in the morning until nine at night and they were exhausted as well as satiated. The sharp consciousness of stern economic conditions was thrust upon us in the midst of the season of good will. (Addams, 1910, p. 148)

Addams also described the dangerous conditions:

> During the same winter three boys from the Hull House club were injured at one machine in a neighborhood factory for lack of a guard which would have cost but a few dollars. When the injury of one of these boys resulted in death, we felt quite sure that the owners would share our horror and remorse, and that they would do everything possible to prevent the reoccurrence of such a tragedy. To our surprise they did nothing whatever, and I made my first acquaintance then with those pathetic documents signed by the parents of working children, that they will make no claim for damages resulting from "carelessness." (Addams, 1910, p. 148)

Although Addams and her staff at Hull House fought hard for changes in these conditions, it wasn't until much later that laws protecting children from unreasonable labor were enacted.

In addition, African-American children were largely excluded from settlement house programs and from the mainly white Charity Organization Societies (Jackson, 1978). As a result, until legislation was later passed, there was little to protect them from being used as laborers.

Sexual Values, Attitudes, and Exploitation

Early History

The definition of *sexual exploitation* has evolved throughout history. Although we might today consider the values and attitudes of the past as exploitive, the fact remains that our current customs exploit children in other ways.

In ancient times, the child, especially the female, was considered the property of her father, to do with as he saw fit. His permission was required for all her dealings. She was something with which he could barter for lands and money. With the father's permission, a betrothal could be sealed by intercourse with the underage (under 12 years) daughter. Marriage of extremely young girls was not uncommon. Since early times, fathers paid dowries for the marriage of their daughters. When dowries could not be provided for all female children, some girls entered the convent, sometimes by the age of 9, to take their vows by age 13. Rush (1980, p. 37) relates a prioress's confession that young nuns were treated like wives by the monks associated with the convent. The girls were threatened with excommunication if they told of this sexual exploitation.

Boys were not immune to sexual misuse in early history either. In Greece, pederasty (men using boys for sexual relationships) was practiced widely. Boys were taken for their attractive appearance, their softness, and their youth but were expected to show strength in battle. In fact, pederasty was the training ground for future soldiers. Most sons of noble families were actually compelled to take adult lovers, and in turn the boys were protected and plied with gifts. The protector was teacher and counselor, accepted and approved by the boy's family (Rush, 1980). In early Rome, however, sex or sexual relationships were not seen as a means of elevating children, as in Greece. In Rome, the rape of a child was a humiliation rather than a means of owning a treasured plaything (Schultz, 1982).

It was not until 1548 that any legal protection from sexual abuse was offered to children. In that year, England passed a law protecting boys from forced sodomy. In 1576, another law was enacted that prohibited the forcible rape of girls under the age of 10 (Conte and Shore, 1982, p. 22). In the 1700s, some educators warned parents to protect their children from abuse by supervising them at all times and by ensuring that they were never nude in front of adults, and in general suggested enforced modesty (Conte and Shore, 1982). This warning was one of the earliest indications that the larger society recognized children could be sexually exploited.

The Nineteenth Century

The rigid standards of the Victorian era also colored society's attitudes toward sexuality and children. Masturbation was vehemently condemned as being a precursor of insanity, growth retardation, and early death for boys; for girls, it was said to promote precocious sexual development, promiscuity, and nymphomania (Olafson et al., 1993). Attempts to curb this practice of self-gratification were extreme—surgery to remove the clitoris, slitting the penis, or cutting the nerves of the genitalia in both sexes (Conte and Shore, 1982, p. 24). With these measures came the message that children should not be seen as sexual beings.

The Victorian era, however, was replete with contradictions. On one hand, society was undergoing unbelievable advances in industrial enterprise and scientific discoveries; it was a time of deep thought and analysis. Yet behind the closed doors of so-called God-fearing homes, sexual abuse apparently flourished. Child molesters, even those who took their interests outside the family, seem to have been well protected. Numerous revered men in the public eye were taken with the charms of little girls, some to the point of acting on their desires. William Wadsworth expounded on his admiration of nubile young girls, and, at age 26, Edgar Allen Poe wed his 13-year-old cousin (Rush, 1980). Victorian morals viewed this union as scandalous, even though girls marrying at a young age had been a common practice. Lewis Carroll was well known for his interest in children. He is said to have had an entourage of whom he took nude photos. Biographers and critics have questioned whether his activities extended beyond taking pictures, telling stories, and playing games with them (Lennon, 1972).

Pornography and child prostitution also increased during the Victorian period. Men who dared not "prevail upon their wives to do their duty too often" and who shielded their children from explanations of sexuality thought nothing of frequenting child prostitutes in city slums. In the early nineteenth century, U.S. slave owners delighted in "breaking in" their young slaves or using them for breeding. Often, 11-, 12-, and 13-year-old girls were impregnated (Rush, 1980; Olafson et al., 1993).

Into this scene came a man who was to be the father of modern psychoanalysis. Sigmund Freud, a therapist in nineteenth-century Vienna, treated women who were diagnosed as having hysterical neuroses and exhibiting a variety of symptoms from compulsive vomiting, sneezing, and coughing to blindness, deafness, and paralysis. In the course of therapy, a large number of patients reported having been sexually abused at a young age. In response to this phenomenon, Freud (1966, p. 584) wrote, "Almost all my women patients told me that they had been seduced by their fathers. I was driven to recognize in the end that these reports were untrue and so came to understand that the hysterical symptoms are derived from phantasies and not from real occurrences."

Note, however, that in 1905, in the case of "Dora," Freud included a vivid description of the 14-year-old girl's seduction by her father and her subsequent use as a "pawn in [his] elaborate sex intrigues" (Herman, 1992, p. 14). From his account, the abuse obviously seems to have occurred so that it is difficult to believe Freud later discounted the credibility of the situation (Rush, 1980). We will never know what caused Freud's reversal of his theories,[1] since he destroyed his notes and diaries. Certainly his attitudes have had an influence on our current denial or reluctance to recognize the symptoms of sexual abuse in children.

The Twentieth Century

Over the years, literature has reflected a preoccupation with sexual activity and children. In 1955, Vladimir Nabokov's novel *Lolita* shocked the public and was banned from numerous bookstores and libraries. People's fascination with this type of story was obvious, and the book became a popular seller and later a movie. At age 12, Lolita is seduced by 50-year-old Humbert Humbert, who had become captivated with her. Unfortunately, the story perpetrated the belief that children—especially young girls—knowingly seduce older men who are helpless to resist. As such, this novel—and later ones like it—likely provided rationalization for incestuous fathers and added to the misconceptions of the general public. *Greek Love,* by J. Z. Eglinton (1965), recounted love and sexual tutelage of boys by adult men and how such a relationship prepares boys for adult sexual experiences. Lawrence Sanders's *The Case of Lucy Bending* (1982) gave the impression of an adult abused by a disturbed child who had instigated the relationship.

It is clear that our current society harbors a contradiction in its view of children and sexuality. On one hand, we state that children should not be exploited sexually; on the other hand, child pornography thrives and the courts are often more likely to believe molesting adults than molested children. Television commercials use nubile girls posed seductively. Such practices can only give molesters and children a mixed message about what society believes about sexual abuse and the sexual exploitation of children.

Newly immigrated cultures bring with them their own contradictory practices. For example, father-daughter incest is rare in India. Rather, an Indian father finds his power in his ability to offer a virginal daughter in marriage—hopefully one that will improve her economic status. However, sexual abuse of young boys is not uncommon though rarely discussed. Indians often bring these taboos and attitudes with them as they immigrate to other cultures.

The Incest Taboo

History

In some form, the taboo against incest appears to be universal. Historically, prohibitions of marriage and sexual relations with one's immediate blood relatives are found even in early writings. In the Bible, Leviticus outlines those individuals whom one could not uncover. "You shall not uncover the nakedness of your father, which is the nakedness of your mother; she is your mother, you shall not uncover her nakedness" (Lev. 18:7). Throughout scripture, sisters, granddaughters, stepsisters, aunts, and daughters-in-law are specifically cited as protected from sexual contact with relatives (Lev. 18:9–18). Marriage with particular individuals was also discouraged. This taboo may actually be the basis of current mores in the United States. The Greeks and Romans prohibited sexual relationships between cousins. Emperor Claudius of Rome married his niece, Agrippina, making uncle-niece marriages acceptable for a time (Weinberg, 1955). In Egypt during the Pharaonic and Ptolemaic periods, brother-sister unions among royalty were not unusual, with Cleopatra's marriage to two of her brothers perhaps the best known. There is some indication that during their conquest of Egypt, Romans also saw sibling marriages as acceptable (Middleton, 1962).

Christianity and the early Catholic church in Europe reestablished and strengthened taboos on incest and intermarriage. Historically, the penalties for incest ranged from severe censure to decapitation (in eighteenth-century Scotland). By the early 1900s, punishment through "penal servitude" or other types of incarceration were favored, and thus the offense became civil rather than religious (Weinberg, 1955).

Reasons for Taboo

Religious laws and legal writings have devoted much attention to the commission of incest. How did this taboo originate? To date there have been several possible explanations for the taboo of incest.

Biological

In *Ancient Society* (1877), L. H. Morgan suggested that incestuous marriages created defective offspring. His information appeared to be based on the experiences of animal breeders who discovered that constant inbreeding created a variety of physical and mental disabilities.

The biological theories of Morgan and his contemporaries were later discounted, however, on the basis of several factors and beliefs. First, geneticists argued that although one can create dysfunctional characteristics by inbreeding and thus giving more opportunity for recessive genes to combine, it is also possible to create superior individuals through the same process. Some breeders practice inbreeding to produce a stronger and better species. Second, it is difficult to detect whether the inferior offspring are a result of weaknesses on the part of the founders of the strain or if the process of inbreeding is at fault. Third, since animals use little selection in mating, they would be extinct if Morgan's theories were true (Meiselman, 1978).

Sexual aversion

Meiselman (1978) discussed the theories of E. Westermarck and J. K. Fox. Despite a fundamental belief in the biological interpretation, Westermarck in 1922 suggested that another explanation could be that people who live together constantly develop a mutual sexual aversion. This theory was later supported by Fox, who in 1962 used the example of children raised in the Israeli kibbutzim. Thrown together from birth, these children seek sexual partners elsewhere.

Family disruption

Family disruption was the basis for Malinowski's theory (1927) of the origin of the incest taboo. This anthropologist suggested that the family could not tolerate the ambiguity, blurred role definitions, and confusion of feelings brought on by the sexual involvement of its members. Interestingly enough, family disruption is considered today to be one of the major causes as well as one of the effects of incestuous behavior.

Multidimensional

In *Incest,* Meiselman (1978) reports that in the 1940s, L. A. White contributed to the incest controversy, and G. P. Murdock created his own multidimensional theory. White contended that survival in early societies was difficult and often depended on ingenuity and cooperation with others. As language developed, people became better able to exchange goods and ideas with other cultures. Marriage with other cultures increased networks and enhanced the possibilities for survival. Intermarriage created isolation and reduced the number of individuals available for marriage outside the tribe, and thus limited the chances of networking.

Murdock later used White's theory but suggested that it be combined with the premise that family members had a repressed desire for each other and that the family itself had to preserve its stability by keeping confusion and sexual jealousy to a minimum. This stability was most likely achieved by prohibiting incestuous behavior.

Subsequently, a variety of theorists reemphasized the importance of the incest taboo to the family structure and suggested the influence of such a taboo on the child's development. As noted by Justice and Justice (1979), Talcott Parsons wrote in 1954 that the incest taboo helped the child develop autonomy and social roles necessary to eventually leave the family. Prohibited from having sexual relations with family members, the child must then seek others outside the family structure. Carl Jung also mentioned the incest taboo as part of the child's vital struggle for individualization. Freud also spoke of the necessity of the child giving up incestuous wishes in order to succeed and procreate outside the family system.

Legal and Social Prohibition

Today, marriages with blood relatives are prohibited by law in the United States. Individual states differ in prohibitions against marriages between cousins, stepparents, and stepsiblings. The penalty for breaking this cultural and legal taboo is a jail or prison sentence. Perhaps more powerful, however, is the social stigma attached. Culturally, Weinberg (1955, p. 31) describes the stereotype as having four components:

1. An inner revulsion to incest
2. Disgust with the participants
3. Perception that participants are mentally or emotionally abnormal
4. Perception of a disorganized or even absent family life

In fact, the taboo is violated in our modern society. Current studies support the idea that incestuous relationships are barriers to children's autonomous development. Incestuous families demonstrate disorganization and dysfunction suggested by early theorists.

Recent History of Helping the Abused and Neglected Child

So far, the historical perspective has not included the individuals and movements that preceded our current child welfare systems. One of the first organized attempts to protect children was the Elizabethan Poor Law. This law was enacted not so much for the children but for society to deal with the impoverished parents. Churches and communities were often expected to provide for children who did not come under the jurisdiction of the law.

Voluntary child welfare services sprang up in isolation during the seventeenth and eighteenth centuries. Convents, churches, and philanthropists led the efforts in early child protection, but the advocates for children did not always arise from the expected quarters of religious and humanitarian groups. From firsthand knowledge, Charles Dickens spoke up for child protection. At age 12, Dickens was sent from his family to a workhouse in London. His father was frequently in debtors' prisons, and his mother's rejection of him was a fact that would greatly influence his life and later writings. In 1838, he wrote *Oliver Twist,* a largely autobiographical novel about a young boy who goes from the poorhouse to apprenticeship and finally to live among a band of juvenile thieves. As Gardner (1980) reports, this book represented Dickens's first social protest and was to be followed by other novels concerned with abused, abandoned, and crippled children. By midcentury, Dickens's work had spread and was influential throughout the United States. In 1858, Dickens began his campaign for child protection with a speech supporting the Great Ormond Street Hospital for Sick Children in London. He graphically detailed a neglected, dying child he had seen in the slums of Edinburgh. His oration had such impact it was published as a pamphlet for distribution.

Several years after Dickens's speech, events were taking shape to transform the course of child protection. New York City was the backdrop for a scene featuring Henry Bergh, who was gaining much attention as the first president of the Society for the Prevention of Cruelty to Animals (SPCA). A writer, lecturer, and administrator, Bergh had so aroused the sentiments of community leaders in intervening in the maltreatment of animals that his efforts were known as Bergh's War. In the midst of this "war" came the case of Mary Ellen Wilson (Watkins, 1990). In 1874, Mary Ellen lived with Francis and Mary Connelly and was the illegitimate daughter of Mrs. Connelly's first husband. On several occasions a neighbor had observed the ill-clad 8-year-old shivering outside a locked door. But Mary Ellen's screams as she was beaten with a leather strap were more than the neighbor could bear. She reported her observations to Etta Wheeler, a church worker from St. Luke's Methodist Mission, who, not knowing where else to turn, took the matter to Henry Bergh at the SPCA.

Although most reports are that Bergh intervened on behalf of the SPCA, more recent sources quote Bergh as saying that he acted as a private citizen. Whatever his motivation, Mary Ellen was removed from the home, and Bergh's close friend, attorney Elbridge Gerry, was asked to prosecute. For Mrs. Connelly, the outcome was a year of labor in prison, and for Mary Ellen, the results were the end of the abuse she had been suffering and eventual placement in the Sheltering Arms children's home.[2] For the nation, however, Mary Ellen

Wilson's abuse set into motion an organized effort to combat child maltreatment. Thus in 1875, the Society for the Prevention of Cruelty to Children (SPCC), under the leadership of Elbridge Gerry, began an impressive movement toward protecting children.

The New York branch of the SPCC was eventually duplicated in Philadelphia and Chicago. The SPCC not only intervened in cases of child abuse and neglect but advocated for child protection in a variety of arenas. Many chapters sponsored shelters for women and children who were in economic distress or victims of family violence. Later, the Boston chapter emphasized *family rehabilitation,* a new concept in protective services. This total family approach would eventually be the predominant philosophy of child protection agencies.

Dedication to this family-centered treatment was obvious from the White House Conference on Dependent Children in 1909. The conference supported the plan for a Children's Bureau, enacted in 1912, to oversee the welfare of children. The bureau did not, however, deal with individual cases of maltreatment but entrusted investigation and treatment of individual children to public agencies, thus diminishing the original strength of the SPCC movement (Wollons, 1993; Nelson, 1984). Another organization dedicated to seeing that children's needs were met was an indirect result of this first White House conference. The Child Welfare League of America (CWLA), a product of Carl Christian's 1915 paper proposing standards for services and aid provided to children, continues to exist today as one of the foremost advocates for children.

Although World War I temporarily diverted attention from child protection as the nation braced itself for a different conflict, the American Humane Association added children to its list of concerns and continued to gather support from anticruelty societies from every part of the United States (Williams, 1983).

By 1930, the cause of children's rights and the treatment of abused children was revived in the Social Security Act that mandated "child welfare services for neglected dependent children and children in danger of becoming delinquent" (Williams, 1983). Although intervention was mandated, the detection of child abuse and neglect was left largely to social workers. Physicians had not entered the war against child maltreatment, possibly because of an unfortunate diagnosis made in 1868 by Dr. Athol Johnson. This London physician observed repeated fractures in hospitalized children and misdiagnosed them as rickets, thus opening the door for almost a century of future misinterpretations (Williams, 1983).

At Columbia University, a radiology professor, John Caffey (1946), noted that the x-rays of some infants demonstrated unexplained multiple fractures. He also noted an increased number of victims with subdural hematoma (a collection of blood under the skull). The case histories did not indicate any falls or events serious enough to explain these medical findings. Caffey wondered if these traumas had been somehow inflicted by the parents. He stated his suspicions:

> In each case unexplained fresh fractures appeared shortly after the patient had arrived home after discharge from the hospital. In one of these cases the infant was clearly unwanted by both parents and this raised the question of intentional ill treatment of the infant; the evidence was inadequate to prove or disprove this point.

Caffey's theory was supported by several other physicians in the early 1950s. Both Williams (1983) and Parton (1985) noted that F. N. Silverman, along with P. V. Wolley and

W. A. Evans, reported they had explored Caffey's work and felt there was strong evidence that parents were responsible for many of these injuries.

Physicians continued to study the phenomenon. Dr. C. Henry Kempe, chairman of the Department of Pediatrics at the University of Colorado School of Medicine, and his colleagues published in the *Journal of the American Medical Association* the now-famous article entitled "The Battered-Child Syndrome." Kempe and colleagues (1962, p. 17) defined this syndrome as "a clinical condition in young children who have received severe physical abuse, generally from a parent or foster parent. The condition has also been described as 'unrecognized trauma' by radiologists, orthopedists, pediatricians, and social service workers." Kempe cited the age of the children involved as under 3 years and suggested that diagnosticians look for a "marked discrepancy between clinical findings and historical data supplied by the parents" as a primary indicator (p. 17). Although experts now include children older than three years, the difference between clinical findings and data supplied by parents is still thought to be significant in the identification of maltreatment (Newman & Lutzker, 1990).

The identification of the phenomenon by name and definition provided a means to publicize the problem. "Battered-baby syndrome" was talked about by almost every professional concerned with children, while an increasing number of studies were undertaken to determine the magnitude of the problem. The studies conducted by Kempe and associates uncovered that in 71 hospitals, at least 302 cases of child abuse had occurred; 33 of these children subsequently died and 85 suffered permanent brain injury. Following Kempe's work, Vincent DeFrancis, the new director of the American Humane Association, discovered that in the year 1962 alone, 662 cases of child abuse were reported to the press (Parton, 1985).

The fervor of the 1960s caused professionals, who had not thought of child abuse as a problem within their particular domain, to recognize their need to be involved. Ray Helfer, a collaborator with Henry Kempe and a fellow physician, outlined the reasons that physicians in the past had been reticent to report abuse. Helfer (1968) felt that physicians were both unaware of their legal obligations and unable to recognize parental abuse because of close ties to the family. By the early 1970s, through the efforts of Helfer and others, physicians had been made well aware of their responsibilities to children and their families.

In 1972, the National Center for the Prevention of Child Abuse and Neglect was established with financial aid from the University of Colorado Medical Center. The purpose of this office was to provide a newsletter, engage in research, and offer training for recognizing and preventing child abuse to interested professionals.

By 1973, the need for a federal stand on the issue became obvious. The Child Abuse Prevention bill (S. 1191) was proposed on March 13, 1973, largely under the sponsorship of Senator Walter Mondale, chairman of the Subcommittee on Children and Youth (Nelson, 1984). Ellen Hoffman (1978), primary author of the Child Abuse Prevention and Treatment Act proposal, was greatly influenced by C. Henry Kempe. Hoffman's proposal to establish a National Center on Child Abuse and Neglect under the auspices of the Department of Health, Education and Welfare (HEW) was in four parts:

1. The center would be responsible for research, establishment of a clearinghouse, and distribution of training materials.

2. Demonstration projects to "prevent, identify and treat child abuse and neglect" would be encouraged by the provision of $10 million in 1973 and $20 million for the next four years to be used for grants and contracts.

3. To study the effectiveness of child abuse and neglect-reporting laws and "the proper role of the federal government" in assisting state and local efforts, a board, known as the National Commission on Child Abuse and Neglect, would be established.

4. States would be required to adopt specific procedures to identify, treat, and prevent child abuse and to maintain information and report to HEW on the efficiency of these procedures. States would also be required to cooperate with state health education and other agencies in the interest of coordinating the treatment of child abuse and neglect cases. Complying with these standards would protect the states' eligibility for certain funds under the Social Security Act.

Hearings for the adoption of this bill went on for four days in Washington, Denver, and New York. Slides of abused and neglected children were shown and experts attested to the need for such a law. A witness who made a substantial impact was Jolly K., the founder of Parents Anonymous. She candidly described how she had at one time beaten her own children. What she did not tell the assembled group, however, was that she had been a victim herself of beatings, abandonment, and rape. Her testimony had a phenomenal impact, and in January 1974, the Child Abuse Prevention and Treatment Act was passed (Nelson, 1984). It was 100 years after Mary Ellen Wilson shivered on the steps of her foster home that the nation officially recognized the need to provide for all children like her.

Child Protection Today

Intervention with abused and neglected children has made much progress since Mary Ellen's day. Several factors have contributed to this progress.

Increased Awareness by Professionals

Kempe and his colleagues led the way in helping fellow physicians and other medical personnel recognize the vital role they could play in detecting and reporting child abuse. Since his 1962 article on the "Battered Baby Syndrome," much progress has been made in the area of recognition and treatment of abuse and neglect. Throughout the 1960s and 1970s, physical abuse and neglect were researched and an increasing number of programs were made available for intervention and treatment. In 1977, Kempe and several of his colleagues created the International Society for the Prevention and Treatment of Child Abuse and Neglect in an effort to:

> …prevent cruelty to children in every nation—whether cruelty occurs in the form of abuse, neglect, or exploitation—and thus enable the children of the world to develop physically, mentally, and socially in a healthy and normal manner.

This organization continues to support efforts in the area of treatment and research largely through the publication of the *International Journal of Child Abuse and Neglect.*

Sexual abuse was not widely studied until the late 1970s when David Finklehor surveyed New England College students to determine if they had been sexually abused as children.

About the same time Diana Russell's study of 940 San Francisco women uncovered that 38 percent reported sexual abuse as children (Olafson et al., 1993). As researchers looked for indications that children were being sexually abused, survivors began speaking out. Butler's *Conspiracy of Silence* and Brady's *Father's Days* recounted abuse perpetuated against children by their fathers. Sexual abuse, once a concept so foreign to most of us, has become a household phrase in the 1980s and 1990s.

As society becomes more aware of the need to protect children, schools must certainly be involved. Over the last decade, educators have become increasingly aware of their responsibilities not only through publications of the U.S. Department of Health and Human Services but also through the efforts of the National Education Association (NEA). In 1984, NEA published a multimedia package to acquaint teachers and other school personnel with their obligation to recognize, and report child maltreatment.

Today all states have mandated reporting laws (each encompassing a variety of professionals), and these have added impetus to professionals' involvement in detection, reporting, and treatment.

Better Communication among Professionals

In the early years, the study and understanding of child abuse was isolated. Professionals now realize that their strength in combatting the problem is through communication. Major national clearinghouses for information have created a ready availability of materials to enhance this communication. In addition to the National Center on Child Abuse and Neglect (P.O. Box 1182, Washington, DC 20013), others, such as the C. Henry Kempe Center for Prevention and Treatment of Child Abuse and Neglect (1205 Oneida St., Denver, CO 80220), the American Humane Association (9725 E. Hampden Ave., Denver, CO 80231), and the National Committee for Prevention of Child Abuse (332 S. Michigan Ave., Chicago, IL 60604) also help coordinate and circulate a wealth of information on child abuse and neglect. Currently, numerous journals in addition to the *International Journal of Child Abuse and Neglect,* serve to keep the professional better informed.

Support for Additional Research

Over the last decade, numerous research projects, funded by grants and private monies, have been undertaken to help professionals understand child abuse and our current methods of combatting it. At each national conference on child abuse a multitude of research projects are represented.

Richard Gelles has continued his studies in the understanding of family violence. David Finkelhor, of the University of New Hampshire Family Studies Program, continues to make a substantial contribution to the understanding of sexual abuse. Kathleen Colburn Faller, John Conte, Lucy Berliner, Lynn Sanford, and John Briere interpret the effects of abuse on both children and adult survivors. Nicholas Groth, Gene Abel, Judith Becker, and Thomas Seghorn strive to present a more understandable picture of the sex offender. Norman Polansky looks at neglectful families and their unmet needs.

During the last few years, NCCAN has funded projects studying remedial prevention for maltreated adolescents, building resources in minority communities, using school systems to prevent maltreatment, dealing with neglect of infants, improving the handling of child abuse cases from initial investigation to litigation, and studying nonprofessional sources of reports of child maltreatment. Other priority areas included aid and respite care projects, recruitment of volunteers for court-appointed advocates, improvement of services for runaway and homeless youth, and providing training for multidisciplinary support in services for abused and neglected children (U.S. Department of Health and Human Services, 1985).

Media Attention

In 1874, the *New York Times* extensively covered the case of Mary Ellen Wilson. In *Violence against Children,* David Gil reported that in a 1965 nationwide survey, newspapers were cited as the main source of information on physical abuse by 72 percent of the respondents, while 56.2 percent cited television, and 22.7 percent said magazines (Gil, 1973, table 5, p. 61). People do depend on the media, especially newspapers, for their information about child abuse.

What impact do the media in fact have on child abuse, prevention, and treatment? Downs (1972) suggests that the interest in and influence of media regarding an issue assumes a five-step cycle:

1. Preproblem stage
2. "Alarmed discovery and euphoric enthusiasm"
3. Disillusionment based on reality
4. Loss of interest
5. Postproblem stage

During the preproblem stage, the problem already exists, usually on a severe and pervasive level, but it has not been given the attention in the press.

During the second stage (as in the 1950s or 1960s for physical abuse or the 1980s for sexual abuse), the press creates a period of alarmed discovery. Newspapers, TV, and radio alert everyone to the horror and indignity of the problem. U.S. society, Downs contends, has a simplistic view of issues, assuming that the problem can be easily solved without too much upset. At this point the government jumps in, mindful of its obligation to its people. Witness the increased federal funds that have, in the last few years, been directed toward child-abuse programs.

The third stage of the cycle is heralded by the painful recognition that the solution will in fact be costly, and to solve the problem, society must in some way be altered. This price is too painful, and the media, perhaps influenced by its disillusioned readers, loses interest during the fourth stage.

The postproblem stage sees the efforts that have been made by the government as institutionalized. Media may provide coverage, but this is often relegated to the back page.

We can question where we currently are, as a society, in Downs's series of stages. Certainly the media has had and continues to have its say by publishing the most sensational stories. We now recognize that society, with its emphasis on violence and sexuality, must change in order to combat the problem of child abuse and neglect.

Some readers protest they have heard enough about sexual abuse, but the public's interest in the total spectrum of child abuse and neglect seems to have increased. Newspapers and television have become more innovative in providing information—about abusers and the victims—to the concerned citizenry.

Responsible advice columnists aid teens or other populations not comfortable or familiar with the social service system. An important service offered by the media is the publication of hotline numbers, books to read, or agency programs. This has provided a valuable link between the helper and the client. There appears to be time before society reaches Downs's fifth stage of indifference. It is necessary to make that time count.

Newspapers, magazines, television, and radio echo ever-increasing evidence of the shift in U.S. values. Proposals for welfare reform, and even outright termination of the welfare system, are common. Parental rights, particularly those of teenage mothers, are hotly debated. Orphanages have been suggested for more effective out-of-home care.

New legislation may well change the philosophy and nature of the child welfare system in the United States. As we view the child protection services of today in the following chapters, it must be from a vantage that recognizes the probability of major changes in the near future.

Current Theoretical Framework

Intervention ideologies in the maltreatment of children are represented by three basic orientations: penal, medical, and social welfare (see Table 1.1). Each of these has a characteristic way of viewing the abuser, the act, and the type of intervention necessary. In reading about child abuse and neglect in this book, it will be important to bear these differences in mind. As the field builds a more multidimensional set of intervention strategies, it is hoped that these views can borrow from and influence one another to some extent.

Summary

The maltreatment of children is a longstanding problem. Since ancient times, children have been viewed as property to be sold, given, or exploited by adults. Throughout history, children have been overworked, prostituted, and physically maltreated for a variety of reasons. Severe beatings administered with religious fervor were inflicted to gain the child's salvation and to exorcise evil. Employers used children to further their own economic interests. Despite the widespread sexual exploitation of children, the one taboo has been incest. The origins of this taboo seem to have been economic. An untouched female child was insurance for later barter with other tribes and cultures. Today we also recognize the family disorganization that the breaking of the incest taboo creates.

There have been crusaders for children throughout history, however. Charles Dickens used his own painful background to speak out against child maltreatment. Then the case of Mary Ellen Wilson and crusader Henry Bergh set in motion a mechanism for the future protection of children. Bergh's efforts on behalf of Mary Ellen gave birth to the Society for the Prevention of Cruelty to Children, which provides help for children even now.

The discovery by radiologists of multiple, unexplained fractures and the coining of the phrase *battered-child syndrome* in the 1960s added impetus to the child protection movement. In 1974, the Child Abuse Prevention and Treatment Act required that states intervene in abuse situations and provided financial and material resources to aid the states.

Today we know that child abuse is seen from the view of three ideologies—penal, medical, and social welfare. Better communication, continued attention from the media, increased support for research, and more community awareness have made child abuse a vital concern. Despite the fact that the field of child protection is young, it continues to mature as we learn to better understand the abuser and the victim.

TABLE 1.1   Alternative Child Abuse Ideologies

Framework	Penal Legal	Medical Scientific	Social Welfare Humanistic (a) traditional	Social Welfare Humanistic (b) radical
Presupposition	individual has free-will	behavior is determined		
Definition	cruelty	battered baby syndrome	child abuse	child abuse
Attitude to problem	punitive; deviance is conscious defiance of rules; moralistic	results from forces beyond control of individual	compassionate; individual/family cannot cope with situation	relative but results from social processes
Social rationale	justice; due process; individual rights	cure; treatment of needs of the child	prevention; rehabilitation by adjustment	social liberation by reorganization
Focus of attention	act of abuse; deprivation	disease process, pathology syndromes	the person; family, social situation; "cycle of deprivation"	social processes, structural inequality
Tools	legal code, courts	medical expertise and technology	counselling, therapeutic relationships, social experts	social change
Conception of parents	responsible	irresponsible or not responsible	psychologically, emotionally and socially inadequate	socially victimized
Stated purpose of intervention	punishment of guilt	treatment of dysfunction	personal, family rehabilitation, physical and emotional safety of child	equality and redistribution
Some practicing groups	police, judiciary	doctors, some psychiatrists	social workers; some doctors, e.g., pediatricians	some social workers and some sociologists

From Nigel Parton, *The Politics of Child Abuse*, Table 1.2, p. 17. Copyright © 1985. Reprinted by permission of Macmillan London and Basingstoke (world rights) and St. Martin's Press (U.S. rights).

Exploration Questions

1. What reasons were given for the maltreatment of children in early history?

2. What were the reasons for infanticide in early history?

3. How did the Greeks and Romans differ in their ideas about the sexual misuse of children?

4. What in today's world gives mixed messages about views of the sexual exploitation of children?

5. Cite early explanations for the incest taboo.

6. What explanations currently support the incest taboo?

7. Why did the case of Mary Ellen Wilson create such a stir in 1874?

8. Why were Caffey's findings so significant? What may have suppressed the assertion of such a theory earlier?

9. Why was the coining of the phrase *battered-child syndrome* so important to the future of the child protection movement?

10. What were the provisions of the Child Abuse Prevention and Treatment Act of 1974, and how are these reflected in protective services today?

Activities for Applied Learning

1. Write to one of the clearinghouses suggested in this chapter to obtain lists of the resources available in child abuse and neglect. Given the number of resources in each area, where does the most emphasis lie?

2. Invite an anthropologist to class to speak about the origins of the incest taboo.

3. Choose a particular type of abuse or an individual case; photocopy newspaper clippings over a period of time and create a scrapbook or mural. Analyze these to determine if Downs's issue-attention cycle applies.

4. Obtain a copy of the *Hearings before the Subcommittee on Children and Youth of the Committee on Labor and Public Welfare,* U.S. Senate, 93rd Congress (from U.S. Government Printing Office, Washington, DC 20402, or your local library). Which of the witnesses presented the most viable reasons for an act to prevent child abuse, and why?

5. Invite a speaker from the Society for the Prevention of Cruelty to Children to outline the history of the movement.

6. Have a lawyer, physician, and social worker join a panel, and analyze the difference in their approaches.

Suggested Readings

Acosta-Belen, E., and Sjostrom, B. (Eds.). *Hispanic Experience in the U.S.* New York: Praeger, 1988.

Billingsley, Andrew, and Giovannoni, Jeanne M. *Children of the Storm: Black Children and American Child Welfare.* New York: Harcourt Brace Jovanovich, 1972.

Cohen, Neil (Ed.). *Child Welfare: A Multicultural Focus.* Boston: Allyn and Bacon, 1992.

Freud, S. *The Complete Introductory Letters of Psychoanalysis.* New York: Norton, 1966.

Hoffman, E. "Policy and Politics: The Child Abuse Prevention and Treatment Act." *Public Policy* 26 (1978).

Kempe, H.; Silverman, F.; Steele, B.; Droegemueller, W.; and Silver, H. "The Battered-Child Syndrome." *Journal of the American Medical Association* 181 (1962):17–24.

Kitano, H. L., and Daniels, R. *Asian Americans: Emerging Minorities.* Englewood Cliffs, NJ: Prentice Hall, 1987.

Nelson, B. *Making an Issue of Child Abuse.* Chicago: University of Chicago Press, 1984.

Olafson, E.; Corwin, D. L.; and Summit, R. C. "Modern History of Child Sexual Abuse: Cycles of Discovery and Suppression." *Child Abuse and Neglect* 17 (1993): 7–24.

Parton, N. *The Politics of Child Abuse.* London: Macmillan, 1985.

Rush, F. *The Best Kept Secret: Sexual Abuse of Children.* New York: McGraw-Hill, 1980.

Takaki, R. *Strangers from a Different Shore: A History of Asian Americans.* Boston: Little, Brown, 1989.

Endnotes

1. Some theorists (e.g., Rush, 1980) attribute Freud's shift to personal experiences, whereas others (e.g., Meiselman, 1978; Olafson et al., 1993) suggest that collegial pressure was the primary reason.

2. Many wondered what happened to Mary Ellen after her much publicized case. The Sheltering Arms was, in fact, a home for disturbed girls—not orphans like Mary Ellen. Thus, Mary Ellen became a victim of the system's mistreatment, as well. Still concerned with her, Etta Wheeler, recognizing the inappropriate placement, petitioned Judge Lawrence to be Mary Ellen's appointed guardian. Lawrence allowed Wheeler to place the child with Wheeler's mother, Sally Angell, on a farm outside Rochester, New York. When Angell died, Mary Ellen continued to be raised by Angell's daughter. Years later, Mary Ellen's own daughter would write to the then director of SPCC, asking to know more of her mother's history (Lazoritz, 1990).

References

Addams, J. *Twenty Years at Hull-House.* New York: Signet, 1910.

Billingsley, A., and Giovannoni, J. M. *Children of the Storm: Black Children and American Child Welfare.* New York: Harcourt Brace Jovanovich, 1972.

Bremner, R., ed. *Children and Youth in America: A Documentary History.* Vol. 1. Cambridge, MA: Harvard University Press, 1970.

Caffey, J. "Multiple Fractures in the Long Bones of Infants Suffering from Chronic Subdural Hematoma." *American Journal of Roentgenology* 56 (1946):163–73.

Conte, J., and Shore, D. "Social Work and Sexual Abuse." *Journal of Social Work and Human Sexuality.* Vol. 1, No. 1–2. New York: Haworth Press, 1982.

Downs, A. "Up and Down with Ecology—'The Issue Attention Cycle'." *Public Interest* 32 (1972):38–50.

Eglinton, J. *Greek Love.* New York: Oliver Layton, 1965.

Freud, S. *The Complete Introductory Letters of Psychoanalysis.* New York: Norton, 1966.

Friedman, A. B. *The Viking Book of Folk Ballads of the English Speaking World.* New York: Viking, 1956.

Gardner, L. "The Endocrinology of Abuse Dwarfism: With a Note on Charles Dickens as Child Advocate." In *Traumatic Abuse and Neglect of Children at Home,* pp. 375–80. Baltimore: The Johns Hopkins University Press, 1980.

Gil, D. *Violence against Children.* Cambridge, MA: Harvard University Press, 1973.

Giovannoni, J., and Becerra, R. *Defining Child Abuse.* New York: Free Press, 1979.

Helfer, R. "The Responsibility and Role of the Physician." In *The Battered Child,* edited by R. Helfer and C. H. Kempe. Chicago: University of Chicago Press, 1968.

Herman, J. *Trauma and Recovery.* New York: Basic Books, 1992.

Hoffman, E. "Policy and Politics: The Child Abuse Prevention and Treatment Act." *Public Policy* 26 (1978).

Inglis, R. *Sins of the Fathers.* New York: St. Martin's Press, 1978.

Jackson, P. "Black Charity in Progressive Era Chicago." *Social Service Review* 52 (1978):400–17.

Justice, B., and Justice, R. *The Broken Taboo: Sex in the Family.* New York: Human Sciences Press, 1979.

Kempe, C. H., and Helfer, R. *The Battered Child.* 3rd ed. Chicago: University of Chicago Press, 1980.

Kempe, H., Silverman, F., Steele, B., Droegemueller, W., and Silver, H. "The Battered-Child Syndrome."

Journal of the American Medical Association 181 (1962):17–24.

Lazoritz, S. "Whatever Happened to Mary Ellen?" *Child Abuse and Neglect* 14 (1990):143–49.

Lennon, F. *The Life of Lewis Carroll.* New York: Dover, 1972.

Lenoir-Degoumois, V. "The Manifestations of Ill-Treatment of Children: Historical Background." *International Journal of Offender Therapy and Comparative Criminology* 27 (1983):55–60.

Malinowski, B. *Sex and Repression in Savage Society.* London: Routledge and Kegan Paul, 1927.

Mass, A. I., and Yap, J. "Child Welfare: Asian and Pacific Islander Families." In *Child Welfare: A Multicultural Perspective,* edited by N. Cohen. Boston: Allyn and Bacon, 1992.

Meiselman, K. *Incest.* San Francisco: Jossey-Bass, 1978.

Middleton, R. "Brother-Sister and Father-Daughter Marriage in Ancient Egypt." *American Sociological Review* 27 (1962):603–11.

Morgan, L. H. *Ancient Society.* Chicago: Kerr, 1877.

Nelson, B. *Making an Issue of Child Abuse.* Chicago: University of Chicago Press, 1984.

Newman, M. R., and Lutzker, J. R. "Prevention Programs" in *Children at Risk; An Evaluation of Factors Contributing to Child Abuse and Neglect,* R. Ammerman and M. Hersen (Eds.). New York: Plenum, 1990.

Olafson, E; Corwin, D. L.; and Summit, R. "Modern History of Child Sexual Abuse: Cycles of Discovery and Suppression." *Child Abuse and Neglect* 17 (1993):7–24.

Parton, N. *The Politics of Child Abuse.* London: Macmillan, 1985.

Popple, P. R., and Leighninger, L. *Social Work, Social Welfare and American Society.* Boston: Allyn and Bacon, 1990.

Rush, F. *The Best Kept Secret: Sexual Abuse of Children.* New York: McGraw-Hill, 1980.

Sanders, L. *The Case of Lucy Bending.* New York: Berkley, 1982.

Schultz, L. "Child Abuse in Historical Perspective." In *Social Work and Child Sexual Abuse: Journal of Social Work and Human Sexuality,* edited by J. Conte and D. Shore. Vol. 1, No. 1–2. New York: Haworth Press, 1982.

Sgroi, S. *Handbook of Clinical Intervention in Child Sexual Abuse.* Lexington, MA: Lexington Books, 1982.

Stadum, B. "The Dilemma in Saving Children from Child Labor: Reform and Casework at Odds with Family Needs (1900–1938)." *Child Welfare* 74(1) (1995), 33–55.

Thomas, J. "Cultural Diversity and Organizational Responsiveness." *APSAC Advisor* 4 (1991): 1–2.

Thomas, M. P. "Child Abuse and Neglect, Part I: Historical Overview, Legal Material and Social Perspective." *North Carolina Law Review* 50 (1972):293–349.

U.S. Department of Health and Human Services. *Child Abuse and Neglect: An Informed Approach to a Shared Concern.* Washington, DC: U.S. Government Printing Office, 1985.

Watkins, S. A. "The Mary Ellen Myth: Correcting Child Welfare History." *Social Work* 35 (1990):500–505.

Weinberg, S. K. *Incest Behavior.* Secaucus, NJ: Citadel Press, 1955.

Williams, G. "Child Protection: A Journey into History." *Journal of Clinical Child Psychology* 12 (1983):236–43.

Williams, G., and Money, J. *Traumatic Abuse and Neglect of Children at Home.* Baltimore: The Johns Hopkins University Press, 1980.

Wollons, R. (Ed.) *Children at Risk in America: History, Concepts and Public Policy.* Albany: State University of New York Press, 1993.

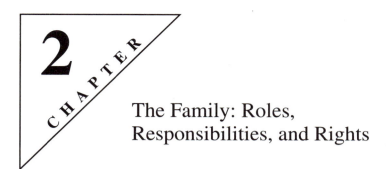

2 CHAPTER

The Family: Roles, Responsibilities, and Rights

The Definition and Function of the Family

The family as an institution has changed significantly over the years. Each culture has a different interpretation of what it expects a family to be. No matter what the culture, society has particular expectations of a family and, in some cases when those expectations are not met, is entitled to intervene. The changes in society itself have put additional pressures on families and can make functioning and meeting societal expectations of a stable unit even more difficult.

What factors in today's culture have altered families' functioning? An industrialized, impersonal climate has increased mobility, as wage earners follow the expansion or relocation of businesses in search of satisfying, better-paying, or continuing positions. Moves frequently promote further isolation of families. Emphasis on faster, more competitive, more affluent lifestyles produces stress.

Amidst the stresses of living in a high-pressured world, the family has had to make adjustments. The nuclear family (mother, father, and children), which for a time had all but replaced the extended family (parents, children often living with grandparents or adult siblings), is now decreasing. The current divorce rate is the highest ever, and the single-parent family represents a large percentage of the parenting population. One in four families is headed by a single mother (Hess et al., 1993). Today there are numerous constellations that can be considered a family—each with its own strengths and weaknesses and issues. In the blended family, husband and wife care for children from their previous marriages and perhaps their children from their present marriage. Within this context, cohabitation, or two people living together without legal sanction and caring for children, is practiced widely today. Communal living, more popular during the 1960s than today, joins several adults and their various offspring in one living arrangement (Goldenberg and Goldenberg, 1980; Hess et al., 1993).

African-American families rely extensively on kinship networks—that is, blood relatives or friends who become "kinsmen" and often take on the duties of family members. African-American children are also more frequently taken into the homes of grandparents to be raised (Staples, 1981). Hispanic families have the institution of *compadres,* or companion parents. Compadres, godparents named at baptism, have an integral part in children's upbringing (Lum, 1992). Price (1981) explains that the Hopi Indian tribe practices *bifurcate merging;* in other words, the father's or mother's relatives are divided into separate lineages. Relatives of the same sex and generation are then grouped together in helping clusters. For example, the mother's sister would be seen as a close relation and would behave toward the child as the biological mother would (Lum, 1992).

Considering this wide variety of family configurations, how can a family be defined? Karpel and Strauss (1983) suggest various contexts:

- The functional family—members who share household tasks, activities, and child care
- The legal family—bound together by its legal structure and altered by divorce or the legal removal of children
- The family by perception—where members see others as being part of the family (e.g., live-in boyfriend, considered to be acting in the role of father and husband, compadres, or kinsmen)
- The biological family—held together by blood relationships
- The family of long-term commitments—where long-term expectations encompassing trust, fairness, and loyalty are present

These definitions may overlap significantly.

Whatever the type, here the term *family* refers to a group of people who live together (or at least have regular contact) and who are expected to perform specific functions, especially in reference to the children involved. In the context of this book, the primary function of the family is the task of raising children. The parents, or parenting adults, are assigned certain responsibilities. Parental responsibilities are not, for the most part, recorded in a book of how-to's. However, mores and customs are passed from generation to generation and now considered by popular opinion to be tasks and roles for parents to undertake. The way in which these responsibilities are characterized may vary widely. Some family texts outline the parental functions as:

1. Reproduction
2. Socialization
3. Assignment of social roles
4. Economic production and consumption
5. Emotional support (Berns, 1985, p. 70)

Katz suggests that parental responsibilities must reflect what the community or the society wants to promote through the parent-child relationship. If this relationship continues to foster the child in the way that society demands, the family unit is promised relative autonomy and freedom from government intervention. Therefore, the parent-child relationship is expected to provide: stability and integrity; financial security; health and education; and morality and respect (Katz, 1971, pp. 6–13).

Stability and integrity mean parents need to provide a secure, stable, constant relationship on which their children can base their expectations and model their future relationships. Within this realm of security, parents have an opportunity to teach their children what society and their own culture will expect from them as adults. To enable the child to learn these lessons, parents are expected to provide comfort—the comfort of being properly housed, clothed, and fed. The assurance of these comforts requires financial security, which should be provided by the parents. Emotional well-being also necessitates being healthy and educated. A healthy future adult will benefit society as a whole.

The Family as a System

The family, especially in its role of raising children, is a complex and ever-changing system. Like any system, families must maintain some type of balance, continue a flow of information, and monitor the communication among their members. Families do this through a series of subsystems, boundaries, roles, and communication patterns.

Subsystems and Boundaries

A subsystem consists of smaller units that carry out specific functions and together make up the whole. In a healthy functioning family, the parents unite in a major subsystem responsible for making decisions and regulating family activities.

Parents are expected to understand and adapt to developmental needs and to explain the rules they impose. They must guide and control, keeping in mind the child's need to mature and gain autonomy. The parents provide models, not only of behavior but of the use of authority. They must also introduce children to their own culture and serve as interpreters to explain differences between that culture and that of the larger society.

The sibling subsystem helps children experiment with the complexities of peer relationships. Here, they have an opportunity to fight, accommodate, isolate, negotiate, compete, and basically learn from each other. In later life, children transfer their interactions with siblings into their dealings with extrafamilial peers (Minuchin, 1981).

In addition to these two major subsystems, the family is composed of numerous others. For example, all the females in the family comprise one subsystem, all the males another, and there may be expectations of each of these. Subsystems exist by virtue of sex, age, interest, and function, and each family member is simultaneously part of several subsystems. Boundaries, which are divisions between subsystems, allow these minisystems freedom to operate (Herbert, 1989). Boundaries also define who can interact with whom and how. For example, in healthy families, the boundary around the spouse or parent subsystem allows children access to each parent but not to interfere in the relationship between these parents. The parents' closed bedroom door is one symbol of this boundary and says to the children that the parents are then maintaining their right to privacy.

In some families where the boundaries are extremely rigid, there is little interaction between subsystems, and family members appear unresponsive to each other. For example, parents whose lives have little involvement with their children and who fail to perform such normal family rituals as eating meals with their children are probably not overly responsive to their children's needs. At the other end, the family with unclear or too flexible boundaries may also present problems. Often the incestuous family has unclear generational boundaries. Relationships, especially those that are sexual and normally kept to the older generation, begin to involve the rest of the family.

Boundaries can also be maintained between the family and the external world. Those that are too rigid create isolation for the family, but if the boundaries with the outside are poorly defined, nonfamily members may float in and out of the family constellation to the confusion of all.

Roles

Each family member is given or assumes a series of roles. These roles may enhance family functioning or may cause dysfunction. Roles in a family shape how we think of ourselves, how others see us, and how we function or behave within a family. One parent may be the breadwinner while the other is the stay-at-home nurturer. In other families, parents share both roles. Sometimes the roles others expect us to take shape how we behave. For example, the mother may respond to her child's misbehavior by saying, "Wait until your father gets home." This sets up her spouse as the disciplinarian, so there is pressure for him to assume this role, which he may do willingly or reluctantly. If, however, he chooses not to take this role and does not confront his wife, the issue is clouded and confusion results.

Some families find that their cultural values impose roles on them that they have difficulty maintaining. For example, Asian/Pacific immigrant parents may find it difficult to maintain the unquestioned position of respect, authority, and leadership given them in their native countries. While their children are learning the value of independence in their U.S. schools, the parents cling to their regard for family and for their "old-world ways." Fathers who worked as engineers and doctors perhaps may find that, due to their inability to speak English well enough to pass licensing exams, they must take jobs that they deem inferior. The respect they were once given is further impacted when their wives find it easier to find work. For these fathers, the experience is one of "losing face" (Mass and Yap, 1992).

Children are often cast in dysfunctional roles. For example, a child can become the scapegoat for the family's stresses and thus sometimes the victim of abuse. Another child may be expected to assume parental roles and is seen as the parent for the rest of the family, including the adults.

The delegation or assumption of roles can be extremely complex. Numerous motivations cause family members to assume or accept roles. Through analyzing the roles in a family, it becomes more clear why one child is abused or why another family is neglectful.

Communication

The regulation of subsystems and boundaries and even the assignment of roles is accomplished through communication patterns. Communication is not always one family member talking to another. Silences, body movements, facial expressions, voice tone, and posture all convey messages. For example, a mother may say, "Stop that," with little conviction in her voice or facial expression. The child gets several messages. Verbally he or she is being told to cease the behavior, but the mother's lack of affect is saying not much will happen if it does not stop. Communication patterns within the total family can become complex and unclear. Using another example, a father's attempt to control his son may be met with his being ignored while the mother looks on smugly, conveying the message, "I told you that kid couldn't be controlled!" In such a situation the child's deviant behavior may well escalate.

Communication patterns in families of different cultures may also differ. Some cultures (e.g., Asian, Hispanic) stress communication patterns that are hierarchical. Young people may be expected to listen to their elders, not contradict them. The feelings and opinions of children are not shared with elders. For example, in Asian tradition, people who show their emotions are considered to lack strength or self-control. The difference in these communication patterns is especially difficult for minority children growing up in the United States. They see their friends or characters on television who openly share feelings with their parents and they may actually feel unloved or neglected by parents who communicate according to a different set of rules (Mass and Yap, 1992).

Part of family communication has to do with family rules. Family rules are repetitive patterns of interaction that family members develop with each other. These patterns begin to be accepted by the family as a code of behavior or assumptions about how to act (Goldenberg and Goldenberg, 1980). For example, a family rule that the son is uncontrollable may have evolved because the mother has been ineffective, and she may even have undermined the father's attempts at discipline.

A family rule in another family might be, "Go to Dad if you're upset; he's more understanding." Incestuous families often develop the rule that no one outside the family can be trusted, so that the family secret of incest can be protected. Rules may be functional or dysfunctional, but they regulate the way the family communicates.

To be truly effective, communication and rules must be clear cut, open, and consistent. Often families with problems practice incomplete communication—that is, sending a partial message that assumes the receiver perceives the remainder of the message. For example, in a voice loud enough to be heard by her husband and children watching TV, a tired mother may say, "Dishes, dishes! As soon as I do them, there are more to do!" On the surface, she is making a statement about the abundance of dirty dishes generated by the family. However, her angry look at the assembled family and the resentment in her voice betray her real feelings of overwork and the need for some help. She assumes that her verbal statement has made the message clear and may be furious that no one offers help. In fact, a more complete message might be, "I'm really tired after doing dishes all day, and I'd like you to help me." Or better still, "Do these dishes so I can relax too." (The mother may also be disrupting the family rule of "Mom's the dishwasher—she'll do the dishes. Just ignore her complaints.") Making a request for help might have to be followed by a command for someone specific to do the job, but the mother will have made her desires known.

When family members communicate unclearly or inadequately yet expect others to understand their meaning and perceive their needs, the result is often frustration, resentment, and anger. Communication is therefore an important element of family functioning or dysfunctioning.

Rituals

When one strives to understand families, especially in the context of their individuality often influenced by their culture, it is important to recognize the presence, absence, or importance of family rituals. Rituals are repetitive behaviors that families may practice as a vital part of their communication. Imber-black and Roberts (1993) identify four types of rituals: *day-to-day essentials* that govern how members eat, sleep, greet each other, and perform other daily tasks; *family traditions* that involve the manner in which families celebrate or choose not to celebrate birthdays, anniversaries, and other milestones as well as vacation times; *holiday rituals* that revolve around calendar holidays such as Christmas, Hanukkah, Ramadan, Three King's Day, New Year's, Fourth of July, and others; and *life cycle rituals* that recognize important birth to death events like naming ceremonies, adoption days, Bar and Bat Mitzvahs, weddings, retirement, and funerals. Understanding what part these rituals play in the life of a given family may enlighten a worker as to how well the family is integrated and functions. Disengaged families may have few obvious rituals, although some rituals may not be as obvious and are even dysfunctional. For example, total inattention to special days may in itself be a ritual and may signify the family's lack of nurture toward its members. Therefore the question may arise: Can this family begin to value itself, or does this lack of value make it unable to protect and care for its children? While there are no stock answers to such questions, the recognition of the place of family rituals, especially in understanding cultural differences, may play an important piece in the intervention with this family.

Minority Family Systems

Families develop communication patterns and roles according to their own cultural values; however, even families of a specific culture may differ. For example, within the Hispanic cultures, Cuban, Puerto Rican, and Mexican families may all have different values. Even among one group (e.g., Puerto Ricans) there will be variations. How a particular family functions will depend on several variables:

1. The culture in which the family has originated
2. The subgroup of that culture (India, Puerto Rico, and many other countries from which immigrants come have caste systems. Individuals from these cultures often feel strongly about not being grouped with those from a lower caste.)
3. The individual characteristics of family members
4. The family's method of adapting to the stresses placed on it by living within the family unit

Leiberman (1990) points out that, in contrast to the individualistic culture emphasized in the United States (i.e., the idea "that a person's highest calling is to be true to him or herself" [p. 107]), many minority cultures value collectivism. Lieberman compares the two value systems by saying:

An individualistic culture is one where a person's social behavior is shaped primarily by personal goals and needs which do not necessarily overlap with the goals and needs of their in-group. Competition is stressed and cooperation is not. In contrast, in a collectivist culture the person's behavior is shaped primarily by the goals, needs, and values of the in-group, even when this involves giving up personal pursuits. These cultures tend to stress cooperation and avoid competition. There is also a high personal identification with the family and a sense of mutual obligation and responsibilities among extended family members. Personal sacrifices are expected on behalf of family welfare.... In individualistic cultures, people who sacrifice important personal goals for the sake of others may be considered masochistic, immature or overly dependent.... In a collective culture a person who *fails* to sacrifice personal goals for the welfare of others is often rebuked as selfish, disloyal, and untrustworthy. (Lieberman, 1990, p. 107)

It is this fundamental difference that creates conflict for many minority families. Due to the extent of these differences, as well as the previously mentioned variables, it is impossible to assume that any one minority family is like another. However, to begin to understand how certain minorities function within the culture, we may generalize the values espoused by each group—recognizing that it is then necessary to be particularly sensitive to the variations of individual families.

African-American Families

Kinship bonds

African-American families rely heavily on the mutual aid of those beyond the nuclear family structure. Extended family members and friends are accepted as kinsmen who provide support for the family, including such things as child care, advice, financial aid, and emotional support (Chapman and Terry, 1984; Lum, 1992; Prater, 1992; Abney and Priest, 1995). Hill (1971) found that African-American families take children from extended families or friends into their households more frequently than whites, and older black women take in the highest proportion of children. It is this reliance on kinsmen and close community spirit—perhaps originating in African tribal cultures and carried into plantation life—that has protected the children to some degree against racism by keeping them within the confines of their own community.

Self-help and self-esteem

The strong reliance on community for support and mutual aid has benefited the development of African-American children's self-esteem. In the African-American culture, children are seen as representing the continuity of life and are prized and nurtured by the whole community (Prater, 1992).

Adaptable family roles

A primary value among African-American families is that everyone is expected to work. There is equality among family members, although over the years it has become the mother who keeps the family together (Lum, 1992; Abney and Priest, 1995). Largely due to the ability of these women to find work more easily than their men, women are often the primary breadwinners. The lower socioeconomic status of African-American families with working mothers has necessitated that children perform a substantial amount of household duties. While their parents work, children may be expected to care for younger siblings, much like their own mother did in her youth. The concept of *parentified child,* with its pejorative connotation, does not take into consideration the need for these families to adjust in any way they can to ensure survival (Abney and Priest, 1995). Indeed, most poor African-American families would fail to understand why expecting so much of their children might be considered neglectful by white social workers.

Achievement and work orientation

Like many minority groups, African-American families realize that the only means for a better life for their children is through achievement and hard work. There are, however, constraints on their ability to achieve. Educational systems are not always receptive to what African-American children have been taught to value. For example, such families often teach children to be assertive and independent at an early age. Such attitudes frequently conflict with the values of modern classrooms. Racism and the failure to be sensitive to cultural differences compounds the picture (Prater, 1992).

Religious orientation

The role of the church in African-American families goes beyond the spiritual. Religion not only provides a social context but a mechanism for survival. Throughout history, religion has fortified blacks against racism from a hostile white world (Staples, 1976; Lum, 1992). Ministers often have close ties with African-American families, serving as spiritual teachers, advisors, counselors, political advocates and spokesmen, and often kinsmen. Church services frequently provide an arena where pent-up emotions can be released and supported by others in the congregation (Abney and Priest, 1995). Solomon (1989) states:

> God is never an abstraction apart from the here and now. He is personalized and included in daily life situations. It is not uncommon to hear Afro-Americans relate a conversation they had with God or with His son, Jesus Christ. Prayer is a frequent response to everyday crisis, even in those who do not profess to any deep religious convictions. (p. 574)

The African-American family's assumption that "the Lord will provide" in the face of crisis is often misinterpreted as a lack of motivation.

Communication

African-American families often communicate in analogies rather than identifying or expressing their feelings. For example, instead of identifying feelings of loneliness or depression, a mother might say, "I feel like I have no one in the world." The abstract nature of such communication is often interpreted as an inability to recognize feelings or as a lack of insight (Solomon, 1989). On the contrary, African-American families are often very much in tune with their feelings and those of others, though this may be expressed in their own characteristic manner. Leigh and Green (1983) sum up the dilemma by saying:

> Black parents appear to be confronted with the dilemma of raising their children in a tradition which is distinctively person-oriented, one that is flexible in its role expectations, in a society where rewards often go to those who are object-oriented, and who find success in highly structured living and working arrangements. (cited in Chapman and Terry, 1984, p. 247).

Hispanic-American Families

Hispanic Americans are from one of several different cultures. The 1989 Children's Defense Fund Report (cited in Delgado, 1992) gave the following demographic profile of Hispanic-American children in the United States today:

Mexican-American	62%
Puerto Rican	13%
Central and South American	12%
Other Hispanic	8%
Cuban	5%

Despite the differences in the origins of these groups, it is possible to make some generalizations about the values and functioning of Hispanic families.

Family ties and values

Hispanic-American families are more likely to be living as single-parent families than the general population (Delgado, 1992), yet there is a strong reliance on the extended family. *Extended families* consist not only of blood relatives but may also include friends (often the children's godparents) and those who share living space. For example, it is not uncommon for families to buy an apartment complex together and maintain strong survival-oriented or cultural bonds.

The *compadrazzo,* or the system of using compadres, is an integral institution among Hispanic-American families, especially Mexican-American and Puerto Rican. Compadres are godparents or sponsors (*padrinos*) to children who are named at baptism and maintain an extremely close relationship to both the parents and children. Children are treated as if they are the compadre's own and even given a home if the need arises (Lum, 1992; Mizio, 1989; Delgado, 1992). Too often these important individuals are overlooked by child welfare workers who instead place children in unrelated foster homes.

Within the family itself, the father is the undisputed authority. He receives respect and allegiance. One value that is much misunderstood is that of *machismo.* This value, often given a negative interpretation by the larger society, is more positively and accurately associated with a male's sense of honor, courage, and responsibility to his family, both nuclear and extended. It is the father's (or older male's) role to keep the family together—to protect and provide for them. Family is all-important to the Hispanic father's role. His inability to have children, especially sons, leads to questions about his maleness (Comas-Diaz, 1995). Unfortunately, this sense of pride and family position is greatly threatened in the Hispanics' adopted culture of the United States. Since it is easier for the women to find employment, Hispanic men often feel depressed and thus unable to command respect from their families (Delgado, 1992; Mizio, 1989). Family tension and sometimes violence may result as aggression is condoned when a man's machismo is challenged (Mizio, 1989).

Comas-Diaz (1995) suggests that the position of the Puerto Rican women is often overlooked. This Latina has more power in her home than her white counterparts and is often vital to family decision making.

Other important values of the Hispanic family are *dignidad, respecto,* and *personalismo. Dignidad* refers to dignity or the inherent unique importance of each individual.

Respecto involves adherence to hierarchical relationships; elders must be respected. *Personalismo* describes the Hispanic value of person-to-person contact and close relationships. Hispanic families shun large impersonal bureaucracies, instead preferring close personal involvements with individuals (Mizio, 1989).

Religion

Catholicism, the predominant religion of Hispanics, plays an extremely important role in family life. The church provides support and comfort as well as often the focus of social activities. Much of *barrio* (Hispanic community) life revolves around the church. Besides teaching about moral and ethical behavior, churches within the community also provide services such as financial aid, housing, rehabilitation programs, and a host of other social services (Lum, 1992; Morales and Salcido, 1989; Delgado, 1992).

Folkhealers

In addition to dependence on organized religion, Hispanic families also espouse the concept of folkhealers. Mexican-Americans, particularly in the southwest, are known for their use of "curanderismo." Perhaps due to the firm belief in folk medicine or the folk healers' understanding of their clients, these practices appear to be especially effective (Delgado, 1992).

Communication

The concept of *respecto,* as it governs attitudes toward authority figures, may distort the Hispanic family's relationship with the larger culture. Lieberman (1990) describes how Hispanic mothers' belief in graciousness and sociability and the social worker's lack of understanding of this interferes with the communication between client and worker. Mothers who were asked to schedule appointments with workers (whom they saw in an authority position) felt compelled to comply but did not keep the appointments. Faced with repeated incidents of this behavior, Leiberman and colleagues finally recognized the cultural implications.

Hispanics, placed under extreme stress and unhappiness, appear to translate their distress into somatic complaints. Rather than openly admitting their psychological suffering, they are more likely to complain of headaches, stomach distress, or other physiological ailments (Derezotes and Snowden, 1990).

Asian and Pacific Island Families

Asian and Pacific Island families are perhaps the most difficult to generalize because of the variety of cultures included in this category. When one speaks of *Asian,* the reference may be to Chinese, Japanese, Filipino, Vietnamese, Cambodian, Thai, Laotian, Indian, Indonesian, Korean, or Pakistani. *Pacific Islanders* encompass Hawaiian, Tamoan, Malasian, Tongon, Guamanian, and Micronesian cultures (Mass and Yap, 1992; Ho, 1989). Mass and Yap (1992) identify two major cultural orientations: "(1) Confucianism, which predominates in northern Asian countries such as China, Japan, Korea and Vietnam and (2) A combination of Hindu Malayan Polynesian cultures that predominate in the southern countries such as India, the Philippines, Indonesia, Malaysia, as well as the Pacific Islands" (p. 111). Although there are some similarities (discussed below), each cultural orientation must also be understood.

Family ties and values

The Asian/Pacific Island culture is another that demonstrates a hierarchical structure with male dominance and well-defined roles. One particular people espousing these values is the Hmongs—one of the newest groups of refugees. Unlike many of those immigrating to the United States, the Hmongs' exodus is involuntary. Most of these immigrants state that they would have preferred to stay in their native Laos or Thailand, where many fled initially, but these countries were unable or unwilling to let them stay. Now, large groups of extended families or clans have settled, primarily in the areas of California, Texas, Minnesota, Wisconsin, and Rhode Island, in numbers that exceed 100,000 (McInnis, 1991). Since the Hmong come from agrarian, isolated areas, their enculturation into the United States has been difficult. They are often seen as part of public assistance caseloads, as they are at a loss for understanding how to survive on their own in this industrialized society.

Clan leaders still maintain a strong hold over family members and act as arbitrators between the clan and the outside world. Family members often will not cooperate with social service systems unless the clan leader is intimately involved in the process. From a subculture that condones severe physical punishment of children, Hmong parents do not understand why protective service agencies intervene. Only by enlisting the support and trust of clan leaders can social workers hope to be effective with these families (McInnis, 1991).

In Asian cultures, the older generation is revered. Whether these individuals are clan leaders, as among the Hmongs, or merely the family's grandparents, family ties bind together each member in an intricate hierarchy of respect. Filial piety (parents are respected and obeyed) is of primary importance, but the male of the oldest generation has the highest rank. Individuals, although important, see themselves in relationship to the family and its well-being. Autonomous behavior on the part of an individual would be considered a rejection of family values. Accomplishments are not individual endeavors, but efforts to bring

honor to the family. Family honor is greatly valued, and shame (over the possible compromise of this honor) is a powerful method used to ensure that children and adults do nothing to disgrace the family. The sometimes intense use of shaming children is often interpreted by non-Asian professionals as emotionally abusive (Mass and Yap, 1992; Ho, 1989; Okamura et al., 1995).

One type of loss of family honor avoided at all cost by Asian families is the sexual misuse of female children. For example, the highest priorities for a Vietnamese female child growing to adulthood are her virginity and good behavior. Many southeast Asian cultures believe that a female who has been sexually violated is not honorable enough to be allowed to marry. Thus she becomes an outcast (Mollica and Son, 1989).

Harmony and self-esteem

Harmony is a dominant aspect especially of the Confucian value system. Individuals are expected to subordinate their needs to the group and to use self-control and self-restraint in the expression of their own needs. Self-esteem is tied into how well one is able to avoid conflict and to submit to the needs of others (Mass and Yap, 1992). Asian/Pacific Islander children are taught that to take a middle position gives them a sense of belonging and togetherness with others (Ho, 1989).

Religion and fatalism

The religions of Asians vary. Confucianism and Buddhism are the foundation for the moral principles of respect for one's ancestors, filial piety, and the avoidance of shame (Lum, 1992). Hindus and Moslems are also often involved with their religions as more of a code of living than any actual worship. More recently, some Asians have been integrated into the Roman Catholic and Protestant faiths (Lum, 1992).

Most Asian cultures practice some type of fatalism—or an adapted philosophical detachment. Whether this is the Indian belief in karma (the belief that behavior in one life affects one's fate in the next) or the resignation of people who have been buffeted by political events over which they have had little control, the Asian may treat events as inevitable. This fatalistic acceptance not only makes the Asian family less likely to seek help but is also often interpreted by nonculturally aware professionals as resistance or a lack of caring (Ho, 1989).

Communication

The hierarchical nature of the family necessitates that communication begins at the top (oldest male) and filters down. Western professionals, schooled by our culture to be direct and open, may find the nature of communication with Asian/Pacific Islanders difficult. In addition to the need to address the highest in authority, direct questions or eye contact are often seen as disrespectful. The Asians' attempt at self-control will keep their affect calm. Some clients' response of "yes" to an idea or suggestion means only "Yes, I heard you," rather than compliance with the suggestion. It is particularly important to understand the cultural values of the particular client in order to facilitate communication.

Native American Families

Native American tribes vary almost as much as the Asians previously discussed. Customs are based on centuries of culture that has been adopted according to geographic location and individual tribal rituals. Once again, an understanding of the particular tribe is important.

Family ties and values

Native American families are structured not so much with the inclusion of extended family members as with total reliance on grandparents as the official and symbolic leaders of the family and their community. Grandparents have the ultimate say in child-rearing practices and are rarely contradicted by parents (Lum, 1992).

Sharing is perhaps the primary value of Native Americans. Accumulation of goods is a foreign concept; what one has is given freely to others. By the same token, child rearing is a shared activity. Children are allowed to roam freely throughout the community, with the assumption that they are the responsibility of the entire group. It is also felt that children learn from experience. Gray and Cosgrove (1985) describe how a very young child, at a powwow, was observed by a number of adults, including his mother, sticking his finger in the fire. The burned finger he received may have prevented future experimentation with fire, but observing this may also have made those not familiar with the Native American philosophy question why no one intervened.

Native American families also believe that one must endure the natural happenings that affect one's life, and thus suffering is an integral part of growing up. They contend that in spite of this suffering, or perhaps because of it, man will triumph because he is ultimately good. This philosophy, perhaps based on the attempts to survive amidst extreme poverty and land disputes, has been called by Lewis and Ho (1989) a kind of "optimistic toughness."

Native American families teach their children to control their emotions. As adults, they are expected to relate to others with poise, self-containment, and even aloofness. Indeed, the family keeps its problems to itself. Noninterference is important. To protest a perceived injustice, the Native American will use silence or withdrawal.

Religion/spirituality

The beliefs of the Native American are based in a complex manner on the healing power of nature. Nature is associated with life itself and the two must remain in harmony. Community religious rites are a fundamental part of living. The type of ceremonies enacted depend largely on the customs of each particular tribe (Lum, 1992).

Communication

Native Americans believe in the dignity of the individual, but that the individual is an integral part of the universe. Each person should respect and revere another.

Another fundamental view is the virtue of patience. With the knowledge and recognition that the universe is unfolding as it should, parents teach their children that one may have to wait for what is desired. In our fast-paced society, with its instant gratification, this quality is sometimes interpreted erroneously by outsiders as laziness (Lewis and Ho, 1989).

Along with patience, Native American children learn a different perception of time. Time is not measured by the clock but rather by natural events (moons, seasons, etc.). Congeniality is more valuable than time; thus if one meets a friend on the way to an appointment, conversation will take precedence (Lewis and Ho, 1989).

Family Problems and Dysfunction

Every family faces problems in its day-to-day life. Many are able to overcome them, but those families that cannot conquer their problems cease to function in a manner that encourages the positive growth of their members. Failing to meet common problems compounds the problems. These failures can be organized into four categories:

1. Failure to complete basic family tasks
2. Failure in dealing with changes associated with developmental tasks
3. Failure to deal with crises
4. Failure to deal with societal pressures (which may include pressures from a different culture)

Failure to complete basic tasks includes the family's inability to provide food, shelter, protection, and education for its members. When they are unable to handle the most basic of needs, such families may come to the attention of agencies.

Other families are able to complete the tasks expected of them until some member or members reach developmental milestones, presenting behavior that upsets the family balance. The most obvious, perhaps, is the family whose children are becoming teenagers. Suddenly the autonomy the children expect and the manner in which they behave to get it is too distressing for the parents, and the family may well have difficulties. The budding sexuality of the teenager can also create problems for other members of the family. For example, one incestuous father described his problems as beginning when his daughter approached adolescence. His wife, unable to cope with the girl's rebelliousness, retreated into her own career. The father began to have quiet talks with his daughter in an attempt to understand her. He described being stimulated by these talks, and suddenly realized she had become quite sexually attractive. The pathology of this abuser and the emotional neediness of the daughter created a family atmosphere that necessitated intervention.

Even before a child reaches adolescence, some parents have difficulty with developmental milestones. The birth of a child, the autonomy sought by a 2-year-old, a child's entrance into school—all have the potential for changing the family balance and creating problems.

Crises can also tax a family's ability to cope (Zastrow, 1993). Illness, death, unemployment, and natural disasters (e.g., fire or flood) force a family to mobilize its resources in order to deal with the event and its consequences. Some families do this well, whereas others are unable to make the necessary adjustments and need outside help.

Another problem confronting some families is prejudice. The minority family faced with the constant need to overcome the societally imposed stigma of color, race, or nationality may have difficulty functioning. For example, some families in a predominantly Puerto Rican neighborhood had adapted themselves to their new society, but Carmen Valasquez had difficulty. Her family had come from Puerto Rico where they enjoyed a certain status in their society. Now, finding herself a member of a minority, she resented what she perceived as her family's "demotion" in social status and was frustrated with the housing and employment she seemed forced to accept. Her depression permeated the family.

The Greybank family experienced similar resentments. Life on the reservation had its own pressures, not totally conducive to a family's well-being. Migrant workers, newly immigrated Asians, and other minorities find that it is not easy to raise children in a culture that does not reflect their views.

Another stigma not related to race or culture is society's attitude about who can and cannot raise children effectively. The mentally retarded and the mentally ill are two populations that have fought hard to prove their ability to be parents.

Sometimes family problems and the failure to cope with them overlap, and the family moves in and out of constant crisis. Often referred to as the *multiproblem family,* these families invariably need help and are frequently the clients of protective services workers.

The Family and Child Maltreatment

Along with the functions, roles, and responsibilities of the family, there are two factors associated with the family's position that actually contribute to the continuation of child maltreatment. These are society's belief in the sanctity of the family and the disproportionate emphasis afforded the rights of parents compared to the rights of children.

Parents' Rights

Goldstein, Freud, and Solnit, in their controversial book *Beyond the Best Interests of the Child* (1973), argue vehemently for the sanctity of the family. The parent-child relationship, they contend, is the basis on which a child's emotional growth depends. Only when parents fail to nurture that child's growth in the most minimal way should intervention be considered.

In 1981, Senators Robert Jepson (Iowa) and Paul Laxalt (Nevada) sponsored a bill that would have made even more private the interactions between children and their parents, even including the parents' right to physically punish at will. Had the bill passed, children might have been even less protected from abuse than they are now (Nelson, 1984, p. 9). The actual consideration of such a bill, however, is indicative of our nation's continued support for the parents' right to do with their children what they will. Our comfort with allowing parents complete jurisdiction over children is based on our expectations of adequate parenting rather than our recognition of the painful statistics of the incidences of child maltreatment and parental failure. Certainly most parents would feel extremely hampered if the government intervened randomly. The assumption is made by parents that "we are doing our job, leave us alone," and in a large percentage of homes this is true. But what of the parents who vehemently contend they are doing their jobs, but are, in fact, subjecting their children to behavior that is considered by the greater society as abusive? What of the child whose premature introduction to adult sexuality is rationalized by a parent as educating or being affectionate toward the child? This is where children's rights enter the picture.

Children's Rights

In an era when society is obsessed with the discussion of individual rights, the rights of children are often overlooked. Despite a few attempts to clearly delineate these entitlements, children's rights are more likely to be defined by virtue of what their parents do or do not do for them. The family, as mentioned, is expected to provide for the basic needs of the child. From the birth of their children, parents have the right to and are entrusted with the care, custody, and control of their children. For young children, parents are also the link with the outside world. These children may, therefore, have no opportunity to have any needs met except those their parents decide are important.

Too young to identify their own needs, too inarticulate to express their hurts, and unable to attract the attention of third parties, a child's access to need, health, or medical care, to adequate food, clothing and shelter rests with the absolute decision of his caretakers. This, in turn rests on the assumption that a child's parents can identify their child's needs and will provide the necessary care and support. From the date that a child is born and leaves the hospital, until the date that the child enters school, the identification of needs (at whatever standard) and the delivery of needed services rests solely with his parent. (Fraser, 1976, p. 328)

Given this reality, what are the rights of children and how do we define them? Goldstein, Freud, and Solnit list some of the child's needs:

The child's body needs to be tended, nourished and protected. His intellect needs to be stimulated and alerted to the happenings in his environment. He needs help in understanding and organizing his sensations and perceptions. He needs people to love, receive an affection from and to serve as safe targets for his infantile anger and aggression. He needs assistance from adults in curbing and modifying his primitive drives (sex and aggression). He needs patterns for identification by the parents, to build up a functioning moral conscience. As much as anything else, he needs to be accepted, valued, and wanted as a member of the family unit consisting of adults as well as other children. (1973, pp. 13–14)

Outlining the child's needs makes the assumption that these will be met by virtue of parental responsibilities. But to what is the child actually *entitled?* What of *society's* obligation to provide for children? A parent may have every intention of meeting his or her children's needs. The problem arises if that parent is poor or of a racial/ethnic minority (which some refer to as *structured racism*) and cannot provide an adequate income or housing. How, then, are children's rights defined?

Gustavsson and Segal (1994) contend that children's only rights are defined by two mandatory services—financial aid and education. But even when it comes to the right to financial support and education, some children fall through the cracks. Children in fact have no clearly established rights. The only rights are negative—rights expressed when the parents fail to meet their responsibilities. Only after parents do not properly care, control, or maintain custody is the child seen to have rights. When the parents have failed to supply this care and if the system works as it should, then the child will be provided with medical care (through Medicaid), financial security through Aid to Families with Dependent Children, and shelter (with foster home placement). Thus children are seen as potential adults, but they do not benefit from the rights given adults. Instead, it is assumed that they have no real rights but only needs, unless the adults to whom they are entrusted are found to have failed. If these adults fail because of the inequities of the society they live in, the children are the ultimate sufferers.

There have been attempts to further delineate the rights of children. The New York State Youth Commission drafted the Young People's Bill of Rights which states:

We The People of New York State Believe In The Right of Every Child To:
1. Affection, Love, Guidance and Understanding from parents and teachers.
2. Adequate Nutrition and Medical care to aid mental, physical and social growth.

3. Free education to develop individual abilities and to become a useful member of society.
4. Special care, if handicapped.
5. Opportunity for recreation in a wholesome, well-rounded environment.
6. An environment that reflects peace and mutual concern.
7. The opportunity for sound moral development.
8. Constructive discipline to help develop responsibility and character.
9. Good adult examples to follow.
10. A future commensurate with abilities and aspirations.
11. Enjoyment of all these rights, regardless of race, color, sex, religion, national or social origin. (New York State Division for Youth).

In 1989, the General Assembly of the United Nations formulated the Declaration of the Rights of the Child (see Figure 2.1). Unfortunately, few have heard of these suggestions of children's rights, nor have they been made into law or operational. In fact, contends O'Hagan (1993), the abuses against children on a national level have intensified.

FIGURE 2.1   Summary of the Universal Declaration of Human Rights

The Preamble states that the child, because of his [or her] physical and mental immaturity, needs special safeguards and care, both before and after birth, and that individuals and groups should strive to achieve children's rights by legislative and other means. [Humanity], it says, owes the child the best it has to give.

In ten carefully worded principles, the declaration affirms that all children are entitled to

1. the enjoyment of the rights mentioned, without any exception whatsoever, regardless of race, color, sex, religion, or nationality;
2. special protection, opportunities, and facilities to enable them to develop in a healthy and normal manner, in freedom and dignity;
3. a name and nationality;
4. social security; including adequate nutrition, housing, recreation, and medical services;
5. special treatment, education, and care if handicapped;
6. love and understanding and an atmosphere of affection and security, in the care and under the responsibility of their parents whenever possible;
7. free education and recreation and equal opportunity to develop their individual abilities;
8. prompt protection and relief in times of disaster;
9. protection against all forms of neglect, cruelty, and exploitation;
10. protection from any form of racial, religious, or other discrimination, and an upbringing in a spirit of peace and universal brotherhood.

Finally, the General Assembly resolved that governments, nongovernmental organizations, and individuals should give this declaration the widest possible publicity as a means of encouraging its observance everywhere.

United Nations Declaration of the Rights of the Child

A five-point Declaration of the Rights of the Child was stated in 1923 by the International Union for Child Welfare, with 1948 revisions in a seven-point document. The League of Nations adopted the IUCW declaration in 1924. The Declaration of the Rights of the Child was adopted by the United Nations General Assembly in 1959.

Based on the United Nations, General Assembly Resolution 1386 (XIV), November 20, 1959, published in the *Official Records of the General Assembly, Fourteenth Session, Supplement No. 16, 1960.*

One of the difficulties in the adoption of a declaration of rights for children is in the interpretation. For example, the Young People's Bill of Rights states that a child has the right to receive "good adult examples." What constitutes a "good" example? This is hardly as tangible as an adult's right to vote or to own a driver's license. It would be difficult, therefore, to protect children when their stated entitlements are subject to interpretation.

Impact on the Child Protection Movement

What impact does our failure to delineate children's rights have on the efforts to protect them from abuse? Perhaps one is to find other methods of primary prevention. Until recently, society assumed that if no one noticed otherwise, the child's growth and development was progressing as expected. Only when contrary evidence was obvious was there intervention. Thus children are not protected until the damage is done. Intervention—before the problem exists—through giving the family more support through primary prevention (see Chapter 18) is clearly needed.

A solution to one type of maltreatment—physical abuse—might be to pass a law, as Sweden has done, prohibiting corporal punishment of children. In this country we are hesitant to limit adult rights or intervene in family life in this manner. Some critics outlining the problems this law has created for Sweden argue against implementing such a statute in the United States. Apparently most people are not ready or able to create a bill of rights for children that can be adopted. Thus people are left with the framework of the family unit as vital to the growth of children but with the need to further protect children where families fail. The debate continues. How can we best protect our children and still continue to give the family room to function? Until this question is answered, professionals can only improve their intervention and treatment practices and look for new methods of prevention.

Summary

The family, despite numerous changes, remains the fundamental societal unit responsible for the care and nurture of children. Today the family may be nuclear, extended, blended, single-parent, communal, or cohabitant. Families can also be defined by virtue of their function, their legal ties, their biological ties, the members' perceptions of who is family, and the members' long-term commitment to each other.

Parents are expected to have specific responsibilities in the areas of reproduction, socialization, assignment of social roles, economic production and consumption, and emotional support. The family is a complex system made up of smaller subsystems. The boundaries between these subsystems give members freedom to operate and promote better functioning of the total family unit. Each family member is assigned or assumes a series of roles that also promote family functioning. Some of these roles are helpful, but others are

dysfunctional and add to or create family problems. Within these roles a family communicates. Communication can be overt or indirect and unclear. Patterns of communication repeated over time become family rules—or the standards that dictate the behavior of family members.

Every family has problems in everyday living, but some fail to solve these problems effectively. The four types of issues that prevent adequate family functioning are (1) failure to complete basic tasks, (2) failure to adapt to changes brought on by developmental tasks, (3) failure to deal with crises, and (4) failure to deal with societal pressures.

Once people understand how the family operates, they see its place in society today. But two factors in the "agreement" between society and the family actually contribute to child maltreatment. The first is society's belief in the sanctity of the family: As long as the family appears to be completing the tasks expected of it (especially in relation to the children), society will not intervene. The problem is that many abusive or neglectful families hide their behavior. The second is that society places little value on children, affording them few rights compared to those for parents. Perhaps the solution lies partly in better prevention efforts, which will be discussed in Chapter 17.

Exploration Questions

1. What types of families are there in today's society?

2. What criteria can we use to define a family?

3. What are the responsibilities of parents?

4. What are subsystems? Boundaries?

5. What are roles?

6. What are family rules?

7. Cite some differences in values or family relationships in the following:
   - The African-American family
   - The Hispanic-American family
   - The Asian/Pacific Island family
   - The Native American family

8. Cite the four problem categories that may face families. Can you think of examples of each?

9. How might societal beliefs or biases in relation to the family contribute to the incidence of child maltreatment?

10. What is meant by the sanctity of the family?

11. Why don't children have rights?

Activities for Applied Learning

1. Make a list of the responsibilities of parents. Interview several parents to determine what they feel their responsibilities are.

2. See if you can list 10 family rules from your family of origin. Discuss and compare these in class or in small groups. How did you know these were rules? How did your ethnic origin affect these rules?

3. Read *Beyond the Best Interests of the Child* by Goldstein, Freud, and Solnit. Why might this book be so controversial?

4. After reading the above book, set up a debate. Have one panel of students espouse the philosophy of the book and the other contend that children have the right to be protected and that their emotional well-being is at greater risk by being with less-than-adequate parents. What are your conclusions?

5. Design your own Bill of Rights for Children. How could you make it operational? What would the implications be?

6. Collect new articles on proposed changes to the welfare system, parental rights, and substitute child care. Discuss as a class what effects these shifting values may have on child protection in the future.

Suggested Readings

Goldenstein, J., Freud, A., and Solnit, J. *Beyond the Best Interests of the Child.* New York: Free Press, 1973.

Herbert, M. *Working with Children and Their Families.* Chicago: Lyceum, 1989.

Karpel, M., and Strauss, E. S. *Family Evaluation.* New York: Gardner Press, 1983.

Mayhall, P., and Norgard, K. E. *Child Abuse and Neglect: Shared Responsibility.* New York: Macmillan, 1986.

References

Abney, V., and Priest, R. "African Americans and Sexual Child Abuse." In L. A. Fontes (ed.), *Sexual Abuse in Nine North American Cultures.* Thousand Oaks, CA: Sage, 1995, pp. 11–30.

Berns, R. M. *Child, Family, Community.* New York: Holt, Rinehart and Winston, 1985.

Chapman, S. B., and Terry, T. "Treatment of Sexually Abused Children from Minority Urban Families: A Socio-cultural Perspective." *Clinical Proceedings Children's National Medical Center.* Vol. 40, pp. 244–59. Washington, D.C.: Children's National Medical Center, 1984.

Comas-Diaz, L. "Puerto Ricans and Child Sexual Abuse." In L. A. Fontes (ed.), *Sexual Abuse in Nine North American Cultures.* Thousand Oaks, CA: Sage, 1995, pp. 31–66.

Delgado, R. "Generalist Child Welfare and Hispanic Families." In *Child Welfare: A Multicultural Perspective,* edited by N. Cohen. Boston: Allyn and Bacon, 1992.

Derezotes, D. S., and Snowden, L. R. "Cultural Factors in the Intervention of Child Maltreatment." *Child and Adolescent Social Work* 7, no. 2 (1990):161–75.

Fraser, B. G. "The Child and His Parents: A Delicate Balance of Rights." In *Child Abuse and Neglect: The Family and the Community,* edited by R. E. Helfer and C. H. Kempe, pp. 316–333. Cambridge, MA, 1976.

Goldenberg, I., and Goldenberg, H. *Family Therapy: An Overview.* Monterey, CA: Brooks Cole, 1980.

Goldstein, J., Freud, A., and Solnit, J. *Beyond the Best Interests of the Child.* New York: Free Press, 1973.

Gray, E., and Cosgrove, J. "Ethnocentric Perception of Child Rearing Practice in Protective Services." *Child Abuse and Neglect* 9 (1985):389–96.

Gross, B., and Gross, H. *The Children's Rights Movement.* Garden City, NY: Doubleday, Anchor Press, 1977.

Gustavsson, N. S., and Segal, E. A. *Critical Issues in Child Welfare.* Thousand Oaks, CA: Sage, 1994.

Harvard Education Review. *Rights of Children.* Cambridge, MA.: Harvard Education Review, 1974.

Herbert, M. *Working with Children and their Families.* Chicago: Lyceum, 1989.

Hess, B. B.; Markson, E. W.; and Stein, P. J. *Sociology.* New York: Macmillan, 1993.

Hill, R. B. *The Strength of Black Families.* New York: Emerson Hall, 1971.

Ho, M. K. "Social Work Practice with Asian Americans." In *Social Work: A Profession of Many Faces,* edited by A. Morales and B. W. Sheafor. Boston: Allyn and Bacon, 1989.

Imber-Black, E., and Roberts, J. *Rituals for Our Times.* New York: Harper Perennial, 1993.

Karpel, M., and Strauss, E. S. *Family Evaluation.* New York: Gardner Press, 1983.

Katz, S. N. *When Parents Fail.* Boston: Beacon Press, 1971.

Leiberman, A. F. "Culturally Sensitive Intervention with Children and Families." *Child and Adolescent Social Work* 7, no. 2 (1990):101–19.

Leigh, J. W., and Green, J. W. "The Black Family and Social Work." *Permanency Planning: The Black Experience—A Training Curriculum.* Knoxville: University of Tennessee, 1983.

Lewis, R. G., and Ho, M. K. "Social Work with Native Americans." In *Social Work: A Profession of Many Faces,* edited by A. Morales and B. W. Sheafor (pp. 511–19). Boston: Allyn and Bacon, 1989.

Lum, D. *Social Work Practice and People of Color,* 2nd ed. Monterey, CA: Brooks Cole, 1992 (1st ed., 1986).

Mass, A. I., and Yap, J. "Child Welfare: Asian Pacific Island Families." In *Child Welfare: A Multicultural Perspective,* edited by N. Cohen (pp. 107–29). Boston: Allyn and Bacon, 1992.

McInnis, K. "Ethnic-Sensitive Work with Hmong Refugee Children." *Child Welfare* 70, no. 5 (Sept.–Oct. 1991):571–80.

Mindel, C. H., and Habenstein, R. W. *Ethnic Families in America: Patterns and Variations.* New York: Elsevier, 1981.

Minuchin, S. *Families and Family Therapy.* Cambridge, MA: Harvard University Press, 1981.

Mizio, E. "The Impact of Macro Systems on Puerto Rican Families." In *Social Work: A Profession of Many Faces,* edited by A. Morales and B. W. Sheafor (pp. 483–519). Boston: Allyn and Bacon, 1989.

Mollica, R. F., and Son, L. "Cultural Dimensions in the Evaluation and Treatment of Sexual Trauma." *Psychiatric Clinics of North America* 12, no. 2 (June 1989):363–79.

Morales, A., and Salcido, R. "Social Work with Mexican Americans." *Social Work: A Profession of Many Faces,* edited by A. Morales and B. W. Sheafor (pp. 543–64). Boston: Allyn and Bacon, 1989.

Nelson, B. *Making an Issue of Child Abuse.* Chicago: University of Chicago Press, 1984.

O'Hagen, K. *Emotional and Psychological Abuse of Children.* Toronto: University of Toronto Press, 1993.

Okamura, A., Hieras, P., and Wong-Kerberg, L. "Asian, Pacific Island and Filipino Americans and Sexual Abuse." In L. A. Fontes (ed.), *Sexual Abuse in Nine North American Cultures.* Thousand Oaks, CA: Sage, 1995, pp. 67–96.

Prater, G. S. "Child Welfare and African-American Families." In *Child Welfare: A Multicultural Perspective,* edited by N. Cohen (pp. 84–106). Boston: Allyn and Bacon, 1992.

Price, J. A. "North American Indian Families." In *Ethnic Families in America: Patterns and Variations,* edited by C. Mindel and R. W. Habenstein (pp. 245–68). New York: Elsevier, 1981.

Skolnick, A. S., and Skolnick, J. H. *Family in Transition: Rethinking Marriage Sexuality, Child Rearing and Family Organization.* Boston: Little, Brown, 1977.

Solomon, B. B. "Social Work with Afro-Americans." In *Social Work: A Profession of Many Faces,* edited by A. Morales and B. W. Sheafor (pp. 567–86). Boston: Allyn and Bacon, 1989.

Staples, R. "The Black American Family." In *Ethnic Families in America: Patterns and Variations,* edited by C. H. Mindel and R. W. Habenstein (pp. 217–44). New York: Elsevier, 1981.

Tower, C. C. "Child Abuse and Neglect." In *Child Welfare: A Multicultural Perspective,* edited by N. Cohen (pp. 157–91). Boston: Allyn and Bacon, 1992.

Vardin, P. A., and Brody, I. *Children's Rights: Contemporary Perspectives.* New York: Teachers College Press, 1979.

Zastrow, C. *Introduction to Social Work and Social Welfare.* Pacific Grove, CA: Brooks/Cole, 1993.

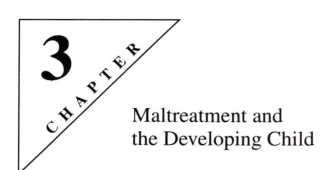

Maltreatment and the Developing Child

Normal development for the abused and neglected child can be a problem. Consider all the motor skills children must learn: crawling, walking, running, speaking, controlling the bladder and bowels, writing, and so on. Helfer, McKinney, and Kempe suggest that to become healthy individuals, children must learn to

1. Set priorities and plan ahead.
2. Trust others.
3. Make friends.
4. Develop a good self-image.
5. Differentiate between feeling and behavior.
6. Get their needs met in an acceptable manner. (1976, pp. 56–57)

Yet learning these lessons necessitates the stable consistent guidance of caregivers, an experience not always available to the abused or neglected child.

In studies with abused and neglected children, researchers and practitioners have found two types of parenting that affect the development of the abused child. The first type of parent-child relationship is fraught with conflict. Unstable, immature parents, whose own childhood needs are still unmet, are faced with children who demand their time and limited psychic energies. The result is impaired bonding, emotional deprivation, and eventually role reversal as these parents place their children in the position of meeting the parents' needs. Neglectful—as well as some sexually and physically abusive—parents often exhibit this type of parent-child relationship. For the physically abused child, this deprivation in parenting has a more profound effect than the physical abuse itself.

The second type of parent-child relationship pattern is more likely to be exhibited by physically, and sometimes sexually, abusive parents. In the physically abusive family, the child is wanted and expected but the desire carries with it a complex set of extremely high expectations. For the physically abusive parent, it can be the child's failure to meet these expectations that creates anger and frustration and results in abuse. Or the abuse is seen by the parent as "normal" discipline designed to create obedience or mold the child to meet the parent's expectations (Martin, 1976b; Tzeng et al., 1991).

For sexually abusive parents, the abuse often results from the parents' disillusionment with themselves and others in their lives, whom they perceive as having failed to meet their expectations. Life is not what they had envisioned. The unmet needs that these parents harbor, but hide so well, surface and return to the child for satisfaction of these needs. Thus the idealized child becomes the target for the sexual exploitation.

Both types of parents have difficulty seeing their children as separate entities from themselves. But this inability to allow room for the child's individual growth[1] creates distinct problems in the child's development. Children learn in several ways: by association, through outcome, and by observation (Helfer, McKinney, and Kempe, 1976). When a child learns by association that a parent's angry voice means that he or she will also be hit, that child may then generalize and demonstrate a fear of all adults. A toddler who attempts to demonstrate his or her autonomy by running when the parent says "come" may discover that the outcome is a beating. The child then learns that autonomy is not encouraged, and an important part of his or her growth suffers. And finally, children who observe their parents using violence to express frustration or anger learn that violent behavior is acceptable. Children, whose parents explicitly demonstrate the answers to sexual questions by rationalizing that they are "lovingly teaching their children," are robbed of the ability to differentiate between sexuality and affection (Howing et al., 1993; O'Hagan, 1993).

How and at what stages are the developmental tasks of childhood arrested by inconsistent or inadequate parenting?

Developmental Stages

Pregnancy and Birth

Even before the birth of a child, the future relationship between parents and child is determined. The atmosphere, attitudes, and expectations surrounding the conception of the baby are the first factors that influence the potential bonding experience. The mother's and father's motivations for conception must be considered. Was conception a planned or hoped-for event? Were the reasons for this anticipation healthy? Is the child a replacement for another or a last effort to solve a failing marriage? Was the pregnancy a mistake, a dreaded inconvenience? Or do the parents disagree on any of these questions? The relationship of the mother and father has an impact on their ability to accept and want the baby, as does the maturity, stability, and mental health of each of the parents. In fact, their own past experiences may have a significant impact on their ability to parent (Weston et al., 1993; Hanson et al., 1994).

Pregnancy can be a time of trauma for many mothers. Not only does a woman's body change but there is a realignment of her perceptions, her needs, and her relationships with others. The mother who finds these changes extremely difficult may attribute her discomfort to her baby. Another mother, feeling a need for nurturing, may welcome pregnancy as a time when she is pampered and coddled, but forget the true significance of her situation—that she is incubating a new life.

Caplan (1960) suggests that pregnancy necessitates a mother adapt in two ways. First, she must recognize the fetus as a part of herself; second, she must accept that the fetus is also a separate individual. The second phase becomes more obvious when the fetal movements begin. The mother's style of handling these adaptations can be significant. Fetal movements impress on the parents that the imminent arrival of the child is a reality. Any conflict the mother has in her attitude toward this new individual can be embodied in her reaction to fetal movements.

The father's contribution during pregnancy should not be underestimated. His presence, his ability to support, and his acceptance of both mother and baby can greatly influence the later parent-child relationships for both him and the mother. Brazelton (1963) suggests that this necessity of supporting the mother creates upheaval for the father as well. Rarely does he feel that he has others available to support him. It should be noted that different cultures see the role of the expectant father differently.

The expectations built up during pregnancy by both mother and father are significant to the later relationship. The potentially neglectful or abusive parent—especially the mother—may not be considering the joys of caring for a helpless dependent baby so much as the satisfaction to be gained from the baby. These mothers have described anticipating how much the babies will love them. They have spoken of reveling in the thought of how good and how idyllic their babies will be. For most of these mothers, reality means disillusionment. The birth itself is not what they had anticipated. Studies show that babies born to these mothers are 2 to 4 times more likely to be premature than other babies. They are 10 times as likely to be born by caesarean section (Martin, 1976a).

Control is an important issue for the abusing parent. Fear of being out of control permeates his or her life. Yet modern technology often takes control from this mother at a time when she most needs it. Anesthesia, emergency or unplanned caesareans, and the often-unexplained procedures of modern medicine render the mother feeling helpless and out of control. The mother who actively participates in her delivery—through natural childbirth or controlled breathing—is more likely to transfer the comfort in her own control over the birth to a positive relationship with her infant (Kennell, Voos, and Klaus, 1976). Again, culture plays such an important role in how the birth process is viewed. Families who are denied their cultural traditions in order to satisfy the policies of a particular medical community may feel the strain in their future relationship with their children.

Studies have underlined the significance of the timing and circumstances of the first contact between mother and child and the effect of this early interchange on bonding. Lynch (1976) found that a significant number of abused mothers and infants were separated early in the child's life.

Other authors stress the importance of how well the child meets the mother's expectations. Does the baby look as the mother had expected? Is he or she attractive? Is he as light or dark as the mother has hoped? Is the mother aware that the baby cannot as yet make eye contact, smile, or behave in what could be perceived as a "loving way"? The father may be influenced by these same factors. His ability to handle the differences between his expectations and his baby can have an influence on the mother's perception as well.

The congenitally malformed infant creates conflicts for any parent, but for the already conflicted mother or father, the effect can be devastating.

Eva is an excellent example of a parent who had difficulty in the early stages of bonding.

Eva Davis, a young African-American woman, was raised by two alcoholic parents and had one older sibling. She had had no experience with babies, but always felt she would "like a baby to love."

At age 17, Eva left high school and got a job as a waitress. She met Joe not long afterwards. Joe was a regular customer, a big brusque Swedish longshoreman who ate lunch and dinner at the restaurant in which Eva worked. Before long, Eva began going home with him after work and staying the night. Accustomed to abusive treatment at home, Eva did not mind when he "slapped her around," and in fact saw it as indicative of his love for her.

Eva heralded her pregnancy with enthusiasm. Although not sure if Joe would "kick her out," she saw a baby as someone who would be totally hers and thoroughly loving. Joe was not as enthusiastic, however, and for the first time questioned their interracial union. Later, Eva observed that despite his anger over the coming baby, "he did stop knockin' me around."

Joe began leaving Eva alone for extended periods. She would return to his apartment but would end up spending the night alone. She described feeling warm and comforted, though, as if "she had company" in the baby. Uneducated about nutrition or the necessity for prenatal care, Eva ate poorly and sought no medical advice. Fetal movement was a surprise to Eva. She had not been prepared for the sensation and found the movement distressing. When assured by a co-worker that this was normal, Eva hesitantly suggested that Joe "feel her belly." The reality of the situation was impressed upon the father and in a fit of temper he threw Eva out, insisting that she "get rid of it or don't come back!"

Overwhelmed, Eva returned to her parents' home and attempted to abort. Her older sister found Eva hemorrhaging and called an ambulance. Assured by hospital staff that she had not lost the baby, Eva cried hysterically. She was referred to the hospital social service, which arranged for a visiting nurse to follow her for the remainder of her pregnancy.

Eva spent the rest of her pregnancy in her parents' home, avoiding their abuse by staying in her room and going to work. She remained depressed and withdrawn. Joe no longer came to the restaurant, perhaps himself dreading a confrontation.

Three weeks prior to her due date, Eva began labor just after arriving at work. Panic-stricken, she had to be calmed down by a co-worker, who took her to the hospital when her labor pains increased in intensity. Once at the hospital, however, her labor stopped. After another 24 hours, the fetal monitors indicated fetal distress and the baby was delivered by caesarean section. For the first few hours after birth, the baby boy remained in "guarded condition." Finally rallying, the infant was brought to his mother the next morning. She greeted him with suspicion, insisting that he was not hers. "He's supposed to be light, like his father!" she protested. The small dark baby had little energy after his long ordeal and lay listlessly in the nurse's arms. He showed little interest in eating and his mother had no inclination to nurse him.

For Eva, what had been initially anticipated as a marvelous event in her life had climaxed in disappointment. She had produced a baby who in no way met her expectations, and was forced to return with him to an environment that gave no support to either mother or child. The result was that 3-month-old Toby Davis was admitted to the hospital after his mother had shaken him severely to "make him stop his damn cryin'!"

Birth to One Year

The average child exhibits certain behaviors throughout the phases of his or her development. These normal developmental milestones (see Table 3.1) depend on the consistency

TABLE 3.1 Developmental Milestones*

Age	Motor	Mental	Language	Social
3–6 months	will bear weight on legs can roll over stomach to back engages hands in midline when pulled to sit, head is steady, does not fall back when on abdomen, can lift shoulders off mat when on abdomen, can lift head and look about will begin to reach for and grasp objects sits with support	looks at objects in hand looks after a toy which is dropped uses a 2-hand approach to grasp toys looks at objects as small as a raisin turns head to voice, follows with eyes	coos gurgles chuckles laughs aloud squeals has expressive noises	has a social smile will pat a bottle with both hands anticipates food on sight
6–9 months	rolls from back to stomach gets feet to mouth sits alone, unsupported, for extended period (over 1 minute) stands with hands held on back, can lift head up beginning attempts to crawl or creep when sitting, reaches forward to grasp without falling	bangs toys in play transfers objects from hand to hand reaches for a toy with one hand picks up a toy he/she drops is persistent in obtaining toys would pull a toy to self by attached string	responds to name vocalizes to social stimulus, i.e., *ba, ka, ma* has single consonants, i.e., *ba, ka, ma* combines syllables, i.e., *da-da ba-ba* likes to make sounds with toys imitates sounds	expects repetition of stimulus likes frolicky play discriminates strangers smiles to mirror image takes some solid food to mouth bites and chews toys beginning to enjoy peekaboo
9–12 months	crawls well can sit steadily for more than 10 minutes stands holding on to furniture	will uncover a toy he/she sees covered up can grasp object small as raisin with thumb and one finger	understands "no," or inflection of "no!" uses *mama*, or *dada*, first inappropriately, then with meaning	cooperates in games will try to roll ball to another person plays patacake and peekaboo

Age	Motor	Play / Cognitive	Language	Social / Self-help
	can pull to sitting position walks, holding on to a hand or to furniture	beginning to put things in and out of containers goes for an object with index finger outstretched likes to drop objects deliberately shows interest in pictures	by 12 months has at least one other word knows meaning of 1–3 words	waves goodbye will offer toy without releasing it likes to interact in play with adult
12–18 months	by 18 months, walks well alone creeps up stairs can get to standing position alone can stoop and recover an object walking, pulls a pull-toy seats self on chair	looks at pictures in a book will scribble spontaneously with pencil or crayon uses spoon drinks from cup will follow one or two directions, i.e., "take a ball to …"	has 3–5 words will point to one body part will point to at least one picture uses jargon, i.e., unintelligible "foreign" language with inflection imitates some words	cooperates in dressing holds own bottle or cup finger feeds points or vocalizes to make desires known shows or offers a toy
18–24 months	can run, albeit stiffly walks up and down stairs with one hand held hurls a ball can kick a ball or object jumps with both feet stands on one foot with one hand held	can tower 2 or more 1 inch blocks turns pages of a book, even if 2–3 at a time will try to imitate what an adult draws with pencil can point to 2–3 body parts	by two years, has at least 20 words by two years, is combining two words in a phrase jargon, which was elaborate by 18 months, is gone by 24 months verbalizes desires with words	uses spoon, spilling very little removes one piece of clothing imitates housework more and more handles a cup quite well

From Harold Martin. *Treatment of Abused and Neglected Children.* Washington, DC: National Center on Child Abuse and Neglect, DHEW (79–30199) 1979.
*If child is not accomplishing two or three of these milestones, consider developmental consultation.

of the child's experience as well as his or her relationship with the primary caregiver—usually the mother.

When mother and child do not make a good adjustment to each other, the infant often develops an irritable high-pitched cry, which can be particularly upsetting to a caregiver, especially an already uncomfortable mother. Not only is the pitch and intensity of the cry unnerving, but it does not vary according to the child's needs. Although most mothers can quickly differentiate their child's cry from hunger from that of being tired or wet, mothers of babies with the high-pitched cry are not given such clues. Thus the mother perceives herself a failure, feels even more out of control of her situation, and may target the child as the cause (Helfer, McKinney, and Kempe, 1976; Tzeng et al., 1991).

Consider too that most new mothers have support systems, people to whom they can go with their problems or fears. It is not uncommon for the neophyte parent to consult her own mother, mother-in-law, friend, other relative, or physician for advice. These individuals provide emotional support or models for the behavior and attitudes necessary to parent. In some cultures, the parenting behavior of others close to the mother allows for the baby's needs to be met. Mothers who are abusive are women who have not developed this important support system. As a result, they feel very much alone and isolated, with no models to emulate. The only models available to them may have been those in their own abusive pasts (Weston et al., 1993). To make matters worse, they are grieving the loss of the attention they received when they were pregnant. Now it is the baby over whom everyone fusses. Mothers within large extended families may feel pushed aside in favor of their babies. Conchita Juarez never felt accepted by the large family she married into. Throughout her pregnancy, she got conflicting messages about how to care for herself and her baby. When the baby was born, it seemed that she no longer mattered. She began to resent her small offspring for the attention he recieved.

The mother's conflicts and sometimes depression may mean the baby's needs are not met adequately by her. The mother may be ignorant of the baby's needs or she may be caught up in her own unmet needs. Sometimes the cries are met with satisfaction, but other times they provoke only anger in the parent, who either shuts out the cries by leaving, ignoring them, or striking out in anger (Martin, 1976a; Factor and Wolfe, 1990).

It is not entirely clear how much of the baby's own inherent personality and how much of the unsupportive environment contribute to this early lack of communication between mother and child. Brazelton's (1969) classic work has demonstrated that there are distinct differences in the personalities of infants from birth. People still can only speculate about the effects of a particular infant's personality on the mother's inability to parent effectively.

Babies' personalities can be influenced by their in-utero environment. Increased research on the effects of perinatal substance abuse indicate that babies whose mothers were using alcohol or drugs during pregnancy have a greater chance of exhibiting such complications as fetal alcohol syndrome, neurological damage, prematurity, or other problems (Inciardi et al., 1993). These babies have been observed to be more irritable, to exhibit high-pitched crying, to have excessive vomiting, diarrhea, seizures, uncoordinated sucking, and to demonstrate either increased or decreased muscle tone (Kropenske et al., 1994). Thus the parent who may either be continuing to abuse substances herself or be dealing with her own attempts to now remain substance free is faced with a baby who is not easy to care for.

For this mother, hampered by her own past or current problems, caring for an infant may seem like an overwhelming task. She may withdraw from this challenge at the baby's expense.

The child who is not sufficiently stimulated may develop a failure-to-thrive syndrome (see Chapter Four for further explanation) and withdraw from a world that he or she sees as hostile. More likely, however, the infant receives inconsistent mothering—with his or her needs being met one minute and not the next. Such treatment creates a child who is wary of the environment. The child's social development—smiling, cooing, and babbling—is delayed. An apathetic infant demonstrates poor muscle tone and is slow to turn over, reach for toys, and (later) sit or crawl (Helfer, McKinney, and Kempe, 1976).

For the abused or neglected child, the lack of social responsiveness between 6 and 12 months becomes more striking. A disturbance in object relations becomes marked. When the child is given a toy, for example, he or she plays with it passively. When the toy is removed, however, the child accepts the loss with the same passivity. Children from inadequately parenting families may also fail to develop separation anxiety and, later, stranger anxiety. Separation anxiety is demonstrated by children crying or acting fearful when their caregiver leaves. Their anxiety is based on their assumption that if out of sight, the caretaker no longer exists. The child must distinguish a loved person or parent from others, which is done by recognizing those who are there to consistently satisfy the needs. Once a child has distinguished the caregiver, he or she fears being abandoned when that person leaves. At the same time, the child fears strangers (stranger anxiety) who have not proved themselves as caregivers and may therefore not be trusted (Martin, 1976b).

A child whose needs are not met consistently does not look to the caregiver as the provider of comforts. And without this directed trust, the child does not see strangers as suspect. Therefore the child seeks the attention of anyone who is a potential need-satisfier. Children who have been inconsistently parented often seek attention indiscriminately. By the same token, they may indicate subtly that they are already convinced that these needs will not be met.

This sense of mistrust becomes obvious in abused children. Again, the development of trust necessitates consistency. Lack of it may convince the child that the environment and those in it are not to be trusted.

Language should be beginning to develop as the child draws closer to the year-old mark. At age 6 or 7 weeks, the first intentional vocalizations (other than cries) lay the ground for language development. When the caregiver talks to the infant, the child watches intently, preparing to mimic these sounds in later months. The child who is not talked to frequently, or whose babblings are not encouraged, learns to take little pleasure in verbalizing. Therefore, language development is slow.

It was mentioned earlier that while one type of parent emotionally neglects, another type stimulates. The latter parent may heavily invest in the child's first year, but with that investment comes great expectations. Before the year is out, the child will be expected to talk, walk, and even be toilet trained. Parents may also have controlled and distinct ideas of what the baby's schedule should be, regardless of the baby's inner timing. Unmet expectations sometimes result in abuse.

What of the baby who is cared for in a large, multiple-generation household? It is possible that another caretaker might meet that baby's need. This fact, in and of itself, might give rise to resentment from the baby's own mother. Or the inconsistency of multiple care-takers may also prove problematic for the young child.

One to Four Years

By age 1 year, the poorly parented baby shows little interest in toys or exploration in general. The ways in which children use toys mirror what they see in others. Children who have nothing to observe—who are not stimulated through mutual play—lack the ability to use toys or to show interest in playing. Many abused adults demonstrate the inability to play and enjoy life. This inability may stem from as early as this first year.

Children also demonstrate *frozen (or passive) watchfulness,* whereby the child lies immobile, watching the actions of others (Helfer, McKinney, and Kempe, 1976; Van der Kolk, 1987). These children have learned that the world is not predictable and sometimes not even friendly. In the course of a day, these children learn that sometimes they are struck for their behavior and that other times that same behavior is ignored. Therefore children from abusive and neglectful homes develop an uncanny knack of "reading" their environment. They become acutely aware of stimuli and what they mean. This ability to assess and often predict their environment requires a skill not always developed by the average child. Unfortunately, this skill is not measurable, so that in later years, when the intelligence of abused children is in question—or felt to be lower than other children—no "points" are given for this demanding ability. In fact, studies done by Rodeheffer and Martin (1976) indicate that *hypervigilance,* as these authors term it, can lower assessment test scores. They describe the child in a test situation:

> His tendency to perceive threat, whenever under close surveillance by an adult, is in dynamic interplay with the intense scrutiny inherent in the evaluation setting. Preoccupation with the examiner and attempts to reduce the anxiety aroused by the evaluation procedures may have a deleterious effect upon the abused child's ability to focus attention on the materials and may reduce his ability to perform. He is alert to the examiner's every move, often focussing attention on the examiner's face rather than on the materials needed for the task. If the examiner moves his hand to pick up a pencil, he may find the child observing him diligently, completely distracted from the task. It appears to be of utmost importance for the child to "read" the whims of this stranger with whom he finds himself. The child is slow to relax and trust the examiner's good will toward him. He behaves as if he is extremely vulnerable and must be in constant readiness for unexpected events. (pp. 116–17)

Thus the young child's ability to read the environment—so basic for survival at home—is a detriment in learning and testing situations.

The child between ages 1 and 3 continues to demonstrate delays in motor activity and social development. He appears to have little investment in relationships and fails to make eye contact. He or she has learned that adults are all-powerful and that autonomy is discouraged. To displease an adult by exerting one's own will may mean abuse.

Around the age of 2, a toddler especially needs a consistent, loving mother (parent) figure. It is a time when the task is to separate from the caregiver and to begin to develop a sense of autonomy. For this, the child needs a mother who is secure enough to encourage individual growth. The mother must be able to send the child off but be available when the child needs to return to her arms—to check if she is still there. Mahler and colleagues (1975) call this the period of rapprochement—a time that is vital for the child's healthy development. The mother, in return, must be confident that her child will return periodically and be pleased by his or her growth, for, indeed, this represents the beginning of the child's final separation and individuation from her (Martin, 1976b; Van der Kolk, 1987).

The child for whom the parent-child relationship has been inadequate may not be comfortable enough to attempt this separation. So the child remains half-involved and half-uninvolved with the withholding parent.

For still other infants, babyhood was a time when the parent was able to give..The tasks of feeding and nurturing were not much of a burden to the mother. After infancy, however, some of these mothers have difficulty. Once the child becomes more of an individual, the mother, who is not confident in her own abilities, may be threatened by her child's need to differentiate. She may see attempts at separation, no matter how brief, as a rejection, and she may either withdraw from her child or strike out in anger.

This inability to wholly test independence also hampers the child's ability to test reality—and to learn to trust himself or herself. When the child is learning the "rules" of his or her environment and is attempting to internalize these rules to eventually become his or her own standards, then the child who is not given full opportunity to test the limits in relative safety will not internalize adequately.

Autonomy in children must also be considered within a cultural context. Lieberman and colleagues demonstrate this in their study of Mexican and Central-American mothers who appeared especially and anxiously attached to their young children, compared to non-Hispanic mothers with their children.

> Most [Hispanic] mothers in our sample believe strongly that parents should be in charge, that disobedience and disrespectful behavior should not be allowed and that good parents should suppress the expression of anger in their children. They also believe that boys and girls should be treated differently. Finally, they tend to have an idealized and self-sacrificing view of motherhood, which of course is very much in line with the importance given to the family rather than the individual. (1990, p. 108)

In contrast, most non-Hispanic-American mothers were more permissive, believing strongly in democratic family relations. The researchers also defend a mother's right to pursue her own interests even if it means "some accommodation by her young children" (p. 108). While these mothers would have seen the behavior of their Hispanic counterparts as

> authoritarian, restrictive, sexist, and self-deprecating…in a Latino cultural context, the mothers in our sample may emerge as confident of their authority, devoted to their family, and selflessly willing to give of themselves and to endure hardship for the sake of their children. It all depends on one's perspective. (p. 109)

Thus, when one sees a child of another culture who does not appear to be developing independence, it is important to look deeper into the values of that culture.

Although much research has focused on the mother's influence on the developing child, paternal influence is also important. Different stages of development are affected differently by paternal absence or by a dysfunctional father-child relationship. These effects are also culture-dependent. One of the most significant areas affected by the absence of a father figure appears to be in intelligence.

Blanchard and Biller (1971) and Landy, Rosenberg, and Sutton-Smith (1969) studied the effect the father's absence had on cognitive development. The consensus was that children deprived of the father (or father figure) show significantly lower academic performance and measure lower on intelligence tests than comparable children with fathers. (These findings could be related not only to the identification with the father but also to the fact that the mother, if alone, might have less time and energy to devote to the stimulation of the children.) Lamb's (1976) studies of young children's affiliative behavior suggest that as the child grew, fathers had progressively more attachment behavior (e.g., touching or wanting to be held) directed toward them. Boys, particularly, by the age of 2 were seeking out their fathers for attention. Lamb suggests this is the beginning of same-sex modeling. It is not surprising that some sons who observe their fathers reacting with violence or with inappropriate sexuality will mirror this behavior (Hilton, 1992; Hanson et al., 1994).

Coopersmith (1967) investigated 85 boys to consider their self-esteem and indicated that a boy's self-esteem is related to his father's positive employment history as is the father's own self-concept. Fathers who were out of work frequently or who had negative attitudes toward themselves and others tended to produce a lower self-concept in their sons.[2]

The importance of the father as well as the mother in sexual development of both male and female children is also worth noting. Between 1 and 3 years, the child's sexual development is progressing. By age 3, the average child will have learned of sexuality through seeing, touching, and doing. He or she may have bathed with children of both sexes and have an early understanding that there are differences. The parents' reaction to toilet training, exposure and touching of the genitals, and masturbation gives the developing child a clear indication of what is "normal" and expected. Most children wonder about their parents' breasts and penises, and ask that the names and functions be identified (Thompson, 1981). The way in which the child's own culture views the discussion of sexuality is also crucial to his/her development in this area.

Sexually abusive parents rationalize that this curiosity necessitates touch or demonstration. The child who experiences this early distortion in teaching is frequently indiscriminate in touching others' genitals, or acts out the "demonstration" on peers.

Finding pleasure in their own bodies is a normal part of development in children. A parent who severely punishes a child for masturbation gives the child a message that that part of the body is "dirty," "sinful," or not to be touched. The sexually abusive parent, on the other hand, may encourage masturbation and develop the practice into mutual manipulation as a progression toward other sexual interplay. The way in which children are treated by the parent of the opposite sex is important in the development of a healthy sexual attitude. Overstimulation impedes the child's ability to incorporate knowledge pertinent to his or her level of understanding. The result is confusion, guilt, and often a later inability to distinguish between sexuality and affection.

By 4 years of age, average children are well within the period when they are attempting to sort out their own concepts of sexuality. Although the boy is attracted to his mother as a love object (Oedipal conflict) and the girl to her father (Electra complex), both are beginning to recognize that these parents are already attached. The solution then is found in modeling the parent of the same sex in the hope of some day finding someone like the beloved opposite-sex parent (Thompson, 1981).

Abuse and neglect impede these vital learnings in several ways. To progress to wanting to identify with the same-sex parent, the child must perceive that the parents condone this growth and that the same-sex parent is emotionally attractive enough to identify with. For example, in order for a girl to model herself after her mother, she must perceive that both her mother and father applaud this behavior. Parents who are threatened in some manner by the child's development may communicate discomfort, thus impeding the child's desire to grow. The mother's attractiveness as a model for the little girl may be diminished if she is emotionally unapproachable, too harsh in her discipline, or is constantly being criticized— or even battered—by the father. In addition, to allow the girl to pull herself away from her immature sexual attachment to her father, he must behave toward her in a nonseductive manner. The female child whose father is not only seductive but sexually abusive does not have an opportunity to develop an appropriate attitude toward sexuality.

The male child sexually abused by the mother faces similar issues. Sexual abuse of a boy by the father often creates fears of homosexuality and gender confusion. Similar conflicts— and apparently more intense—are evident in the female abused by her mother (Forward and Buck, 1978).

By age 4, abused and neglected children demonstrate difficulty in relating to others— especially in the area of trust, a diminished capacity for play, low self-esteem, and often fears and phobias. Language development is not comparable to other children their age. One of the most marked observations of children who have experienced inadequate parenting, however, is their extreme passivity. Their disinclination to reach out or explore makes the scope of their activities extremely limited. Survival has taken so much energy that they have little left for other pursuits (Helfer, McKinney, and Kempe, 1976).

Four to Eight Years

The developmental delays continue to be obvious in the child between ages 4 and 8. The hallmark of this period should be learning, but the child whose early development has been punctuated with abuse or neglect may not have sufficient energy or interest for this activity. These children come to school unable to trust the teacher, and the success of their education often depends on the quality of this relationship. Their relationships with peers are frequently poor.

By age 8, children who have experienced consistency in their lives are beginning to develop the concept of cause and effect. For the abused child, however, causal relationships may not be clear. A particular action or event one day elicited a specific response from the mother or father, but the next day the same action caused a totally different result. Thus the child's sense of predictability has been distorted, and an inability to understand some of the most basic learning principles has been created (Martin, 1976a).

Verbal explanations may be difficult for the understimulated child to comprehend. Used to one-word commands at home, the teacher's complicated set of instructions creates only confusion in the child's underdeveloped mind. (See Chapter 4 for a further explanation.) The hypervigilance developed for survival again proves more of a liability than an asset at school. The child becomes so preoccupied with the teacher's perceived intention that he or she has difficulty grasping cognitive material.

The "rules" of life and games, including the cultural context on which these are based, are firmly embedded in most children's minds by the development of the superego (i.e., the incorporation of past parental restrictions that eventually form a conscience and a concept of the ideal self). These rules may be hazy for the abused and neglected child. Whether you get caught or not is often of more concern than any inner morality. "Getting caught" is symbolic of failure, and there is little remorse about the actual deed. This is the experience of the child deprived of consistency and adequate nurturing.

Another type of child—a member of the rigid, physically abusing family—has developed a superego, but it too is faulty. Rigid and uncompromising, this child's superego outlines strict rules, but again the control is external. The child may comply because he or she has learned that not to comply brings on abuse. The child may have begun to internalize some of these unrealistically high expectations—not through any sense of independence but because the parents' admonishments echo in his or her mind. These children often demonstrate an intense need to succeed in their school work. Failure is totally unacceptable.

> *"Craig reminded me of a little robot," remarked the teacher of a compulsive 8-year-old. He was immaculately dressed, right down to the unfailingly white section of the saddle shoes he wore. His movements were definite. Each task would be undertaken with intense concentration. I often felt he was "programmed" at home to do superior schoolwork. When hard work and concentration were the only prerequisites to a job well done, Craig was fine. But when the task required deductive reasoning, Craig faltered. Failure to answer a question correctly or a low grade on a paper resulted in a rigid body posture so intense that I was concerned. Several "failures" in one day usually brought on an asthma attack.*
>
> *Craig's parents had high expectations of their son. Their own fear of failure (his father was in sales with a company that pitted its employees in fierce competition with each other for quotas) had translated into physical abuse when Craig displeased them. (It was later learned that his numerous bruises were not the result of accidents but caused by this abuse.)*
>
> *Craig was indeed a child whose internalized expectations, as well as the abuse he suffered, left him all but unable to learn.*

Eight to Twelve Years

The abused or neglected child, whose parents have difficulty in nurturing, is probably well established as the nurturer by now. The parents have long since indicated their expectations that the child assume their roles and meet their needs. The unsure child thus cares for younger siblings, assumes household tasks, and caters to parental whims. While this role reversal usually commences as soon as the child is able (often as early as age 4 or 5), the preadolescent becomes skilled in these tasks. To complete these tasks often requires returning home right after school or taking days off. Already feeling alienated from peers, the child's isolation is intensified by his or her lack of opportunity to participate in peer activities. The child who has been having school problems may be beginning to be disillusioned with the educational system. Behavior problems within school and truancy are indications of the inability to cope. The way in which the school deals with these issues can be of utmost importance in the child's future attitude toward learning and toward authority figures. Suspension or expulsion provides the isolated maltreated child with one more proof of rejection and failure. It is important to note that some cultures expect that children will care for younger siblings at an early age. The need to work several jobs, for example, might mean that a mother leaves her 9-year-old as the sole caregiver of a 6-, 4-, and 2-year-old from 7:00PM to 3:00AM when the mother returns home. Although protective agencies state that under the law this practice is neglectful, parents like this mother argue that it is a necessity.

A parentified child (one who takes the parents' place as caregiver), especially the pre-adolescent girl, is particularly vulnerable to the onset of sexual abuse. She has often been placed in a position at home where she has assumed more and more household responsibilities, culminating in a role reversal with her mother. This role reversal, as well as her budding sexuality, are perceived by the abusive father as signals of her availability. Since incest is a family issue, it is important to examine the dynamics of family life for the preadolescent and adolescent girl. Several factors influence the onset of an incestuous affair.

1. The current sexual adjustment of the parent
2. The child's developing sensuality and later overt sexual development
3. The psychological impact of the child's sexual development on the parents' sexual adjustment and their subsequent response to the child
4. The interactional effect which results in the parents' reexperiencing their own early childhood memories and feelings related to their own sexual development (Mzarek and Mzarek, 1981, p. 23)

The parents of a sexually abused child are caught up in their own marital disputes, which often originate or culminate in their sexual adjustment. At the same time, the female child is developing sexually and is realizing her own sexuality. Threatened by this aspect of her child's development, the mother may further alienate herself from the parent-child relationship (some degree of alienation usually exists prior to this time). The father, at the same time, is attracted by his daughter's sexuality and sees her as a nonconflictual sexual substitute. So complex are the patterns of this dysfunctional family that it is difficult to outline in other than a simplistic manner. The problems inherent in a father's seduction of his daughter and a mother's further isolation are present prior to the child's overt sexual development. While in most families there exists the inclination toward such feelings, the censoring mechanism of the healthy ego quickly represses them. The potentially incestuous father and his mate, however, are plagued by remnants of childhood scars that inhibit this censoring (Mzarek and Mzarek, 1981; Horton et al., 1990).

Adolescence

The same factors just mentioned operate during adolescence. But during adolescence the sexually abused girl is likely to try to extricate herself from an incestuous relationship—especially if the onset of the abuse occurred after she had established some peer connections. Her desire for age-appropriate peer relationships and her guilt over her perceived complicity, along with the normal adolescent quest for identity, often cause her to attempt to stop the behavior herself or to tell someone else. The boy who has witnessed his sister's abuse may either identify with the aggressor—acting out abusively on either his sister or other siblings, or, less frequently, attempting to be protective of his sister. The boy who is being sexually abused himself may feel the same need to free himself for reasons of peer connections. Abuse by a male often elicits myriad homosexual fears, desires, and conflicts.

> *Todd was abused by his father from the age of 9. The middle of three brothers, he also remembers his older brother approaching him sexually. This angered Todd, and after initially complying, he rebuffed his older brother's attention. Todd does remember, however, that on several occasions he instigated sexual contact between his younger brother and himself.*
>
> *The main recipient of his father's attention, Todd remembers feeling "special" and "loved." At age 13, however, he was attracted to an older girl but worried that he was homosexual. His father ridiculed his concerns, causing Todd to feel "belittled and humiliated." In a fit of anger, he told his mother of his relationship with his father. She became angry and apparently confronted the father, but the subject was never discussed again.*
>
> *Angered by Todd's "betrayal," the father ceased all attention to his son. He ignored the boy in every way. Todd was devastated. In desperation, he became involved with drugs, but his mother was delegated to handle any trouble he got into. Finally, two years later, Todd reapproached his father sexually in a desperate attempt to terminate the silence. The relationship became sexual once again and lasted well into the boy's twenties.*
>
> *Todd "resolved" his conflicts by bartering sexuality for the attention he received from his father. This was the first of a series of homosexual relationships in which he chose the attention of men rather than chance trusting a woman again.*

Body image is another important dynamic for adolescents and plays a particular role in the behavior of the sexually abused child. In a conscious or unconscious compulsion to feel less sexual in response to their developing bodies, some sexually abused girls develop anorexia nervosa. When this condition persists, it can inhibit menstruation and the further development of secondary sex characteristics (Masterson, 1977; Hendrick, 1983). Other types of self-abuse are also common among this age group (deYoung, 1984; Briere, 1992).

For the adolescent, sexual abuse has a decided impact on development in other ways. Finkelhor and Browne (1985) postulate that sexual abuse has four types of traumatic effects:

1. Traumatic sexualization
2. Betrayal
3. Powerlessness
4. Stigmatization

Traumatic sexualization is a result of a child's exposure to sexual behavior inappropriate to the level of development. She or he has been rewarded for participation in this activity and therefore sees sexuality as a method of manipulating others to meet his or her needs. The adolescent may also view his or her own value as synonymous with being sexual. Promiscuity is often a part of the abused adolescent's pattern.

The adolescent has also developed cognitively, recognizing the possibility of alternatives and choices. The abused adolescent begins to recognize that the perpetrator also made choices, and, in choosing to exploit, has betrayed the victim's trust. The sense of betrayal felt by the developing adolescent can be profound and can contribute to self-abusive or rebellious behavior.

Having been unwillingly violated again and again and, compounding the assault, not having been believed when trying to tell someone, the sexually abused adolescent feels a sense of powerlessness. The stigmatization comes when the adolescent recognizes that being abused makes him or her different. The resulting shame and guilt further intensify the isolation and low self-esteem, which are already a burden for the developing child.

Control and self-mastery are issues not only for the sexually abused but for all maltreated children. The child who has received inadequate parenting may not have learned to internalize control. Neglecting families do not provide sufficient role models for standards and moral development. Overly rigid, abusive families maintain the locus of control that makes it difficult for the adolescent to do anything but mimic their rigidity. For physically abused adolescents, control has been ensured through violence. It is not surprising, therefore, that Green (1981) and Howing et al. (1993) found that exposure to violence predisposes children to delinquent behavior.

Separation is difficult for the adolescent whose needs have not been met. For these children, the break with parents is often abrupt—through running away, early pregnancy, premature marriage, or total alienation. Although unequipped with the proper models, these adolescents often promise they will be better parents than their own.

The search for identity, pursued with full force during adolescence, is built on testing internalized values and the final resolution of an individualized code of ethics. Such a hazardous emotional pilgrimage necessitates some degree of self-esteem, room for growth, and positive models to emulate. For the child whose family life has been disorganized and dysfunctional, the search for identity can be exceedingly painful. Too often this adolescent, hampered by insecurity and robbed of good self-esteem,[3] gives up the pursuit and immerses himself or herself in the parents' values. Thus the cycle of abuse and neglect may repeat itself.

Fortunately, in adolescence, children have access to other role models. Contact with a concerned teacher, relative, friend, or counselor may enable the child to develop alternative values.

Developmental Differences

Statistics show that each year a multitude of children are abused and neglected. Yet all abused and neglected children do not demonstrate severe language or emotional difficulties. Many of these individuals do not seem severely disturbed in later life. What accounts for these differences?

Martin suggests that several factors account for the variations in the reported effects of abuse and neglect on children:

1. The equipment (personality differences inherent in an individual child) of the child
2. Neurological damage to the child
3. Important others in the child's life

     4. Biological considerations in addition to neurological damage from trauma

     5. Malevolent environmental factors (1976b, pp. 139–40)

Martin also points out that therapeutic intervention may have positive (or negative) effects on the child's personality.

Brazelton studied the differences in personality (what Martin refers to as "equipment of the child") of infants at birth. Brazelton's (1973) neonatal assessment scale provides a method of considering the child's activity level, responsiveness, loveableness, and irritability. Perhaps the "match" between infants and mothers based on these factors should be considered. The mother and father who have no difficulty nurturing a quiet cuddly infant, who takes readily to a schedule and sleeps through the night, may find it impossible to adjust to an irritable, colicky baby, who requires a great deal of rocking and attention just to become quiet enough to fall asleep.

Children who develop hypervigilant behavior have a much better chance of survival in the abusive home (Martin 1976b; Briere, 1992). A certain amount of creativity and the will to survive—characteristics the origin of which have not been determined—give the young child a better chance. Other studies (Lynch, 1976) confirm that children who are hampered by prematurity, are handicapped, or suffer the stigma of being different are more at risk for abuse.

Damage to the central nervous system through battering can create permanent neurological impairment in children. The central nervous system controls defense mechanisms, the development of social behavior, and impulse control, so the child who has experienced damage may be less able to cope (Martin, 1976b).

The individuals in a child's life are important. From these people he or she receives attention, learns to test reality, gets an indication of self-worth, and selects models. The abused and neglected child sometimes seems trapped in a dysfunctional bubble that consists only of parents, but the other people who touch the child's life—teachers, neighbors, relatives, group leaders—are important. As the child grows, it is possible to use a variety of models to enhance development. With one or more concerned consistent individual in life, the child may succeed in diluting significantly the negative effects of being maltreated.

Biological and environmental influences are other variables that can affect differences in development. Malnutrition and persistent illness significantly influence memory, learning, thinking, and language (Chase and Martin, 1970). Untreated medical issues can create permanent disabilities. Martin (1976b) suggests untreated middle-ear infections—a frequent childhood complaint—can cause deafness and therefore affect speech development. Other factors in the environment, such as economic disadvantage, significant psychiatric disturbance in one or both parents, and maternal deprivation, compound the problem of maltreatment and perhaps impede the child's ability to cope. Substance abuse by one or both parents adds to the problem of child abuse.

Finally, Martin considers the effects of treatment on the developing child. It is difficult to determine if protective intervention will have the desired effect. Placement of the child in a foster home, accompanied by the separation from the parent, often becomes part of the treatment plan. Is this intervention indeed more detrimental, as Goldstein, Freud, and Solnit (1973) suggest? The lack of consistency of intervention, hampered by case reassignment, lack of total case coordination, and the changes in the court system mirror the chameleon-like world the child experiences at home. It is still too early to assess accurately how effective intervention has been. Many theorists contend there is a long way to go in protecting the abused and neglected child's opportunity to grow with some degree of normalcy.

Summary

Developing normally is a difficult task for the abused and neglected child. Two parenting patterns occur in maltreating families, both of which hamper the development of the child. One type of family is composed of adults who continually strive to get their own needs met, neglecting the needs of the child and eventually forcing the offspring into the role of nurturing them. A second type of family is rigid in its standards with unrealistically high expectations for the child. Although they are able to give the child more nurturing, the result of their unmet demands is abuse and confusion for the developing child.

Each developmental period provides new conflicts for the maltreating family. Pregnancy is marked with hopes for an infant who will be miraculously loving and giving in every way. The relationship between mother and father frequently determines the couple's ability to accept the infant. Birth and early bonding are complicated by the emotional immaturity of the mother, the relationship or lack of relationship between the mother and significant others, and other environmental factors. Inadequate bonding leaves the child at risk for abuse.

The abused or neglected child between birth and 1 year demonstrates poor motor control, a lack of social responsiveness, slow language development, and a general mistrust of the environment. From 1 to 4 years of age, the child develops a passivity combined with hypervigilance about his or her surroundings. This child is slow to reach out or explore and has little interest in developing autonomy.

Fathers, too, have an effect on the child's development. Studies indicate that young children demonstrate affiliative behavior with their fathers, and fathers who are absent or unavailable can negatively influence their children's cognitive development and self-esteem.

Early sexual development is impeded by inappropriate exposure to sexuality during these years. Children who are sexually abused develop confusion about their own sexuality and the way in which they are expected to relate to others.

By 4 to 8 years, the child's development delays appear more significant. He or she has difficulty relating to peers and is unable to make the transition to structured learning in the classroom. Abused children have difficulty internalizing standards—some because they have observed no consistent standards at home and others because the rigidity in their home life does not allow them the autonomy to be self-directed.

The maltreated child between ages 8 and 12 may well have developed into the nurturer of the parents. School problems and behavior problems may be part of the child's life. Preadolescence is a classic age for sexual abuse to commence. The child's budding sexuality augments the parents' own conflicts, and abuse may be the result. Maltreated children of this age group often feel isolated and alienated from their peers.

Adolescence marks the quest for control, separation, and identity—a quest hampered by maltreatment. The abused child demonstrates poor self-esteem and a poor body image, which often leads to self-injurious behavior. Adolescents frequently separate abruptly from the family of origin through running away, becoming pregnant, or some other method of separation.

Why does abuse and neglect affect some children profoundly and others to a lesser degree? Some reasons for the differences are the child's own personality, neurological damage from abuse, the influence of significant people in the child's life, and other biological and malevolent environmental factors. The impact of society's efforts toward intervention can also affect the child's chances for normal development.

Exploration Questions

1. What are the critical tasks children must accomplish in their growth?

2. Cite the types of parents usually found in abusive and neglectful homes. How do their patterns of behavior affect their children's development?

3. What expectations of pregnancy might an immature mother have? What fears?

4. What is the importance of the father during pregnancy and birth? What type of impact might he have on the child's bonding?

5. What factors prohibited Eva Davis from bonding with her infant?

6. What are the developmental problems faced by a child between birth and age 1? Ages 1 to 4? Ages 4 to 8? Ages 8 to 12?

7. What is meant by "frozen watchfulness"? How does it help the abused child? How does it hinder?

8. What impact does an absent father have on child development?

9. How can a child be inhibited in the development of his or her own set of standards?

10. What factors lead a family to become incestuous?

11. What are the tasks of adolescence? How are they impeded by maltreatment?

12. What factors go into the determination of how maltreatment affects a particular child?

Activities for Applied Learning

1. Create a chart that outlines the developmental tasks of each stage; note what could go wrong in each stage. (Consult a child development book for detailed information on tasks.)

2. Write an autobiography of your childhood. Who were the people in your life, other than your parents, who had an influence on you? How did these models alter your development? Did your ethnic/racial orientation or values have an impact on your development?

3. Read *One Two Three: Matt a Feral Child* by Eleanor Craig (Penguin, 1979). Why did Matt's development go so totally astray? What factors in the mother-child relationship inhibited his growth?

Suggested Readings

Brazelton, T. B. *Infants and Mothers: Differences in Development.* New York: Dell, Delacorte Press, 1969.

Briere, J. N. *Child Abuse and Trauma.* Newbury Park, CA: Sage, 1992.

Craig, E. *One Two Three: Matt a Feral Child.* New York: Penguin, 1979.

Lamb, S., and Coakley, M. "Normal Childhood Sexual Play and Games: Differentiating Play from Abuse." *Child Abuse and Neglect* 17, 4 (1993):515–526.

Le Francois, G. R. *Of Children: An Introduction to Child Development* (4th ed.). Belmont, CA: Wadsworth Publishing, 1983.

Mahler, M. *The Psychological Birth of the Infant: Symbiosis and Individuation.* New York: Basic Books, 1975.

Endnotes

1. Within the confines of the culture. In some cultures, families are more enmeshed than in others, but even here the child's need to grow is respected.

2. In some cultures (e.g., Asian, American Indian), the self-esteem of the child is enhanced by his or her acceptance into the group rather than the behavior of his or her parents alone.

3. Orr and Downes (1985) saw self-esteem as a major problem among the sexually abused victims they studied. Fisher and colleagues (1980) also noted that the self-concept of abused adolescents was severely impaired.

References

Blanchard, R., and Biller, H. "Father Availability and Academic Performance among Third-Grade Boys." *Developmental Psychology* 4 (1971):301–305.

Brazelton, T. B. "The Early Mother-Infant Adjustment." *Pediatrics* 32 (1963):931–38.

Brazelton, T. B. *Infants and Mothers: Differences in Development.* New York: Dell, Delacorte Press, 1969.

Brazelton, T. B. *Neonatal Behavioral Assessment Scale.* Philadelphia: J. B. Lippincott, 1973.

Briere, J. N. *Child Abuse Trauma.* Newbury Park, CA: Sage, 1992.

Caplan, G. *Emotional Implication of Pregnancy and Influences on Family Relationships in the Healthy Child.* Cambridge, MA: Harvard University Press, 1960.

Chase, H. P., and Martin, H. P. "Undernutrition and Child Development." *New England Journal of Medicine* 282 (1970):933–39.

Coopersmith, S. *The Antecedents of Self-Esteem.* San Francisco: Freeman, 1967.

deYoung, M. "Self Injurious Behavior in Incest Victims: A Research Note." *Child Welfare* 63 (1984):577–84.

Factor, D. C. and Wolfe, D. A. "Parental Psychopathology and High-Risk Children." In *Children at Risk,* edited by R. T. Ammerman and M. Hersen. New York: Plenum Press, 1990.

Finkelhor, D., and Browne, A. "Traumatic Impact of Child Sexual Abuse: A Conceptualization." *American Journal of Orthopsychiatry* 55 (1985):530–41.

Fisher, B.; Berdie, J.; Cook, J.; and Day, N. *Adolescent Abuse and Neglect: Intervention Strategies.* Washington, DC: U.S. Department of Health and Human Services, 1980.

Forward, S., and Buck, C. *Betrayal of Innocence.* New York: Penguin, 1978.

Gil, E., and Johnson, T. C. *Sexualized Children.* Rockville, MD: Launch Press, 1993.

Goldstein, J.; Freud, A.; and Solnit, A. *Beyond the Best Interests of the Child.* New York: Free Press, 1973.

Green, A. H. "Child Abuse and the Etiology of Violent Delinquent Behavior." In *Exploring the Relationship between Child Abuse and Delinquency,* edited by R. J. Hunner and Y. E. Walker, pp. 152–60. Montclair, NJ: Abner Schram, 1981.

Hanson, R. F.; Lipovsky, J. A.; and Saunders, B. E. "Characteristics of Fathers in Incestuous Families." *Journal of Interpersonal Violence.* 9(2), (1994): 155–169.

Helfer, R. E.; McKinney, J. P.; and Kempe, R. "Arresting or Freezing the Developmental Process." In *Child Abuse and Neglect: The Family and the Community,* edited by R. Helfer and C. H. Kempe, pp. 55–73. Cambridge, MA: Ballinger, 1976.

Hendrick, S. "The School Counselor and Anorexia Nervosa." *The School Counselor* 31(5) (1983):428–32.

Hilton, N. Z. "Battered Women's Concerns About Their Children Witnessing Wife Assault." *Journal of Interpersonal Violence.* 7(1), (1992): 77–86.

Horton, A. L.; Johnson, B. L.; Roundy, L. M.; and Williams, D. *The Incest Perpetrator.* Newbury Park, CA: Sage, 1990.

Howing, P. T.; Wodarski, J. S.; Kurtz, P. D.; and Gaudin, J. M. *Maltreatment and the School-Age Child.* New York: Haworth Press, 1993.

Inciardi, J. A.; Lockwood, D.; and Pottieger, A. E. *Women and Crack-Cocaine.* New York: Macmillan, 1993.

Kennell, J.; Voos, D.; and Klaus, M. "Parent-Infant Bonding." In *Child Abuse and Neglect: The Family and the Community,* edited by R. Helfer and C. H. Kempe, pp. 25–53. Cambridge, MA: Ballinger, 1976.

Kropenske, V., and Howard, J.; with Breitenbach, C.; Dembo, R.; Edelstein, S. B.; McTaggart, K.; Moore, A.; Sorenson, M. B.; and Weisz, V. *Protecting Children in Substance-Abusing Families.* Washington, DC: U.S. Department of Health and Human Services, 1994.

Lamb, M., ed. *The Role of the Father in Child Development.* New York: Wiley, 1976.

Landy, F.; Rosenberg, B.; and Sutton-Smith, B. "The Effect of Limited Absence on Cognitive Development." *Child Development* 40 (1969):941–44.

Lieberman, A. "Culturally Sensitive Intervention with Children and Families." *Child and Adolescent Social Work* 7(2) (1990):101–19.

Lynch, M. "Risk Factors in the Child: A Study of Abused Children and Their Siblings." In *The Abused Child,* edited by H. P. Martin, pp. 43–56. Cambridge, MA: Ballinger, 1976.

Mahler, M., et al. *The Psychological Birth of the Infant: Symbiosis and Individuation.* New York: Basic Books, 1975.

Martin, H. P. "The Environment of the Abused Child." In *The Abused Child,* edited by H. P. Martin. Cambridge, MA: Ballinger, 1976a.

Martin, H. P. "Factors Influencing the Development of the Abused Child." In *The Abused Child,* edited by H. P. Martin, pp. 139–62. Cambridge, MA: Ballinger, 1976b.

Masterson, J. F. "Primary Anorexia Nervosa in the Borderline Adolescent—An Object Relations View." In *Borderline Personality Disorders,* edited by P. Hartocollis. New York: International Universities Press, 1977.

Mzarek, D. A., and Mzarek, P. B. "Psychosexual Development Within the Family." In *Sexually Abused Children and Their Families,* edited by P. B. Mzarek and C. H. Kempe, pp. 17–32. Elmsford, NY: Pergamon, 1981.

O'Hagan, K. *Emotional and Psychological Abuse of Children.* Toronto: University of Toronto Press, 1993.

Orr, D., and Downes, M. "Self-Concept of Adolescent Sexual Abuse Victims." *Journal of Youth and Adolescence* 14 (1985):401–10.

Rodeheffer, M., and Martin, H. "Special Problems in Developmental Assessment of Abused Children." In *The Abused Child,* edited by H. Martin, pp. 113–28. Cambridge, MA: Ballinger, 1976.

Thompson, A. E. "Normal Child Development." In *Social Work with Abused and Neglected Children,* edited by K. Faller, pp. 219–37. New York: Free Press, 1981.

Tzeng, O. C. S.; Jackson, J. W.; and Karlson, H. C. *Theories of Child Abuse and Neglect.* New York: Praeger, 1991.

Van der Kolk, B. A. *Psychological Trauma.* Washington, DC: American Psychiatric Press, 1987.

Weston, J. A.; Colloton, M.; Halsey, S.; Covington, S., Gilbert, J.; Sorrentino-Kelly, L.; and Renoud, S. S. "A Legacy of Violence in Nonorganic Failure to Thrive." *Child Abuse and Neglect.* 17(6), (1993):709–714.

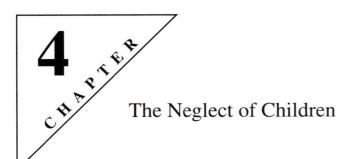

The Neglect of Children

A 5-year-old child sits on a Chicago doorstep in early January clad only in a thin dirty sweater, ragged slacks, and holey sneakers. With grimy fingers, she listlessly picks a potato chip from a half-empty bag. Her hair is matted and her eyes stare into the distance; she is indifferent to her surroundings. Beside her sits a 2-year-old, pulling idly at the threads on his already frayed socks. He, too, is ill clad despite the temperature. In the apartment above no one is home. In fact no one has been home since morning. Small, emaciated, dirty representatives of a world that pays little heed to their welfare, the children appear oblivious.

Neglect Defined

Defining *child neglect* in legal or social terms can in no way give an accurate picture of the neglected child. Such children must be seen to appreciate the true hopelessness of their existence. For years social workers and legal authorities have debated the definition of *neglect* and the magnitude of the problem.

Neglect is seen, by most experts, as an act of omission which some divide into three categories: *physical neglect, educational neglect, and emotional neglect* (DePanfilis and Salus, 1992). Zuravin and Taylor (1987, as cited in Pecora et al., 1992) broke neglect down into eight separate parental omissions:

1. *Physical health care,* failing to provide or delaying the provision of it
2. *Mental health care,* failure or delay in obtaining
3. *Supervision,* inadequate supervision both in and out of the home (includes truancy and depends on age of child)
4. *Substitute child care,* abandons child or does not return within 48 hours to substitute care provider without notifying provider
5. *Housing hazards,* does not protect child from hazards such as dangerous substances or objects
6. *Household sanitation,* does not insure that child is protected from spoiled foods, garbage, or human excrement, including malfunctioning toilets, etc.
7. *Personal hygiene,* does not keep the child's person and clothes clean and free from dirt and excrement
8. *Nutrition,* failure to provide regular and ample meals and failure to protect child from spoiled products or a diet which could cause physical health problems (pp. 17–18)

Admittedly the definition of *neglect* at any given time in history is influenced greatly by the mores and values of that particular period. Not only the contemporary standards but the cultural values significantly frame the definition. Our current society holds parents responsible for giving their children adequate food, shelter, and clothing; medical care; education; supervision and protection; and moral and social guidance (Kadushin and Martin, 1988; Gustavsson and Segal, 1994)

Polansky, Hally, and Polansky, who have done an extensive amount of research in the area of neglect, provide a more concise working definition:

> Child neglect may be defined as a condition in which a caretaker responsible for the child either deliberately or by extraordinary inattentiveness permits the child to experience available present suffering and/or fails to provide one or more of the ingredients generally deemed essential for developing a person's physical, intellectual, and emotional capacities. (1975, p. 5)

In 1967, to further define the concept of *neglect,* Norman Polansky and his colleagues developed the Childhood Level of Living Scale (CLL), originally as a result of research done among families in rural Appalachia and later applied to low-income families in Philadelphia. The CLL was designed to assess families with children between the ages of 4 and 7, but has also been used for a wider range of ages. Geared predominantly toward maternal care—because in a majority of households only the female parent was available for study—the CLL presents nine descriptive categories, five of which assess physical care and four the emotional, cognitive, or psychological factors. Under physical care, consideration is given to such factors as meal planning, medical care, safety issues, leaving the child alone, house or shelter adequacy and safety, appropriateness of sleeping and living conditions, and cleanliness. The psychological assessment considers the type of stimulation the child is given, the parents' emotional availability to the child, quality of discipline, the mother's concern for the child, and her own stability (Hally, Polansky, and Polansky, 1980, pp. A-2–A-8).

Despite the fact that Polansky and his fellow researchers purportedly used different types of families to draw the composite that became the CLL, experts in multicultural studies protest that the scale would make some functional minority families appear neglectful. For example, Amy Iwasaki Mass, an expert in Asian/Pacific studies, comments that the CLL would be totally inappropriate in assessing an immigrant Hmong family.

> The Hmongs are hill people from Laos who do not have a written language. Their culture and history have been passed orally from generation to generation. After the fall of Saigon, they had to leave their country to come to America because many of their men were used by the American armed forces during the Vietnam conflict. They have not been exposed to urban life, modern plumbing, transportation, electronics, or housing in their villages in Laos. They are not Christian. It would be highly unlikely that Hmong families would have magazines available, or that they would take their children to see some well-known historical building [see numbers 49 and 61 on CLL scale] when they find it challenging just to shop in a supermarket or taking public transportation to tend to essential business. (Mass, 1991)

Native American, Hispanic-American, and African-American families also often place emphasis on child-rearing practices that do not conform to the CLL scale. Certainly these cultural differences should not be enough to label them neglectful.

Polansky and his colleagues then field tested Magura and Moses' "Child Well-Being Scale" to determine if this scale could be validated as an adequate measure for detecting neglectful families. The Childhood Level Living Scale was lengthy and the Child Well-Being Scale offered a more concise tool if it proved valid. The author's sample included 53 neglectful families (who had already been deemed neglectful by child protective services) and a control group of 80 non-neglectful families. The scale assessed such areas as physical health care, personal hygiene, sanitation, supervision, safety, and arrangements for substitute care. Although these researchers felt that this scale was indeed a valid measure (Gaudin et al., 1992), Seaburg (1990) and Doueck (1991) voice reservations about the scale's sensitivity to such issues as cultural diversity.

Recognizing the limitations of the CLL scale, a panel of experts on child maltreatment in Ontario developed the Child Neglect Index to aid protective workers in Ontario as they make determinations of neglect. Although geared specifically to Ontario statutes, the scale can be applicable to other geographic locations (Trocmé, 1996).

The Child Neglect Index (CNI) (see Figure 4.1) assesses neglect in the following areas: (1) supervision, (2) food and nutrition, (3) clothing and hygiene, (4) physical health care, (5) mental health care, and (6) developmental/educational care (Trocmé, 1996). The index was originally tested by intake workers dealing with neglect cases and was found to be as reliable, if not in some instances more reliable, than the field trials used with the Child Well-Being Scales. Perusal of the short instrument attests to the latitude available to see cases in cultural contexts rather than imposing upon clients a particular cultural bias. However, Trocmé (1997) comments that the brevity of the index is both a strength and a weakness. Use of the CNI presupposes some degree of training on the part of the protective worker in order to make judgments. It is especially important that the worker be familiar with the cultural background of the family in question.

Polansky and his colleagues' studies were largely based in lower socioeconomic areas. But what of the family of the busy professionals whose 6-, 8-, and 10-year-old children let themselves in from school and prepare their own meals before the parents return home? The neighborhood is affluent and supposed to be idyllic. Yet these parents and children have little contact, and while well provided for materially, the children lack the attention necessary for healthy growth. However, the more affluent family, even if the parents were not able to meet the children's needs adequately, probably has many more resources available to them than a poor family. There may be more support within neighborhoods, among families, and friends. Families with money may be more able to pay for the care of their children (Trocmé, 1997). Thus status and income level may not only protect children from not having their needs met but may also protect a family from being defined and therefore reported as neglectful. The chances for this more affluent white family being reported to a protective agency are probably quite slim. Poor or minority families, on the other hand, are more likely to come to the attention of the social service system. Therefore, this chapter deals with the families more likely to be reported—those with lower incomes and with fewer resources.

Thus it becomes increasingly perplexing as to how to develop a scale to measure neglect which will encompass all socioeconomic and ethnic groups. Neglect is a type of

FIGURE 4.1   Child Neglect Index

20	15	5	0

CHILD'S NAME: _____   AGE: 0–2   3–5   6–12   13–16

FILE #:

WORKER' NAME: _____   DATE: _____

SUPERVISION

The two factors to be considered in assessing level of supervision are avoidability (i.e. extent to which a caretaker can be expected to anticipate and prevent) and severity of harm, or potential harm. CFSA identifies three specific types of harm that may result from failure to supervise:

Physical Harm S.37(2)(a&b)	**Sexual Molestation** S.37(2)(c&d)	**Criminal Activity/Child Under 13** S.37(2)(k)

na	Unknown/Does not Apply
0	1. Adequate; provisions made to ensure child's safety, caretaker knows child's whereabouts and activities, clear limits set on activities.
25	2. Inconsistent; child is occasionally exposed to situation that could cause moderate harm (e.g. young school-aged child occasionally left alone, parents do not monitor whereabouts of adolescent who occasionally comes home late in evening).
50	3. Inadequate; child is often exposed to situations that could cause moderate harm, or there is a slight possibility that child could suffer serious harm (e.g. young school-aged child often left unsupervised, or infant occasionally left alone while sleeping).
60	4. Seriously Inadequate; child is often exposed to situations that could cause serious harm; (e.g. abandonment, home used as "crack house" & drugs left within reach of child, child often left to wander in dangerous neighbourbood, toddler often exposed to hazardous situations).

PHYSICAL CARE

Physical harm or substantial risk of physical harm due to the caretaker's "failure to care and provide for...the child adequately" CFSA 37(2)(a&b).

FOOD/NUTRITION

na	Unknown/Does Not Apply
0	1. Regular and nutritional meals provided.
20	2. Meals irregular and often not prepared, but child's functioning is not impaired.
40	3. Meals irregular and often not prepared, child's functioning is impaired (e.g. child is hungry and has difficulty concentrating in class).
50	4. Inadequate food provided, there is a substantial risk that the child will suffer from malnutrition (e.g. infant given diluted formula).
60	5. Child displays clinical symptoms of malnutrition; medical attention and/or rehabilitative diet required (e.g., weight loss, anaemia, dehydration, etc.).

CLOTHING & HYGIENE

na	Unknown/Does Not Apply
0	1. Child is clean and adequately clothed.
20	2. Inadequate clothing or hygiene, but this does not appear to affect child's functioning.
40	3. Inadequate clothing or hygiene limits child's functioning (e.g. unable to go outdoors because of lack of clothing, isolated by peers because of hygiene or appearance).

50	4. Inadequate clothing or hygiene likely to cause illness requiring medical treatment (e.g. infestation of head lice).
60	5. Illness requiring medical treatment due to inadequate clothing or hygiene (e.g. serious infection due to poor diaper care, intestinal disorder).

PROVISION OF HEALTH CARE

For the following three scales "not provided" means "does not provide, or refuses or is unavailable or unable to consent to…" (CFSA S.37(2)(e, f, g, h, & j). The extent to which harm could be avoided should be carefully considered in rating these three scales. Three factors should be examined: (a) whether a reasonable layman would recognize that a problem needs professional attention; or (b) whether a professional has recommended services or treatment; or (c) availability and/or effectiveness of treatment or services (e.g. the questionable effectiveness of services for chronic teen runners).

PHYSICAL HEALTH CARE   CFSA S.37(2)(e)

na	Unknown/Does Not Apply
0	1. Basic medical care provided.
20	2. Preventive medical care not provided (e.g. no regular checkups).
40	3. Medical care not provided for injury or illness causing avoidable distress.
50	4. Medical care not provided for injury or illness causing avoidable distress and interfering with child's functioning (e.g. chronic absence from school due to untreated illness).
60	5. Medical care not provided for injury or illness which could lead to permanent impairment or death (e.g. infant vomiting or diarrhea leading to dehydration).

MENTAL HEALTH CARE   CFSA S.37(2)(f, g, & j)

na	Unknown/Does Not Apply
0	1. Parents anticipate and respond to child's emotional needs.
25	2. Inconsistent response to emotional distress (e.g., responds only to crisis situations).
50	3. Services or treatment not provided in response to emotional distress, child at substantial risk of severe emotional or behavioural problems (anxiety, depression, withdrawal, self-destructive or aggressive behaviour, child under 13 engaging in criminal activity).
60	4. Services or treatment not provided in response to emotional distress, child experiencing severe emotional or behavioural problems.

DEVELOPMENTAL AND EDUCATIONAL CARE   CFSA S.(2)(h)

na	Unknown/Does Not Apply
0	1. Child's developmental and educational needs are met.
25	2. Child's developmental and educational needs are inconsistently met (e.g. limited infant stimulation, child could benefit from remedial help in one or two subjects, child having academic difficulties due to poor school attendance).
50	3. Services or treatment are not provided in response to identified learning or developmental problems (e.g. learning disability diagnosed but caretakers refuse remedial help).
60	4. Child has suffered or will suffer serious/permanent delay due to inattention to developmental/educational needs (e.g. Non-Organic Failure To Thrive identified but caretakers refuse remedial help).

For further information contact Nico Trocmé (416–978–5718; nico@fsw.utoronto.ca), Faculty of Social Work, University of Toronto (Version 5: Toronto,1995)

Funding provided by the Child, Youth & Family Policy Research Centre & the Social Sciences & Humanities Research Council Reprinted with permission from Nico Trocmé, "Development and Preliminary Evaluation of the Ontario Child Neglect Index," *Child Maltreatment,* 1(2) (1996) p. 145–155. pp. 153–154.

maltreatment which is so dependent on cultural child rearing values as well as variations in the neighborhood, the community, and indeed by the cultural, economic, and political values of society itself (Hally, Polansky, and Polansky, 1980).

Causes of Neglect

Where does neglect begin? Does it commence when a family resigns itself to experiencing poverty or struggling to live with inadequate welfare benefits? Does neglect emanate from a decaying neighborhood that attracts those who care as little for themselves as they do for their surroundings? Or is neglect an individual phenomenon practiced by a parent or parents for whatever complex psychological reasons, resulting perhaps from their own unmet needs, stresses, or mental health problems?

Polansky and colleagues suggest that the causes can all be grouped within three theories:

> The *economic,* emphasizing the role of material deprivation and poverty; the *ecological,* in which a family's behavior is seen as responsive to the larger social context in which it is imbedded; and the *personalistic,* which attributes poor child care to individual differences among parental personalities, particularly their character structures. (1991, p. 21)

Economic Causes

Proponents of the economic view suggest that neglect is a response to stress, and poverty is an all-pervasive stress. Although she stresses the infantile personalities of parents as the major contributor to neglect, Young (1964) noted that poverty was widespread among the families studied. The most overwhelming feature in Katz's (1971) observations was the extreme level of poverty of these families; many were receiving welfare funds or aid from some other governmental or private program. Giovannoni and Billingsley (1970) and Pelton (1989) concluded that poverty had a deleterious effect on the parents' ability to care for their children. It cannot be denied that these families are among the poorest. Does neglect then stem from poverty? Or is poverty inevitable, given deficits in personality structure and the ability to cope with everyday tasks?

It should be noted in a discussion of the correlation between neglect and poverty that being poor may cause the onlooker to suspect neglect. Weissbourd (1996) notes that African-American children are nearly three times more likely than white children to be poor and for longer periods of their childhood. Hispanic children, the fastest-growing population of poor, actually outnumber African-American children. And yet, according to the Children's Defense Fund (1996) 58.5 percent of the abused and neglected children were white while 27.4 percent were African American and 10.1 percent Hispanic (p. 94). Thus, to be poor does not mean that a child is neglected. Why then do some poor families neglect while the majority do not? The answer must be found in other variables.

Ecological Causes

The ecological view originated with similar questions. According to a study by Wolock and Horowitz (1979), neighborhoods of maltreating parents appeared to be more run-down and more unfriendly, creating low morale among respondents. Again, does the low morale of unfriendly, poorly kept neighborhoods severely stress parents and sap their strength for adequate child care? Or does the obvious lethargy in those unable to parent lead to other undone tasks, such as proper housekeeping and adequate home repair, and to their inability to support and communicate with neighbors? Do neighborhoods fail to understand the practices of newly immigrated parents and therefore isolate them? When vulnerable families fall prey to slum landlords, are they too overwhelmed to band together and protest? Or has their own development hampered their ability to relate to others, even in this basic way? If parents' ability to care for their children is influenced by the total social context in which they live, then feeling unsupported by their surroundings could well create parents who neglect.

Today, the ecological perspective is widely favored as a sufficiently encompassing theory to deal with a form of maltreatment that has as many variables as neglect. Fostered largely by Germain (1991), the ecological view in social work practice sees the individual as part of and interacting with the environment. From the perspective of neglect, this view would lead to several assumptions. First, the neglectful family must be seen within the context of the neighborhood, their culture and society. An understanding of cultural and racial values is vital in assessing the family's ability to function. The family is seen as a complex system and the strengths they exhibit are as important as the problems they have. And finally, the family's issues are seen in relation to the community's ability to provide resources and social supports for them (Kadushin and Martin, 1988). The ecological approach to neglectful families puts more emphasis on interventions which stress social supports.

Societal Causes

The ecological perspective invites us to look at how society contributes to neglect. From a societal perspective, we have difficulty accepting that our values and institutions actually stimulate neglectful situations. For example, several years ago a state decreased its eligibility categories for Aid for Dependent Children recipients from three to two: potential and current need. Thus, if only lack of daycare services prevented a mother from working, she was eligible for free care. If she was currently receiving AFDC, she could also benefit. But if she had been on assistance in the past and had gotten a job, she was now cut off from the child care support. The result is obvious: Societal values and work-incentive programs espouse the work ethic, but the system actually discourages the mother's self-sufficiency and perpetuates the problem. The result for some mothers is depression, frustration, and possibly the neglect of their children's needs. For others it means working and leaving young children alone or inadequately supervised.

The welfare system is not the only contributor to neglect. The conversion of low- and moderate-income apartments into high-priced condominiums and the construction of condominiums, shopping malls, and professional buildings on formerly affordable housing sites leave families homeless or force them into decaying neighborhoods. These injustices burden the family with additional stresses. As immigrant and minority populations are forced into confined areas, their bitterness and frustration increase, and the energy they have available for child rearing decreases. Lives punctuated by long-term oppression often prevent parents from performing their roles adequately.

The contributors to neglect are many. Not only are neglectful families difficult for society to accept but they present problems for the system in its attempts to intervene.

Problems in Intervention

First, neglectful families are numerous. An average social worker's caseload has a considerable number of neglect cases. Second, many neophyte workers find these cases elusive; they don't know what to expect from the parents, and the neglect is difficult to document. Too often neglect is equated with material deprivation. If a family appears affluent, it is easier to ignore the emotional and physical neglect of the children. Third, coordination of these cases is extremely difficult. The organization that social workers feel is so desperately needed is alien to these clients. Social workers describe acute frustration with clients who have few skills or little ability to carry out the plans recommended for them. And frustration mounts because neglect often permeates generation after generation in these families. Fourth, when professionals do recognize neglect and mobilize the families, they have few tangible resources to offer them. With cutbacks in funds, programs, and personnel, how can they hope to meet the ever-growing needs?

Yet amidst frustration with the parents and insufficient resources, professionals are constantly motivated to try to intervene so that at least the children will have a chance.

Neglected Children

Neglect is a phenomenon which usually involves the entire family. If one child is neglected, usually all will be. Certainly as children grow older and are more able to care for themselves, they are less likely to be dependent on parental care, but the neglect of earlier years has usually taken its toll emotionally. The National Center on Child Abuse and Neglect found, in their 1993 study of child maltreatment, that children were significantly more likely to be neglected from birth to 1 year than at any other time in their lives. Of these, boys were slightly more frequently neglected than girls. From 1 year, the incidence of neglect declines with age until only a small percentage of adolescents are reported as neglected (U.S. Department of Health and Human Services, 1994).

Physician Vincent Fontana became concerned about neglected children when he came to the New York Foundling Hospital in the late 1960s. Although some of the 320 children then sheltered at the hospital had been battered, a substantial number showed signs of neglect. Fontana describes making the rounds:

> What my associates and I saw were dull-eyed children who turned their faces to the wall, who could not respond to a friendly touch. Children with infections that had gone untreated. Children who had had lice removed from their hair. Children who were slightly bruised, perhaps had a minor dislocation or two, whose eyes were big in hollow faces. Children who had been dehydrated almost to the point of death. Small children barely capable of speech who used the most incredible gutter language. Children who had been fed totally unsuitable foods. Children who showed traces of medication

never intended for children. Children who gave every appearance of being physically healthy, yet looked terribly lost and who never laughed and seldom cried. (1976, p. 20)

Symptoms of Neglect

Children who have been neglected demonstrate numerous symptoms including those described by Fontana. Some physical symptoms are not obvious, but others are—to a painful degree.

The *nonorganic failure to thrive syndrome* (NFTT) is a condition found in infants and diagnosed by the presence of several factors: (1) The infant has fallen below the fifth percentile in weight and often in height (Faller, et al., 1981). (The percentile scale is used by physicians to determine normal height and weight of infants and children. Below the fifth percentile means that 95 percent of babies weigh more than this.) (2) The baby was once of a weight and height within the expected norm. (3) The infant demonstrates a delay in psychomotor development (English, 1978; Weston et al., 1993).

NFTT may be caused by parental inexperience in not knowing how to feed properly or how much babies eat, or by diluting the formula for lack of money. NFTT can also be a more deeply rooted problem. Infants quickly sense the feelings and attitudes of caregivers. If the parent feels ambivalence or hostility toward the infant, lacks attachment, or sees the child as too demanding, the infant may react negatively. NFTT infants often exhibit little affect. They are difficult to feed because of poor ability to suck and little interest in food. Some infants vomit after feedings (Faller et al., 1981). These babies appear to turn inward, and parents describe them as unlovable or unwilling to be held. If untreated, the syndrome can result in death as the infant depends less and less on the environment and simply wastes away. Maternal deprivation has largely been held accountable for the NFTT syndrome. Family systems proponents suggest this condition is symptomatic of total family maladaptation, of family disengagement characterized by distancing and lack of communication within the total family unit (Alderette and deGraffenreid, 1986; Weston et al., 1993). In neglectful households, poor communication and the inability to get one's needs met are typical.

NFTT infants who are removed from home are likely to gain up to a pound a week when fed and stimulated properly. There is some controversy, however, about the maximum level of normalcy that can be attained.

Psychosocial Dwarfism

Children from 18 months to 16 years may suffer from a related syndrome known as *psychosocial dwarfism* (PSD), or by a variety of other terms including *hyposomatotropism, deprivational dwarfism,* or *abuse dwarfism.* The symptoms are similar to NFTT in that emotional deprivation promotes abnormally low growth. PSD children are also below the fifth percentile in weight and height, exhibit retarded skeletal maturation, and have a variety of behavioral problems. Bizarre eating patterns, which may include voracious overeating, indiscriminate eating, or stealing food, are compounded by failure to sleep, night wanderings, hyperactivity, or extreme fatigue. Enuresis (uncontrolled urination) or encopresis (fecal soiling) may further complicate the condition. Underlying the physical symptoms, children afflicted by PSD have reacted to the disturbed environment in which they live by their own disturbance of growth, development, speech, and social relationships. Removed from the distressing environment, most PSD victims recover (Faller et al., 1981).

Not all symptoms of neglect are as pronounced. Lack of emotional stimulation and poor nutrition affect weight gain but are not always immediately discernible. Nor are all children neglected from infancy, but to understand this is to comprehend the parental needs and patterns of neglect discussed later in the chapter.

Effects and Affects of Neglect: Infancy to Adolescence

Infancy

Infants who are neglected demonstrate poor muscle tone and an inability to support their own weight in later months. If the infant lies unattended for long periods, hair is rubbed off the back of the head, and the back of the head may become flattened. The infant fails to gain weight properly. Infants who have little confidence in their environment are unwilling to make eye contact and do not smile, babble, or squeal as normal babies do. Babies who are not changed or who are left in their own excrement or vomit develop rashes and infections that may go untreated.

Poor motor skills and language development delays appear in neglected children. Continued lack of attention to diet as well as to emotional needs creates a child with poor skin clarity and dull hair. Severe malnutrition creates the distended stomach and emaciated limbs that are associated with children from countries experiencing famine. Lack of emotional stimulation promotes flat affect or extreme passivity.

Under normal circumstances these impairments in development would be detected by the child's physician. Physician Henrika Cantwell (1980, p. 187) suggests that the following is the *minimum* number of preventive visits expected: from birth to 2 months, the child should be seen at least twice; 6 to 12 months, the child should be seen twice; 12 to 18 months, at least once; 18 to 24 months, at least once; 2 to 5 years, at least once; 5 to 11 years, once; and 11 to 18 years, at least once. Neglectful parents, however, often leave medical problems unattended let alone attend to regular checkups. Immunizations, as well as screenings for anemia and lead poisoning, may never be completed, and avoidable childhood diseases often become a painful part of the neglected child's life.

Another persistent medical problem in the neglectful home is *pediculosis,* or lice. Children's lice-infested hair may infect the body as well. Getting rid of these pests is a time-consuming process of shampoos and combings, which can be beyond the abilities of the already overwhelmed parent.

Young Children
Behaviorally, neglected children present a sad picture.

> *Lori Sue Samson sits in front of an old TV, rocking her frail body while sucking on two fingers and clutching a dirty, tattered blanket. The blanket, much loved and fiercely guarded, is her only memory of a time when her mother rewarded her spasmodically with fervent attention. But by the time Lori Sue was 18 months, Mama had another baby, and then another two years later, and the last six months ago. Now 5-year-old Lori Sue is the designated caregiver while Mama shops, visits, and meets friends at their hangout, the bowling alley. Small for her age, the child twists dull, tangled hair around one finger. After occasional admonishments about not combing her hair, both mother and child have tired of the struggle. Lori Sue has not yet lost a tooth and her baby teeth are fragile and decayed. Idly she drags the blanket with her as she retreats to the kitchen, searching for something to eat.*
>
> *In a crib at the far side of the kitchen is 6-month-old Franny, naked but for an undershirt. The baby is awake, but pays little attention to her older sister. She is listless and small. A full bottle of now-curdled milk lies beside her, but the infant makes no move to reach it. The mattress on which she lies is soiled and lacks a sheet. Lori Sue gazes at her baby sister and goes quickly into the next room to assure herself that her 3-year-old brother is still asleep on his mattress.*
>
> *The Samson children are alone and have been for several hours. It is not that 21-year-old Ella Samson does not care about her children. She does, in her own inconsistent way. She did not think that parenting would be too much for her. When she became pregnant with Lori Sue at age 16, Ella had been jubilant. She hadn't expected that her boyfriend would leave her after impregnating her once again, nor that a new boyfriend would later do the same. Ella Samson is sure she is a victim— just as others feel her children are.*

Within the year, Lori Sue Samson will go to school. Her hair, too tangled to comb, will have to be cut. Her teacher will report that she is dirty, smells, has lice, and an impossibly short attention span. And Lori Sue will have difficulty understanding the most basic commands given her at school.

Cantwell (1985) suggests that neglected children do not do well in school partly because their home environment has robbed them of the ability to understand the messages being given in the classroom. The teacher may say, "Now sit in your seats, put your feet on the floor, take out your notebook, and copy this word off the board." Children like Lori Sue who are accustomed to hearing one-command statements (e.g., Sit down! Shut up! Shut the door!) do not have the experience to conceptualize the number of commands given in the teacher's instructions. But they have also learned that not to respond to a command may result in being hit or at least a stern admonishment. So the child complies with as much of the message as he or she has heard—"Sit in your seat." How this seeming lack of compliance is handled by the teacher differs. If the teacher reacts with annoyance, the child, in time, will conclude that nothing he or she does is correct. In time, this child may experience school as a series of frustrations. If the teacher recognizes the child's lack of comprehension, there may be a happier ending.

Impaired socialization is not uncommon in neglected children. Impairment in language development manifests itself in the child's inability to conceptualize beyond the most basic level. This lack leads to poor communication with others who have the ability. Thus as the neglected child grows older, he or she feels isolated from all but those who are similarly lacking in this ability.

Another aspect of socialization is the internalization of standards. Due to the inconsistency in the home setting, the neglected child is never sure what to expect. Without defined and consistent rules, neglected children face punishment when their actions annoy the caregiver. Little attention is given to what is best for the child. Therefore neglected children do not develop an internalized set of standards to guide them. Instead, they respond to external stimuli. For these children, whether stealing is wrong is less important than the prospect of getting caught.

Along with this impaired thinking goes a need to "have it now." Neglected children are never sure if their pleasures or prizes will be available tomorrow. If Mom fixes dinner one day it does not mean she will the next— or the next. Therefore the children learn to take it when it comes. Thus, these children develop an inability to delay gratification, which in turn results in impulsive behavior, stealing, promiscuity, and a variety of other frustrations for both the individual and for society.

Adolescents

It is not uncommon in neglectful homes for older children to strike out on their own at an early age. Thus early emancipation through moving out, running away, or becoming pregnant often sets the cycle of neglect in motion once again. Neglected children with unmet needs are isolated from those who have learned to compete in society. They seek out others with similar backgrounds and begin the pattern again with their children.

Neglectful Parents

The neglectful parent has long been an enigma to the greater society. It is difficult for most of us to understand how a family can slip to the level of disorder, confusion, indifference, and filth exhibited by some neglectful households. Yet there is a segment of our population that knows little else, and being sufficiently isolated from others save those with similar values, they have little chance to learn another style of living. The typical neglectful parent is an isolated individual who has difficulty forming relationships or carrying on the routine tasks of everyday life. Burdened with the anger and sadness over unmet childhood needs, this parent finds it impossible to consistently recognize and meet the needs of her or his children. Most neglecting households are headed by women due largely to the inability of these women to maintain lasting heterosexual relationships. Always at the commencement of a relationship is the hope that this new lover or helpmate will meet the unmet needs from childhood. When neither the man nor woman is able to ease the burden of sorrow carried by the other, the man moves on, leaving the woman to try to mother the children they have created.

In the mid-1960s, Young studied families involved with child welfare agencies in both urban and rural areas. She describes the neglectful parents as wearing "blinders imposed by their own unsatisfied needs; they can rarely appraise reality apart from themselves" (1964, p. 23). Young found these parents to be emotionally detached from and indifferent to their children. Yet they never refused their children permission to join in school activities. If they slapped their children, it was done in a fit of emotion or a burst of impulsive irritation. Young wrote:

> If the behavior of neglecting parents toward their children could be summed up in one word, that word would be indifference. Children themselves, they reacted as children to the demands and obligations of parenthood and of adult life. They had little wish to hurt their children but most of them had small capacity to help them. (1964, p. 31)

One of the biggest issues in intervening in neglectful households is the parents' inability to plan.

> Carrying responsibility, fulfilling obligations, planning for the future are actions. They require a goal, a direction, and the active effort to move in that direction. Without continuity of effort there can be no direction and without planned action there can be no progression. Inherent in neglect is a lack of continuity, and therefore direction; without direction parental action is likely to be little more than blundering in the dark. The neglecting parents in this study did not plan and so their lives and the lives of their children showed no consistent direction except for the drift toward personal and family disintegration. What actions they did take were nearly always those impulsive responses to pressures and problems that seek escape not solution. For the rest the parents drifted passively, convinced of their helplessness and of the hostility of the outside world. (Young, 1964, p. 18)

In addition, Hally, Polansky, and Polansky (1980, 1991) suggest that neglectful parents are less involved with others, less able to control impulses, less verbally accessible, and less equipped with pride in their accomplishments or workmanship. In these studies, neglectful parents were found to test lower on intelligence scales and higher on scales for anomie, or an absence of social norms or values.

Cantwell (1980, p. 184) suggests that "neglectful parenting can be attributed to a lack of knowledge, lack of judgment, and lack of motivation," and outlines some examples:

Parents *lack knowledge* in the areas of attending to their children's needs (e.g., a baby must be fed every three to four hours), housekeeping and cooking skills, nutrition, child development including the need for stimulation and nurturing, medical care, and the need to set limits for children. Parents may also *lack judgment* in perceiving when a child is really ill, knowing when to leave a child alone, recognizing when children are unable to act like adults, and knowing what roles are appropriate for parents and what roles belong to children. They may also *lack motivation* in the form of energy to attend to their children, or because they feel that they are the best judge of what is best for their children. These parents may have little desire or energy to learn. Their behavior may well be based on the fact that they have no standard for comparison. If they were raised in neglectful families, they may not see that anything is wrong. Once again, it is vital that the assessment of parental limitations be seen within their context of their culture.

Whether or not we understand the apparent indifference of these parents toward their children, many theorists feel that parents who neglect have disturbances in their personality structure.

Polansky, Borgman, and DeSaix (1972) describe these parents as having *infantile personalities.* The word *infantile,* despite its negative connotation, refers simply to a regression or fixation to childhood concerns or being burdened with remnants of unfinished business of one's childhood. The parents' need to attain or mourn the love and concern expected but not given them in their family of origin explains, to some extent, their inability to give to their own children.

Perhaps another reason why these parents present themselves as infantile is not only that they have not had their needs met in childhood, but also because their parenting career has begun prematurely. Hampton (1991) in his study of African-American families found that neglectful parents were more likely to have their children at a younger age, more likely to have more live births spaced close together, and that these births were more often unplanned (p. 55). The comparison group of white neglectful parents was similar except that white mothers had their children at a slightly older age. Zuravin and DiBlasio (1992) studied teen mothers who were found to be neglectful and found that these mothers were likely to have additional children during their teen years. Thus we find overburdened parents, usually a mother, who finds herself unprepared and unsupported in the important task of parenting. It is not surprising, therefore, that, given the likelihood of coming from a dysfunctional family herself, the pattern of neglect repeats itself.

Personalities of Neglectful Mothers

In 1972, Polansky, DeSaix, and Sharlin developed a set of types of neglectful mothers which some still find useful today. These types are: (1) apathetic-futile; (2) impulse ridden; (3) mentally retarded; (4) women in reactive depression; and (5) women who are borderline or psychotic.

Of these types, the authors felt that most women fell into the apathetic-futile and impulse-ridden categories. Little emphasis was at first placed on neglectful fathers in Polansky's studies, as households were most often of single-parent women. Later the influence of the father was researched (Polansky et al., 1991). The results showed that the quality of child care and whether a family is considered neglectful or not still rests largely on the personality structure of the mother.

Apathetic-futile

The women who are characterized as apathetic-futile (Polansky et al., 1991) seem to have given up on living. They are withdrawn, flat in affect, with a feeling that nothing is worth doing. "What is the point of changing the diaper?" the mother asks. "She'll just get it dirty again." She is lonely, emotionally numb, and isolated. The relationships she does attempt are superficial and chaotic, giving her little real pleasure. She is typically stubbornly negative. This mother fears commitment but may comply with requests in a hostile passive-aggressive manner. Her thinking is doggedly concrete. She thinks in terms of black or white because she lacks the ability to conceptualize except on the most basic level. Her limited conceptualization ability and underdeveloped language skills make her verbally inaccessible. She may be annoyed when people don't understand her when she uses inappropriate words. One mother described how the lifeguard gave her son "artificial perspiration," and was openly angered when a social worker didn't immediately comprehend. Yet inherent in her problem is an inability to gain insight. She is almost incapable of self-observation.

The Brent family exemplifies the apathetic-futile syndrome.

The Brents came to the attention of social services when City Hospital reported that 2-month-old Gordon had just died. The cause of death was determined to be severe neglect.

The Brent family lives on the second floor of a run-down, three-story house in an urban area. There is trash on the porch, and the backyard is cluttered with car parts, an old refrigerator, and assorted items. The social worker encountered a very dirty little boy, probably about age 4 or 5, standing outside. He was dressed in a tattered, soiled undershirt and shorts. He did not greet the worker but watched furtively.

There was no response to the knock at the door. The worker knocked again and still no response. Wordlessly the little boy came forward, opened the door, and went in, leaving the door open. It appeared to be an invitation, so the worker followed him into the kitchen, which was strewn with various bits of food. A strong smell appeared to be a combination of garbage and urine. Another child about 3 years old was crawling on the floor after a cat, but showed no reaction to the social worker. The older child went over, picked up the younger, and sat him on a chair.

They both stared at the worker. On the table were several beer cans and an empty potato chip bag. A sound from a bedroom made it obvious there was someone else in the house. At the same moment, a child cried in another room off the kitchen. The worker observed a baby about 1 year old sleeping on a bare mattress badly soiled with urine and feces. The baby was naked from the waist down and wore only a dirty shirt. Mrs. Brent emerged from the bedroom and wondered at the worker's presence. Mrs. Brent did express sorrow when told of Gordon's death, and explained that he had always been sickly. When questioned about the 1-year-old's lack of a diaper, the mother stated there was no point in keeping a diaper on as the child would only get it dirty.

At 5 years old, Ricky Brent is small for his age. He appears to be the primary caregiver for Peter, 3, and Alfred, 11 months, who rests on his mattress for hours without making a sound. Mrs. Brent rejected any suggestion that she might be having trouble coping with her children or the home situation, but accepted the agency's intervention in a hostile, but passive, manner.

Mrs. Brent is a small stocky woman who appeared to be in her 30s, but in fact is barely 20. She was dressed in a torn bathrobe and apparently nothing else. She was disheveled and somewhat incoherent and had apparently been sleeping, as she reported doing much of the time. She immediately lit a cigarette and continued to chain smoke, flicking her ashes on the floor.

Lorraine Blake Brent is the youngest of 13 children. Her family of origin had a history of involvement with the welfare system, and as a child Mrs. Brent was placed in a foster home for a short time as a result of "deplorable conditions" in her mother's home. Mrs. Brent calls herself her "mother's mistake," the result of her mother's attending a party for a group of sailors. At an early age Mrs. Brent was left alone while her mother and older siblings pursued their own interests.

Currently Mrs. Brent is a single parent. Her husband, Richard, age 29, worked sporadically, sometimes collecting unemployment or welfare. He reportedly is able to accept little or no responsibility and is currently serving a jail term for auto theft. He is the middle of seven children and his family also had frequent contacts with social service agencies. The Brents grew up in the same neighborhood and have known each other since childhood. When Lorraine became pregnant at age 14, the couple was married, and since that time Richard has come and gone as he pleased.

The difficulty for social workers is that such a mother's feelings of futility are quite contagious. Her lack of insight creates doubts in the inexperienced worker's mind as to the diagnosis. Even the most experienced workers relate the contagion of "nothing is worth doing." Without using the simplest language, the worker will not be understood (and even then may be blocked out), and intervention is extremely difficult.

Impulse-ridden

The impulse-ridden mother is one who has a low frustration tolerance, little ability to delay gratification, and uses extremely poor judgment in her actions (Polansky et al., 1991). She may demonstrate more energy in her undertakings, but this energy is usually directed toward getting her own needs met rather than meeting the needs of her children. Her home may not be as dirty and disorganized as the apathetic mother, but her consistency is in question. Characteristically she has used faulty judgment and is erratic in her treatment of her children. She fails to protect or nurture her children adequately. Over the years the children have learned that the only thing they can count on is that tomorrow will be different. Today their mother may be loving, tomorrow irritable and rejecting. Millie exemplifies such a parent.

The school voiced its concern over the Harper family, alleging that 7-year-old Alice and 6-year-old Karen had not been in school for most of the past two months. Both girls had severe coughs, which appeared to be untreated.

The social worker was greeted by Beverly Harper, an attractive African-American woman, who said she was the children's grandmother. She recounted with some annoyance that her 28-year-old daughter Millie, the children's mother, had just gotten home after being away for several days. Millie apparently had no address of her own and dropped the girls off unannounced and left them for extended periods.

Millie Harper was an attractive young woman who behaved more like a teen- ager than the mother of two. She was neatly dressed, relatively clean, and babbled enthusiastically about her latest boyfriend, with whom she and the girls "were going to live." In fact, they had stayed there several times "just to try it out." Ms. Harper appeared extremely nervous and bit her nails. She reported having had several addresses over the last year, usually taking the girls with her to stay with her boyfriend of the moment. She did not perceive this as a problem for the girls. She spoke of the girls' fathers. Alice's was a migrant worker from Puerto Rico, whom she had dated for a short time, and Karen's was a white college student, with whom she had been particularly impressed.

When it was pointed out that the girls had persistent coughs, she seemed gen- uinely concerned and said she might take them to the clinic. Assuming that the school had made the report, Ms. Harper embarked on a tirade of perceived injus- tices by the school personnel. These perceived injustices caused her to rationalize not sending the children to school more often. She felt that her children were being discriminated against in the predominantly white school.

Discussion was difficult with this nervous, flighty young woman. The girls' welfare reminded her of a myriad of other stories, which she recounted excitedly. Throughout the meeting, Ms. Harper's mother grumbled to herself, picking up accumulated clutter in the small apartment, all the while smoking incessantly. At one point Millie Harper suggested that if social services preferred, she would leave the children with her mother until she became "settled." "Like hell you will!" came almost inaudibly from her mother.

Although she obviously cares for her children, Millie Harper has difficulty perceiving and meeting their needs. Her inability to recognize inappropriate situations and living con- ditions exposes her children to an erratic, potentially harmful lifestyle. Despite her caring for the girls on numerous occasions, Millie's mother appears to give little real support.

Mentally Retarded

Mental retardation certainly does not negate the possibility of adequate parenting. In fact, only a small percentage of neglectful mothers are mentally retarded. However, without proper supervision and education, it is possible for neglect to become an issue.

Terry Taylor and her infant daughter Michelle came to the attention of social ser- vices when Michelle was hospitalized after being fed whole milk rather than a for- mula. The baby was also extremely thin and had a severe diaper rash that had become infected. Ms. Taylor, at age 23, had the mental age of 12. She reported liv- ing on her own in an apartment across town. Extremely distraught and agitated over the illness of her baby, whom she obviously adored, Ms. Taylor was difficult to talk with, but her background was eventually uncovered.

Brain-damaged at birth, Terry Taylor had attended a series of schools and programs for the mentally retarded. Her older parents were obviously so pleased with her progress that they repeatedly told her older married siblings how self-sufficient Terry was. The parents died in quick succession 18 months ago, and Terry's care was relegated to her older sister who lived in a small town some distance away. "I didn't want her to have to leave her sheltered workshop," the sister later reported, but also admitted that she "didn't trust my bum of a husband" around attractive Terry.

For whatever reasons, the sister set Terry up in her own apartment in the city and returned home. Confused, lonely, and disoriented, Terry did not return to the workshop and was befriended by a male neighbor who subsequently impregnated her and left. Disgusted by Terry's plight, the sister arranged to have a family care for her during her pregnancy. She delivered a healthy baby girl and returned to her own apartment. Why neither the foster family nor the hospital intervened for support is unclear. A visiting nurse did stop by on several occasions, but felt the young mother was doing fine.

Lonely and depressed Terry had difficulty caring for her infant. When money was not forthcoming from her sister, she tried to feed the baby whole milk. The baby became ill, and Terry, in frustration and panic, began screaming hysterically. A neighbor urged her to open the door and, alarmed by the baby's overall poor condition, took the mother and child to the hospital.

With supervision, Terry Taylor might have been able to care for infant Michelle. Without it, however, this young mother was overwhelmed and unable to adequately parent.

Reactive depression

Characterized by the mother's inability to adjust to some aspect of her life and the resultant depression over that inability, the reactive-depressive mother is left incapable of parenting adequately. Other factors such as the birth of another child, desertion by a spouse, or death of a loved one can trigger such a depression. For Jane Wales the depression was a result of a change in lifestyle.

The building is extremely run down and situated over a liquor store. There is no glass on the outside door and the stairs up to the third floor are extremely dirty. When the worker arrived at the apartment, Mrs. Wales had apparently just returned and was wearing a soiled, torn housedress. She stated that she had been downstairs at a neighbor's "getting her husband cigarettes." Mrs. Wales is an obese young woman who looks much older than her 23 years. Her hair is uncombed and appears dirty. She is softspoken with little or no affect, and in fact, expresses little emotion about anything.

Mrs. Wales made no objection when the worker suggested they go into the apartment. Inside were two children, a baby about 18 months old and a girl about 2. Both were in cribs in one section of a small, unlighted apartment, which appeared to have only one large room, an alcove containing a double bed and the two cribs, and a kitchen. There were tattered curtains at the windows and several broken panes of glass that had newspaper over them. There was only a couch and one table in the main room, and a dinette set in the kitchen. The smell in the apartment was overwhelming. The kitchen table was cluttered with dishes and there were piles of dirty dishes on the sink and on the stove. The entire kitchen was lit-

tered with scraps of food; the chairs and table were crusted. The couch had a ripped and dirty cover. On the table were several packs of cigarettes and matches. The floor appeared not to have been cleaned for some time.

Both children were scantily clad, the baby in a diaper and light shirt and the little girl in a light sleeveless nightgown and diaper. Sitting in her crib, the little girl played with her toes. The baby was crying and banging his head against the bars of his crib. The mother made no attempt to comfort either child, but finally got a bottle from the table and gave it to the baby. He retired to the far side of the crib to drink it. The little girl fussed and was given a cupcake. Both cribs were sheeted but quite dirty.

Mrs. Wales answered the worker's questions but volunteered little. She spoke in an even, quiet tone with little or no inflection. She stated that her husband worked at a nearby mill, and although he had changed jobs frequently in the past, he was a fairly steady worker and provided a meager income for the family. She also stated she did occasionally go to the neighbors and leave the children alone, but thought they were fine if left in their cribs. At no time did she look at her children until the baby, bottle finished, began to cry again. Mrs. Wales picked him up and put him on the floor. She then did the same for the little girl, who began searching for crumbs to eat.

At one point the mother looked furtively at the clock and suggested that the worker leave before her husband got home. When asked why, she could only respond that he would not like finding the worker there. Mrs. Wales agreed that the worker might return on another occasion. During the next few visits the worker learned the following about the Wales family.

Jane Foster Wales, mother of Marlene, 23 months, and Ronald, Jr., 8 months, is a daughter of Mary and Harold Foster, successful real estate brokers in town. Mrs. Wales has not seen her mother nor father since her marriage four years ago. Mrs. Wales is a high school graduate who completed one year of college before her marriage. She was an excellent student and reportedly of above-average intelligence.

Mrs. Wales is the younger of two children. Her brother, she assumes, is still in business with their father, but she has not seen him since her marriage either. She reports that she met her husband while he was working in a gas station. Her car broke down on her way home from college one weekend, and Mr. Wales was the attendant at the garage. They dated for several months, and Mrs. Wales discovered she was pregnant. The couple's decision to marry met with the complete disapproval of Mrs. Wales's parents, who said they would never see her again. They kept their word, and Mrs. Wales's several attempts to contact them have been to no avail. "My father wanted me to be a doctor," Mrs. Wales once said, "and he was really angry when I quit school."

The Waleses had a baby boy who was born with a heart problem. His death at 3 months brought about severe depression for Mrs. Wales. She gained more than 100 pounds, stayed at home, and remembers feeling alone and isolated at first. After a while "it didn't matter." Now Mrs. Wales rarely goes out of the apartment building and only occasionally goes to the neighbors, who buy cigarettes for her husband. She is obviously a very depressed young woman.

Ronald Wales, 23, is the oldest of 10 children. He left home at age 16 when he felt put upon because his alcoholic father had disappeared, leaving him again to help support his mother. He states he was "sick of it" and longed to be on his own. The local welfare department records numerous contacts with the family, including several for severe neglect. There has been no contact between Wales and his family.

After leaving home, Mr. Wales had numerous odd jobs, the longest of which was attendant in the gas station. He appears to be an extremely immature young man who requires that his wife wait on him hand and foot. Although there is no evidence that he has ever abused his wife, Mrs. Wales seems afraid to displease him. She makes sure that he is always well stocked with cigarettes. Mr. Wales seems oblivious to his wife's depression, weight problem, or insufficient care of the children. He pays little attention to the children except to make sure they are out of his way.

Psychotic

Psychosis is present in only a small percentage of neglectful families. Frequently the neglect stems from the parents' inability to see beyond their delusional world. Detection is not always easy. When the parent is not hallucinating, she or he may be conscious of the needs of the child. This inconsistency is damaging in and of itself. Some parents have a borderline reality orientation. Such individuals drift in and out of psychosis or practice delusional thinking, once again causing confusion for the child.

Social Services received a call that Norma Spitz needed immediate hospitalization and a placement for her 3-year-old son, Georgie. When the worker arrived at the Spitz home, the police were already there, having been summoned by neighbors. The house was dark, and shrieks were heard from behind the locked doors. A small naked boy dashed excitedly from window to window calling inaudible phrases to the assembled group. He was finally prevailed upon to open the door and turn on the lights.

The small house was extremely dirty and scattered with a mixture of food, dog food, and animal feces. Mrs. Spitz, dressed in shorts and a torn blouse in spite of the mid-winter chill, sat on a stool in the kitchen, rocking and mumbling to herself, "God is dead. God is dead." Georgie dashed about in a frenzy repeating his mother's exclamation and asked the worker, "Did you know God is dead?"

This was not the first time social services had been involved with the Spitz family. At 35, Norma Spitz was the mother of five children, all of whom had spent their lives in and out of foster homes. Mrs. Spitz had been in and out of hospitals since she was 15 years old. During her first stay, she had met Herman Spitz whom she later married. Spitz was diagnosed schizophrenic and was himself hospitalized on several occasions. He also frequented detoxification centers for treatment of his alcoholism. Twenty years older than his wife, Herman Spitz had drifted away and was now assumed by Mrs. Spitz to be dead.

Mrs. Spitz had been treated as an outpatient during several periods of her motherhood. During visits with her children, she appeared to be a concerned, loving mother. Returning the children to her, however, usually resulted in her rehospitalization.

> *At his birth, Georgie had been cared for by an itinerant sister of Mr. Spitz's.*
> *At 18 months, Georgie was returned to Mrs. Spitz when the sister moved to another*
> *city. Seen regularly at a community mental health center, Mrs. Spitz had appeared*
> *to do well with her son. It was unclear exactly what had sparked her breakdown*
> *but a reorganization at the health center caused a change in her treatment.*

It is often extremely difficult to work with or predict the future behavior of psychotic parents. Hospitalization causes interruptions in child care and can be extremely confusing for children. If the parent is capable of stabilizing, it is usually only through close supervision and support from community agencies.

Substance-Abusing Families

Substance abuse on the part of parents, like domestic abuse, can lead to any type of child maltreatment. Parents under the influence of drugs or alcohol could physically, sexually, or emotionally abuse their children and often do. It is certainly true that even if they do not abuse their children in one of these ways they are not fully available to be adequate parents. For this reason, that the influence of substances hampers parents in parenting and therefore implies neglect, the subject of substance-abusing parents is included in this chapter.

> *Dolores, 18 years old and five months pregnant, appeared at the free prenatal*
> *clinic at the insistence of her AFDC social worker. This was the girl's second preg-*
> *nancy. During her first pregnancy she had been "kicked out" of her closely knit*
> *Puerto Rican family. She began to use alcohol and drugs. When the baby was born*
> *she gave it up for adoption after it was diagnosed with fetal alcohol syndrome. The*
> *social worker advised the clinic that not only was Dolores continuing to drink, but*
> *the father used cocaine and had "turned on" Dolores to the drug. Despite staff*
> *counseling, Dolores continued to drink and use drugs until she gave birth to a pre-*
> *mature baby who was diagnosed with fetal alcohol syndrome and went through*
> *drug withdrawal at birth.*

Prenatal Abuse

Although, over the years, some women have ingested substances known to be harmful to unborn fetuses, it is only recently that this has been identified as child abuse. Kropenske et al. (1994) identify numerous medical complications which can be caused by prenatal substance abuse. Children born of substance-abusing mothers may be premature, have infectious diseases, be infected with Human Immunodeficiency Virus (HIV) or AIDS or demonstrate such syndromes as Fetal Alcohol Syndrome (FAS), failure to thrive (FTT), Sudden Infant Death Syndrome (SIDS), intrauterine growth retardation (IUGR), or central nervous system disorders. Neurological disturbances may cause babies to demonstrate such symptoms as: irritability, tremors, high-pitched crying, increased or decreased muscle tone, problems with sucking or frantic sucking, seizures, diarrhea, excessive vomiting, rapid and unusual eye movements, or disturbed sleep patterns (Kelley, 1992, Kropenske, et. al., 1994).

Fetal Alcohol Syndrome (FAS) or *Fetal Alcohol Effects* (FAE—not the full syndrome but several effects associated with it) are conditions which have frequently been seen by protective services workers over the years. The diagnosis of FAS is based on three criteria: low birth weight, an abnormally small head, and prenatal and postnatal growth retardation. Later the child will be identifiable by abnormalities of the face, intellectual impairment, developmental delays, and neurological problems. These children have difficulty learning, remembering, problem solving, and being aware of cause and effect. They are often uncoordinated, hyperactive and impulsive (Kelley, 1992, Inciardi et al., 1993, Kropenske et al., 1994). Dorris (1989) in his book, *The Broken Chord,* describes his experiences with a fetal alcohol syndrome child who he had adopted from an Indian reservation in the Dakotas. The story makes clear the impact of this condition and how it affects both the child's and the parents' ability to function.

It is also important to mention, in this context, the incidence of the *HIV virus* or of *AIDS* among young children. The virus can be not only transmitted in utero, but also at delivery or through breast milk. Mothers who are injection drug users, prostitutes, or who have had multiple sexual partners have the ability to transmit this disease to their babies before or at birth. The prognosis for these infants is poor. Or newborns may test negative and later show evidence of infection. Currently, the outcome for these children is uncertain (Kropenske et al., 1994).

Substance Abuse and Children

Not all mothers abuse substances during pregnancy. For some, their abuse does not become problematic until the child is older.

> *Penny was 14 when she had her first baby, Joanne. At 16, when she became pregnant with her second child, Eddie, the father of this child, suggested that they get married. After the birth of Amy, Penny and Eddie found that parenting was not what they had imagined. When a friend suggested they try crack, it seemed like an exciting new experience. Smoking crack, using devices that Eddie made from old beer cans, provided a unique form of entertainment. Penny found that she could get extra money for crack through having sex with dealers. Eddie didn't seem to mind as long as she brought home the crack to him. Neither noticed when their lives changed. They became absorbed in their habit to the point where they cared little about themselves, each other, and their two children. When four-year-old Joanne was found wandering the neighborhood by a local police officer, protective services was called in. What social workers found was two ill parents who in no way could cease their bingeing on drugs to care for their children.*

Inciardi et al. (1993) describe drug users such as Penny and Eddie when they say:

> This tendency to "binge" on crack for days at a time, neglecting food, sleep, and basic hygiene, severely compromises physical health. As such, crack users appear emaciated most of the time. They lose interest in their physical appearance. Many have scabs on their faces, arms, and legs—the result of burns and picking on skin (to remove bugs and other insects believed to be crawling *under* the skin). Crack users have burned facial hair from carelessly lighting their smoking paraphernalia; they have burned lips and tongues from the hot stems of their pipes; and they seem to cough constantly. (p. 11)

Although other drugs are equally as damaging to one's ability to parent, crack is perhaps one of the most popular street drugs due to its availability and affordability. Heroin, hallucinogens, cocaine, and morphine are also available. The effects of any of these substances are that the parents under their influence become ineffective caretakers. Their dulled reactions, euphoria, sleepiness, or general neglect of their children's needs can also expose these children to possible sexual or physical abuse. Often drug- and alcohol-abusing parents are so addicted to the substance and their way of life that social service intervention can do little to effect change. It is only when the parent sees a reason to be helped that change can occur. For some, their children may not be reason enough.

Plight of the Parent and the Social Worker

When professionals see the effects that parents' problems and deficits have on their children, it is easy to condemn the neglectful parent as the adversary or enemy. This attitude must be counteracted because the parent is all the child knows, and children see the condemnation of their parents as a rejection of themselves. It is important to remember the parent is like a child. Given a neglectful family of four, there are not two adults and two children but rather four children. Children grow emotionally when their needs are met. Unmet needs result in retarded emotional growth. Only by seeing the omissions of the neglectful parent as a cry for help can we truly understand them.

New social workers, especially, want to remove the children from their neglectful families. In some situations, this is the only solution. Yet in a great number of neglectful homes, the solution is not that simple. The cycle must be broken to ensure that the next generation has a chance to grow into healthy adults. To achieve this, it is not so much placement that is needed as "parenting" of the parents so they can take care of their children. Unfortunately, this takes time and a great deal of energy. Neglectful families elicit the same feelings of futility and hopelessness in those who try to help them. The degree of stress experienced by neglecting parents often strikes the worker as overwhelming. Progress with this type of client is extremely slow. Since the average worker has more neglect than abuse cases, it is vital to understand the neglectful parent.

Summary

Neglect of children is a result of parental failure to meet basic human needs—adequate food, shelter, safety, and affection. Several authors have attempted to define *neglect*—first by the creation of the Childhood Level Living Scale, developed by Polansky and colleagues, and second by the creation of the Child Well-Being Scale.

It is difficult to determine the cause or causes of neglect. Some theorists feel the economic factors should be considered, along with deficits in the personality structure of the parent. Today, many theorists favor an ecological view—that is, the parent within the context of the environment.

Children who have been neglected demonstrate retarded growth, poor motor and language development, flat affect, indications of malnutrition, unattended medical problems, and an inability to conceptualize. Older children often seek early emancipation and may begin the cycle all over again. Neglectful parents are largely children themselves. Their infantile personalities seem to be largely the result of their own unmet childhood needs. They are isolated, have difficulty maintaining relationships, are verbally inaccessible, and lack the knowledge, judgment, and maturation to adequately parent their children. From their studies of neglectful mothers, Polansky and colleagues identified five types of personalities: the apathetic-futile, the impulse-ridden, the woman in reactive depression, the mentally retarded, and the psychotic. Parents may also neglect (or abuse) under the influence of drugs or alcohol.

Although knowledge about maltreatment is increasing, we need to strive to understand the large numbers of neglectful families, and by understanding, hope to break the cycle.

Exploration Questions

1. How can *neglect* be defined? Why must a client's cultural background be considered when defining *neglect?*

2. What theories explain the causes of neglect?

3. What is community neglect?

4. What makes neglectful families difficult to treat?

5. What are symptoms of neglect in infants? In older children?

6. What is meant by NFTT and PSD? What are their causes and how are they different?

7. Why might neglected children have difficulty in school?

8. What are some characteristics of neglectful parents? What appears to be the underlying reason for these parents' neglect?

9. Cite the categories of neglectful mothers, as described by Polansky and colleagues and describe each.

10. What effects might their parents' substance abuse have on children?

Activities for Applied Learning

1. Cite instances of community neglect within your own community. What could be done to remedy them? What could you personally do?

2. Listen to "Corinne's Story" on the tape *Abusive and Neglectful Parents* (available through National Education Association Professional Library, 1201 16th St. NW, Washington, DC 20036).

3. Roleplay an interview with Mrs. Brent or Mrs. Wales. What else might these women tell you about their lives?

4. Research the life of James Earl Ray (assassin of the Reverend Martin Luther King) or Arthur Bremer (would-be assassin of Gov. George Wallace), both of whom were victims of neglect. What led them to commit their crimes? Are there other notorious neglected children you can research?

5. Invite a speaker from the local alcohol/drug treatment program to talk on the effects of parental substance abuse on children.

Suggested Readings

Cantwell, H. B. "Child Neglect." In *The Battered Child,* edited by C. H. Kempe and R. E. Helfer, pp. 183–197. Chicago: University of Chicago Press, 1980.

Dorris, M. *The Broken Chord.* New York: Harper Perennial, 1989.

Kropenske, V.; Howard, J.; Breitbach, C.; Dembo, R.; Edelstein, S. B; McTaggart, K.; Moore, A.; Sorenson, M. B.; and Weisz, V. *Protecting Children in Substance-Abusing Families.* Washington, DC: U.S. Department of Health and Human Services, 1994.

Tzeng, O. C. S.; Jackson, J. W.; and Karlson, H. C. *Theories of Child Abuse and Neglect.* New York: Praeger, 1991.

Zuravin, S. J. and DiBlasio, F. A. "Child Neglecting Adolescent Mothers: How Do They Differ from Their Non-Maltreating Counterparts?" *Journal of Interpersonal Violence.* 7(4), (1992):471–489.

References

Alderette, P., and deGraffenreid, D. F. "Nonorganic Failure-to-Thrive Syndrome and the Family System." *Social Work* 31 (1986):207–11.

Cantwell, H. B. "Child Neglect." In *The Battered Child,* edited by C. H. Kempe and R. E. Helfer, pp. 183–97. Chicago: University of Chicago Press, 1980.

Cantwell, H. B. "Neglect Responses and Solutions." Paper presented at the 7th National Conference on Child Abuse and Neglect, 10–13 November 1985, Chicago.

Children's Defense Fund. *The State of America's Children Yearbook, 1996.* Washington, DC: Children's Defense Fund, 1996.

Davis, J. *Help Me, I'm Hurt.* Dubuque, IA: Kendall/Hunt, 1982.

DePanfilis, D. and Salus, M. *A Coordinated Response to Child Abuse and Neglect: A Basic Manual.* Washington, DC: U.S. Department of Health and Human Services, 1992.

Doueck, H. J. "Review of Magura and Moses: Outcome Measures for Child Welfare Services." *Research in Social Work Practice.* 1 (1991):214–222.

English, P. C. "Failure to Thrive without Organic Reason." *Pediatric Annals* 7 (1978):774–80.

Faller, K. C.; Bowden, M. L.; Jones, C.; and Hildebrandt, H. M. "Types of Child Abuse and Neglect." In *Social Work with Abused and Neglected Children,* edited by K. Faller, pp. 13–31. New York: Free Press, 1981.

Faller, K. C., and Ziefert, M. "Causes of Child Abuse and Neglect." In *Social Work with Abused and Neglected Children,* edited by K. Faller, pp. 32–51. New York: Free Press, 1981.

Fontana, V. J. *Somewhere a Child is Crying.* New York: New American Library, 1976.

Gaudin, J. M.; Polansky, N. A.; and Kilpatrick, A. C. "The Child Well-Being Scales: A Field Trial." *Child Welfare.* LXXI, 4 (1992):319–328.

Germain, C. B. *Human Behavior and the Social Environment: An Ecological View.* New York: Columbia University Press, 1991.

Giovannoni, J. M., and Becerra, R. M. *Defining Child Abuse.* New York: Free Press, 1979.

Giovannoni, J. M., and Billingsley, A. "Child Neglect among the Poor: A Study of Parental Inadequacy in Families of Three Ethnic Groups." *Child Welfare* 49 (1970):196–204.

Gustavsson, N. S. and Segal, E. A. *Critical Issues in Child Welfare.* Thousand Oaks, CA: Sage, 1994.

Hally, C.; Polansky, N. F.; and Polansky, N. A. *Child Neglect: Mobilizing Services.* Washington: U.S. Department of Health and Human Services, National Center on Child Abuse and Neglect, revised 1991.

Hampton, R. L. *Black Family Violence.* Lexington, MA: Lexington Books, 1991.

Inciardi, J. A.; Lockwood, D. and Pottieger, A. E. *Women and Crack-Cocaine.* New York: Macmillan, 1993.

Kadushin, A. and Martin, J. A. *Child Welfare Services.* New York: Macmillan, 1988.

Katz, S. N. *When Parents Fail.* Boston: Beacon Press, 1971.

Kelley, S. J. "Parenting Stress and Child Maltreatment in Drug-Exposed Children." *Child Abuse and Neglect.* 16 (3), (1992):317–328.

Kropenske, V.: Howard, J.; Breitenbach, C.; Dembo, R.; Edelstein, S. B.; McTaggart, K.; Moore, A. Sorensen, M. B.; and Weisz, V. *Protecting Children in Substance-Abusing Families.* Washington, DC: U.S. Department of Health and Human Services, 1994.

Mass, A. I. Personal communication, July 11, 1991.

Pecora, P. J.; Whittaker, J. K.; Maluccio, A. N.; Barth, R. P.; and Plotnick, R. D. *The Child Welfare Challenge.* New York: Aldine De Gruyter, 1992.

Pelton, L. H. *For Reasons of Poverty.* New York: Praeger, 1989.

Polansky, N. A.; Borgman, N. D.; and DeSaix, C. *Roots of Futility.* San Francisco: Jossey-Bass, 1972.

Polansky, N.; Chalmers, M. A.; Buttenwieser, E.; and Williams, D. P. "Assessing Adequacy of Child Caring: An Urban Scale." *Child Welfare* 57 (1978):439–49.

Polansky, N.; Chalmers, M. A.; Buttenwieser, E.; and Williams, D. P. *Damaged Parents: An Anatomy of Child Neglect.* Chicago: University of Chicago Press (1980, revised 1991).

Polansky, N. A.; DeSaix, C.; and Sharlin, S. *Child Neglect: Understanding and Reaching the Parent.* New York: Child Welfare League of America, 1972.

Polansky, N. F.; Hally, C.; and Polansky, N. A. *Profile of Neglect: A Survey of the State of Knowledge of Child Neglect.* Washington: Community Services Administration, Department of Health, Education and Welfare, 1975.

Seaburg, J. R. "Child Well-Being: A Feasible Concept?" *Social Work* 35 (1990):267–272.

Trocmé, N. "Development and Preliminary Evaluation of the Ontario Child Neglect Index." *Child Maltreatment* 1(2), (1996):145–155.

Trocmé, N. Personal communication. Oct. 14, 1997.

Tzeng, O. C. S.; Jackson, J. W.; and Karlson, H. C. *Theories of Child Abuse and Neglect.* New York: Praeger, 1991.

U.S. Department of Health and Human Services, National Center on Child Abuse and Neglect. *Child Maltreatment 1992: Reports from the States to the National Center on Child Abuse and Neglect.* Washington, DC: U.S. Government Printing Office, 1994.

Weissbourd, R. *The Vulnerable Child.* Reading, MA: Addison-Wesley, 1996.

Weston, J. A.; Cooloton, M.; Halsey, S.; Covington, S.; Gilbert, J.; Sorrentino-Kelly, L.; Renoud, S. S.; "A Legacy of Violence in Nonorganic Failure to Thrive." *Child Abuse and Neglect.* 17 (6), (1993):709–714.

Wolock, I., and Horowitz, B. "Child Maltreatment and Maternal Deprivation among AFDC Recipient Families." *Social Service Review* 53 (1979):175–84.

Young, L. *Wednesday's Children.* New York: McGraw-Hill, 1964.

Zuravin, S. J. and DiBlasio, F. A. "Child-Neglecting Adolescent Mothers: How Do They Differ from Their Nonmaltreating Counterparts?" *Journal of Interpersonal Violence* 7 (4), (1992):471–489.

Zuravin, S. J. and Taylor, R. *Family Planning Behaviors and Child Care Adequacy.* Final report submitted to the U.S. Department of Health and Human Services, Office of Population Affairs (Grant FPR 000028-01-1) as cited in P. J. Pecora et al. *The Child Welfare Challenge.* New York: Aldine De Gruyter, 1992.

The Physical Abuse
of Children

The physical abuse of children is a phenomenon that can only be defined by considering the total social context with special emphasis on some specific factors. Chapter 1 discussed the historical prevalence of physical abuse, and the influence different historical periods had on the definition of *abuse*. The structure of society must also be considered. For example, as part of their heritage, other cultures have practices that by Western standards would be considered abusive. Finding a definition, therefore, depends largely on the source culture or the prevailing sentiment. It is agreed, however, that the physical abuse of children refers to non-accidental injury inflicted by a caregiver. Although protective services tries to understand different cultural practices, the fact remains that those living in the United States must live within state and federal statutes.

The medical community sees abused children by virtue of the bruises, welts, broken bones, and burns they present in a hospital or other medical setting. Spurred on by the adoption of the term *battered-child syndrome,* medical professionals define abuse in light of the child's ailments, which must be healed, and the parents' "illness," which must be treated.

The legal community, including the police, defines *child abuse* more in terms of intent. Parents have particular legal (and moral) responsibilities. Failure to comply with the acceptance of these duties is to defy the statutes set up by society and is therefore punishable. The child is the victim; the parent is either the perpetrator or accomplice. This is not to imply that compassion does not enter into the disposition of abuse cases. Nevertheless, the legal definition is deeply entangled with the debate over individual rights.

Amidst the healing of the injured and the punishment of the guilty appears the social worker, taught over time to see the family as a total system—a system influenced in turn by larger and more complex systems (i.e., the neighborhood, the social strata, the state, and the culture). Thus *child abuse* is again defined with respect to anticipated outcome—that is, to restore in some manner the delicate balance of family continuity so that the nurturing of children can continue. If this is not possible—if the family system is too grossly distorted by stresses or individual pathologies—placement of the child may be the only solution. Thus three very different approaches to the nonaccidental injury of children combine to create the helping climate of today.

Several agencies have been involved in the compilation of statistics on child abuse and neglect. From 1976 until 1987 the children's division of the American Humane Association was largely responsible for collecting statistical data. More recently, however, both the National Committee to Prevent Child Abuse and the National Center on Child Abuse and Neglect (NCCAN) in Washington, D.C. have assumed the primary responsibility for this service.

The National Center on Child Abuse Prevention Research, a program of the National Committee to Prevent Child Abuse, found, in a survey of state child protection agencies, that in 1993 there were 2,989,000 reported cases of child abuse and neglect nationwide. Of the reported cases, approximately 47 percent were neglect, 30 percent physical abuse, 11 percent sexual abuse, 2 percent emotional abuse and 9 percent other forms of maltreatment. (*Other* is a category used by some states to classify abandonment, substance abuse and domestic violence effects, etc. Other states group these cases into either physical abuse or neglect.) While these statistics went up only slightly since 1992 the increase in overall population means that the incidence of reported abuse and neglect—45 children in every 1000—has remained the same. However, the rate of reported child maltreatment since 1976, when statistics were first kept, has gone up by 330 percent. And in 1993, 1,299 children died from maltreatment (National Center on Child Abuse Prevention Research, 1994).

The National Center on Child Abuse and Neglect (NCCAN), as part of its newly created National Child Abuse and Neglect Data System (NCANDS), surveyed fifty states, the District of Columbia, Guam, the Virgin Islands, and all branches of the military to determine the incidence of *substantiated* abuse reports. From the 51 jurisdictions reporting on their 1992 abuse statistics, 993,000 children were substantiated as victims of child maltreatment. Of these the greatest majority (55.2 percent) were white, 25.8 percent African American, 9.6 percent Hispanic American, 1.4 percent Native American, 0.8 percent Asian/Pacific Island and 7.3 percent either other or unknown (NCCAN, 1994).

What do these statistics mean? It is important to remember that these figures are based on the reports made to state protective agencies and do not reflect the abused children whose abuse is never reported. In addition, because most courts do not find sufficient evidence to take action in emotional abuse cases, many protective agencies do not encourage the reporting of these. In some states, the disposition of prenatal substance abuse (when mother is abusing substances during pregnancy) is still in controversy. Whatever we choose to assume from statistics, the fact remains that there are at least a possible 2,989,000 children too many being subjected to some form of abuse and neglect in the United States today. The question remains: why?

Causes of Physical Abuse

The search for an explanation for the causes of physical abuse has created several models.

Justice and Justice suggest that the findings of a variety of studies can be framed in terms of seven models—more complete in and of themselves but overlapping to a degree with each of the others. These are

> ...(1) the psychodynamic model, (2) the personality or character-trait model, (3) the social-learning model, (4) the family-structure model, (5) the environmental stress model, (6) the social-psychological model, and (7) the mental-illness model. (1976, p. 37)

These authors then conclude that none of these models gives an accurate explanation of the causes of abuse. They contend that only a model that "approaches the problem from a systems point of view, incorporating host, agent, environment and victim, can properly represent the interplay of multiple forces that result in child abuse" (p. 38). The authors offer an eighth model that combines a psychological perspective—the social or environmental pressures brought to bear on the family, interactional factors, and cultural expectations. They call this eighth model the psychosocial systems model.

More recently, Tzeng et al. (1991) have identified nine paradigms, each encompassing several theories or models. These paradigms are: (1) the *Individual Determinants Paradigm* which includes several theories concerned with the abnormal characteristics of the perpetrator; (2) the *Sociocultural Determinants Paradigm* covering the Social Systems theory; (3) the *Individual-Environment Interaction Paradigm* which involves theories considering the interaction between the abuser and his/her environment; (4) the *Offender Typology Paradigm* which fits abusers into specific categories; (5) the *Family Systems Paradigm* which views the abusive family as a social system; (6) the *Parent-Child Interaction Paradigm* which includes five theories outlining parental interaction with the abused child; (7) the *Sociobiological Paradigm* which emphasizes the role that genetic factors play in human behavior; (8) the *Learning Situational Paradigm* which applies learning theory to abuse situations asserting that abusive/violent behavior is learned; and (9) the *Ecological Paradigm* which brings together theories that use the variables of the individual, the family, the community and all societal and cultural factors to explain abuse.

Given the abundance of all the above theories and that several overlap, it is necessary to create three categories, each encompassing several of the above models: (1) the *psychopathological,* or those theories that stress the characteristics of the abuser as the primary cause of the abuse (psychodynamic, mental-illness, and character-trait models); (2) the *interactional,* or those models that see abuse resulting from a dysfunctional system (e.g., family-structure model); and (3) the *environmental-sociological-cultural,* or those theories that see the primary contributing factors to abuse as stresses from the immediate environment, society, or culture (social-psychological and psychosocial systems).

To understand the full significance of these causal models, each is considered here.

Psychopathological Categories

Psychopathological categories encompass models that see the primary cause of abuse as residing within the parent. The abuser's personality characteristics predispose the child to being abused. All that is needed is a stimulus.

Psychodynamic Model

Referred to by Gelles (1973) as the psychopathological model, this model stems largely from the work of C. Henry Kempe and Ray Helfer, proponents of the psychodynamic model, who blame a lack of bonding as an important factor in the disturbance in the nurturing relationship between mother (or father) and child. Further, the abuser is said to have particular traits of lack of ability to trust, low frustration tolerance, immaturity, and involvement with the abuse of drugs or alcohol. These parents are part of a vicious cycle of parental inadequacy (Factor and Wolfe, 1990). Often they were battered by their own parents or at least came from a home characterized by tension and unhappiness. The inner conflicts produced by this unsatisfactory childhood manifest themselves in the battering of their own children (Fontana, 1974; Mufson and Kranz, 1994). It is therefore assumed by this theory that the parent has the potential to abuse based on his or her rearing, is faced with a particular child with whom he or she cannot adequately bond, and experiences a crisis that sets the abusive act in motion (Helfer, 1974; Tzeng et al., 1991). This model assumes all but the individual's potential to abuse as secondary. The condition of a potential abuser exists, lying in wait for the particular child and a crisis. Without the specific disposition toward abuse, the same child and same crisis would fail to produce maltreatment.

Still another aspect of the psychodynamic model is role reversal—that is, when parents expect their children to nurture them and assume their roles. This need to be "parented" by one's children can be traced to the rejection or unmet needs of the parent in his or her own family of origin. Galdston (1974) says the parents "speak of the child as if he were an adult with all the adult's capacity for deliberate, purposeful and organized behavior.... The parents then proceed to spontaneously associate their reactions to the child with personages and experiences from their own childhood." Galdston refers to the parents' problem as a *transference neurosis,* or the parents' rejection of the child as a result of feelings left over from childhood and more appropriately directed toward the parents' own parents.

Gelles (1973) argues against what he calls the psychopathological model, stating that sociological as well as psychological factors must be given attention. Gelles notes that much of the literature has been based on medical research, by psychiatrists, clinical psychologists, and psychiatric social workers. The emphasis has been placed on the need for treatment: for medical practitioners, the treatment of childrens' injuries, and for the psychiatric practitioners, the treatment of the pathological parent.

Mental-illness Model

Whether mental illness of parents as a primary underlying cause can actually be framed into a model, as Justice and Justice propose, is debatable. With the advent of the DSM IIIR and more recently the DSM IV the definition of mental illness has been expanded. Certainly some abusive parents would fit into categories such as Borderline, Bi-Polar, etc., but today child protection theorists would probably argue that these problems, though related to the abuse of their children, are not the total cause. Kempe found that only 5 percent were actually psychotic. Although the authorities espousing the psychopathological theories describe the abuser as disturbed, psychopathological, or personality-disordered, many others say that abusive parents do not fit any psychiatric classification (Justice and Justice, 1976; Tzeng et al., 1991). Galdston uses the term *transference neurosis* to describe the residual anger of the abuser (Gelles, 1973). Delsordo (1963) refers to the mentally ill in his classifications, but admits that only 4 of the 80 casework studies fell into this category. Some parents do torture, burn, maim, and kill children as part of their own delusional patterns, but fortunately the number is small.

Character-trait Model

The character-trait model is similar to the psychodynamic model in that it attributes particular traits to the abusive parent with no concern about the etiology of those characteristics. For example, abusive parents are seen to be self-centered, immature, and impulse ridden, but little consideration is given to how they become this way.

In his categorization of abusive parents, Merrill proposed four classifications of abusers based on particular characteristics. The first group of parents felt generally hostile toward the world. Their lives were filled with hostility and anger that could erupt with the slightest provocation and manifest itself in abuse. The second group of parents were rigid, compulsive, cold, and unbending in their beliefs. They demanded complete obedience and cleanliness from their children and were not at all amenable to compromise. Parents in this group saw their children as property, and it was their right to abuse them if they chose. Strong attitudes of rejection were seen among these parents (Spinetta and Rigler, 1972).

Passivity and dependence characterized Merrill's third group of parents; they were often depressed, moody, and immature. There was a sense of competitiveness between the abusers and their children, especially for the love and attention of the spouse. The last group was based on characteristics found in fathers. Young and intelligent but somehow disabled, they stayed home while their wives worked. Their frustrations over their role led to anger directed toward their children in the form of rigid discipline.

Delsordo (1963) also categorized parents by character traits in an effort to explain their behavior and the causes of the abuse. Abuse, he felt, stemmed from five types of parenting:

1. Mentally ill parents saw the child as part of their delusionary process. Some parents described exorcising the devil as they abused their children. Others saw the child as trying to harm them and the abuse as self-protection.

2. Overflowing frustration, irresponsibility, and lack of confidence promoted abuse by pleasure-seeking parents who felt little or no guilt about the abusive behavior.

3. A nonspecific disturbance is a catch-all phrase for the parents of battered children seen in hospitals.

4. Overly severe and rigid discipline for failing to match up with parental expectations was seen as cause for abuse reports. The homes of these parents were spotless, and order was maintained at all costs.

5. Misplaced abuse was the last category. These parents were often feeling the stress of conception before marriage, a handicapped child, marital disputes, an interruption in parent-child bonding, or prolonged separation and subsequent return of a particular child. Unable to cope with their lives, the parents abused their children.

Unlike many theories in the study of child abuse, Delsordo's theories were tested by Boisvert (1974) who found them applicable. Boisvert combined Delsordo's work into classifications under two typologies. The first typology was *uncontrollable abuse,* which included:

1. The psychotic personality or the parent who sees the child as having a role in his or her fantasies

2. The inadequate personality who is irresponsible and immature and has a low frustration tolerance

3. The passive-aggressive personality who resents meeting the demands of others and displays this resentment through anger and hostility often directed toward the child

4. The sadistic personality who has a history of sadistic behavior

Boisvert labeled his second typology *controllable abuse* and included in this those who displaced aggression and the cold, compulsive disciplinarian.

Interactional Categories

Martin's theory may be a natural transition between the psychopathological and the interactional categories.

Martin and Zimrin's Theories

In his discussion of causes, Martin (1976) espouses the theory of Kempe and his colleagues, but expands it somewhat. He suggests that the abusive act necessitates not only a certain type of adult, a crisis, and a special child but also the role of that child. A child seen by everyone else as attractive and lovable may, for some egocentric reason, be perceived by the parent as abnormal or different. In fact, within the same family some children are more likely to be abused than their siblings because of their parents' perception of them. Because of the parents' perception of the child's inadequacy, the child is unable to derive adequate parenting. In parenting, an individual is influenced by his or her expectations of the particular child, desire for the child, capacity to give to that child, ego strength to adapt to stress, ability to accept imperfections, and realistic fantasies about the child. The parent must perceive that the child is free from defects or imperfections, matches the parents' expectations, is relatively healthy, and can exhibit what the parent perceives as loving behavior (e.g., smiling, cuddling, and thriving). For most parents there develops a balance between their needs and the needs of their infant. For the abusive parent, however, some aspect (or aspects) has upset the delicate balance in his or her ability to properly nurture the child. The parent may be capable of loving behavior for a time, but at some point the anger at a less than satisfactory relationship manifests itself.

Zimrin (1984) describes, in similar fashion, what he calls the encounter theory in which the traits and characteristics of the parents interact with those of the children in such a way that abuse is the result. For example, a nervous or anxious parent who is convinced that he or she will not succeed in parenting may have a colicky, crying baby who does not seem to be able to be comforted. Thus, the parent feels unsuccessful and is perhaps angered by this while the baby feels unable to gain comfort. The crying then escalates. The result of this scenario may well be abuse.

Another issue bears on the mother-child relationship—a factor which, for lack of a better term, can be called *chance events*. There are events that hamper the parents' ability to attach. Lynch (1976) describes difficulties in pregnancy, labor, and delivery as sometimes having a negative effect on the attachment process. Particular changes in the mother's body or in her life—those that she perceives as attributable to her pregnancy or the child's birth—may hamper her ability to bond. Disruption in attachment can be precursors of physical abuse. Phenomena such as illness of the infant or mother, significant changes in the mother's life, and significant stresses are capable of breaking the tenuous bond. A mismatch of the child and the parents' expectations can be a significant factor in abuse. Parents who abuse often have expectations that are beyond the developmental capacity or ability of their children. The ensuing frustration, the sense of loss, and the feeling that the perceived failures of the child reflect the parents' weaknesses are translated into abusive behavior (Martin, 1976; Tzeng et al., 1991).

Family-structure Model

The family-structure or family-systems model is based largely on the influence of family-systems theory. In this view the family is an intricate system that must maintain some degree of balance in order to continue to exist. Child abuse is the result of dysfunctional family patterns, such as severe enmeshment (the symbiotic dependence of the family members on each other in the fervent hope that others in the family will meet their unmet needs) or disengagement (the distancing or lack of communication among family members). Two other family patterns in abusive families are parentification and scapegoating. The parentified child is entrusted with the role of caregiver at an early age. The child is not only expected to act like an adult and take on the tasks of adulthood but he or she is expected to nurture the parents as well. The cost of this type of family balance is that the child is deprived of a childhood while the parents strive desperately to have their own needs met. The family scapegoat "saves" the family in another manner. The scapegoated child represents something or someone with which the family cannot deal. Beset with other problems that they prefer to keep secret, the family offers the scapegoat as "the problem." Having someone to blame, the family can then feel blameless (Karpel and Strauss, 1983; Tzeng et al., 1991).

Environmental-Sociological-Cultural Categories

The predominant view of proponents of sociological theories is that the stresses in society are the primary causes of child abuse.

Environmental Stress Model

This model suggests that environmental stress is largely responsible for child abuse (Gil, 1970; Farrington, 1986). Factors such as poor education, poverty, racism, unemployment, or occupational stress weaken the parents' control and the result is abusive behavior. Gil attributes abuse to the lower socioeconomic levels of society. Some critics discount his theories, saying that only the reports of abuse come from lower socioeconomic groups. The more affluent, it is assumed, can cover up their abusive behavior. Gil insists that the higher the environmental stresses, the more significant the rate of abuse. Gil holds there is a predisposition to violence toward children in society today, and other authors agree. Farrington (1986) contends that family violence is based on the facts that families experience a great deal of stress today, that they are not equipped to handle this stress, and that society accepts violence as a reaction to stress.

Until recently, physical punishment of children was practiced widely. When children became adults and were beset with stresses, they fell back on the only type of discipline they knew, often expanding the degree of force used by their parents (Giovannoni and Becerra, 1979).

Social-learning Model

Related to Gil's theories about parents retreating to previously learned modes of discipline, the social-learning model emphasizes parental inadequacy in a variety of other areas. Abusive parents have not learned effective, nonharmful methods of discipline and, knowing little about child development, they do not know what to expect from their children. As a result of their own childhoods, they have developed inappropriate expectations of their children and are ill equipped to guide them in their growth. Many feel parenthood is a burden and are unready and unsuited for the task. Their frustration over their own ineptness or their children's failure to meet their expectations leads to the abuse (Justice and Justice, 1976).

Social-psychological Model

Not fully integrated is Gelles's (1973) social-psychological approach. The social-psychological theory assumes that frustration and stress resulting from such factors as marital disputes, unemployment, social isolation, unwanted or too many children, and difficult or special children are all contributors to child abuse. Gelles contends that seeing merely the stressors does not present the total picture. His model also suggests that the parents are predisposed, by virtue of their own individual pathology, to manifest abusive behavior. Their pathology in turn relates to their faulty socialization experiences as children. Thus Gelles suggests that when an ill-equipped parent, with particular traits that he or she carries as scars from childhood, is faced with a series of societal and child-produced stresses compounded by a crisis, abuse will be the result. Gelles's theory did not consider the symbiotic interaction between the abused and the abuser nor family patterns that are generated by and result from the abuse.

Psychosocial Systems Model

Using a transactional analysis family systems perspective, Justice and Justice (1976) say that abuse results from a system of interactions between the abuser and his or her spouse, the parents and the child, the child and his or her environment, the parent and the environment, and the parent and society. The family is the primary arena in which the action takes place. The precursors of the abuse are not in fact found solely in individual pathology or stressful events but in the systems themselves: the family system and the family as part of the environmental and cultural systems.

In abusive families, the family system is out of balance. The parents are seen as *undifferentiated,* a term used by family-systems proponents to describe an individual who is so fused to others that he or she has no separate self (Bowen, 1966). The more the stress on the undifferentiated individual, the more he or she becomes dependent on and fused with others.

Justice and Justice stress symbiosis in their model, suggesting that undifferentiated parents become so as a result of the influence of symbiosis in their own childhoods. Symbiosis is, in fact, the natural, healthy process by which an infant is nurtured by his or her mother. The infant depends totally on the mother. She benefits emotionally from being needed and responds by caring for, stimulating, and loving the child. Undifferentiation stems from the abuser's own childhood when he or she was (1) the victim of insufficient or inconsistent symbiosis, not receiving the nurturing for which he or she continues to hunger; or (2) subjected to prolonged symbiosis, robbing him or her of the ability to function autonomously (Justice and Justice, 1976). (When considering this model it is important to take into consideration the family enmeshment expected and condoned in some cultures.)

The victims of insufficient nurturing will, as adults, seek someone to care for them as their parents did not. So needy are these individuals that they tend to attract mates who can understand their plight or are also undifferentiated adults. Thus begins the battle to see whose needs will be met. When neither spouse is capable of being emotionally satisfied by the other, marital discord ensues. If one partner appears to be winning the attention, the other may develop illnesses that demand care. Both see the child as a potential caregiver and compete for his or her attention. The participants are so deeply fused by their neediness that they are unable to perceive the family dysfunction. The tension becomes too great for the system to absorb, and the abuse directed toward the child is a combination of anger and frustration—and a cry for help.

Other parents who experienced intense or prolonged symbiosis in childhood felt smothered and suppressed their anger over the lack of opportunity for autonomy. Yet this type of relationship is all they know, so in marriage they shift their attachment to a mate, carrying with this function all the festering anger from childhood. Single parents often fall back into fusion with their family of origin or other relatives. The child needs to be dependent and his or her vulnerability predisposes him to be the recipient of his parents' anger about not being separate individuals. Abuse is often the result (Justice and Justice, 1976).

Environmental stresses compound the problems for this dysfunctional system. As the family system is unable to meet the needs of its members, the adults subject themselves to change, in an unconscious desire to relieve tension. Change is constant—a new home, a new job, new crises. Yet the family exists in isolation, lacking the vital support systems that could enable them to cope with these frustrations. Two cultural assumptions complete the picture. First, society assumes that parents will unfailingly love their children. Pictures of mothers adoringly watching their children appear in every family magazine. Television shows profile the "super parents" armed with a solution for every crisis. When parents do not experience this unfailing love for their children or do not feel able to meet every crisis, the hostility they feel cannot be owned. Instead, the child—the perceived symbol of their failure—becomes the target.

Second, our culture provides a clear message that physical punishment is a sanctioned form of discipline. But for overwrought parents the line between discipline and abuse is not always clearly discernible (Justice and Justice, 1976).

In the view of Justice and Justice, abuse is the result of a complex system of variables, thoroughly interrelated and influential in the family system of the abused and abuser.

The Abused Child

Characteristics of the Abused Child

There has been much debate in the literature about the contribution of the child to physical abuse. Although one can hardly assume that initially a child intentionally invites abuse, there are some characteristics that predispose a child to being abused.

Children conceived out of wedlock are particularly vulnerable to being abused because of the stress their birth created for the parents. Illegitimate children represent a variety of conflicts for their parents. The unwed mother may be seeking to produce an individual who will love her where others have failed. The pregnancy may be symbolic of a dysfunctional relationship with her parents or other intimates. Once the child is born and he or she does not meet the mother's unrealistic expectations, she may feel disappointed, angry, and hostile. Men brought into a union as a result of pregnancy may harbor the same resentment and see the child as the source of the problem.

Premature infants present less than comfortable parents with a dependent who needs extra care, thus putting additional stresses on the caregiver. The baby may be particularly sensitive to stimuli, cry more, be smaller, perceived as more fragile, and be generally more difficult to care for than a full-term baby. In addition, the mother may perceive the child as being somehow abnormal because it is premature (Elmer and Gregg, 1967). And finally, parental expectations about behavior at specific stages may not take into consideration that a premature infant is not as advanced, developmentally, as a full-term child.

Congenitally malformed babies, mentally retarded babies, and twins are three types of infants that again subject parents to added stresses. Since the groups are "different," they may be perceived as an added burden.

Children conceived during a mother's depressive illness may remind the family of this fact. The parents may even see the child as the cause of the mother's disturbance. In fact, any type of trauma around the time of conception or during pregnancy can cause the child to be viewed as a contributor to the problem and therefore rejected and possibly battered. The last child born to a mother who already feels overwhelmed can also be in jeopardy.

Gold (1986) suggests that numerous factors related to specific children predispose them to being abused. Inadequate bonding, mentioned by other authors, impedes the development of a positive relationship between parents and child and places the child at higher risk. The child who is colicky, difficult to feed, and resists being held may add to the parents' discomfort. Health problems in both parents and children, as well as allergic reactions and nutrition deficits, may also produce irrationalness, nervousness, or hyperaggressive symptoms, the misunderstanding of which causes potentially abusive situations.

In later years, learning problems, whether based on sensory difficulties, neurological damage, or psychological connections, may place children at risk from parents who are unaware or misunderstand their child's behavior. And finally, the adolescent years—marked by children's striving toward autonomy, which may take on rebellious overtones, and their reliance on peer cultures, which are not always positive in their influence—once again set up children to seemingly invite their parents' abuse (Gold, 1986).

The consensus among most authors is that children do not actually invite abuse, but some of the reasons above cause them to be at higher risk for abuse.

Physical Symptoms of Abuse

Bruises

Although play can cause bruises, particular bruises are indicative of abuse. Bruises prior to a child becoming ambulatory are suspect. Granted, it is possible to bruise an infant accidentally, but it is not as likely as with an older child. Bruises on various parts of the body may indicate that a child has been hit from several directions. Bruises on the backs of the legs, the upper arms and chest, neck, head, or genitals are often manifestations of abuse. Investigators are cautioned to look for bruises that are covered by clothing and that indicate a clear pattern—a hanger, a palm print, a buckle print, or an imprint going around the body that would suggest the child had been hit with a rope, belt, or cord (Davis, 1982).

Bruises that vary in color indicate they have been inflicted at different times. On white or light pigmentation, a new bruise is red and turns blue after 6 to 12 hours. About 12 to 24 hours later, the injury becomes blackish-purple, and in 4 to 6 days, a dark greenish tint appears. In 5 to 10 days, the bruise looks pale green or yellow (Davis, 1982). Bruises are not always easy to detect, however. On darker skin pigmentation, for example, bruises may be less discernible or not follow the above-mentioned patterns. Human bite marks (especially adult size) are of concern. Other indications of abuse can be choke marks, pinch marks, grab marks (often indicating that the child has been grabbed to be shaken), and fingernail scratches (Schmitt, 1980).

Fractures

Fractures in infants under age 12 months are a strong indication of abuse. Spiral fractures (especially in children under age 3) should be studied carefully. Many abusive parents' explanations do not fit the injury and cause investigators to be suspicious. Numerous fractures, either healed or current, may indicate repeated battering. Radiologists can detect previously healed breaks by the calcium deposits formed around them. A number of these, improperly healed, give support to findings of abuse. There are specific medical terms for certain types of fractures, including

1. Multiple fractures, *in which there are two or more lines of fractures on one bone.*
2. Spiral *or* torsion fractures, *in which there is evidence that the bone has been broken by twisting.*
3. Greenstick fractures, *in which one side of the bone is broken while the other side is bent.*
4. Subperiosteal fractures, *in which a bone is broken but there is no change in its contour. This leads to increased calcium deposits around the break.*
5. Dislocations, *in which the bone is separated from the joint. (Faller et al., 1981, pp. 18–19)*

In general, small children do not demonstrate numerous fractures under nonabusive conditions. Toddlers are most likely to exhibit greenstick fractures when they fall in play. For most children, however, a broken bone is accompanied by swelling, discomfort, discoloration, and a need to be comforted. It is unlikely that such an injury could be overlooked. If a parent displays little knowledge of previously acquired breaks picked up by x-rays, there should be further investigation (Faller et al., 1981).

Head and Internal Injuries

Head injuries can be extremely serious, and are often associated with abuse, especially in infants. Skull fractures may result from hitting the head against an object or throwing the child. In a depressed fracture, the bone fragments are pressed into the skull cavity. This type of injury is produced by a severe blow. Hematomas are collections of blood that form around the surface of the brain. In a subdural hematoma, blood collects between the brain and the tissue (dura) surrounding the brain. This is usually caused by a jolt (such as a slap) or severe shaking, which breaks veins and releases blood. The child may vomit, feel listless, or have seizures before the injury is diagnosed. In an epidural hematoma, the blood collects beneath the skull; this is caused by the rupture of an artery covering the brain. The child may vomit or lose consciousness soon after the assault (Faller et al., 1981).

Retinal detachment or hemorrhages are often caused by severe shaking. Black eyes, especially in small children, should be considered suspect (Davis, 1982).

Abused children may also experience injuries to the abdomen, such as a ruptured liver or spleen, intestinal perforation, kidney or bladder injury, torn arteries, or injury to the pancreas. Physicians note that peritonitis (inflammation of the abdominal lining) has often set in by the time the child is seen in a medical facility (Schmitt, 1980).

Burns

Burns are also common in child abuse, but not always easy to evaluate. The infant or small child is most likely to be a victim of burning. One of the most common types are those inflicted by cigarettes. While it is possible for burns to be accidental, cigarette burns that appear on the abdomen, genitals, bottoms of feet, or other more inaccessible spots are more likely to be intentionally inflicted. The recent popularity of the wood-burning stove has created more frequent reports of burns made by pressing the child's hands, legs, or buttocks on a hot stove.

Tap water burns (which can be inflicted with water over 130°F) often result from parents' frustrations over child behavior—especially problems with toilet training. The child may be forcibly immersed in hot water. If the child's buttocks touch the bottom of the receptacle, they may not be burned, thus creating an unusual looking donut-shaped burn (Schmitt, 1980). Burns more pronounced in the middle and radiating out represent hot liquid having been poured on the spot. Glovelike or sacklike burns indicate that the hand or foot has been immersed in hot liquid (Davis, 1982). If the burn occurred accidentally, there are likely to be splash marks from the child's attempt to avoid the spill or the parents' attempt to protect the child. Some children show signs of burns from steam or direct contact with flame.

Patterned burns indicate that a hot object has been used on the child. Hot pokers, irons, heating grates, or other utensils are sometimes used (Schmitt, 1980). Rope burns are also common. Again, attention should be given to the location of the burn. Is it feasible in light of the parents' explanation?

It may not always be easy to differentiate the accidental injury from the intentional one. The wise investigator, however, armed with a knowledge of indicators, considers other factors as well. It is vital to have a complete explanation of how the injury occurred. Is it possible for the injury to have occurred in the proposed manner? Is the parent willing to discuss the injury or does he or she seem secretive and defensive? (Certainly the interviewer must guard against putting the family on the defensive.) It is also important to consider the family's cultural background, where some practices may have indications of abuse.

Behavioral Indicators of Abuse

Children's behavior often mirrors the atmosphere at home. Abused children exhibit particular behaviors that are indicative of their dysfunctional environment.

Some of the first behavioral indicators of abuse were observed by physicians in hospital settings. Young children brought in with broken limbs, bruises, welts, and other suspect injuries appeared different from the normal pediatric patient. The abused children cried little, on the whole, but cried hysterically when being examined. They were apprehensive when other children cried, and demonstrated a passive watchfulness—lying quietly in their cribs and observing their surroundings intently. These children showed no expectations of being comforted by parents, but constantly searched for candy, favors, and prizes from staff members (Martin, 1972). One nurse described the release of such a child:

> *I knew there was something wrong, but we couldn't quite put our finger on it. He just lay there in his crib, with one leg in a cast and those big eyes just staring at everyone. Two years old and he never smiled, never talked. At first I thought he was just homesick, but the day his parents came to get him was a real mystery. They seemed excited to pick him up, but he hardly reacted. He almost seemed reluctant to go with them. It was only later when we learned that the broken leg was a result of abuse, that I understood.*

Children who are abused early in their infancy may develop a shrill cry that is not differentiated according to their particular need. The high-pitched quality of this cry is described by abusive parents as extremely unnerving, often precipitating further abuse. The motor development and social development of these infants is slow. They do not begin to crawl, sit, or reach for toys when others of their age do. The passive watchfulness described earlier is especially obvious among abused infants. Passivity permeates their attitude toward their world. They show little interest in toys and accept losses with little reaction. As they grow, this same passivity demonstrates itself in their attitude toward school work (Helfer, McKinney, and Kempe, 1976).

Martin and Beezley (1976) studied more than 50 children between 2 and 13 years of age with a mean age of 6½ years. In all cases, at least three examiners found that these abused children consistently demonstrate nine categories of traits. The most striking of these characteristics is the child's impaired capacity to enjoy life. The children studied seemed old for their years (pseudo-mature); they lacked the ability to play. Life for them had been unrewarding and they demonstrated this clearly in their attitudes. Symptoms such as enuresis (inability to control bladder functions), encapresis (fecal soiling), temper tantrums, and bizarre behavior were classified under psychiatric symptoms. Low self-esteem became obvious not only at home but in the school setting as well. Children had little confidence in their own abilities, and school learning problems were the result.

Withdrawal was another common characteristic of abused children. Often used as a defense to avoid further punishment, abused children carry this withdrawal into every aspect of their lives. What Martin and Beezley (1976) referred to as *opposition* has been termed *aggression* or *overt hostility* by others. Abused children harbor a suppressed anger over their lack of control of their lives. In addition, they see their parents using violence as a way of handling problems and taking out aggression. Some children act out their anger against peers, animals, or even adults, while others harbor it and turn their anger inward.

Hypervigilance is the term used by Martin and Beezley (1976) to describe the quality of passive watchfulness. They also note that some children demonstrate *compulsivity*. If abuse is an issue of control, and children cannot control the abuse, it follows that they may attempt to control other aspects of their lives. Children may reason (more unconsciously than consciously), "I cannot control Daddy's hitting me, but I do have control in my own room or in my play. I can fix my room just as I want it or I can stack the blocks precisely one on another. In this way *I* can maintain *some* control." Many abusive families have immaculate homes and lead well-ordered lives—both manifestations of their intense need to control. Feeling out of control is disturbing to all the family members.

One characteristic of abused children is their unusual ability to adapt to a variety of people and settings. For these children, this ability has meant survival. It has been important for them to perceive, with almost psychic ability, the needs of those around them, and adapt accordingly. "If Dad doesn't want to see you after a hard day at work, get out of his way." "If Mom doesn't want to be disturbed, leave her alone." One particularly adaptive 5-year-old boy discovered that if his father had several beers when he got home, he would fall asleep and thus spare the family his tirades and possible abuse. The boy soon learned that greeting Dad with a beer, and following that by several more, was all that was needed to ensure the family a relatively peaceful evening.

Researchers Rodeheffer and Martin (1976) noted that abused children were particularly fearful of failure. Again, this quality may relate to being adaptable and not wishing to displease the examiner. It may also be that children perceive abuse as a deserved retribution for their failure. The children tested also demonstrated difficulty attending to instructions, a behavior that carries over into school and is a frustration to both teacher and pupil. This behavior may exist for several reasons. First, there are numerous stimuli in a test situation. The hypervigilance of the child means that he or she has taken in all of these stimuli and may be confused. Further, the child is faced with a collection of objects that are not his or hers. The admonishment at home has been not to touch without first asking. Therefore, the child's anxiety is raised. Similar situations in the school setting add to the child's learning problems.

The abused child may also demonstrate verbal inhibition. At home, talking too much can be dangerous. Verbalization is also a step in cognitive development. Organizing thoughts and conceptualizing increase in complexity as the child matures. If a child's development, self-esteem, opportunity to converse, and trust are hampered by abuse, poor language development may be the result (Rodeheffer and Martin, 1976).

Regression is often used by abused children as a defense. Children may find it more comfortable to return in some way to an earlier stage—a stage perhaps where they did feel nurtured and loved. Baby talk, wetting the bed, and sucking fingers or thumb are methods children sometimes unconsciously use to cope with their situations.

Poor peer relationships are often marked among maltreated children. These children with poor object relations have not learned the give-and-take of relationships and they may be hesitant to share lest friends uncover the magnitude of their unhappiness. Abused children sometimes exhibit behavior that does not appeal to other children—pugnaciousness or extreme shyness. And finally, what if they attempted to make a friend and were rejected? The anticipation of this hurt is enough to prevent abused children from even trying.

Parents may prohibit their children from participating in activities—keeping the child even more isolated from others of their age. With their own insecurity and lack of support system, the parents do not allow their children to have friends. Lacking confidence to make friends themselves, these parents feel threatened when their children do. Abusers are also fearful that confidences between children and their friends will uncover the abuse. Poor peer relationships carry into adolescence.

The abused adolescent was, until recently, all but overlooked. It may have been assumed that adolescents were not as vulnerable to abuse because of their strength, weight, size, and age. Adolescents are also seen as being able to run away, avoid the abuse, protect themselves, or get help (Fisher et al., 1980).

Yet every year numerous adolescents are abused. The abuse may have been long-term, persisting throughout childhood and continuing into adolescence, or the maltreatment may begin or intensify during adolescence because of the parents' own current conflicts, which are possibly brought on by the stresses of adolescence (Ziefert, 1981). Separation and control are important factors in the life of the adolescent as well as the parents. Abuse often represents the battle being waged over these issues. A fervid attempt at control used by the abused adolescent is running away. Feeling deeply fused with his or her family yet unable to stop the abuse, the desperate teen forces the separation by escape. Some adolescents run to someone or some place, but most, aware of their own isolation, run aimlessly and are often picked up by pimps and drug dealers. Another form of escape for abused adolescents is through drugs and alcohol. These substances dull the mind or heighten the fantasy world and allow adolescents to ignore or deny the abuse.

Other adolescents, rather than escaping, conversely provoke abuse from adults or peers. The underlying need is again to maintain control. To provoke abuse is to bring it on one's self or to control the situation. Such adolescents may be assaultive, aggressive, or pugnacious. Their acting out causes schools and parents to label them incorrigible. The mood swings of adolescents are especially visible in the abused child. Acute hostility gives way to withdrawal as the adolescent strives to cope with the abuse as well as the conflicts of development (Fisher et al., 1980). The same type of attention-seeking devices seen in the younger child are obvious in the adolescent. Low self-esteem and depression are hallmarks of adolescent abuse.

Green suggests that child abuse is also a precursor of delinquent behavior.

The usual restructuring of superego, ego ideal and ego identification from childhood fails to occur in these adolescents after disengagement from their parents. In the normal adolescent, changes in these structures are effected through contact with new peers and adults who provide models for identification quite different from the parents. In the case of child abuse, fixation to the sadomasochistic identifications from childhood limits the freedom of the abused adolescents to experiment with new object identifications. Their compulsion to repeat the original trauma propels them toward violent and aggressive peers and adults who are extensions of the sadistic, "bad" parents. Thus the adolescent process perpetuates the earliest pathological identifications of these children, rather than modifying them. (1981, p. 157)

"Trigger" Collins, so-called because he had gained the reputation of being the faster to "trigger his switchblade," is an example of an abused adolescent who turned to delinquency.

Trigger Collins, a handsome, tall, African-American, 16-year-old, remembers little else of his home life except the abuse. The youngest of five children, Trigger knew from his early years that he was unplanned and unwanted. His father was an alcoholic who beat the boy regularly. His mother took a job as an elevator operator to provide an income for the family.

His siblings, the youngest of whom was 10 years his senior, paid little attention to him unless they required errands to be run. Oldest brother Jake thought it amusing, and later profitable, to teach his brother to shoplift. When he was 8, Trigger's mother interrupted the transaction of stolen goods between brothers, and when Jake denied knowledge of the theft, she beat Trigger severely with a strap. His refusal to continue stealing was met by his older brother's assaults.

Trigger, the only child still at home, was also expected to maintain the house in his mother's absence. This often meant finding his father's hidden bottles and putting his father to bed when he came home drunk. Mrs. Collins was a compulsively well-organized and immaculate housekeeper. She found Trigger's attempts at housekeeping totally unacceptable. Failure to maintain her standards meant "a walloping" and admonishments about being a "stupid, lazy, dirty kid."

The abuses Trigger suffered for his own apparent misdeeds were compounded by the marital discord of his parents. Parental fights meant thrown pots, broken bottles, and an array of verbal assaults. The victor, usually his mother, accused the bystanders of being "just like your father," and sent them "out of my sight" while she recuperated. If pressed, Trigger remembers some calm periods when his father stopped drinking and his mother was more amenable.

At age 13, after a particularly painful beating by his father, he decided he had had enough. He stole money from his father's pants pocket and his brother's switchblade, which had been carefully hidden from his mother, and ran. A bus ride took him into the city, where his large size and his agility with the switchblade quickly brought him to the attention of Arnold, a small-time thief who maintained an apartment for homeless boys and required them to steal for him to earn their keep. Trigger, already an adept thief, thanks to the tutelage of Jake, fit in well. Brief skirmishes with the police brought his whereabouts to the attention of his parents, but by mutual consent he did not return home. With Arnold's final arrest came Trigger's chance to assume his place at the head of the small gang of boys. Fierce street fighting and a myriad of different crimes punctuated his career for the next year, until at age 17 Trigger was arrested for armed robbery.

Throughout his childhood, Trigger Collins had been written off as difficult, unwilling to learn, and developmentally slow. His later actions, therefore, mirrored the only behavior he knew—violence.

Like Trigger, isolated, withdrawn, or aggressive attention-seeking children mature into individuals much like their own parents.

In the detection of abuse, it is extremely important that one be aware of the child's culture heritage (Fontes, 1995; Leigh, 1998). Lieberman (1990) suggests guidelines that could be used in detecting maltreatment among cultural minorities. First, it is important for the helper to discover what are the practices and/or customs of a particular culture. For example, in a culture where children are expected to be obedient and respectful, the Wu family found that 4-year-old Byron's hyperactivity was impossible for them to understand and difficult for them to cope with. In the detection of abuse, one must assess the mother's (and father's) own history and background in a cultural context. Lieberman (1990) recounts a Samoan woman who described being "punished severely" and made to "walk barefooted in the mountains carrying such heavy burdens that her feet bled" (p. 116). The mother's tearful recounting of the story let Lieberman and her colleagues know that this type of treatment was also considered abusive in Samoa.

And finally, cultural sensitivity also necessitates that one look at the current environment of the family. The Samoan mother mentioned above was further stressed by the fact that her husband had left her and thus forced her to live with unwelcoming relatives in very crowded quarters. She felt humiliated and unwanted. The added stress brought her to the point where she severely bruised her 18-month-old son (Lieberman, 1990).

Abusive Parents

Although the abusive family is a complex system influenced by sociological, cultural, psychological, and interactional variables, many authorities feel that parents who abuse demonstrate some particular personality characteristics. Low self-esteem is universal among abusive parents. These parents feel unloved and unworthy themselves. Their lives have usually been fraught with rejection and losses, with the loss of nurturing in childhood as the foundation. Other parents may have had relatively accepting childhoods, but find they must now cope with circumstances for which they feel totally unprepared. For example, parents who are newly immigrated from a different culture may not know what is expected of them. Or, Rodriguez and Murphy (1997) point to the difficulty for mothers raising children with developmental disabilities as a possible stressor that could correlate with abuse in some instances.

Both types of parents, those with dysfunctional childhoods and those thrust into a totally foreign environment, are excessively dependent on others and often have symbiotic attachment to their spouse or family of origin. Feeling incapable of autonomous behavior, the parents cling to others. When their needs are not met, frustration ensues.

By the same token, isolation from the outside—the absence of an adequate support system—is of vital importance in understanding abuse. Overwhelmed by the tasks of parenting, these parents have few outlets through which to vent their tensions. To compound these stresses, many abusive parents have rigid superegos and feel they need to tightly control their behavior and the behavior of those around them. Their inability to control themselves and others causes them great distress.

Helfer stated that there are five tasks abusive parents have not learned: (1) To get their needs met in appropriate ways; (2) to separate feelings from actions; (3) to determine they are responsible for their own actions and not for the actions of others[1]; (4) to make decisions; and (5) to delay gratification (Helfer et al., 1976, pp. 59–60).

Each of these will be considered here.

Parents' Unlearned Tasks from Childhood

Getting Needs Met
Through their own childhoods, abusive parents learned that to have their needs noticed, they had to express them in the extreme. For example, a quiet request for attention from their own parents was ignored, but a tantrum was acknowledged—if only by a slap. Becoming extremely ill or trying to commit suicide also elicited a response. Thus the now-abusive adult learned that if you want to be heard you must exhibit behavior that cannot be ignored. Because they learned early to overact or overreact, abusive parents do not know how to make their wishes and feelings known in appropriate, less dramatic ways. They feel so insignificant that they are sure no one will listen if they merely tell how they feel. These parents find themselves directing these attitudes in their children. More than one abusive parent has said, "But my child doesn't listen if I just *tell* her no!"

Separating Feelings from Actions
Hitting instead of telling a child about the misbehavior is also related to the parents' inability to separate the feelings from the action. In childhood, when the mother was angry, she

hit. Anger for these parents translates into action. Verbally expressing the anger is a foreign concept to them.

Determining Limits of Responsibility

"I don't know how many times my mother told me," recounted one abusive mother, "If it hadn't been for you, your father wouldn't have left. For years I was convinced that I was the cause of every rotten thing that happened to our family."

Unable to accept the responsibility for their own actions, abusive parents blame everyone else, especially their children: "If you hadn't done that, I wouldn't have beaten you." There is a stage in development when children feel all-powerful—able to cause or affect anything in their environment. Eventually, healthy children recognize they are not that powerful and, in fact, that people make choices about what they do. The child who is constantly blamed continues to believe that he or she is the cause—especially of unpleasant happenings. Because the events are always negative, the child would like to deny his or her contribution but feels powerless to do so. Thus begins one more conflict in the area of control. As an adult, the individual feels inherently responsible for the negative aspects of life regardless of the role others play. For example, a wife is liable to believe she drove her husband away, not that her husband left because he was irresponsible and couldn't settle down. Overwhelmed by blame and in a last attempt at control, a parent projects the blame on his or her own children and the cycle repeats itself.

In cultures where an individual's actions *are* expected to affect the family or community, abuse may result from the child's failure to meet these expectations. For example, 9-year-old Jon Chen's theft of candy from a local store was seen by his father as a deliberate attempt to make the family "lose face." The abuse that resulted was an effort to tell Jon that he too was responsible for the family's honor.

Making Decisions

Healthy families teach children how to make daily decisions. "What kind of cereal would you like for breakfast?" asks a mother of her sleepy charges. So fearful are some parents of losing control, however, that they do not allow their children to make decisions. When the children become adults, they may lack the ability to make decisions. Since every aspect of life requires decisions (frequently immediate ones), the indecisive individual again feels powerless and out of control.

Delaying Gratification

Children presented with consistency in their lives learn that life is predictable; a pleasure one would like now will be attainable if one has patience. Yet the childhoods of abusive parents have not been characterized by consistency. One minute their parent was loving while the next he or she struck out in anger. Pleasurable things make one feel good, but abusive parents, unable to trust what will come in the future and needing so desperately to feel good now, have difficulty putting off until tomorrow what can be had today. They live in a world geared toward instant results—instant solutions to their problems and instant obedience from their children. When these instant results are not forthcoming, the parents once again feel powerless and react.

These five factors promote unrealistic expectations of the child. Abusive parents expect their children to nurture them, perform household tasks, excel in school, and, generally, be mini-adults (the parent becomes involved in role reversal with the child). These parents demonstrate impulsivity and tenuous control, and are easily provoked to anger. Since abusive parents have usually sought mates who were developmentally similar, both expect the other to meet their needs. When this is not possible, marital discord is the result. Yet the family is so deeply fused that neither parent can leave. In fact, as one parent abuses, the other stands by (a kind of coabuser) unable to significantly intervene. Perhaps conflicts go unaddressed because neither of the spouses has learned to handle issues except with violence. Much of the therapy practiced with abusing dyads involves teaching these parents how to communicate their frustrations and resolve conflicts verbally and without excessive hostility.

Munchausen Syndrome by Proxy

An increasing number of protective service agencies are becoming aware of a syndrome referred to as *Munchausen by proxy*. Affecting predominantly mothers and their infants or young children, this distortion in parenting has caused a sufficient amount of public attention to be the theme of Kellerman's novel, *The Devil's Waltz* (1993). Related to adult Munchausen, this syndrome nonetheless has variations.

Adult Munchausen involves an adult who seeks attention at a hospital for symptoms which are often self-induced. This individual is extremely demanding of drugs and hospital attention but seems also resentful of those who attend him or her. The conclusion made by those studying this syndrome is that it is based on rage directed toward what the patient has perceived (symbolically) as abandoning parents (Schreier, 1992).

Munchausen by proxy is manifested by mothers (although fathers may demonstrate this pathology, the incidence is rare) who have sometimes been Munchausen patients themselves. These mothers present a picture to the world of caring and concerned caretakers while, at the same time, they are administering to their children large doses of such substances as ipecac (producing vomiting), phenolphthalein (causing diarrhea), insulin or glucose (affecting blood sugar), or even fecal matter. Some mothers try to smother their children. Children may also appear to be failure-to-thrive. The intent on the mother's part is to induce a condition which necessitates hospitalization and the attention rendered by medical staff. Because this mother seems so attentive, albeit demanding, and so intensely interested in hospital procedures during the child's hospital stay, it often requires several hospitalizations and sometimes results in the death of the child before medical personnel recognize what is occurring (Stone, 1989).

It may be difficult to understand the mother who would inflict harm on her child so that she could benefit from the attention the child receives. But this mother has developed, usually as a result of her own childhood, a pathological way of getting her needs met. This mother

> …uses her child to forge a relationship with a physician in which lying is the essential mode of interaction…. The mother becomes the "perfect" mother in a perverse, fantasized relationship with a symbolically powerful physician, in which the harm that she inflicts on her infant is but a *by-product* of the needs of her relationship. (Schreier, 1992, p. 442)

While physical abuse is often not discernible in the childhoods of these mothers, emotional abuse and abandonment is. Feeling the rage over not having her needs met, this mother uses her child to gain attention and protection from the figure who is associated with life and death. At the same time, she resents this professional feeling that nothing he does (usually a male physician) is enough (Schreier, 1992).

The emotional impact on the infant who survives Munchausen by proxy has not been studied extensively. It may be that the syndrome is too newly recognized as a form of child abuse.

Abusive Parents and Adolescents

Adolescence is a difficult period for abusive parents. For all parents, adolescence marks the time when they watch their children blossom with sexuality and autonomy just at the time they themselves are beginning to face or anticipate middle age. For example, immigrant parents may find that their adolescents have become well acclimated to the new culture, often accepting values that are foreign to their parents. Recognizing perhaps what they have not accomplished in their own lives, parents see their children as now having the opportunity to accomplish these or similar things. Healthy parents may see this as an extension of their own accomplishments, but abusive parents, in competition with their child, see the child's growth as a threat. For these parents the frustration and fear of losing control manifests itself in striking out at the perceived symbol of their failure—the adolescent. Separation is also an important factor for parents and their teenagers. Anxious to be on their own, teens pull away from home in a manner that may be especially difficult for the insecure parent. Abusive parents, often hopelessly fused with their offspring and scarred by previous rejections, see separation as a major crisis often surrounded by much emotional conflict. Perhaps an element of guilt enters into the already complex picture. Determined to exert control over the child and confused by anger, guilt, and fear over the impending loss, the parent abuses.

Sheri and her mother were locked in a conflict stimulated by the girl's adolescence:

"I don't know what happened!" protested Sheri tearfully in the therapy session. Sheri had been abused from ages 14 to 16 by her 40-year-old mother. She had run away at age 16 and was for a period of time placed in a foster home. Now at 17, she was living at home and was, with her family, in therapy. Sheri's attempted suicide necessitated individual therapy as well.

"It was like she turned into a mad woman," recounted the pretty, full-figured teenager referring to her mother. "We never got along too well, but one day she caught me drinking and she just spaced out. She took this belt and started hitting me and hitting me. She wouldn't stop! I was really afraid of her!"

Sheri's mother had been treated for severe depression a year before the abuse began. Mrs. Meade had supported herself and her daughter since her divorce 5 years before. Dependent and immature, Mrs. Meade clung to her daughter for support. Sheri had always been immature, but at age 13 she suddenly blossomed and began an intense interest in boys. She went out often and became sexually active. Mrs. Meade admitted being desperately lonely and felt unable to handle Sheri's flippant attitude and rebellious behavior.

She met and, within three months, married Frank Meade in the desperate hope that together they would solve her problems with Sheri. Meade, a retired army officer, set down firm rules in an attempt to control his new stepdaughter.

Feeling rejected by her mother's marriage and overwhelmed by her new stepfather's intensity, Sheri ran away and went to live with a boyfriend. She returned of her own accord, however, and was met by a violently angry stepfather and a hysterical mother. The next few months Sheri describes as "pure hell." Her stepfather ignored her and attempted to regiment his now bewildered wife. Mrs. Meade's hospitalization for depression created even more tension between Sheri and her stepfather, and Sheri began once again staying out late.

When her mother returned, Sheri said she "felt bad." Although they had never been close, the adolescent now felt a need to make amends and became "really nice" to her mother. Annoyed by "this pretty picture that leaves me out," Frank Meade left the home. Mrs. Meade was devastated, feeling that she couldn't possibly survive without him. The feeling was apparently mutual because Meade called her daily but refused to return until "that kid gets out." A month later, Mrs. Meade smelled liquor on her 14-year-old daughter's breath when Sheri returned from a party. A beating ensued, leaving Sheri bruised and crying and Mrs. Meade hysterical. Finally composing herself enough to call her husband, she begged him to return.

The next two years were marked by episodes of abuse, Mr. Meade's leaving and returning, and Sheri's more and more rebellious behavior. Eventually Sheri sought help from a teacher who reported the situation to social services. So enraged were her parents that the resulting arguments led Sheri to attempt suicide.

Not unlike other abusive families, the Meades represent a complex system of confused, unhappy individuals. Mrs. Meade, the product of an extremely close family, transferred her need to be taken care of to her first husband. When he failed and even eventually left her for another (equally needy) woman, she turned to her daughter. Adolescent Sheri, however, was just beginning to come into her own and found her mother's dependence too intense. Sheri began pulling away in the only way she knew—her interest in boys and staying out late. It is not surprising that Mrs. Meade then discovered another individual on whom she felt she could depend.

For parents new to this culture, the separation expected of adolescents takes on more complexities.

Eduardo Hernandez had immigrated to the southwestern United States as a young man. He was easily accepted into the closely knit Mexican-American community. He met and married Carmelita, who had newly immigrated from another part of Mexico. Together they raised three sons.

Eduardo had no complaints about his new life. Originally a clerk in his uncle's small grocery store in the Mexican community, Eduardo eventually became the owner when his uncle died. The community was a strong one—perhaps protecting itself from the discrimination they saw outside. Eduardo's two older sons naturally began working at the store. But with Alphonso, the youngest, the family reached an impasse. Alphonso had long questioned the family's values. He had learned English early—unlike his parents who still had difficulty conversing in anything other than Spanish. At age 13, he had become rebellious and argumentative— qualities not accepted by his patriarchal community. Initially Eduardo managed to punish his son in ways that would not be considered abusive. The father found himself greatly conflicted. On one hand, he admired his son's ability to acclimate to the non-Hispanic culture and to make non-Hispanic friends; on the other hand, Eduardo feared that he was losing his son and resented the boy's failure to recognize his authority. The result was that Eduardo began severely beating his son. After one such beating, Alphonso fled to a friend's house. The friend's parents contacted protective services.

Only a small percentage of abusive parents are actually psychopathic. They too have experienced an interruption in nurturing in early life and have difficulty when faced with parenting. Psychotic parents see the child as part of their delusional system and present a high risk of abuse.

From the characteristics suggested here, it becomes obvious that abusive parents are themselves in need of help. With the exception of a few sadistic individuals, they do not intend to harm their children. However, their own conflicts, compounded by the stresses of day-to-day living, result in abuse.

Domestic Violence and Other Abuse Within the Family

Domestic Violence

It is difficult to determine where to include the issue of domestic or family violence in a book on child abuse and neglect. Certainly violence in the family has a severe emotional impact on the children and can be seen as a form of *emotional maltreatment*. There is also the possibility that abused women will be so caught up in their own survival that they will *neglect* their children's needs. And finally there is a high correlation between the incidence of the physical abuse of wives and the simultaneous *sexual abuse* of their female children. But because family violence is predominantly a physical act, it has been included in this section on physical abuse.

There is increasing evidence that children who witness physical violence within their homes between their mothers and the adult male figure (father, step-father or boyfriend) demonstrate a number of reactions and lifelong effects (Kolbo et al., 1996; Brewin and Vallance, 1997). Some children identify with the victim, becoming withdrawn, fearful, and depressed. Others demonstrate a phenomenon called *identification with the aggressor* in which the child is so fearful of also being harmed that he or she chooses consciously or unconsciously to join with the abuser in the aggressive behavior. This may take the form of criticizing the mother (the usual victim) for not standing up to the abuse or the child may actually abuse the victim himself or herself or assault a younger sibling (Hampton, 1991; Hilton, 1992; Gustavsson and Segal, 1994; Kolbo et al., 1996). For all children brought up in violent homes the seed of aggression has been planted—a seed which may well mature into violence in future generations (Cappell and Heiner, 1990).

Kanisha was in high school before she was able to remember the full extent of the violence which had gone on in her home when she was a small child. Now she confided to a trusted teacher that she was afraid to go home. "I can't stand what Jerome's doin' to Mama!" she wailed. Jerome, her 22-year-old brother, had recently returned home after a brief stay in jail for drug trafficking. Influenced by a very violent father who had left several years before, Jerome had now taken on the role of batterer. Although Kanisha was at first fearful for her mother's safety, she later admitted that she too was a victim of her brother's assaults.

For children like Kanisha and Jerome, childhood was a nightmare. They worried about their and their mother's safety. They viewed their father with hatred and fear, but were confused by the moments when he could seem kind and loving. They watched their mother with a mixture of compassion, pity, and resentment, realizing that she was too fearful for herself to give them much comfort. Although Hampton (1991) found that African-American families like this one had a higher incidence of domestic violence, the reality is that children of any ethnic group may be victims. For these children low self-esteem, developmental delays, depression, conduct disorders, acute anxiety, and violence against others are their legacy from their homes. The effects of violent homes can be equally as emotionally damaging to children as assaults perpetrated on them directly.

Abuse by Siblings

When Laura Allen found 2-year-old Stephen screaming and observed his cut and bleeding head, she could not imagine what had happened. Grabbing the wounded child to her quickly, she frantically surveyed the scene. It was not until she saw the metal truck with one bloody corner and 8-year-old Aaron sitting nearby, that she realized what had happened.

"Did you hit your brother?" she accused angrily. Aaron looked up unperturbed. "He was bothering me!" the older child responded calmly. It was not the first time Aaron had injured Stephen and Laura now realized that, if she did not get him some help, it would not be the last.

Every year the amount of violence between siblings increases. This is not to say that siblings, over the years, have not expressed their rivalry in physical terms, but today, in a society which is obsessed with violence, there is no doubt that children are learning that this is the way to deal with disagreements (Gustavsson and Segal, 1994). A survey of 2,143 families in the United States found that sibling physical abuse actually occurs more frequently than abuse by parents. It is estimated that 53 out of 100 children attack a sister or brother each year. Further, 138,000 children from ages three to seventeen used a weapon on their sibling. While this abuse may begin as hitting, biting, slapping, shoving and punching, it may escalate to life-threatening action such as choking, smothering, or using guns and knives (Weihe and Herring, 1991).

What underlies such behavior? Weihe and Herring (1991) contend that sibling violence is about power. In our fast-paced, power-oriented world, violence is an easy way to take control. These authors also believe that power is a

...male-oriented issue in today's society. Many men still mistakenly believe that they must be in control. Feeling powerless creates problems for some of them. They think they are expected to be powerful, and they seek to satisfy that idea.... The sense of power they get from being abusive makes them want to repeat the experience. (p. 18)

While it is more likely for male children to physically abuse younger siblings, especially sisters, some females are also abusive. Children who abuse may also be mirroring the abuse in their family. For example, boys who see the father figure assaulting their mother may identify with the aggressor and abuse siblings.

Parental reaction to abuse by siblings is extremely important. Parents like Laura Allen (mentioned earlier) who perceive the behavior as problematic and respond by trying to help the abuser offer a chance for healing. But parents who are abused themselves, who perceive the extremes as *normal* sibling rivalry or who are so caught up in their own issues that they can be of no help to their children, may be sanctioning an abuser who will continue to fall back on this behavior as an adult.

Summary

Physical abuse is a concept that is difficult to define. Its definition depends largely on the mores and values of the times. Today most specialists agree that abuse involves the nonaccidental injury of a child at the hands of the caregiver. Four professional fields are intimately involved in the investigation and treatment of child abuse: medical and psychiatric, legal, social services, and law enforcement. Causal theories are numerous, but can be divided into three categories: the psychopathological, the interactional, and the environmental-sociological-cultural categories.

Particular children may be at higher risk for abuse than others: Children born illegitimately, premature infants, children who are congenitally malformed or mentally retarded, twins, and children born during a mother's depressive illness are the most vulnerable to abuse. Bruises, fractures, head injuries, and burns are the primary physical indicators of abuse. Behaviorally, children demonstrate a variety of symptoms such as passive watchfulness or hypervigilance, developmental delay, passivity, enuresis, encopresis, aggression, compulsiveness, regression, and fear of failure. Adolescent runaways are often overly aggressive, turn to drugs or alcohol, or become delinquent in behavior.

Abusive parents carry into their adulthood the unmet needs of their own childhood. They exhibit low self-esteem, excessive dependency, a failure to meet the challenges of parenting, unrealistic expectations of their children, role reversal with their children, and impulsivity. Parents abusing adolescents are frequently working out their own developmental conflicts. It is not only parents who are abusive. Siblings, too, can become abusers. Some children also observe violence within their homes and this too can take its toll.

Physical abuse, whether perpetrated by parents or siblings or observed within the home, is difficult to understand. Once society fully understands the abuser and the family that harbors that abuse, however, people will be better able to help the abused child.

Exploration Questions

1. Discuss the problems of defining *abuse.*

2. Discuss the problems of knowing the demographic characteristics that describe the abusive family.

3. What are the major categories into which most abuse models fall?

4. Cite physical and behavioral indicators of abuse.

5. Why might adolescents be abused?

6. What are some characteristics of abusive parents?

7. What appear to be the underlying causes for parents to abuse their children?

8. Why might siblings abuse?

9. What effect does family violence have on children?

Activities for Applied Learning

1. Obtain statistics from your local social services agency on how many children have been maltreated in the last five years. How many of these cases were physical abuse? Have the numbers increased? Decreased? By what percentage? What do you think may explain this?

2. Show the videotape (general version) called "Lee's Story." (The tape is available through the National Education Association Professional Library, 1201 16th St. N.W., Washington, DC 20036.) Discuss the pressures that pushed this mother to abuse her children. What characteristics does she appear to exhibit?

3. Read a novel that involves physical abuse (e.g,. *Mommie Dearest* by Christina Crawford; *When Rabbit Howls* by Truddi Chase). Numerous others are available. What characteristics does the abuser demonstrate? What are the consequences for the child?

4. Invite someone from a battered women's center to speak. Ask how children are impacted by domestic violence.

Suggested Readings

Barth, R. P. and Derezotes, D. S. *Preventing Adolescent Abuse.* Lexington, MA: Lexington Books, 1990.

Briere, J. N. *Child Abuse Trauma.* Newbury Park, CA: Sage, 1992.

Chase, Truddi. *When Rabbit Howls.* New York: Jove Books, 1987.

Faller, K. (ed.) *Social Work with Abused and Neglected Children.* New York: Free Press, 1981.

Hampton, R. L. (ed.) *Black Family Violence.* Lexington, MA: Lexington Books, 1991.

Hayden, T. *One Child.* New York: Avon, 1980.

Milner, J. S. and Chilamkurti, C. "Physical Child Abuse Perpetrator Characteristics." *Journal of Interpersonal Violence.* 6 (3), (1991): 345–366.

Tzeng, O. C. S.; Jackson, J. W.; and Karlson, H. C. *Theories of Child Abuse and Neglect.* New York: Praeger, 1991.

Endnote

1. There may be some cultures in which it is accepted that individuals are responsible for each other's actions.

References

Azar, S. T. "A Framework for Understanding Child Maltreatment: An Integration of Cognitive, Behavioral, and Developmental Perspectives." *Canadian Journal of Behavioral Science* 18(4), (1986): 340–355.

Boisvert, M. "The Battered-Child Syndrome." In *The Battered Child,* edited by J. Leavitt, pp. 141–46. Fresno, CA: General Learning Corp., 1974.

Bowen, M. "The Use of Family Theory in Clinical Practice." *Comprehensive Psychiatry 7* (1966):345–74.

Brewin, C. R., and Vallance, H. "Self-Discrepancies in Young Adults." *Journal of Interpersonal Violence.* 12(4) (1997):600–606.

Cappell, C., and Heiner, R. B. "The Intergenerational Transmission of Family Aggression." *Journal of Family Violence* 5 (1990): 135–152.

Child Welfare League of America. *Too Young to Run: The Status of Child Abuse In America.* New York: Child Welfare League of America, 1986.

Davis, J. *Help Me, I'm Hurt.* Dubuque, IA: Kendall/Hunt, 1982.

Delsordo, J. D. "Protective Casework for Abused Children." *Children* 10 (1963):213–18.

Elmer, E., and Gregg, G. "Developmental Characteristics of Abused Children." *Pediatrics,* 40 (1967):596–602.

Factor, D. C., and Wolfe, D. A. "Parental Pathology and High-Risk Children." In *Children at Risk,* edited by R. T. Ammerman and M. Hersen. New York: Plenum Press, 1990.

Faller, K.; Bowden, M. L.; Jones, C. O.; and Hildebrandt, M. "Types of Child Abuse and Neglect." In *Social Work with Abused and Neglected Children,* edited by K. Faller, pp. 13–31. New York: Free Press, 1981.

Faller, K., and Ziefert, M. "Causes of Child Abuse and Neglect." In *Social Work with Abused and Neglected Children,* edited by K. Faller, pp. 32–51. New York: Free Press, 1981.

Farrington, K. "The Application of Stress Theory to Family Violence: Principles, Problems and Prospects." *Journal of Family Violence* 1(2), (1986): 131–147.

Fisher, B.; Berdie, J.; Cook, J.; and Day, N. *Adolescent Abuse and Neglect: Intervention Strategies.* Washington, DC: U.S. Department of Health and Human Services, 1980.

Fontana, V. "Which Parents Abuse Children?" In *The Battered Child,* edited by J. Leavitt, pp. 195–99. Fresno, CA: General Learning Corp., 1974.

Fontes, L. A. "Culturally Informed Interventions in Child Sexual Abuse" in L. A. Fontes (ed.). *Sexual Abuse in Nine North American Cultures,* pp. 259–266. Thousand Oaks, CA: Sage (1995).

Galdston, R. "Observations on Children Who Have Been Physically Abused and Their Parents." In *The Battered Child,* edited by J. Leavitt, pp. 52–55. Fresno, CA: General Learning Corp., 1974.

Gelles, R. "Child Abuse as Psychopathology: A Sociological Critique and Reformation." *American Journal of Orthopsychiatry* 43 (1973):611–21.

Gelles, R., and Straus, M. "Is Violence Toward Children Increasing? A Comparison of 1975 and 1985 National Survey Rates." Paper presented at the Seventh National Conference on Child Abuse and Neglect, 5 November 1985, Chicago, IL.

Gil, D. *Violence Against Children.* Cambridge, MA: Harvard University Press, 1970.

Giovannoni, J. M., and Becerra, R. M. *Defining Child Abuse.* New York: Free Press, 1979.

Gold, S. *When Children Invite Abuse.* Eugene, OR: Fern Ridge Press, 1986.

Green, A. H. "Child Abuse and the Etiology of Violent Delinquent Behavior." In *Exploring the Relationship Between Child Abuse and Delinquency,* edited by R. J. Hunner and Y. E. Walker, pp. 152–60. Montclair, NJ: Allanheld and Schram, 1981.

Gustavsson, N. S. and Segal, E. A. *Critical Issues in Child Welfare.* Thousand Oaks, CA: Sage, 1994.

Hampton, R. L. (ed). *Black Family Violence.* Lexington, MA: Lexington Books, 1991.

Helfer, R. "Child Abuse and the Private Physician." In *The Battered Child,* edited by J. Leavitt, pp. 199–203. Fresno, CA: General Learning Corp., 1974.

Helfer, R. From an untitled lecture given in New Bedford, MA, March 1979, as cited in Tower, C. C. *Child Abuse and Neglect.* Washington, DC, National Education Association, 1984, pp. 59–60.

Helfer, R.; McKinney, J.; and Kempe, R. "Arresting or Freezing the Developmental Process." In *Child Abuse and Neglect: The Family and the Community,* edited by R. Helfer and C. H. Kempe, pp. 55–73. Cambridge, MA: Ballinger, 1976.

Hilton, N. Z. "Battered Women's Concerns about their Children Witnessing Wife Assault." *Journal of Interpersonal Violence* 7(1), (1992): 77–86.

Howing, P. T.; Wodarski, J. S.; Kurtz, P. D.; and Gaudin, J. M. *Maltreatment and the School-Age Child.* New York: The Haworth Press, 1993.

Justice, B., and Justice, R. *The Abusing Family.* New York: Human Services Press, 1976.

Karpel, M., and Strauss, E. *Family Evaluation.* New York: Gardner Press, 1983.

Kellerman, J. *The Devil's Waltz.* New York: Bantam, 1993.

Kolbo, J. R., Blakely, E. H., and Engleman, D. "Children Who Witness Violence." *Journal of Interpersonal Violence.* 11(2) (1996): 281–293.

Lieberman, A. "Culturally Sensitive Intervention with Children and Families." *Child and Adolescent Social Work* 7(2) (1990):101–119.

Leigh, J. W. *Communicating for Cultural Competence.* Boston: Allyn and Bacon, 1998.

Lynch, M. "Risk Factors in the Child: A Study of Abused Children and Their Siblings." In *The*

Abused Child, edited by H. P. Martin, pp. 43–56. Cambridge, MA: Ballinger, 1976.

Martin, H. "The Child and His Development." In *Helping the Battered Child and His Family,* edited by C. Kempe and R. E. Helfer, pp. 93–114. Philadelphia: J. B. Lippincott, 1972.

Martin, H. P., ed. *The Abused Child.* Cambridge, MA: Ballinger, 1976.

Martin, H. P., and Beezley, P. "Personality of Abused Children." In *The Abused Child,* edited by H. P. Martin, pp. 105–11. Cambridge, MA: Ballinger, 1976.

Milner, J. S. and Chilamkurti, C. "Physical Child Abuse Perpetrator Characteristics." *Journal of Interpersonal Violence* 6(3), (1991): 345–366.

Mufson, S. and Kranz, R. "A Family History of Abuse Contributes to Child Abuse." In *Child Abuse: Opposing Viewpoints,* edited by K. de Koster and K. L. Swisher, pp. 107–113. San Diego, CA: Greenhaven Press, 1994.

National Center on Child Abuse and Neglect, *Current Trends in Child Abuse Reporting and Fatalities: 1989 Survey,* Washington, DC: NCCAN, 1990.

National Center on Child Abuse Prevention Research, *Current Trends in Child Abuse Reporting and Fatalities: The Results of the 1993 Annual Fifty State Survey.* Chicago, IL: National Committee to Prevent Child Abuse, 1994.

Rodeheffer, M., and Martin, H. "Special Problems in Developmental Assessment of Abused Children." In *The Abused Child,* edited by H. P. Martin, pp. 113–28. Cambridge, MA: Ballinger, 1976.

Rodriguez, C. M., and Murphy, L. E. "Parenting Stress and Abuse Potential in Mothers of Children with Developmental Disabilities." *Child Maltreatment,* 2(3) (1997): pp. 245–251.

Schmitt, B. "The Child with Non-Accidental Trauma." In *The Battered Child,* edited by C. H. Kempe, pp. 128–46. Chicago: University of Chicago Press, 1980.

Schreier, H. A. "The Perversion of Mothering: Munchausen Syndrome by Proxy." *Bulletin of the Menninger Clinic* 56(4), (1992): 421–437.

Spinetta, J. J., and Rigler, D. "The Child-Abusing Parent: A Psychological Review." *Psychological Bulletin* 77 (1972):296–304.

Stone, F. B. "Munchausen-by-Proxy: An Unusual Form of Child Abuse." *Social Casework* 70(4), (1989): 243–246.

Thomson, E. M.; Paget, N. W.; Bates, D. W.; Mesch, M.; and Putnam, T. *Child Abuse: A Community Challenge.* East Aurora and Buffalo, NY: Henry Steward and Children's Aid Society for the Prevention of Cruelty to Children, 1971.

Tzeng, O. C. S.; Jackson, J. W.; and Karlson, H. C. *Theories of Child Abuse and Neglect.* New York: Praeger, 1991.

U.S. Department of Health and Human Services, National Center on Child Abuse and Neglect. *Child Maltreatment 1992: Reports from the States to the National Center on Child Abuse and Neglect.* Washington, DC: U.S. Government Printing Office, 1994.

Weihe, V. R. and Herring, T. *Perilous Rivalry: When Siblings Become Abusive.* Lexington, MA: Lexington Books, 1991.

Ziefert, M. "Abuse and Neglect. The Adolescent as Hidden Victim." In *Social Work with Abused and Neglected Children,* edited by K. Faller, pp. 162–69. New York: Free Press, 1981.

Zimrin, H. "Child Abuse: A Dynamic Process of Encounter between Needs and Personality Traits within the Family." *The American Journal of Family Therapy* 12(1), (1984): 37–47.

The Sexual Abuse
of Children

Is there anything wrong with sex between children and adults? Some researchers argue that not only are children unharmed but that sexual relationships with adults can be educational. Perpetrators contend their sexual tutelage is actually beneficial to the victims' development. DeYoung (1982, p. 46) cites a 1937 article by Lauretta Bender and Abraham Blau, in which they comment that "the experience of the child in its sexual relationship with adults does not seem always to have a traumatic effect.... The experience seems to satisfy instinctual drives.... The experience offers an opportunity for the child to test in reality an infantile fantasy.... The emotional balance is thus in favor of contentment." Although some agree, many researchers argue against sexual activities between children and adults. First, some say a small girl's vagina is too small to accommodate an adult male's penis. Since sexual abuse often does not progress to the point of vaginal intercourse, this argument is not always valid. Second, many people are disgusted by the idea of child-adult sexual involvement, and prefer to see children as innocent and untouched by adult sexuality. And third, most societies have some type of taboo against such a sexual liaison. Researchers and therapists alike feel that early sexual involvement with adults exposes the child to premature sexualization and may have long-term negative effects. Indeed, studies of survivors attest to the scars left by sexual abuse.

Researcher David Finkelhor presents the most convincing argument against adult-child sexual involvement. He contends (1984a) that our society is based on consent and free will, and in order to consent one must have knowledge and authority. Children do not have knowledge of the meanings of sexuality, information to enable them to anticipate the direction of the sexual relationship, or any idea of how others will react to their sexual involvement. Further, children have no authority in either a legal or psychological sense. Their natural awe of adults, perpetuated by their elders, renders them subject to the whims of these adults. Legally, children are unable to marry, drive a car, or enter into contracts prior to their maturity. Therefore, children are in no position to consent to relationships that carry so many implications as sexual liaisons with adults.

Two Groups' Approaches to Child Sexual Abuse

Sexual abuse of children is not new to our culture. (The historical aspects of exploitation were outlined in Chapter 1.) Today, child sexual abuse is a major problem. The concern is heightened when adult survivors report its impact on their lives. Two groups have been instrumental in bringing this issue to the attention of the public and in championing the efforts toward effective treatment and prevention: the child protection movement and the feminist movement. Although currently the two groups show evidence of combining their efforts in the interest of children and adult survivors, their fundamental difference must be understood (Finkelhor, 1984a).

Child Protection Movement

The child protection movement sees sexual abuse as the third form of child maltreatment in addition to physical abuse and neglect (Giovannoni and Becerra, 1979). Protective agencies deal primarily with in-family abuse or incest, which is perpetrated by family members, surrogate parents, or caregivers. The etiology of this problem is believed to be in the family pathology, a problem to which all family members contribute in some way (deYoung, 1982). Theorists describe family patterns that may repeat themselves if no intervention takes place. Although extrafamilial abuse is of concern, most protective agencies are legally bound to report this exploitation to law enforcement or judicial institutions. Protective agencies become involved in the treatment of parents of children abused outside the home. Alleviating parental guilt and strengthening the family unit provides protection for the child in the future. Thus child protection advocates place emphasis on the family as the seat of pathology as well as the medium responsible for the child's protection.

Feminist Movement

Feminists, on the other hand, espouse the sociological view that considers the assault of children as representative of societal values (see Table 6.1). Because of the patriarchial social structure, women and children have inferior status and are subjected to male dominance (Herman and Hirschman, 1981; Herman, 1992). Struve (1990) adds that patriarchy has not only set up boys to be sexually abused but has caused abused boys to keep silent, because they fear that disclosure or their victimization will prevent them from being seen as "man enough" to eventually assume the role of patriarch. Further, advertisements in the media and the prevalence of child pornography suggest that children are exploitable. Although Finkelhor's studies have shown that healthy strong mothers can apparently prevent incest, Russell (1984) states, "Mothers should not have to protect their children from their fathers!" (p. 264). Thus feminists see child sexual abuse as more of a societal than a familial issue.

TABLE 6.1   How Society "Sets Up" Children as Victims

Girls	Boys
Taught by society to be "vulnerable"	Taught to believe they're "powerful"
Taught to feel guilt and shame	Taught not to be seen as victims
Taught to be clean and attractive	Taught molestation may lead to homosexuality or
Taught to be manipulative	others to question manhood
Taught to please others	Taught to think it "cool" to be initiated by a female
	Taught to fear no one will believe them
	Taught to be "free" and "freedom" repressed if
	molestation reported to parents

By virtue of their particular perspectives, each group portends a different approach to treatment. The child protective philosophy sees protection of the child as paramount and the family as the unit responsible for this protection. Toward this end, the whole family is seen in treatment, with emphasis on redefining generational boundaries and role definitions and enhancing communication. The ultimate goal is reuniting the family if the perpetrator is able to take responsibility for his actions and the mother is able to protect her child in the future. Some agencies use the threat of prosecution of the perpetrator to engage him in treatment. Only when his cooperation is not forthcoming or when required by state law do most agencies favor incarceration.

Feminists favor a rape crisis model with an emphasis on victim advocacy. Use of the criminal justice system to punish the perpetrator is seen as a deterrent to future abuse. The victim is helped through this process by a concerned advocate who also strives toward the establishment of protection for the child in the future. Family reconciliation is viewed with some reservation and favored only if protection of the child can be ensured (Finkelhor, 1984a).

It is not always easy to discern the orientation of a helper in the area of child sexual abuse. Although some workers concentrate on family dynamics, they may feel that separation and even incarceration of the perpetrator is better for all involved. Many also see the victim in need of a strong advocate. Whatever the position, both perspectives agree that protection of the child in the future is vital.

Definition of Child Sexual Abuse

Child abuse, for reporting purposes, was defined in the 1974 Child Abuse Prevention and Treatment Act. In 1984, however, the U.S. Congress amended the previous definition to read:

> The term sexual abuse includes: (i) the employment, use, persuasion, inducement, enticement, or coercion of any child to engage in any sexually explicit conduct (or any simulation of such conduct) for the purpose of producing any visual depiction of such conduct, or (ii) the rape, molestation, prostitution, or other form of sexual exploitation of children, or incest with children, under circumstances which indicate the child's health or welfare is harmed or threatened thereby. (Child Abuse Prevention and Treatment Act 42 as Amended by Public Law 98–457, 98th Congress, 9 October 1984)

The National Center on Child Abuse and Neglect defines *sexual abuse* as "any childhood sexual experience that interferes with or has the potential for interfering with a child's healthy development" (1985, p. 3). More simply, *sexual abuse* is the use of a child for the sexual gratification of an adult. Numerous other words are used synonymously with sexual abuse. *Sexual exploitation,* for example, can be not only the actual genital manipulation of a child and the request to touch an adult but also compelling the child to observe sexual acts or have pictures taken for pornographic purposes. Some authors use the terms *assault* (Burgess et al., 1978), *molestation* (Sanford, 1980), *victimization* (Finkelhor, 1979), and *child rape* (Rush, 1980). *Rape,* in the commonly understood sense, denotes sexual intercourse usually undertaken with violence to the victim. The laws of many states, however, define *child rape* as the intrusion of any part of the perpetrator's body (e.g., penis, fingers, tongue) into an orifice of the child's body.

The use of specific terms is debatable. For example, Finkelhor argues against the terms *sexual assault* and *sexual abuse* because they imply physical violence, which is usually not a part of the pattern. *Sexual harassment,* he contends, is too weak, while *sexual misuse* implies the child is an object instead of a person. Finkelhor suggests the term *victimization* to stress that by virtue of age, naivete, and relationship, the child becomes victim to the sexual behavior (Finkelhor, 1979).

Geiser, on the other hand, favors the term *sexual misuse. Sexual abuse,* he feels, is a legal term, while *sexual misuse* emphasizes the mental health perspective, suggesting that normal process has gone astray. In this view, the focus should be on treatment rather than punishment. Geiser writes,

> Abuse implies an exclusive relationship between abuser and victim, which is often not the full picture. Sexual abuse is often a symptom of family dysfunction. The term misuse is a reminder of the need to study the entire system of human interrelationships. The consequences of sexual misuse will show up somewhere in this system as physical and/or behavioral symptoms in the child or as psychic distress in other family members. (1979, pp. 7–8)

Types of Sexual Abuse

Whether termed *child sexual abuse* or *misuse,* this type of maltreatment is usually divided into categories based on the identity of the perpetrator.

Familial Abuse

Incest is sexual abuse by a blood relative who is assumed to be part of the child's nuclear family. An individual assuming the role of a surrogate parent, such as a stepfather or live-in boyfriend, may be included in a functional definition of *incest.* Older siblings, who differ significantly in age or by virtue of their power and resources, may also be considered abusive.

Mayer (1983) cites categories of incestuous activity in families and to each attaches an assessment of harm to the child. The first and least damaging to the child is *sexual molestation.* This includes noncoitus sexual contact, petting, fondling, exhibitionism, and voyeurism, all of which result in the sexual stimulation of the perpetrator. The second category, *sexual assault,* consists of manual, oral, or genital contact with the genitals of the victim, masturbatory activities, fellatio (oral stimulation of the penis), and cunnilingus (oral stimulation of the clitoris). The last and most damaging category is called *forcible rape* and includes forced sexual contact resulting in assault with the penis. Fear, violence, and threats are used to ensure compliance from the victim. Mayer states that the latter two categories produce the most trauma for the child, but past victims of abuse say this is not so. Despite Mayer's contention that the degree of trauma is dependent on the type of sexual abuse, victims and survivors experience things very differently. A survivor who has been a victim of molestation may be as severely impacted as one who has been forcibly raped. Many more variables (discussed in a later section of this chapter) affect the degree of trauma to the child (Tower, 1988).

Extrafamilial Abuse

Extrafamilial abuse, perpetrated by someone outside the child's family, represents only about 40 percent of reported abuse. The abusing adult is often called a *pedophile,* that is, an adult whose primary sexual orientation is toward children. *Pedophilia* literally means "love of children" (deYoung, 1982). *Pederasty* is sexual relations between an adult male and a male child (Rush, 1980; Struve, 1990).

Child pornography uses children to produce sexually explicit material such as graphics, photographs, films, slides, magazines, and books (O'Brien, 1983; Trivelpiece, 1990; Pecora et al., 1992). Using the child for pornography may be part of the engagement process—a form of initiation of the child by the perpetrator—or the pornography may be an end in and of itself. New evidence gives credence to the possibility that child pornography actually stimulates perpetrators to commit a sexually abusive act (Finkelhor, 1984b; Trivelpiece, 1990).

The Progression of Sexual Abuse

There is usually a progression in the sexual abuse of a child. The perpetrator may "try out" behaviors to measure the child's comfort. If the child allows the abuser to continue, the abuse is intensified. Such a progression may be

1. Nudity (on the part of the adult)
2. Disrobing (of the adult in front of the child)
3. Genital exposure (by the adult)
4. Observation of the child (bathing, undressing, or excreting)
5. Kissing the child in a lingering, inappropriate manner
6. Fondling (of the child's breast, genital area, thighs, or buttocks)
7. Masturbation (mutual or solitary)
8. Fellatio—oral stimulation of the penis (to the perpetrator or the child)
9. Cunnilingus—oral stimulation of the vulva or vaginal area (to the child or the perpetrator)
10. Digital penetration (of anus or rectum)
11. Penile penetration (of the vagina)
12. Digital penetration (of the vagina)
13. Penile penetration (of anus or rectum)
14. "Dry intercourse" (the rubbing of the perpetrator's penis on the genital or rectal area, inner thighs, or buttocks of the child) (Sgroi, 1982, p. 71)

Not every case of sexual abuse progresses in the same manner, but generally there are five separate phases of child sexual abuse. Certainly, a longer-term relationship between the child and the perpetrator allows for a more leisurely progression over a period of time.

Engagement Phase

During the engagement phase, the perpetrator gains access to the child, engages him or her, and conveys to the child that the behavior is acceptable. (The pronouns *he* and *his* are used here for *perpetrator* because more than 95 percent of those reported are men.) Often this is accomplished by his misrepresentation of moral standards. For example, he may say to a child, "This is what every father does with his daughter," or "This is the way adults teach kids about sex." Perpetrators use a variety of methods to elicit cooperation. Basically, perpetrators play on children's need for human contact and affection, their need for adult approval, their enjoyment of games, and their interest in material rewards. Children's awe of adults and recognition of their own powerlessness provide the perfect opportunity for the perpetrator. This process is referred to as *grooming*. Groth (1979) classifies the method in which the perpetrator grooms the child according to that individual's motivational intent or the psychological aims underlying his behavior. Groth places these aims in two categories: pressured sex contacts and forced sex contacts.

Pressured Sex

In a pressured sex contact a perpetrator uses enticement, trying to persuade or cajole the child. "Come see the game I have for us to play" might be a lead line. Entrapment suggests that the perpetrator attempts to make the child feel indebted or obligated. He might say, "After I gave you that nice toy, the least you can do is make me feel good." This type of offender encourages the child to cooperate with the sexual activity by means of bribing or rewarding the child with attention, affection, or material goods. If the child refuses, he will not use force; he is attracted by the child as a loving, innocent, undemanding love object, and frequently knows the child prior to the assault (Burgess et al., 1978).

Forced Sex

Forced sex contacts, on the other hand, involve the threat of harm or the use of force to complete the abuse. A perpetrator may attempt to intimidate the child, using his position as an adult for this purpose. Although he does not intend to injure the child, his use of force to complete the sexual act sometimes harms the child. To him, the child is an object—a tool to carry out his sexual gratification or his need for control. As a result, he makes no attempt to engage his victim. A very small number of child molesters gain pleasure from hurting their victims. This sadistic child abuser sees the child as a target for his anger and cruelty. His crime is premeditated, and his intent is to degrade, hurt, or even destroy the child (Burgess et al., 1978).

Sexual Interaction and Secrecy Phases

The second phase is sexual interaction, or the actual sexual contact. The abuse may range anywhere from watching or fondling a child to sexual intercourse. Often the longer the abuse has gone on, the more advanced and complex it becomes. The third, or secrecy phase, ensures that the abuse can continue as the perpetrator uses his power to dominate, bribe, emotionally blackmail, or threaten the child into keeping the secret.

Disclosure Phase

Disclosure may or may not occur during childhood. Many adult victims of child sexual abuse attest that this phase may not be realized until adulthood. During disclosure, the abuse is uncovered either purposefully (the child tells an adult or the perpetrator seeks help) or accidentally (the participants are observed or the child demonstrates physical or emotional trauma resulting from the abuse). Children with genital or vaginal tears, venereal disease, or age-inappropriate sexual behavior or knowledge often give clues that are interpreted as indicators of abuse.

Suppression Phase

The final phase, or suppression stage, occurs when those close to the child, as a result of their own abhorrence of the issue or fear of scandal, stigma, or consequences, encourage and often compel the child to recant or forget the abuse. The pressure the child feels often elicits a recantation, and treatment or prosecution becomes difficult or impossible.

> *Georgia's abuse followed the classic progression. Soon after her divorce, Georgia's mother's boyfriend, Chip, moved in with the family. Alone with Georgia and her infant brother while the mother worked evenings, Chip appeared to be the ideal babysitter. He engaged 7-year-old Georgia in games and encouraged her trust. After several months of tickling, fondling, and bathing—interspersed with a variety of innocent games—Chip suggested they play a new game. He demonstrated to Georgia the "inflatable quality" of his penis and encouraged her to "play with it." Such play was followed by Chip's statement that this was "their little game" and she mustn't tell anyone. If she did, he told her, he'd have to leave, and her mother would never forgive her.*
>
> *When her mother observed Georgia rubbing her baby brother's penis sometime later, she questioned her. Georgia's response was that she "wanted to see if it got big like Chip's." Not wanting to admit to herself that her boyfriend could be guilty of any wrongdoing, the mother passed off the remark by telling her daughter that she "shouldn't talk like that." Several years later, when Georgia developed extreme tenderness in her vaginal area, the mother took her to a doctor who, in conference alone with Georgia, managed to uncover the story. The mother reacted in disbelief and sobbingly ordered Georgia to "take back your awful lies." Fortunately, the mother was eventually able to support her daughter, but once social services closed the case, she told Georgia "to put it all out of your mind."*

For such abused children there are interviewing techniques that include preparing children for the possibility they will be asked to recant. With this preparation and support from the helping system, fewer children are placed in the position of feeling they must deny what has happened to them.

Whatever the semantics or the categories citing its damage and progress, *sexual abuse* is the use of sex by an adult to gain power, dominance, and control over a child. The child is manipulated through force, coercion, cajoling, enticement, and threat to comply with the adult's desires. It is natural for children to "participate" because of their awe, trust, respect, or love for the adult.

Incidence of Sexual Abuse

Studies of Abuse

Studies to determine the scope of child sexual abuse have been undertaken in numerous countries and some date to 1914. One of the earliest studies was done in 1919 by deFrancis (Finkelhor, 1979) in association with the American Humane Association (Children's Division). From 263 cases studied in the New York City area, deFrancis discovered a much higher incidence of sexual abuse than had been previously assumed. Kinsey and his associates, in their random survey of 14,000 women in the 1950s, discovered that at least 25 percent had had some sexual encounter prior to the age of 13 (Kinsey et al., 1953, p. 21).

Pursuing adults' experience of abuse in their childhoods, Finkelhor (1979), of the University of New Hampshire Family Violence Program, studied 796 college students in the 1970s and disclosed that of the 530 females, 19.2 percent reported having been victimized in childhood, as did 8.6 percent of the 266 males. In her survey of 930 San Francisco women, Russell (1984) found 647 cases of child sexual abuse but only 30 had ever been reported to the police.

In Finkelhor's 1981 study of 700 households in Boston, researchers conducted interviews with 521 parents to discover whether they or their children had ever been victimized. Of the 63 people 21 percent (15 percent female and 6 percent male) reported that they, themselves, had been sexually abused. Parents reported that 4.5 percent of their children had been abused and another 4.5 percent of their children had been victims of attempted abuse. Overall, 47 percent of the subjects studied had some knowledge or experience of sexual abuse[1] (Finkelhor, 1984a). From the various studies of adults reporting their own past experiences, it was found that between 9 and 52 percent of the females and between 3 and 9 percent of the males had some sexual abuse exposure as children (Finkelhor, 1984a).

With the recognition that males are abused almost as frequently as females have come recent studies on male victimization. In 1988, Urquiza found that, of the 2,016 male students studied at the University of Washington, 17.3 percent reported some type of sexual abuse prior to the age of eighteen. Murphy, in 1989, conducted 777 telephone interviews in Minnesota and came up with an 11-percent abuse rate among males. Many theorists and clinicians would argue that these statistics are extremely low compared to the actual suspected incidence of abuse (Urquiza and Keating, 1990).

The National Center on Child Abuse and Neglect (NCCAN) and the National Center on Child Abuse Prevention Research, a program of the National Committee to Prevent Child Abuse (NCPCA), have provided important data on the current incidence of child sexual abuse. NCCAN (1994) reports that in 1992, 14 percent of the 918,263 reported maltreatment cases nationally were sexual abuse (p. 6). In 1993, according to NCPAC (1994), 15 percent of *substantial* cases of 1,016,000 were sexual abuse (p. 8). (The differences in total numbers of these reports is related to data collection sources and methods.) Of these numbers the majority of *reported* sexual abuse victims are female. Males are still sexually exploited at younger ages with the highest incidence of boys abused at age 4–6 years and the highest number of girls between ages 11–14 (NCCAN, 1994, p. 26).

There are a few statistics to indicate the prevalence of children involved in pornography and prostitution. Campagna, in the "Meat Rack Investigation" conducted with Poffenberger, considered a variety of forms of exploitation of children. Based on a nationwide survey of 596 police departments, Campagna (1985, p. 6) estimated that 100,000 to 200,000 children (average age of 15 years) are involved in full-time prostitution. Considering runaways, Campagna suggests that at least 10 percent of the nation's runaways are victims of violence or abduction by strangers, much of which may be sexual (p. 135). Campagna offered no statistics on child pornography, but O'Brien (1983) states that of the $5 billion grossed in the sale of pornographic materials in the United States in 1980, perhaps 5 to 10 percent was from child pornography.

Sgt. Lloyd Martin of the Los Angeles Police Department estimates that in the three states of California, Texas, and New York, 40,000 to 120,000 children are involved in pornography or prostitution each year (O'Brien, 1983). The difficulty in obtaining more accurate statistics is based on several factors: (1) the public is naive to the existence of such a problem; (2) there is no national standardization in data-gathering or reporting; (3) few, if any, agencies have units specifically designed to study and uncover this type of sexual exploitation; and (4) there has been little funding for research and little, if any, legislative attention to the problem (O'Brien, 1983; Campagna, 1985).

Reporting of Abuse

Although the incidence of sexual abuse of children seems significant, the reported cases represent a very small portion of the children actually abused. There are several reasons for this:

1. Sexual abuse is difficult to identify and prove and easy to deny.

2. Children are given few legal rights and are often not believed.

3. Efforts to treat focus on punishing the offender. In family situations, the other family members are less likely to report because prosecution upsets the family balance both economically and physically.

4. Those investigating cases feel discomfort in talking about sexual issues and do not screen cases properly or do not recognize signals that sexual abuse is occurring.

5. Treatment methods are not coordinated or sufficiently effective to elicit a desire for treatment on the part of families or victims. Investigators, too, feel treatment is not effective enough to warrant the trauma children are exposed to when the case is reported.

6. Society's taboo on sexual deviations places a stigma on both victim and perpetrator, and, therefore, not to report is not to suffer disgrace (Urquiza and Keating, 1990; Pecora et al., 1992).

Family members and other private citizens describe personal reasons for not wanting to report sexual abuse. Some people do not want to inform on or interfere in the affairs of others, especially when the perpetrator may be a respected member of the community or even a family member. Parents may feel they can handle the situation of their child's abuse on their own. Even if the fact of the abuse is accepted and help seems warranted, many adults do not know where to report. Perhaps the most universal reason why more reports are not substantiated is adults' reluctance to believe children and their hesitancy to attribute such behavior to other adults (Sanford, 1980; Sgroi, 1982; Finkelhor, 1984a; Urquiza and Keating, 1990).

False Allegations Movement

Currently there is a movement which may also hamper the reporting of abuse now and in the future. This movement charges that the incidence of sexual abuse has been greatly exaggerated or even fabricated. While this sentiment has existed among some of the public and a few professionals for some time, it became formalized into what is known as the *False Memory Syndrome Foundation,* when one particularly controversial case sparked supporters of an accused couple to protest their innocence.

Gardner (1991), a forensic psychiatrist, is one believer in the idea that our society has become preoccupied with sexual abuse to the point of obsession or hysteria. He contends that "...[T]he ubiquity of environmental sexual stimuli is playing a role in the epidemic of false sex abuse allegations that we have witnessed in the last decade." (Gardner, 1991, p. 19). Further, he suggests that several common mechanisms lead parents (often within the context of custody disputes) to influence their children to make false accusations. These, Gardner explains, are: *vicarious gratification* (where the parent forms a visual image of a sexual encounter and attributes that encounter to the child); *projection* (where unacceptable thoughts or feelings are attributed to others); *reaction formation* (when an individual consciously takes on feelings which are the opposite of what he or she really feels); *voyeurism* (which is a compulsive need to observe sexual happenings or people); *a release of anger or displacement of blame* (which enables the parent to get back at the perpetrator by the accusation); and *substitution* (which allows the child to be substituted for the sexual object) (Gardner, 1991, pp. 25–37). Through these mental processes, the parent either suggests to the child that he or she has been abused or assumes that he or she has been.

Gardner goes on to characterize the evaluators of sexual abuse allegations as being untrained, with no certification and often little knowledge or experience. He also questions the use of anatomically correct dolls, the assumption that children never lie, and whether indicators of sexual abuse are in fact reliable. (See Gardner, 1991, p. 46–68.) It is his contention that not only do children lie, but that they may seek notoriety and want to ingratiate themselves to adult authority figures. Some may also make reports because others of their peers have reported or embellish these reports for the same reasons (pp. 92–97).

Although some authors believe that these ideas require additional debate, other clinicians and authors express concern that voicing such arguments only serves to prevent those who might otherwise have sought help for their abuse from doing so (see also Ofshe and Watters, 1994; Ney, 1995).

Profile of the Abused Child

Is there, in fact, a typical kind of child who is sexually abused? Research shows that girls are more likely to report as the victim of abuse than boys (NCCAN, 1994). This fact appears to be not so much indicative of who is abused but of our culture that tells males to be strong and run from danger (see Table 6.1). In the role of victim, boys may feel like sissies. Boys are less likely to have to account for their whereabouts and, therefore, not as likely to be confronted by parents about unusual behavior (Groth, 1979; Nasjleti, 1980; Sanford, 1980; Finkelhor, 1984a; Urquiza and Keating, 1990). Based on reports and stereotypes, the assumption has been that girls are the most frequent victims. It is now shown that boys are almost equally as vulnerable.

Recent studies (Urquiza and Keating, 1990) show the incidence of abuse among male children is significantly higher than reported. Porter (1986) reports that Henry Giarretto, executive director of the Institute for the Community as Extended Family (ICEF) in San Jose, California, points out that only 5 percent of child sexual abuse victims, treated between 1970 and 1975, were males. In 1986 the percentage of males being treated by ICEF rose to over 22 percent. Porter estimates that the true ratio of sexually abused boys to sexually abused girls would be 1:1, even though significantly fewer boys than girls report the abuse. Urquiza and Keating (1990) suggest that until more research has been done on male victimization we cannot gather accurate statistics.

The average age of those abused is between 4–6 years for boys and 11–14 years for girls (NCCAN, 1994). There may be more abused adolescents, but statistics are difficult to formulate for several reasons. First, adolescents are especially reluctant to report because they fear their parents will curb their freedom to punish or protect them in the future. Further, because of age, the offense, if reported, may very likely be categorized as adult rape. Our dating culture (i.e., early, unchaperoned dating as well as the popularity of singles bars) makes teens especially vulnerable to strangers, acquaintances, and the so-called date rape.

Children at Risk

It is difficult to determine why some children are abused while others are not. Several factors put children at risk for sexual victimization. Social isolation is one reason. Children who are left alone, are unsupervised, and who do not have the physical presence of numerous friends and neighbors are more likely to be abused (Sgroi, 1982; Finkelhor, 1984a). The mother has an influence on the child's vulnerability. Studies show that the mother who is absent, who is not close to her child emotionally, who is sexually punitive or religiously fanatic, who never finished high school, or who keeps herself isolated is more likely to have a child who will be abused (Sgroi, 1982; James and Nasjleti, 1983; Finkelhor, 1984a). Finkelhor suggested that the presence of a stepfather in the home made a child more vulnerable, not only for abuse by the stepfather himself but for abuse by others. He theorized that statistically a girl, especially one whose mother had remarried, was probably exposed to a variety of men (i.e., the mother's previous boyfriends) who may have had an opportunity to abuse her. Further, friends of a stepfather may not perceive as strong a taboo against molesting the adopted daughter of a friend as against a blood relative. This perception may result from the belief that the stepfather does not have as great an emotional investment in the child (Finkelhor, 1984a).

Faller (1988) found that the stepfather was the abuser in only 17.3 percent of her sample, compared to 28.1 percent of biological fathers married to the mother at the time of the abuse (p. 30). Faller also considered other factors related to the victim's family. She found that 29 percent of the mothers of victims reported having themselves been abused as children (p. 32). In 52.7 percent of the families studied, there was some substance abuse or addiction (p. 3). Families of victims reported significant marital problems with 35.8 percent of the perpetrators as the dominant figure in the household (p. 34). Children came from families who tended to be isolated and have few supports.

Vander May (1988) outlined the risk factors associated primarily with male children. This author concluded that boys are at higher risk for sexual abuse in either father-son or mother-son incest if the parents abused alcohol. Mothers were likely to abuse their sons if they were single parents or the dominant parent, if the household was low income, and if these mothers exhibited other emotional or mental problems. Fathers were more likely to abuse their boys sexually if they were the dominant parent, if there was marital discord, if they had physically abused the wife or other children, if the household was low income, if the mother was emotionally distant and hostile toward males and if the father feared homosexuality.

Female Victims

Why a child is chosen to be abused has long been a subject of debate. In incestuous situations, deYoung (1982) found that of her sample of 60 victims of paternal incest, 83 percent were oldest daughters and 5 percent were only children. Others theorize that a father may approach his eldest daughter and if she refuses, he may go on to abuse other daughters (Justice and Justice, 1979; Sgroi, 1982). Children with disabilities (physical limitations or emotional disturbances) are particularly vulnerable to victimization (deYoung, 1982).

Although actual physical attractiveness of the daughter in incest situations seems to have little influence on whether or not she is abused, there is some debate as to the seductiveness or promiscuity of the female incest victim prior to victimization. Although offenders often describe their victims as seductive, this allegation is usually viewed as part of the perpetrator's rationalization. Recent studies that question the promiscuity of the daughter as a contributor to incest (Maisch, 1972; Meiselman, 1979) show that the daughter's behavior was predisposed by her already character-disordered family. The patriarchal nature of the incestuous family may also have created a child limited in her ability to say no and thus vulnerable to all types of sexual exploitation (Meiselman, 1979; Herman and Hirschman, 1981; deYoung 1982; Herman, 1992).

Male Victims

A composite of male victims is less easy to formulate. From five studies of adult men conducted to assess the incidence of abuse among boys, Finkelhor estimated that the prevalence of abuse reported among boys under 13 years was between 2.5 percent and 5 percent. "This should mean a total of 550,000 to 1,100,000 of the currently twenty-two million boys under thirteen (census estimate, 1980) would eventually be victimized" (Finkelhor, 1984a, p. 155). Yet, despite these figures it is difficult to get a picture of the boy involved or the abuse he experiences.

The research thus far indicates that boys are abused at a younger age. Earlier research cited the median age for boys to be sexually abused was 8.46 years (as opposed to girls at 12.4 years) (Finkelhor, 1984b). However, NCCAN (1994) reports that during 1992 the majority of boys were abused between the ages of 4 and 6 years (p. 26). The abuse takes place for shorter periods of time and is more likely to take place outside the family. Statistically, abused boys are from poorer socioeconomic backgrounds than girls. There is more likely to be physical abuse in their families, but why a particular boy is chosen (youngest, eldest) has not been

fully researched. Some theorists believe that the less assertive boy is more likely to be victimized (Finkelhor, 1984a; Porter, 1986; Urquiza and Keating, 1990; Chandy et al., 1997).

Degree of Trauma

Not every child is affected by sexual abuse in the same way. The degree of trauma the child experiences depends on several variables:

1. *The type of abuse.* Some victims of family incest appear to be more deeply affected than those who were abused by someone outside the family. Yet abuse by nonfamily members who have either meant a great deal to the victim or who have been sadistic or violent can also have profound effects.

2. *The identity of the perpetrator.* When the relationship with the perpetrator was close, the victims describe being more significantly traumatized. This trauma is based on the betrayal of trust that abuse by a family member or trusted individual represents. Daughters abused by fathers demonstrate less trauma in adulthood than those abused by mothers. Sons molested by mothers reported fewer effects of the abuse, but researchers are now finding abuse by mothers in the backgrounds of many rapists and homosexuals (deYoung, 1982). The experiences of boys abused by fathers appears to be more negative (Finkelhor, 1979). Sibling incest is drawing increased attention as producing more trauma than previously recognized.

3. *The duration of the abuse.* Most abuse in incestuous families takes place from one to three years before disclosure. Abuse that continues for a period of time, rather than a one-time incident or series of incidents, seems to create more trauma. The exception is when the one-time incident involved violence or sadism (Beitchman et al., 1992).

4. *The extent of the abuse.* Although any type of misuse can cause traumas for children, a perpetrator who takes a child further along the progression, or does more physical damage to the child, creates more residual effects.

5. *The age at which the child was abused.* Developmentally, children pass many milestones. Each interrupted developmental stage will cause its own particular effects (Beitchman et al., 1992).

6. *The first reactions of significant others at disclosure.* Most children attempt to tell at least one adult of the victimization. Individuals who decide to tell a trusted adult may receive help that can lessen the impact. Securing therapeutic aid is often based, however, on the reactions of those who first hear of the abuse. If the adults in the child's life are not willing to believe the child, he or she may be blamed or forced to keep the guilty secret into adulthood (Burgess et al., 1978).

7. *The point at which the abuse was disclosed.* Children who try to tell and are not believed, or who do not have the confidence in their protection to disclose, may keep their secret to adulthood. Treatment of adult survivors indicates that the secret keeping does, in fact, compound the trauma.

8. *The personality structure of the victim.* Children differ in as many ways as perpetrators. One child abused in a similar manner as another might react totally differently.

Profile of the Perpetrator

Much debate surrounds the treatment and the personality of the perpetrator. Between 95 and 98 percent of known perpetrators are males (Maisch, 1972; Walters, 1975; Rush, 1980; Groth, 1979). In a later study and analysis of the data, however, Finkelhor (1984b) questions whether there are not more cases of female perpetrators than previously recognized. Between 50 and 70 percent of the offenders were themselves victims of sexual abuse as children (Seghorn and Boucher, 1979; Groth, 1979). Cohen, Seghorn, and Mehegan (1979) described offenders as having a lack of "joy and [having] a relative absence of non-sexual emotional qualities of human relationships such as warmth, tenderness or caring. Although many manifest a severe self-deprecatory attitude, some appear grandiose; some present themselves as weak, passive and helpless, but there are others who affect a super-normal autonomous picture." While these authors concluded there were no typical offender characteristics, more recently theorists are attempting to generate a profile to be used in assessment and treatment (see Conte, 1990; Prendergast, 1991; and Hanson et al., 1994).

Familial Perpetrators

Fathers
The incestuous father is more widely described in the literature. These abusers have usually experienced mild to extreme levels of childhood deprivation with dysfunctional, chaotic

families of origin. Many have been sexually abused themselves as children and have often left home at an early age (Faller, 1988; Hanson et al., 1994). Some authors (Herman and Hirschman, 1981) depict these fathers as overbearing and tyrannical; others describe them as passive, immature and dependent (Ballard et al., 1990). Intellectually, these men present an average picture (Meiselman, 1979; Faller, 1988), but they may appear to have poor impulse control, low frustration tolerance, social and emotional immaturity, faulty ego operation, and frustrated dependency needs. In addition to a passive-aggressive expression of affect, low ego strength, low self-esteem, and the use of rationalization, denial, and manipulation, they may also use or abuse alcohol (Conte, 1990; Prendergast, 1991). The individual incestuous father has a proclivity for rationalization: He rationalizes about alcohol (alcohol caused him to abuse); that he is mentally ill (feels he must be "crazy"); that his daughter is his possession (and may therefore be used as he wishes); and that it is his daughter's duty (daughters should be dutiful to fathers, even to the point of having sexual relations). Another type of father also rationalizes that he and his family must be sexually liberated from archaic social mores (deYoung, 1982).

Justice and Justice (1979) categorized incestuous fathers. The first of these major categories is the *symbiotic* personality who hungers for the closeness, sense of belonging, and intimacy lacking in childhood. These personalities confuse sexuality with affection and try to satisfy their need for closeness with sex.

They further characterized these symbiotic men into four types. The *introvert* closes his family into a womb. He remains totally isolated and within this isolation derives pleasure from his child. He feels under attack from the outside world. The *rationalizer* is one who "uses lofty words and sentiment or plausible sounding, but specious reasoning for establishing an incestuous affair with his daughter" (p. 67). Some rationalizers see themselves as lovers, others as teachers, and others as protectors of their daughters. The *tyrant* is another subtype of symbiotic personality. This man rules his home and is very much the type of individual that Herman and Hirschman (1981) describe. The *alcoholic* has a need to be dependent and be taken care of.

The other two major categories of incestuous fathers described by Justice and Justice are more pathological. The *psychopathic* father is not looking for affection but is seeking to "get even" for his own deprived childhood. He chooses the sexual exploitation of his daughter as a way of expressing his hostility. The *pedophiliac's* primary interest is in sex and his incestuous behavior is a manifestation of this disturbance. These categorizations by Justice and Justice refer primarily to father-daughter incest. Others describe fathers who abuse sons as having latent homosexual desires that they have repressed. Usually these fathers have married and appear to be heterosexual (Meiselman, 1979; deYoung, 1982; Urquiza and Keating, 1990).

Mothers

Mothers who abuse tend to be less intelligent and more emotionally disturbed than their male counterparts (Peterson, et al. 1993). The incestuous mother who abuses her son is often looking for the closeness of another "man" in her life. She usually has an emotionally or physically absent husband and wants her son to fill her needs. The woman who abuses her daughter is a more disturbed individual and sees her daughter as an extension of herself. Mother-daughter sexual acts often have a masturbatory quality (Forward and Buck, 1978; James and Nasjleti, 1983; Mayer, 1993).

Siblings

Researchers have studied the trauma from sexual interaction between siblings (beyond age-appropriate exploration). Data suggest it is the exploitive nature of sibling incest that creates negative residual effects (deYoung, 1982; Weihe and Herring, 1991). If the older sibling has greater power, knowledge, and resources, the younger often feels victimized (Sanford, 1980). The sibling abuser is either modeling the role of an abusing parent or is seeking to dominate or punish the younger child (Weihe and Herring, 1991). To engage a brother or sister, the abuser often initiates the abuse in the form of play (Meiselman, 1979).

Extrafamilial Perpetrators

The outside abuser exhibits similar characteristics in terms of a disturbed family history. There appears to be more childhood physical abuse present among these individuals (deYoung, 1982; Prendergast, 1991). Many experienced sexual abuse as children, but data indicate that some pedophiles witnessed rather than experienced the abuse and may be modeling their behavior in this manner (deYoung, 1982). Interesting data from a study of incarcerated male sex offenders by Seghorn, Pretky, and Boucher (1986) suggest a higher number of men had been sexually abused as children than was reflected in earlier studies. Further, in a comparison of rapists and child molesters, the researchers found that child molesters were more likely to have been victimized by someone outside their family, although the family at the time of victimization appeared to be in turmoil. Such information causes us to seriously consider the impact of abuse on the males who later perpetrate. An assault from a family member appears to produce aggressive behavior—such as rape—directed toward adults. Assault from a nonfamily member creates an individual who abuses children. The research is too recent to draw final conclusions or postulate any explanations. It should also be emphasized, however, that not all males who were abused become perpetrators.

Sexual Addicts

Carnes (1983) places the sexual abuser of children in the category of *sexual addict*. The addict develops a delusional thought process that is supported by a distorted belief system. He denies, rationalizes, and eventually begins to believe his own lies. This theory equates sex with an addiction to alcohol or drugs. In a fashion similar to substance addiction, the addict undergoes a four-step cycle. Preoccupation is a time when his mind focuses completely on sex. So pervasive is the idea that it becomes obsessive. He then begins ritualization, or the development of a ritual that leads up to the behavior. One addict, for example, cruises in his car in a certain neighborhood. When he finds a child to molest, he goes into a familiar routine of engagement. Another addict reports giving his daughter a bath in the same manner as a prelude to every molestation. He reads to her after her bath, tucks her in, and begins to fondle her. Both these sexual addicts have developed a ritual that differs only slightly from abuse to abuse. The compulsion cycle includes the actual act, which the addict feels unable to stop or control. *Despair* often follows, and he feels powerless over his behavior and hopeless about his ability to change. This cycle then perpetuates itself (see Figure 6.1) until the addict feels unable to tolerate his behavior or is discovered. In the meantime he has retreated from his family and isolated himself.

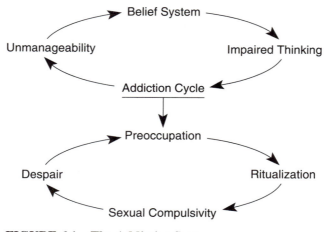

FIGURE 6.1   The Addictive System

From Patrick Carnes, *Out of the Shadows.* Minneapolis, MN: CompCare, 1983. Reprinted with permission.

Pedophiles

Although sexual addiction may be one way of explaining the behavior of perpetrators, the most widely used categorization to explain the motivations of perpetrators is Groth's typology of the fixated and regressed pedophile (see Table 6.2). The *fixated offender* is one whose primary orientation is to children, predominantly male children. His compulsive, premeditated abuse is based on his need to repeat his own past victimization. Emotionally, he is fixated in adolescence and his maladaptive resolution of life issues creates an individual who is not distressed or guilty about his behavior. He has little heterosexual interest in agemates unless the woman has children of the age (usually the age at which he himself had been abused) that interests him (Groth, 1979).

The *regressed offender* is one who has achieved a tenuous developmental level in adulthood, but who is motivated by crises and conflicts to regress to an interest in children. He chooses primarily female children in an attempt to find an undemanding adult female substitute and sees this child as a miniadult ("She looked older than her alleged 3 years."). This individual's abuse is impulsive and episodic, precipitated by stress. He often seeks closeness and an "all-loving mother." The regressed offender may also coexist sexually with an agemate, often appear to maintain a relatively normal relationship, and may be involved in the use or abuse of alcohol (Groth, 1979).

Although Groth's categories can be used to describe incestuous fathers as well as pedophiles, his studies were based on work with incarcerated individuals, the majority of whom were pedophiles. Researchers, including Maisch (1972), insist there are primary differences in the categories. For example, pedophiles' interests are in children of a particular age—that when the pedophile himself was traumatized (or ceased to develop emotionally); the interest often only continues until the child begins to develop secondary sex characteristics. The incestuous father (Justice and Justice, 1979; Meiselman, 1979; Conte, 1990), on the other hand, bonds with his victim and continues the relationship into her adolescence

TABLE 6.2   Typology of Pedophilia

Fixated	Regressed
1. Primary sexual orientation is to children	1. Primary sexual orientation is to agemates.
2. Pedophilic interests begin at adolescence	2. Pedophilic interests begin at adulthood
3. No precipitating stress/no subjective distress	3. Precipitating stress usually evident
4. Persistent interest—compulsive behavior	4. Involvements may be more episodic
5. Pre-planned, premeditated offense	5. Initial offense may be impulsive, not premeditated
6. Identification: offender identifies closely with the victim and equalizes his behavior to the level of the child; and/or may adopt a pseudo-parental role to the victim	6. Substitution: offender replaces conflictual adult relationship with involvement with the child; victim is a pseudoadult substitute and in incest situations the offender abandons his parental role
7. Male victims are primary targets	7. Female victims are primary targets
8. Little or no sexual contact with agemates; offender is usually single or in a marriage of "convenience"	8. Sexual contact with child co-exists with sexual contact with agemates; offender is usually married/common-law
9. Usually no history of alcohol or drug abuse	9. In more cases the offense may be alcohol related
10. Characterological immaturity/poor socio-sexual peer relationships	10. More traditional lifestyle but under-developed peer relationships
11. Offense—maladaptive resolution of life issues	11. Offense—maladaptive attempt to cope with specific life stresses

From *Men Who Rape*, by A. Nicholas Groth. New York: Plenum Press, 1979. Reprinted with permission.

(and perhaps into adulthood, unless she protests). Further, some theorists point out that while the pedophile can be considered in the light of his own pathology, the incestuous father must be seen in the context of the total family dynamics (Justice and Justice, 1979; Meiselman, 1979; Sgroi, 1982; deYoung, 1982; Faller, 1988; Conte, 1990). New research also shows that the incestuous father, once thought to contain his abuse within the family, may, in fact, abuse outside the family circle. This seems to contradict previous findings and highlights the need for more research in the area of perpetrator motivation and personality (Conte, 1990).

Juvenile and Adolescent Offenders[2]
One population that, until recently, has been inadequately studied is the juvenile or adolescent perpetrator. Adolescents are not likely to be reported as offenders due to their age and society's concept of typical adolescent issues. Teenagers explore their sexuality during these years. As a result, most parents and even mental health professionals do not take sexual molestation by a teen seriously, even though its impact on the victim may be significant. The abusing adolescent may be someone who is close to the family or knows the victim well, which again causes adults to discount the likelihood of the abuse occurring. Yet at least 20 percent of the offenders seen by Groth described assaulting a child when they were adolescents (Groth, 1979). In addition, Finkelhor (1979) found in his study of college students that one-third of the 119 women reporting a past history of abuse said the perpetrator was a male between 10 and 19 years old. Of the 23 men in the study, 9 (or 40 percent) were

victimized by a male between 10 and 19 years of age. Barbaree et al. comment that approximately 50 percent of all adult offenders report beginning their abuse careers as adolescents. (Barbaree et al., 1993).

In 1966, Shoar, Speed, and Bartlet examined 80 adolescents who had abused children under the age of 10. They depicted the typical adolescent abuser as

> …a "loner" who is socially and sexually immature and lacking suitable sex education. He has minimal social peer group activities with boys and girls and prefers playing with younger children. Not surprisingly, his main work experience is babysitting with younger children. (Knopp, 1982, p. 14)

Adolescents who abuse may do so for a variety of reasons. Most, if not all, have been victims of abuse (either sexual or physical) themselves. Many have witnessed parental conflict and possibly substance abuse. They may be modeling what was done to them or to their siblings, or using sexuality to exert power over those younger or less powerful. Ryan et al. (1987) found that many of these teens had been involved in other delinquent acts as well.

It is not just adolescents who act out sexually against others. Gil and Johnson (1993), in their combined research, have found an increasing number of children under the age of twelve who molest others. Although the authors compare these *"sexualized children"* to their adolescent counterparts, they draw several distinctions.

> …children who molest, and their parents, across the board, have more highly disturbed interpersonal relationships, levels of family disruption, sexual confusion, and victimization. In contrast to adolescent sex offenders, most children who molest have severe oppositional disorder…have significant disruptions of development in their core self, as well as their capacity to make meaningful attachments. In addition, the thrust of sexual behaviors in young children is less frequently toward obtaining sexual pleasure, and more frequently toward expressing internalized anger and tension. (p. xv)

Preconditions for Perpetration

Perhaps the most convincing research in the area of understanding the perpetrator is that of Finkelhor (1984a) who states there are four preconditions for sexual abuse to take place (see Table 6.3). The first is that the perpetrator must be motivated to abuse. Motivation is based on three factors: emotional congruence, sexual arousal, and blockage of normal outlets. *Emotional congruence* is the need of the perpetrator for the child to satisfy some emotional need. His choice of a child is a result of his need to feel powerful and in control because of his arrested emotional development or his reenactment of his own childhood trauma. Society contributes to this need by its emphasis on male dominance in sexual relationships. A child is a person over whom dominance is assured. The perpetrator must then be *sexually aroused* by the child. Again, a sexual trauma in his own childhood or his modeling of another's interest in the child can create such arousal. Some perpetrators misinterpret children's need for affection and attention and assume they are being sexually seductive. Child pornography as well as the male tendency to sexualize emotions may contribute to the perpetrator's sexual interests.

TABLE 6.3   Preconditions for Sexual Abuse

	Level of Explanation	
	Individual	Social/Cultural
Precondition I: *Factors Related to* *Motivation to* *Sexually Abuse*		

Emotional congruence	Arrested emotional development
	Need to feel powerful and controlling
	Re-enactment of childhood trauma to
	    undo the hurt
	Narcissistic identification with self as a
	    young child
		Masculine requirement to be dominant
		    and powerful in sexual relationships

Sexual arousal	Childhood sexual experience that was
	    traumatic or strongly conditioning
	Modeling of sexual interest in children by
	    someone else
	Misattribution of arousal cues
	Biological abnormality
		Child pornography
		Erotic portrayal of children in advertising
		Male tendency to sexualize all emotional
		    needs

Blockage	Oedipal conflict Castration anxiety Fear of adult females Traumatic sexual experience with adult Inadequate social skills Marital problems	Repressive norms about masturbation and extramarital sex

Precondition II:
Factors Predisposing
to Overcoming
Internal Inhibitors
	Alcohol
	Psychosis
	Impulse disorder
	Senility
	Failure of incest inhibition mechanism in
	    family dynamics
		Social toleration of sexual interest in
		    children
		Weak criminal sanctions against offenders
		Ideology of patriarchal prerogatives for
		    fathers
		Social toleration for deviance committed
		    while intoxicated
		Child pornography
		Male inability to identify with needs of
		    children

Precondition III:
Factors Predisposing
to Overcoming
External Inhibitors
	Mother who is absent or ill
	Mother who is not close to or protective
	    of child
	Mother who is dominated or abused by
	    father
	Social isolation of family
	Unusual opportunities to be alone with
	    child
	Lack of supervision of child
	Unusual sleeping or rooming conditions
		Lack of social supports for mother
		Barriers to women's equality
		Erosion of social networks
		Ideology of family sanctity

Precondition IV:
Factors Predisposing
to Overcoming
Child's Resistance
	Child who is emotionally insecure or
	    deprived
	Child who lacks knowledge about sexual
	    abuse
	Situation of unusual trust between child
	    and offender
	Coercion
		Unavailability of sex education for
		    children
		Social powerlessness of children

From *Child Sexual Abuse: New Theory and Research* by David Finkelhor. Reprinted with permission of The Free Press, a Division of Macmillan, Inc. Copyright © 1984 by David Finkelhor.

Further, the perpetrator's motivation to abuse is a result of a *blockage of normal outlets* for his sexual and affectional needs. A fear of adult females, based perhaps on an unresolved Oedipal conflict, castration anxiety, or early trauma, complicated by inadequate social skills, can create such a blockage. Marital problems and society's norms, which censure masturbation and extramarital sex, can also create an atmosphere of frustration for the potential perpetrator.

The second precondition to child sexual abuse is based on the perpetrator's lack of internal inhibitors. Alcohol, psychosis, senility, and an impulse disorder can all prevent his "inner voice" from prohibiting him from acting on the desire to abuse. He may not have received a clear message in his family of origin that sexual activities with children are prohibited. Society's weak sanction against offenders, support of patriarchal prerogatives, and toleration for acts committed under intoxication give a confused and easily rationalized message to the perpetrator.

The third precondition describes the external inhibitors that the perpetrator must overcome for the abuse to take place. The role of the mother of the potential victim is an important factor. Mothers who are emotionally distant, ill, absent, or who fail to supervise present less of a deterrent to the perpetrator. The lack of privacy and unusual opportunities for the abuser to be alone with the child can also contribute to the abuse. Families who are socially isolated are also more vulnerable to sexual abuse.

In the fourth precondition, the perpetrator must overcome the child's resistance to the abuse. Children who have a poor self-concept and lack knowledge of abuse are more vulnerable. The closeness between child and perpetrator may also place a child in a position where the abuse can take place. Children learn early that they have no rights or power.

Powerlessness makes children extremely vulnerable; a group of sex offenders describe this vulnerability.

Six inmates in a maximum-security prison agreed to speak with the small group of students, assembled as part of a community awareness program. All convicted child molesters, these men spoke openly of their backgrounds and motivations.

"What kind of child do you look for?" asked one young coed.

The handsome, slightly built young man scratched his beard thoughtfully and smiled.

"I look for the kid who looks like he needs attention. The one who hangs back; he reminds me of me a few years ago, thinking I was garbage and figuring I wasn't good enough to ask for anything."

Another inmate spoke up. "I used to be awed at the power I could have over my victims, like they had no idea what I was doing. I couldn't believe someone hadn't told them something about sex! But at that time, I'm sure I was glad no one had."

"What do you think could have protected kids from you?" baited an involved student.

"Someone should have told them about guys like me. A couple of kids I approached said, 'No,' and I just backed off. I didn't want no hassle, you know. If someone had told them about sex and sex abuse or even watched them better, I'd have been sunk."

Who Become Perpetrators

Finkelhor has outlined the reasons why an individual male might perpetrate, but what is it about certain men that they will abuse a child while others will not? Why do some, who were themselves molested as children, molest other children while other survivors find other ways to make sense of this trauma? Gilgun (1990) has outlined a four-factor risk model which offers an explanation to this question. In her research, Gilgun, looking at men who were abusive and those who were not, found that differences in four areas seemed to account for why some went on to abuse and others did not. In *confidant relationships,* Gilgun discovered that abusers had had no one to confide in growing up and felt isolated or excluded by others. The non-abusive males (known as the controls) had these intimate relationships. Abusers, in the area of *sexuality* used sex to maintain equilibrium, masturbated prior to the age of twelve, and had repetitive, coercive, sexual fantasies. Controls began to masturbate later in adolescence and used the practice to release sexual tension along with appropriate peer-related and non-coercive sexual fantasies.

The *families of origin* of the sex offenders tended to be filled with maltreatment, and domestic violence. If these offenders had not been abused themselves, they may have witnessed the abuse of a sibling or parent. Non-abusive controls had much more stable family environments. And finally, *peer relationships* for abusers growing up tended to be centered around antisocial activities. Masculinity was also equated with sexual conquest. Controls, on the other hand, were involved in more social behavior and equated masculinity with a respect for women. As Gilgun and others continue their research, we will hopefully learn more about why some men abuse and some do not.

Gilgun's research was carried out with men. Finkelhor created his four-precondition model based on his own studies and on the work of many other theorists. His compilation of research into a precondition model appears to be based largely on the reports of male perpetrators. There is some question as to why women are not reported as perpetrators and whether they are, in fact, not as likely to abuse. The issue of female abuse (see Table 6.4) can be examined from several perspectives: (1) women may be able to mask their behavior through normal nurturing activities, such as bathing and dressing the victim; (2) victims are less likely to report because of their dependency on females, especially their mothers; and (3) the targets are often boys who are the most reticent to report (Groth, 1979; Justice and Justice, 1979; Kasl, 1990). Finkelhor (1984a) estimates that, of sexual abuse perpetrated by females, about 20 percent is directed toward male children and 5 percent toward female children. These findings contradict earlier statistics in terms of actual percentages, but do

TABLE 6.4   Why Women Are Less Likely to Abuse

1. Women are trained to be nurturers; they learn the "total child."
2. Traditionally, the child is always neat and clean and smells good when turned over to Dad.
3. Because of nurturing, a mother is more likely to have empathy for the child.
4. Men are trained for smaller, weaker partners.
5. Women are trained for bigger, stronger partners.
6. Men are trained to equate affection with sex.

support the premise that most perpetrators are male. Carlson (1990) found that 39 percent of the men she studied reported abuse by a female.

The reasons for this are worth considering. Perhaps women are not as likely to abuse based on their socialization; women are socialized to prefer older, larger, more powerful sexual partners who initiate the relationship. Children do not fit this picture. Women are socialized to be more maternal, caring for needs of children and identifying with the pain they feel when harmed. Women are less likely to perpetrate harm (Finkelhor, 1984a). Our culture teaches women that they are subject to domination and that they must sublimate their needs for sexual stimulation (Rush, 1980; Herman and Hirschman, 1981; Mathews et al., 1990). And finally, Finkelhor (1984a) suggests that the basic differences between men and women (men are more easily aroused by sexual stimuli such as pornography and men appear to sexualize their emotions more than women) account for the higher percentage of male perpetrators.

In reviewing the long-term effects of sexual abuse, there is evidence that some men tend to act out their victimization in later life by becoming perpetrators (Groth, 1979; deYoung, 1982; Finkelhor, 1984a), while women are more likely to repeat the role of victim (Herman and Hirschman, 1981; Sgroi, 1982; Sanford and Donovan, 1984).

Of those women who do abuse, comparatively little is known. Mathews et al. (1990) feel that these women are motivated to abuse for one (or more) of several reasons: (1) they were abused themselves as children, (2) they went along with abusing male partners, (3) they reported needing closeness, attention, or acceptance, (4) they were displacing anger, jealousy, feelings of rejection, or a need for power onto their victims, or (5) they viewed children as a safe target for their displaced feelings. Most women were not motivated primarily by sexual arousal, and many fantasized that their victim was a "perfect adult man." Unlike male perpetrators who usually project blame onto the victim, only one of the offenders blamed the child (pp. 276–277). Mathews et al. (1990) have created a preliminary typology of offenses perpetrated by females. These authors believe that the offenses fit into two categories: self-initiated offenses and accompanied offenses.

Self-initiated offenses include acts by women who have been abused themselves and who are repeating their own victimization. Also in this category are offenses committed by adolescent girls who are experimenting with or exploiting younger children. And finally, there are some women who see themselves as teaching children about sexuality or have a distorted view of these children as their lovers. *Accompanied offenses* are committed with or prompted by the men in these women's lives. Often the women observe the abuse by the male and then join in. Or these women feel so insecure in their relationship with the man that they will do his bidding even if it is to abuse a child (Mathews et al., 1990; Mayer, 1992).

Whether abuse is perpetrated by a male or female it can be equally traumatic for the child. The next two chapters will cover familial and extrafamilial abuse by both sexes and the implications for the victims of each type of abuse.

Summary

The understanding and study of child sexual abuse has been promoted largely by two movements—the child protection movement and the feminist movement. The first sees abuse as part of total family dysfunction, or a failure of the family to protect, while the second holds that society victimizes its weaker members. Most authors agree that sexual abuse—whether through molestation within or outside the family, pornography, or prostitution—takes place for the gratification of the adult. Sexual abuse progresses over time, usually in five specific phases.

In the last few years, experts have seen an increasing number of sexual abuse cases, despite society's hesitancy to recognize its existence. Girls are more likely to report their victimization, although it is beginning to be known that more boys are abused than is reported. The degree of trauma a child experiences is based on a variety of factors, such as the identity of the perpetrator,

the extent and duration of the abuse, and the point of and reactions to disclosure.

Several typologies describe the perpetrator (most likely a male), but the most widely used is Groth's fixated and regressed categories. The fixated abuser appears developmentally fixated in his interest in children, while the regressed abuser turns to children in response to the stresses and conflicts in his relationships with adults. Finkelhor describes four preconditions to sexual abuse: motivation on the part of the perpetrator, lack of internal inhibitors, weak external inhibitors, and overcoming the child's resistance. Gilgun discusses why some men abuse and some do not. There is also increased emphasis on the study of female offenders.

Exploration Questions

1. What two approaches have characterized the study of child sexual abuse to date? How does each see the victim?

2. Why is child pornography so difficult to document?

3. What are the phases sexual abuse takes in a given case? How would you guess these phases could be interrupted?

4. Why might a particular child be abused? What factors might protect a child from abuse?

5. Why might male victims be less likely to report than female victims?

6. What are the two major categories of perpetrators? How are these perpetrators most likely to engage their victims?

7. Cite Finkelhor's four preconditions for child sexual abuse. Explain them.

8. Why, according to Gilgun, might some men abuse and some not?

9. Why might women abuse children? Why are they less likely to than men?

Activities for Applied Learning

1. How many agencies are there in your community that deal with child sexual abuse? Invite personnel from one or more agencies to speak to the class, or arrange to visit the agency. Which agency is mandated to take reports of sexual abuse? What is the function of the agency once the abuse is reported?

2. Invite a panel from agencies involved with investigation, assessment, and treatment to discuss their roles.

3. Invite a representative from a rape crisis center to discuss how the center becomes involved with

child sexual abuse. How do the techniques differ between rape and child-abuse cases? Include in this discussion a protective social worker. Do the viewpoints differ?

4. Invite a police officer or court official to discuss the investigation or prosecution of child sexual abuse.

5. Listen to "Leonard's Story" (a perpetrator) on the tape *Profiles of Abusive and Neglectful Parents* (available from the National Education Association, 1201 16th St. NW, Washington, DC 20036) and discuss it in light of this chapter.

Suggested Readings

Adams, C., and Fay, J. *No More Secrets.* San Luis Obispo, CA: Impact, 1981.

deYoung, M. *The Sexual Victimization of Children.* Jefferson, NC: McFarland, 1982.

Faller, K. C. *Child Sexual Abuse.* New York: Columbia University Press, 1988.

Finkelhor, D. *Child Sexual Abuse.* New York: Free Press, 1984.

Horton, A. L.; Johnson, B. L.; Roundy, L. M.; and Williams, D. (eds.). *The Incest Perpetrator.* Newbury Park, CA: Sage, 1990.

O'Brien, S. *Child Pornography.* Dubuque, IA: Kendall-Hunt, 1983.

Ofshe, R., and Watters, E. *Making Monsters: False Memories, Psychotherapy and Sexual Hysteria.* New York: Charles Scribner's Sons, 1994.

Endnotes

1. The researchers in Finkelhor's study noted that children abused by their own parents were less likely to have been reported by those parents. Therefore, the statistics reflecting sexual abuse are assumed to be higher than calculated.

2. More information on adolescent perpetrators is available from the Adolescent Perpetrator Network, C. Henry Kempe Center, 1205 Oneida St., Denver, CO 80220.

References

American Humane Association. *Highlights of Official Child Neglect and Abuse Reporting, 1983.* Denver: American Humane Association, 1985.

Barbaree, H. E.; Hudson, S. M.; Seto, M. C. "Sexual Assault in Society: The Role of the Juvenile Offender", in H. E. Barbaree; W. L. Marshall; and S. M. Hudson, *The Juvenile Sex Offender,* pp. 1–24, New York: Guilford Press, 1993.

Ballard, D. T.; Blair, G. D.; Devereaux, S.; Valentine, L. K.; Horton, A. L.; and Johnson, B. L. "A Comparative Profile of the Incest Perpetrator: Background Characteristics, Abuse History, and Use of Social Skills," in A. L. Horton; B. L. Johnson; L. M. Roundy; and D. Williams (eds.). *The Incest Perpetrator,* pp. 43–64, Newbury Park, CA: Sage, 1990.

Beitchman, J. H.; Zucker, K. J.; Hood, J. E.; DaCosta, G. A.; Akman, D.; and Cassavia, E. "A Review of the Long-Term Effects of Child Sexual Abuse," *Child Abuse and Neglect.* 16 (1) (1992): 101–118.

Burgess, A.; Groth, A. N.; Holstrom, L.; and Sgroi, S. *Sexual Assault of Children and Adolescents.* Lexington, MA: Lexington Books, 1978.

Campagna, D. *Sexual Exploitation of Children: Resource Manual.* Southwick, MA: Daniel S. Campagna, 1985.

Carlson, S. Personal communication as cited in C. D. Kasl, "Female Perpetrators of Sexual Abuse: A Feminist View," In M. Hunter, *The Sexually Abused Male, Vol. 1,* pp. 259–274. New York: Lexington Books, 1990.

Carnes, P. *Out of the Shadows: Understanding Sexual Addiction.* Minneapolis: CompCare, 1983.

Chandy, J. M., Blum, R. W., and Resnick, M. D. "Sexually Abused Male Adolescents: How Vulnerable Are They?" *Journal of Child Sexual Abuse* 6(2) (1997): 1–16.

Cohen, M.L.; Seghorn, T.K.; and Mehegan, J. "The Sexual Offender Against Children." Paper presented at a meeting of The Association for Professional Treatment of Offenders, 1979.

Conte, J. "The Incest Offender." in A. L. Horton; B. L. Johnson; L. M. Roundy; D. Williams (eds). *The Incest Perpetrator,* Newbury Park, CA: Sage, 1990.

deYoung, M. *The Sexual Victimization of Children.* Jefferson, NC: McFarland, 1982.

Faller, K. C. *Child Sexual Abuse,* New York: Columbia University Press, 1988.

Finkelhor, D. *Sexually Victimized Children.* New York: Free Press, 1979.

Finkelhor, D. *Child Sexual Abuse.* New York: Free Press, 1984a.

Finkelhor, D. "How Widespread Is Child Sexual Abuse?" *Perspectives on Child Maltreatment in the Mid 80's.* Washington: National Center on Child Abuse and Neglect, Department of Health and Human Services, 1984b.

Forward, S., and Buck, C. *Betrayal of Innocence.* New York: Penguin, 1978.

Gardner, R. A. *Sex Abuse Hysteria: Salem Witch Trials Revisited,* Cresskill, NJ: Creative Therapeutics, 1991.

Geiser, R. *Hidden Victims.* Boston: Beacon Press, 1979.

Gil, E. and Johnson, T. C. *Sexualized Children: Assessment and Treatment of Sexualized Children and Children Who Molest,* Rockville, MD: Launch Press, 1993.

Gilgun, J. F. "Factors Mediating the Effects of Childhood Maltreatment." In Hunter, M. *The Sexually Abused Male, Vol. 1,* pp. 177–190, New York: Lexington Books, 1990.

Giovannoni, J., and Becerra, R. *Defining Child Abuse.* New York: Free Press, 1979.

Groth, A. N. *Men Who Rape.* New York: Plenum Press, 1979.

Hanson, R. F.; Lipovsky, J. A.; and Saunders, B. E. "Characteristics of Fathers in Incest Families," *Journal of Interpersonal Violence,* 9 (2), (1994): 155–169.

Herman, J. *Trauma and Recovery,* New York: Basic Books, 1992.

Herman, J., and Hirschman, L. *Father-Daughter Incest.* Cambridge, MA: Harvard University Press, 1981.

James, B. and Nasjleti, M. *Treating Sexually Abused Children and Their Families.* Palo Alto, CA: Consulting Psychologists Press, 1983.

Justice, B., and Justice, R. *The Broken Taboo: Sex in the Family.* New York: Human Services Press, 1979.

Kasl, C. D. "Female Perpetrators of Sexual Abuse: A Feminist View." In M. Hunter. *The Sexually Abused Male, Vol. 1,* pp. 259–274, New York: Lexington Books, 1990.

Kinsey, A.; Pomeroy, W.; Martin, C.; and Gebhard, P. *Sexual Behavior of the Human Female.* New York: Pocket Books, 1953.

Knopp, F. *Remedial Intervention in Adolescent Sex Offenses.* Syracuse, NY: Safer Society Press, 1982.

Maisch, H. *Incest.* New York: Stein and Day, 1972.

Mathews, R.; Mathews, J.; and Speltz, K. "Female Sex Offenders." In M. Hunter, *The Sexually Abused Male, Vol. 1* pp. 275–293, New York: Lexington Books, 1990.

Mayer, A. *Incest: A Treatment Manual for Therapy with Victims, Spouses, and Offenders.* Holmes Beach, FL: Learning Publications, 1983.

Mayer, A. *Women Sex Offenders.* Holmes Beach, FL: Learning Publications, 1993.

Meiselman, K. *Incest: A Psychological Study of Causes and Effects with Treatment Recommendation.* San Francisco: Jossey-Bass, 1979.

Nasjleti, M. "Suffering in Silence: The Male Victim." *Child Welfare* 59 (1980):269–75.

National Center on Child Abuse and Neglect. "Profile of Sexual Abuse-Attachment B." *The National Center on Child Abuse and Neglect: A Fact Sheet.* Unpublished report, Washington, DC, March 15, 1985.

National Center on Child Abuse Prevention. Research of the National Committee to Prevent Child Abuse. *Current Trend in Child Abuse Reporting and Fatalities: The Results of the 1993 Annual Fifty State Survey.* Chicago, IL: National Committee to Prevent Child Abuse, 1994.

Ney, T. *True and False Allegations of Child Sexual Abuse.* New York: Brunner/Mazel, 1995.

O'Brien, S. *Child Pornography.* Dubuque, IA: Kendall-Hunt, 1983.

Ofshe, R., and Watters, E. *Making Monsters: False Memories, Psychotherapy and Sexual Hysteria.* New York: Charles Scribner's Sons, 1994.

Pecora, P.; Whittaker, J. K.; Maluccio, A. N.; Barth, R. P.; and Plotnick, R. D. *The Child Welfare Challenge.* New York: Aldine DeGruyter, 1992.

Peterson, R. F.; Basta, S. M.; and Dykstra, T. A. "Mothers of Molested Children: Some Comparisons of Personality Characteristics." *Child Abuse and Neglect* 17 (3), (1993): 409–418.

Porter, E. *Treating the Young Male Victim of Sexual Assault.* Syracuse, NY: Safer Society Press, 1986.

Prendergast, W. E. *Treating Sex Offenders in Correctional Institutions and Outpatient Clinics.* New York: Haworth, 1991.

Rush, F. *The Best Kept Secret.* New York: McGraw-Hill, 1980.

Russell, D. *Sexual Exploitation.* Beverly Hills, CA: Sage, 1984.

Ryan, G.; Lane, S.; Davis, J.; and Isaac, C. "Juvenile Sex Offenders: Development and Correction." *Child Abuse and Neglect* 11 (1987): 385–395.

Sanford, L. *The Silent Children.* New York: Doubleday, 1980.

Seghorn, T., and Boucher, R. "Sexual Abuse in Childhood as a Factor in Adult Sexually Dangerous

Offenses." Paper presented at the International Symposium on Childhood and Sexuality. University of Quebec, Montreal, 1979.

Seghorn, T.; Pretky, R.; and Boucher, R. "Childhood Sexual Abuse in the Lives of Sexually Aggressive Offenders." *Journal of American Academy of Child Psychiatry.* Bloomington: Indiana University Press, 1986.

Sgroi, S. *Handbook of Clinical Intervention in Child Sexual Abuse.* Lexington, MA: Lexington Books, 1982.

Struve, J. "Dancing with the Patriarchy: The Politics of Sexual Abuse." In M. Hunter (ed.). *The Sexually Abused Male: Vol. 1,* pp. 3–45, New York: Lexington Books, 1990.

Tower, C. C. *Secret Scars: A Guide for Adult Survivors of Child Sexual Abuse,* New York: Viking\Penguin, 1988.

Trivelpiece, J. W. "Adjusting the Frame: Cinematic Treatment of Sexual Abuse and Rape of Men and Boys." In M. Hunter (ed.) *The Sexually Abused Male: Vol 1,* New York: Lexington Books, 1990.

Urquiza, A. J. and Keating, L. M. "The Prevalence of Sexual Victimization of Males." in M. Hunter (ed.). *The Sexually Abused Male: Vol 1.* pp. 89–103. New York: Lexington Books, 1990.

U.S. Department of Health and Human Services, National Center on Child Abuse and Neglect. *Child Maltreatment 1992: Reports From the States to the National Center on Child Abuse and Neglect.* Washington, DC, U.S. Government Printing Office, 1994.

Vander May, B. J. "The Sexual Victimization of Male Children: A Review of Previous Literature." *Child Abuse and Neglect.* 12 (1988): 61–72.

Walters, D. *Physical and Sexual Abuse of Children.* Bloomington: Indiana University Press, 1975.

Wiehe, V. R. and Herring, T. *Perilous Rivalry: When Siblings Become Abusive.* Lexington: MA: Lexington Books, 1991.

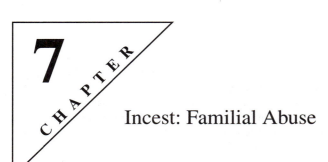

Incest: Familial Abuse

Incest has long been an issue in our culture. (The incest taboo and its roots in early civilizations were discussed in Chapter 1.) It is not always possible, however, to define inappropriate sexual behavior between adults and children within families. Sexual intercourse and even overt handling of the genitalia are inappropriate in most cultures. Family nudity, however, is more controversial. Perhaps the difficulty lies in the fact that child rearing involves aspects of sexuality. In many cultures, children are nurtured by their parents with hugs, kisses, and physical closeness. Nursing, some say, promotes sexual feelings. It is disturbing to know that these well-intended and emotionally necessary components of child rearing can become sexual, when, in fact, kept at the appropriate level, they are beneficial to the child and the parent (Rosenfeld, 1980). It is the abuse of these normal activities that differentiates the incestuous from the nonincestuous family. Rosenfeld lists aspects of normal family life:

- There is no attempt by the parents to satisfy their adult, genital-sexual needs through their children.
- No seduction or overstimulation of the child takes place.
- There is an ability to tolerate social and personal intimacy between parents and children without actual sexual involvement.
- A culturally acceptable degree of warmth, affection, and stimulation without either discomfort or inhibition in doing what is unusual, and without disregard for subcultural standards, is in effect. Parents must be comfortable with these standards.
- There is adequate privacy for both parents and children in overt sexual matters, and a willingness on the parents' part to transmit honest information about sex to their children. This information should be consistent with the parents' personal and cultural standards.
- There is an ability to change and adapt family practices so that they remain suited to the child's changing age and stage of psychosexual development. (1980, p. 94)

Incestuous families have not been able to keep their touching within Rosenfeld's definition of a *normal range.*

Incest as a Problem Today

Prior to the late 1970s, *incest* was a word in our vocabulary but was little used. It may have been the subject of jokes, but it rarely entered the consciousness as being a national problem.

Today, incest figures prominently in the media, and what Butler (1978) called the "conspiracy of silence" is slowly being uncovered. Each year a large number of incest cases come to the attention of protective services. Researchers like Diana Russell (1986), who studied 930 California women, and David Finkelhor (1979), who surveyed 796 college students in New England, proved that incest has gone unreported by victims for years. This realization brings so many questions to mind. What causes incest? Why are some victims more traumatized than others? Why are some children chosen as victims and others are not? We are just beginning to find answers to these questions—but asking them has stimulated some excellent research.

Who Is to Blame?

In Chapter 1 the incest taboo and how it originated was discussed. In most people's minds such a taboo is still sacred. Why, then, is it so often broken?

Part of the answer lies in society's preoccupation with sexuality. Attractive young bodies sell jeans, and sexy women drape themselves over cars and mattresses to provide more appealing advertisements. Many people feel we have sexualized our young female children for years. Butler comments:

> Our culture teaches young girls, implicitly and explicitly, that seductive behavior is a way to get what they want. Acting cute or sexy, even when they are quite young, garners compliments and attention. Furthermore, a girl's socialization teaches her at the same time to internalize guilt for such learned behavior. Therefore female incest victims in effect have been programmed to blame themselves—they feel they must have done something "bad" to have caused the abuse to happen. (1978, p. 36)

Thus society not only teaches female children that sexuality is useful but plants the seeds for the child to feel she is to blame for whatever comes of acting sexual.

Society itself has fewer rules about sexual behavior. At one time people could count on more clearly stated mores. Now with changing sexual values, confusion is rampant. Amidst this confusion about the rules, the perpetrators more easily justify their behavior or are themselves even unsure of appropriate limits.

Along with a shift in rules and an increased preoccupation with sexuality has come a greater emphasis on sexual performance. Magazine articles discuss improving sexual relationships and numerous paperback books offer ways to enhance one's sexual prowess. For the average individual, this emphasis on sexual performance may create casual interest, but for a man already concerned about his own incompetence and powerlessness, the effect can be damaging. To compensate, he looks for a partner who is adoring and who will not measure his sexual competence. Often that person is his daughter.

The stresses and constant changes in society provide another clue to why incest occurs. High technology also places emphasis on performance. Businesses grow quickly and employees must frequently move. Immigrants still flock to our shores in search of better economic conditions. Families are often transferred from one location to another or immigrate from other cultures and are left with few roots and insufficient support systems. Some families adjust easily, making new friends and building new alliances. Other families are not so quick to respond, and their sense of isolation intensifies. The stresses of everyday life augment the feelings of failure these individuals already carry with them. The members find comfort within their own family structure—sometimes turning to children to meet their needs.

The characters in this drama are varied. The most widely discussed type of incest is perpetrated by fathers against their daughters. But mothers, siblings, uncles, grandfathers, and cousins are also abusers. The victims may be sons, daughters, or other siblings, and the degree of trauma each experiences depends on numerous variables.

Father-Daughter Incest

Incest, especially when it involves a father and his daughter, is about family dysfunction and pathology. The family as a system gives up its dedication to the growth of each of its members and instead holds sacred the family "secret"—incest. So exhausting is the guarding of the secret that the family has little time or energy for other pursuits. It is not surprising that children's needs go unmet. Instead, the perpetrator rationalizes that sexual attention is what the child desires. The family presents a picture of an isolated, enmeshed system, balancing precariously in what they perceive as a hostile environment. The role and characteristics of each family have been studied and restudied in an attempt to understand and intervene.

Family Patterns

Although there is generalization in the literature about family patterns in father-daughter incest, the dynamics of this type of abuse can be more easily studied through the typology of Stern and Meyer (1980). They suggest three interactional patterns among incestuous families: the possessive-passive, the dependent-domineering, and the dependent-dependent.

Possessive-passive
The possessive-passive pattern is often referred to in feminist literature as the *patriarchal family.* Herman and Hirschman describe the fathers as "perfect patriarchs."

> Their authority with the family was absolute, often asserted by force. They were also the arbiters of the family's social life and frequently succeeded in virtually secluding the women in the family. But while they were often feared within their families, they impressed outsiders as sympathetic, even admirable men. (1981, p. 71)

Justice and Justice describe the father who

> ...rules over the family with strict discipline and accountability. He brooks no opposition and relies on intimidation. He may use threats of physical force or actual beatings in demanding submission. (1979, p. 77)

Faller (1990) found that 29 of the 60 fathers in her sample fit this profile (p. 67).

In the possessive-passive family, the father sees his wife and children as possessions. The mother tends to be passive, insecure, and often withdrawn. She acquiesces to her husband's domination and is often unable to protect her daughter, because she learned through her own childhood that this is the way men behave. Since the daughter has also learned to see her father as undisputed head of the family, she is vulnerable. The father turns to his daughter for sex for a variety of reasons but largely as an abuse of power (Faller, 1990; Deblinger et al., 1993).

Dependent-domineering

This pattern is characterized by a strong, domineering woman and a weak, inadequate man. The father looks to his wife for support and nurturing, and she treats him as she does their children. The father often allies himself with his children much as he would siblings, so that many children of these liaisons describe their fathers as sharing and loving and their mothers as cold and rejecting. This father may be prone to outbursts of anger and spend much of his energies compelling others to meet his needs. Eventually the mother feels that her own needs are not being met and withdraws from the husband and the children. Because she is more outgoing than a dependent wife and has developed better social skills, she often seeks gratification outside her home through a job, activities, or education. The more the mother is absent, the more the daughter is required to perform housekeeping tasks, and the father then turns to her for his emotional and sexual needs (Stern and Meyer, 1980).

Dependent-dependent

The third pattern is that of a dependent-dependent relationship between spouses. Two needy, dependent individuals come together, each with the anticipation that his or her needs will be magically met by the spouse. Both the mother and father experienced abuse or deprivation in their childhoods. The women have frequently been abused while the men, if not themselves abused, have observed maltreatment in their families of origin. As they escape from the deprivations of childhood, they unconsciously seek out individuals with similar backgrounds, not recognizing that other needy individuals cannot meet their needs (Hanson et al., 1994). The couple clings to each other in desperation, but since they are of no emotional support to each other, they turn to their children for nurturance. Often the oldest daughter assumes the role of surrogate mother and sees her task as keeping the family together. As she continues in her role, the father sees her as a rival to his wife, and because his daughter appears to be more nurturing, he turns to her for comfort. The daughter in such a family is endowed with a great deal of power and status. Her siblings are liable to resent her for the position she holds. In turn, the victim represses anger toward her mother for not protecting her (Stern and Meyer, 1980).

The abusive behavior in each type of family serves some purpose for the equilibrium of the system. Furniss (1985) suggests that in some families the abuse is a conflict-avoiding mechanism while in others it is a conflict-regulating mechanism.

Conflict-avoiding

In conflict-avoiding families, the mother sets the emotional tone. Sexual and emotional problems are not discussed. In an effort to avoid problems, the mother tends to distance herself. Thus the daughter emerges as nurturer and mother figure. The father and mother covertly agree with the arrangement rather than bring up the role-reversal problem for discussion or confrontation. The daughter in turn recognizes that she cannot go to her mother for help and has in fact been abandoned despite her mother's outward appearance of competence.

Conflict-regulating

Conflict-regulating families "sacrifice" the daughter to regulate conflict and avoid family breakdown. In these families the mother gives little or no support to her children. The daughter feels rejected by her mother and resentful of her lack of protection. There may be overt conflict in the family, and although there is more discussion and awareness of the problems, the family allows the daughter's abuse and does not seek help.

It is not surprising that children who are unnurtured and who are forced into pseudomaturity feel robbed of their childhoods. Emotionally deprived, they spend their adulthoods searching for someone who will meet their needs. When two people with these problems marry, the cycle of abuse may begin again.

From the numerous studies on incest, profiles of each of the participants have been developed.

Profiles of the Family

The Father

Incestuous fathers share common characteristics—a deep-seated feeling of helplessness, a sense of vulnerability, and dependency. They are unprepared for adulthood, marriage, or fatherhood. Newly immigrated fathers are also unprepared for what *our* culture expects of them; failure in these roles only serves to intensify their feelings of inadequacy (Hanson et al., 1994). The picture they present in their fervent attempts to control the demands of their life may differ, however. As Meiselman wrote,

> The typical incestuous father is not mentally retarded, psychotic, or pedophilic, but is characterized by some sort of personal disturbance that interferes with his ability to control his impulses in a situation where the temptation to commit incest exists. (1978, p. 106)

The type of father most commonly described in the literature is one who overcompensates for his feelings of powerlessness by adopting an extremely rigid, controlling, authoritarian position as the undisputed head of his household (Groth 1982; Faller, 1990). He was described as the primary participant in the possessive-passive family pattern. He has frequently learned his behavior from his own father, since a large number of abusive fathers were parented by overbearing and often physically abusive fathers, themselves. In 1982 deYoung reported that 43 percent of the fathers in her sample were physically abused as children.

Sometimes tyrannical behavior is a father's exaggerated response to feeling he has lost his importance within the family.

> *The Lees were comfortably situated in their native Korea. Dr. Lee was on the staff at a large hospital. When the political situation necessitated that they leave the country, the Lees came to live with cousins in the United States. Dr. Lee soon*

discovered that his medical license was not readily recognized in this country. His wife, however, was offered secure employment as a companion housekeeper for an elderly woman. Dr. Lee was very much against his wife's working, especially in the role of a domestic. He argued that they had had servants in Korea, and his wife would not be one here. It went against family honor. But seeing no other way to support themselves, Mrs. Lee acted for the first time against her husband's wishes and took the job.

As Mrs. Lee became more involved outside the home, her husband grew more and more depressed at home. For the first time he was forced into the role of caregiver of his two daughters, aged 5 and 9. The more out of control he felt, the more tyrannical he became. He was convinced that although his wife had "left him," his daughters were his to do with as he would. Eventually he began to see his oldest daughter as a nurturing—and finally sexual—substitute for his wife.

"The tyrant" is the term Justice and Justice (1979) use for this type of father. Power and control are bywords in this abuser's orientation to the world. Some of these fathers have not had the success that Dr. Lee had once had. Many of them fit the profile of the man who, throughout his life, has felt out of control because of a father who dominated and used his power and a mother who was cold, unloving, and failed to protect (Meiselman, 1978; Faller, 1988, 1990). It is not unlikely that this abuser witnessed the sexual abuse of his own siblings (deYoung, 1982; Gilgun, 1990). In short, this individual never learned to share with a mate, to nurture, or to parent. His insecurity in his own masculinity convinced him that he must rule his family in every way. This father may also physically abuse his children (deYoung, 1982; Faller, 1988).

Studies show that this father is alienated from his wife. An individual as needy as he, she was scarred by her own childhood trauma and turned to him for nurturance and comfort. His unreasonable demands on her intensify her own sense of inadequacy, and she withdraws emotionally—unable to meet his needs and unable to nurture her children.

The second orientation is markedly different from the "the tyrant." This type of man appears in the dependent-domineering and dependent-dependent family patterns. He does not project his insecurity through aggressive or violent behavior, but instead withdraws from adult responsibilities and maintains a passive-dependent role, often seeming like a child himself (Groth, 1982; Prendergast, 1991). Although Groth and others contend that "this stance permeates all his dealings," Herman and Hirschman (1981) argue that this father has the ability to assess situations and determine who has the power. In the face of other authority figures (such as police, prosecutor, therapist, or researcher), he presents himself as passive, helpless, and dependent. Reports of daughters seem to substantiate that their mothers are in the dominant role and the perpetrators are more like siblings. Other survivors describe families in which both mother and father characteristically assume the role of nurtured children.

Art was raised by his mother and two aunts. He vaguely remembers his father but believes he left when Art was quite young. One of the aunts was divorced and the other had never married. Art's mother was extremely overprotective, not wanting him to go out with friends or participate in school activities. She did everything for him, allowing him to do little for himself. Art remembers that his mother chose his clothes and bought all his toiletries until he left home. She also bathed him until his teen years, seemingly with little resistance on Art's part.

When Art was 18, he joined the army with, surprisingly, his mother's blessing. One of his aunts had recently died, and he thinks his mother was having difficulty coping. "I think she thought I'd be taken care of," he commented. Army life was extremely difficult for him; he had been surrounded by women, and being thrust into an all-male society created problems. He was teased about his indecisiveness, his lack of assertiveness, and his meticulous mannerisms.

After a year, Art was hospitalized after confessing suicidal feelings and demonstrating a severe inability to cope with everyday tasks. He received a medical discharge and went home to live. His mother suggested he enter the seminary, but remembering his past experiences living with males he refused. Instead, Art got a job in a shoe store. Shortly thereafter his mother developed cancer; her health rapidly deteriorated and she died. While his mother was ill, Art's aunt constantly berated him about "how thoughtless he was about his poor mother, who had done so much for him." He was confused and hurt by these admonishments, convinced that his presence was all his mother needed.

After his mother's death, Art was at a loss. He lived with his aunt for a short time, but found this intolerable and moved to his own apartment. He continued at the shoe store, which was owned by a family who pampered and fussed over him. Art found living on his own difficult. He knew little about cooking or housekeeping, so when Sally, the young woman in the next apartment, started inviting him over for dinner, he was overjoyed. He praised her cooking and commented favorably on her every action. After a brief courtship, they were married. Art was sure he'd be taken care of; Sally was convinced she had found someone to adore her as her parents never had.

The marriage was far from idyllic. Art demanded that their lives revolve around him. If Sally did not cater to him, he would develop an ailment to gain her pity and elicit her attention. The birth of twin girls further taxed Sally's coping abilities, and she invited her sister to live with them and help her. Once again, Art heard how lazy and ungrateful he was—this time from Sally's concerned sister. Her criticism drove him further into his own world emotionally. His relationship with Sally deteriorated and they ceased sexual relationships.

Art turned instead to the twins, especially Gabrielle—the younger of his daughters who had always been smaller and more timid. "She reminded me of myself," he commented. When the twins were 7, Sally's sister left to marry her long-time boyfriend. Sally found herself once more in the mothering role—mothering Art as well as their children. Art intensified his demands on her time and energies, but Sally had adopted her sister's habit of berating him.

Through the crisis of the family's attempt to rebalance, Sally became particularly involved in the church. She attended church meetings regularly and left Art to care for the girls. Gretchen, more assertive than her sister, would frequently antagonize her father, at which point he would send her to bed. This left Art and Gabrielle watching TV together and gave him the opportunity for sexual abuse.

Despite Art's more passive behavior, he too ruled his family by insisting that they meet his needs.

In describing incestuous fathers, Mayer (1983) and Prendergast (1991) note particular characteristics: These fathers tend to demonstrate *poor impulse control, low frustration tolerance,* and *the need for immediate gratification.* They often *regress,* exhibiting sexual or emotional immaturity and *frustrated dependency needs.* Such men have *low ego-strength and self-esteem* often to the point of *identity confusion.* They may be *passive-aggressive* in their demonstration of anger, denying, rationalizing, and projecting blame for their actions. In their feelings of powerlessness and *faulty super ego operation* they seek to *manipulate* both the victim and other family members. In general their *interpersonal relations are poor* (Mayer, p. 29; Prendergast, p. 4).

Groth contends there are no unique personality features distinguishing incest offenders from other individuals, but that offenders tend to have some characteristics in common. These characteristics relate to each other as follows:

1. A general relating to life in which fantasy and passive dependency (submissiveness) replace active strivings (assertiveness), especially in interpersonal relationships, with the result that the offender experiences himself more as a helpless victim of external forces and events than as a person in control of himself and in charge of his life, producing

2. An intrinsic feeling of isolation, separateness, and apartness from others—the offender experiences himself psychologically as a loner, lacking any consistent sense of intimate attachment, belonging, or relatedness to others, which in turn results in

3. An underlying mood state of emptiness, fearfulness, and depression which combines with a sense of low self-esteem and poor self-confidence to make him oversensitive to what he interprets as criticisms, put-downs, exploitations, and rejections from a hostile and uncaring world; then

4. This lack of psychological comfort, security, and pleasure in life, and his deficient empathetic skills, prompt him to regress from anxiety-producing adult relationships, to substitute fantasy for reality, and to replace adults with children who symbolize his own immaturity. (1982, pp. 229–30)

We have considered characteristics of the perpetrators, but what motivates them to abuse children? Most authorities agree that this abuser is motivated by emotional rather than sexual needs. This man finds that adult relationships are too taxing on his already low self-esteem. He therefore misuses his power as an adult in an attempt to bolster his own ego. Groth suggests that incestuous behavior serves a number of motivations simultaneously for the father. It may serve to *validate his sense of worth and bolster his self-esteem,* as he tries fervently to *compensate for the perceived rejection* of him by his wife and other women. It often gives him an *illusion of power and control* and gratifies his *need for attention, affiliation, and recognition.* In short, it *strengthens his sense of identity* (1982, p. 228).

Incestuous fathers present strangely different pictures. Some inspire empathy, others disgust. Regardless of an abuser's manner of presentation, and despite the family dynamics surrounding his abusive behavior, this individual is still responsible for his actions and cannot be exonerated. Much blame has also been placed on the mother in abusive situations.

The Mother

Elizabeth Ward, author of *Father-Daughter Rape,* comments:

> A woman's main role in life is presented as the reproduction and production of a Happy Family. The wife-mother role also assumes emotional mediation between the husband and their children; ensuring that the father is seen as a "good man" by his children and at the same time, that the children do not put too many demands on him. She is also expected to mediate within the child's personality development so that her children are, and are seen to be "good." It is seen by others, and felt by her, as a measure of failure if anything goes wrong in the complex web of balancing acts required to create the reality and/or image of the Happy Family. It is always her fault. (1985, pp. 162–63)

Ward and others (e.g., Herman and Hirschman, 1981; Russell, 1986; Faller, 1990; Schonberg, 1992; Deblinger et al., 1993) contend that the mother is (unjustly) blamed for causing the incest affair and for not intervening. Some victims harbor as much, if not more, resentment toward their mothers for not protecting them than toward their fathers for molesting them, so the motivation of the mother must be considered in more depth. Lustig sums up the usual attitude that much of the literature has adopted toward the mother.

> It is interesting that despite the formal innocence of the mother in the actual incestuous event, she seems to emerge as the key figure in the pathological transaction involved.... Despite the overt culpability of the fathers, we were impressed with their psychological passivity in the transactions leading to incest. The mother appeared the cornerstone in the pathological family system. (1966, pp. 38–39)

Groth (1982) suggests that wives of incestuous fathers are either dominant or dependent. Regardless of their manner of presentation, both tend to lack self-esteem and feel trapped by an unsatisfying marriage. Other differences are noted in Table 7.1.

TABLE 7.1   Wives in Incestuous Families

Dominant Wives	Dependent Wives
More social skills	Few social skills
Self-assertive	Passive
Capable, but unwilling to make it on their own	Highly dependent on husbands; fear outside world
Consciously turn away from spousal relationship	Remain dependent but may withdraw unconsciously
Feel in control and like mother to both father and children, often resentfully	Feel more like a child than a wife
Husband describes them as "cold" and "unforgiving"	Husband describes them as "dumb" or "silly"

Reprinted by permission of the publisher, from *Handbook of Clinical Intervention in Child Sexual Abuse* by Suzanne M. Sgroi, M.D. (Lexington, MA: Lexington Books, D.C. Heath and Company, Copyright 1982, D.C. Heath and Company).

Johnson (1992) categorizes mothers of incest victims somewhat differently. She identifies three categories of mothers: the collusive mother, the powerless mother, and the protective mother. The *collusive mother* is one who is withdrawn, cold, ill, or psychologically impaired and who pushes her daughter into her own role in the family. In her withdrawal from the family communication, this mother fails to enforce limits, so that not only are generational boundaries blurred, but the perpetrator is afforded more opportunity to abuse when another adult is not supervising. The daughter is then identified as the delegate to take over household tasks and decisions, eventually evolving into a pattern of role reversal between mother and child. Anger permeates this relationship. As the actual sexual abuse commences and then continues, the daughter then harbors anger at her mother for failing to protect her. At the same time, the mother may see that she has become isolated, unnecessary, and replaced, and as a result she feels anger toward her daughter (Faller, 1988; Schonberg, 1992; Jacobs, 1994; Joyce, 1997).

The *powerless mother* is one who feels helpless, defeated, victimized, and unable to protect herself, let alone her daughter. The incestuous father in this home usually fits the pattern of the tyrant and may be physically abusive to his wife as well as sexually abusive to his daughters. Although some theorists have called this a collusive stance, others point out that the fear that this mother feels totally paralyzes her and renders her unable to act (Schonberg, 1992; Johnson, 1992). The feminist perspective would say that women are taught by society to be victims so that this role becomes natural for them. Traditional female sex roles dictate the subservience, say feminists, that secures the victim role from one generation to the next.

The *protective mother* profile is one which is only recently emerging in the literature. Johnson (1992) suggests that our lack of a clear picture of this mother is based on an inability to define *protection*. Is protection, protection *from the incest* or protection from *future victimization* once the incest has been disclosed? Obviously, when dealing with reported cases, the mothers have not been able to protect their children from the abuse. Therefore, it is post-disclosure behavior by the mother which comes under scrutiny. Does the mother believe her daughter, condemn the father's actions, report the incest, and protect her child in the future? Mothers may be empowered to take these actions for several reasons: she may have had the resources or support outside the marriage to allow her to follow through with her protective stance; she may have been ready to end the marriage and this gave her the impetus to do so; or the mother's love for her child was greater than her need or love for her husband (Johnson, 1992, p. 5). Mothers' ability to do any of the above may be based on economics. If she is financially dependent on the abuser, she may not feel as free to be protective of the victim. Cultural values may also influence the mother's ability to protect. In cultures where the father is more dominant, there may be even more at stake for this mother.

Can the mother be blamed for her daughter's abuse? Whether she is collusive or powerless, many professionals feel that the answer is no—for several reasons. First, society unrealistically expects the mother to maintain the family balance; when she is ill-equipped by her own deprived background to nurture appropriately, this is an impossible task. She is in need of nurturing herself. In addition, mothers of these families usually have few employment or social skills. These factors cause her to be financially dependent on her husband (Schonberg, 1992; Peterson et al., 1993).

Ward comments about these mothers, *"Their very sense of survival* is predicated on keeping going what they have got, since the unknown yawns like a void" (1985, p. 166).

Along with the problem of her dependence is the way the mother views sexual abuse. If she herself was victimized, her husband's abuse of the daughter is too painful for her to acknowledge. Victimization is a reality for her. Not only does she live in a society that communicates that women are to be victims but she has developed a self-image in which she sees herself as vulnerable. If she was not a victim of sexual abuse, the idea of such a thing happening may not be within her frame of reference. How many women ever consider that their husbands could abuse their child? Such things are "not supposed to happen" according to the societal stereotype. Therefore the least painful defense for this confused, needy woman is to deny that the abuse is taking place (Ward, 1985).

Does the mother know, consciously or unconsciously, that her husband is abusing her daughter? Some mothers do know. When professionals observe the signals of incest, they assume that the mother must know. The mother who found blood and semen on her 7-year-old daughter's underwear must have suspected that something was very wrong. Yet so intense is the mother's need to deny that she can often block out all the signs.

Whether or not the mother recognizes the signals of her daughter's abuse becomes secondary, at the time of disclosure, to her ability to protect her child by believing her and insisting the perpetrator stop the abuse. Her ability to do this, even if it means her separation from her husband, depends on how much ego strength she has (Russell, 1986; Deblinger, 1993).

It is difficult to assign blame to anyone but the perpetrator in an incestuous family, and yet his behavior is often based on his own victimization. The fact remains that every member of the abusive family contributes to the homeostasis of that system and is therefore a principal figure in the pathology.

The Daughter

The victim of a father-daughter incest, like her parents, usually has a poor self-concept. She is deeply in need of attention and nurturing and becomes a hostage in the conflict between her parents. As her mother withdraws, her father seeks her out as his undemanding partner. She may bask in the attention, for with the abuse may come gifts, money, or other special treats. She feels special, and it becomes easier to accept the sexual activity. In fact, the daughter begins to confuse sexuality with affection (Mayer, 1983). Experts in incest (deYoung, 1982; Mayer, 1983; Downs, 1993; Jacobs, 1994) provide several reasons as to why the daughter accedes to the abuse. She has the natural *awe of adults* instilled in most children in our society. Taught to submit to authority, she may *fear physical or emotional retaliation* if she does not submit. Her father may actually *physically force her,* and she is powerless to resist. Or this girl *may love and trust her father.* In her *need for attention,* she *becomes engaged in the games* he plays with her. She may also see herself as providing help to her troubled family by *keeping her parents' marriage* together or, by her submission, *protecting her younger siblings* from abuse.

Not all daughters are cajoled into incestuous activities. Beth describes how her father raped her when she was 5 years old:

> *He just came in one night. I think I was half asleep. He frequently tucked me in, but this night he took me out of bed, not too gently, laid me on the floor, and raped me—or at least tried penetration. I only know I was stunned; we were close and I loved him.*

Later I found I was bleeding and asked what I should do. He just said, "You're disgusting, go wash!" I felt so hurt and so abandoned. I'd never felt close to my mother—even at that young age. I thought my father was wonderful. I couldn't fit that piece of behavior into my picture of him. So I blocked it out until it happened again—and again. When I was older, I convinced myself that he'd been drinking and that explained it for me.

A few daughters also experience violence with the abuse. Doreen's father stood her on a chair in the attic with a hangman's noose around her neck:

First he'd fondle my genitals; I was afraid to move for fear the chair would tip. I was so scared. He'd masturbate and then when he was finished he'd run down-stairs. He told me when he came back he'd pull the chair out and I'd hang. He would run up the stairs—just to the top, and then go back down. I never knew if he was coming in. I became more and more anxious and wet my pants. Then he'd beat me for wetting myself.

The daughter in incest usually has a poor relationship with her mother. Her father may be a nurturer—or a tyrant—or somewhere in between. Whatever his approach, she is completely vulnerable when unprotected by her mother.

The victim of abuse may develop symptoms from stomach problems to enuresis (wetting). She exhibits behavior such as passivity, acting out, truancy, and promiscuity. She may become involved with substance abuse (Mayer, 1983). Daughters present a picture of pseudomaturity, appearing older than their years, yet they are very vulnerable, nonassertive children who blame themselves for the family disruption. They also harbor repressed anger against both of the parents, but especially toward the mother for failure to protect them (Sgroi and Dana, 1982; Briere, 1995).

The burden of keeping the secret to herself is a heavy one for the abused child. For this reason she isolates herself from her peers—a fact that intensifies her loneliness and forces her to turn once more to her abusing parent.

Daughters are abused at various ages, although the average age at onset appears to be between 8 and 10 (Finkelhor, 1984) while the highest percentage of girls are abused between 11 and 14 (NCCAN, 1994). Often these victims try to tell someone of the abuse but are frequently not believed. The ensuing feeling of powerlessness sets the girl up for victimization in later life (Finkelhor and Browne, 1985). The incest experience can be so disturbing to the daughter that she continues to exhibit symptoms in her adulthood. (See Chapter 17.)

The Siblings

In a family that cannot properly nurture its children, it is not surprising that more than one child is starved for attention. The siblings of the victim are often resentful of the attention given to the abused daughter. They are also conscious of the abusive behavior. They may not be aware that the victim feels her submission protects them from abuse. Therefore, the siblings may, in their resentment, "set up" the victim for further abuse. If violence is part of the family system, it may be "safer" for a sibling to aid the aggressor than to advocate for the victim (deYoung, 1982).

The importance of their own sense of security in the collusion behavior of siblings is undeniable. These brothers and sisters recognize that keeping the secret is necessary for the continuation of the family unit. If the abuse is disclosed, the family might be separated, and their fear of this is often enough to ensure their silence. This failure to protect the victim creates a feeling of guilt that siblings carry through adulthood. This guilt, combined with their witnessing the abusive behavior, may lead them to victimize or be victimized in their own adult years (deYoung, 1982; Faller, 1988).

Some siblings attempt to intervene on behalf of the victim, but because of their powerlessness as children, they are usually thwarted.

Father-Son Incest

The victim of father-son incest suffers from the consequences of not only the broken incest taboo but the violation of the taboo against homosexuality. Since this type of abuse often includes sodomy (anal intercourse), the victim suffers physical pain as well as emotional conflicts. Unlike other forms of incest, this type emerges from the individual pathology of the perpetrator. His conflicts are usually scars from his childhood—disturbed reactions to feelings of inadequacy, an overbearing mother, or conflicts over homosexuality (Forward and Buck, 1978). Dixon, Arnold, and Calestro (1978) found that none of the fathers in their sample were practicing homosexuals. Meiselman (1978) agreed with this finding, but felt that their homosexual desires had been masked by marriage and a seemingly heterosexual orientation. Interestingly enough, the fathers in deYoung's sample (1982) did not see victimization of their sons as being homosexual. In fact, they had definite ideas about what was homosexual—equating it with a lack of masculinity. Nor did these fathers see their victimization by males in their childhood as homosexual. Some fathers involved with their sons also abuse, or have abused, their daughters.

Instead of being motivated by a sexual orientation, the father in this type of incest is often trying to feel more powerful. He finds power in sexual exploitation.

Family Dynamics

While the father is seeking power through his relationship with his son, the mother in this family usually plays the role of silent partner. She may even have a vested interest in the abuse continuing—her husband's sexual interest in her son relieves her of his sexual demands (deYoung, 1982). Whatever her motivation, this mother fails to protect her son, sometimes after she has been told of the abuse.

> *"I think I blame my mother almost as much as my father," recounted Todd bitterly. Todd's relationship with his father began when he was 12 years old.*
>
> *"We were out camping. I had been thrilled when he'd wanted to take me and not my older brother. We began talking about sex and he said he'd show me some things that I didn't know. He showed me his penis along with a kind of lecture on how big I'd get and what I could do when I was older. Then we started fondling each other. I thought it was fun at first. The rest of the camping trip was great. My father was a really quiet guy; he'd been dominated by his own mother and I guess*

that made him sort of meek. He really knew about the woods, though, and that knowledge plus the sexual stuff with me made him seem more alive—more forceful!

"I didn't think a lot about it when we got home, but then he started coming to my room when no one else was home. He got home around 4:00 and my brother was usually out and my sister at a friend's. My mother worked and didn't get home until 5:30.

"So, he started asking me to perform oral sex—actually, not asking—almost forcing. It was like he was on a power trip. But I just got sort of philosophical about it. I liked the attention, and if it made him feel good, it was okay. It went on occasionally for a few years.

"Then I heard some older guys at school talking about guys who fooled around with other guys being homosexual. That sort of shook me up. I asked my Dad, and he said that I was being silly. Did he look like a 'fag'? He talked in a high voice, lisping and looking really effeminate, and strutted around the room. We laughed, and I said I guess we weren't like that. But it must have still bothered me because I asked my older brother one day. The first thing he said was, 'Has Dad been messing around with you?' I was shocked. How did he know? But he said that Dad had tried it with him and he'd said no. I was really hurt. I thought I was so special, and I was angry too.

"I wanted to hurt my father, so I told my mother. We never got along too well. I'd describe her, in retrospect, as kind of cold. She didn't seem too surprised when I told her, but she must have said something to my father because suddenly he stopped coming to my room. As a matter of fact he stopped everything—he no longer gave me any attention at all. He sort of ignored me. Then one day he said, 'You know, maybe you are a fag—only a fag would wreck a good thing like we had!' It didn't occur to me that the logic of that was screwy. I think he knew that a comment like that would really hurt and it did. I became really depressed. Some of my friends were on drugs and I got into that scene for a while. I tried to make it up to my father, but he was really angry at me I think.

"When I was 16, my father had a stroke and was paralyzed for the next five years until he died. I tried to help him then, but he'd just glare at me and I'd know he didn't want me around.

"In my teens I dated a few girls, but something was missing. Finally after my father died, I started going to gay bars, but I hated that scene. Finally I met a great guy at work. He's a lot older than me, but we get along good. We have a great apartment together. Sometimes the closeness we have reminds me of the good times between my father and me. But those memories are mixed with a lot of anger and bitterness, too."

Unlike Todd, many victims do not disclose the secret. Often they are too afraid that they will be labeled homosexual. The father-son affair usually terminates without outside intervention. It is usually the son who refuses to participate.

Effects of Father-Son Incest

Finkelhor (1979) concluded that the victimization by males had more residual effects than victimization by females regardless of the sex of the child. Like female victims, boys too tend to exhibit poor peer relations and self-destructive behavior (Dixon, Arnold, and Calestro, 1978; Froning and Mayman, 1990; Brown, 1990; Briere, 1995). Some note, however, that while female victims turn their anger inward, males express it outwardly. Dixon, Arnold, and Calestro cite a case in which the victim fantasized murdering, and suggest that violence toward others may be an outlet for the repressed anger. Some authors also point to sexual dysfunction, depression, substance abuse, and perpetration of sexual assaults as residual effects of this type of abuse (Brown, 1990; Briere, 1992).

Most experts agree that an early introduction to homosexual activity predisposes a boy to later fears of or to homosexual acting out. Justice and Justice (1979) state that a significant percentage of boy prostitutes in large cities were at one time victims of father-son incest. Father-son incest is not the only cause of homosexuality, but some victims, like Todd, later prefer a homosexual lifestyle (Parker, 1990). While not actively homosexual, others fear they will become so.

Mother-Daughter Incest

Mother-daughter incest is an abusive relationship that researchers and clinicians find to be rare. Russell (1986), in her study of 930 women, uncovered only 10 cases of incestuous abuse by females, only one of which was by a mother. Although Finkelhor (1979) notes that victims of female perpetrators reported less trauma than those abused by males, deYoung (1982) and Mayer (1992) suggest that the victims they saw experienced disruption (e.g., self-abusive behavior, suicide attempts, and depression) in later life. Perhaps the contradiction in the findings of various researchers depends on (1) the overall quality of the relationship between mother and daughter, (2) how much the daughter incorporated her mother's pathological attitudes and was therefore not traumatized by them, and (3) whether the activity was masked in otherwise maternally acceptable activities such as bathing or prolonged breast feeding.

This type of incest is underreported in a general population survey, and because of its rarity has not been fully explored. It is known that in general women tend to be less likely to abuse children than men. According to Russell (1986, p. 308), "Only five percent of all sexual abuse of girls and about twenty percent of all sexual abuse of boys is perpetrated by older females." Of this seemingly small population, what is known about the participants in mother-daughter incest?

Family Dynamics

Perhaps the most striking characteristic of the abusive mother is what many victims describe as her *differentness* (Sanford, 1980). These mothers usually come from dysfunctional, depriving families themselves. Their own childhood trauma has rendered them incapable of adequately dealing with everyday living. Forward and Buck (1978) describe these mothers as "severely disturbed, possibly psychotic" (p. 118), while deYoung (1982) describes the women in her sample as not being psychotic but "very clearly unhappy, chronically depressed women, with dismally low self-esteem" (p. 92). Feeling inadequate, these women view their daughters as extensions of themselves—as their completion. Often unable to distinguish between their daughters and themselves, their abuse becomes almost masturbatory. The mother views her attention to her daughter as affection. Since this type of abuse often begins at a very young age, the daughter begins to equate sexuality with affection. She may bask in her mother's attention. She sees her mother's neediness and feels compelled to take care of her. Thus the mother becomes the nurtured and the daughter the nurturer, which she may or may not resent (deYoung, 1982; Mayer, 1992; Schwartz and Cellini, 1995). The daughter feels she cannot hate this woman or even break away. She is so caught up in their symbiotic relationship that hating her mother seems like hating herself. Despite feeling trapped, the girl sees abandoning her mother as the ultimate rejection.

Ruby recounts her experience:

"I don't remember when it began—probably when I was really young. I just know that my earliest memories of my mother were of sleeping with her. I think it started out because my father was away a lot. He had a small orchestra and was on tours. It's all very muddled in my mind, but I know that my mother used to sing. He really encouraged her. I think he pampered her and they worked together. She was his prize. Then she had some kind of throat operation and couldn't sing. I know she felt my father abandoned her. She was really unstable, I think. She always was, I guess, but my father kept her going so she would sing. I was just a baby when all this happened. I used to think I'd done something to her though, but she assured me I hadn't.

"Anyway, we'd sleep together when my father was away—well even when he was home, for that matter. My mother would masturbate me and get me to do it to her. And she wanted me to pamper her like my father had. We'd play little games— like she'd want her breakfast in bed with silver and a rose on the tray, sort of like a prima donna. She wanted me to sing. She really pushed me. It was as though she saw me as her chance.

"I really liked the attention—especially since when he was home, my father treated us the same. One minute he'd "humor" us, the next minute he'd be yelling. Finally he just left—I think with the cellist from his orchestra. That was when I was 12. It was also about then that I began feeling trapped—suffocated. I think I pulled away. My mother started taking tranquilizers and she began drinking. It worried me. I felt I needed to take care of her, so I did. She was usually "out of it," so the sex stuff stopped. But sometimes I'd get in bed with her and just stroke her hair. She seemed so vulnerable."

Ruby finally attempted to leave home at age 17. Her mother overdosed on tranquilizers and was hospitalized. Ruby returned home and pursued a singing career until her mother died when Ruby was 28. Ruby married, but was divorced five years later. She tried to return to her singing, but had little success. She went through a period of extreme depression, but after treatment seemed to recover. At 38, Ruby is currently engaged in a lesbian affair with an older woman and describes herself as "relatively happy."

The fathers in the family supporting mother-daughter incest are, like Ruby's, either absent or emotionally unavailable. Their unavailability seems to support the need for the mother to cling to her daughter.

Effects of Mother-Daughter Incest

As mentioned earlier, there seems to be some controversy over the effects of this type of abuse. The women described by Forward and Buck (1978) demonstrated "extremely self-degrading and hostile" behavior, and one sister sexually abused her younger sister in a "humiliating violent manner" (p. 125). Both sisters in one case had a series of homosexual and heterosexual relationships, sometimes dedicated toward seducing the husbands of other women as a kind of "sexual vendetta" (p. 125). Another woman Forward and Buck described seems to have adjusted much more favorably, but feels that her relationships with the males in her life are confused because she had learned to associate sexuality with the attention given her by her mother.

DeYoung (1982) suggests that the daughters in her sample had problems associated with becoming independent. They remain dependent on others to the point of having difficulty functioning and often experience depression and suicidal tendencies as part of their conflict over these feelings.

Finkelhor (1979) and Russell (1986) conclude that past victims of mother-daughter incest are not as severely traumatized. This contradiction with the findings of other researchers suggests the need for another explanation. When a child is deprived of adequate mothering as a result of mother-daughter incest, the problem is compounded by this maternal deprivation. The trauma or lack of trauma resulting would therefore be dependent on the overall quality of the mother-child relationship aside from the incestuous behavior.

Mother-Son Incest

Although romanticized and eroticized in literature and movies, mother-son incest appears to have as deleterious an effect on the victim as father-daughter incest. Only a small number of cases of this type of abuse have actually been reported. This may be the result of three factors: mothers statistically do not abuse their sons as often as fathers do their daughters; mothers are able to mask (through bathing and caressing for instance) some activities that might be considered sexual to a degree; and sons are not as likely to report mother-son incest because of the severity of the taboo. Lawson (1993) also suggests that improved research methodologies would uncover a great number of these cases.

Forward and Buck (1978) suggest that there are three patterns of mother-son incest. The first describes a seemingly benign arrangement where mother and son dress and undress together, sleep in the same bed, and possibly bathe together. The trauma is related to the son's perception of these activities, and is often based on the absence of the father. The son sees himself in his father's role and his mother does nothing to prevent this assumption. The second pattern involves overt sexual contact but not actual intercourse. The mother bathes her son long after he can perform this task himself. In later years she stimulates him often to the point of ejaculation. Enjoying this new sexual stimulation, the boy participates but is confused by the relationship and frustrated by its limits (see also Kasl, 1990). The last type of mother-son incest involves regular intercourse and is found to be exceedingly rare.

Family Dynamics

Usually no father is present in the family where a mother abuses her son. In the very few cases where a father is involved, he is inconsistent, unavailable, and, on learning of the incestuous relationship, is seemingly indifferent to it (deYoung, 1982; Kasl, 1990). It is the absence of a father figure that often motivates the mother to abuse and encourage the boy to comply. Feeling his mother's sense of loss and needing to protect her, the boy responds to her overtures of "affection." His own Oedipal desires stimulate his need to be "the man of the house," so with his sexual involvement with his mother comes a pattern of role reversal. Promiscuity may be a dynamic in the mother's personality. Many theorists feel that the mother's indiscriminate relations with other men are actually provocative for the son. Once their relationship begins, however, the mother becomes extraordinarily dependent on her son emotionally. For her the relationship may, in fact, be more emotional than physical.

> Conrad Simons was 6 years old when his parents were divorced. It had been a stormy marriage, but his mother's reaction was one of acute grief. After several years of strife with the mother, Conrad's 15-year-old sister had chosen to live with her father. Conrad believes this was a double blow for his mother. Financially comfortable, Mrs. Simons remained home and showered her son with attention. She started getting a neighborhood girl to come over after he was in bed and while she went out. Conrad remembers numerous men frequenting their apartment, and it was not uncommon for one of these men to be there in the morning when he got up. Despite the attention he got during the day, Conrad described feeling "very left out" by his mother's evening activities.
>
> Whether actual or fabricated he cannot remember, but the boy began complaining of fears—of the dark and of being alone. His mother confessed that she too was "afraid to sleep alone" and invited her son to sleep with her. Conrad was delighted, especially since their arrangement seemed to preempt the invitations to other men. He felt safe and secure with his mother and eagerly participated in mutual body rubs. Conrad continued to sleep with his mother on a regular basis, but her ministrations to him evolved into fondling his penis and encouraging him to touch her genitals. She assured him of his importance to her, and, in retrospect, Conrad realizes how "crushingly dependent" she was on him. Their relationship evolved to include mutual masturbation, and Conrad was convinced of his role as her emotional as well as sexual partner.
>
> During this time Mrs. Simons was also a regular and avid church-goer. She took Conrad along and frequently pointed out pictures and statues of the Virgin Mary and Jesus, telling the boy how special the relationship between mother and son could be. She suggested that others might "taint" the purity of that relationship, and urged him to tell no one of their "special moments" together.
>
> When Conrad was 13, Mrs. Simons met a widower through church and began to date him. When they married a short time later, Conrad remembers feeling enraged but "afraid to show it for fear I'd lose her altogether." His difficulties with his stepfather resulted in a mutual decision that he be sent to boarding school. Although quiet and somewhat sullen, Conrad managed to repress his anger and remain an average student. He went directly to college and married shortly after

graduation, maintaining very little contact with his mother and stepfather throughout.

At the birth of his first child, a boy, Conrad's mother suggested they see more of each other. Conrad feels that he had repressed much of their previous relationship, so he agreed. Seeing his mother with his infant son made him extremely anxious, however, and he always felt a "need for air" when she was in his home.

Conrad began taking walks on evenings when his mother came over. One evening he saw through a window a young woman dressing. She emerged from the apartment with a young man, who had obviously just come to get her. Several nights later he returned to the apartment, crawled through an open window, and raped the girl. "I just kept thinking about how mad that guy would be to see what I'd done," he later remarked. This began a pattern of finding women who were involved with a man and raping them. Conrad's primary motivation seemed to be "taking something" that belonged to another man. The rapes were always followed by extreme remorse and severe depression. Soon after the first rape, he began to experience impotence with his wife. Only when he raped could he reach a climax. Conrad's rapes also began to take on bizarre religious overtones and he would often fantasize raping the Virgin Mary.

Finally, when his wife threatened to leave if Conrad did not get over his depression, he sought the aid of a therapist.

Most incest of this type is initiated by the mother or occurs as a pathological extension of the mother's nurturing. Meiselman (1978) discusses son-initiated incest. The mother in this relationship is less disturbed than her son. Although many of these sons are found to be schizophrenic, the incest seems not to be a causal factor in this illness. The advances toward his mother may be part of an episode or, in some other manner, representative of his disturbance.

Effects of Mother-Son Incest

Finkelhor (1979) felt that men were not as deeply affected by this type of incest. The fact that the women used no force and inspired cooperation, combined with the fact that the boys were eager to explore sexuality, is what may account for this finding. In addition, society tends to view young males' involvement with older women as a form of initiation into sexuality rather than a form of abuse. In reality, however, studies show that male victims of abuse by mothers do feel extreme guilt which can create later problems. These sons report feelings of worthlessness, betrayal, rage and fear (Kasl, 1990).

Nasjleti (1980) suggests that victims of mother-son incest exhibit aggressive problems such as rape, child molestation, or wife battering. Meiselman (1978) and Kasl (1990) relate that the victims in their experience have exhibited sexual problems such as impotence.

For many cultures, sexual abuse by the mother causes additional conflict and trauma. For example, the Hispanic culture sees mother as "…precious above all things" (Carrasco and Garza-Louis, 1995, p. 13–8). She is supposed to be granted the child's absolute love and devotion. Imagine the confusion for the Hispanic boy who learns that the sexual contact between him and his mother is not acceptable. His confusion will be profound. Unfortunately not enough data exist on the mother-son relationship or on the effects for the victim, so until more research is conducted, only speculation is possible.

Brother-Sister Incest

Brother-sister incest is surrounded by what Russell (1986) calls the "myth of mutuality." Despite this assumption that sexual contact between siblings is more than likely benign, 48 percent of the women in Russell's study reported that their experience with brothers was at least somewhat upsetting. Finkelhor (1980) found that 30 percent of his sample were left with negative feelings after an incestuous relationship with their brothers. Distinguishing between peer sexual play and abusive incest is not always easy. Several authors have attempted to define what is incestuous and what is exploratory, as in this example from Forward and Buck.

> Under certain very specific circumstances sibling incest may be a traumatic or even unpleasant experience. If the children are young and approximately the same age, if there is no betrayal of trust between them, if the sexual play is the result of their natural curiosity and exploration, and if the children are not traumatized by disapproving adults who stumble upon their sex play, sibling sexual contact can be just another part of growing up. In most such cases both partners are sexually naive. The game of show-me-yours-and-I'll-show-you-mine is older than civilization and between young siblings of approximately the same age it is usually harmless. (1978, p. 85)

Therefore what factors create trauma for some children? Perhaps there are two styles of initiation in brother-sister incest. One type of brother is curious about sexuality and uses his sister as a kind of sexual guinea pig (Forward and Buck, 1978; Wiehe and Herring, 1991). If she resists, he may cajole or even threaten in order to elicit her compliance. The sister, too, may be curious and perhaps even participate initially. At some time during the interaction, however, the sister may resist because she is confused or frightened by the intensity of the sexual experience, which is beyond her developmental years, or because she is overcome by the shame and guilt that the taboo of these activities arouses. Although one brother may be deterred from further exploration, another may intensify the pressure on his sister to continue.

Another personality type is characterized by Mayer (1983) as fraught with unconscious conflict. This aggressor is a number of years older than his sister and knowingly exploits her for complex intrapsychic reasons. Brothers initiate incest with bribes or threats in addition to capitalizing on their sisters' regard for them. Although only 12 percent of the brothers in Russell's sample actually used physical force (though none with weapons), 44 percent used a less severe type of force such as pushing or pinning the sister down. This type of perpetrator seems motivated by his need to in some way dominate his sister. Often he is in the role of surrogate father because this parent is absent, incapacitated, or emotionally unavailable. Sisters often describe their abusing brothers as "bullies" who teased them, used trickery, and liked to demonstrate their superior strength (Meiselman, 1978; Weihe and Herring, 1991).

> *Nicki was the youngest child and had three brothers. Her mother, divorced from Nicki's alcoholic father, worked long hours, entrusting Nicki's care to Will, her oldest brother. Although her two brothers were allowed by the domineering Will*

to go to a nearby playground after school, Nicki was not. Instead, Will invaded every aspect of her life, giving her little privacy. When she complained to him, he assured her that it was "only because he wanted to protect her." Complaints to her mother were met with defensive remarks such as, "You kids don't know how hard it is for me to work all those hours and come home to this. Can't you get along?"

When Nicki was 9 and Will 17, he suggested they "play a game," which consisted of Will touching her genitals and her touching his. At first she resisted, but discovered that the sensation was not unpleasant. It wasn't long before she noticed that Will's attitude toward her changed during these sessions. He was almost loving despite his commands for her to "try different things." She learned that she could "buy" freedom and privacy by complying with her brother's demands. "After a while," she commented, "the price got too high. He threatened all kinds of stuff, but I just wouldn't do it. Then he and my mother had a big fight and he left. My next oldest brother took care of me—but he never tried anything."

In retrospect, Nicki is extremely angry with Will. She feels she was exploited and that it colored her later attitude toward sex.

There are several motivations of the perpetrators in sibling incest. Exploration is the most common. This exploration is often framed in a game or in play (Weihe and Herring, 1991). Although the activities may begin as "games," Finkelhor (1980) makes the distinction that the brothers in his sample were too developmentally advanced to be involved in play. At least one of the partners in 35 percent of his sample was older than age 12, and in 73 percent of the cases one partner was over 8 years old.

Laredo noted that retribution was not an uncommon motivator for abusers. The brother sought to humiliate his sister—to make up for perceived past injustices. His anger was expressed in his abuse of his sister. Power and control were also motivators. This brother sought to motivate and control more out of his need for dominance than for retribution. A few sisters described sadistic relationships with brothers. Such attacks were motivated by the brothers' own severe disturbances and often produced long-term effects for the victim.

Why does the sister become involved in sibling incest? Since most researchers (Finkelhor, 1980; deYoung, 1982; Russell, 1986; Weihe and Herring, 1991) described the sisters in their samples as younger than the brothers, the difference in power and resources might be the reason, and, undoubtedly, the ties of siblinghood, punctuated perhaps with affection, mutuality, and trust, give the perpetrator a significant edge. Older siblings are persuasive; they can convince younger, more naive children about sexuality or the possible physiological, pleasurable sensations of sexual exploration. Some victims describe their belief that the threats of their brothers—of harm or of telling the parents—frightened them sufficiently to ensure cooperation or at least compliance.

Family Dynamics

Most incest victims describe parents who are either absent or uninvolved in their children's lives. They certainly have not adequately protected their children or provided the familial restraints to prevent incestuous behavior. According to Meiselman (1978), 50 percent of the fathers were unavailable because of death, alcoholism, or psychosis. Other theorists found the fathers were physically in the home, but described as emotionally absent. Families, in general, appeared dysfunctional, and were either unaware or discounted the incest. (de Young, 1982; Laviola, 1992).

The mothers in these situations were of two types. One type was not available to the victim. Some of these mothers were physically absent from the home, but those who were not were passive and ineffectual, apparently lacking the energy or inclination to supervise the children (de Young, 1982). The other type of mother, described even more frequently by de Young's respondents, was one whose extremely rigid, puritanical attitudes toward sex led her children to experiment on their own, rather than ask for information.

> *Dora described her mother as a cold and unyielding fundamentalist who saw her religion as her life. (Dora's father died when she was a baby.) Dora's mother spent most evenings going to some function at the church while Dora and her brother, three years her senior, were left at home. "She used to preach to us on the 'evils of sin,'" recounted Dora.*
>
> *"I believed her, but my brother apparently was talking to friends. He'd sneak out with his buddies when my mother was at church meetings, and I wasn't supposed to tell. When I was 11 he said he wanted to show me something. He showed me his penis and wanted me to undress. I was really naive. I was sure I'd burn in Hell. But finally he convinced me. For a while it was fun—if you can call it that. Then I started feeling guilty again and wanted to stop. But he didn't; he threatened to tell my mother, and that really scared me. If I'd had any smarts, I'd have realized that he would have been in as much trouble as me—but that never occurred to me. Anyway it kept on for a couple of years. He tried intercourse, but it hurt too much and I got really upset. I think he found some girl in the neighborhood after that, because he left me alone. It really changed our relationship. I still think of it when I see him today."*

Unlike Dora's, families of the participants of sibling incest tend to be large, providing less privacy but less supervision as well. Meiselman (1978) found that the perpetrator often tended to be the oldest brother in this large family. Finkelhor (1980) found that his respondents were from large families, and Russell (1986) reiterated this finding by documenting that 77 percent of the victims of sibling incest in her sample of 930 San Francisco women came from families of six or more. This is especially understandable, considering that the greater the number of brothers in a girl's family, the higher the statistical chance of brother-sister incest (Russell, 1986).

Effects of Brother-Sister Incest

Although some authors contend that brother-sister incest leaves little lasting effects, the latest research argues otherwise. An immediate effect of this type of sibling incest appears to be an increase in alienation from the parents. The siblings' recognition of their need to protect themselves from disclosure and the possible consequences of that disclosure accounts for some of this alienation (de Young, 1982; Weihe and Herring, 1991). The victim who feels exploited from the onset may also resent the lack of protection her parents have afforded her (Laviola, 1992).

Promiscuity was found to be a problem for some past victims. As it turned out with Dora, many lapsed into multiple relationships with married men following the cessation of their affairs with their brothers. Meiselman (1978) reported that 71 percent of her sample were promiscuous prior to reaching adulthood. Conversely, some adult past victims described an aversion to sex. Many have severe mistrust of men (deYoung, 1982; Weihe and Herring, 1991; Laviola, 1992).

Perhaps related is Russell's (1986) finding that 47 percent of her sample of victims never married. Of those who did marry, a high percentage (50 percent) were physically abused by husbands. Revictimization and the fear of revictimization are also obvious among past victims. Of Russell's respondents, 58 percent were sexually victimized by an authority figure, 90 percent were upset by a man's sexual comments or advances on the street, and 32 percent were asked to pose for pornographic pictures. Also, 79 percent of the victims of brother-sister incest in Russell's study expressed fears about being further sexually assaulted.

In contrast to the negative effects of brother-sister incest, Finkelhor (1980) discovered a higher level of self-esteem in the young women who had been involved in such a relationship. Finkelhor concluded that learning to combine sex and friendship is a crucial developmental task in adolescence and young adulthood. Women who had already learned to do this saw themselves better able to cope with new relationships. How this finding relates to Russell's suggestion that a high percentage of past victims do not marry is subject to speculation.

Not every girl involved sexually with her brother reports long-term traumatic effects, despite the increased number who have. If the intent is exploration not exploitation and the girl continues to maintain a trusting relationship with her brother, then traumatic effects are avoided.

Homosexual Sibling Incest

Little has been written on either brother-brother or sister-sister incestuous relationships. Raybin (1969) cited brother-brother incest occurring in the same family as father-son incest. The presence of this type of incest within the family may well indicate the permeation of sexuality between males as a result of the father's pathology. Incestuous behavior between brothers is often motivated by experimentation, a need for power on the part of the older brother, or homosexual leanings. If both participants are under age 7, the behavior is more likely to spring from sexual exploration and awakening. When the power differences between the participants become greater, or when the brothers are over 7 years old, there is a possibility of homosexuality or bisexuality. Forward and Buck (1978) suggest that even if homosexual preference does not stimulate the incest, sibling same-sex interaction can lead to homosexuality. In Tower's (1988) sample of survivors of child sexual abuse, two were found to be victims of brother-brother incest. One was more traumatized by the simultaneous incestuous relationship with his father than by the seemingly incidental interaction with his brothers. This young man later pursued a homosexual lifestyle. The second victim was abused at an early age by a brother only. Despite feeling exploited, the individual continued the relationship with his brother intermittently, and secretly, well into mid-life. His orientation, however, appeared to be heterosexual as he married, fathered children, and gave no indication of his relationship with his brother for many years.

With so few reported cases, the data about brother-brother incest are inconclusive. The victims who have disclosed reported suffering depression, self-loathing, and confusion over sexual identity in later life (Forward and Buck, 1978).

Sister-sister incest seems to have less impact on the participants than other types of sibling incest. The sisters in Russell's (1986) sample did not see this type of sibling incest as creating problems for them in their lives. "Not only are girls much less likely to be sexually abused by a sister than a brother, but it appears that when sister-sister incestuous abuse occurs, it may be less upsetting and may have a less negative impact on the victim's lives" (p. 306). Some 50 percent of the women reporting sister-sister incest in Russell's sample saw it as a nonabusive relationship.

Since others have not researched sister-sister incest, it is not possible to draw any conclusions as to its frequency or the extent of trauma.

Incest with Uncles, Grandfathers, and Cousins

The most common type of incestuous behavior, according to Russell's (1986) study, occurs between uncles and nieces. Uncles, in fact, represented the primary perpetrator in slightly more cases than fathers. Kinsey and colleagues (1953) in their earlier study of female sexual behavior also concluded that uncles abused their nieces in more instances than fathers abused their daughters. The degree of trauma experienced by these nieces has been the subject of controversy.

Meiselman (1978) speculated that numerous women had been victimized by uncles but had experienced little trauma. She supposed that in these cases the uncle was distant from the family and therefore did not play a significant role in the child's upbringing. On the other hand, where the uncle is closer to the family circle and perhaps more trusted, or if he employed violence, more trauma would be expected. Russell (1986), however, stated that in 96 percent of her cases the abuse by uncles was unwanted, and that 48 percent of the respondents reported being very or extremely upset by the incidents. The uncles involved appeared to have a variety of different relationships, ranging from surrogate parents to intense involvement with the family to infrequent interaction with the family. For those who saw their nieces infrequently, greetings and departures often provided opportunities for the uncles to overstep their bounds and fondle or inappropriately kiss their nieces (Russell, 1986).

An interesting statistic uncovered by Russell was that nieces who were abused by their uncles were more likely to be raised by surrogate parents, such as grandparents or the uncles' own families. Certainly if an uncle was functioning as a surrogate father, the quality of the incest and its resultant trauma would more closely approximate father-daughter incest.

Uncles who abuse nieces, for whom they were not surrogate parents, are usually described as abusing other relatives as well. Family members frequently see them as trouble-makers or problems apart from the abusive behavior. The victimized nieces tended to be dependent children often attached to their mothers (Browning and Boatman, 1977; deYoung, 1982). Frequently the uncle is able to ensure compliance based on the niece's experience with domineering authority figures who insist on obedience. It is also highly likely that the girl's mother was herself an incest victim.

Gloria's uncle was in the service during the years when the abuse first began. She describes her father as domineering and her mother as passive and docile, but basically loving. Mother and daughter appeared to see their alliance as a protection against the father's wrath. Gloria's older sister was more like her father, "assertive and often overbearing." On occasion this created real friction between the sister and her father.

When Uncle Harry first started coming to their house on his leaves, Gloria was pleased. He was a carefree kind of person quite different from her father. He would spend time with her, take her to a nearby playground, and push her on the swings. Sometimes he'd reach his hands in her shorts as he pushed her. Gloria doesn't remember being traumatized by this, thinking it was all part of the game.

Uncle Harry was reassigned to a base near the family's home and frequently came over on weekends. He started engineering activities so that he and Gloria were alone. The abuse intensified as he would openly touch her genitals and encourage her to touch him. "It began to frighten me," reports Gloria, "and finally I told my mother." The mother was angry, but said that Gloria's father could not be told lest "he kill Uncle Harry." Gloria was so frightened that Uncle Harry, whom she did like, would be harmed that she felt terribly guilty about her disclosure. She withdrew from contacts with her uncle, and soon after he stopped coming to the house. Gloria became extremely depressed and is still convinced she "drove him away."

In later years Gloria's mother recounted that her brother had also abused her as a child. At the time she felt powerless to stop it, but when her daughter was abused she was able to intervene by suggesting he no longer come over.

Girls who are abused by uncles may develop a variety of after-effects. Some complain of psychosomatic ailments and their inability to openly handle the conflict (deYoung, 1982). Still others report sexual difficulties or a general mistrust of men. Often this trauma is not experienced until later in life (Russell, 1986).

Grandfather-granddaughter incest is another frequent type of abusive relationship. This abuse often takes place because society views the older person as nonsexual, beyond the age of interest in sexuality. In fact, age is often a contributor to the incest. Already unsure of his power and worth, the incestuous grandfather's self-doubts are intensified as society begins to view him as a less capable individual because of his age. He feels infanticized—especially if he lives with his adult children and needs to be looked up to. His granddaughter provides affection and attention, asks little of him, and usually looks up to him (Sanford, 1980). The relationship provides him with an opportunity to assert his manhood, and his sexual performance will not be judged. It may be this need for his granddaughter's approval that explains another finding. While grandfathers usually use tenderness with their granddaughters, many abused their own daughters with brutality (deYoung, 1982).

Not every grandfather is in the older-age range. A grandfather may be in his 40s or 50s and still at the height of his career and capabilities. For these men the motivation is much like father-daughter incest. Often their marriage has broken down and they are seeking a less-demanding, less-conflictual relationship. The man may also have incestuous wishes toward his own daughter—the child's mother—and find it easier not to break so clear-cut a taboo. A relationship with a female one generation removed appears to be less guilt-provoking (Forward and Buck, 1978).

Grandfathers frequently abuse other relatives within their family circle. Eight out of ten grandfathers, in the study done by Goodwin, Cormier, and Owen (1983), had abused their own daughters. By the same token, the victims of grandfather incest tended to be involved in multiple victimizations, often also being abused by uncles or cousins. It was not unusual for the grandfather, however, to be the first in a string of abusers (Russell, 1986).

Many researchers feel that granddaughters are not as likely to experience trauma from abuse by a gentle grandfather as through other types of incest. Russell's (1986) respondents described fewer long-term effects, due perhaps to the grandfather's gentleness or only mild level of abuse. It would be a mistake, however, cautions Russell, to assume that all grandfather-granddaughter incest is benign. Goodwin, Cormier, and Owen (1983) concur that this type of incest can in fact have severe long-term effects, especially if it has been an introduction to abuse by other family members.

Victims who report trauma from their grandfathers' abuse blame themselves rather than the perpetrators.

Diona was 7 years old when her grandfather began his abuse of her and her sister. When the girls stayed at their grandparents for the weekend, he would intentionally leave his robe open as they breakfasted. He would suggestively rub Diona's legs under the table while their grandmother fixed the food in the adjoining kitchen. The activity progressed to touching Diona's legs and breasts and finally her genitals, when he was able to coax her into being alone with him. He had apparently not touched her sister, and although Diona felt pleased at the attention, she also felt enormous guilt that she had somehow provoked it. (She later learned that her sister was also abused.)

The abuse lasted over the course of a year until Diona refused to comply. Her grandfather stopped, and they remained relatively close but she describes "feeling weird about it" and wondering what was "wrong" with her. Everyone loved her grandfather, so Diona concluded she must be at fault.

In her teens, Diona began to binge and use laxatives excessively. She sought therapy for this behavior but never associated it with the abuse. When she became engaged in her early 20s, the bulimic behavior intensified. Again in therapy, she finally recognized that her new sexual relationship with her husband had intensified her self-guilt over the abuse.

Although the incest taboo is not quite as strong, sexual abuse by first cousins can also create conflict for the victim. The degree of conflict caused by male cousins' abuse appears similar to the conflict created by brothers' abuse. Cousins, however, are more likely to molest once (although some did abuse over extended periods), and significant long-term effects are less likely. Certainly the degree of force used and the closeness of the perpetrator's relationship to the victim are important variables in considering the degree of trauma experienced (Russell, 1986).

Why Incest Stops

Intervention is not always the reason incestuous relationships cease. Other factors can also account for its cessation. As the victims grow to adolescence, they may begin to feel trapped and constrained by the abuser's inability to let go. Victims describe a need to be involved in more peer activities, but the perpetrator, afraid to lose the relationship, may hold on even tighter. At some point the adolescent refuses to continue. The price is too high. In *Father's Days,* Katherine Brady describes that it was her engagement that finally enabled her to terminate the relationship:

> Finally my father was willing to relinquish me. Something had taken precedence over his need for sexual gratification: ownership, custody of me by another man. That was something he could understand, however, much as he resented it. (1979, p. 120)

As adolescents grow in stature and strength, they also feel powerful enough to stop the abuse: "I told my father when I was 17, that if he touched me again, I'd kill him," reported Ed. "I think I would have, too. I was much bigger than he was by then and I'd had enough of being used and abused by him."

The perpetrator may also lose interest in the child who is becoming more like an adult. When this happens, abusers, especially fathers, turn to younger siblings.

For some older victims, leaving home is the only solution. Often harboring guilt that they leave their younger siblings vulnerable to the abuse, the victims flee in an attempt to resist further exploitation of themselves. The progression of abuse has been discussed. When the activity begins to include actual vaginal penetration, some children become frightened. Truly concerned about the child, the perpetrator may not continue. Or the abuser may perceive that a girl nearing puberty might become pregnant.

Recall that parents, especially, often abuse their children as a result of their own inability to cope with stressful situations, so when the stress subsides the abuse may also.

> *Geri described the abuse she suffered from her father when he was unemployed. The family was in a great deal of conflict, especially when her mother, with great reluctance, was forced to work outside the home. A year later, the family pressures were somewhat relieved. Her father had been working for several months, had a renewed and more positive outlook on life, and her mother had given up her job. The abuse ceased.*

Not all situations are as clear cut as Geri's. Easing family conflict can, however, lessen or alleviate abusive behavior in some families.

Opportunity is another essential ingredient in abusive situations. If the perpetrator is robbed of the opportunity to sexually exploit, the abuse will stop. Geri's father's return to a job with long hours decreased her availability for the abuse. Better supervision of children minimizes the opportunities of the abusers.

And finally, some mothers recognize the problem and are able to intervene either by better supervision and protection of the child or by actual confrontation with the perpetrator. Individuals for whom there was no overt intervention and treatment appear to suffer more profoundly from the effects of incest (Russell, 1986; Faller, 1990; Jacobs, 1994).

Summary

Child rearing is accompanied by closeness and touching, which in most families serves only to provide the child with a sense of security and the feeling of being loved. Some families, however, are not able to confine their touching to appropriate limits and hence sexually abuse their children. Familial abuse or incest has become recognized today as a national problem. Part of the explanation for the high incidence of incest lies in society's emphasis on sexuality and performance as well as its training little girls to see sexuality as a means to gain attention and favors. Increased mobility and confused values also lay the groundwork for sexually abusive behavior.

The most frequently discussed type of incest involves fathers and their daughters. This type of incestuous family exhibits three patterns: possessive-passive, dependent-domineering, and dependent-dependent. The incestuous father tends to be either controlling, rigid, and dominant, or passive, dependent, and submissive. Underlying both these styles are a deep-seated vulnerability, helplessness, and low self-esteem. Mothers whose husbands abuse are either domineering or extremely dependent and passive. Some mothers appear to collude in the abuse while others are powerless to stop it. Both mother and father are usually from emotionally deprived families and both are seeking to be nurtured. Where the parents are unable to meet each other's needs, they both turn to their daughter—the mother through role reversal and the father through sexual abuse. As the mother withdraws from the family, her daughter feels abandoned and isolated. She looks to her father for support, and is sexually exploited. Daughters then become hostages in the conflict between their parents. The siblings in this family also suffer. They are forced to choose between their father and their sister, and suffer guilt as a consequence. Often these siblings carry scars into their adult years and may later victimize or be victimized themselves.

Other types of incest include father-son (a pathological orientation of the father, based, perhaps, on his own latent homosexual drives or on his need for power); mother-daughter (the mother's overidentification with her daughter results in a masturbatory type of abuse); mother-son (the mother sees her son as the surrogate adult male in her life); and brother-sister (a brother uses his superior power over his sister as a means of meeting his exploration or exploitation needs). The incidence of homosexual sibling incest is relatively underreported and therefore difficult to document. Uncles, grandfathers, and cousins are also known to be abusers. The degree of trauma to the victim of each type of abuse depends largely on the relationship between abuser and victim, as well as on other variables.

Intervention is not the only reason why abuse ceases. Victims may be able to protect themselves as they grow older. Opportunity may be denied the perpetrator. Or the stressful situation that prompted the abuse may abate.

Incest, past victims tell us, often leaves scars. The residual effects will be discussed in Chapter 17.

Exploration Questions

1. Cite several societal contributors to the incidence of incest today.

2. Describe the three patterns of father-daughter incest.

3. What type of father sexually abuses his daughter?

4. Can mothers in families supporting father-daughter incest be held responsible for the abuse? Why or why not? What are these mothers like?

5. What are the effects on the victim of father-daughter incest?

6. Why would a father sexually abuse his son? What effect would this relationship have on the son?

7. Why might a daughter have difficulty terminating the relationship with her sexually abusive mother?

8. Under what conditions does a mother abuse her son?

9. What two motivations would an abusive brother demonstrate in the abuse of his sister? What are the effects on her?

10. What variables explain the degree of trauma caused by incest perpetrated by uncles, grandfathers, and cousins?

11. If no intervention takes place, what might cause the abuse to stop?

Activities for Applied Learning

1. Read *Father's Days* by Katherine Brady or *Daddy's Girl* by Charlotte Vale Allen. From your reading in this chapter, how would you characterize the father in each of these stories?

2. View the film *Something about Amelia*. Analyze the family dynamics. What type of pattern did this family exemplify?

3. Listen to "Ruth's Story" on the tape *Profiles of Abusive and Neglectful Parents* (available through the National Education Association, 1201 16th St. NW, Washington, DC 20036).

4. Create a chart comparing and contrasting the various types of familial abuse. Consider such topics as Why does the abuser victimize? Why does the victim comply? You may want to read *Secret Trauma* by Diana Russell or *Child Sexual Abuse* by David Finkelhor for additional statistics to use in your chart.

Suggested Readings

Faller, K. C. *Child Sexual Abuse.* New York: Columbia University Press, 1988.

Friess, D. L. *Cry the Darkness: One Woman's Triumph Over Incest.* Deerfield Beach, FL: Health Communications, 1993.

Herman, J., and Hirschman, L. *Father-Daughter Incest.* Cambridge, MA: Harvard University Press, 1981.

Hunter, M. *The Sexually Abused Male, Vol 1 and 2.* New York: Lexington Books, 1990.

Johnson, J. T. *Mothers of Incest Survivors.* Holmes Beach, FL: Learning Pub., 1992.

Russell, D. *Secret Trauma.* New York: Basic Books, 1986.

Sgroi, S. *Vulnerable Populations.* Lexington, MA: Lexington Books, 1988.

References

Brady, K. *Father's Days.* New York: Dell, 1979.

Briere, J. N. *Child Abuse Trauma.* Newbury Park, CA: Sage, 1992.

Brown, J. "The Treatment of Male Victims with Mixed-Gender, Short-Term Group Psychotherapy." In M. Hunter, *The Sexually Abused Male, Vol 2,* pp. 137–169. New York: Lexington Books, 1990.

Browning, D. H., and Boatman, B. "Incest: Children at Risk." *American Journal of Psychiatry* 134 (1977): 69–72.

Butler, S. *Conspiracy of Silence.* San Francisco: Volcano Press, 1978.

Carrasco, N., and Garza-Louis, D. "Hispanic Sex Offenders—Cultural Characteristics and Implications for Treatment" in B. Schwartz and H. Cellini, *The Sex Offender,* pp. 13-1–13-10. Kingston, NJ: Civic Research Inst., 1995.

Deblinger, E.; Hathaway, C. R.; Lippman, J.; and Steer, R. "Psychosocial Characteristics and Correlates of Symptom Distress in Nonoffending Mothers of Sexually Abused Children." *Journal of Interpersonal Violence.* 8 (2), (1993): 155–168.

deYoung, M. *The Sexual Victimization of Children.* Jefferson, NC: McFarland, 1982.

Dixon, K. N.; Arnold, L. E.; and Calestro, K. "Father-Son Incest: Unreported Psychiatric Problem?" *American Journal of Psychiatry* 135 (1978): 835–38.

Downs, W. R. "Developmental Considerations for the Effects of Child Sexual Abuse", *Journal of Interpersonal Violence,* 8 (3), (1993): 331–345.

Faller, K. C. *Child Sexual Abuse.* New York: Columbia University Press, 1988.

Faller, K. C. "Sexual Abuse by Paternal Caretakers: A Comparison of Abusers Who Are Biological Fathers in Intact Families, Stepfathers, and Noncustodial Fathers." In A. L. Horton; B. L. Johnson; L. M. Roundy; and D. Williams (eds.). *The Incest Perpetrator.* Newbury Park, CA: Sage, 1990.

Finkelhor, D. *Sexually Victimized Children.* New York: Free Press, 1979.

Finkelhor, D. "Sex Among Siblings: A Survey of the Prevalence, Variety and Effects." *Archives of Sexual Behavior* 9 (1980):171–94.

Finkelhor, D. *Child Sexual Abuse.* New York: Free Press, 1984.

Finkelhor, D., and Browne, A. "The Traumatic Impact of Child Sexual Abuse: A Conceptualization." *American Journal of Orthopsychiatry* 55 (1985):530–41.

Forward, S., and Buck, C. *Betrayal of Innocence: Incest and Its Devastation.* New York: Penguin, 1978.

Froning, M. L. and Mayman, S. B. "Identification and Treatment of Child and Adolescent Male Victims of Sexual Abuse." In M. Hunter, *The Sexually Abused Male,* Vol. 2, pp. 199–224. New York: Lexington Books, 1990.

Furniss, T. "Conflict-Avoiding and Conflict-Regulating: Patterns in Incest and Child Sexual Abuse." *Acta Paedopsychiatrica* 50 (1985):6.

Geiser, R. L. *Hidden Victims.* Boston: Beacon Press, 1979.

Gilgun, J. F. "Factors Mediating the Effects of Childhood Maltreatment." In M. Hunter, *The Sexually Abused Male, Vol. 1,* pp. 177–190, New York: Lexington Books, 1990.

Goodwin, J.; Cormier, L.; and Owen, J. "Grandfather-Granddaughter Incest: A Trigenerational View." *Child Abuse and Neglect* 7 (1983):163–70.

Groth, A. N. "The Incest Offender." In *Handbook of Clinical Intervention in Child Sexual Abuse,* edited by S. Sgroi, pp. 215–39. Lexington, MA: Lexington Books, 1982.

Hanson, R. F.; Lipovsky, J. A.; and Saunders, B. E. "Characteristics of Fathers in Incest Families." *Journal of Interpersonal Violence* 9 (2), (1994): 155–169.

Herman, J., and Hirschman, L. *Father-Daughter Incest.* Cambridge, MA: Harvard University Press, 1981.

Jacobs, J. L. *Victimized Daughters.* New York: Routledge, 1994.

Johnson, J. T. *Mothers of Incest Survivors.* Bloomington, IN: Indiana University Press, 1992.

Joyce, P. A. "Mothers of Sexually Abused Children and the Concept of Collusion: A Literature Review." *Journal of Child Sexual Abuse* 6(2), 1997: 75–92.

Justice, B., and Justice, R. *The Broken Taboo: Sex in the Family.* New York: Human Services Press, 1979.

Kasl, C. D. "Female Perpetrators of Sexual Abuse: A Feminist View." In M. Hunter, *The Sexually Abused Male, Vol. 1,* pp. 259–274. New York: Lexington Books, 1990.

Kinsey, A. C.; Pomeray, W.; Martin, C.; and Gebhard, P. *Sexual Behavior in the Human Female.* Philadelphia: W. B. Saunders, 1953.

Laredo, C. "Sibling Incest." In *Handbook of Clinical Intervention in Child Sexual Abuse,* edited by S. Sgroi. Lexington, MA: Lexington Books, 1982.

Laviola, M. "Effects of Older Brother-Younger Sister Incest: A Study of the Dynamics of 17 Cases." *Child Abuse and Neglect* 16 (3), (1992): 409–421.

Lawson, C. "Mother-Son Sexual Abuse: Rare or Underreported? A Critique of the Research." *Child Abuse and Neglect* 17 (2), (1993): 261–269.

Lustig, N.; Dresser, J. W.; Spellman, S. W.; and Murray, T. B. "Incest." *Archives of General Psychiatry* 14 (1966):31–40.

Mayer, A. *Incest: A Treatment Model for Therapy with Victims, Spouses and Offenders.* Holmes Beach, FL: Learning Publications, 1983.

Mayer, A. *Women Sex Offenders.* Holmes Beach, FL: Learning Publications, 1992.

Meiselman, K. *Incest.* San Francisco: Jossey-Bass, 1978.

Nasjleti, M. "Suffering in Silence: The Male Incest Victim." *Child Welfare* 49 (1980):269–75.

Parker, S. "Healing Abuse in Gay Men: The Group Component." In M. Hunter, *The Sexually Abused Male, Vol. 2,* pp. 177–198. New York: Lexington Books, 1990.

Peterson, R. F.; Basta, S. M.; and Dykstra, T. A. "Mothers of Molested Children: Some Comparisons of Personality Characteristics." *Child Abuse and Neglect* 17 (3) (1993): 409–418.

Prendergast, W. E. *Treating Sex Offenders in Correctional Institutions and Outpatient Clinics.* New York: Haworth Press, 1991.

Raybin, J. B. "Homosexual Incest." *Journal of Nervous Mental Disease* 148 (1969):105–10.

Rosenfeld, A. "Sexual Misuse and the Family." In *Sexual Abuse of Children: Selected Readings,* edited by B. Jones, L. Janstrom, and K. MacFarlane, pp. 91–95. Washington: U.S. Department of Health and Human Services, 1980.

Russell, D. *Secret Trauma: Incest in the Lives of Girls and Women.* New York: Basic Books, 1986.

Sanford, L. *The Silent Children.* Garden City, NY: Doubleday, 1980.

Schonberg, I. J. "The Distortion of the Role of Mother in Child Sexual Abuse." *Journal of Child Sexual Abuse* 1 (3), (1992): 47–61.

Schwartz, B. K., and Cellini, H. R. *The Sex Offender.* Kingston, NJ: Civic Research Institute, 1995.

Sgroi, S., and Dana, N. "Individual and Group Treatment of Mothers of Incest Victims." In *Handbook of Clinical Intervention in Child Sexual Abuse,* edited by S. Sgroi, pp. 191–214. Lexington, MA: Lexington Books, D. C. Heath, 1982.

Stern, M., and Meyer, L. "Family and Couple Interactional Patterns in Cases of Father-Daughter Incest." In *Sexual Abuse of Children: Selected Readings,* edited by B. Jones, L. Janstrom, and K. MacFarlane, pp. 83–86. Washington: U.S. Department of Health and Human Services, 1980.

Tower, C. C. *Secret Scars: A Guide for the Survivor of Child Sexual Abuse.* New York: Viking/Penguin, 1988.

U.S. Department of Health and Human Services, National Center on Child Abuse and Neglect. *Child Maltreatment 1992: Reports from the States to the National Center on Child Abuse and Neglect.* Washington, DC: U.S. Government Printing Office, 1994.

Ward, E. *Father-Daughter Rape.* New York: Grove Press, 1985.

Weinberg, S. K. *Incest Behavior.* Secaucus, NJ: Citadel Press, 1955.

Wiehe, V. R. and Herring, T. *Perilous Rivalry: When Siblings Become Abusive,* Lexington, MA: Lexington Books, 1991.

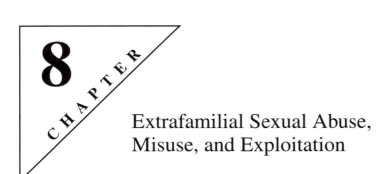

Extrafamilial Sexual Abuse, Misuse, and Exploitation

The prevailing myth has been that children are sexually abused by strangers. It is now known that a significant percentage of sexual abuse is perpetrated by family members or by surrogate caregivers who are close to the child. Yet there is also danger that friends, acquaintances, and, yes, even strangers abuse and exploit children.

Child sexual abuse in the broadest sense encompasses not only the inappropriate touching of children but also using children in sexual trafficking, pornography, and prostitution. Often perpetrators abduct their victims. This chapter covers the wide range of extrafamilial sexual abuse—from molestation by acquaintances and strangers to the sexual exploitation of children through a variety of misuses of adult power. For the purpose of this chapter, *abuse* refers to the touching or molestation of a child by a perpetrator, whereas *misuse* and *exploitation* refer to the perpetrator's encouraging sexual contact with or photographing of the child for the perpetrator's own financial gain.

Sexual Abuse Outside the Family

It has been concluded that the greater the emotional bond between the perpetrator and the victim, the greater the potential for harm, but the trauma precipitated by an abuser outside the family cannot be minimized. Several factors (mentioned in Chapter 7) are said to cause the greatest trauma in children who have been abused. Consider how each of these factors (adapted from Groth, 1978a and MacFarlane, 1978) can be seen in relation to incest and to extrafamilial abuse.

From Table 8.1, it would seem obvious that children do experience trauma from extrafamilial abuse. The degree and types are explored later in this chapter.

It should be noted that there are cultural implications that also affect the degree of trauma felt by children who are sexually abused both within and outside the family. For example, children of a culture that has experienced a great deal of oppression or prejudice might be either hypervigilant to abuse from the outside or emotionally numb due to having dealt with non-familial emotional assaults throughout childhood (Ertz, 1995). This is important to consider when making an assessment of the degree of trauma experienced by an individual child.

Children are vulnerable to abuse from many different individuals. Of the women who were abused prior to the age of 18 by males outside the family, Russell (1984) found that 15 percent were molested by strangers, 40 percent by acquaintances, 14 percent by friends of the family, 2 percent by unclassified authority figures, and 18 percent by a friend or date

TABLE 8.1   Factors Influencing Degree of Trauma

		Extrafamilial	
Factor	Incestual	Acquaintance	Stranger
Continues for a long period of time	Probable	Possible, but often not as long as in familial	Usually not
Close emotional bond	Almost always	Possible, but not always	No
Involves penetration	More likely, due to progression and duration	Possible, but may not	Possible, but may not. If penetration, usually rape
Is accompanied by aggression	Majority of cases are not	Possible	Often
Child's "participation" to some degree	Usually	Possible	Unlikely, but possible
Child is cognizant of taboo against or violation	Possible in older children	Possible	Probable (due to admonishments about strangers)

of the victim. Of those women who reported being abused by females, 2 percent named acquaintances and 2 percent cited friends of the family or of the respondent.

The perpetrator's ability to molest in an extrafamilial situation often depends on lack of parental judgment or inadequate parental supervision. This statement seems to imply blame, but parents allow access to their children for different reasons, some unrelated to intent or irresponsibility. Why might a parent not perceive potential harm from a perpetrator?

First, the *perpetrator has an emotional bond* with the parent. The individual may be a family friend who has gained the trust of the parent, or the abuser may be a babysitter who is assumed to be reliable. Or abuse is *not within the parents' frame of reference.* Parents who have had no experience with abuse, or who have blocked the memory of their own experiences, do not expect other adults to sexually abuse children. Native American families, for example, give children a great deal of freedom on the reservation, not expecting that they will come to any harm. Because of current media attention, parents may be more cautious, but even cautious parents often tell themselves their fears are groundless. Some parents *need the services of the potential abuser.* The increased reports of abuse in daycare settings, in schools, and by babysitters point out that parents are not always discerning about the providers of those services. Even with thorough checking of references, it is not possible to know that these individuals are reliable. Financial constraints may necessitate using whatever facility or person is available. And finally, the *parent trusts the potential abuser.* Parents who trust coaches, youth-group leaders, or even ministers and priests, for example, may not realize that these individuals could be harmful.

Parents may not provide adequate supervision for several reasons: They may *feel their children can care for themselves.* Parents who allow children freedom in walking home from school or playing in the neighborhood may not even consider the danger of potential abuse or may feel that the children can take care of themselves. Some parents have unrealistic expectations about their children's ability to care for themselves. Parents *may feel unable to provide supervision.* Latchkey children, who come home to an empty house and remain alone until the parents return from work, are becoming the trademark of two-career families. Child care is expensive, and some parents feel financially unable to provide an alternative. In addition, the parents may not be able to find a program or a sitter to supervise. Or parents *may be unaware of unsupervised periods.* The child who misses a ride, or for some reason is left unsupervised, is vulnerable despite the parents' good intentions. Some parents *may be otherwise occupied.* Caring for a child is a demanding and full-time job. For some parents the responsibility is sometimes overwhelming. Others may be so involved in their own crises or conflicts that they are not able to concern themselves with their children's whereabouts. And finally, the *child may initiate the separation.* Children who wander off, run away, or become distracted sometimes separate themselves from supervising caregivers.

All of these conditions make children vulnerable to abuse. These children may be exposed to one or more of the variety of types of abuse, misuse, or exploitation—from abuse at the hands of one perpetrator to involvement in sex rings and prostitution. Let us consider some of these forms of sexual deviation.

Pedophilia

Pedophiles are individuals who have a sexual interest in children. Although some incestuous fathers may be pedophiles in their orientation, the term is mostly reserved for the abuser whose victim is outside the family. Perhaps one difference between the pedophile and an incestuous father is that incest is indicative of family dysfunction, and the perpetrator is a participant in a complex web of dysfunctional relationships. Pedophilia is related to the individual pathology of the abuser. A pedophile may be either fixated or regressed (see Chapter 6), and his choice of victim may reflect his particular type of pathology. Pedophiles seek a relationship with a child because they see children as nonconflictual partners who can satisfy their unmet emotional needs. The fixated perpetrator has probably nurtured his interest in children for some time. He has become expert at engaging children. He becomes emotionally involved with these children and sees himself at their level. Outside of his relationship with children, the fixated pedophile views himself as helpless and ineffective (Prendergast, 1991; Schwartz and Cellini, 1995).

Fantasy is an important part of this individual's life. He may fantasize sexual and emotional involvement with children, and often acts out his fantasies. Interestingly, the perpetrator projects his feelings of powerlessness and often perceives that it is the child who initiates the relationship (Prendergast, 1991; Schwartz and Cellini, 1995).

The victim is usually vulnerable to the advances of the pedophile. In the movie *Fallen Angel,* a male softball coach befriended and molested Jennifer, whom he called Angel, a needy and isolated young girl. Concerned but caught up in her own conflicts, the girl's mother was emotionally unavailable to her. "Angel's" primary motivation for not disclosing the abuse before she did was her need for attention and affection and her trust in Howie, the perpetrator. Howie lured his victim with great skill. He provided companionship, a sense of belonging, and affection to the emotionally starved, confused child. Gradually he cajoled her into the abuse, demonstrating his consideration for her feelings but pressuring her with gifts and thinly veiled threats.

This type of relationship is not uncommon between the abused and the abuser. The fixated pedophile suffers from a "temporary or permanent arrestment of psychosocial maturation resulting from unresolved formative issues that persist and underlie the organization of subsequent phases of development" (Groth, 1978b, p. 6). This molester has failed to develop normally; he sees himself as a child and finds no gratification in the accomplishment of adult tasks. As children, these perpetrators' needs were unmet, and having lost faith in adults they now look to children to meet their dependency and nurturing needs. They find themselves at ease with children and become "sexually addicted" to them (Groth, 1978a).

The regressed pedophile usually does not demonstrate his interest in children until his relationship with adults breaks down. He is often married, and, in fact, may prefer an adult partner if she validates his need to feel adequate. When relationships with peers are too conflictual, he chooses children. Frequently the onset of his molestation behavior can be traced to a crisis in his life. His relationship with a child becomes an impulsive act that underlies his desperate need to cope.

> *Perry was 35 years old when his sexual abuse of children was discovered. He was married and had three sons, all of whom were good athletes and did well in school. Perry was proud of them but vaguely resentful, as he had never excelled at anything. His wife Trudy was employed by a large company where she had worked herself up to a position of some importance. She frequently attended corporate meetings in the evenings and left Perry alone and feeling neglected. His sons were rarely home either, so he'd often go out for a walk or a drive "to think." He was trained as a plumber and made good money. He was much in demand because his customers liked his efficiency and his quiet, friendly manner. Customers' children often watched him work, and he would explain what he was fixing.*
>
> *As Trudy became less and less of a companion, Perry's depression increased. One night on one of his drives, he saw the daughter of a customer walking home. He pulled over and offered her a ride. The child had talked with him on numerous occasions and got in readily. The offer of an ice cream cone was also accepted, and Perry found himself stopping on a deserted road and molesting the child. When she became frightened, he took her home and urged her not to tell. When he arrived home several hours later, an irate Trudy and the police greeted him. The girl had told her parents.*
>
> *After his arrest, Perry admitted that he had "maybe done the same kind of thing before." He remembered molesting a girl while he was in the service, but she apparently never told anyone. He also remembered a brief relationship he had had with a child, when Trudy was pregnant with their last child. Neither he nor his wife had wanted another child, and there had been considerable friction between them. Perry described his relationship with these children as "comforting." He said they gave him something no adult could.*

In deYoung's (1982) sample of pedophiles, 42 percent were regressed. All had had some degree of success relating to adults prior to their "setback" and subsequent abuse of a child. The types of setbacks were most frequently divorce, separation, or marital problems, followed by sexual problems or the pregnancy of their wives. Regressed pedophiles may abuse less frequently than fixated pedophiles because the assaults are usually triggered by some event. If their lives are relatively conflict free, the abusers may act only infrequently.

As mentioned in Chapter 6, both fixated and regressed pedophiles approach children in a variety of ways. Some pressure their victims and others threaten or physically force them.

The pedophile who pressures does so without using physical force. He may use *enticement* in which he cajoles the victim with gifts, treats, and affection. Or he may convince the child of how important he or she is to him. *Entrapment* is also used by abusers who try to make the child feel indebted or obligated to them in some manner. The pressuring pedophile hopes to gain the child's "consent" in the relationship and thus convince himself that the union is mutual rather than abusive or exploitive. If the child refuses, the perpetrator may intensify his efforts to cajole or entrap, but will rarely force the child (Groth, 1978a).

The abusers who force their victims use either *intimidation* or *physical aggression*. Children are in awe of adults. The perpetrator who intimidates uses his power as an adult to commit the abusive act.

> *"He didn't say much," remembers Suzannah. "In fact, I'm not sure he spoke English well; but he was so overpowering." She spoke of the man who had worked at her father's ranch for a short while. Suzannah's family was strict. Her parents insisted that she respect adults. She describes not knowing what to do when the workman took her into the cabin and began undressing her. "His size scared me; he was so big. It was just understood that I'd comply." Suzannah was molested on several occasions by the 6-foot, 7-inch ranchhand. Only after the man had drifted away at the end of the season was she finally able to tell her parents, who admonished her for "making up stories." Suzannah tried to forget; the memories, however, continued to haunt her.*

The motivation of abusers who force themselves on their victims is to complete the sexual act. Force is used when the abuser perceives it necessary. Most likely, he intends no injury to the child, but sees her or him as an object to be exploited and manipulated to his own satisfaction. He is not concerned about the trauma for the victim and he will usually not take no for an answer (Groth, 1978a).

Other abusers actually prefer physical aggression. They, too, are exploiting and plan to do so without the child's consent. This type of abuser is often called a child rapist because of the likelihood that his assault includes penetration. Any type of pedophile may reach the point of intercourse with his victim, but this individual's act more closely approximates the rape of an adult female. Two motivations seem to play a role in child rape—anger and the need for power.

Anger toward a child or something that the child symbolizes may cause the perpetrator to use sex as a weapon. His purpose is to hurt the victim and he often combines physical battering with the sexual assault. Often he does not anticipate abuse, but acts instead on impulse or emotion (Groth, 1979; Prendergast, 1991; Schwartz and Cellini, 1995). One abuser was apprehended after raping the 6-year-old daughter of his girlfriend.

> *"I was so angry when she [the child's mother] broke up with me," he said, "that I just had to find a way to hurt her. The kid was there and it wasn't 'til after I raped her that I realized what I'd done."*

The power rapist sees the child as weak, vulnerable, and unable to resist. The child once again is seen as an object that he uses and discards. Some rapists who have unsuccessfully tried to take their aggression out on adults may make children their targets (Groth, 1979).

A small minority of child molesters are sadistic in their assaults. They are sexually stimulated by hurting the child. Their act is totally premeditated, often taking on an almost ritualistic pattern. The sadistic abuser uses more force than necessary to overcome the child and sometimes kills the child. The child sometimes symbolizes something the abuser hates in himself or perhaps evokes a memory of his disturbed childhood (deYoung, 1982).

Today, according to the National Incidence Studies on Missing, Abducted, Runaway, and Throwaway Children in America (1990), there are between 43 and 147 thousand children abducted and murdered each year. Many of these crimes have a sexual component.

The age of the pedophile can vary, but heterosexual abusers tend to be adolescents, in the mid-30s, or over 60.

Pederasty

Chapter 1 briefly discussed the practice of pederasty among early Greeks. But this practice is not confined to ancient times; pederasty thrives in our culture today.

Geiser (1979) speaks of pederasts as "eternal adolescents in their erotic life. They become fixated upon the youth and sexual vitality of the adolescent boy.... Pederasts love the boy in themselves and themselves in the boy" (p. 83). Rossman (1976) describes pederasts as males over age 18 who are sexually attracted to and involved with young boys who are between ages 12 and 16.

Are pederasts considered pedophiles? In England the answer is affirmative. In the United States, however, the answer lacks clarity. Geiser (1979) differentiates by saying that pedophiles exploit children, whereas pederasts prey on "willing children." Many might disagree with this premise and the semantics, but most agree that pederasty is the abuse of boys, especially those between 12 and 16 years old.

To research the problem of pederasty, Rossman (1976) used questionnaires and interviews with 300 adolescent boys who were sexually involved with adult men, and reviewed the writings of more than 1,000 pederasts. Although there is a small fraction of promiscuous pederasts (called *chicken-hawks*) who seek out boys between ages 12 and 16 for sexual exploitation, Rossman's study found a larger percentage drifted into sex play or sexual relationships with boys as a result of their fantasies or contacts with these youths. Rossman estimated that at least 1 million men in the United States have been sexually involved with teenage boys. Further, he calculated that one of every eight men has pederastic inclinations. From his study, Rossman created a composite of the "typical" pederast.

> He is young or in middle adulthood. He has an above-the-average education, a good job, and is not yet married. He became aware in his young adolescence that he was erotically attracted to boys thirteen or fourteen years old. As he has grown older he has continued to be smitten with boys of that age, one after another. When he had the chance to carry on mutual masturbation with one of these boys, his infatuation and fantasies increased the pleasure and power of the experience over what it would have been for another boy. If he had other adolescent sex play or experience it was with relatives or very close friends. In mid-adolescence he began to date girls, perhaps a bit more than other boys his age, because he was anxious to prove to himself as well as to others that

he was normal. At that time he still hoped that his crushes on boys were a temporary phenomenon and that he would grow out of it.

...In mid and late adolescence he developed a generalized fondness for the company of boys which led him to concentrate his activities in areas of interest to younger boys.... He intended to put his sex play with boys behind him, but every now and then a younger boy he was enamored of would respond with affection and sexual gestures. One or more of these relationships—each lasting a year or more with increasing involvement—would be so happy and emotionally rewarding as to set a pattern for future such relationships. (1976, pp. 197–198)

The pederast usually accepts his interest in boys as a reality, and he may discover other men interested in the same type of relationships. The underground network, therefore, becomes the pederast's form of self-definition. Contact with other pederasts enables him to assert he is not gay but dedicated instead to a particular interest. Such contact may also confirm his ability to marry and in other ways lead a "normal" life.

Rossman suggests there are several behavioral types of pederasts and that these can be placed on a continuum from the more passive and feminine to the aggressively masculine. These behavioral types are characterized by motivational differences.

The *substitute pederast* initiates sexual interaction with a boy when he is temporarily without a female partner. Often a tourist or prisoner, this individual pretends the boy is a woman. The sexual act may be performed with an emotional undertone of warmth or it may be aggressive or sadistic.

The *teacher pederast* sees himself as a tutor for young boys. He initiates a platonic involvement that slips into sexual involvement, sometimes accidentally and sometimes with forethought. Once the sexual acts evolve, he emphasizes giving pleasure to the boy (as well as to himself) as an initiation into sexual activity. Pederasts demonstrating this motivation argue that they are encouraging the adolescent to explore his own sexuality. They see themselves as nurturing and as playing an integral role in the boys' development. Since the boys they engage are often emotionally deprived, the boys often appreciate the attention they receive and seemingly validate the pederast's claims.

The *sports or comrade pederast* sees himself as exceedingly masculine and trains young boys to emulate him. He initiates sexual activities with a rough playful orientation and usually engages them in mutual masturbation, which, he assures his victims, is acceptable behavior "among the guys." Such a pederast would be scandalized by oral or anal sex. Masturbation, on the other hand, he sees as an integral part of individual development. The boys can frequently rationalize this involvement. They are encouraged to sublimate sexual energy in sports activities where their masculine identity is affirmed and strengthened. Therefore, the stereotype of sex between males as being less than masculine is quickly denied.

The *adventurer pederast* is looking for new types of sexual experiences. Although a small percentage of adventurer pederasts in Rossman's sample was promiscuous, many formed relationships with boys and pursued their search for variety in this context. The *sensuous pederast* uses boys for his own pleasure. Boys are sometimes trained by pimps to become experts in appealing to men who crave a pederastic sexual experience. Some pederasts exploit boys in sadistic, neurotic, and physically harmful ways. Fortunately the percentage is small, but the harm to the boys is often great.

Not all men act on their desires for involvement with boys. The *fantasy or fetish pederast* uses pornography or voyeurism to satisfy his needs. He may engage in ritualized spanking of boys or other horseplay, which falls short of actual sexual contacts.

No one cause has been isolated to explain pederasty. Most of the men involved have been aware since adolescence of their interest in boys. For many, masturbation plays a significant role, but apparently does not cause the behavior. Pederasts describe being stimulated by the fact that a boy can be sexually aroused by them and see their ability as a "special gift" (Rossman, 1976).

A variety of boys become victims of the pederast. In their attempts to discover what predisposes boys to this type of liaison, researchers have concluded that inadequate supervision, inadequate sex education, adherence to societal values involving heterosexuality, and social adjustment appear to have little significant influence on boys' likelihood of being part of pederasty. Based on his 300 respondents, Rossman (1976, p. 143) developed a composite of the "typical" boy involved with a pederast. This boy, often one who is relatively self-confident and willing to take risks, has more freedom than the average person to take athletic trips or to go hunting or fishing with someone other than a family member. He is rebellious and "fun-oriented," frequently seeking kicks from drugs, alcohol, stealing, or sex. He probably developed early, has a surplus of sexual energy, and is is sophisticated and experienced in sexual matters. Often from a broken home, this boy is bored with school and with conventional activities. He is not homosexual, expects to marry and have children, but sees recreational sex as a "fun thing" which is different and exciting. This boy is the pederast's dream.

Since pederasty is illegal in our society, men and boys practice it through underground movements. Several organizations currently exist that are only half-hidden from the public. The North American Man Boy Love Association, known as NAMBLA, was created in 1979 in response to the break-up of the "Revere Ring" outside of Boston. The ring had operated for many years and included numerous professional men and more than 60 boys. After several of the men were charged of illegal sexual acts with boys, 32 men and 2 teenage boys organized to protect these kinds of sexual relationships and to defend the "rights" of these youths (Rush, 1980; deYoung, 1982). NAMBLA publishes newsletters and provides a network for pederasts. The René Guyon Society believes that sexuality between men and boys is a natural type of education. Based in Los Angeles, the group argues that the age of consent should be lowered, as reflected in their motto, "Sex by eight is too late" (Geiser, 1979; deYoung, 1982; Kempe and Kempe, 1984). Such groups sometimes appear on TV talk shows to argue for a lower age of consent or the importance of such sexual education for children.

Should pederasty be considered abusive? Since there is so little research available on male sexual victimization, it is only possible to speculate. Organizations of pederasts argue that their proponents neither abuse nor exploit boys. Some say that, unlike the fixated pedophile, the pederast is not reliving the trauma of a sexual assault in his own youth but rather is seeking a reciprocal relationship of sexual pleasure with a boy (Rossman, 1976). Because of this difference in motivation, the pederasts interviewed by researchers indicate that they see themselves as guided by a particular code of ethics:

1. Boys should not be treated as sex objects to be used at the whim of the pederast.

2. Pederasts should know the boy's feelings and interests before a sexual relationship is initiated.

3. A pederast must not cruise to pick up strange boys because that encourages boys to hustle.

4. Protect your reputation as well as the reputation of the boy.

5. At all times be truthful and honest with the boy.

6. Any photographs taken of the boy are for your own use.

7. The boys must consent to the sexual relationship.

8. No alcohol or drugs may be given to the boys.

9. Encourage the boys to initiate and maintain heterosexual relationships.

10. Encourage the boys to stay in school and avoid crime.

11. Teach the boys a code of behavior conducive to respectable social living.

12. Do not share your boys with other pederasts.

13. Never harm the boy. (Rossman, 1976, pp. 192–193; deYoung, 1983, p. 155)

Also, according to Rossman (1976, p. 194), pederast organizations contend that a boy should have the right to

- Privacy for his own personal thoughts, ideas, dreams, and explorations of his body.
- Accurate sex information.
- Enjoy fully whatever sensual pleasures he chooses.
- Learn the art of lovemaking from adequately interpreted experiences of his own choice.
- Affirmative, affectionate relationships with adults of his own choice.

On the other hand, many argue that a child under age 18, by virtue of his insufficient knowledge and lack of authority, cannot consent, and that to ask consent is taking unfair advantage. Another issue for consideration is that of harm to the child. It is known that many boys involved with pederasts do not see themselves as exploited or harmed. The possibility of trauma increases when a boy has been forced. If he agrees to the alliance and is treated gently and with respect, is trauma precluded (Geiser, 1979)? Burgess, Groth, and McCausland (1981) suggest trauma results from the inclusion in and/or disclosure of child sex-initiation rings. Their sample tended to include boys who were younger than Rossman's identified ages of 12 to 16. Tindall (1978) considered long-range effects of pederasty and concluded that there were few of any significance. Clearly, more research must be undertaken in the area of pederasty before any assumptions can be made about the trauma or lack of it.

Sexual Misuse and Exploitation

Sexual Abuse by Clergy

An increased amount of attention has been given in the news media to the abuse of children by religious figures such as priests and ministers. (Currently, no major news story has surfaced about a rabbi.) In August 1993 *Newsweek* featured major coverage of "Sex and the Church" with a discussion of priests who abuse. Jason Berry's book *Lead Us Not Into Temptation* (1992) met with much controversy as it chronicled the abuse by a number of priests during the 1980s. Berry supports the need for such a book by commenting that:

[B]etween 1983 and 1987, more than two hundred priests or religious brothers were reported to the Vatican Embassy for sexually abusing youngsters, in most cases teenage boys—an average of nearly one accusation a week in those four years alone. In the decade of 1982–1992, approximately four hundred priests were reported to the civil authorities for molesting youths. The vast majority had multiple victims. By 1992, the church's financial losses—in victim settlements, legal expenses, and medical treatment of clergy—had reached an estimated $400 million. (p. xix)

The Catholic church should not be singled out as the only religious organization to be plagued by deviant activities among its clergy (despite the fact that in the relatively new body of literature, most has been aimed at abuse by priests). Across the nation, other religious orders and denominations are being disillusioned by reports of clergy abuse.

"When our minister was arrested," reported one mother, *"I couldn't believe it! He used to run the youth group. He was so great with the kids. He'd taken them on trips and was even involved with a Boy Scout troop. I refused to believe that this minister who we all loved could have molested kids. That is until my own son told me that he'd been abused too."*

Some critics contend that the reports of abuse by clergy are "manufactured panic" (Jenkins, 1994, p. 167). Jenkins (1994) points to the issue as providing an "…excuse for a frontal assault on celibacy" (p. 173). This author believes that the magnitude of reports is really a movement, led to some extent by feminists, to question the authority of the church.

The panic is in a sense a perfect weapon, because so few are prepared to question this orthodoxy and hence to challenge its practical consequences. Realizing this, the liberals and feminists have used the abuse ideology as Trojan Horse to enter and subvert many traditional institutions. (p. 175)

Others would say that abuse by priests and clergy has been a fact for years and is only now coming to the surface (Katchen, 1992). For example, James Porter, the former priest, who later left the priesthood and married, admitted to abusing between 50–100 children over a period of 30 years. (He was eventually convicted of molesting his children's babysitter in Minnesota.) Frank Fitzpatrick, investigator and former victim of Porter's, finally confronted the ex-priest, who was living with his wife and children while his former victims sought to repair their lives (Berry, 1992). (Fitzpatrick now offers support and a newsletter as a method of communication to others who were abused by clergy.)

Motivation of Perpetrators

What could possibly motivate a priest, minister, or other religious leader to sexually abuse children? This is a question which has not been well explored to date. Perhaps the only way to deal with this conundrum is to consider what religious life offers and how this fits into the needs of a perpetrator. First and foremost, church leadership brings with it respect and often unquestioned authority. Ministers and priests are usually held up as people who are trustworthy, loyal, and who want the best for those to whom they minister. For an insecure individual, which perpetrators appear to be (Prendergast, 1991), this lauded position would hold great appeal. Further, the trust with which a clergyman or woman is surrounded, offers opportunity to be alone with children, often in a close or nurturing role. Until recently, when abuse by clergy has come under scrutiny, being a religious leader also offered one some degree of protection. The church community will often go to great lengths to deny that their leader is guilty of any deviance. Like the mother quoted earlier, most parishioners find abuse by their priest or minister unbelievable. And finally, Freudian interpretation might suggest that the perpetrator, often abused, neglected, or abandoned by his own mother, is searching for the "all-loving mother." What better candidate for this role than the "mother church"? Some might also argue that celibacy in the Catholic church provides the perpetrator, who is not interested in adult women, with an acceptable alternative.

It should be made clear that despite the fact that the perpetrator may find a haven in the church for the above reasons, there are many healthy members of the clergy who have never and will never be abusive to children. Perpetrators seek out, whether consciously or unconsciously, situations and positions which give them opportunities to be with children. The position of church leader, like numerous other positions, provides that vehicle.

Impact on Victims

Abuse by a minister or priest brings with it the same trauma as abuse by any other trusted adult. There may, however, be an additional factor compounding the trauma. As one survivor put it:

> I was so invested in the church as a kid. To me, being an altar boy was a big deal. It made me feel like somebody. At home things weren't great. My Dad left us when I was little. My Mom had a whole string of boyfriends, most of whom had drug problems. And here was the church where the minister made a big deal of me and I loved the attention. When he started touching my genitals, I didn't know what to think. Before it had gone too far, I found out that he was doing it to other kids. It made me feel like I didn't really count. It also rocked my faith. How could a man of God do that to me?

Survivors often report losing their faith and the desire for a spiritual life after they have been abused by a priest or minister. As many from troubled homes have sought the church as a form of comfort, these victims feel especially shaken by this betrayal. In addition, many wonder how their parents have not known. Why did these parents continue to allow them and even urge them to go to church? Some survivors describe feeling alienated from parents as a result of these feelings (Berry, 1992).

Sexual Abuse in Daycare Settings

In the last few years much publicity has been given to the sexual abuse of children in daycare settings. The Manhattan Beach, California, case, one of the largest and most publicized, involved numerous children and their parents in lengthy investigation and court proceedings. Some of these daycare settings involved ritualistic abuse (see Chapter 6). From this and other such situations evolved a near hysteria over daycare.

Is daycare a safe alternative for child care? asked many parents. Daycare facilities, in general, became suspect. The reality is most adults have a sincere interest in taking care of children, but unfortunately those who have the potential to be or are abusive gravitate to settings where children are available.

The daycare scare stimulated changes—some positive and some negative—in the provision of the service. On the negative side, daycare centers found their insurance rates rose significantly. Centers may pass on this cost in their fees, so they become beyond the financial reach of some parents. Especially vulnerable to insurance hikes were those facilities based in private homes. The increased rates meant that some of these providers were no longer able to operate.

Relationships between children and staff members are also under closer scrutiny. Once available for comforting pats and hugs, some childcare workers express fear about touching their charges and thus deprive the children of a valuable means of communication and demonstration of caring. Although both men and women have been found guilty in recent abuse trials, men seem to be more suspect. Children who have no male contact outside of daycare centers may be denied this opportunity because of the center's hesitancy in hiring or retaining male employees. In addition, more stringent licensing regulations may be decreasing the number of centers available to parents.

On the other hand, some providers applaud the changes brought about by concerns of abuse. Many parents have become more positively involved in their children's substitute care arrangements (Burgess et al., 1990). The media, as well as concerned organizations, have published guidelines for choosing a daycare center. Parents are cautioned to interview staff attentively and be cognizant of policies about discipline, nap time, bathroom visits, and off-limit areas. Protective workers postulate that if just one child can be protected by such publicity, then it is warranted.

Sex Rings

A *sex ring* is an arrangement in which at least one adult is involved sexually with several underage victims (Burgess, Groth, and McCausland, 1981; Lanning and Burgess, 1989; Lanning, 1992). Campagna (1985, p. 61) suggests that these adults may be engaged in

- Production of pornography
- Prostitution
- Molestation by adults of children in the ring (group)
- Sale or transportation of minors for sexual purposes
- Use of juveniles to recruit other youths into the ring
- Use of blackmail, deception, threats, peer pressure, or force to coerce or intimidate children into sexual activity.

Lanning (1992) characterized sex rings as having four dynamics: (1) multiple young victims, (2) multiple offenders, (3) fear as a controlling tactic, and (4) bizarre and/or ritualistic activity (p. 126).

The organization of such rings ranges from small, informal neighborhood groups to intricate, national networks. One of the largest and best-publicized child sex rings was uncovered in December 1977 in Revere, Massachusetts. The media reported that 24 men, including a psychiatrist, a psychologist, and several educators, were indicted. The ring had allegedly exploited 63 boys between the ages of 8 and 13. The boys were reportedly plied with beer and marijuana to induce them into sexual activities. The adults paid between 30 and 50 dollars for their visits with the boys, and of this the boys were allowed to keep 5 to 10 dollars. Along with the arrests, the police confiscated more than 100 pornographic photographs and films of young boys. The ring was obviously well organized and had been in operation for several years. The case rocked conservative Boston and brought to light a phenomenon that few had ever considered. The reactions prompted the Massachusetts House Subcommittee on Children in Need of Services to establish a statewide hotline to deal with other potential victims. A backlash of a different sort gave rise to Boston's North American Man Boy Love Association, which argued for the justification of sexual experience between men and boys (Geiser, 1979).

Sex rings are not reserved exclusively for male victims. Burgess, Groth, and McCausland (1981) described six such rings, three of which concentrated on boys, two involved girls, and one where both girls and boys were exploited. In 1984, Burgess, Groth, and McCausland studied sex rings involving 66 children—49 boys and 17 girls. From their research, these authors concluded there were different types of rings. The *solo ring* consisted of one adult involved with a small group of children whom the perpetrator kept to himself or herself. The *syndicated ring* was a more sophisticated and better-organized network with several adults engaging the children in pornography and prostitution. The *transitional ring* was less organized but might include more than one adult with a number of children.

Sex rings—especially those that are better organized—involve children in a variety of activities and indoctrinate them into a particular mode of thinking. Characteristics of these rings are:

1. *A belief system.* Children are taught that the activities are normal and desirable. This distortion serves to protect the group from revelation to other adults.

2. *Premature sexuality.* Curiosity, awe of adults, and the need for attention are exploited as children are initiated into a variety of sexual activities. Peer pressure is encouraged, which escalates the involvement and ensures that the secret is kept.

3. *Inclusion in pornography and other illicit activities.* Children are encouraged to model what they see in pornographic films and pictures. In turn, they are compelled to become involved in the manufacture of pornographic materials. Often drugs are used as incentives or rewards or to ensure compliance. The fact that pornography and drugs are illegal is used by ringleaders as insurance against disclosure. The children realize that to tell means they, as well as others in the ring, will suffer censure or prosecution.

4. *Recruitment of new members.* Children are encouraged to and rewarded for bringing in other children. (Burgess, Groth, and McCausland, 1984; Holmes, 1991)

Perpetrators gain access to children in a variety of ways. Most often these adults were already involved in the lives of the children. Some had met children in their capacities as teachers, coaches, youth-group leaders, or as neighbors. Sex rings have also been discovered in daycare centers.

How do children become involved in sex-ring activities? Exposed to adults who play roles in their lives, children are often initiated into sex rings without recognizing the implications. They may observe sexual activity between adults and other members and be presented with the idea that such activities are part of group membership. Perpetrators may approach children by showing them pornographic pictures or allowing them to see the perpetrator nude. The perpetrator works to increase the cohesiveness of the group, often building in an element of fear for these are keys to encourage cooperation and discourage disclosure (Lanning, 1992). There seem to be no significant characteristics of children involved in these rings. Burgess and her colleagues in both studies (1981, 1984) found that children involved in sex rings come from different family backgrounds and vary in age from 6 to 16.

Disclosure comes about in various ways. Some children tell adults of their activities either accidentally or in order to extricate themselves. One crisis hotline worker talked frequently with an anonymous youth. He was afraid to tell anyone about his involvement but did not want his young brother to become involved in the ring. Eventually he was convinced to go to the police. The victims may also act out their message through running away or delinquent behavior. Perpetrators are often investigated for other deviant acts, or concerned adults become suspicious of the activities of the perpetrator (Burgess, Groth, and McCausland, 1981; Burgess et al., 1984).

The impact on the victims of sex rings and their disclosure is still being researched. Because children are encouraged to participate and they gain peer support and attention from the rings, the degree of trauma is usually reported to be minimal. Burgess, Groth, and McCausland (1981) did find that parents and children cited genital irritation (urinary infections, soreness), sleep disturbances, altered behavior, appetite problems, and increased daydreaming during the operation of the sex ring. At disclosure, however, the impact for many children increases. It is difficult to determine whether trauma is affected more by the activities of the ring or by the reactions of parents and other adults to what the child has experienced. Some children show little reaction at disclosure. Others experience flashbacks of the events. Vivid memories and dreams cause stress and anxiety for some. Children may suffer ridicule from other children when their involvement in the ring becomes known. Increased risk taking (to affirm masculinity) is often observed in boys who were formerly in rings. Both boys and girls may develop symptoms such as enuresis, fears and phobias, school problems, and somatic problems (Burgess et al., 1984; Lanning, 1992).

Parents, in Burgess's studies, reacted to the disclosure of child sex rings. Initially most reacted with shock or extreme anger or both. Later their reactions appeared to fall into several categories (Burgess, Groth, and McCausland, 1981):

1. *Rationalization.* Parents found ways to rationalize the activity. They assured themselves that at least the activity had taken place in a group and other children besides their own had been involved.

2. *Avoidance.* Some parents preferred not to hear the details, and thus they could deny the full extent of the abuse.

3. *Minimizing.* Parents minimized the degree of seriousness of the events. They were thankful that their children were not maimed, killed, or seriously hurt physically.

4. *Concealment.* Parents often sought to keep the information from spouses, friends, and relatives. The implication was they or their children would be stigmatized by having others know.

5. *Blaming.* Given their anger and feelings of guilt, parents sought someone to blame. Usually they blamed the perpetrator. Sometimes, however, they chided the child with being in the wrong place—or not saying no. Other parents blamed themselves for not knowing or protecting their children.

Involvement in sex rings can have long-term effects on children. Their early indoctrination into adult sexuality certainly distorts their sexual development. Possible outcomes of this sexual trauma are prostitution, sexual dysfunction, delinquency, and substance abuse (Burgess, Groth, and McCausland, 1981). Some research also suggests that sex ring participants may later act out sexually against others (Groth, 1979).

Child Pornography

The production and consumption of child pornography is deeply interwoven in the activities of pedophiles, pederasts, and those involved in rings, sexual trafficking, and child prostitution. Pornography is a stimulant and a byproduct, in many forms, of sexual exploitation of children. Sometimes referred to as *kiddie porn,* child pornography is currently a multi-million dollar business. In his 1976 study, Lloyd estimated that more than 260 child pornography magazines were being sold in the United States. Indications are that this figure has increased. Available for 10 to 15 dollars from pornography dealers, magazines with titles such as *Torrid Tots, Succulent Youth,* and *Dirty Games for Little Girls* advertise their content. One magazine poses children from 3 to 8 years old in suggestively sensual scenes. Paperbacks depict erotic meetings and are designed to stimulate their readers. Travel guides suggest where young people can be found. Publications are filled with ads looking for sexual encounters with children. Films and videotapes are among the most lucrative. Child "actors" demonstrate or observe a variety of sexual encounters (O'Brien, 1983). Attempts to control pornography date back to the 1800s, yet child pornography is very much a part of our culture today.

It is difficult to define *child pornography.* The most inclusive appears to be "sexually explicit material with children as the subject" (O'Brien, 1983, p. 3). The National Center for Missing and Exploited Children (1986) explains that pedophiles collect two types of materials to support their sexual interest in children—child pornography and child erotica. Child pornography, according to NCMEC, is the "sexually explicit reproduction of a child's image, voice, or handwriting—including sexually explicit photographs, negatives, slides, magazines, videotapes, audiotapes, and handwritten notes" (p. 17). The NCMEC further classifies pornography as commercial (produced for wide distribution and sale) or homemade (intended for individual consumption). Child erotica is "any material relating to children that serves a sexual purpose for a given individual" (p. 18). Types of erotica include souvenirs, letters, toys, games, and sexual aids. The difference between erotica and pornography is that in the production of the latter, children are victimized.

Pornography represents specific uses to the pedophilic consumer. First, it provides him with a means of sexual arousal. With pornographic pictures, films, and tapes, he stimulates his fantasies, often as a prelude to masturbation or sexual activity with children. Child molesters also use pornography to lower children's inhibitions. Children who see peers engaging in sex and apparently enjoying it may be more likely to comply with the molester's demands. The exploitation of a child may include taking pictures or movies of the child, which the pedophile subsequently uses as a form of blackmail to compel the child to keep the sexual activities a secret.

Second, the NCMEC (1986) also notes that pornographic collections are important to pedophiles. Some perpetrators use the materials they have produced as a medium of exchange. By trading pornography with others, the pedophile broadens his own collection and varies his stimuli. And finally, pornography is used for profit. Those who reap the most significant profit, however, do not appear to be pedophiles. Although those interested in children consume and sometimes produce the materials, commercial dealers, who reproduce and distribute, amass the bulk of the financial gains (Jarvie, 1992).

True collectors of pornography place a great deal of emphasis on the acquisition of materials, never feeling that they have quite enough. Collections are often organized, filed, documented, or catalogued—even on computers. Currently computers, especially E-Mail, figure largely in the communication system between pornographers and victims. Concealment is necessary because the illegal nature of much of this business makes collectors vulnerable. Yet others take pride in their collection and share the materials with other pedophiles. The risk of sharing versus concealment often provides a bonus in the way of excitement.

Who is the perpetrator of child pornography? To survive and flourish, child pornography depends on a producer (or perpetrator) and a collector. Campagna describes such a collector:

> The pedophile collector of kiddie porn is the archetype of sexual exploitation; his is a world of sexual obsessions and, in a sense, moral consumption. The deeper he plunges into the market, buying, selling, and trading duplicate and triplicate films and photos of child pornography, the harder it is for him to recognize and accept legal and social bans. Like a stamp or coin collector, he devotes a sizeable portion of his discretionary income toward the purchase of pornography. To that end, he will actively seek out new contacts and sources of materials. By a process of communication with other fellow collectors and through trial and error, he will eventually insure a steady flow of fresh materials. (1985, p. 68)

O'Brien (1983) cautions that perpetrators are not all alike. She suggests, however, that a composite points to a white male between the ages of 25 and 40, who is married and has children. He may be of any socioeconomic status, but is usually involved with and respected in the community. Producers of pornography are not just individuals. Sex rings, organized crime, and business groups seek to profit from the production of pornographic materials. For the freelance pornographer or the leader of a sex ring, pornography is combined with a sexual interest in children. The perpetrator enjoys watching children and he photographs them. He may involve himself sexually with his subjects. Most of the production of child pornography is undertaken by pedophiles and pederasts. In the film *Fallen Angel,* the perpetrator, Howie, began his relationship with Jennifer, his female victim, by snapping her picture and commenting on her attractiveness. Eventually he molested Jennifer, but first he engaged her by showing her explicit photos of children involved in sexual activity. He continued to photograph her in various poses and in varying degrees of undress, until he had desensitized her sufficiently to involve her in the production of pornographic films. The actual filming was done by others, but it was Howie's role to engage and supply the child "actors." At his apartment, Howie also kept a group of boys who participated in illegal films. This male sex ring provided a home base for the boys, and their affiliation with and affection for the perpetrator strengthened their belief in their "business."

Such a scenario is not unusual. Perpetrators are skilled in engaging children to participate by appealing to their need for attention, enjoyment of belonging to a group, and their enthusiasm over "earning a living." (Children are not frequently paid in cash, but rather with gifts, housing, and attention.)

Much of pornography is produced at a local level by men who are pedophiles or who run sex rings. They use low-grade equipment of retail quality and engage their victims from among their acquaintances. Their materials are sold directly or by mail to interested parties. In addition to local production, pornography is also developed on a regional, national, and international scale. Regional producers hire freelance photographers who use low-grade equipment but develop materials in their own studios. Sometimes parents are encouraged to volunteer their children through bribes or blackmail. The producers may be transient, moving their business if disclosure seems imminent. The material is distributed by mail, direct purchase, or through adult book stores.

National and international production of child pornography is undertaken on a large scale. Equipment is sophisticated and mass production techniques are more advanced. Nationally, organized crime as well as freelance photographers are involved. Internationally, syndicate sex rings and entrepreneurs in addition to freelance people are responsible for the actual photography and reproduction. Mobile production sites and intricate business fronts are used to ensure secrecy. Materials are mailed, sold in adult bookstores, and purchased through catalogues (Campagna, 1985). For these producers, child pornography is a sophisticated, smooth-running business.

There are few common characteristics to identify the victims of child pornography. Most fall between the ages of 10 and 16, but younger and older models are also used. Blondes are often preferred.

Debbie is an example of a girl involved in pornography. At age 9, she frequented a local shopping mall, mainly to escape from her alcoholic mother who often beat her. From the age of 3 to 5, Debbie had been molested by an uncle. When he was killed in a bar, Debbie was freed from his exploitation. Adult sex wasn't new to Debbie, either. She had observed her mother's activities with boyfriends on numerous occasions.

At the mall, Debbie hung around the arcade. She was bored and lonely and quite vulnerable to a nice-looking man who began to pay attention to her and treat her to candy bars and soda. Before long he was taking her to his apartment and videotaping her in various activities. She met his other "young friends" and heard how they "made movies." By the time her benefactor offered her "a movie contract" to do pornographic films, Debbie was thoroughly enmeshed in his way of life. For her, the type of acting required of her meant little, but the attention and status she gained for doing it meant everything.

Male victims are often engaged by peers. Certain characteristics make some boys vulnerable to being lured into pornography: boys without close religious affiliation, with no strong father figure, in need of money, or upset by family unrest (such as death, divorce, or a recent move). Boys and girls who are runaways, come from broken or impoverished homes, or who are estranged from their families make excellent targets for the pornographer (O'Brien, 1983).

O'Brien (1983) described several steps in the cycle of child pornography (see Figure 8.1). First, the perpetrator uses *enticement* through psychological or material rewards. He gives time and a great deal of energy to engaging children. He seeks to understand them—discern their likes and dislikes—so that he knows exactly what will appeal to them. The perpetrator acts concerned about the child and plies him or her with gifts and affection. *Excitement* is the next step. Self-conscious children with fragile egos and awkward, growing bodies find excitement in the perpetrator's assurances that they are "movie star quality." The perpetrator encourages them to pose for pictures, flattering them and encouraging them to display more and more of their bodies. Eventually they pose nude with other victims or even with adults until they become comfortable with "action shots" of sexual acts (Lloyd, 1976). Drugs are often used to heighten the excitement and diminish inhibitions. *Entrapment* occurs when the child begins to feel that it is impossible to escape the relationship. "After all I've done for you," the perpetrator insists, and the child feels compelled to continue and keep the activities secret. Perpetrators use a variety of methods to avoid detection. They may threaten harm or blackmail, or play on the child's fondness for them. Pressure from peers in the pornography circle also encourages the child to keep the secret. By now the child has begun to feel there is nothing wrong with the pornographic activities, and the perpetrator encourages this belief.

Exit or disclosure takes place in many ways. In the earlier discussion of sex rings, disclosures were described in Burgess's (1981, 1984) studies. By the point of disclosure, the

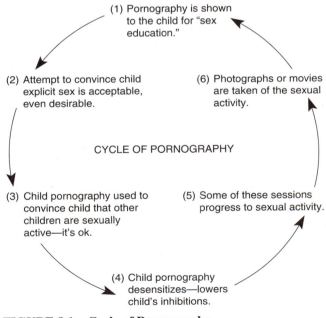

FIGURE 8.1   Cycle of Pornography

pornographic production group has become much like a sex ring. The most difficult part of disclosure for a child is overcoming the guilt of having "voluntarily" participated.

The long-term effects for children engaged in pornography are not unlike those of children in the sex rings. The most significant problems in the victims' futures seem to involve the direction and values in their lives. They may have difficulty separating love and sex, gaining a true sense of their own worth, and seeing themselves on a par with their peers. Because their experiences differ so completely from "normal" children, pornography victims often find themselves becoming reinvolved in a deviant lifestyle. Sex is something they know; using sex for attention or for a feeling of importance or to make money is part of their history. It is not surprising that pornographic "stars" often continue in the business or turn to prostitution. It is not unlikely for such individuals to later become involved in the production of child pornography (O'Brien, 1983).

Child Prostitution

After three years of study, Lloyd (1976) estimated there were 300,000 males under age 16 prostituting in the United States. The studies by Densen-Gerber and Hutchinson (1978) and Densen-Gerber (1980) suggested that there were equally as many girls. In a nationwide survey of 596 police departments, Campagna (1985) and his associate Don Poffenberger conservatively estimated that between 100,000 and 200,000 juveniles, with an average age of 15, are engaged in full-time prostitution. Child prostitution is rooted in antiquity. More recently, the history of various cultures abounds with reports of child prostitution. For example, early Chinese immigrants included girls who were sold by their fathers and brought to America to serve as prostitutes (Mass, 1991). Why, then, has it only recently come to the attention of researchers, therapists, and theorists? Perhaps several factors contribute to its incidence and to its study.

The so-called hippies and the counterculture of the 1960s was one that brought this type of exploitation into focus. In the Haight-Ashbury district of San Francisco, the urban working class residences gave way, in the mid-1960s, to the hippies—middle-class young people dedicated to the overthrow of the political and social views of the previous generation. Approximately 7,000 young people were said to have inhabited this one district. The hippies espoused the power of innocence, the importance of "doing one's own thing," as well as a life of instant gratification, which encompassed sexual permissiveness. This sexual laissez-faire attitude, compounded by the transient nature of their lifestyle and the often immediate need for food, shelter, and money to live, created a vulnerability for involvement in prostitution. Groups seeking to deal with the burgeoning problem were faced with epidemics of venereal diseases and drug abuse. Although the hippie problem died out quickly, their existence had a great impact on our culture (Weisberg, 1985).

The hippie population was commonly made up of teens who had fled their homes. The problem of runaways began to take on its own identity, as the media told the story and social agencies explored new solutions. In the early 1970s, the mass murder in Houston of young runaways further highlighted the problem. The general public was alerted to the issues by countless articles and by Ambrosino's popular book, *Runaways* (1971). The attention given the problem culminated in the Runaway Youth Act in 1974. The legislation offered funds and technical assistance to communities seeking to combat the problem (Weisberg, 1985).

Lloyd's *For Money or Love* (1976) illuminated the prostitution of male children as a byproduct of the runaway problem. Lloyd's book made a formal connection between runaways and prostitution and intensified the focus on both.

The child abuse movement has helped reveal the widespread problem of child prostitution. As professionals explored the after-effects of maltreatment, prostitution was noted as a major consequence. Prostitution was also found to be intertwined with pornography, physical abuse, and other types of exploitation. In 1974, the Child Abuse Prevention and Treatment Act expanded the definition of *sexual abuse* to include "negligent treatment or maltreatment," which, by many, is interpreted to include child prostitution.

The children's rights movement is the last significant influence on our attitude toward child prostitution. Surfacing in the mid-1960s, children's rights have been the basis for a variety of court decisions. The Gault case in the late 1960s had a major impact on the recognition of the rights of children. When 15-year-old Gerald Gault was placed in a detention center after allegedly making an obscene phone call, neither he nor his parents were offered legal counsel. The result was Gault's incarceration in the Arizona State Industrial School, ostensibly until his majority. The American Civil Liberties Union eventually brought the case to the U.S. Supreme Court on May 15, 1967, and established the precedent that children—like adults—have constitutional rights to counsel, to face the accuser, and the right to avoid self-incrimination (Giovannoni and Becerra, 1979). The Gault decision alerted the public and the legal system to the importance of children's rights.

Throughout the 1970s, the movement for the rights of children blossomed. Today, the recognition of these rights includes protection from exploitation and abuse.

In 1977, Congress considered the sexual exploitation of children as an extension of the concerns over child abuse as well as children's rights. The conclusions reached stressed the harm done to children through their engagement in prostitution and the inefficiency of current laws dealing with the problem. Since that time, the National Center on Child Abuse and Neglect has awarded four grants to study child prostitution and pornography, through which more has been learned about child prostitution and exploitation (Weisberg, 1985).

Profile of the Prostitute

Background

Juveniles who enter prostitution are often from similar backgrounds. Most are from dysfunctional family systems. James (1980) discovered that 70 percent of the girls in prostitution reported the absence of one or more parent during childhood. Silbert and Pines (1981) stated that 75 percent, or three-fourths of the girls in their study, were raised by one parent. Juvenile prostitutes report poor relationships with parents and other family members. Some girls had mothers who were themselves prostitutes (Newman and Caplan, 1981).

Sexual abuse in the family of origin has long been associated with later prostitution in adulthood (see Figure 8.2). Juvenile prostitutes also report incestuous experiences in their younger years (James, 1980; Silbert and Pines, 1981). Campagna (1985, p. 12) comments, "Typically the victims of sexual abuse at the hands of their father, stepfather, or uncle, girl hustlers see prostitution as an exit from an intolerable home life." The sexual abuse they

FIGURE 8.2   Steps to a Way of Life

From O'Brien, *Child Pornography*. Copyright © 1983 by Kendall/Hunt Publishing Co. Reprinted with permission.

suffered at home was often of long duration. Acquaintance with sexuality in this exploitive manner teaches the young girl that sex can be used. She learns to separate her feelings from the sexual experience—a technique that accounts for her survival and now enables her to prostitute herself. James (1980) noted that a large percentage of girl prostitutes were raped at least once in their lives. Mollica and Son (1989) describe rape of Asian and South American women who were held as political prisoners or in their first flight as refugees. Certainly some of these women were young enough to be considered children. Some of these children fell into prostitution when they reached this country. The association between sex and violence further insulates the prostitute from emotional involvement. Between 60 and 70 female child prostitutes were physically abused—many with extreme brutality—prior to their emancipation (James, 1980; Silbert and Pines, 1981). Other girls are from neglectful homes. Some spent their lives in institutions and see prostitution as a means of escape (Densen-Gerber, 1980; Campagna, 1985).

Boys enter prostitution from similar backgrounds. Many are raised by one caregiver. The indifference or hostility in their family of origin is marked. It is not unusual for boy prostitutes to have had different caregivers during their younger years. A few may have spent time in institutional care (Weisberg, 1985). Physical and emotional abuse are often significant elements in the boys' backgrounds. Weisberg identified 34 percent as victims of physical abuse and 38 percent of emotional abuse. The emotional abuse tends to center on belittling the youth or derisive comments about his budding homosexuality.

An even larger percentage of young male prostitutes are victims of neglect. Some felt compelled to leave their homes, whereas others were forceably evicted by unconcerned parents. Some 29 percent of Weisberg's sample of young male prostitutes were sexually abused by a family member; 15 percent were abused by nonfamilial perpetrators. Weisberg suggests that the relatively low percentage of those reporting abuse as children is misleading. It may be that many more boys who go into prostitution were exposed to early sexual experiences, but the victims themselves have not labeled these experiences as abusive (Lloyd, 1976; Weisberg, 1985).

> When he was 9 years old, Teddy was molested by a man in the men's bathroom at a park. As Teddy started to come out of the bathroom, the man pushed him back in, locked the door, pulled a knife, and insisted that Teddy comply with his demands. At first Teddy was frightened. Once the man felt Teddy would not resist, he began to be more gentle and even talkative. On several other evenings, Teddy found himself returning to the park—almost hoping to meet the man. Anything was more enjoyable for him than listening to the fights of his alcoholic mother and her equally drunk boyfriend. On the fourth meeting, Teddy's acquaintance gave him five dollars. That was the last time he saw the man, but this was Teddy's initiation into prostitution. Teddy does not see his experience as abusive. Rather, he sees it as a bright spot in his childhood.

Boys and girls seem to have somewhat different reasons for going into prostitution. Girls are reported to be motivated by the rage, depression, and a sense of helplessness they experience as a result of deprived childhoods. They feel worthless and can therefore be easily exploited by pimps, who praise their worth as sex objects (Newman and Caplan, 1981; Jarvie, 1992). Flight from dysfunctional homes often leads to being picked up by pimps who provide some security. Police estimate that a runaway seeking to exist on the streets of a city will be driven to prostitution within four days. Although some authors suggest that girls usually start prostituting themselves when they are on their own and need money to survive, James (1980) argues that although economic issues are important, the meeting of other needs is more influential in their entrance into prostitution.

Boys, on the other hand, cite money as the primary factor in choosing to prostitute. This is especially interesting in light of Campagna's (1985, p. 11) contention that "the world of boy prostitutes is characterized by lower earnings than girl hustlers, free-lance studies and fewer tricks per night." Weisberg (1985) indicates that 87 percent of her respondents engaged in prostitution for the money. Many youths described their earnings as "easy money." Boys who consider themselves homosexual reported that they were drawn to prostitution for the sexual contacts (27 percent), for adventure (19 percent), and for sociability (11 percent); only a few boys in Weisberg's study prostituted to obtain drugs (3 percent) or to seek attention (5 percent).

Lifestyle

Not all juvenile prostitutes pursue their trade full time. Weisberg cites four types of prostitute styles; situational (those who only engage in prostitution under certain circumstances); habitual (those who are full-time participants of street life); vocational (those who consider prostitution a skilled profession); and avocational (those who also see themselves as professionals but not on a full-time basis). Most juvenile prostitutes are habitual or situational.

Sometimes called *weekend warriors,* the part-time or situational prostitutes devote themselves to the "trade" while maintaining a seemingly normal life. The youths work on weekends, evenings, or perhaps when an old customer or a new referral comes along (Campagna, 1985). Full-time prostitutes use this activity to survive rather than to make extra money. This need to survive makes them much more vulnerable as they are not as apt to "screen" clients.

The setting of the hustling also varies. Street solicitation takes place in truck stops, on roadways (hitchhiking), arcade game rooms, tourist locales, bus and train terminals, city parks, bars, convenience stores, and military bases. Sheltered settings include sex clubs, adult book stores, homes, escort services, hotels, massage parlors, and pornographic theaters (Campagna, 1985).

The life of a boy prostitute or "chicken" varies according to his age, his degree of experience, and the setting of his activities. While one boy waits on the street for customers or "chickenhawks," another is "on call" at his apartment, waiting for his client to come to him. Lloyd describes how many boys meet their customers. Boys in New York City wait for their Johns in one of many arcades. The John stops by the machines one particular boy is playing and appraises him. Eye contact means that the complex ritual is about to begin.

> The boy asks for a quarter. A "no" indicates no interest in that particular boy. With a "yes" the man makes his interest known. While the boy plays the machine, he and the man look each other over. The man offers encouragement—and increasing interest—with additional quarters.
>
> The second stage is usually initiated by the boy. He says he's hungry and would like to eat.... If the adult and boy agree to use each other, they will then check into a hotel. In that midtown section of New York, there are many cheap hotels that depend on prostitutes for much of their business.... By the time the chicken and chickenhawk start to undress the man knows just what he's going to get for the fifteen dollars he must pay. The boy has detailed just what he will and won't do though it's not uncommon for the "won't do" to be done in return for supplemental payment. (1976, pp. 12–13)

Other boy prostitutes pick up customers in movie houses or at train or bus stations. If the men do not choose to rent a hotel room, boys are adept at servicing their customers in a darkened theater or restroom. The street boy is often of lower socioeconomic origin. Middle-class boys often use hitchhiking as their introduction to clients (Geiser, 1979).

Violence is a constant threat for young male prostitutes. Unprotected by pimps, they must be constantly watchful of the men they accommodate. It is not uncommon to be assaulted by a customer. On the other hand, boys have been known to rob their clients, often with the help of a juvenile colleague.

Boys may very well be taking or selling drugs. In fact, prostitution may be the way they support their habit. Drugs not only relax the defenses but also may be a medium of exchange, instead of money (Lloyd, 1976).

The girl prostitute or "hustler" usually depends on a pimp for her connections and her protection. She may engage in one or more types of prostitution. Some girls are "on the street," meaning they solicit their own customers. The encounter is often brief, lasting only about 30 minutes from the initial contact until parting. The girl attracts her customers, and the two agree on a price as well as the services that will be provided. The prostitute directs the customer to a location—often an inexpensive hotel catering to by-the-hour traffic. Young prostitutes learn to service customers in cars and other settings as well (James, 1980).

Another girl may be involved in the "circuit" or in a bordello. The circuit is a string of cities in which a child prostitute works—usually for a period of two to four weeks. A booking agent, or sometimes the girl's pimp, arranges where she will go, transportation, and the length of the stay. The agent is compensated for this service by a commission; in the case of the pimp, his girl's "take" is enough. The girl is met immediately when she arrives to ensure that she keeps the agreement. This type of arrangement is difficult to intercept because investigation requires a lengthy, costly, and cumbersome cross-state search (Campagna, 1985).

Bordellos are often used to house girls who work the circuit. Bordellos are especially favored by pimps because the girl can be easily watched and cared for by the owner of the house. The prostitute's earning power increases as she need not hunt for customers on the street.

Donald Poffenberger, researching child sexual exploitation along with Daniel Campagna (1985, pp. 17–18), interviewed 16-year-old Eve, a veteran prostitute who had experienced circuit and bordello life. The product of a lower-class family, she preferred prostitution to the sexual violence at the hands of her stepfather.

Don: *Your first time on the streets; what was it like?*

Eve: *My pimp, a bartender, took me to Pittsburgh. I was on a corner in a pink skirt and he was in a cafe nearby. I was very scared but I did it for the money.*

Don: *What kind of money are we talking about? Did he tell you how much to charge?*

Eve: *Oh, not in so many words. He told me the price ranges and it's really up to you how much you charge.... For certain things you'd never go for under twenty dollars. Or, in other cases, you'd never go under fifty dollars. There was always a certain rate for different things.*

Don: *Did you set the price by a guy's looks, his car, or by the sex act?*

Eve: *By the act. Prostitution made me feel real low but safe. Like nothing would happen to me that I didn't want to have happen. I made about $400 the first few days.*

When asked if she'd ever worked in a bordello, Eve responded affirmatively (pp. 18–19). A friend had arranged it for her in response to police pressure on street prostitutes.

Eve: *When I first got there an old lady…sat me down at a table and explained everything about the house…. There were two other girls working. One girl was thirteen and the other was sixteen. The lady said we were supposed to lie about our age if the cops ever came. They never did.*

Don: *Tell me about the working routine.*

Eve: *You wear a body suit. When tricks come they ring the doorbell; the lady asks for identification, talks to them, finds out how many times they've been there before. Just procedures so no one new ever gets in.*

Don: *They had to have new customers, didn't they?*

Eve: *Yeah, usually old customers bring new people. Anyways, we would stand in the line-up while the trick checked us out. If he picked me we'd go upstairs, he'd paid [sic] me, and I would shove the money down a pipe to the downstairs money box. Then you check him out for V.D. You always worried about someone coming in you know….*

Don: *What about prices?*

Eve: *Prices are exactly like those on the street, but at the house there are more tricks and it's a lot easier.*

Don: *On a Friday or Saturday night, how many tricks would you have?*

Eve: *My first day I'm pretty sure I had at least thirty.*

Although somewhat safer than the street girl, the bordello girl still worries about violence. Customers may beat her or rob her. Possession of large sums of money makes girls vulnerable to violence and robbery. Pimps, too, use violence to keep their girls in line. This can be particularly difficult as she depends on her pimp for managing and keeping her money, clothes, protection, and making her feel important. Pimps are often loved by their girls (known as their "stable"), and pimps guide and teach them during their earlier years. The girls turn over their earnings; he in turn protects them from the police, violent customers, and sometimes pregnancy (Silbert and Pines, 1981).

Campagna (1985) identifies several types of pimps—the "Sweet Mac," the "Gorilla," and the "Business Manager."

A Sweet Mac is the street equivalent of a child psychiatrist. His expertise in human nature, its strengths and foibles, enables him to discover a child's needs or weak spots. Without resorting to outright violence, the Sweet Mac manipulates a juvenile into a state of total dependency. To do so requires forethought and planning. The goal of the Sweet Mac is to lead her away from her family and friends by exposing her to parties, drugs, and new clothes. He convinces her that she is important to him, and he becomes a surrogate parent or boyfriend.

For several days he entertains her and often takes her to another state to complete her separation from all she knows. He suggests that she get an apartment of her own, but first moves her in with a friend of his (often called his "booster lady"), who encourages the girl and convinces her that having sex with strangers is not a bad way to make money. The booster lady may even provide demonstrations with her own tricks. After several weeks, the young girl is ready. The pimp arranges that her first customer is gentle and loving. The initiation of a new girl is often referred to as "turning out."

The Gorilla uses brute force and fear instead of the subtle coercion of the Sweet Mac. He either purchases his girls from alcoholic parents or blackmails them into service. Eventually he compels his young victims to recruit others. Often he drugs a hesitant or unwilling girl, takes her to his apartment, and has a friend sexually abuse her while he films the event. Blackmail ("You wouldn't want Mom and Dad to see this, would you?") usually serves to ensure her cooperation.

The Gorilla makes a business out of his pimping. He carefully assesses the area in which he hopes to place his girls. Connections are made with local bartenders and others who get a commission for their referrals. The Gorilla is adept at paying off police and others who might interfere with his operation.

This pimp does not particularly like children. He sees them as his financial future and has no compunctions about beating them, getting them on drugs, or killing them if need be.

The Business Manager trains his girls to appeal to middle- and upper-middle-class professionals. He often hails from this background himself. Quality is his most important product, and the prostitutes he provides are far superior to those working the streets. He uses legitimate investments and businesses to cover his activities. To get his girls, the Business Manager does not resort to trickery but rather buys them from willing parents. The promise of large fees frequently appeals to the greed of the guardians. The girl is thrown directly into prostitution, but often agrees in the expectation of financial rewards. Her on-the-job training sets her up for a future of soliciting. The girls are "on call" and not forced to work the streets. In addition to his juvenile call girls, the Business Manager may also have adult prostitutes and deal in pornography. His seeming legitimacy and status in the community reduces significantly the possibility of exposure.

Both male and female prostitutes lead precarious and often short lives. Their earnings may be significant, but they rarely have the opportunity to fully enjoy them.

Missing Children

Every year thousands of children turn up missing from their homes. The National Center for Missing and Exploited Children (1985) suggests these children fall into four categories: (1) voluntary missing or runaways, (2) parental kidnappings, (3) abduction by unknown individuals or nonfamily members, and (4) unknown missings. Custody disputes in divorce cases often lead to one parent taking children from another. Some see parental kidnapping as a form of emotional maltreatment, and such a problem must be addressed by courts settling divorce and custody cases.

The other three categories, however, often cause a child to be raped or sexually molested, or lead to pornography, prostitution, and even murder. The problem of missing children should be influenced by the movement to protect children against physical and sexual assault and exploitation (see Figure 8.3). Only by recognizing the need to join forces can society truly ensure the protection of its children.

FIGURE 8.3   Don't Let Your Child Be among the Missing

1. Have your child fingerprinted and keep the card in a safe accessible place, along with pictures updated every 6 months and an accurate description, including scars.

2. Teach your children their telephone number, area code and address.

3. Show your children how to dial the operator and what to say. (Tell them to stay on the line, if possible.) Practice this.

4. Know where your child is at all times.

5. Don't let your child go to a public restroom alone.

6. Don't leave your child alone in the car.

7. Don't put your child's name—first or last—on hats, caps, jackets, bikes, wagons, etc. Remember, a child responds to a first name. A person using that name will automatically not be thought of as a stranger.

8. Teach your children to avoid strangers. A stranger is someone they don't know very well.

9. Don't leave your children in the toy section of a store or wandering in a mall. If they do get lost or bothered, tell them to go to the cashier for help.

10. Know your child's friends.

11. Be involved in your child's activities.

12. Practice with your child ways he/she may walk to and from friends' homes or school.

13. Make it clear to your child to whose home he/she may go to play or visit.

14. Teach your child which homes are "safe" to go into near your home when you are not around.

15. Listen when your child tells you that he/she doesn't want to be with someone. Find out the reason.

16. Notice if someone pays undue attention to your child.

17. Teach your child that it is okay to say "no" to unwanted touching. Believe what your child says about unwanted touches. Reassure the child that what happened was not his/her fault.

18. Encourage parent-child communication.

19. Never belittle any fear or concern your child has—real or imaginary.

20. Tell your children that if anything happens, you will look for them no matter how long it takes to find them.

21. Organize safe houses in your neighborhood with signs in the windows. Teach the children to go there if they are frightened.

TO REPORT A MISSING CHILD OR TO GIVE INFORMATION ABOUT A MISSING CHILD, CALL:

1-800-235-3535
(The Missing Child Network),
in affiliation with the Society for Young Victims
or
1-800-THE LOST (843-5678)
(National Center for Missing and Exploited Children)

From the National Center for Missing and Exploited Children.

Summary

Recognition that a significant percentage of children are abused by family members does not negate the need to consider those children abused or misused outside the home. The first component necessary for a child to be abused outside the family is for the perpetrator to gain access to the child or have the opportunity. Children are abused by pedophiles—individuals who either prefer children sexually or for whom sexual contacts with adults have become too conflicted. Pedophiles could have contact with children in a variety of ways—as friends, teachers, coaches, or even ministers or priests. Pederasty is another type of exploitation of children. Pederasts prey on young boys whom they befriend and initiate into sexuality. Since pederasty is illegal in this country, pederasts often operate in underground groups such as NAMBLA or the René Guyon Society. Organizations of pederasts are guided by a code of ethics and see themselves as benefiting rather than harming the child. There is some controversy over whether or not inclusion in pederasty has lasting traumatic effects for the young victim.

Children are also sexually exploited through sex rings, pornography, and prostitution. A sex ring is a group of children brought together by the perpetrator for the purpose of molestation, pornography, prostitution, or other sexual purposes. Sex rings are characterized by a belief system, premature introduction to sexuality, and the exposure of children to a variety of illicit activities. Trauma resulting from these activities may be based, in part, on the reaction of concerned adults at disclosure. Parents understandably deny, avoid, rationalize, and minimize their children's involvement in such rings, often blaming their children as well as the perpetrator and themselves.

Child pornography is a significant problem in the United States. Efforts have been made since the 1800s to curb this type of exploitation of children. Pornography is used to engage children in sexual abuse relationships and may also be the end product of the perpetrator's exploitation. Both male and female chil-

dren are used in pornography. The child is enticed and entrapped by the skillful perpetrator and may find that the only alternative is through continuing in the career, often as a producer or through prostitution.

Child prostitution, although an old form of exploitation, has more recently been brought to light by several groups: (1) the hippies in the 1960s, (2) runaways and their helpers, (3) the child abuse movement, and (4) the children's rights movement. Both male and female children, often seeking refuge from disturbed or abusive homes, become involved in prostitution. Boys are less likely to be sponsored by pimps but are more subject to violence. Girls typically are "managed" by adult males who do so either as surrogate fathers or lovers or from a purely business perspective. Some pimps are abusive and use threats and blackmail to ensure cooperation. Children are indoctrinated into prostitution by skilled adults. Boys are promised money and freedom, while girls value the attention and a sense of belonging provided by pimps—as well as the promise of financial gains. While boys are often able to exit from prostitution and lead relatively normal lives, girls are more likely to go into adult prostitution as a means of survival.

Our nation continues to be concerned over the plight of missing children. Children are abducted by parents, and many run away or are lured away by perpetrators. Until society fully understands the dangers to children who are separated or unsupervised by caregivers, it will be difficult to provide our children with the protection they need and deserve.

Exploration Questions

1. What might make a child vulnerable to being abused outside of the family?

2. What causes pedophiles to be interested in children? In what ways might a pedophile engage a child in sexual activities?

3. Why might clergy abuse children?

4. What is a pederast? On whom do pederasts prey? What types are there?

5. What argument do pederasts give as to why their contacts with children should not be considered abusive?

6. What is a sex ring? What characteristics do sex rings have?

7. What are the reactions of parents at the disclosure of their child's involvement in a sex ring? What problems does this create?

8. What is child pornography? What efforts have been made to curb it?

9. What are the uses of child pornography for perpetrators?

10. What is the cycle of child pornography?

11. What factors created the current public awareness of child prostitution?

12. What are some similarities and differences between male and female child prostitutes? What types of prostitutes are there?

13. What types of pimps are mentioned in the chapter? What effect might each have on the prostitute?

14. What are some residual effects of a child's involvement in prostitution or pornography?

Activities for Applied Learning

1. See the movie *Fallen Angel*. Discuss the engagement of the victim, the personality of the perpetrator and his relationship with his victim, the origination of the pornography activities, the reaction of the parent on disclosure, and the residual effects on the victim.

2. Through newspapers and magazines, research the subject of a major sex ring, such as the Revere Ring (see *Boston Globe* from 11 November 1977 through 2 May 1978) or of abuse by priests. Consider the perpetrators and victims. In addition, what influence does the media have on such stories?

3. Keep a notebook of news clippings on incidences of child pornography and or prostitution. How prevalent is the problem?

4. Obtain a copy of *Protection of Children Against Sexual Exploitation,* Hearings before the Subcommittee to Investigate Juvenile Delinquency of the Committee on Judiciary of the U.S. Senate, 95th Cong., 1st sess., 1978; and *Sexual Exploitation of Children,* Hearings before the Subcommittee on Crime, U.S. House of Representatives, Serial #12, 95th Cong., 1st sess., 1977. Both are available from the Government Printing Office, Washington, DC. How effective were these hearings? How would you design a law to protect children without disregarding the rights of adults?

5. Obtain a copy of your state's child protection laws. How is pornography addressed? What is the penalty for pornography? for prostitution? for child molestation?

Suggested Readings

Able-Peterson, T. *Children of the Evening.* New York: Putnam, 1981.

Ambrosino, L. *Runaways.* Boston: Beacon Press, 1971.

Berry, J. *Lead Us Not Into Temptation,* New York, Doubleday, 1992.

Burgess, A.; Hartman, C.; McCausland, M.; and Powers, P. "Response Patterns in Children and Adolescents Exploited Through Sex Rings and Pornography." *American Journal of Orthopsychiatry* 141 (1984):656–62.

Geiser, R. L. *Hidden Victims.* Boston: Beacon Press, 1979.

James, J. *Entrance into Juvenile Prostitution.* Washington: National Institute of Mental Health, 1980.

Linedecker, C. L. *Children in Chains.* New York: Everest House, 1981.

Lloyd, R. *For Money or Love: Boy Prostitution in America.* New York: Vanguard, 1976.

National Center for Missing and Exploited Children. *Child Molesters: A Behavioral Analysis.* Washington: National Center for Missing and Exploited Children, 1986.

O'Brien, S. *Child Pornography.* Dubuque, IA: Kendall/Hunt, 1983.

Rossman, P. *Sexual Experience between Men and Boys.* Wilton, CT: Association Press, 1976.

Weisberg, K. *Children of the Night.* Lexington, MA: Lexington Books, 1985.

References

Ambrosino, L. *Runaways.* Boston: Beacon Press, 1971.

Berry, J. *Lead Us Not Into Temptation.* New York: Doubleday, 1992.

Burgess, A.; Groth, A. N.; and McCausland, M. P. "Child Sex Initiation Rings." *American Journal of Orthopsychiatry* 51 (1981):110–19.

Burgess, A. W.; Hartman, C. R.; McCausland, M. P.; and Powers, P. "Response Patterns in Children and Adolescents Exploited Through Sex Rings and Pornography." *American Journal of Orthopsychiatry* 141 (1984):656–62.

Burgess, A.; Hartman, C. R.; Kelley, S.; and Grant, C. A. "Parental Response to Child Sexual Abuse Trials Involving Day Care Settings." *Journal of Traumatic Stress* 3 (3), (1990): 395–405.

Campagna, D. *Sexual Exploitation of Children: Resource Manual.* Southwick, MA: Daniel S. Campagna, 1985.

Densen-Gerber, J. "Child Prostitution and Child Pornography: Medical, Legal and Societal Aspects of the Commercial Exploitation of Children." In *Sexual Abuse of Children: Selected Readings,* edited by B. Jones, L. Jenstrome, and K. MacFarlane, pp. 77–82. Washington: U.S. Department of Health and Human Services, 1980.

Densen-Gerber, J., and Hutchinson, S. "Medical, Legal and Societal Problems Involving Children—Child Prostitution, Child Pornography and Drug-Related Abuse: Recommended Legislation." In *The Maltreatment of Children,* edited by S. Smith, pp. 317–50. Baltimore: University Park, 1978.

deYoung, M. *The Sexual Victimization of Children.* Jefferson, NC: McFarland, 1982.

Ennew, J. *The Sexual Exploitation of Children.* Cambridge, UK: Polity Press, 1986.

Ertz, D. J. "The American Indian Sexual Offender" in B. Schwartz and H. Cellini. *The Sex Offender,* pp. 14-1–14-12. Kingston, NJ: Civic Research Inst., 1995.

Geiser, R. L. *Hidden Victims.* Boston: Beacon Press, 1979.

Giovannoni, J. M., and Becerra, R. *Defining Child Abuse.* New York: Free Press, 1979.

Groth, A. N. "Guidelines for Assessment and Management of the Offender." In *Sexual Assault of Children and Adolescents,* edited by A. Burgess, A. N. Groth, L. Holstrom, and S. Sgroi, pp. 25–42. Lexington, MA: Lexington Books, 1978a.

Groth, A. N. "Patterns of Sexual Assault Against Children and Adolescents." In *Sexual Assault of Children and Adolescents,* edited by A. Burgess, A. N. Groth, L. Holstrom, and S. Sgroi, pp. 3–24. Lexington, MA: Lexington Books, 1978b.

Groth, A. N. *Men Who Rape.* New York: Plenum Publishing, 1979.

Holmes, R. M. *Sex Crimes.* Newbury Park, CA: Sage, 1991.

James, J. *Entrance into Juvenile Prostitution.* Washington: National Institute of Mental Health, 1980.

Jarvie, J. C. "Child Pornography and Prostitution." In W. O'Donohue and J. H. Seer (eds.). *The Sexual Abuse of Children,* pp. 307–328. Hillsdale, NJ: Lawrence Erlbaum Assoc., 1992.

Jenkins, P. "Accusations of Abuse are Anti-Catholic Propaganda." In K. deKoster and K. L. Swisher (eds.). *Child Abuse: Opposing Viewpoints,* pp. 167–175. San Diego, CA: Greenhaven Press, 1994.

Katchen, M. H. "The History of Satanic Religions." In D. K. Sakheim and S. E. Devine, *Out of Darkness: Exploring Satanism and Ritual Abuse,* pp. 1–19. New York: Lexington Books, 1992.

Kempe, R. S., and Kempe, C. H. *The Common Secret: Sexual Abuse of Children and Adolescents.* New York: W. H. Freeman, 1984.

Lanning, K. V. "A Law-Enforcement Perspective on Allegations of Ritual Abuse." In D. K. Sakheim and S. E. Devine, *Out of Darkness: Exploring Satanism and Ritual Abuse,* pp. 109–146. New York: Lexington Books, 1992.

Lanning, K. V. and Burgess, A. W. "Child Pornography and Sex Rings." In Zillman, D. and Bryant, L. (eds.). *Pornography: Research Advances and Policy Considerations,* pp. 235–255. Hillsdale, NJ: Lawrence Erlbaum Assoc., 1989.

Lloyd, R. *For Money or Love: Boy Prostitution in America.* New York: Vanguard Press, 1976.

MacFarlane, K. I. "Sexual Abuse of Children." In *The Victimization of Women,* edited by J. R. Chapman and M. Gates, pp. 81–109. Beverly Hills, CA: Sage, 1978.

Mass, A. I. Personal communication, July 11, 1991.

Mollica, R. F., and Son, L. "Cultural Dimensions in the Evaluation and Treatment of Sexual Trauma." *Psychiatric Clinics of North America,* 12(2) (1989):363–79.

National Center for Missing and Exploited Children. *Investigator's Guide to Missing Child Cases.* Washington: National Center for Missing and Exploited Children, 1985.

National Center for Missing and Exploited Children. *Child Molesters: A Behavioral Analysis.* Washington: National Center for Missing and Exploited Children, 1986.

Newman, F., and Caplan, P. "Juvenile Female Prostitution as a Gender Consistent Response to Early Deprivation." *International Journal of Women's Studies* 5 (1981):128–37.

O'Brien, S. *Child Pornography.* Dubuque, IA: Kendall/Hunt, 1983.

Prendergast, W. E. *Treating Sex Offenders in Correctional Institutions and Outpatient Clinics.* New York: Haworth, 1991.

Rossman, P. *Sexual Experience Between Men and Boys.* Wilton, CT: Association Press, 1976.

Rush, F. *The Best Kept Secret: Sexual Abuse of Children.* New York: McGraw-Hill, 1980.

Russell, D. *Sexual Exploitation.* Beverly Hills, CA: Sage, 1984.

Sanford, L. *Silent Children.* Garden City, NY: Doubleday, 1980.

Silbert, M. H., and Pines, A. M. "Sexual Child Abuse as an Antecedent to Prostitution." *Child Abuse and Neglect* 5 (1981):407–11.

Tindall, R. H. "The Male Adolescent Involved with a Pederast Becomes an Adult." *Journal of Homosexuality* 3 (1978):373–82.

U.S. Dept. of Justice. "Missing, Abducted, Runaway and Throwaway Children in America: 1990." Washington, DC: U.S. Dept. of Justice, Office of Juvenile Justice and Delinquency Prevention.

Weisberg, K. *Children of the Night.* Lexington, MA: Lexington Books, 1985.

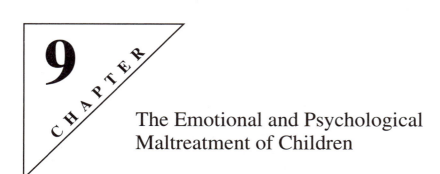

The Emotional and Psychological Maltreatment of Children

"You're a stupid, lousy kid and I wish you'd never been born!" shrieked Delvina at her wailing toddler. Motherhood was more than she had ever imagined and Delvina, at age 17, felt ill prepared to deal with it. Perhaps sharing her frustration in their less than satisfactory relationship, 2-year-old Allen cried frequently or banged his head against any available surface. His behavior stimulated his grand-mother's screams at his mother.

"What's your problem, girl? You too dumb to take care of a baby? Well, I just can't abide that wailing no more!" Invariably these words preceded her exit and Delvina once more turned her angry words on her plaintive child.

The pattern in baby Allen's family was one of emotional abuse—a pattern that had long preceded his birth.

Emotional and Psychological Maltreatment Defined

Emotional and psychological maltreatment remains the most difficult type of abuse or neglect to define or isolate. Some child development experts argue that almost all parents are guilty of emotional maltreatment of children at some time or other. The ambiguous messages we give to children in our culture have even been considered to be abusive. For example, consider these mixed messages: A mother teaches her children not to lie but then comments, "Do not tell Dad I bought this today!" A father belittles his child by saying, "I don't understand why you can't do better in school. In my day, I worked to buy my books and walked three miles to school. *I* realized the value of an education." The clear message to the child is "What's wrong with *you?*"

At the 1990 Symposium on Child Abuse and Neglect in Atlanta, "Rites and Reason" (a group sponsored by Research and Development, Afro-American studies of Brown University) presented a series of vignettes depicting a collection of abusive messages given to children in many households across the United States. As those in the audience heard and saw these messages portrayed, there were murmurs of surprise, disbelief, and perhaps even guilt at the all too familiar refrains. Others dismissed many of the messages as "benign" compared to "real" emotional abuse. What exactly constitutes emotional maltreatment has been the subject of controversy for years.

In fact, emotional/psychological maltreatment underlies all types of abuse or neglect. Survivors tell us that the results of the physical blows do not last as long as the messages that accompany them. By the same token, it is the psychological manipulation on the part of the perpetrator of sexual abuse that creates and/or intensifies the scars for their victims.

The attempt to define *emotional/psychological maltreatment* has led many theorists to separate the definition into two parts: emotional/psychological abuse (including verbal or emotional assaults, threatened harm, or close confinement) and emotional/psychological neglect (including inadequate nurturance, inadequate affection, refusal to provide adequate care, or knowingly allowing maladaptive behavior such as delinquency or drug abuse) (Garbarino, Guttmann, and Seeley 1986; Wiehe, 1990; O'Hagan, 1993). Such fine distinctions are often muddled in the face of reality, however. Some parents both emotionally abuse and emotionally neglect, and in some situations it is difficult to discern one from the other.

Garbarino, Guttmann, and Seeley (1986) have suggested the definition that is currently the most widely used. They conclude that emotional maltreatment—or what they term *psychological maltreatment*—is not an isolated event, but rather a *pattern* of psychically destructive behavior that may include any of the following:

1. *Rejecting* (The adult refuses to acknowledge the child's worth and the legitimacy of the child's needs.)
2. *Isolating* (The adult cuts the child off from normal social experiences, prevents the child from forming friendships, and makes the child believe that he or she is alone in the world.)
3. *Terrorizing* (The adult verbally assaults the child, creates a climate of fear, bullies and frightens the child, and makes the child believe that the world is capricious and hostile.)
4. *Ignoring* (The adult deprives the child of essential stimulation and responsiveness, stifling emotional growth and intellectual development.)
5. *Corrupting* (The adult "mis-socializes" the child, stimulates the child to engage in destructive and antisocial behavior, reinforces the deviance, and makes the child unfit for normal social experience.) (1986, p. 8)

Wiehe (1990) adds two additional behaviors to this list: destroying personal possessions and torturing or destroying a pet. He also suggests that siblings as well as parents can be emotionally abusive.

Although all of these may be seen in conjunction with or as an integral part of physical abuse, neglect, or sexual abuse, emotional/psychological maltreatment is perhaps the only type of assault on children that can also stand alone. The hurtful words, the serious inattention, or the hostile attitude can be enough to leave severe scars.

Alicia never felt "good enough." She was convinced that her mother's departure in her (Alicia's) infancy was a direct result of her birth. The youngest of six girls, Alicia knew without a doubt that the fact that she was not a boy had sealed her fate. Her father virtually ignored her, leaving her care to her oldest sisters. When one sister left home, her nurturance passed to the next oldest, but these sisters seemed incapable of giving much either. Perhaps they too blamed her for her mother's leaving. At age 16, Alicia became involved with a friend of her father's— a man her father's age. She knew he was married, but it didn't matter. When their affair ended she drifted from the arms of one older man to another, never quite able to find the love and approval she lacked. By age 25, she had attempted suicide four times.

In defining this type of maltreatment, O'Hagan (1993) makes a stronger case than Garbarino, Guttman and Seeley for the use of the term *psychological abuse* instead of the less easily defined emotional abuse. He suggests that the following terms currently used in the literature are more in the realm of the psychological: (1) *psychological torture* (frequently seen in ritualized abuse); (2) *psychological terror* (creating extreme fear in the child); (3) *mental injury* (acts which have an impact on the child's mental well-being); and (4) *psychological unavailability* (being absent in the care of the child). This author goes on to distinguish between the terms emotional abuse and psychological abuse in the following manner:

> Emotional abuse is the sustained, repetitive, *inappropriate* emotional response to the child's expression of emotion and its accompanying expressive behavior. *(p. 28)...*
> *Psychological abuse is the sustained, repetitive, inappropriate* behavior which damages, or substantially reduces, the creative and developmental potential of crucially important mental faculties and mental processes of a child; these include intelligence, memory, recognition, perception, attention, language and moral development (p. 33–34). (Italics or lack thereof are the author's).

Certainly the term *psychological abuse* is gaining recognition (Brassard et al., 1993), but some authors fail to distinguish between the two as has O'Hagan (1993). It would seem, therefore, that the use of both terms in the discussion of this type of maltreatment would be the most inclusive.

The clear definition of *emotional/psychological maltreatment* is further complicated when one considers the different practices of the cultures that make up the melting pot of this country. Several cultures use shame as a powerful tool to ensure obedience and acceptable behavior from their children. Ho (1989) reports, "Shame (*tiu lien* in Chinese) and shaming are used traditionally to help reinforce familial expectations and proper behavior within and outside family. If an individual behaves improperly, he or she will 'lose face' and also may cause the family, community or society to withdraw confidence and support" (p. 528).

Some families of African or Native American origin threaten their children with the cultural approximate of the "bogeyman" when they perceive the need arises. As previously mentioned, the behavior of ethnic minorities closely tied to their origins must be seen in that context. In other words, psychologically abusive behavior conveys "a culture-specific message of rejection or impairs a socially relevant psychological process, such as the development of a coherent positive self concept" (Garbarino, Guttmann, and Seeley, 1986, p. 5).

In this same vein, Garbarino, Guttmann, and Seeley (1986) ask the question: Is there a difference between psychological maltreatment and "growth inducing challenge" (p. 20)? These authors contend that there is. "Growth inducing challenge," when it occurs in the context of a caring supportive relationship, is designed to enhance the sense of self and build the character. Psychological abuse, on the other hand, attacks or fails to nourish the individual in fundamental ways. Thus the culturally accepted practice intended to strengthen the child's character is probably not abusive in the eyes of the parents and children and therefore not likely to leave scars.

Another problem arises, however, when parents, closely tied to ethnic origins, use techniques long employed by their culture with a child who has become acclimated to a different value system. Mass and Yap (1992) describe the care of an 11-year-old third-generation Chinese-American boy who was sent to a child guidance clinic as a result of his development of an involuntary facial tic. The diagnosis determined that the boy's tic had developed as a result of the intense pressure his more traditional Confucian family had put on him over grades. For this family, their son's Bs and Cs were tantamount to his failure—and to the family's "losing face" (pp. 123–124).

To further define *emotional/psychological maltreatment* in a way that helps us take into consideration cultural variations, Garbarino and Gilliam (1980) state that psychological maltreatment involves acts or omissions by parents that jeopardize "the development of self esteem, of social competence, of the capacity for intimacy, of positive and healthy interpersonal relationships" (p. 7).

Even after one has defined emotional and psychological abuse operationally, intervention can be hampered by the fact that protective services must have proof that the abuse has occurred. There must, therefore, be three observable components: (1) identifiable parental behavior; (2) demonstrable (here and now as opposed to the future scars) harm to the child; and (3) a causal link between the parental behavior and the harm to the child (Bross et al., 1988, p. 544). Many child rearing practices, as previously mentioned, are so imbedded in our cultural values that we find it difficult to discern when they are abusive. Thus, it may not be easy to determine that the child who has a poor self concept and does poorly in school is doing so *because* of the extreme pressure being put on him or her to succeed rather than as a result of some other factors. Given this difficulty in identifying cause and effect in a psychological sense, it is not surprising that the National Committee to Prevent Child Abuse (1994) indicated that only two to four percent of the reported or substantiated cases of maltreatment, in their 1993 survey, fell under the category of emotional abuse (p. 8).

The Roots of Emotional/Psychological Maltreatment

Our children are victims of the increasingly prevalent view that parenting is a messy, frustrating job that gets in the way of one's own growth and life, rather than enriching it.... To ask a young woman who is raising two toddlers, "But what are you *doing* with your life?" is to tell this mother that what she is doing—the job of parenting—is not worthy of respect. When a culture removes status from the role of mother or father, the self esteem from assuming that role is lessened. It is as if society is punishing parents rather than respecting them for tackling a tremendous task. Only jobs in the "real world" seem to earn such respect. (Covitz, 1986, pp. 6–7)

The prevailing attitude of much of society that parenting is an unrewarding task certainly sets the stage for psychological maltreatment. Even families where the family unit is the most valued social structure find themselves in conflict as their children adopt the predominant lifestyle of this country and question (or totally reject) old-world values. But Covitz (1986) goes on to say that beyond the societal atmosphere, emotional/psychological maltreatment results from "the healthy narcissistic needs" (p. xi) of the parents not being met. Garbarino, Guttmann, and Seeley (1986) contend that psychological maltreatment is rooted not only in dysfunctional family communication patterns but also in the societal pressures impacting on the family. Family disruption, an inharmonious marital relationship, divorce, and outside stressors such as poverty, unemployment, mobility, and isolation can provide an atmosphere for this type of maltreatment. Prejudice too takes its toll.

> *The Roa family, Brahmans (the highest caste in Indian culture), were well-educated professionals, newly arrived in the United States. All light complected, the Roas were extremely distressed when their third child was born. His dark complexion was met by his maternal grandmother with the comment, "Where did he come from? Our family has never been dark! He looks like the village people!" (often from a lower caste). While the Roas at first tried to overlook their son's different coloring, they felt that he was rejected by relatives. The subtle pattern of ignoring this child, which they developed, and their practice of keeping him away from others as much as possible, was detected by teachers when he reached school age. The family was referred for counseling. Although initially they denied any differences in their feelings for this child, they were eventually able to deal with their issues around his coloring.*

How much do children themselves contribute to being emotionally and psychologically maltreated? As in physical abuse, psychologically abused children are often perceived by their parents as more difficult, different, or representing something that stimulates the parent to anger. Thus the child may trigger his or her own maltreatment, but he or she is not necessarily the cause. Rather, it is how this child is perceived by the abuser. The hyperactive child, for example, while stimulating abuse by one type of parent may find understanding and help from the other parent. Once again, it is often the parents' expectations of their children that determine how well they are able to deal with the children.

There has always been a tendency to link emotional disturbance to maltreatment by parents. Garbarino, Guttmann, and Seeley (1986) contend that "emotionally disturbed children are not by definition psychologically maltreated. There are multiple possible origins for disturbed personality development" (p. 5).

Characteristics of the Emotionally Maltreated Child

Children who are emotionally maltreated by a parent or even siblings suffer feelings of being inadequate, isolated, unwanted, or unloved. Their self-esteem is low and they consider themselves unworthy (Jenewicz, 1983; Krugman and Krugman, 1984; Burnett, 1993; Brassard et al., 1993; O'Hagan, 1993).

Children respond to such messages in one of two ways: They fight back, becoming hostile, aggressive, and behavior problems, or they turn their anger inward, becoming self-destructive, depressed, withdrawn, or suicidal. Some of these children also develop somatic complaints (e.g., headaches, asthma, colitis, nervous habits, etc.) or sleep disturbances.

> *Gil was a child who responded to his abuse by striking out. In his 12 years he had been constantly belittled and rejected at home. Feeling he and his accomplishments were worthless, Gil began sabotaging the efforts of other children. At school*

he destroyed other children's papers and broke into and vandalized lockers; he wrecked the contents of lunch boxes, returning them crushed, soggy, and filled with insects or in some other way spoiled.

Inga, on the other hand, reacted to her parents' rejection by turning inward. She frequently scratched herself with sharp objects, seemingly mesmerized by watching the marks she made bleed. Every week at school was punctuated by at least two visits to the nurse's office with a myriad of medical complaints. When she was pronounced well, or given some type of treatment, Inga wanted to be allowed to sit and talk with the nurse. The nurse soon realized that this emotionally starved child needed psychological treatment more than physical.

The negativity expressed by emotionally/psychologically maltreated children is often pronounced. Their behavior seems designed to draw attention. Some develop eating disorders, attempt suicide, or drift into delinquency. By the time the child is an adolescent, the consequences of maltreatment have often become an integral part of his or her personality (Garbarino, Guttmann, and Seeley, 1986; O'Hagan, 1993).

Family Dynamics and Parental Characteristics

The scene is often set for emotional abuse and neglect long before children are born. Covitz (1986) suggests several situations that make the family ripe for maltreatment of their children. Parents "marry the wrong mate" (p. 29), become disillusioned with their partner, and consciously or unconsciously look for substitutes on whom to vent their anger and disillusionment. Parents who have unwanted pregnancies or desire children for unrealistic reasons may find their frustrations are vented on these children. Parents whose own needs have not been met in childhood may be so involved in finding an outlet for their neediness that a child becomes a burden to them (O'Hagan, 1993).

> *Edith, the child of an alcoholic mother and a father no one had seen in years, saw Rick as the "answer to her prayers." He was a steady worker and seemingly reliable. But two children later, Rick found Edith's extreme neediness too draining and asked for a divorce. Furious, Edith refused, but paradoxically took the children and left. For several months they were homeless, living in shelters. Shelter staff complained that Edith left her children often and expected whoever was there to care for them. "And those children do nothing right in their mother's eyes," a shelter worker complained. Feeling harassed by the complaints, Edith moved in with a man she met at the unemployment office. Once again she felt she would be cared for, but he disliked children. At first Edith bullied the children into silent compliance. Eventually she took them to a neighbor—saying she'd return soon— and disappeared with her new boyfriend.*

This mother's search for emotional fulfillment meant psychological abuse for her children and eventually abandonment.

Morrow (1987) contends that psychological abuse can be the natural by-product of alcoholism. "Children in alcoholic families suffer all forms of abuse, but they feel most keenly the emotional deprivation, alienation from their parents, and their own social isolation" (p. 115). Children in alcoholic and drug-addicted families are not only subject to possible emotional abuse by their parents but also suffer a secondhand emotional abuse in the form of shame and humiliation.

> *I never knew what my father would do. Sometimes, when he was drinking he'd be as sweet as could be, and sometimes he was even funny. But he was also cruel and inappropriate. One time he threw the cat across the room in front of my friend. Another time he came into my party wearing a lampshade on his head and nothing else. I was so embarrassed. I never knew whether to trust him. In fact, I never knew whether to love him or hate him.*

Today, with the high incidence of separation and divorce, children may become the innocent victims of psychological warfare between their feuding parents. Certainly the dissolution of the parental union has an impact on children in any case. Children are torn by their loyalties to each parent, they fear for their futures and they feel guilt over what they perceive they must have done to cause this unrest (Klosinski, 1993). Handling by concerned, caring parents can help children to weather this storm to some degree. However, it is the parents who are so caught up into their own anger and bitterness who may inflict upon their children additional psychological abuse. These parents may not only be unaware of the daily needs of their children, but may insist that the children take sides. They may also lose sight of the fact that the spouse that they so despise and criticize is one half of the child's heritage. Therefore, to continually slander this partner is to do so to the child as well (O'Hagan, 1993).

O'Hagan (1993) also suggests that some parents with mental illness may be more likely to exhibit "inappropriate emotional responses to their children's emotional expressions"

(p. 89). In addition, the very fact that these parents may be in and out of the home, due to hospitalizations, will have an impact on their children.

And finally, adolescent parents who are children themselves may find that the demands of parenthood are too great.

> *"The baby just needed so much!" said 15 year old Tanya. Although usually attentive to her baby's needs, Tanya found that she was frustrated by having little time to herself. She began screaming at her son, assuming that as long as she was feeding and changing him, she was a good caretaker. "He's too young to know how I feel," she argued. She was surprised when, several months later, she noticed that the baby cringed when she came near him.*

It is fairly safe to say that parents who emotionally/psychologically abuse do so either because they had inappropriate (emotionally abusive) models of parenting or because they are waging their own internal emotional battles. Unfortunately their children become the innocent victims of the parents' confusion.

Difficulty in Detecting and Treating Emotional Abuse

Often emotional abuse is expertly hidden amidst the child-rearing practices of our culture. It is therefore very difficult to recognize what is actually abusive. Usually the recognition comes from the results—a child who cries out, withdraws, or lets us know he or she needs help. Unfortunately, intervention by protective services often depends largely on the ability of agencies to document and perhaps support the existence of the abuse in court through tangible, observable, or concrete evidence. Emotional abuse is not easy to prove or document and thus may go unnoticed or untreated. Increasingly, however, states and protective agencies are developing statutes or policies that address emotional abuse. These certainly represent progress. It may be that our children will not be protected from emotional abuse until we, as a society, learn to value them more. Then the rights children deserve as well as their protection will follow.

Ritual abuse is another type of maltreatment which has an emotional impact on children. Due to the relatively new recognition of this form of child abuse, it is often difficult to diagnose and treat.

Summary

Emotional/psychological maltreatment has long been the subject of debate. What *is* emotional/psychological abuse? Although this maltreatment underlies physical and sexual abuse and neglect, it may also exist alone. Some authors, in an effort to define *emotional maltreatment,* divide it into emotional abuse and emotional neglect. Garbarino, Guttmann, and Seeley (1986) include rejecting, isolating, terrorizing, ignoring, and corrupting in their definition. Wiehe (1990) adds destroying personal possessions and torturing pets to the list.

Because the United States is a compilation of many cultures, it is sometimes difficult to determine when cultural practices are emotionally abusive. One question to ask may be: What effect do these practices have on the children involved? Emotional/psychological maltreatment has its roots in a variety of societal and personal deficiencies. Children who are emotionally/ psychologically abused demonstrate anger, behavior problems, depression, withdrawal, and somatic complaints. Negativity is pronounced.

Parents who emotionally maltreat are often disillusioned with their own lives, emotionally needy, or per- haps substance abusers. Often these parents have had inadequate models of parenting from their own parents. Because emotional/psychological maltreatment is so difficult to document, children who are abused or neglected do not always get the services to which they are entitled.

Exploration Questions

1. How can *emotional maltreatment* be defined? Psychological?

2. What are some of the issues involved in defining *emotional/psychological maltreatment*?

3. What are the components of what Garbarino, Guttmann, and Seeley call *psychological abuse*?

4. What is the difference between psychological abuse and a "growth inducing challenge"?

5. Cite some ethnically based situations that might appear to be emotional abuse or neglect.

6. How does society set the stage for emotional abuse or neglect?

7. What symptoms do emotionally abused or neglected children demonstrate?

8. Why might parents emotionally maltreat children?

9. What is meant by ritual abuse?

10. What is the impact of ritual abuse on children?

Activities for Applied Learning

1. Brainstorm and make a list of the sayings and behaviors that might be considered emotionally abusive or neglectful.

2. Look up the child abuse laws of your state. Is emotional/psychological maltreatment mentioned? Is it spelled out?

3. Invite an attorney familiar with child welfare and a protective services worker to class. How does the system—court and social services—address emotional maltreatment?

Suggested Readings

Covitz, J. *Emotional Child Abuse: The Family Curse.* Boston, Sogo Press, 1986.

Garbarino, J.; Guttmann, E.; and Seeley, J. W. *The Psychologically Battered Child.* San Francisco: Jossey-Bass, 1986.

Jenewicz, W. J. "A Protective Posture Toward Emotional Neglect and Abuse." *Child Welfare,* 62 (1983):243–52.

O'Hagan, K. *Emotional and Psychological Abuse of Children.* Toronto: University of Toronto Press, 1993.

Sakheim, D. L. and Devine, S. E. *Out of Darkness: Satanism and Ritual Abuse.* New York: Lexington Books, 1993.

References

Brassard, M. R.; Hart, S. N.; and Hardy, D. B. "The Psychological Maltreatment Rating Scales." *Child Abuse and Neglect* 17 (6), (1993):715–729.

Bross, D. C.; Krugman, R. D.; Lenherr, M. R.; Rosenberg, D. A.; and Schmitt, B. D. (eds.). *The New Child Protection Team Handbook.* New York: Garland, 1988.

Burnett, B. B. "The Psychological Abuse of Latency Age Children: A Survey." *Child Abuse and Neglect* 17 (4), (1993):441–454.

Covitz, J. *Emotional Child Abuse: The Family Curse.* Boston: Sigo Press, 1986.

Garbarino, J., and Gilliam, G. *Understanding Abusive Families.* Lexington, MA: Lexington Books, 1980.

Garbarino, J.; Guttmann, E.; and Seeley, J. W. *The Psychologically Battered Child.* San Francisco: Jossey-Bass, 1986.

Ho, M. K. "Social Work Practice with Asian Americans." In *Social Work: A Profession of Many Faces,* edited by A. Morales and B. W. Sheafor, pp. 521–41. Boston: Allyn and Bacon, 1989.

Jenewicz, W. J. "A Protective Posture Toward Emotional Neglect and Abuse." *Child Welfare* 62 (1983):243–52.

Klosinski, G. "Psychological Maltreatment in the Context of Separation and Divorce." *Child Abuse and Neglect.* 17 (4), (1993):557–563.

Krugman, R. D., and Krugman, M. K. "Emotional Abuse in the Classroom." *American Journal of Diseases of Children* 138 (1984):284–86.

Lloyd, D. W. "Ritual Child Abuse: Definitions and Assumptions." *Journal of Child Sexual Abuse* 1 (3), (1992):1–14.

Mass, A. E., and Yap, J. "Child Welfare: Asian and Pacific Islander Families." *Child Welfare: A Multicultural Perspective,* edited by N. Cohen, pp. 107–129. Boston: Allyn and Bacon, 1992.

Morrow, G. *The Compassionate School: A Practical Guide to Educating Abused and Traumatized Children.* Englewood Cliffs, NJ: Prentice-Hall, 1987.

National Committee to Prevent Child Abuse. *Current Trends in Child Abuse Reporting and Fatalities: The Results of the 1993 Annual Fifty State Survey.* Chicago, IL: National Committee to Prevent Child Abuse, 1994.

O'Hagan, K. *Emotional and Psychological Abuse of Children.* Toronto: University of Toronto Press, 1993.

Ryder, D. *Breaking the Cycle of Satanic Ritual Abuse.* Minneapolis, MN: CompCare Publ., 1992.

Sakheim, D. K. and Devine, S. E. *Out of Darkness: Exploring Satanism and Ritual Abuse.* Lexington, MA: Lexington Books, 1992.

Wiehe, V. R. *Sibling Abuse: Hidden Physical, Emotional and Sexual Trauma.* Lexington, MA: Lexington Books, 1990.

Intervention: Reporting and Investigation

The dynamics of child maltreatment are complex, and the complexity is heightened when the social service system becomes involved. These helping professionals strive to refine the intervention process so as to cause the least harm and upset for the already traumatized child. These efforts will become more successful as the professionals continue to assess the intervention process.

Culturally Sensitive Intervention

Child abuse or neglect is not an easy subject to discuss with any parent, and when cultural differences exist between worker and client, the picture becomes even more complex. Effective intervention—that is, to intervene so as to cause the least damage and prove the most helpful—with culturally diverse populations necessitates several areas of expertise on the part of the worker and agency (Leigh, 1998). First, workers must become acquainted with cultures other than their own. If the agency has numerous potential clients from a particular culture, it is vital that the agency educate workers about the values, customs, and attitudes of those clients. For example, one city's demographics indicated that there was an increasing Hispanic-American population. Efforts were originally made by the social service agency in the area to hire Hispanic caseworkers. After a year of recruitment, there was only one Spanish-speaking caseworker within 50 miles. Concerned about the increasing demands of Hispanic-American clientele, several agencies joined together to establish training in the values and customs of this particular culture (predominantly South American) and required workers to take part in this training. Also, Spanish-speaking paraprofessionals were recruited from the community to work with non-Spanish-speaking caseworkers as translators.

While learning more about broad ethnic groups is important, Thomas (1992) stresses the need to not generalize completely. In other words, workers must know about Hispanic or Asian-Pacific Islander values in general, but if their caseloads are peopled by Mexican or Filipino clients, workers must learn more specifically about these cultures. Another pitfall in the pursuit of becoming culturally diverse in case management and treatment of victims and families is the assumption that because something happens within a cultural context, it is normal. One worker reported having a case of a pregnant African-American fourteen-year-old. The girl had been raped by her aunt's white boyfriend. The worker wanted to file a sexual abuse complaint, but the girl adamantly refused.

"My Mama says that Black women has always been raped by white men, right back to slave time. She was raped by a white man, her Mama was, and her Mama. Way back. So why is it so different for me? That's just the way it is."

It was difficult for the worker to communicate to this teen that just because something seemed to have happened, it need not be considered right (Young, 1993).

The language values and customs of particular groups may also be affected—in the case of new immigrants—by the situations from which they came. For example, many refugees from totalitarian countries are extremely suspicious and even fearful of any government or institutional representative (Mass, 1991; Heras, 1992). A social worker who has the power to intervene may well be seen as just that—a government representative.

Heras (1992) cites several other cultural values of ethnic families which may be difficult for workers not familiar with the culture to understand. The emphasis on *family cohesion* may mean that the family would rather stick together ignoring or discounting the abuse than to be separated. Often the family is dependent on the abuser and can see no other way than to tolerate whatever he is doing. The *family also takes precedence over the marital dyad.* The American culture sees the marital couple as the cornerstone of the family while other cultures view alternative family subsystems as equally as important. Trying to strengthen the marital dyad may mean weakening the family structure. Another dynamic for many Asian cultures is the need to *save face*. If family members feel shame over something that they or another family member has done, they may deny it at all costs in order to save face. To the uninitiated worker this may look like denial and resistance. And finally, the *indirect communication style* employed in many cultures may be confusing. Clients who are urged to express their feelings or tell someone something directly may leave the agency rather than behave in a manner so foreign to their value systems (Heras, 1992; Root, 1993).

The importance of having interventionists who understand the practices and history of such cultures cannot be stressed enough. Areas where there is a large Asian population (such as Los Angeles County, California) have established a specialized Asian unit in the Department of Children's Services to investigate and serve Asian clients who are referred because of suspected abuse and neglect. When it is not feasible or practical to provide bilingual, bicultural staff for direct service, it is important to have consultants who can be available to line staff to advise and educate on the cultural aspects of the case (Mass, 1991; Root, 1993).

In addition to participating in training groups or using consultants, the worker who is not bicultural must be aware of his or her own values and attitudes. No matter how aware a worker may be of cultural differences, if he or she has preconceived negative attitudes toward a particular population, the client will not receive optimum service. Agencies should be responsible for effective as well as cognitive training of staff before these workers become involved in the intervention process.

The Intervention Process

Before considering the process, it is important to consider intervention itself. The goal of intervention is to stop the abuse and neglect of the child or children in question. The children's current safety is paramount. But there are also several future dimensions to the effort. The children's future safety must be ensured. Ideally, parents can be helped to change—to adopt different coping skills and perhaps even alternative values about child rearing. Another goal—too often overlooked—is that the children be given positive parenting models so they can grow into nonabusive adults.

Although these ideals are not always attainable, given the limited resources and the relatively young art of protective social work, it is toward these ends that the system strives. The way in which the system functions to help abused children and their families differs from state to state. Figure 10.1 charts the usual process protective cases follow. Variations depend on numerous legal and human factors.

In this and the next chapter, the role of reporters, social service workers, physicians, police, nurses, and teachers is considered. Chapter 12 explores the influence of the legal system, primarily the courts. The remainder of the intervention process—treatment—will be outlined in Chapters 13 through 15.

Reporting

Changes in the 1970s brought legislation that mandated the identification and reporting of child maltreatment to designated social service agencies. States enacted their own laws and identified specific professionals who were mandated to report child abuse and neglect. The term *mandated reporters* refers to individuals who, in their professional relationship with the child and family, may encounter child maltreatment. Some states are more specific than others as to those who are mandated, but those who list these professionals usually include physicians, other medical professionals, counselors, social workers, and school personnel. According to a nationwide study done through the National Education Association (NEA), 20 states, for example, specifically mention teachers in their list of mandated reporters, whereas all others include them under school personnel or indicate that "anyone" should report (Tower, 1984).

In addition to who shall report, most state laws spell out several other guidelines for mandated reporters. Tower's (1984) study for the NEA provides a basis for comparing these state guidelines using teachers to represent mandated reporters. Most state laws indicate the following: (1) *To whom the report should be made.* Departments of social services, child welfare, family services, or public welfare were usually designated to be the recipients of these reports. Some states indicated that a report to a law enforcement agency was also appropriate; (2) *Under what conditions a mandated reporter must report.* States gave one of three answers: suspicion of abuse and neglect, reasonable cause to believe, and reasonable cause to suspect; (3) *A time period during which the report must be investigated by social services.* Some 45 states in the NEA study indicated there was a particular time period in which the report should be investigated. These periods ranged from 2 hours to 30 days; (4) *The type of action taken if mandated reporters do not report.* Of the 45 states responding to this question, most indicated that a mandated reporter who did not report would be subject to a fine or imprisonment, or be charged with a misdemeanor. Only one state had no penalty for nonreporting; and (5) *The type of immunity provided mandated reporters who make a report.* All states indicated some type of immunity from civil or criminal action.

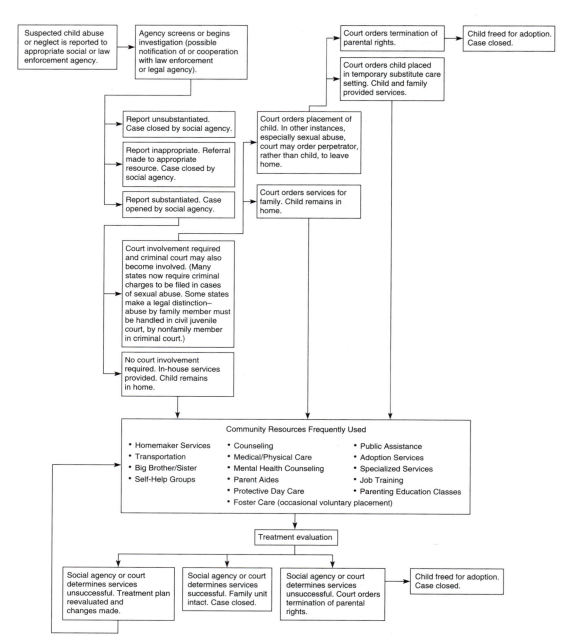

FIGURE 10.1   What Happens When Suspected Child Abuse or Neglect Is Reported

Copyright 1984 by the National Education Association Reprinted with permission. (Adapted from "Open the Door—on Child Abuse and Neglect: Prevention and Reporting Kit." Ohio Department of Public Welfare, Children's Protective Services, under a grant from NCCAN, n.d.)

While the law compels mandated reporters to disclose child abuse and neglect, other citizens are encouraged to do so. This often presents problems for the average person. Many people have no idea where to report. Although phone directories list protective agencies, people who have not had experience with social services may not know what these agencies are called. In fact, any law enforcement office, welfare office, or school can provide the name of the appropriate protective agency.

Another dilemma for people is whether or not to become involved. Abuse and neglect are not always easily recognizable and clearly defined. Even if they are, people wonder if they have the right to intervene in another's life. What would you have done in the following instance?

I was in an ice cream shop in mid-January. It was extremely cold and it had recently snowed. Incongruous as it may seem, those of us waiting in line for ice cream were well bundled in coats, scarves, and mittens. As we waited, a mother and her toddler came into the store. The child was probably about 2 years old and wore only a diaper and a short-sleeved cotton shirt. She was barefoot. Her legs and arms looked chapped and red. Her face was dirty and her nose encrusted. The mother, dressed in slacks and a long-sleeved cotton blouse, paid little attention to the child, who coughed and snuffled her way to a nearby spot on the floor where she sat quietly.

In addition to not knowing where to report and not feeling the right to intervene in other's lives, most people prefer not to entangle themselves in the workings of a bureaucracy. Yet it is important that the average individual become better informed about reporting and take the risk in order to save a child from potential or continued harm.

Most agencies accept anonymous reports of child abuse and neglect, but they prefer not to for several reasons. Having the name of the reporter enables the agency to call back, if necessary, to clarify information. Some agency staff believe that giving one's name indicates more commitment to help the family. Agencies are quite familiar with vindictive calls from feuding neighbors, relatives, and ex-spouses, although fortunately these calls are rare.

Well-meaning mandated reporters have asked if they can report anonymously rather than chance having the family discover their identity. Although some states allow this, anonymity creates problems. First, many agencies require the staff to investigate reports from mandated reporters but allow them to use their own judgment on anonymous calls. Second, the mandated reporter could actually be fined or imprisoned for not reporting, and anonymity would provide no later proof of the reporter's identity. Thus, mandated reporters are always encouraged to give their name with the understanding that most agencies do not disclose their identities. Certainly the reporter has the right to request anonymity.

To reporters who are hesitant to identify themselves, Hill stresses the importance of telling the family of the referral. She suggests that if the reporter has not told the family, he or she should be helped to do so:

> The referrer will be helped in this and future referrals to see that this material can be discussed in a constructive way once feelings are dealt with, that he can present the referral as helpful to the family, and that this will enhance his future working relationship with them. The family, in turn, will benefit in self-esteem from being treated with the respect they deserve, will be given an opportunity to respond to the material in the report, and even if they are angry and defensive, will have experienced the referrer as direct and honest, thus building a modicum of trust. It is particularly helpful if the referrer can cite a concrete need that he knows the family views as a problem and which has contributed to their stress, telling the family he has mentioned it to the protective worker. (1983, p. 46)

Hill feels the clients' knowledge of the identity of the reporter allays amorphous fears and minimizes the energy family members might use expressing anger toward numerous others. Instead, the worker can help focus these energies on solving the problem that brought them to the attention of social services.

Disclosure of the reporter's identity to the family should depend not only on the anticipated casework relationship but on other more immediate factors. For example, would telling the family of the report prior to the actual involvement of social services put the child at greater risk? Or is the family more likely to flee without the recognized authority of social services or the courts? Mandated reporters have also wondered about retaliation by the family. Although reporters are sometimes subjected to verbal abuse by clients, it is unusual, in child protection situations, for family members to physically harm reporting professionals. An abuser's choice of a child, rather than another adult, as a target of his or her aggression makes clear that the abuser likely fears adults and their authority.

Reporting suspected child abuse and neglect is not easy, but the step is vital to securing help for children and their families. (See Figure 10.1.)

Investigating and Validating

A report to a social service agency starts a complex chain of events. Substantiation is the determination by the initial or intake social worker that abuse or neglect is in fact present. The decision whether to substantiate is usually made after the social worker has made some basic inquiries. Reports come in by phone or through written referrals. The reporter is questioned on the phone or sometimes interviewed to determine the validity of his or her concerns. If the report is anonymous and little information is available, the screening or intake worker's job may be extremely difficult. This preliminary investigation requires the worker to talk with the children and their parents, and perhaps other family members as well. Children are often interviewed at school or in another neutral setting, providing an opportunity for the worker to see the child alone. This is important to prevent the child from feeling overwhelmed or inhibited by the presence of the parent(s) who may also be the abuser(s).

In the course of the investigation, the intake worker may conclude that the report was inappropriate. For example, in a housing rather than a protective situation, the case would be referred to a different agency. If the worker determines that there is too little information to conclude that abuse or neglect exists or if the family appears to be coping without evidence of maltreatment, the case is "unsubstantiated," and no further contact is made. Some agencies keep the report on file for a period of time to see if other reports are made. New legislation protecting individual privacy in some states requires that the report be destroyed after a specific interval.

A substantiated report requires further investigation to determine how best to intervene in the maltreatment cycle. Protective social workers not only see involuntary clients but must conduct the interviews in the clients' homes instead of in the perhaps more secure setting of their offices.

Home Visiting

Traditionally the home visit has been the realm of the protective social worker. The abusive and neglectful parents are mostly involuntary clients. In most cases, they resent social service intervention and therefore are unlikely to seek it out or to respond to a call or letter requesting they keep an office appointment. On the other hand, sophisticated or aggressive clients (especially in sexual abuse cases) decide the best way to fight the intrusive system is with a good offense. These clients often appear at the office with little or no notice. Some cultural groups (e.g., Native Americans) protest by withdrawal or silence and most likely will not come to the office. Therefore, the worker must go to them. For most protective workers, the first client contact is in the parents' home, which offers several advantages. First, the clients perhaps feel greater comfort and protection in their own familiar setting. The family may actually gain strength from this setting. From the worker's perspective, the home is an ideal diagnostic arena (Bloom, 1973). The family drama is played out daily in this setting, and aspects of this interaction will continue, regardless of the presence of an outsider.

> *It became clear from visiting the Jenks's home that the primary rule was to pacify Mr. Jenks. Running of the household revolved around his return from work at 5:30. Whatever energy the severely ill mother, Kitty, was able to muster was directed toward her husband's comfort. But the furniture and the holes in the wall attested to the father's rage when his needs were not met by his wife and four children. Only 9-year-old Herbie, reported to the agency as a victim of severe abuse, did not subscribe to the family's mission, and had obviously suffered for it. After visiting on several occasions and at different times of the day, the worker realized that the family dynamics changed significantly depending on the presence or anticipated presence of Mr. Jenks. Midday was marked by relative calm, while the closer to 5:30 the family was seen, the more intense were their interactions.*

In some cultures, one does not take problems outside the home. Thus being in the client's home may enable the investigator to learn more about what originated the report.

Family patterns emerge as one observes members in their home. The quality of relationships becomes more clearly discernible; the unpredictable behavior of children and their parents' candid response to them provide workers with valuable information. Client strengths can be identified (Bishop, 1983). For example, noticing a flair for creativity in home decoration may give a worker the opportunity to encourage outside interests for an isolated mother. Severe neglect of the home may indicate depression or a feeling of being overwhelmed by life and responsibilities. On the other hand, clients' compulsive and rigid neatness may reflect control, anger, or extremely high expectations that manifest themselves in child management. Less experienced workers may find that their own values about housekeeping standards must be acknowledged and not allowed to affect their view of the client's. It is important for workers not to generalize on the appearance of the home. The impressions gleaned from the home visit should instead be mentally filed for future use in diagnostic assessment.

Visits in the home also provide clients with an element of control as well as comfort—a fact that is not without frustrations for many social workers. Clients, for example, may not answer the door or not be home for appointments. In some instances unannounced home visits are made, but a letter is usually sent to clients alerting them to the worker's intention to visit.

Consistency and a caring attitude seem the best way to work with a resistant client. Sometimes a note, saying that the worker is sorry to have missed Mrs. Jones but will be back at the same time next week, will indicate to the client that the worker intends to be persistent. The frustration itself represents interaction, and the engagement of the client has indeed begun. The worker hopes that consistency and persistence will be rewarded by some degree of client cooperation. If, however, the child is perceived to be at too much risk, court intervention may be immediately necessary.

Through the frustration of missed appointments and unopened doors, it is vital to remember the attitudes and motivations that underlie the resistance of protective clients. Resistance is, in fact, based on fear. We all fear unwanted intrusion in our lives, especially if it is accompanied by the perceived admonishment that we are not assuming responsibility as we should. Although workers are trained not to tell clients they are not parenting effectively, the fact of social service intervention nevertheless conveys the message. Further, clients often see protective services as the agency that takes away children. Although hampered perhaps in child rearing by their own childhoods, their attitudes, inabilities, or incapacities, most parents do love their children. Suggesting that children cannot stay at home makes parents feel branded as failures.

For the most part, protective clients have histories of deprivation and betrayals. Much of their relationship with the protective worker will be colored by the client's fear of being betrayed and abandoned once again. Clients who learn to trust the worker may become greatly dependent on him or her. Thus, allowing a social worker to enter one's life can provoke anxiety.

Clients control and resist during interviews. They also control by missing them. The too-loud TV, ringing phone, or frequent demands of children provide distractions behind which some clients hide. Again, perseverance and the polite and patient suggestion that these issues are important and must be discussed may help. Clients often surround themselves with neighbors or relatives who either speak on their behalf or ensure that the conversation remains superficial. The worker may need to request to see the client alone. It is important to remember, however, that the kinship values of some cultures means that the presence of relatives and intimates is not as much resistance as inclusion. In these situations, recognition of these cultural variations may actually enhance the relationship between worker and client.

Clients use a variety of resistance techniques. A young social worker describes her experience with a neglectful mother whose child had been placed in foster care by the courts.

> *Dot was sullen and withdrawn during our interview. We talked about the action she would need to take to have her daughter returned. Suddenly she got up, walked through a nearby door, and shut it. I heard the lock click. I assumed she had gone to the bathroom until I saw that the bathroom door was open—and the room was empty. I waited and waited. All I could think of was, "No one ever told me what to do about this!" I must have sat there for 20 minutes and finally called to her. No answer. I knocked on another door and asked, "Are you okay?" No answer. I then realized that Dot had no intention of coming out. I wrote her a note telling her when I would be back and left it on the table. Not knowing what else to do, I left.*

The home visit provides opportunities to engage the client; befriending a much-loved pet, admiring a possession, or appreciating a cup of coffee helps clients witness the worker's concern. Hispanic-American clients may actually be more cooperative if they see the worker as a warm, friendly individual who could be part of the family. Above all, however, it is important to remember that seeing clients at home is entering their sanctuary. The home is the most intimate area of one's life. Respecting this sanctity while still effecting protective work is the art of home visiting.

Assessing Aspects of Risk

Assessment begins the moment the social worker assumes a case. Discussions with the reporter, reading old files and new reports, and contacts with collaterals (e.g., teachers, neighbors, therapists, or others involved with the family) are all important. However, the first interview with the client must provide information pivotal to the case. Initially, the social worker must answer four questions:

1. Is the child at risk from abuse or neglect and to what degree?
2. What is causing the problem?
3. Are there services that could be offered to alleviate the problem?
4. Is the home a safe environment or must the child be placed? (DePanfilis and Scannapieco, 1994).

Risk to the child must be fully investigated. Can the child remain at home? It is vital to look at risk in the context of the type of abuse, the family history, and the family's attitude toward the child. Neglect, although disturbing, usually has been going on for years, if not for generations. Unless the family decides to flee to avoid intervention or unless the child's health is severely endangered, the situation is perhaps not overly volatile. Physical abuse, on the other hand, is much less predictable. The report itself can precipitate further abuse. Yet for some families, the intervention of authority, represented by protective services, is enough to give the child some protection.

Familial sexual abuse has probably gone on over a period of time and, short of pregnancy, venereal disease, or physical harm, the child may not be in immediate danger. However, several factors tend to cause protective service agencies to see sexual abuse as a high-risk situation. First, society in general believes sexual contact between adults and children so abhorrent that it must be stopped. Second, once disclosure has taken place, with its initial crisis, confusion, and disorganization, an incestuous family tends to mobilize itself to preserve its existence. If intervention does not begin immediately at disclosure, the family may persuade the child to recant, protect itself with legal help, or even flee. And finally, after disclosure, the chance of suicidal thoughts or actions on the part of the child or the perpetrator or both is high, and immediate intervention may be needed (Faller, 1988).

The next few sections cover interviewing to further assess risk. Before this interviewing is undertaken, it is important that the worker determine which conditions present low risk and which present high risk for dependent children. Risk may be assessed according to several interdependent, yet situation-specific, factors: child specific, caregiver related, perpetrator specific, incident related, and environmental factors. Table 10.1 outlines these factors and provides a method of assessing the degree of risk to the child or children.

Children

The child-specific factors to consider are age and physical or mental abilities. The younger the child, the more vulnerable he or she is to the abuse; the same force may cause more injury to an infant, for example, than to an older child. Further on the continuum, the worker considers the mental and physical capacities of the child to protect himself or herself. Children who are mentally retarded, physically disabled, congenitally malformed, premature, chronically ill, or physically affected by the parents' use of drugs or alcohol during pregnancy are at higher risk for maltreatment (DePanfilis and Scannapieco, 1994).

Caregivers

Initially the worker notes the level of cooperation and capabilities shown by the caregivers, remembering to frame this within a cultural context. Parents who recognize there is a problem present a better prognosis and less risk to the children than those who demonstrate hostility or refuse to cooperate. The physical, mental, and emotional capabilities of the parent—as evidenced by their expectations of the child, ability to protect the child, ability to control anger, or other impulses—indicate the degree of risk to the victim. Parents who are unaware of children's needs or demonstrate poor judgment or concept of reality present a high risk to the dependent child.

Perpetrators

Here, the worker is concerned with the abuser's rationality of behavior and access to the child. The adult who intentionally abuses or who has a history of abusive or sadistic behav-

TABLE 10.1   Assessment of Risk

Factors	Low Risk	Intermediate Risk	High Risk
Child			
Age	Adolescent	Lower elementary school age	Infant
Physical and mental abilities	Cares for and protects self without adult assistance	Requires adult assistance to care for and protect self	Completely unable to care for or protect self without assistance
Caretaker			
Level of cooperation	Aware of problem; works with social service agency to resolve problem and protect child	Overly compliant with investigator	Doesn't believe there is a problem; refuses to cooperate
Physical, mental, and emotional abilities or control	Realistic expectations of child; can plan to correct problem	Poor reasoning abilities; may be physically handicapped; needs planning to protect child	Poor conception of reality or severe mental or physical handicaps
Perpetrator			
Rationality of behavior	Accidental injury; adequate supervision	Minor injury, resulting from excessive corporal discipline	Injury, the result of irrational desire to harm the child permanently
Access to child	Out of home; no access to child	In home, but access to child is difficult	In home with complete access to child
Incident			
Extent of permanent harm	Abuse or neglect has no discernible effect on child	Abuse or neglect results in physical injury or discomfort; no medical attention needed	Abuse or neglect may result in death or permanent dysfunction of an organ or limb
Location of injury	Bony body parts, knees, elbows, buttocks	Torso	Head, face, genitals
Previous history of abuse or neglect	No previous reported history of neglect or abuse	Previous abuse or neglect of child	Previous abuse or neglect of child
Physical condition of home	Home is clean with no apparent safety or health hazards	Trash and garbage not disposed; animal droppings in home	Structurally unsound, leaky roof and windows, wall bending under weight, holes in exterior walls
Environmental			
Support system	Family, neighbors, friends, available; good community	Family supportive but not in geographic area; some support from friends	Caretaker or family have no relatives or friends and are geographically isolated from community
Stress	Stable family, steady employment, nonmobile	Birth of child	Death of spouse

Adapted from Massachusetts Department of Social Services, *Reference Guide for Child Abuse and Neglect Investigations,* Boston: Massachusetts Department of Social Services, 1985, p. 59.

ior places the child in greater danger than the accidental abuser. Further, the greater the perpetrator's access to the child, the more likely the abuse is to be repeated.

Incidence and Environment

The incident itself is weighed in the light of future potential harm to the child. The worker determines the likelihood of permanent harm, the location of the injury, the previous history of abuse or neglect, and the physical conditions of the home. Environmental factors provide additional information. Parents who do not use support systems place the child at higher risk, for example, than those who can reach out for help. The degree of stress in the home also affects the likelihood of abuse. Death, divorce, incarceration of a parent, unemployment, career change, residence change, and birth of a child can all place a child at greater risk (Massachusetts Department of Social Services, 1985). Again, all these factors must be evaluated within a cultural context.

Assessing Causes and Services

The causes of child maltreatment are myriad. Assessment begins at the first meeting with the client and continues throughout treatment. Whether there are existing services to provide aid or otherwise help the situation is a factor in assessing risk to the child. A family for whom little can be done—because of the severity of their problems or their unwillingness to use services—provides greater risk for the child. Removal of the child may therefore be indicated.

One particularly difficult aspect of assessment is that it is usual for the family to initially deny the report of maltreatment. Subsequent interviews will be much more productive if the worker is able to identify with the client's underlying feelings and need to deny rather than with the denial itself. Recognizing feelings rather than assigning blame often elicits the client's recounting of his or her perception of the situation. During the client's presentation of the facts, the worker gathers clues in order to "begin where the client is." Does the father feel overwhelmed by the problems of inadequate housing? Does the mother see her frustrations increased by an alcoholic husband? Does the parent try to cope with new cultural mores combined with the stresses of finding a place for himself or herself in a seemingly hostile culture? Worker-client engagement can be enhanced by the worker's ability to give direct support to the client (DePanfilis and Salus, 1992).

For example, Mrs. Clemens, defensively recounting her problems, mentioned the difficulty of feeding her seven children. Being sure Mrs. Clemens would be eligible, given what was already known about the family, the worker suggested food stamps. "Oh, I've heard of them little coupons," the mother responded, "but I never knew where you got 'em." The worker arranged to take Mrs. Clemens to get food stamps, and the mother was then more amenable to discussing the problems of her children.

Some parents do not deny the report, and instead feel they were justified in their actions. Mr. Alverey, for example, acknowledged that the belt marks on his son's legs were punishment for the boy's misbehavior. "My father punished me that way," he contended, "and I turned out okay." The worker was able to identify with this father's concern for his son, but tried to help him use less forceful disciplinary methods. Met with Mr. Alverey's resistance to change, the worker had to firmly stress that the beatings must stop or court intervention would be necessary. If the practice that caused the abuse is accepted in another culture, but not in the United States, the family must be helped to understand this.

On the first visit, an assessment of immediate risk to the child is vital. If the worker begins to engage the parents by recognizing their feelings and needs, future intervention should go more smoothly.

Handling Emergencies

At the onset or at any time during the intervention process, the protective case may reach the point of emergency. What constitutes an emergency is debatable, but agencies generally acknowledge three conditions: imminent danger of physical harm to the child, a dangerous home situation, or abandonment of the child. Immediate responses may include the police taking custody or hospital staff detaining children whom they deem to be in danger. In some states, protective services workers may also remove children from their homes in an emergency. Immediately following the emergency removal, a court order (authorizing custody) must be obtained. According to the Model Child Protection Act (U.S. Department of Health, Education and Welfare, 1977), a child taken into custody must not only be in danger but there must be no time to obtain a court order. Most states recommend that if the emergency is during working hours, a court order be obtained prior to removing the child.

In some emergency situations, protective services workers rely on police to aid them in the removal of children. For example, if the home situation is volatile or there is danger to the worker as well as the child, police may be asked to help. A worker who fears violence or retaliation from the parent, or who has reason to believe that the parents will flee, may seek police support. Police officers can be invaluable in handling hostile or aggressive parents while the worker attempts to calm and pack for overwrought children.

Emergencies require particular skills of protective workers. Assessment must be made quickly while weighing carefully the risk of the child and the rights of the parents. Actions must be purposeful while still recognizing the feelings of those involved. In most cases, the worker has time to interview and assess, but emergencies do occur.

Interviewing Adults

Validating the existence of abuse or neglect without antagonizing parents (and thereby closing the door to their help in the future) or precipitating an emergency is not easy. Not only does the worker have particular questions that should be answered to assess risk to the child but he or she must also use good interviewing skills to elicit the responses and engage the client. The investigative worker must seem confident, skilled, relaxed, and be assertive without losing the ability to communicate concern and compassion.

How an interview progresses depends on the worker's style and attitudes as well as on the client's responses. Table 10.2 lists interviewing techniques. Several other factors go into successful interviewing.

The worker must recognize the level of sophistication of the parents. In Polansky's studies (1972, 1981), he and his colleagues observed that neglectful mothers demonstrated verbal inaccessibility or a limited ability to communicate, especially in relation to their thoughts and feelings. It was important, therefore, to use simple language to explain things carefully, and to encourage client feedback to test for understanding. Although more sophisticated clients have a better command of language, they may still be unfamiliar with the process of the social service system or with social work jargon. Certainly a worker must be careful to refrain from language that implies blame or connotes particular values.

TABLE 10.2   Skills Used in Interviewing

1. Listening
   Attending — The process by which the interviewer communicates interest and encouragement to the client. Attending involves
   Establishing eye contact*
   Maintaining a posture indicating interest;
   Using gestures to communicate message; and
   Verbalizing statements that relate to the client's statements.

   Paraphrasing — The method of restating the client's message to test the interviewer's understanding of what has been said.

   Clarifying — The process of bringing the client's message into clearer focus by the interviewer's restating or asking for clarification.

   Perception-checking — The process of the interviewer verifying his or her perceptions by paraphrasing what was heard, requesting feedback on the validity of the perception, and then correcting the perception as necessary.

2. Leading
   Indirect Leading — Inviting the client to tell his or her story by saying, for example, "What would you like to discuss?" or "Tell me more about that."

   Direct Leading — Focusing the topic by a suggestion to do so, for example, "Can you tell me about the last time you saw welts on Johnny?"

   Focusing — Bringing the client back to the topic that the interviewer needs to discuss, for example, "Could you think about what it is that annoys you about his behavior?" or "What are you feeling right now after we've been talking?"

   Questioning — Using open-ended questions (those that require more than a yes or no answer) to further explore the client's message.

3. Reflecting
   Reflecting Feelings — Paraphrasing the client's feelings in an effort to make clearer those that were vaguely expressed. The clients are thus given an opportunity to own their own feelings by hearing what they said.

   Reflecting Experience — Relating to what the client is experiencing as he or she talks, the interviewer comments on body language, such as rapidity of speech, gestures, eye contact, or postures.

   Reflecting Content — Repeating in fewer words the ideas expressed by the client. Through the use of additional vocabulary words—to help the client express himself or herself better, or through more concise phrasing—to get to the point, which has been lost in an abundance of words, the worker clarifies the client's ideas.

4. Summarizing — Trying to aid the client by picking out various themes or overtones as the client speaks. The interviewer can aid the client by picking out the major ideas and feelings in a total interview, which helps both interviewer and client focus on the essence of the interview.

5. Confronting — Pointing out to the client what is actually happening by giving feedback about his or her behavior. The risk in confronting is that the client may not be ready to hear what the interviewer has observed.

Continued

TABLE 10.2 *Continued*

6. Interpreting	— Explaining the meaning of events to clients to enable them to see their problems in a new light. The interpretations may be given in terms of the particular philosophy or model of the interviewer. For example: "You are concerned that your daughter favors her father and seems to reject you. Many little girls at three are going through a stage when this is very natural." Sometimes the interviewer uses metaphors or stories to help interpret the client's behavior or feelings.
7. Informing	— Giving information, the most common of which is advice. Although it is often tempting to give advice, the interviewer must be aware of the client's readiness to receive it. For a variety of reasons, clients frequently ask for advice and then do not follow it. Advice may be based on the interviewer's values and not conform to the client's.
8. Guiding	— Informing clients about what to expect in certain instances, for example, when they go to court. Guidance provides clients with information that may direct their actions and responses.

Adapted from L.M. Brammer, *The Helping Relationship: Process and Skills,* 4th ed., © 1988, pp. 66–94.
Adapted by permission of Prentice-Hall, Inc., Englewood Cliffs, New Jersey.
*Where culturally appropriate.

Clients for whom English is a second language or who are relatively new to the culture may also need to have things explained slowly and carefully. Workers (in interviewing) must also be aware of cultural variations. For example, most people have been taught that eye contact is important, but some cultures (e.g., Asian) see it as disrespectful. Many cultures (e.g., Hispanic) will be resistant unless the worker has taken time to become acquainted through answering questions about himself or herself and chatting. The Hispanic is looking to respect this person before he or she will disclose (Lum, 1992; Comas-Diaz, 1993).

The purpose of the interview is to gather facts or information in order to assess the danger to the child. Direct questioning is likely to put the parent on the defensive. A series of open-ended questions or reflections, or giving the parent an opportunity to express his or her own feelings and attitudes toward the child, is more effective. Another technique to uncover previously hidden facts or discrepancies is to ask the parent to recount in detail the incident that resulted in the child's injury. For example, "Could you show me what happened when Susie fell off the bed?" Careful observation not only of the parent's description but also of his or her emotional response and manner in telling the story will help the worker to gather more information.

Mrs. Hall tearfully explained how she had been in the other room when she heard 1-year-old Susie scream. Her husband had been there with the baby. When asked to describe the fall, Mr. Hall responded angrily, "What do you mean describe to you how she fell? If you fall off a bed, you just fall off a bed." As the worker discussed the situation further with this father and mother, she recognized the inconsistencies in their accounts. A fall from the height of the bed could not have caused

Susie's type of injury. The mother often confused facts and seemed more concerned with her story than with Susie's welfare. She was defensive, although the worker had implied no blame. Finally, Mrs. Hall tearfully admitted that she had been with Susie and had been so angered by her constant crying that she had slapped her. The blow was so hard the child was thrown off the bed with enough force to fracture her arm. The father's inability to explain the accident, in addition to other discrepancies, had given the worker her first clue.

Although the facts of abusive incidents are important, there are particular areas that should also be explored during the first few interviews in order to gather information for validation.

Parental History and Functioning
- How does the parent feel about the parental role? Are there cultural variations to this role?
- How did the parent's own parents discipline? Has the parent adopted the same methods that result in physical abuse or neglect?
- Was the parent sexually abused as a child?
- Did the parent experience early deprivation (which may hamper the parent's own ability to nurture) or abuse?
- Did the parent experience abandonment, death, or divorce as a child?
- Were the parent's parents alcoholic, drug-dependent, or involved in criminal activity?
- Does the parent show evidence of extreme rigidity, excessive dependency needs, or borderline or state of psychosis?
- Has the family newly immigrated?

Parent's View of the Child
- What kind of expectations does the parent have of the child?
- Does the parent appear to understand the child's developmental needs?
- Does the parent see the child as difficult, unusual, hard to care for, or even "evil"?
- Does the parent describe the child in negative terms?
- Does the parent touch the child lovingly or talk to the child with affection? Or does the parent seem unable to comfort the child and perhaps stiffen when touched?
- Can the parent provide a history of the child's developmental milestones?
- Does the parent ignore the child or talk negatively about him or her in the child's presence?
- Is the parent frequently frustrated with the child? Is the child a scapegoat?
- Is the parent jealous or extremely overprotective of the child?
- Does the parent compare the child negatively to anyone else in the family?
- Does the parent describe the child as having any significant health or behavior problems?
- Is the parent overly seductive with the child?
- Does the parent engage in role reversal with the child? Is the child expected to assume adult responsibilities and take care of the parent?

Functioning of the family
- Does one parent significantly dominate the other? (Is this culturally appropriate?)
- Are the parents openly antagonistic to each other?

- Are the conflicts between parents taken out on the children?
- Do there appear to be no family rules or extremely rigid rules?
- Is there marked role reversal between parents and children?
- Are the generational boundaries blurred?
- Do the parents appear to be covering up for one another?
- Is there undue stress on the family (e.g., significant losses, unemployment, alcoholism, residential moves, prejudice, or one parent absent)?
- During stress do family members appear to abandon each other or do they become neurotically overdependent on one another? (Keep in mind that some cultures are more family oriented than others.)
- Do family members engage in eye contact or physical contact?
- Do family members engage in activities together?

Environment
- Are there chronic environmental stresses or long-term problems that sap the parents' energies? (Are there, for example, feuds with relatives or neighbors, poverty, discrimination, infestation by rodents, inadequate sanitation, significantly different cultural mores, or inadequate space and privacy?)
- Are there neighborhood factors that threaten the child's safety? (Is there, for example, drug trafficking, unsafe housing, an unprotected body of water or wells, a condemned building, or a high crime rate?)
- Are there conditions around the home that endanger the child's safety? (For instance, are there easily accessible poisons, sharp objects, broken glass, exposed electrical wiring, rotten or moldy food, or small objects dangerous to a child under 2 years old?)

Family's Support System
- Does the family appear to be isolated either geographically or in terms of having someone close they could call on?
- In a time of crisis, does the family have friends or relatives they feel they can ask for help?
- Does the family depend more on formal social service systems than on informal systems?

An assessment of the family's support system—that is, who they have available to go to in time of crisis or to share good times—is particularly important. Research attests that a major cause for abuse is isolation. A family that is isolated is more vulnerable to intrafamily and environmental stresses. Later treatment may help family members make connections with others who can be of support emotionally, especially in times of crisis.

Although not all these questions can be answered in one interview, the astute protective worker gains a great deal of insight by careful observation as well as from verbal interchange on this interview.

Interviewing Children

Children—both victims and their siblings—provide valuable information in the investigation of protective cases. It is important to remember several important facts about children, however.

Expression

Children often speak in metaphors, whereas adults usually give a more literal interpretation of a situation. Children often relate their experiences in stories (especially in cases of sexual abuse). Children's drawings, especially, symbolize what they are attempting to express (see Sgroi, 1982, pp. 298–303). With this in mind, the investigative interviewer takes care to consider what the child has said at many levels.

Time

Children may have difficulty understanding time in the way adults do. A day, a week, or a year may mean little to a young child. On the other hand, the interviewer learns to use milestones such as "the time you got up" or "how long before Christmas."

Attention

Children are not used to being interviewed in the way we traditionally talk with adults. Indeed, their attention spans may not be sufficient to cover the entire story at one time. For this reason, a variety of techniques are used with children. They may be encouraged to draw or to act out the incident themselves or use dolls or talk to puppets.

Setting

Children perceive adults as authority figures and this may color their responses. The wise interviewer engages the child in a nonthreatening manner, often sitting on child-sized chairs or even on the floor to come down to the child's level.

Memories

Children's memories differ from adults. Does fantasy distort children's memories? Although it is often assumed that children recall at poorer rates than adults, this seems to be related more to their insufficient experience and lesser ability with the language than to their ability to retain information. In fact, because children's heads are less cluttered with extraneous details, they may have a better recall of certain events (Jones and McQuiston, 1985).

It is often debated whether children are able to differentiate between fact and fantasy. This has been an especially controversial topic in the consideration of the testimony of children in sexual abuse cases. Jones and McQuiston state:

> Young children may indeed have problems distinguishing their own thoughts and dreams from what actually did happen, but only in a specific way. That is, children do not appear to be more likely to confuse what they have dreamed of doing with what they actually saw; on the other hand, young children do have problems distinguishing between what they have actually done and what they have thought of doing. (1985, p. 11)

Developmental Level

If one considers the developmental level of a young child and the child's understanding of sex as witnessed by their play (see Table 10.3), it is not likely that the details of oral and genital sex, for example, would be in the child's frame of reference. Therefore, the child has not imagined doing it and does not have these imaginings to confuse with reality.

TABLE 10.3   Stages of Sex Play

0–18 months	Child begins awareness of ability to experience pleasure from own body, including genital exploration.
2½ years	Child shows interest in different postures of boys and girls when urinating and interest in physical differences between the sexes. Genital exploration continues.
3 years	Verbally expresses interest in physical differences between sexes and in different postures in urinating. Girls attempt to urinate standing up. May feel increased need for genital masturbation.
4 years	Extremely conscious of the navel. Under social stress may grasp genitals and may need to urinate. May play the game of "show." Also, verbal play about elimination. Interest in other people's bathrooms; may demand privacy for self, but be extremely interested in bathroom activity of others.
5 years	Familiar with but not too much interested in physical differences between sexes. Less sex play and game of "show." More modest and less exposing of self. Less bathroom play and less interest in unfamiliar bathrooms.
6 years	Marked awareness of and interest in differences between sexes in body structure. Questioning. Mutual investigation by both sexes reveals practical answers to questions about sex differences. Mild sex play or exhibitionism in play or in school toilets. Game of "show." May play hospital and take temperature. Giggling, calling names, or remarks involving words dealing with elimination functions.
7 years	Less interest in sex. Some mutual exploration, experimentation, and sex play, but less than earlier. Sexually oriented dreams and fantasies begin, commonly resulting in "wet dreams." Strong feeling of modesty and privacy needs beginning to be expressed.
8 years	Interest in sex rather high, though sex exploration and play is less common than at six. Interest in peeping, smutty jokes, provocative giggling. Children whisper, write, or spell "elimination" or "sex" words.
9 years	May talk about sex information with friends of same sex. Interest in details of own organs and functions; seeks out pictures in books. Sex swearing and sex poems begin.
10 years	Considerable interest in "smutty" jokes. Feelings of modesty. Privacy continues. Onset of secondary sex characteristics may begin.

From Ilg, Ames, and Baker, *Child Behavior.* Copyright © 1980 by Harper and Row Publishers, Inc. Reprinted with permission.
Note: Some cultures differ markedly from this chart. Cultural variations must be considered.

Language

Children use different terminologies and language. During an interview, especially when validating sexual abuse, the interviewer needs to verify the child's terminology, especially about body parts. This can be done by having the child point to areas of his or her own body or by using anatomically correct dolls or pictures. Once the meaning is clear, it may be more comfortable for the child to use his or her own terminology (Sgroi, 1982; Everson and Boat, 1994; Faller, 1996).

In addition to the above, the interviewer of children must take into consideration the child's age, maturity, language and communication skills, and emotional readiness to be interviewed.

Setting up an interview with a child necessitates more care than for an interview with an adult. Children are usually seen alone or sometimes with a "functioning ally," that is, a concerned adult who takes the child's side and protects him or her from further abuse. Workers often try to see the child at school or in another neutral setting where parental intervention will not cause the child undue concern. In this case, to alleviate guilt, the child is often assured that the parent will be told of the interview. The parent is subsequently notified.

Sometimes it is necessary to see a child in the home. The parents' cooperation will then need to be secured. Certainly the child is entitled to as much confidentiality as an adult, and the parents are helped to understand this. The setting of the interview (if one has control over this) should be free of distractions but equipped with a few necessary resources—such as paper, crayons, dolls and other toys, and materials designed to enable the child to explain what has happened. Interviewers are usually cautious about having too many toys in the room, as this can serve to distract. Older children are often aided in their talking by playing board games.

The actual interview usually involves engaging the child, establishing the interviewer's credibility, fact finding, allaying the child's anxiety, and helping the child to anticipate the future.

Engaging begins with helping the child feel comfortable by letting the child explore the room, ask questions, or talk about school, friends, or activities. This spontaneous small talk makes the child feel comfortable and also assists the interviewer to discern the child's emotional style, maturity, and ability to communicate. The interviewer explains to the child why he or she is there. This may lead naturally into establishing the credibility of the interviewer. Comments, such as, "I've talked to many other boys and girls who had this kind of problem" help the child see the worker as someone others have trusted. The child may also feel less alone in his or her problem (Sgroi, 1982). During these opening phases, the worker should be especially sensitive to any anxiety the child is feeling and reflect on this. By feeling that he or she has agreed to give this information, the child is helped to feel in control. The abused child is one who has felt out of control for a long time, so giving the child an element of control through the interview can be the beginning of the therapeutic process.

Fact finding is not as simple and straightforward as it may be when interviewing adults. Children have short attention spans. They may not want to discuss the abuse. As a result, they may change the subject frequently or want to end the interview. Such an interview takes mental agility and creativity. One 5-year-old boy, being interviewed by a worker and observed behind a one-way mirror by a team of professionals, refused to discuss the "games" his mother's boyfriend played with him. After undressing anatomically correct dolls and asking the child to identify the body parts, as well as numerous other techniques, the worker was at a loss. She assured the child she would return, and went to talk with her colleagues. As soon as she left, the child scrambled under the table with the male doll and furtively sucked on its cloth penis. He then took out his own penis and attempted to insert it in the doll's mouth. With this obvious demonstration of what had been done to the boy, the worker returned and began gently questioning him about male penises, without disclosing what she had seen. Eventually the boy began to talk about the boyfriend's sexual abuse of him.

Although open-ended questions are a good place to begin, the worker may need to be more direct without leading the child into specifics. For example, the interviewer might say, "I've talked with children who have had adults touch them in the private places of their bodies. Has that ever happened to you?" Or, in the case of physical abuse, "Some kids say that they had accidents because they are afraid to say that someone had hit them." It may seem natural to the interviewer to ask the child direct questions that will confirm what the worker believes has happened. However, it is important that questions be kept nonleading. Although small children do not usually lie, especially about sexual abuse, they may easily be led to make erroneous statements by their desire to please adults. For example, one interviewer believed that a child had been sexually abused by her father and communicated this belief to the child. With anatomically correct dolls, the worker placed the adult male doll on the girl doll and asked, "Is this what your father did to you?" The child—having roughhoused with her father in the past—was confused. She had not felt what she and her father had done was wrong. She sensed, however, that the worker did and wanted her to respond affirmatively. Her mother, too, had pressured her, so the child decided she had better agree that this had happened.

Such obvious leading of a child to accuse the father, who turned out to be innocent, causes great pain for all involved. Prejudicing juvenile witnesses jeopardizes court cases that are brought against guilty perpetrators. For this reason, interviewers are being taught to be especially careful. Some agencies videotape or record the interview to ensure that they have an accurate record of what—and how—the child was asked.

Instead of talking to the worker, the child may prefer to draw what happened without saying anything. The interviewer then encourages the child to explain the picture. Puppets are useful because a child can engage in a conversation with the worker's puppet or through his or her own puppet without having to talk to the interviewer directly.

The worker must be particularly sensitive to the feelings of the child during the telling of the abuse. Children experience fear, anxiety, guilt, shame, and a myriad of other emotions. In addition, children do not always have the same view of the abuser that an adult may. An abusing parent may still be beloved because the child internalizes the guilt. On the other hand, expressions of extreme rage and hatred may be difficult for the worker to accept.

Other validating information to assess the further risk to the child may be necessary after the interview, but the child's own assessment of safety is often quite accurate. Questions about what precipitated the abuse may indicate what steps will be needed to protect the child in the future.

Sometimes it is useful to ask the child to reconstruct the event. The effectiveness of this technique must be weighed against possible trauma to the child of remembering in such detail. If remembering appears to be beneficial rather than detrimental, the worker might ask the child to recall the setting, what he or she was wearing, where the abuser was, where others were, and how the abuse occurred (Jones and McQuiston, 1985). If the child is from a culture with distinct taboos against talking about sex, the interview may be more difficult.

Sgroi (1982) and Faller (1988, 1996) suggest that in the case of sexual abuse, the worker should consider certain validating factors: multiple incidents over a period of time, progression of sexual activity, elements of secrecy, elements of pressure or coercion, and explicit details of sexual behavior. Since most sexual abuse includes multiple incidents over time, the interviewer can discover from the child if this was the case. As discussed in previous chapters, sexual abuse usually involves a progression of sexual activity that becomes more intimate over time. In almost all situations, the perpetrator of sexual abuse pressures or coerces the victim and then compels secrecy. And finally, the child who recounts in explicit detail would not have sufficient knowledge for such a description unless he or she had been abused.

DeYoung (1986) suggests a variation on this framework as a means of judging the truthfulness of the allegations of young children in sexual abuse. She cites clarity, celerity, certainty, and consistency as indicators of the validity of the reports. But children between the ages of 2 and 7 (the ages of her study) demonstrate problems in these areas. In terms of clarity, children of these ages may have difficulty in expressing themselves accurately. They must rely on their limited experience for elaboration. Thus "ejaculation" becomes "urination," as the latter is the only function of the penis with which they are familiar. Their thinking is concrete, and has insufficient subtlety to recognize objects in an altered form. The relationship between the erect and flaccid penis therefore confuses them. Children may also delay telling anyone about their abuse. Such delays actually give credence to the child's report, as delay is the rule rather than the exception. It must also be noted that delays are not a result of the child's doubt of what has happened but of the perpetrator's demands for secrecy.

The lack of certainty, often pointed to in the testimony of abused children, relates to their perception of reality. The abuser may have told the child that the sex interaction was normal, while other adults are now saying it is not. The child, therefore, is required to sort out or reinterpret the abuse and is often confused.

The last factor deYoung cites as considered in the testimony of sexually abused children is consistency. There is a great deal of pressure on the child to recant or amend the accusation. Further, the way in which the child tells the story to a given adult may differ according to the adult's style and manner of interviewing.

If these four validation points are compromised with young children, how then can the allegation be verified? DeYoung (1986) suggests that the answer is found in specific details: The child who is asked to describe the acts of sexual abuse and can do so in detail—especially if these details exceed the child's level of understanding and maturity—is more likely to be believed. The context of the abuse should also be described. Asking the child to describe exactly where the abuse occurred and where others were at the time elicits further specific details. In addition, the more specific the child can be about how the perpetrator elicited secrecy, the better. Did the abuser threaten or bribe the child or suggest harm to others?

And finally, the way in which the child recounts the abuse—the child's affect—is important. Did the child experience pleasure, pain, confusion? The child will often describe mixed emotions—pain at the penetration, but happiness and warmth at the amount of attention received from the perpetrator. The victim may not feel negative toward the abuser. And this fact can confuse the less experienced or even the informed interviewer.

In validation, much use can also be made of the past trauma factors suggested by Finkelhor and Browne (1985) and deYoung (1986): An abused child will demonstrate traumatic sexualization (using sexual behavior to manipulate others or demonstrating age-inappropriate sexual knowledge); indicate a feeling of betrayal (by those previously trusted); evidence disempowerment (by feeling that all his or her needs will be overridden and by exhibiting fear and anxiety about the sense of powerlessness); and indicate a feeling of being stigmatized (evidenced by shame, guilt, blame, and low self-esteem). If these factors are present, a child is more likely to be believed.

Although most researchers and practitioners report that young children, especially, rarely fabricate stories of sexual abuse on their own and should be believed, the court system, in prosecution of perpetrators, has required more attention to the validity of allegations. A particular concern is still expressed over the accusation of sexual abuse by adolescents. Are adolescents more likely to fabricate the sexually abusive experience? Because adolescents are engaged in battles for control and separation, some may use allegations of sexual abuse as tools in this conflict (Ziefert, 1981). Although there is certainly this possibility, the skilled interviewer concentrates on adolescents' details and considers their clarity, celerity, certainty, and consistency that smaller children tend to distort. If it is found that the adolescent has used the accusation as a weapon, some investigation should be undertaken as to why this particular weapon was used. Was the adolescent traumatized at an earlier time by someone else?

Once the child or adolescent has told the interviewer about the abuse in depth, he or she may feel anxious, fearful, and guilty about having disclosed so much or about what the abuser might do. The child needs assurance of protection. Fears must be allayed—not that the situation will immediately improve but that the worker is willing to help. The child should be told that he or she is not to blame, and that it was important that he or she was able to talk with the interviewer.

Children wonder, and should be helped to anticipate, what will happen in the future. Sgroi (1982) refers to this type of preparation as *anticipatory guidance*. The thorough interviewer finds out what the child expects or wants to happen. Despite some assumptions, the child may not want to return home. The worker makes clear to the child, however, that what does happen depends on many factors and not just the interview. Children should not be given false hopes that their desires will prevail, nor should they be left with the feeling that they are to blame for the outcome. In the balance between assisting children in feeling somewhat in control and recognizing that they are still children, and therefore subject to the decisions of parents, social services, and the courts, workers face a difficult problem. Some element of control can be found, however, in knowing what might happen. The child can be told that the worker will see the parents and may talk with the child again. If the worker is sure that the court will be part of the process, the child may be helped by seeing the courtroom and knowing who will stand where. The worker's encouragement of the child's questions may strengthen the bond and elevate the trust between worker and child.

Interviewing a child necessitates skill, calm, self-assurance, and both cultural and personal sensitivity. The worker who does not enjoy or appreciate children or who is not familiar with the particular child's culture is not a good candidate for this task. For this reason, the worker who interviews children should be carefully chosen.

Anticipated prosecution of abusers in sexual abuse situations has stimulated the search for more accurate methods of validation that will not put increased stress on the victim. Videotaping of the allegedly abused child is one area in which advances are being made to alleviate the stress on the child. Prior to videotaping, a child is asked to repeat the account to numerous people—social workers, police, therapists, the judge, and a myriad of others. Videotaping places the child and just one experienced interviewer in a room with anatomically correct dolls, drawing materials, puppets, and other tools through which the child can find expression. The interview can be watched behind a one-way mirror by police, district attorneys, psychiatric or medical consultants, or other professionals who are or will be involved in the case. The tape provides visual evidence to assess the child's credibility. There has been much controversy over whether or not such a tape can be used in court in lieu of the child's testimony. The justice system grants the right to everyone accused to face his or her accuser and has not yet settled on a provision for the unique situation of abused children.

Some states are, however, addressing this issue with specific legislation. The Texas legislature, for example, in 1983 passed a bill that not only allows sexually abused children to be videotaped but declares the tape as admissible evidence in criminal and civil procedures. To ensure the protection of all parties, the bill stipulated several requirements. No attorney may be present at the taping of the interview. The video equipment must be operated by competent, experienced operators and the voices on the tape must be fully identified. The child must not be asked leading questions and the worker interviewing the child must be experienced and trained in interviewing. The requirements stipulate that the interviewer must be available to testify or be cross-examined at the court proceedings. The child too may be called to testify if the court deems it necessary, although this would be done in the judge's quarters rather than the open court. And finally, the defendant should be allowed to see the child, but the child need not be required to face him/her (through the use of closed-circuit TV or a one-way mirror) (Colby and Colby, 1987). So far, such a ruling seems to be effective and is, in fact, being employed or explored in other states.

Not only can videotapes prevent children being needlessly and repeatedly interviewed but they can demonstrate to the nonabusing parent or to the perpetrator the validity of the child's story. This is done with much preparation and care, however, by ensuring the child knows the adults will see the tape and ensuring that the child is protected from pressure or harm after the viewing.

Another much-debated issue is the ownership of the videotape. Since the tape is an important and confidential piece of evidence, it is often retained by the district attorney or the court, which regulates its viewing. The efficacy, ethics, and usefulness of videotaping are still under discussion, and only time will tell what the outcome is.

Innovations are made not only in the legal arena but also in medical research. *The New York Times* of 28 December 1986 reported that two Baltimore researchers, Dr. Jeanne McCauley and Dr. Richard Gorman, had discovered that a dye used to detect cervical cancer could also illuminate abnormal skin breaks and irregularities that could be indicative of sexual abuse in small children. Use of such a substance, described as "similar to the ink used in cartridge pens [is] easy to apply, inexpensive, rubs off, and has no side effects," would add to the validation of physical trauma caused by sexual abuse. These are but two of the efforts being made to improve the system and help the victims of child maltreatment.

Summary

The trauma caused by child abuse and neglect can, unfortunately, be increased by the intervention system. For this reason, professionals continue to evaluate and change the intervention process so that it can be as helpful as possible to victims and their families.

The intervention process involves a series of complex steps: recognition, reporting, initial contact, investigation, and assessment. Case management, treatment planning, treatment, and evaluation and follow-up are discussed in the next chapter. The intent of this process is to stop the current abuse and neglect. Hoped-for outcomes include protecting the child from future maltreatment, teaching the parents coping skills, and possibly even changing their attitudes toward child rearing.

The first step of the process falls on the reporters. Many professionals, such as physicians, counselors, social workers, police, and teachers, are designated by law as mandated reporters. The mandated reporter is required to report the abuse or neglect to the appropriate agency—usually to the state or county department of social services—and can be penalized for failure to report.

Following the report, the social service agency decides whether or not maltreatment is present. This may necessitate talking with the alleged victim, with the parents, and with other knowledgeable people about the situation. If the case is substantiated or the conclusion made that maltreatment is a fact, further investigation ensues. A unique aspect of protective services is that much of the interviewing is done in the client's home. Home visiting involves a variety of issues not present in office interviews, and requires a worker to develop additional sensitivity along with a different set of diagnostic and interviewing skills.

Protective workers involved in the assessment process learn to ask specific questions designed to assess the potential risk of the home situation to the child and the capacity of the parents to cope with child rearing. The interviewing process is an integral part of assessment. Different skills are required for interviewing adults than for children.

Sometimes the social worker has time to investigate and assess a particular case. In other instances, however, the child is in too much danger or the parents will not cooperate. Such cases are considered emergencies, and require an immediate decision of whether to involve the court system, remove the child from the home, or both.

Validation, especially in the area of child sexual abuse, is not always easy. New techniques to improve the quality of intervention are constantly being explored. Two such techniques are videotaping the child's testimony and using a new dye that uncovers trauma to the genital area of female victims.

The next chapter considers the family's reactions to intervention and the roles of various professionals in the intervention process.

Exploration Questions

1. What is the goal of intervention in child abuse and neglect cases?

2. What is a mandated reporter? Cite several mandated reporters.

3. What information do most reporting laws or policies include?

4. What are the dilemmas for mandated reporters?

5. What is substantiation?

6. What is unique about home visiting? What are the advantages and disadvantages of home visiting? What are some cultural implications of home visiting?

7. When does assessment begin? What is the protective worker trying to assess?

8. What factors are considered in risk assessment?

9. What is an emergency in protective services? What are the options in an emergency?

10. What is the purpose of interviewing parents? Cite some areas the worker will want to explore.

11. What special factors must be considered when interviewing children? What methods are used in interviewing children?

12. What must be considered when seeking validation through an interview with a child? Are children

reliable in their information? What guidelines can be used in assessing credibility?

13. What are the advantages of videotaping a child's testimony? What legal safeguards must be considered?

Activities for Applied Learning

1. Send for a copy of the child abuse reporting laws for your state (available through the mandated reporting agency or statehouse).

2. Who in your state are listed as mandated reporters? What is the penalty for not reporting? How are mandated reporters protected if they do report?

3. Invite a member of the staff of a local protective agency to speak to the class, or interview this person on tape. Explore such issues as the procedure for making an abuse or neglect report, the length of time it takes to investigate, and the procedures for investigating an abuse or neglect case. On what other professionals in the community do protective services depend? How?

Suggested Readings

Atkinson, D. R.; Morten, G.; and Sue, D. W. *Counseling American Minorities,* Dubuque, IA: Wm. C. Brown Comm., Inc. 1993.

Brammer, L. M. *The Helping Relationship: Process and Skills.* Englewood Cliffs, NJ: Prentice-Hall, 1988.

Campbell, J. C. *Assessing the Risk of Dangerousness.* Thousand Oaks, CA: Sage, 1994.

DePanfilis, D. and Scannapieco, M. "Assessing the Safety of Children at Risk of Maltreatment: Decision-Making Models." *Child Welfare.* LXXIII 3, (1994):229–245.

Morgan, M. *How to Interview Sexual Abuse Victims.* Newbury Park, CA: Sage, 1995.

Sgroi, S. *Handbook of Clinical Intervention in Child Sexual Abuse.* Lexington, MA: Lexington Books, 1982.

References

Bishop, E. B. "The Art of Home Visiting." In *Child Abuse and Neglect: A Guide with Case Studies for Treating the Child and Family,* edited by N. Ebeling and D. Hill, pp. 61–80. Boston: PSG Publishing, 1983.

Bloom, M. L. "Usefulness of the Home Visit for Diagnosis and Treatment." *Social Casework* 54 (1973).

Brammer, L. M. *The Helping Relationship: Process and Skills.* Englewood Cliffs, NJ: Prentice-Hall, 1979.

Colby, I., and Colby, D. "Videotaped Interviews in Child Sexual Abuse Cases: The Texas Example." *Child Welfare* 66 (1987):25–34.

Comas-Diaz, L. "Hispanic\Latino Communities: Psychological Implications", in D. R. Atkinson: G. Morten; and D. W. Sue, *Counseling American Minorities,* pp. 245–263, Dubuque, IA: Wm. C. Brown Comm. Inc., 1993.

DePanfilis, D. and Salus, M. K. *A Coordinated Response to Child Abuse and Neglect: A Basic Manual.* Washington, DC: U.S. Department of Health and Human Services, 1992.

DePanfilis, D. and Scannapieco, M. "Assessing the Safety of Children at Risk for Maltreatment: Decision-Making Models." *Child Welfare.* LXXIII 3 (1994):229–245.

deYoung, M. "A Conceptual Model for Judging the Truthfulness of a Young Child's Allegation of Sexual Abuse." *American Journal of Orthopsychiatry* 56 (1986):550–59.

Everson, M. D. and Boat, B. W. "Putting the Anatomical Controversy in Perspective: An Examination of the Major Uses and Criticisms of the Doll in Child Sexual Abuse Evaluations." *Child Abuse and Neglect* 18 (2) (1994):113–129.

Faller, K. C. "Interviewing Children Who May Have Been Sexually Abused: A Historical Perspective and Overview of Controversies." *Child Maltreatment* 1(2) (1996): 83–95.

Faller, K. C. *Child Sexual Abuse.* New York: Columbia University Press, 1988.

Finkelhor, D., and Browne, A. "The Traumatic Impact of Child Sexual Abuse: A Conceptualization." *American Journal of Orthopsychiatry* 55 (1985):530–41.

Heras, P. "Cultural Considerations in the Assessment and Treatment of Child Sexual Abuse." *Journal of Child Sexual Abuse* 1 (3) (1992):119–124.

Hill, D. "The Initial Interview: Alliance Building and Assessment." In *Child Abuse and Neglect: A Guide with Case Studies for Treating the Child and Family,* edited by N. Ebeling and D. Hill, pp. 43–60. Lexington, MA: PSG Publishing, 1983.

Howing, P. T. and Wodarski, J. S. "Legal Requisites for Social Workers in Child Abuse and Neglect Situations." *Social Work* 37 (4) (1992):330–335.

Jones, D., and McQuiston, M. *Interviewing the Sexually Abused Child.* Denver: C. Henry Kempe National Center, 1985.

Leigh, J. W. *Communicating for Cultural Competence.* Boston: Allyn and Bacon, 1998.

Lum, D. *Social Work Practice with People of Color,* 2nd ed. Monterey, CA: Brooks/Cole, 1992.

Mass, A. I. Personal communication, July 11, 1991.

Massachusetts Department of Social Services. *Reference Guide for Child Abuse and Neglect Investigations.* Boston: Massachusetts Department of Social Services, 1985.

Polansky, N.; Borgman, N. D.; and DeSoiz, C. *Roots of Futility.* San Francisco: Jossey-Bass, 1972.

Polansky, N.; Chalmers, M. A.; Buttenweiser, E.; and Williams, D. *Damaged Parents: An Anatomy of Child Neglect.* Chicago: University of Chicago Press, 1981.

Root, M. P. P. "Guidelines for Facilitating Therapy with Asian American Clients." In D. R. Atkinson; G. Morten; and D. W. Sue. *Counseling Cultural Minorities.* pp. 211–224. Dubuque, IA: Wm C. Brown Comm. Inc. 1993.

Sgroi, S. *Handbook of Clinical Intervention in Child Sexual Abuse.* Lexington, MA: Lexington Books, 1982.

Thomas, J. N. "Cultural Considerations in Assessment and Treatment of Child Sexual Abuse: A Commentary." *Journal of Child Sexual Abuse.* 1 (3) (1992):129–132.

Tower, C. C. "Questions Teachers Ask About Legal Aspects of Reporting Child Abuse and Neglect." In *Child Abuse and Neglect: The NEA Training Program,* edited by C. C. Tower. Washington: National Education Association, 1984.

U.S. Department of Health, Education and Welfare. "Model Child Protection Act with Commentary." Washington: U.S. Government Printing Office, 1977.

Young, C. "Psychodynamics of Coping and Survival of the African American Female in a Changing World." In D. R. Atkinson; G. Morten; and D. W. Sue. *Counseling American Minorities.* pp. 75–87. Dubuque, IA: Wm. C. Brown Comm. Inc., 1993.

Ziefert, M. "Abuse and Neglect: The Adolescent as Hidden Victim." In *Social Work with Abused and Neglected Children,* edited by K. Faller, pp. 162–69. New York: Free Press, 1981.

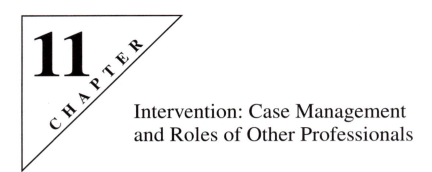

Intervention: Case Management and Roles of Other Professionals

Case Management Considerations

Once a case of abuse or neglect has been validated, the social worker must consider what services will be needed by the family. This is not decided in a vacuum, however, as validation itself often generates additional problems. Family members have a variety of needs and reactions, as they begin to recognize the inevitability of social service interaction.

Family Reactions

It is safe to assume that the family is in a state of crisis or disequilibrium when validation or disclosure takes place. Hill and Knox comment that individual balance is usually maintained by

> ...(1) one's current sense of well-being; (2) one's resources and strength of recuperative power; and (3) the quality of fundamental mothering one received. Given that the client has very likely had inadequate basic parenting, has little reserve and is presently acutely overwhelmed, it is little wonder she/he is in a state of crisis. (1983, p. 86)

Certainly fear is very much a part of the clients' experience—fear of what will happen next, fear of authority, fear of having their children removed or of family breakup, and fear of their own feelings of helplessness. Yet clients respond to this fear in different ways. Denial is a common defense, especially in abusive situations and regardless of clear-cut evidence attesting to the abuse.

Often clients project their problems or the cause of their problems onto others. A sexually abusive father responds, "If my wife had stayed home and had been there for me, I wouldn't have turned to my daughter." A mother accurately identifies the myriad stresses in her life as the cause of her battering her child. Some clients see the system as the problem rather than their behavior or the behavior of a family member.

Incestuous families frequently displace their anger onto the helping system rather than face the threat of losing the perpetrator and the dissolution of the family unit (Joyce, 1997). The nonabusing mother demonstrates a

> ...strong loyalty toward her husband of many years. Her low self-esteem and marked dependence lead her to make a distinction between her husband's abusive behavior and his "true" character. She rationalizes that he is essentially a good person and that the

sickness from which he suffers is something which can be exorcized. (Solin, 1986, p. 571)

Some children also feel loyalty toward the perpetrator and want him to stay home. Unable to accept their underlying anger and repulsion for him, the family members instead develop antagonism for the social service system that has forced them to open this painful wound. These negative feelings are further augmented if the social worker in any way speaks out against the perpetrator. The family then sees this worker as unfeeling, uncaring, and unconcerned with the pain the perpetrator feels at his own victimization by the system. Such an unfeeling individual, the family deems, could not possibly be of any help to them. This reaction should be considered in the context of the family's desperate need to regain a balance (Solin, 1986; Faller, 1988).

The abusive and neglectful family may demonstrate its fear through withdrawal or hostility. Withdrawal may take the form of missed appointments, inhibited affect, or refusal to talk. All of these reactions reflect an effort at self-protection and control. For Asians, it may be to "save face." Hostility, although based on the same needs, may manifest itself in threats, verbal abuse, or passive resistance.

> *Mrs. Basil greeted the worker with an angry, "Oh, it's you again." Although she allowed the worker to enter, the door was slammed forcibly, and followed by a tirade: "I don't know why you damn nosy people can't leave us alone." Mrs. Basil responded to the worker's questions with angry one-word answers, and hurled verbal admonishments at her three young children.*

Although this client felt she had to cooperate to some extent, she nevertheless needed to express her frustration and helplessness through her verbal attacks.

> *Mrs. Desmond, on the other hand, expressed her hostility by compulsivity. She compulsively cleaned and demonstrated a rigidity with her household and communicated a message to the worker that Mrs. Desmond was finally able to verbalize: "I'll show you I can be a good mother." The worker recognized her extreme vulnerability, and rather than pointing out that her rigidity was actually producing an opposite effect, was able to identify with her underlying feelings of powerlessness.*

Some clients experience and demonstrate depression, often precipitated by their feelings of failure and hopelessness. An easing of this depression can be translated into an attachment or overdependence on the worker. The message becomes, "I can't take care of things. I'm overwhelmed. Take care of me." For some clients, this initial clinging to the helper provides the basis for a trusting relationship on which they can build their future independence. Others feel so incapable that they can only transfer their dependence from one worker to another over the years.

Developing a case management or service plan for some clients can be a challenge. One of the most important aspects of deciding what type of services will be necessary is to assess the client's strengths, within the context of his or her cultural values.

Since trust is the fundamental basis for the helping relationship, the worker must initially assess the client's ability to trust. One way to determine this is to explore the quality of significant relationships he or she has had in the past. Have there been some people on whom the client could count? Or have all the past relationships been punctuated with betrayals? Certainly the client who has had some close trusting relationships will have a better capacity to invest in treatment. There are also cultural implications in the client's ability to trust. African-American, Hispanic-American, and Asian clients, faced with a predominantly white system, may feel they cannot trust. The client whose life has been permeated with disappointments, whether involving intimates or related to prejudice, will necessitate a long, patient period of engagement that may be characterized by an approach and avoidance dance as he or she learns that it is possible to trust. But trust is not always easy to establish between protective social worker and client.

Although the worker is fundamentally interested in helping the client, protective services also functions as part of the legal system. A worker has the power to remove children, and most clients are very much aware of this. Further, the worker cannot sacrifice accountability to the legal system in the interest of establishing a relationship. If the client chooses not to cooperate, the worker must take a legal role and possibly render a further trusting relationship impossible.

The concern the client demonstrates for the children is also significant. Poor judgment can cause parents to inadvertently harm their children. Stress may have the same effect, but if the parent has a fundamental love for the child, this love can be strengthened. Some recognition of their children's needs provides a useful strength on which to build. In addition to caring, the parent who expresses pride in his or her children can be helped to accept disappointments and adjust unrealistic expectations. Pride frequently derives from a sense of self. Although most protective clients exhibit poor self-esteem, many have some sense—albeit small—of their own worth. Self-esteem often can be enhanced if the client has had some previous successes of which he or she is proud. Further, clients who demonstrate an absence of chronic self-destructive patterns have a better prognosis for treatment (Hill and Knox, 1983).

Many workers find that clients demonstrate determination. The same manipulation of the system, so often seen in multiproblem families who enlist the support of numerous agencies, can be used, with direction, as a strength to marshal community resources such as advocacy, housing services, financial aid, and so on.

Most workers hope for a willingness to change as an important ingredient in treatment planning. Unfortunately, this is not always likely at the onset—and sometimes clients are never willing to change. Above all, case management and treatment requires patience. The rewards for the concerned worker, who sees a client finally able to cope with and care for the children, however, are significant.

Custody of the Children

The custody and possible placement of children during the investigative process is controversial, and it therefore entails careful scrutiny of a number of factors. The infant requiring a consistency in caregivers for bonding and the toddler's needing comfort in expressing individuality and autonomy are just two such factors. The 3- to 5-year-old's pursuit of identity through continuity and feeling loved by the caregiver is also recognized. The school-age child seeks stability in order to form a healthy conscience and self-concept and begins to seek relationships outside the family, while adolescents need to know they can return to dependency even as they pursue their painful journey from childhood to adulthood (Noonan, 1983). Amidst the recognition of these different needs, the debate centers on whether constancy with parents who are functioning at a barely minimal level is preferable to separation and placement in a setting where the children's needs will be met more adequately.

Theoretically, children are placed during investigatory periods only when it is deemed that the risk to the child's remaining home is inordinately high. Someone—whether worker, supervisor, or both—must decide that the danger to the child outweighs the need for constancy. Who makes this choice and on what basis? Katz and colleagues (1986) examined the existing research and their own sample of 185 children, at Children's Hospital in Boston, for suspected child abuse and neglect to explore this question. The existing research pointed to lower socioeconomic or minority status, unemployment, and substance abuse as factors associated with physician and social service decisions to remove a child from parental custody. But Katz and colleagues discovered a variation. The researchers found that children with nonphysical injuries, such as failure to thrive or neglect, were more likely to be removed than those with physical injuries. The exception proved to be with lower-income families. Although social class was not a significant variable in the overall disposition of cases, it was concluded that low-income families were more likely to lose their physically injured children. The explanation for this seems to be the propensity for clinicians to attribute abusive behavior to these families while assuming that more affluent families have had "accidents."

The severity of the abuse did not appear to contribute to removal but perceived future risk did. In this particular study (Katz et al., 1986), no attention was given to the abuser's intent. The other significant factors in the decision to recommend removal of children were the degree of parental stress exhibited and the parents' past history of abusive behavior.

The researchers recognize the limitations of a hospital-based study, but offer several recommendations they feel are universal. First, a more formal decision-making process is necessary. A single clinician, be it a physician or a social worker, should not be invested with the final decision for removal. Further, cultural implications suggest that racial and cultural minorities be involved in the decision-making process. Input from other agencies is significant in the assessment of a particular family situation. And finally, to avoid removal, families should be helped to use available resources to minimize risk to the child.

In addition to the potential danger to the child, protective service agencies cite as significant in the decision to remove the family's inability to use existing services or its unwillingness to cooperate. But social workers are criticized for their perceived lack of creativity and perseverance in eliciting cooperation from parents. Although this criticism may be justified in some instances, the protective services case can be extremely frustrating and draining on an individual worker.

Currently much attention has been paid to the traumatic effects of separation on the children. Littner (1956) contended that children feel abandoned, rejected, helpless, worthless, and humiliated as a result of being removed from their homes. These feelings produce anger, which is sometimes directed toward the parent but more often is turned inward. Children may feel inherently bad or tend to isolate themselves. This sense of isolation sometimes combines with an intense need to retaliate. Fantasies about retaliation give rise to the fear of punishment that the child perceives will result from this retaliation (Littner, 1956).

Attempts are now being made to find alternative methods to separation in order to protect the child. Abusers, especially in sexual abuse cases, are being separated from the family rather than the child. The problem with this intervention exists when the nonabusing parent does not cooperate in the enforcement of the separation. Certainly the preference of protective services agencies is, whenever possible, to keep the family unit intact. In cultures with strong kinship ties, it is vital that social services explore the feasibility of placing children with relatives or friends of the family rather than strangers. Being placed with people the child knows can minimize the separation trauma.

After the difficult decision to remove a child, the social worker must prepare the child for removal, which ideally includes, over time, familiarization with the foster home (or institutional setting), meeting the family, preliminary visits, explanations about the placement, conveying the child's likes and dislikes to the foster parents, and finally placement (Noonan, 1983). The reality is that most placements during the preliminary stages of the social services process (i.e., investigation and initial case management) are emergencies. These increase the trauma for the child and require sensitivity on the part of the worker and foster parents to manifestations of this trauma.

Early placement produces trauma for the child and adds to the helplessness of the parent. Removal has different effects on the future of the client-worker relationship. For some parents, removal forces them to realize they must cooperate in order to regain custody of their children. Other parents, however, see the loss of their children as the ultimate failure and withdraw by total noncooperation or even flight. The effect of child removal on parents is often difficult to predict.

Removal of children is, in most cases, involuntary for the parents. In an attempt to protect the children, the court authorizes placement. There are instances, however, when placement is a voluntary, preplanned, and therapeutic event. Some states allow voluntary placement of children when the ego strength of the parent is sufficient to allow them to contract with protective services. In these cases, placement permits the parents to mobilize their own resources toward the reunification of the family unit. During the agreed-upon time, the parents receive treatment or in some other way prepare themselves so that the risk to their children is minimized. Because significant motivation on the part of the parents is necessary, this solution is often impractical.

Although involuntary placement is painful for both children and their parents, it is in some instances necessary to protect the victims during the preliminary stages of casework. Chapter Fifteen considers placement in the context of treatment rather than as an emergency measure and discusses the implications for foster parents.

Other Professionals Involved in the Intervention Process

Protective service social workers depend heavily on other professionals within the community for reporting, assessment, and treatment of abused and neglected children and their families. It is important to consider the contributions of all these professionals in order to appreciate what their concerted efforts might achieve.

The Medical Team

Recognition and reporting of child abuse owes much to the medical community. From radiologist John Caffey, who first brought to the attention of others what he felt could only be explained as nonaccidental injuries, to C. Henry Kempe, who labeled the phenomenon the battered child syndrome, physicians, nurses, and medical social workers have been vital in shaping the services now provided for child maltreatment cases (Parton, 1985).

Physicians

The physician's main role in child abuse and neglect is to be an accurate diagnostician. His/her other roles are to report confirmed cases to the local child protection service, to hospitalize the child in need of diagnosis and protection, and to fully arrange for the evaluation of the abused child's personal medical and psychological needs. (Schmitt, Gross, and Carroll, 1976, p. 91)

Physicians, whether private family practitioners or pediatricians on the hospital staff, provide input into the social service process in three important ways: (1) as reporters when they discover cases of child maltreatment, (2) as diagnosticians to aid in validation of maltreatment, and (3) as consultants in planning treatment.

The physician is mandated in all states to report suspected child abuse and neglect (Hildebrandt, 1981). Many physicians are hesitant, however, to report their suspicions to social services for several reasons. First, they may be unsure that the injury or condition is undeniably attributed to abuse. Second, they may not have faith in the social service system because of lack of knowledge or because of past situations they deemed were not handled well by social service staff. Physicians may fear that reporting the maltreatment will put the child in more danger or that it will negatively affect the doctor-patient relationship. Many physicians fear that a report will involve them in court proceedings, which will take time from their other patients. Some private physicians are so involved with their patients that it is difficult for them to even consider that those individuals could be abusive.

Although there may be some truth behind these reasons of hesitancy, the problems can be circumvented. Renewed dialogue among social service agencies, physicians, and other medical personnel has improved communication. In addition, physicians such as Ray Helfer and Suzanne Sgroi have assumed leading roles in the training of their colleagues. With an understanding of the system, the physician can assess it much more effectively. Clearer laws mandating reporting by physicians have compelled their increased involvement.

The physician's role in validation cannot be understated. Radiology plays an important role in the documentation of physical abuse (see Oestreich, 1986). Skeletal abnormalities, unexplained fractures, and multiple fractures are conditions that necessitate further study to rule out abuse. A skeletal survey aids the physician in gathering validating material. Radiologic findings that are seen frequently in abused children include spiral fractures (often from twisting); transverse fractures in the middle of long bones or fingers (from the extremities being "rapped"); unusual fractures, such as rib or clavicle breaks in infants; traumas to the head, such as skull fractures; and other unusual fractures (Shubin, 1984). All of these can be detected through x-rays.

Physicians can diagnose symptoms of neglect. Comparison with normal growth curves may validate the suspicion of the failure-to-thrive syndrome. Long-unmet medical needs attest to the neglect of the child's health care. The physician may also confirm the social worker's concerns over the child's inappropriate affect.

A physical examination often validates sexual as well as physical abuse. Sgroi (n.d.) suggests that "every child has the right to receive a complete examination by a competent and knowledgeable examiner if sexual assault is suspected." The thoroughness and type of examination, however, depends on the nature of the sexual abuse. If the abuse has continued for a considerable period of time, there is less likelihood of force or violence and thus the chance of observing vaginal or rectal tears is minimized. Or if the abuse took place some time before, evidence of physical trauma may no longer be obvious.

For these reasons, a complete physical exam should be considered only if the abuse has just occurred and physical damage to the child is likely. Certainly the physician should screen for venereal disease and possible pregnancy in all cases, whether by an actual physical exam or through asking the child or parents pertinent questions.

Some physicians contend that an examination allows them to assess the degree of physical harm. Since almost all children fear that physical harm has been done to them, an exam allows the professional to assure the unharmed child that no damage has been found. Whether or not to do a physical exam should be considered carefully to ensure that the child's best interests are served.

If an examination is done, Sgroi (n.d., 1978, 1982; Sgroi, Porter, and Blick, 1982; Kerns, 1981) directs physicians to screen for such evidence as

1. Sperm in the vaginal, genital, or rectal region
2. Trauma to the genital or rectal area
3. Gonorrhea infection of the vagina, rectum, urethra, and throat
4. Foreign bodies in the vagina, urethra, or rectum
5. Syphilis
6. Symptoms of pregnancy
7. Signs of other type of maltreatment, abuse, or neglect

The medical examination should be done by a physician who is knowledgeable about the signs of sexual abuse, and who is relaxed, calm, and can offer reassurance to the child. An internal examination for a small girl can be especially anxiety provoking unless accompanied by a great deal of sensitivity toward the child. The physician will want to develop a rapport with the child, answer any questions, and provide some explanation as the examination progresses (Sgroi, 1978; Sgroi, Porter, and Blick, 1982).

Whether examining for physical abuse, sexual abuse, or neglect, the physician is mindful of the child's need for control. Although the victim is not often given the opportunity to consent to the exam, an explanation of what will take place may help the child feel more in control. In sexual abuse situations, especially, the child is often concerned about having been damaged. Assurances that the physical examination will help to determine this and will not be painful often elicits the child's cooperation (Sgroi, 1978; Shubin, 1984).

The physician is also a valuable consultant in planning treatment for abused and neglected children. Broken bones or other medical problems that require frequent visits afford medical personnel time to observe the child's affective behavior as well as tend to the physiological needs. Pregnancy or venereal disease will require continual involvement. Physicians can maintain contact with social services to aid in case management. The sensitive physician can be a vital part of the total therapeutic team.

Nurses or Nurse Practitioners
Nurses see abused and neglected children in many areas other than the office or the hospital emergency room. School nurses are in one of the best positions to recognize maltreatment.

Public health and visiting nurses often enter an abusive or neglectful home, long before social services becomes involved. Thus, nurses should be well versed in not only the symptoms of abuse and neglect but in the necessity and procedure for reporting.

Since the nurse is often the first medical contact with the family and child in the office or hospital setting, she or he is in a unique position to gather important information about the injury, the family history, the parent-child interaction, and the affect of both parents and children. For example, clues about the abusive or neglectful behavior can be gleaned by attention to such details, as suggested by Heindl et al. (1979) and McCleery and Pineyard (1988).

- How does the parent speak to the child?
- Does the parent comfort the child, or in other ways react to his or her crying?
- Does the parent hold the child and, if so, how?
- Is there obvious role reversal between parent and child?
- Does the parent seem aware of the child's needs?
- Does the parent speak negatively about the child?
- Can the parent provide a history of the child's development?

The nurse can also set the tone for later interviews with the child and parent. The nurse can engage, comfort, and generally put the child at ease. The child can be helped to realize that he or she is not to blame for the abuse and is welcome to talk and ask questions. Calming the child will be extremely beneficial for the later examination. In fact, the nurse can explain to the child in a soothing manner exactly what the examination will entail.

The nurse can engage parents as well. Since the parents probably feel vulnerable, unsure, and perhaps even guilty, the nurse is in a position to empathize with them and make them feel as comfortable as possible. It may be difficult not to make judgments on these parents, but careful observation of their behavior, especially with the child, can be an important part of the assessment done by the total medical team. Some nurses are asked to explain the legal responsibility of the office or the hospital to report abuse and neglect. Although false assurances as to the outcome are not possible, it is important to allay parents' fears about the process—for example, their fears that their children will be immediately whisked away from them (if, indeed, that does not seem warranted).

In talking with the parent, the nurse often secures certain important information (Heindl et al., 1979; McCleery and Pineyard, 1988), such as the parents' explanation of the injury or condition, the history of previous health problems or trauma, the preventive health measures such as immunizations and tests that have been done to date, the dietary history, and the parents' assessment of the child's general health and temperament.

Although many of the questions asked and assurances given may fall within the realm of the physician's exam, the nurse is usually the first professional seen and is, therefore, in a pivotal role to set the stage for a productive and comfortable relationship between the patient and the medical team.

The office or hospital nurse also provides a valuable service in preventive medicine. Often abuse or neglect can be predicted by prenatal, perinatal, or postnatal indicators. Parents who present extremely negative attitudes toward pregnancy or attempt to deny the pregnancy, parents who lack emotional support, mothers who wanted to terminate the pregnancy but did not, and parents who do not appear to want their child can be at high risk to abuse or neglect.

Studies have shown that some experiences at birth place children at higher risk for abuse. A difficult delivery, combined with a lack of support for the mother, a negative response to the baby evidenced by not wanting the baby, and an inability to attend to the infant's needs, especially with a high-risk infant—all are factors that may indicate later maltreatment. Parental behavior that should be noted includes anxiety around the baby, negative reactions to the baby, withdrawal from the baby, complaints about nonexistent problems, and maternal depression (Heindl et al., 1979; McCleery and Pineyard, 1988). Another indicator is apparent isolation or lack of support for the parents.

According to the laws of most states, little can be done about child maltreatment until it actually happens. However, parents who appear to be at risk can be referred to support services and, perhaps, helped to prevent maltreatment.

Nurses have long been valued in child abuse prevention for their teaching role with parents. Modeling of appropriate infant and child care as well as education on nutrition and health issues for unsure parents is especially helpful. Education for professionals on how to recognize bruises that do not fit the explanation, untreated medical problems, and venereal disease is valuable in the validation and treatment of child abuse by social service workers, teachers, lawyers, and others.

Medical Social Workers

The duties of the social worker employed in the hospital or other medical setting differ from institution to institution. Theoretically, the social worker is the coordinator for information pertaining to a case of abuse or neglect and the liaison with the social service system. The worker should be well versed in the questions protective services will ask and the procedures that will be undertaken. The social worker may be in a position to provide support to the child or family during the investigation process. A vital part of the role may be pulling together existing evidence such as x-rays, various physicians' opinions, test results, records, and diagnoses for the protective services personnel. It may fall to the medical social worker to explain to the parents the process both at the hospital and in the protective services system.

If the child returns home, the medical social worker may be instrumental in treatment planning. Placement in a foster home may warrant an interview with foster parents to acquaint them with the child's needs and medical treatment. When protective services dismisses a case, because it is deemed neither abuse nor neglect or because there is insufficient evidence, the social worker on the hospital staff may want to ensure that the parents are referred to services that will aid them in practicing more effective child care (e.g., parent support groups, visiting nurses, or homemaker services).

The responsibility for coordination of an abuse or neglect case is not always clear. Medical professionals may prefer to deal with protective services directly. The medical social worker needs to be guided by the knowledge of hospital policy and the political atmosphere. Also, abusive or neglectful situations sometimes elicit counterproductive negative or emotional feelings from hospital staff. Ideally the medical social worker should be in a position to help other medical professionals come to grips with their feelings. In some hospitals, this professional is adequately utilized. In others, however, the medical hierarchy takes precedence, and medical professionals themselves report or deal with the abuse without the intervention of social services. The best possible solution for the abused or neglected child and the family, however, is for the medical team to function as a unit, providing valuable validation, case management, and treatment planning material to the protective services workers.

The Legal Team

Police

The police officer's involvement in cases of child abuse and neglect differs from state to state and from community to community. Traditionally the public assumes that "police officers are responsible for the protection of life and property and for the preservation of peace in the community" (Swanson, 1974, p. 112). But where child abuse is involved, there are vast differences in the duties of the police officer. In some areas, the police have the primary responsibility for taking reports and investigating allegations of abuse and neglect, while in the majority of jurisdictions the police play a supportive role to protective services agencies. How states address the maltreatment of children in their legal statutes also varies. In New York, for example, sexual assault is covered under a variety of categories ranging from second- or third-degree misdemeanors to felonies (Keefe, 1978). In many states, sexual abuse by a family member or relative comes under the jurisdiction of social services, whereas abuse by a nonrelated perpetrator is solely a police matter. Prostitution and pornography usually are considered the realm of law enforcement, yet the victims of these crimes are often eligible for services from child protective workers. Thus, any attempt to generalize the exact role of the police officer is fruitless. In most communities, however, the police play some role in intervention on behalf of abused and neglected children.

The police officer is an important member of the intervention process for several reasons. First, the officer is easily identifiable (much more so than a protective social worker) and is frequently well known in the community. Children are taught, for the most part, to see the police as protectors. Second, the police are easy to locate and can be quickly dispatched to the scene of an emergency. And finally, no community is without some police service, but some smaller communities are quite far removed geographically from protective services offices (Kean and Rogers, 1988).

Police officers (Graves, 1983; Kean and Rogers, 1988) in general perform three functions: take reports of abuse and neglect, investigate reports (either independently or in a supportive role to the department of social services), and respond to emergencies (e.g., domestic violence, severe abuse, or abandonment). Most individual officers will, at some time, take reports and respond to emergencies, but some precincts have special child abuse units trained to investigate allegations of abuse.

A report comes to a police office in one of several ways. The direct report is made by the victim who is willing to describe the abuse and give information; the victim can often lead the officer to the scene or to the perpetrator. If a child reports, the parents must be notified as soon as possible. The department of social services may also be contacted if state law dictates. (In every state the police are mandated reporters to the designated agency, and if that agency is social services, they must be notified.)

An indirect report is made by a parent or other caregiver. These are made after the victim has disclosed the abuse and often after some time has elapsed (Keefe, 1978; Kean and Rogers, 1988), or when the parent has observed an injury and has become concerned. It is not uncommon for reports to be made in custody cases, when one parent perceives that the estranged spouse or ex-spouse has in some way harmed the child. Obviously such cases are difficult to handle and not always clearly defined.

The referral report comes from a community agency such as a school, hospital, or other social service agency. The proactive report is one in which the police officer discovers child abuse or neglect in the process of investigating another complaint, such as a domestic disturbance, a suicide attempt, or a runaway child.

Several problems exist in the police detection of child abuse. The first is that police are becoming increasingly hesitant to intervene in cases of domestic violence, partly because this situation is certainly the most volatile and dangerous to the police themselves. If a call appears to be spousal violence rather than child abuse, the police are sometimes less willing to intervene. A second issue concerns runaways. Only fairly recently has the connection between running away and abuse at home been clearly demonstrated. In the past, runaways were not taken so seriously. The assumption was that the child would probably return or that the likelihood of the child's running away again was fairly slim. As a result, the symptom—running away—was passed over with little exploration of the cause. The well-trained and competent police officer should evaluate the situation (to the extent possible) to determine if child abuse is indicated.

Once a report is received, the police officer must decide what action should be taken. The case can be closed, based on the assumption that no abuse or neglect actually existed or because of insufficient evidence. Recognition that the child is abused or neglected necessitates further action—through referral to the police department's child abuse unit for investigation, or a referral to the local department of social services, or both. If the situation requires removal of the child or if the child is abandoned by his or her caregiver, the officer may need to refer the case directly to juvenile or family court (Swanson, 1974; Kean and Rogers, 1988).

Rarely are abusive and neglectful parents arrested. Exceptions exist when the injury to the child is extremely severe or obviously sadistically inflicted, when a crime has been committed, when the parents present a danger to others, or when arrest is the only way to preserve peace (Broadhurst, 1984). New regulations in some states, however, require the arrest of sexual abusers. If prostitution or pornography is involved, arrest is also indicated.

Child abuse and neglect investigation is an area that is not usually expected of police by the public and one that in many ways seems to contradict the other roles performed by police. As a result, their involvement in abuse and neglect investigations raises problems for police agencies. First, police officers must have adequate training to recognize and deal with child abuse situations (Tocchio, 1974). According to her study of child abuse and the role of police officers, Graves (1983, p. 70) points out that "ninety percent of the decisions to dismiss or refer child abuse cases for further investigation were based upon the personal judgment of the officer involved rather than adherence to a criminal justice code." Yet most officers receive only a minimum of training, if any, in the dynamics of child abuse. Second (and in relation to the first problem), more personnel are needed for units established specifically to deal with juvenile matters such as child abuse. These officers should receive more comprehensive training. Third, there is a need for social service agencies and police agencies to work more closely together in coordinating their roles in child abuse cases. Although this does exist in some communities, the cooperation could be much more widespread. Fourth, police agencies should keep abreast of new abuse legislation and its implications in their practice. And finally, police and other community agencies should participate in interdepartmental planning for the protection of children and the prevention of child abuse and neglect (Tocchio, 1974; Kean and Rogers, 1988). Although many police departments provide safety training (including children's personal safety from abuse) in schools, there is often little coordination with social service prevention programs. More coordination would provide a better opportunity for the effective education of children.

The role of the police and their place on the child protection team is a vital one. Graves (1983) found that most child abuse reports were made between 3:00 P.M. and 9:00 P.M., four hours of which most child protective workers may not be available to respond. (Some agencies do have workers on call.) The response time of police officers averages about 26 minutes. In emergencies, responsive service is important to adequately protect children. Police authority cannot be minimized, and social workers often benefit from police protection from difficult clients. The incentive to cooperate with the police is therefore mutual.

The police have long been recognized as protectors; without their input, along with others on the child protection team, a vital part of the process is overlooked.

Courts

The role of the courts will be covered extensively in Chapter 12.

The Educational Team

Teachers

The teacher is in a unique position to detect and report child abuse and neglect. Teachers are in closer contact with children for more hours in the day than any other adult—often more than the parents. Those dedicated to the teaching of the "whole" child perceive impediments to the child's learning. New legislation mandates attention to the perceptual learning problems in children. Schools spend many hours addressing the needs of and teaching children who are disabled. And yet the residual effects of child abuse and neglect can be just as detrimental to learning as other types of disabilities (Tower, 1989, 1992).

As stated earlier in this chapter, the teacher is also a mandated reporter in every state. Until recently teachers were not sufficiently educated to either the signs of abuse and neglect or to their responsibility to report and the importance of their role in child abuse prevention. The National Education Association's recognition of this need resulted in a multimedia child abuse prevention package published in 1984 (soon to be revised) and made available for purchase to schools across the country. Teachers are now benefiting from increased training in not only the recognition and steps to reporting but also the necessity and use of prevention programs.

Despite increased training, many teachers still verbalize fears and problems about their role in the intervention process. One fear is that they will not really be able to recognize abuse and neglect in any given child. Further education of teachers appears to be the key: Teachers take courses or extensive training in child maltreatment intervention and learn to look for specific physical and behavioral clues in both children and their parents. This education emphasizes that all state statutes dictate that teachers who suspect abuse or neglect *must* report, but also leads to the understanding that trained protective workers investigate and validate rather than the teachers themselves.

Teachers also fear the responsibility involved in reporting an abusive or neglectful family. The responsibility may seem overwhelming, but compared to the guilt over a seriously injured child, whose situation was not reported before additional abuse occurred, reporting can easily be seen in perspective.

Some teachers are concerned that reporting will destroy their relationship with the child's parents. Although this is a possibility, it need not happen. Intervention by protective services is often frightening for parents. Teachers can provide supportive relationships to help them through the process. Teachers may also have observed problems that inhibit the parents' child-caring abilities. Relating these problems to the social worker can help the parents.

> *A concerned teacher filed a report regarding 7-year-old Anita Reynaldi, who appeared to be severely neglected. The teacher had had her brother Roberto in class several years before and had found Mrs. Reynaldi a concerned and cooperative mother. Why this mother now ignored requests to come in to talk about Anita or to remedy the situation in any way was a mystery. However, in talking with the social worker, the teacher outlined the mother's strengths and her previously cooperative attitude. The teacher was also able to reach out to the mother once the social worker had visited. Totally overwhelmed by recent developments in her life and by Anita, a hyperactive child whom she felt she could not handle, Mrs. Reynaldi responded to the teacher and, through her, gained support during the intervention and treatment.*

Unfortunately not all parents are as cooperative as Mrs. Reynaldi. Teachers describe parents who are angry and hostile when a report has been made. However, the safety of the child is of more importance than the teacher's relationship with the parents. If that safety requires intervention, the concerned teacher should act.

The administration is not always supportive of teachers' reporting. (The reasons for this are discussed in the next section.) Teachers who feel they should file a report of child abuse or neglect have met with opposition from school principals or vice-principals. The teacher is in a difficult position, and must decide whether to abide by the superior's wishes or to report independently, and thus jeopardize the relationship with the superior or even his or her own job. Some teachers do not know that reporting to an administrator does not constitute the teacher's legal responsibility of reporting. Nor does reporting anonymously cover the teacher as a mandated reporter.

Another major fear teachers have expressed is that nothing will be done by social services once the report is made. Teachers complain that they never hear from the social worker or that the family situation does not appear to change. More communication between teachers and social workers greatly enhances the trust each has for the other. If treated as an integral part of the child protection team, the teacher is a valuable resource in keeping the social worker up to date on the child's progress.

Teachers learn of abuse or neglect situations in one of several ways. First is through their own observation of the child in class. Children who are abused or neglected manifest behavioral indicators that can be detected by the sensitive teacher. Although many behavioral problems can be associated with other disturbances, some point more specifically to maltreatment. Sometimes children themselves disclose to those concerned educators with whom they have developed a trusting relationship. In these situations, the teacher must take the responsibility for seeing that the child is protected from further abuse. Immediate involvement with protective services ensures this protection. The child's peers may recognize abusive or neglectful situations and tell their teacher. In some instances, contacts with the parents have uncovered practices of inappropriately severe discipline or other forms of abusive behavior.

Once teachers receive reports, they should be aware of the procedure or protocol followed by their particular school system. Sometimes reports are made to the school nurse, the counselor, or an administrator who then files a report with protective services. In other schools, teachers must notify the administration but are expected to make the actual contact with the social services agency themselves. In many states, the social service agency responds to the reporter and assures the reporter that the case is being investigated. Rules of confidentiality usually prohibit that specific information be given to the teachers.

Reporting is not the only area in which teachers are involved. During the course of treatment, the social worker monitors the child's progress. A mirror to this progress is the child's behavior in school. Teachers provide valuable input in helping determine the direction for treatment.

Recently teachers have also become increasingly involved with the prevention of abuse. Since the child trusts this adult and since these adults often provide a constant influence in what is sometimes a chaotic life otherwise, teachers are in an ideal position to introduce abuse- and neglect-prevention materials into the curriculum.

The teachers' influence on and importance to children make them particularly important members of the intervention team.

Administrators

Administrators see themselves as responsible for the effective running of their educational community. Yet an educational community is not effective unless the rights of each child to an education are being protected. Although the attention to individual children is usually left to line workers—in this instance, teachers—it is the administrator's role to lend support to the staff. Therefore the detection and reporting of child abuse is as much a responsibility of the administrator as it is of the teacher.

As mentioned, teachers sometimes complain that administrators are not supportive of their need to file reports of child maltreatment. Administrators appear cautious about reporting for several reasons. First, they may fear that reports of child abuse will reflect on their school. Will reporting antagonize parents? Will reporting abuse gain the principal or the school a reputation for "making trouble," and perhaps cause funds to be cut in the future? Yet concerned principals, vice-principals, superintendents, and assistant superintendents realize that most parents value consideration of the "whole" child—including attention to learning barriers.

Some administrators are not fully aware of their reporting responsibilities or of their liability when they do not report. More and more, supervisory staff have begun to attend training for teachers, as well as training geared specifically toward administrators. And finally, administrators, like teachers, voice frustration that not enough is being done in child protection cases. Again, only effective communication with community agencies and recognition of the options available to protective services can fully dispel these frustrations.

Pupil Personnel Services

Pupil personnel services include those professionals involved in enhancing a child's education: the school nurse, guidance counselor, school adjustment counselor, psychologist, and other staff.

The school nurse is in the school system. It is often the nurse to whom teachers turn for support in the process of recognizing and reporting child abuse and neglect. Nurses are asked to examine bruises and talk with children, and often invited to give their opinions as to whether to report. Because of their medical training, school nurses can validate that a bruise does not fit the explanation, or, in some other manner, give the teacher confidence in the ability to recognize abuse. Nurses are also frequently involved in prevention education, and some feel more comfortable discussing topics such as sexuality than some teachers. The nurse can help by teaching hygiene to children whose parents are not meeting this need.

In some schools, the nurse has the responsibility of reporting child abuse and neglect. This removes the teacher, who is in constant contact with the child and may see the parents, from the role of reporter (although the teacher is still legally mandated to see that a report is made). In some instances, this distance allows the teacher more flexibility in the ability to relate to the parent in a helpful way.

School counselors and psychologists are used in a variety of ways. Traditionally the guidance counselor helped with scheduling and career choices, the adjustment counselor provided a link with the parents, and the psychologist administered testing. As funds became limited and the number of personnel decreased, the roles merged or overlapped in many schools. Today it is difficult to generalize as to who sees the child for counseling or has contact with the parents. Counselors who see children in a guidance or counseling capacity frequently learn that a child has been maltreated. In fact, teachers often send children to counselors to validate their own suspicions. Children may reach out to counselors either to report the abuse or to seek help with issues that are symptoms of the abuse.

By functioning as a team along with teachers and administrators, nurses and counselors help to ensure that the child's right to learn without the impediment of abuse or neglect is more fully protected.

The Mental Health Team

The term *mental health professional* refers to a variety of professions: psychologists, psychiatrists, clinical social workers, expressive therapists, and possibly other therapists responsible for clinical intervention.

Mental health professionals may become involved in child abuse and neglect cases in several ways. Their juvenile patients may disclose that they are currently being or have been abused or neglected, or other patients (parents, spouses, relatives, or friends) may report that the child is being abused by someone with whom they are involved. Abusers may report their own acts of maltreatment, although this is the exception rather than the rule. And finally, protective service agencies may refer children for counseling or for psychological testing (Smith and Meyer, 1984; Peterson and Urquiza, 1993).

Mental health professionals, like physicians, police, and educators, are mandated reporters under the child abuse reporting laws. Since reporting can be somewhat controversial, some mental health facilities designate a particular staff member to be the liaison with protective services and in that capacity be responsible for reporting as well as accepting referrals.

Psychiatrists, psychologists, psychiatric social workers, and other counselors often voice concerns over the obstacles to reporting from a therapist's perspective. Some therapists prefer not to become involved. Others argue that the reporting laws jeopardize the therapeutic relationship between therapist and client. Smith and Meyer (1984) address this point and cite several particulars. First, they contend that therapists are in a position to be told highly personal material. The client's comfort in disclosing this material is based on the assurance that it will be kept confidential. The act of reporting a disclosure of child abuse is, in the opinion of these authors, a gross breach of confidence. In addition, the definitions of abuse in the laws are vague, so that much of what therapists are told might or might not be deemed abusive or neglectful. And finally, Smith and Meyer argue that abusers who might seek voluntary treatment would be discouraged from doing so if they thought they might be reported to social services.

From the point of view of a therapist, these concerns may be justified. Peterson and Urquiza (1993) argue, however, that telling the therapist is a plea for help. Further, failure of mental health professionals to report may place children in dangerous situations. Encouraging clients to self-report is one method of circumventing this problem. In addition, some states allow agreements between mental health professionals and protective services by which abusers, who continue to seek therapy and receive treatment, are exempt from services other than periodic case review by protective social workers (Lauer et al., 1975).

Mental health professionals provide a valuable resource for protective service agencies. It is often helpful to the validation process or in the course of treatment planning to refer a child, an abuser, or a nonabusive parent for psychological testing. In addition, psychiatrists, psychologists, psychiatric social workers, and other counselors are often asked to use their skills in the treatment of victims, perpetrators, and families.

Toward a Total Team Approach

Certainly the most effective method of combating child abuse and neglect within a particular community is to employ the skills of all of the medical, legal, educational, and mental health professionals in the formation of a communitywide child protection team. In addition to including a variety of professionals, the team must include racial and cultural representatives of the clientele served. Numerous communities have demonstrated the effectiveness of such an approach by improving communications among professionals, eliminating unnecessary and costly overlap of agency services, and coordinating more effective prevention programs. (For examples of team approaches, see Goldstein and Griffin, 1993, and Pence and Wilson, 1994.) Only through a total team effort can children be adequately protected from future abuse and neglect.

Summary

In considering case management and plans for treatment, the protective services worker must assess several factors. The first of these is the family's reaction to intervention. Not only must workers look at the family's fears and the defense mechanisms they use but they must evaluate the family's strengths as well. Throughout this process the custody of the children may come into question. Ideally, children should be allowed the continuity of life at home, but there may be instances in which harm at home is more detrimental than removal. The decision to remove often falls to the protective worker and involves several factors relating to that worker's assessment of the family.

A variety of professionals are involved in the intervention process, and each of their roles must be understood individually. The medical team, consisting of the physician, nurse or nurse practitioner, and medical social worker, is in the position to report, validate, and sometimes treat maltreatment cases. Police officers are often the first to discover child abuse or neglect, through reports from children and adults or in the course of their investigation of other police matters.

The educational team, consisting of teachers, administrators, and pupil personnel services staff, is a vital link in the intervention process. As a result of their constant contact with children, these professionals are more frequently in a position to recognize abuse or neglect, provide valuable input during the intervention and treatment process, and participate in prevention programs to educate children about abuse and neglect.

Although mental health professionals may be in the position to recognize child maltreatment in their cases, some are reluctant to report. Mental health services play an important role, however, in validation and treatment of protective situations.

As a society, our best hope of intervention in cases of child abuse or neglect is for community professionals to communicate and work as a team. The team approach has been implemented in many communities and appears effective.

Chapters 13 and 14 cover treatment and evaluation as the final stages of the intervention process.

Exploration Questions

1. What are some possible family reactions to early intervention?

2. What factors should be considered when deciding who should have custody of the children in a protective case?

3. What effect does separation have on a child?

4. What is the role of the physician in maltreatment cases?

5. What is the role of the nurse or nurse practitioner?

6. What is the role of the medical social worker?

7. What are three possible functions of the police in abuse and neglect situations?

8. How do reports come to the attention of the police?

9. Why are teachers important in the intervention process?

10. How can other professionals within the school system support teachers in their role?

11. What is the primary concern of many mental health professionals in regard to reporting child abuse and neglect?

Activities for Applied Learning

1. Invite representatives from the police and the medical, educational, and mental health community to form a panel. Have these professionals discuss their roles in child abuse and neglect prevention and treatment.

2. Design a questionnaire to assess the knowledge of reporting statutes and procedures. Secure permission to administer it to community professionals such as teachers, police, and representatives of mental health services. Compare and contrast the knowledge of each group. Which group is the best informed?

Suggested Readings

Boss, D. C.; Krugman, R. D.; Lenherr, M. R.; Rosenberg, D. A.; and Schmidtt, B. *The New Child Protection Team Handbook.* New York: Garland, 1988.

Brammer, L. M. *The Helping Relationship: Process and Skills.* Englewood Cliffs, NJ: Prentice-Hall, 1988.

Pence, D. and Wilson, C. *Team Investigation of Child Sexual Abuse.* Thousand Oaks, CA: Sage, 1994.

Peterson, M. S. and Urquiza, A. J. *The Role of Mental Health Professionals in the Prevention and Treatment of Child Abuse and Neglect.* Washington, DC: U.S. Department of Health and Human Services, 1993.

Sgroi, S. *Handbook of Clinical Intervention in Child Sexual Abuse.* Lexington, MA: Lexington Books, 1982.

Tower, C. C. *The Role of Educators in the Prevention and Treatment of Child Abuse and Neglect.* Washington, DC: U.S. Department of Health and Human Services, 1992.

References

Delaney, J. J. "New Concepts of Family Court." In *Child Abuse and Neglect: The Family and the Community,* edited by R. Helfer and C. H. Kempe, pp. 335–58. Cambridge, MA: Ballinger, 1976.

Faller, K. C. *Child Sexual Abuse.* New York: Columbia University Press, 1988.

Goldstein, J. and Griffin, E. "The Use of a Physician-Social Worker Team in the Evaluation of Child Sexual Abuse." *Journal of Child Sexual Abuse.* 2 (2), (1993): 85–97.

Graves, J. D. *Early Intervention in Child Abuses: The Role of the Police Officer.* Saratoga, CA: R & E Publishers and Joy Dan Graves, 1983.

Heindl, C.; Krall, C. A.; Salus, M. K.; with Broadhurst, D. D. *Nurses' Role in the Prevention and Treatment of Child Abuse and Neglect.* Washington: U.S. Department of Health, Education and Welfare, 1979.

Helfer, R. E., and Schmidt, B. "The Community-based Child Abuse and Neglect Program." In *Child Abuse and Neglect: The Family and The Community,* edited by R. E. Helfer and C. H. Kempe, pp. 229–65. Cambridge, MA: Ballinger, 1976.

Hildebrandt, H. M. "The Role of Physicians." In *Social Work with Abused and Neglected Children,* edited by K. Faller, pp. 177–80. New York: Free Press, 1981.

Hill, D. A. and Knox, E. C. "Ego Assessment and Treatment Planning." In Ebeling, N. B. and Hill, D. A. *Child Abuse and Neglect: A Guide with Case Studies for Treating the Child and Family,* pp. 83–111. Boston: John Wright, 1983.

Katz, M. H.; Hampton, R. L.; Newberger, E. H.; Bowls, R. T.; and Snyder, J. C. "Returning Children Home: Clinical Decision Making in Cases of Child Abuse and Neglect." *American Journal of Orthopsychiatry* 56 (1986):253–62.

Kean, R. and Rogers, E. J. "The Law Enforcement Officer as a Member of the Child Protection Team." In D. C. Bross et al. *The New Child Protection Team Handbook,* pp. 199–212. New York: Garland, 1988.

Keefe, M. L. "Police Investigation in Child Sexual Assault." In *Sexual Assault of Children and Adolescents,* edited by A. N. Groth, L. L. Holstrom, and S. M. Sgroi, pp. 159–70. Lexington, MA: Lexington Books, 1978.

Kerns, D. L. "Medical Assessment of Child Sexual Abuse." In *Sexually Abused Children and Their Families,* edited by F. B. Mrazek and C. H. Kempe, pp. 129–41. Elmsford, NY: Pergamon Press, 1981.

Joyce, P. A. "Mothers of Sexually Abused Children and the Concept of Collusion." *Journal of Child Sexual Abuse* 6(2) (1997): 75–92.

Lauer, J. W.; Lourie, I. S.; Salus, M. K.; with Broadhurst, D. D. *The Role of the Mental Health Professional in the Prevention and Treatment of Child Abuse and Neglect.* Washington: U.S. Department of Health, Education and Welfare, 1975.

Littner, N. "Traumatic Effects of Separation and Placement." *Proceedings of the National Conference in Social Work.* New York: Family Service Association of America, 1956.

McCleery, J. T. and Pineyard, B. J. "Nursing Evaluation and Treatment Planning." In D. C. Bross; R. D. Krugman; M. R. Lenherr; D. A. Rosenberg; and B. D. Schmidtt. *The New Child Protection Team Handbook,* pp. 127–135. New York: Garland, 1988.

Noonan, R. "Separation and Placement." In *Child Abuse and Neglect: A Guide with Case Studies for Treating the Child and Family,* edited by N. Ebeling and D. Hill, pp. 207–27. Littleton, MA: PSG Publishing, 1983.

Oestreich, A. E. "Radiology and the Battered Child." *Hospital Physician* 22 (1986):93–100.

Parton, N. *The Politics of Child Abuse.* London: Macmillan Ltd., 1985.

Pence, D. and Wilson, C. *Team Investigation of Child Sexual Abuse.* Thousand Oaks, CA: Sage, 1994.

Peterson, M. S. and Urquiza, A. J. *The Role of Mental Health Professionals in the Prevention and Treatment of Child Abuse and Neglect.* Washington, DC: U.S. Department of Health and Human Services, 1993.

Schmitt, B. D.; Gross, C. A.; and Carroll, C. A. "Child Protection Team: A Problem Oriented Approach." In *Child Abuse and Neglect: The Family and the Community,* edited by R. Helfer and C. H. Kempe, pp. 91–113. Cambridge, MA: Ballinger, 1976.

Sgroi, S. M. "Comprehensive Examination for Child Sexual Assault: Diagnostic Therapeutic and Child Protection Issues." In *Sexual Assault of Children and Adolescents,* edited by A. W. Burgess, A. N. Groth, L. L. Holstrom, and S. M. Sgroi, pp. 143–57. Lexington, MA: Lexington Books, 1978.

Sgroi, S. M. "Pediatric Gonorrhea and Child Sexual Abuse: The Venereal Disease Connection." *Sexually Transmitted Diseases* 9 (1982):154–56.

Sgroi, S. M. "Examination for Child Sexual Assault." Mimeographed (no date).

Sgroi, S. M.; Porter, F. S.; and Blick, L. C. "Validation of Child Sexual Abuse." In *Handbook of Clinical Intervention in Child Sexual Abuse,* edited by S. M. Sgroi, pp. 39–79. Lexington, MA: Lexington Books, 1982.

Shubin, C. A. "Child Abuse and Neglect: The Physician's Role." *Maryland State Medical Journal* 33 (1984):46–50.

Smith, S. R., and Meyer, R. G. "Child Abuse Reporting Laws and Psychotherapy: A Time for Reconsideration." In *International Journal of Law and Psychiatry* 7 (1984):351–66.

Solin, C. "Displacement of Affect in Families Following Incest Disclosure." *American Journal of Orthopsychiatry* 56 (1986):570–76.

Swanson, L. D. "Role of the Police in the Protection of Children from Neglect and Abuse." In *The Battered Child,* edited by J. Leavitt, pp. 112–16. Fresno, CA: General Learning Corporation, 1974.

Tocchio, O. J. "Procedural Problems Inhibiting Effective County and Community-Wide Resolution of Battered Child Problems." In *The Battered Child,* edited by J. Leavitt, pp. 117–22. Fresno, CA: General Learning Corporation, 1974.

Tower, C. C. "Questions Teachers Ask About Legal Aspects of Reporting Child Abuse and Neglect." In *Child Abuse and Neglect: The NEA Training Program,* edited by C. C. Tower. Washington: National Education Association, 1984b.

Tower, C. C. *How Schools Can Combat Child Abuse and Neglect.* Washington, DC: National Education Association, 1989.

Tower, C. C. *The Role of Educators in Prevention and Treatment of Child Abuse and Neglect.* Washington, DC: U.S. Department of Health and Human Services, 1992.

The Legal Response
to Child Abuse and Neglect

In dealing with protective cases, the hope is that intervention is sufficient to protect the child until treatment is established and implemented, and that parents see the need for their cooperation with social services—an ideal that is frequently difficult to achieve. It may be necessary, therefore, to bring the structure and authority of the court system into the overall picture.

Figure 10.1 in Chapter Ten showed that referral to the court system is one type of intervention available. Court action is generally considered when the child is in imminent danger or the parents are unable or unwilling to cooperate with the social service agency in improving the care of their children. There are other instances, however, when involvement with the court system might also be considered:

- The parents are unable to provide the child with proper care because of the hospitalization, incarceration, or physical or mental incapacity of one or both parents.
- The parents abandon their children, and an emergency placement must be arranged.
- Treatment is necessary and can only be obtained by a court order and not through the informal resource channels of social services (Caulfield, 1978).
- The parents are denying the child medical attention, and the lack of this attention may be life threatening.
- The case involves death of a child or severe physical injury inflicted on the child by the parent.
- The case involves sexual abuse and state statutes indicate that sexual abuse is punishable by law.

Before deciding definitely on court action, the concerned caseworker weighs the positive and negative aspects. Could this case be handled in another manner than those already tried and that does not involve court proceedings? There are some definite disadvantages to involvement in the court system. First, whether juvenile or criminal court, the proceedings have adversarial overtones (Caulfield, 1978). Parents feel antagonistic and want to mobilize their resources against the social service agency. Lawyers arguing for their clients may seem, for some, reminiscent of Perry Mason fighting to win for his client. Although juvenile court, especially, is quite unlike the TV version of courtroom scenes, the fact remains that court intervention can be an upsetting experience and one that may make the participants feel they must take sides. Second, the authority of the court and its decisions can be anxiety provoking for parents and children alike. Third, after all the preparation and emotional upheaval, the court may find insufficient grounds for further intervention, leaving the parents mistrustful of social services and the caseworker with few other options.

From the agency's perspective, the preparation of evidence, the writing of the court report, and the interviewing of witnesses accounts for a significant output of time for the social worker. Further, court delays and postponements require long hours of waiting and schedule changes. However, the caseworker and the agency may find that the positive aspects of court action—that is, the protection of the child and possible rehabilitation of the parents—outweigh all the negatives.

The Legal Rights of Parents and Children

In the court process, participants have particular rights (Caulfield, 1978; National Legal Resource Center for Child Advocacy and Protection, 1981; Stein, 1991; Haralambie, 1997). Those of the parents include the right to notice, counsel, a hearing, be informed of their rights, and to confront and cross-examine.

The right to notice means notification that the parents are suspected of being abusive or neglectful and will need to appear in court. Parents are encouraged to engage an attorney, or one can be appointed for them by the court. Parents also have a right to demand the specifics of the allegations from the individual(s) who brought the case to court attention. In criminal court, parental rights increase. Here, parents have the right to a jury trial, the right to face their accuser, and the privilege against self-incrimination. Hopefully, non-English speaking clients will have access to a translator or someone who can help them understand what is taking place. Rather than being a right per se, this service more often depends on the particular court or social agency involved.

Although children also have rights in court proceedings, these are not always as clear. They definitely have a right to counsel, and an attorney is usually assigned to them by the court. Technically, they have the right to notice of the hearing dates, but once an attorney or guardian has been appointed, notice usually goes to the surrogate. Children have the right to a hearing and cannot be removed from their home without a hearing. Some states, however, allow removal on parental consent or in an emergency, followed by a court order when necessary. Children, like their parents, are allowed the right to a hearing (Caulfield, 1978; Duquette, 1990; Haralambie, 1997).

Another right, interpreted in different ways by different states, is the child's right to a family life. Some states mandate that attempts be made to rehabilitate and reestablish the family unit. Some legal codes insist that a permanent, stable plan be made for the child whether it be to remain in the biological home or to be placed in substitute care. Children also have the right to a hearing in most states, although the case may be settled out of court before this occurs. Once in court, however, the child's lawyer, on behalf of the child, may cross-examine or confront witnesses (Caulfield, 1978; Stein, 1991).

Intervention with Native-American children is guided by the 1978 Indian Child Welfare Act. This federal legislation supplants normal state procedures, as well as substantive law, when dealing with Native-American children. Failure to meet the requirements of this act can have extensive repercussions, including the invalidation of court action years after it is supposedly final. The Indian Child Welfare Act is based on years of research, which uncovered the fact that Native-American children had long been removed from their homes by social services because of the misapplication of middle-class norms to such families (Thorne, 1991). Through the Indian Child Welfare Act, the federal government has empowered some reservations to establish legislative bodies, such as courts, to handle abuse cases. Different tribes interpret their rights under this law differently. Some handle cases totally independently, whereas others work closely with non-Native-American agencies (Wichlacz and Wechsler, 1983).

Types of Court Intervention

Civil courts usually deal with child abuse and neglect. Most courts have within their civil court system a juvenile or family court that holds a session at least one day a week, or whenever needed. Juvenile courts are usually responsible for juvenile matters—delinquency, statute offenses (such as running away or truancy, which, if committed by adults, would not come to the attention of the court), and the acceptance and disposition of protective petitions on behalf of children. Such a petition, often initiated by the protective services worker, attorney, or probation officer, brings to the attention of the court a child who is in need of protection from abuse and neglect. How each juvenile court or session addresses the filing of a protection petition differs greatly and can only be generalized. In general, juvenile court is more informal than other court settings. Hearings are closed to the public and emphasize planning for the best interests of the children.

Some states prefer to address the protection of maltreated children through a guardianship procedure in probate court. In this instance, gaining legal guardianship of the child enables the protective worker, as the agency's representative, to regulate the quality of care available and the place of residence, based on the child's best interests.

In both of these proceedings, emphasis is on the child's needs rather than censure of the parents. In very few situations are physically abusive or neglectful parents involved in criminal procedures. Criminal court action would usually be taken in instances of severe or sadistic abuse or death, and some states' criminal court procedures are initiated when otherwise deemed necessary.

A recent trend, however, has been to prosecute sexual abuse cases. States cannot agree on whether all sexual abuse should come to the attention of criminal court or on what constitutes criminal sexual abuse. While sexual intercourse with a juvenile is a crime in all states, variations (e.g., age, identity of partner, etc.) may or may not be covered by the law.

The initiation of criminal proceedings may go directly through the police or district attorney, or the protective service agency may initiate the complaint after initial screening. In juvenile court matters, the individual who investigates the case usually has a great deal of input in the decision or the outcome of the case, but this is not always true in criminal cases. The primary purpose of criminal proceedings is to punish the perpetrator and the court deems to know the best method. In this instance, the victim serves as a witness to facilitate conviction, and in the past only a minimum of attention (if any) was given to the needs of the victim (Fraser, 1981). Fortunately, there is now a trend toward supporting the child through the court process.

Given the differences in the types of court action that address abuse and neglect, one must consider the process in each, keeping in mind that each state differs in its interpretation of the legal statutes and the execution of the process.

Juvenile Court

The Process

The juvenile court process is initiated by filing a petition on behalf of the child and follows a sequence (see Figure 12.1), depending on the variables in the case. The petition is a formal document that alleges that on a specific date, at a certain time, and in a designated place, events occurred that placed the child in question in danger from abuse or neglect. The filing of this petition gives the parents notice that court action is being taken. The signer of the petition—usually the child protective worker—is referred to as the petitioner. In many states those other than the protective worker may file a petition. If the case has gone directly to juvenile court and has not been initiated by a protective services agency, the agency must be notified and is usually then involved in the process.

The petition is reviewed in some states, often by the clerk of the court, to determine its clarity and seriousness. In some instances, a conference or a pretrial hearing is held (sometimes called a show-cause hearing), often in conjunction with the probation department, to determine the credibility of the petition. Although all those represented in the petition must be present at such a hearing, they need not then be represented by counsel. Although the hearing is geared toward fact finding, sometimes decisions are made. The petition may be *withdrawn* because of insufficient facts or evidence, or the child may be ordered to receive medical care or psychological *evaluation*. Also, the child may be placed temporarily *in foster care*.

Occasionally, agreements or settlements preclude the need to carry the process further, but more often the case proceeds to an adjudicatory hearing (Fraser, 1981; Landau et al., 1980; Owen and Hershfang, 1983; Duquette, 1990).

Sometimes the protective services worker deems that between the filing of the petition and the adjudication, emergency removal of the child is warranted. A hearing must then be held to present the facts to support the removal and obtain an official removal order from

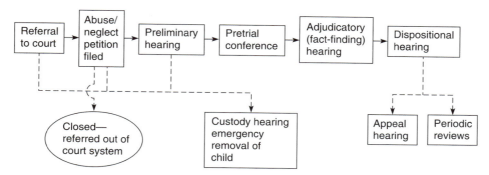

FIGURE 12.1   Juvenile Court Process

From Landau et al., *Child Protection: The Role of the Courts*. Washington, D.C., U.S. Department of Health and Human Services, 1980.

the judge. The way in which emergency removals are handled differs greatly from state to state.

At the adjudicatory hearing, the petitioner must prove the facts in the petition are accurate. The petitioner does this by providing the court with written documentation or records and by calling witnesses to testify to the validity of the allegations. These witnesses provide an important multidimensional view of the case. The parents can in turn bring forth their own evidence or refute the charges. This procedure is usually presided over by a judge (although a very few states allow a jury trial). Some states also require that the child be present at this initial hearing to be identified by the court as the individual on whose behalf the petition has been filed. For small children, especially, this argument over their welfare, and seemingly against their parents, can be quite upsetting. Recognizing this, courts often allow the children to be taken from the courtroom once the identification has been made.

The layperson frequently pictures a formal and forbidding courtroom setting for this and other juvenile hearings. To minimize the trauma to children, juvenile court is much less formal than its sister courts, and may look like a classroom or a meeting room. Of course, when the civil court holds a juvenile session or when space is limited in juvenile court, a standard courtroom may be used. Even so, the atmosphere tends to be more relaxed and informal.

At the adjudicatory hearing, attorneys who have been appointed for both parents and children (if the parents have not chosen to secure their own attorney) present each side of the case. For the most part, the protective services agency is not represented by legal counsel. In complex situations, a member of the agency's legal staff may attend. The purpose of the adjudicational hearing is fact finding. Based on these facts, several important decisions are made at this hearing (Landau et al., 1980; Mintzer and Casaly, 1980; Stein, 1991; Peters, 1997; Ichikawa, 1997). First, the validity of the case is determined. If the judge concludes that the petition is not supported by testimony, the case is dismissed. Then, an investigator is appointed by the court and given a prescribed period in which to complete a report of his or her findings. The investigator may be a social worker, an independent attorney, or an employee of the court who handles such investigations.

If the petition appears to be supported, the process continues as follows: The custody of the child is determined. Once abuse or neglect is found, the court takes jurisdiction over the child and then reserves several options: (1) Both legal and physical custody of the child can be given to the protective agency. The child would, in these circumstances, be placed in a foster home pending the next hearing. (2) The child can be placed with relatives. (3) The child can be allowed to return home during the investigation. If the child does return home, custody is often awarded to the protective agency to facilitate emergency removal should it be necessary.

Much discussion surrounds the placement of children during the investigatory period. Although an investigator can not make a clear assessment of parenting skills if the children are not in the home, some child protection advocates still feel that a case that necessitated court action is usually serious enough to require removal. Because of this debate, it is difficult to predict where the children will reside during the investigation.

The investigation is that period between the adjudicatory hearing and the dispositional hearing in which the appointed investigator gathers additional facts to determine the severity and the causes of maltreatment. In addition, the investigator formulates recommendations for treatment or future actions to present to the court. The role of investigator is an important one. This individual should be fair and competent in searching out collaterals (e.g., teachers, neighbors, and others interested in the case) and exploring all the factors in the case.

The court may have ordered medical or psychological evaluations of the parents or child or both, and the results are included in the investigator's report at the next hearing.

While the investigator seeks information to determine what will be in the best interests of the child, the parents' attorney seeks to help his or her clients form a plan whereby the child remains in or is returned to their care. Some attorneys encourage the parents to seek treatment during this interim period so they might argue more convincingly at the hearing. Indeed for some parents, the reality of the court experience is enough to motivate them toward positive action.

Once the investigation is completed within the specified period, all the participants—usually excluding the child—again appear in court for the dispositional hearing. This proceeding is designed for decision making (Stein, 1991). It determines the custody of the child and the steps the parents must take to eventually resume the full care of their child if it is felt that this is possible. To make these determinations, several things happen at this hearing. First, the investigator's report is presented (Landau et al., 1980). (If the report is written, the judge and perhaps the attorneys have had some time to read it before the hearing.) The report includes

- A description of the type of harm done to the child
- Background information on the family
- Information supplied by collaterals
- Recommendations of services for the family
- Possibly a time frame in which these goals should be accomplished

Witnesses may be called to support the information in the report. Other types of evidence (e.g., records, letters, and medical files) may be entered to support the report. And finally, the parents' attorney has the right to cross-examine witnesses or produce evidence to refute the allegations that the parents have abused or neglected their child.

Witnesses in this type of hearing can be few or many, depending on the complexity of the case. The layperson may testify from direct observation of the situation and may express opinions or make assessments. Witnesses are encouraged to recount as much direct observation as possible, however. For example, a teacher may be able to recount how he or she saw the bruises on Johnny or that Johnny confided that he had been beaten. These witnesses are asked to testify as to what they smelled, heard, saw, or touched. Neighbors, teachers, social workers, and others with firsthand knowledge may be called to testify. Only rarely is a character witness for the parents brought in to testify on their behalf.

The next most frequently used witness in protection hearings is one who gives expert testimony. This expert's credentials give him or her the sanction to give opinions in his or her area of expertise and answer hypothetical questions (Caulfield, 1978). For example, a psychologist, who has tested the child in question, might be asked, "In your expert opinion and having done extensive testing with Johnny, would it be emotionally damaging for this child to continue to reside in this home?" Physicians, psychologists, some social workers, and others in specialized fields can appear as expert witnesses. Recently some courts have allowed more controversial experts, such as graphologists (who are able to detect character traits from handwriting), to untangle the often complex factors in a case.

Sometimes children are allowed to testify, but very young children may be in question as to their competency. In some states, especially in sexual abuse situations, evidence may include information told to a qualified third party by the child. This prevents the child from having to testify. Other states prefer to use videotaped interviews with the child.

The testimonies and the evidence must prove that harm was done to the child. It is not enough to prove that the parents' behavior is abusive. Rather, the effect this behavior has had on the child must be established (Arthur, 1984).

Several dispositions can be made as a result of this proceeding (Landau et al., 1980). These also vary considerably from state to state.

- The case can be dismissed if the judge deems that insufficient evidence has been presented to support the allegations of maltreatment.
- The judge may suspend judgment based on the parents' willingness to comply with the court's recommendations. In other words, the court may order the parents to undergo treatment or follow some other prescribed plan. They are given a time frame—usually six months to a year—in which they must meet certain conditions; at the end of this time another hearing is held. If the parents have failed to comply with the order, a judgment is made. If they have complied, the case may be dismissed or it may be continued to a later date to ensure the parents' compliance or consistency over time.
- The judge may order custody of the child to the protective agency. The child will then either (1) remain at home, but be visited regularly by a social worker who assures the court of the safety of the child; or (2) be placed in a foster home pending the parents' compliance with treatment.
- The judge may terminate parental rights based on the court's perception that the parents are unable to adequately care for their child. If this step is imminent before the hearing, the parents are notified of the court's intent. The termination of parental rights is not an arbitrary decision but rather is based on specific conduct or inaction. In other words, the court observes that the child would be further harmed if the parents regained custody. In some states, this termination of parental rights frees the child immediately for adoption. In some other states, an additional petition outlining the best interests of the child and possibilities for future placement is necessary to set into motion the actual adoption procedure.

Throughout the court protection process, the parents have the right to appeal to a higher court, although procedures on such an appeal differ from state to state. If the appeal is heard, it is designed to review the case to ensure that the trial court correctly interpreted and followed existing law. The higher court may uphold the juvenile court decision, overturn its decision, or order the juvenile court to hear the case again if there was a violation of due process (Caulfield, 1978; Landau et al., 1980; Thorne, 1991; Haralambie, 1997).

The juvenile court process is usually lengthy. Courts attempt to keep to a minimum the time between filing the petition and the adjudicatory hearing, but because of multiple dispositional hearings and delays and cancellations, the process can drag on into years. During this time, the child may be moved from home to foster home in a seemingly endless cycle of separation and loss. This unfortunate situation can be somewhat ameliorated by competent social workers preparing and supporting the child during this period.

The Participants

Before examining criminal court intervention, it may be helpful to look at the participants in the juvenile court process. While many have an idea (albeit colored by TV and other media, and fiction) of the role of judges, lawyers, and prosecutors in criminal court, few understand the differences and subtleties of a juvenile court hearing. The informality, the fact that children are involved, and the fact that juvenile court is not specifically concerned with adversary proceedings changes the style in which participants operate.

Judges

The role of the judge in juvenile court is not easy. Most judges are aware they serve as authority figures but understand that children should not be intimidated more than they already are. From the initial petition, it might be easy for judges to see parents as cruel and intentionally hurting their offspring. A closer look often promotes the understanding that the parents are frightened, deprived, overburdened individuals who may not have had the models to parent properly themselves. The judge must both protect the constitutional rights of the parents and consider the child's rights as well (Ward, 1992).

Deprived of the support of a jury (in most cases), the judge must base the final decision on the report of the investigator, on what has been heard in the courtroom, on the judge's own experience, and often on an assumption of what will be best for all concerned. The judge is also aware that the ruling may be subject to public outrage or overturned by a higher court.

Courts seek to determine guilt or innocence, but the juvenile court process emphasizes treatment. The judge must be able to assess how amenable the parents are to treatment and what resources are actually available in the community to help them. The judge must also face the shortage of placement and treatment resources for children (Polier and McDonald, 1972).

Since people's motivations are never predictable, the juvenile court judge realizes there is no assurance that a child will be safe when returned home or happy in placement. Using only best judgment and the hope that it is correct, the judge renders the decision.

Children's Advocates

The attorney who represents the child has an important role in protecting the child's interests, but often works with little or no information or feedback from the underage client. Representation of infants requires the attorney's judgment of what will be best for the child. With an older child, the counselor may adopt an approach that explores the child's feelings and hopes for the outcome. Then the attorney is faced with deciding whether the child will be more at risk at home or more traumatized by placement. Understanding the impact on the child, not only of the abuse or neglect but of the implications for staying in the home, is essential. This attorney must be singleminded and constantly aware of the effects of the treatment suggested or the decisions made for the young client (Isaacs, 1972; Duquette, 1990). Attorneys for children do not assume the adversary role of attorneys in other proceedings, but act here, as their alternate title implies, as guardians of the children's best interests. The lawyer is in close contact with the protective services agency to ensure what they propose for the child will indeed be the best plan (Peters, 1997; Litzelfelner and Petr, 1997).

Lawyers representing children sometimes function in an advisory role, acquainting their clients with what will transpire in court or even giving a tour of the courtrooms to minimize the intimidation when the child must be present. Some lawyers prefer to leave this preparation to social workers. Not every lawyer is interested in representing children. In fact, counsel for children are chosen differently depending on the state and court. Some attorneys specialize in representing children and become proficient in balancing the needs of the children with their obligations to the court. Others are appointed—often as part of a training process when they first begin with a firm or an agency. The attorneys' feelings about child representation can greatly affect their manner of dealing with their clients.

Children are not always represented solely by lawyers. Some courts appoint a specially trained volunteer to protect the child's interests. One such volunteer program, known as CASA (Court Appointed Special Advocate), was created by Judge David Soukup, of the King County Superior Court in Seattle, Washington. In 1970, Soukup was concerned about the children in the cases coming through his court. His idea of using trained volunteers became established in January 1977. During the first year of this program (then known as the G.A.L., or *guardian ad litem,* program), there were 110 volunteers serving 498 children. The program is now nationwide, and by 1986 there were 201 CASA programs in 43 states.[1]

The concept of using special advocates arose from the fact that many lawyers did not feel comfortable being the sole representatives of children. There was little consistency in how this representation was carried out, and few lawyers were trained for child welfare responsibilities. Many felt ill prepared for the untraditional legal responsibilities of interviewing and sometimes counseling children (Duquette, 1990; Litzelfelner and Petr, 1997).

The court-appointed special volunteer (who may be a layperson) plays a part in both juvenile and probate court proceedings. In probate court custody cases, CASA volunteers investigate the home situation and follow up to ensure the children's welfare until the case is decided by the court. In juvenile court cases, even though an investigator has already been appointed, the CASA volunteer continues to monitor the home once the investigation is over. The goal in this monitoring is to be sure the child is safe and that the parents are doing what they can for the child's well-being.

Although this program has been successful in many areas, some attorneys feel uncomfortable using lay volunteers. Volunteers, in turn, often complain that they are not being taken seriously by the courts. Those programs using volunteers hope that increased training and communication will ameliorate this problem.

Parents' Attorneys

While the children are being represented by an attorney, a CASA volunteer, or other court-appointed advocates, the parents also have representation. The parents' attorney is either hired by them or appointed by the court. This attorney may need to overcome negative feelings about what has been done to the child in order to understand and defend the needs and rights of the clients. Considering that neglectful and abusive parents often have difficulty trusting others, forming relationships, and following through, the lawyer's role is often marked with frustration.

The main role of the parents' attorney will be to refute the allegations brought by the petition and convince the court that the parents do have their children's interests in mind. This counselor attempts to evaluate the clients' problems and helps them and the court discover ways to minister to these problems. The lawyer advises the clients as to what might help minimize the court's concerns. For example, the lawyer might suggest that the court would look more favorably on the case if the clients secured housing not so structurally dangerous and rat infested as their current dwelling. Further, the counsel may help the clients get in touch with a housing agency through which better accommodations could be found. The parents' attorney may also advise them to cooperate with the protective services agency by following the prescribed treatment plan.

The attorney who fights vigorously for abusive or neglectful clients is not always popular. Yet this advocate serves to ensure that the court consider all sides of the problem. The presence of this counsel protects the parents' rights to due process (Duquette, 1990). The attorney may also be operating as a spokesperson for those inarticulate parents who otherwise might not be given a fair hearing.

Agency Attorneys

The protective services attorney does not always follow the case into the courtroom. More often this individual functions in an advisory role to the protective services worker on whom the burden of proof has fallen. This attorney is familiar with the court system and recognizes how to use it to the best advantage in securing an equitable plan for the child. The attorney is also familiar with the functioning of the protective services agency and can help to interpret this to the court. Knowing both areas, this attorney is better able to aid caseworkers in preparing reports and assisting them in the preparation of their testimony. In more complex legal situations, the attorney may also go into the courtroom to provide firsthand legal advice to agency representatives.

Social Workers

Social workers serve several roles in a court hearing. The roles they take differ greatly from state to state and agency to agency. The original reporter may have been a social worker who then came to court to testify, or a social worker may have been assigned to either the family or the children separately. This worker may then be asked to provide support to his or her clients and pertinent information during the hearing. It is often extremely difficult for workers who have been giving service to a family to seemingly "choose sides" in court.

Some agencies assign one or more social workers to advocate for either parents or children just before, or following, the initial hearing. These social workers are usually responsible for helping the clients to carry out the directives of the court (e.g., receive treatment, find adequate housing, etc.). Social workers may be in the employ of state, county, or private agencies, depending on who has responsibility for the case.

One of the most widely described problems for social workers going into court is that their views usually conflict with that of the attorney. Attorneys are trained to listen for facts and to search out evidence, but social workers are often trained to make judgments on experience, psychological analyses, and even intuition. For this reason, some attorneys complain that social workers cannot articulate in a manner that is beneficial to their case (Stein, 1991).

Since each profession has its strengths, there is an increased trend toward dialogue between these two professionals. Social workers are learning to be more comfortable and articulate in court proceedings, while they strive to make attorneys more aware of how to interview children and how to determine what will be in the best interest of these children.

Witnesses

Anyone, but especially those involved with child welfare services, may be called to appear in juvenile court as a witness. First-time experiences in court can be anxiety provoking, but the witnesses should remember they are there on behalf of the child (or the parent) and not on trial themselves.

Caulfield (1978) suggests pointers for those who must appear in court. A witness should prepare ahead. Notes about dates and events can help with recall, but these should not be read verbatim. Nor should the testimony be memorized. Appropriate dress is essential. Courts are still often conservative.

It is natural to be nervous. The stress of an unfamiliar courtroom, combined with the requirements that the witness answer under oath, often makes the witness uncomfortable. Speaking more slowly and somewhat louder and more distinctly than usual will help get the testimony across. Most attorneys prefer to develop the case without having witnesses furnish extraneous details. Therefore the attorney may ask questions that can easily be answered by yes or no. On the other hand, an attorney may direct the witness to furnish a good deal of information at once. For example, the witness may be told, "Tell us what you observed and what happened when you went to the Jones's home on March 15th." Answers should be factual and contain a minimum of hearsay or secondhand information. (In the event of an undue amount of hearsay, the opposing attorney may object.) A witness should confine himself or herself to that which is known rather than guess or assume.

Cross-examination can be especially anxiety provoking. Although the witness must tell the truth, words can often be twisted to appear to mean something else. This is especially true if a question is in two parts or is meant to be a trick question. Experienced witnesses learn that it is important not to be rushed. They consider the question calmly and then answer it as positively as possible. Two-part questions, for example, can be broken into their parts before being answered. If there is an objection, witnesses learn to stop talking until a ruling has been made (Caulfield, 1978).

With experience, court appearances become considerably easier and can actually make one feel involved and helpful in the cause of protecting children.

Alternatives

Settlements resulting from negotiations between attorneys sometimes preclude the need for a hearing. Unlike negotiations in other types of cases (e.g., criminal), these negotiations are often more complex. The fact that there are more participants, each perhaps with different viewpoints, and that the children cannot speak for themselves adds to this complexity (Mintzer and Casaly, 1980; Ichikawa, 1997).

Settlements usually take the form of what the parents will do in order to avoid a court appearance and have the children remain with them. The advantages of these settlements to the children must be fully weighed. For this reason, the agreements made are often written up in the form of a treatment plan.

There are advantages to settlements in juvenile court cases. First, a hearing may make the participants feel they are in an adversary relationship; people feel forced to take sides even though the issue for everyone should be what is in the best interest of the child. Second, a recapitulation of the facts surrounding the abuse may increase the parents' feelings of guilt and elevate their defenses to compensate. Third, hearings and the preparation for them can be lengthy and require an inordinate amount of time for lawyers, social workers, and other court personnel (National Legal Resource Center, 1981).

The disadvantages to settlements, however, include the instances of parents who later regret that they had not presented their side. They may have felt pressured into negotiating. Without a hearing, pertinent information that could have a profound impact on the case may not be uncovered. It is vital, therefore, that the ramifications of the case be studied thoroughly prior to or during negotiations and that all parties feel comfortable with the settlement agreement (National Legal Resource Center, 1981).

Some states use voluntary placement of children to circumvent juvenile court hearings. An agreement is made between the parents and the protective agency that the children will be placed in a foster home while the parents undergo treatment or make other arrangements for their return.

> *Rochelle Duclas, a 22-year-old mother of two, entered into such an agreement with the department of protective services. Rochelle maintained an apartment that she frequently shared with a boyfriend, Al, who was subject to extreme bouts of temper. The year before, Rochelle's two children, ages 2 and 3, had been removed by the juvenile court after it was discovered they had been severely abused by Al. It was the decision of the court that this mother could not, or would not, separate from her boyfriend long enough to ensure the safety of her children. The children therefore remained in foster care while the department petitioned to have them legally freed for adoption.*
>
> *When Rochelle gave birth to a third child, she recognized the danger to the infant from Al, who had recently returned. She thought she could get her boyfriend to leave but needed more time. Rochelle approached the department and asked that she be allowed to place her child, temporarily, while securing a better apartment and a restraining order against Al. Feeling that this plan was preferable to the possible abuse of the baby, the department agreed.*

One of the problems with voluntary agreements is that in many jurisdictions they can be easily broken by the parents. The protective agency is then left with little alternative but to seek court action.

Not all states use the juvenile court in every instance. Sometimes a guardianship petition is filed in probate court to avoid the lengthy juvenile court process. Guardianship is provided for a child when the parent is absent, incapable, or unfit to care for him or her. This course of action is usually undertaken when the parent seems unlikely to be able to resume care of the child. Guardianship is also used to protect the child when agreements to voluntary placements are broken (National Legal Resource Center, 1981).

Advantages and Disadvantages of Juvenile Court

The consideration of advantages and disadvantages of the juvenile court system prompts a look at this system from a historical perspective. Prior to the late 1800s, children were rarely considered in courts as anything other than extensions of their parents. In 1899, due largely to the efforts of child advocates, the first juvenile court was established in Chicago. Advocates of this seemingly new progressive system felt that children should be separated from adults in court proceedings for three reasons. First, when children committed infractions or crimes, they did so not because they were evil (a common perception about adults) but because they were in pain or conflict. These attention-seeking behaviors warranted help, not punishment. Second, children whose families abused or neglected them required careful evaluation and help that would protect their interests. Careful attention must be given to the rights of the children as well as the rights of the parents. And finally, those responsible for making these legal decisions about the welfare of children should have an interest in and expertise about children (Dziech and Schudson, 1991; Noel, 1998).

Over the years, juvenile courts have taken on more informality and less dependence on rigid legal protocols. There has been an attempt to keep in focus the needs of the children and their welfare. In abuse and neglect situations, petitions are brought on *behalf* of children rather than *against* their parents. This shifts the emphasis from punishment of parents for their actions or lack of action toward treatment that will strengthen the home environment if at all possible.

Yet, as the sexual abuse of children became one of the most pervasive issues of this era, some authors argue that juvenile court may actually benefit the perpetrator as much, if not more, than the child. Dziech and Schudson contend that sexual abusers have benefited in two ways from having their case brought to juvenile court.

> First, and most obvious, they enjoyed confidentiality. The law prohibited disclosure of juvenile court proceedings even when neighbors or relatives might have been able to protect children had they known the identity of the abuser.... Less apparent, but more significant is the fact that once juvenile courts became the primary place for child abuse cases, adult criminal courts could ignore the issue. (1991, p. 26)

Thus, continue Dziech and Schudson, while on the one hand the child's privacy is protected, the offender also escapes having the community know the "sensitive, unsavory, embarrassing offense" (1991, p. 27) he or she has committed.

For these reasons, more and more states are passing legislation that mandates the report of sexual abuse cases to district attorneys. In this way, criminal courts will often also be involved.

Criminal Court

Increasingly, and especially in cases of sexual abuse, criminal courts deal with perpetrators. Occasionally, when a child dies as a result of abuse or neglect or is severely harmed, parents are also prosecuted. The goals of criminal prosecution are, theoretically, rehabilitation, removal of the perpetrator from society, deterrence from future crimes, or retribution. The problem is that it is only the defendant, if found guilty, who is required to receive treatment. In family situations, such a remedy ignores the fact that abuse is usually a family system problem (National Legal Resource Center, 1981).

Criminal prosecution may be used instead of, or in conjunction with, juvenile court. When this occurs, the juvenile court judge suspends decision pending the outcome of the criminal proceedings. Unfortunately this often leaves the child and other members of the family in uncertainty for an extended period. In many states, nonfamilial sexual abuse is not within the responsibilities of protective services agencies, and the issue is handled only as a criminal matter.

Criminal procedures differ significantly from those in juvenile court. Figure 12.2 depicts this complex legal process.

As in other criminal cases, a perpetrator can be released on bail. Plea bargaining (an agreement made between all the parties to minimize the charges or avoid going to trial) is another option—and a controversial one in many cases. While in both instances the lawyer for the perpetrator is seeking to get the "best deal" for the client, the child and others concerned hope for adequate protection for the child (Arthur, 1986). Therapists or victim-witness advocates are often used to ensure that the child's best interests are protected.

Threat of prosecution is used as leverage, especially in sexual abuse cases. In these situations, the perpetrator pleads guilty with the understanding that the sentence will be suspended or reduced if he cooperates with a treatment program.

Prosecution in criminal court is not without drawbacks for the child and the family. The court process can be traumatic to the victim. Many appearances in the courtroom are often required and thus extend the procedure. The participants' lives seem consumed with preparing for and then enduring the court experience. The assault(s) must be relived again and again in the presence of a jury and amidst a possibly crowded courtroom. Victims who testify often feel fatigue and may begin to doubt their own stories (Burgess and Holmstrom, 1978). Videotaping (described in Chapter 11) spares victims the numerous appearances. Yet for the duration of the trial and often long afterwards, the family feels the pressure of scrutiny.

Much depends on the actions and attitudes of the important figures in the criminal court process. The district attorney emerges early as a professional whose style can have an effect on the participants. Burgess and Holmstrom (1978) describe the district attorney who appears indifferent to the witnesses and gives them little direction or support. Another district attorney may be extremely authoritative and matter of fact, and indicate that he or she knows how to proceed and is not willing to deviate. Fortunately for most families and victims, many district attorneys take a more humanistic approach. As abuse cases have become more frequent, district attorneys have sought training to become more sensitive to the needs of children and families. Many district attorneys take time to prepare the participants in order to minimize the trauma of appearing in court.

Another source of help for families is the increasing number of victim-witness advocates. Operating out of the district or county attorney's office, victim-witness programs supply workers to offer support to the child and the family, to provide transportation, and to prepare the participants for their roles in court. The victim-witness advocate is a friend for the child and a counselor on whom the child can depend when others in the child's life may feel under too much pressure to offer support (Mayer, 1985).

Despite the delays, the uncomfortable cross-examination, and the trauma of feeling put on the spot, the trial comes to an end. The possibilities for outcome are varied. The abuser may be fined for damages or be required to undergo treatment (see Chapter 13). If the family is to remain intact or if this is the eventual plan, family counseling may be ordered or recommended. In some instances the perpetrator will be incarcerated and treatment may or may not be available (Arthur, 1986). Perhaps one of the most difficult rulings for the plaintiff is to have the case dismissed. The child may be vulnerable not only to future assaults but to the guilt of family disruption.

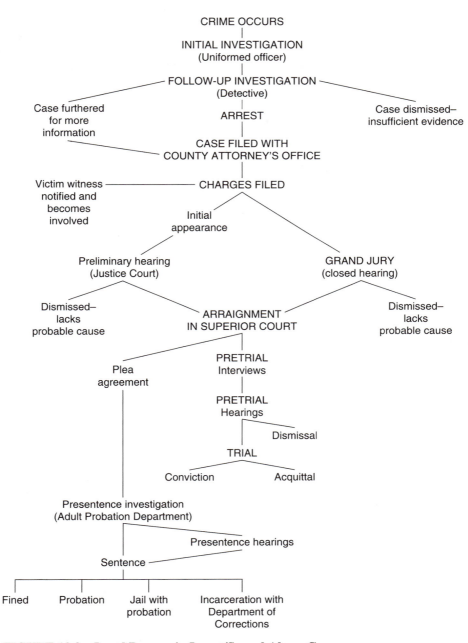

FIGURE 12.2   Legal Process in Incest/Sexual Abuse Cases

From Mayer, A., *Sexual Abuse: Causes, Consequences and Treatment of Incestuous and Pedophilic Acts.*
Learning Publications, Inc., 1985. Reprinted with permission.

Whether the perpetrator is convicted or not, therapy for the child is usually advisable. Unlike adults, who may try to forget the unpleasantness of what has happened, children are frequently more affected by the process. Even when the perpetrator was not a family member, the child may fear retaliation or carry guilt because of testifying.

The criminal process is not always a smooth one and can be painful for those involved. The system, however, has come a long way in becoming sensitive to the needs of the parties in this all-too-frequent type of case.

The Impact of Court on Children

A child who has been abused or neglected and who is then faced with the experience of going to court has an additional adjustment. Once children were the pawns to be moved to and fro in the legal maze. With attention to children's rights, more focus has been put on the children and their reactions to the court experience.

How traumatized are children by the experience of going to court? Lipovsky (1994) compared three studies to determine the degree of "system-induced" trauma to children. She found that when children do testify in court, which is not as frequent as one might imagine, they are in fact not unduly traumatized. Older children have more difficulty with the experience than their younger counterparts, and children who are exposed to lengthy court battles may show more negative effects. Maternal support was found to be a key factor. Children who had mother as an advocate fared better (Lipovsky, 1994).

Time delays are one issue which can compound trauma for children. Bishop et al. (1992) found, in their Massachusetts-based sample, that 38 percent of the children studied were involved in the court on their case for 8 years with 10 percent of the children involved for more than 10 years. The majority of the cases in this study were in court process, from the initial filing to the close of the court case, for 5 years (p. 471). Many of these children (45 percent) remained in foster care. Some were moved from foster home to foster home. For children whose future rests in the hands of the legal system, a few years can seem like an eternity.

To minimize the trauma to children, Lipovsky suggests several interventions that courts and social workers should keep in mind. *Education* is an effective tool to decrease children's anxiety about the court experience. Both children and their parents can be educated about court process complete with trips to familiarize themselves with a courtroom. *Stress management procedures,* such as teaching deep breathing, muscle relaxation and focusing, helped children to cope. Children respond well to role plays which let them practice using these techniques. *Improving parental attitudes about court* was another method of providing support to children. Parents who were fearful of or extremely negative about the experience communicated this to their children. *Improving maternal support* (or support from the non-offending parent) is vital in enhancing the child's ability to feel safe and protected. And, finally, Lipovsky stresses that helping professionals should *keep in mind the individual characteristics of the child.* Older children, who studies show are more traumatized by court experiences, are often overlooked with the assumption that because they are older they can take care of themselves. Each child should be seen individually from the perspective of age, gender, reactions to stress, and general psychological makeup. Through these simple procedures children can be helped to cope with their court experiences (Lipovsky, 1994).

The Media and the Court

As child abuse and neglect cases appear more and more frequently in both juvenile and criminal court, the media have given greater coverage to the issue. Media interest stimulates the controversy over the public's right to know about these proceedings and the child's and family's rights to privacy. Media attention can also aggravate an already emotionally charged atmosphere. Critics of media coverage have expressed the opinion that perpetrators are condemned by public outrage and therefore have less than a fair hearing. The stigma is attached to the abusive and the nonabusive parent as well (National Legal Resource Center, 1981).

In general, juvenile court hearings are open only to the participants and are closed to the media. Criminal hearings, however, may be opened to public scrutiny. Although it may be important to educate the public about what is being done in the area of court involvement in child abuse and neglect, the effect on children of not only the legal proceedings but of the attendant coverage cannot be minimized. Therefore, it should be with a great deal of sensitivity that the media be allowed to fully cover these cases.

Summary

Court action in cases of child abuse and neglect takes place as a last resort when parents abandon their children, severely injure or kill them, place them in imminent danger, sexually abuse them, or fail to cooperate with the protective services agency. Going to court is not easy for the child or the family, and the positives and negatives must be considered carefully in the context of the entire case. Both parents and children have similar legal rights. These are the right to counsel, the right to be given notice, and the right to confrontation and cross-examination.

An abuse or neglect case may be handled in one of several courts. Civil court houses juvenile sessions or courts in which a petition can be brought to request protection for dependent children. Criminal courts prosecute the perpetrators. In some states, probate or superior courts hear different types of maltreatment cases.

The juvenile court process differs from state to state. For the most part, it consists of three stages: the petition, the adjudication, and the disposition. Between each stage there can be variations, such as fact-finding conferences, an investigation, or out-of-court settlements. The parents and the child are each represented by counsel, and the hearings are tried on merits to determine what is in the best interest of the child. The juvenile court hearing is usually somewhat informal. Once the case has been investigated, the facts are presented

and a plan of treatment for the parents may be required. The court also determines that the custody of the child be with the parents, relatives, or through the protective services agency.

The professionals involved in juvenile court are an important part of the process. The judge hears the case and makes the final decision based on the recommendations of the investigator, the protective agency, and the attorneys. The attorney for the child assumes the role of counselor for the client as well as represents the child's best interest. More recently, court-appointed special advocates provide support for the families and monitor the cases to ensure that court recommendations are followed.

The parents' attorney attempts to refute the allegations of abuse and neglect and represents the interests of the clients. Often this role extends to helping the parents by making referrals for services that will enable them to provide a better environment for their children. The attorney for the protective service agency usually functions in an advisory capacity but may attend the hearings to provide support in more complex situations.

There are some alternatives to juvenile court hearings. Settlements resulting from negotiations between the attorneys of involved parties sometimes preclude a court hearing. Voluntary placement gives parents time to receive treatment or mobilize their resources in order to provide a better home for their children. Some protective agencies use probate court guardianship as an alternative to juvenile court.

When children have been killed, severely injured, or sexually abused, perpetrators are usually prosecuted in criminal courts. One of the most significant drawbacks about criminal court is the effect it can have on children and their families. Often it is the participants' relationships with the district attorney, their own attorneys, and the victim-witness volunteers that minimize the trauma caused by this complex process.

Although court action can create a strain for the participants, it does provide a useful mechanism through which society can protect abused and neglected children.

Exploration Questions

1. When might a protective services worker opt to initiate court action?

2. What are the legal rights of parents or abused or neglected children?

3. Outline the types of court intervention available in child abuse and neglect cases.

4. How does the juvenile court process begin?

5. What is the adjudicatory hearing? What happens at this time?

6. What is the role of the investigator? What is included in the investigator's report?

7. What is a dispositional hearing? What happens at this time?

8. Cite the role of each of the participants in the juvenile court process.

9. What are some of the guidelines suggested for witnesses?

10. Cite several alternatives to juvenile court.

11. What is the goal of criminal prosecution?

12. What are the disadvantages of using the criminal justice process in abuse and neglect cases?

Activities for Applied Learning

1. Research the procedures of the juvenile court and the criminal court in your area.

2. Invite a court investigator to class. How does this person see the role of investigator? What does he or she look for in conducting an investigation?

3. Invite a representative from a CASA program to speak to the class. How does this volunteer view CASA and his or her own role?

4. Contact the local victim-witness advocacy program. When was it begun and how does it function?

5. Visit a juvenile or criminal court. Talk with court personnel about their roles.

6. Create a scrapbook of media coverage of legal proceedings in abuse and neglect cases. Is this coverage helpful or harmful to the participants? To other members of society?

Suggested Readings

Arthur, L. G. "Judicial Procedures." *Juvenile and Family Court Journal* 35 (1984–85): 15–22.

Arthur, L. G. "Court Procedures." *Juvenile and Family Court Journal* 37 (1986): 27–36.

Caulfield, B. A. *The Legal Aspects of Protective Services for Abused and Neglected Children.* Washington, DC: U.S. Department of Health, Education and Welfare, 1978.

Duquette, D. N. *Advocating for the Child in Protection Proceedings.* Lexington, MA; Lexington Books, 1990.

Dziech, B. W., and Schudson, C. D. *On Trial: America's Courts and Their Treatment of Sexually Abused Children.* Boston: Beacon Press, 1991.

Landau, H. R.; Salus, M. K.; Stiffarm, T.; with Kalb, N. L. *Child Protection: The Role of the Courts.*

Washington, DC: U.S. Department of Health and Human Services, 1980.

Lipovsky, J. A. "The Impact of Court on Children." *Journal of Interpersonal Violence* 9 (2), (1994): 238–57.

Endnote

1. Based on an interview with Sue Scrogin, project director, The CASA Project, Worcester, Massachusetts.

References

Arthur, L. G. "Judicial Procedures." *Juvenile and Family Court Journal* 35 (1984–85): 15–22.

Arthur, L. G. "Court Procedures." *Juvenile and Family Court Journal* 37 (1986): 27–36.

Bishop, S. J.; Murphy, J. M.; Jellinek, J. S.; Quinn, D.; and Poitrast, F. G. "Protecting Maltreated Children: Time Delays in a Court Sample." *Child Abuse and Neglect* 16 (4) (1992): 465–474.

Burgess, A. W., and Holmstrom, L. L. "The Child and Family During the Court Process." In *Sexual Assault of Children and Adolescents,* edited by A. W. Burgess, A. N. Groth, L. L. Holmstrom, and S. M. Sgroi, pp. 205–30. Lexington, MA: Lexington Books, 1978.

Caulfield, B. A. *The Legal Aspects of Protective Services for Abused and Neglected Children.* Washington: U.S. Department of Health, Education and Welfare, 1978.

Duquette, D. N. *Advocating for the Child in Protection Proceedings.* Lexington, MA: Lexington Books, 1990.

Dziech, B. W., and Schudson, C. B. *On Trial: America's Courts and Their Treatment of Sexually Abused Children.* Boston: Beacon Press, 1991.

Fraser, B. G. "Sexual Child Abuse: The Legislation and the Law in the United States." In *Sexually Abused Children and their Families,* edited by P. B. Mrazek and C. H. Kempe, pp. 55–74. Elmsford, NY: Pergamon Press, 1981.

Haralambie, A. "Current Trends in Children's Legal Representation." *Child Maltreatment* 2(3) (1997): 193–201.

Ichikawa, D. P. "An Argument on Behalf of Children." *Child Maltreatment* 2 (3) (1997): 202–211.

Isaacs, J. L. "The Role of the Lawyer in Child Abuse Cases. In *Helping the Battered Child and His Family,* edited by C. H. Kempe and R. E. Helfer, pp. 225–41. Philadelphia: J. B. Lippincott, 1972.

Landau, H. R.; Salus, M. K.; Stiffarm, T.; with Kalb, N. L. *Child Protection: The Role of the Courts.* Washington: U.S. Department of Health and Human Services, 1980.

Lipovsky, J. A. "The Impact of Court on Children." *Journal of Interpersonal Violence* 9 (2), (1994): 238–257.

Litzelfelner, P., and Petr, C. "Case Advocacy in Child Welfare." *Social Work* 42(4) (1997): 392–402.

Mayer, A. *Sexual Abuse: Causes, Consequences and Treatment of Incestuous and Pedophilic Acts.* Holmes Beach, FL: Learning Publications, 1985.

Mintzer, B. L., and Casaly, J. P. *Representing the Abused and Neglected Child in Massachusetts.* Boston: Commonwealth of Massachusetts, Office for Children, 1980.

National Legal Resource Center for Child Advocacy and Protection, American Bar Association. *Child Abuse and Neglect Litigation.* Washington: U.S. Department of Health and Human Services, 1981.

Noel, J. "Court Services on Behalf of Children" in C. Crosson-Tower, *Exploring Child Welfare,* pp. 266–287. Boston: Allyn & Bacon, 1998.

Owen, J. T., and Hershfang, H. H. "An Overview of the Legal System: Protecting Children from Abuse and Neglect." In *Child Abuse and Neglect,* edited by N. B. Ebeling and D. A. Hill, pp. 229–57. Littleton, MA: PSG Publishing, 1983.

Perry, N. W. and Wrightsman, L. S. *Child Witness: Legal Issues and Dilemmas.* Thousand Oaks, CA: Sage, 1991.

Peters, J. K. "The Lawyer for Children at the Interdisciplinary Meeting." *Child Maltreatment* 2(3) (1997): 226–244.

Polier, J. W., and McDonald, K. "The Family Court in an Urban Setting." In *Helping the Battered Child and His Family,* edited by C. H. Kempe and R. E. Helfer, pp. 208–24. Philadelphia: J. B. Lippincott, 1972.

Stein, T. *Child Welfare and the Law.* New York: Longman, 1991.

Thorne, W. A. Personal communication, July 15, 1991.

Ward, M. H. "Insuring the Voice of the Child Be Heard." *Journal of Child Sexual Abuse* 1 (3), (1992): 109–113.

Wichlacz, C. R., and Wechsler, J. G. "American Indian Law on Child Abuse and Neglect," *Child Abuse and Neglect* 7 (1983): 347–50.

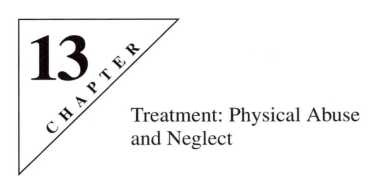

Treatment: Physical Abuse and Neglect

The identification and assessment of abusive and neglectful families has one end, and that is that the child will be protected. In years past, some people believed that the solution was to remove the child from the family if it was not providing appropriate care. Now, we realize that this alternative, in some instances, may actually be more damaging to the child. We have also learned that some families, with adequate supports, can begin to parent effectively. Treatment of families, therefore, becomes more essential in providing children with a safe and nurturing atmosphere. Unfortunately, if funds are cut from social services it is often in the area of treatment. It is hoped that, as more effective treatment methods are developed, funding sources will recognize how vital this area of the helping system is to children.

Preparing to Provide Treatment

Professionals who are involved in treatment of abusive and neglectful families must be aware of several aspects of their work. First is in the area of *countertransference,* that is the worker's reaction to the client (feelings, attitudes, thoughts, and behaviors) which is brought about by the helper's own past life experiences. These reactions may be based upon the worker's own history of abuse, past relationships with parents or caretakers, previous life experiences, and relationships with intimates (Peterson and Urquiza, 1993; Jackson and Nuttal, 1997). If clients "push our buttons," we, as professionals, must become aware of it so that our actions do not negatively influence the service being provided.

A second area of importance is *confidentiality.* Every client has the right to privacy when he or she shares thoughts or feelings with a helping professional. In protective work, the parameters of confidentiality become more problematic. There are three areas, in treatment, which the client cannot expect the worker or therapist to keep confidential. These are: if the client has threatened or attempted suicide; if the client threatens to kill another; or if the client abuses or neglects a child. These situations should or must be reported. What if a worker is treating a mother who admits in an interview that she has begun to beat her child *again* and asks the worker to keep this secret? After all, she is participating in services for the original report of abuse. For treatment to be effective, no secrets can be kept between worker and client. This would not be confidentiality but collusion. The skilled worker learns the difference.

Providing Treatment

The recognition and reporting of abuse and neglect accomplishes little for the victim and the family unless prompt, effective treatment follows. Treatment often takes the form of intensive case management during which the services needed by the family are overseen by a social worker. Sometimes families also participate in group or individual counseling (DePanfilis and Salus, 1992). Unfortunately, prompt and effective treatment does not always become a reality for several reasons.

Client Resistance

Engaging families in treatment can be extremely difficult. Communicating to a family that its methods of child care are considered inadequate does not always convince them of the need for change. Families may resent the intervention and are concerned only with escaping from the scrutiny of the social service system.

> *Mike Forrester was particularly resistant to treatment. He did not consider beating 5-year-old Timmy with a belt as abusive. His father had disciplined him in this manner. But social services insisted that he refrain from hitting Timmy. Mike therefore agreed with whatever was suggested, hoping "they'd get off his back." He agreed to see a counselor, but never quite made the appointments, citing as excuses transportation and sick children, whom he had to watch while his wife worked. It was not that Mike Forrester did not love his son. The 35-year-old father had been raised with particular values and with set methods of discipline. He could not believe that these would be any more harmful to Timmy than he felt they had been to him.*

Some parents mistrust services and treatment methods or feel they will do no good. It should be remembered that seemingly negative patterns of interaction can keep families together. The sexually abusive family, for example, thrives on keeping the secret. Two isolated parents with extremely low self-esteem are threatened by exposure to the outside world. They have taught their children to be like them. Exposure to treatment means possible change and an upset of the delicate family balance. Treatment may force them to break their dependencies on one another. Family members feel this will intensify their isolation and leave them even more helpless. Cultural differences may actually be perceived as resistance. If professionals do not take time to understand the culture and therefore fail to engage a minority client, the client is often labeled as resistant or difficult. For example, the African-American client who believes that she should "leave things in the hands of the Lord" is often perceived as unmotivated to cooperate with treatment (Chapman and Terry, 1984; Atkinson et al., 1993).

Parents have expressed the fear that seeing a social worker or a counselor will label them. A young, neglectful mother was asked to take her son to a child guidance clinic to evaluate his multiple learning problems. Despite the fact that transportation was provided, alleviating her first concern, the mother refused to go. "My son ain't crazy!" she protested, "and I ain't takin' him to no shrink."

Individuals who have had difficult, deprived childhoods themselves have difficulty trusting. Establishing trust with a helping professional may be extremely hard for them.

Some parents perceive that there is still a threat of removal of their children and they are afraid to disclose too much.

Above all, treatment must be seen within a cultural context: How can the client be helped to parent more effectively within her or his own culture? How can a compromise be reached between the client's cultural values and the laws which govern this nation? When clients perceive that they are not being robbed of their cultural values, their resistance may be considerably less.

Client Response

Even after becoming engaged in treatment, families do not always follow through. Consistency may be a problem for many families who abuse and neglect children. They also have difficulty delaying gratification or looking toward final goals. For these families, participating consistently with the services provided to them can be frustrating and unrewarding. As one neglectful mother said, "If I'm such a lousy mother, either fix me NOW or forget it" (Williams, 1998). Parents who have been able to recognize their need for change may not understand why it doesn't happen more quickly. They do not comprehend that change can involve pain, and at the first twinges of pain they want to flee.

> *Mrs. Hooper found it extremely difficult when 10-year-old Betty began to act like the child she was. Betty had been sexually abused by her father since she was 5, but had cared for her sickly mother despite their poor relationship. Betty's father had been ordered out of the house by the court, and now the mother and daughter agreed to try to pick up the shattered fragments of their relationship. Since Betty had taken on all her mother's responsibilities and domestic roles, the change in this arrangement was difficult for both mother and child. Mrs. Hooper, who was able to see that her hypochondria was a bid for attention, recognized Betty's need to be a little girl. But the tasks and decisions that now fell to the mother seemed overwhelming to her. In reaction, she blamed the therapist for "causing her so much trouble" and refused to return to therapy.*

In their discussion of treating neglectful parents, Polansky, DeSaix, and Sharlin (1972) suggest that personality problems, such as extreme immaturity and difficulty with verbal communication, present major barriers to treatment. These authors characterize a majority of chronically neglectful mothers as "playing games" to resist treatment. One such game is "look-how-hard-I'm-trying." The client with this outlook appears to do whatever is suggested by the worker but continually fails in her efforts to change, often because she sabotages her own efforts. There may be several reasons why the treatment does not work for this mother. Changing may be too difficult for her. Or she has been asked to change in a way that has not fully engaged her cooperation and has instead antagonized her. This mother may not even recognize the importance or necessity for change and her apparent efforts only because she has been told she must alter her lifestyle. It is important to recognize that agreeing with the worker but not acting as promised may not be a game per se—as Polansky describes. For example, Asians value harmony; they would not contradict someone in authority. Therefore, rather than saying no to the worker, some Asians might agree to change behavior but do nothing. This is another cultural nuance (Lum, 1992).

Another game cited by Polansky and colleagues (1972) is the "Yes, but" maneuver. A client asks for advice but to every suggestion she counters with the reason why she cannot possibly carry it out. Another scenario includes clients who continue their old patterns of behavior, and when this is pointed out, one type of client protests she did not understand what was expected of her. A difficult type of client enlists the worker's sympathy by apologizing profusely, but claims the worker cannot expect much more from someone so incapable. The result of any of the preceding maneuvers is frustration on the part of the worker, who may want to transfer the case, close it, or invoke court action to remove the children.

Other clients respond to treatment with other defenses.

Mrs. Moss was being seen by a social worker and a private therapist. Because of busy schedules, these two professionals conferred only infrequently about Mrs. Moss's progress. Then the irate therapist called the social worker to complain that the worker was sabotaging Mrs. Moss's therapy. It took a good part of the conversation before the professionals recognized that their client had been playing them against each other, by telling each suggestions that Mrs. Moss said the other had made. Until the worker and therapist finally talked, Mrs. Moss's therapy had been in severe jeopardy.

It is not uncommon for some clients to lure professionals into disagreements with each other. For this reason, open communication within the helping network is vital.

Clients resistant to treatment sometimes present their need as one involving a concrete service. For example, the client who requests housing assistance, welfare, or food stamps may agree to counseling to ensure that the concrete service is provided. Yet once the money or food stamps are in hand or the family moves into the new dwelling, the client no longer goes for counseling, despite telling the worker that he or she would. These clients have difficulty seeing help as anything except the tangible. To them, change is having some commodity they did not have before. These clients, like the ones who play games and have difficulty following through, present a particular problem to those offering treatment.

Eligibility Criteria

Limited funding forces agencies to have clear eligibility criteria. Families who do not fit into these guidelines may not receive adequate service. The Sung family, for example, was not eligible to receive group therapy at a clinic that served only low-income families, because their income was above the guidelines. The only other similar program for abusive families was at an agency that served an area outside the Sungs' neighborhood. The solution to this problem, perhaps, is for agencies to exercise as much flexibility as possible.

Limited Community Resources

There are often limited resources within the community to treat families (especially those who have difficulty with English). Until recently there were very few programs in smaller communities to treat incestuous families. With increased publicity and more training in treating sexual abuse, this problem is slowly being remedied. Services in still other areas may be in short supply. For example, respite daycare openings for the abusive mother who needs time away from her child to enhance her coping capabilities are not always available. Groups for physically or sexually abusive parents are all too few. Some therapists prefer not to accept clients for whom a sliding fee scale is necessary. Programs to train parents in their role or offer them support, such as parent aide programs or Parents Anonymous, cannot always find sponsorship.

The reasons for these shortages are many; cuts in federal and state funding have been somewhat but not entirely responsible. Volunteers to sponsor parent aide groups are much needed, but they cannot always be found. In fact, private citizens are often not aware of the need for their involvement, and, if aware, frequently prefer not to become involved.

Treatment Methods

While the social service system has developed somewhat adequate methods of recognizing, validating, and initially intervening in child abuse or neglect situations, treatment methods are still, in many cases, in the development stages. Despite the progress that has been made in the area of treatment, some types of clients are difficult to help. Some cultural minorities are newly represented in this country, and many workers know little about working with them. The multiproblem family, for example, living from crisis to crisis, takes a great deal of time and consistency on the part of the helpers. In turn, the workers experience frustration and often burnout. Such families must be monitored, but programs continue to explore the most effective methods of treatment for the sexual offender with little real consensus. As new monies become available and new ideas are generated, the difficult cases become less overwhelming for the workers.

Logistics

Who actually treats families depends largely on the availability of services, finances, and expertise. Some protective agencies with certain types of clients undertake treatment themselves in addition to case management. On the other hand, if more expertise exists elsewhere and the service can be funded in some way, treatment may be referred to another agency.

For example, a particular protective agency had traditionally assigned ongoing workers to see neglectful families regularly to help them provide better care for their children. These cases were extremely time consuming; clients often missed appointments. Crises were a way of life for these clients and necessitated immediate response from the workers. Transportation had to be provided, workers had to accompany clients to medical appointments, and so on. A large caseload of such families made the social worker relegate other cases to lower priority status. The worker was also unable to perform those necessary administrative tasks such as dictating and writing reports, completing authorization forms, and attending consultation, supervision, or staff meetings.

To combat this problem, several agencies wrote and received a grant to form a service for this multiproblem client population. Currently this new agency provides a complete range of treatment services for multiproblem families. One worker supplies the family with a "friendly visitor" with whom to talk, respond to crises, or provide transportation. Another professional within the agency provides counseling for clients on an individual, group, family group, or family basis. Because caseloads are kept small and communication between those involved in a case is scheduled regularly, the approach seems to be particularly effective.

Although some agencies are now setting up in-house treatment programs, sexually abusive clients and families are often referred to other treatment agencies. Treatment for sexual abusers may be undertaken in prison or may be done at private agency facilities. Groups—currently the treatment of choice for not only offenders but for mothers and daughters—are sponsored by a wide variety of agencies and programs.

If treatment is referred out of the protective agency, the social worker maintains a case-management role, which means monitoring the case, keeping communication open among all parties, documenting progress, connecting the clients with additional sources of help, and eventually determining when the case can be closed.

Phases

Length of treatment is impossible to estimate. Some families find that the resources available through social services and the knowledge of how to tap such resources in the future is sufficient. For these families, the process may be short. At the other end of the continuum are clients whose lives will be constantly intertwined with social services, as were the lives of their parents and grandparents. Their cases may be open for extended periods or once the immediate service is provided, the case is closed only to be opened again sometime later.

As in any type of treatment, therapeutic efforts with abusive and neglectful parents go through phases. In the early 1970s, a team of researchers with the National Society for the Prevention of Cruelty to Children (1976) undertook a study to consider the process of treatment with 20 families who physically abused their children. They found that the goals of treatment and the reaction of parents could be separated into phases. During the first three months, the families were in crisis. They had been identified as abusive and were at various stages of readiness to comply with treatment. Working predominantly with mothers, the researchers found that some of these women were able to acknowledge their problems and were ready to address them. Other mothers were ambivalent about receiving help. They blamed their children and had difficulty cooperating consistently. The last group of mothers were openly resistant. They missed appointments and were reluctant to talk when they did meet with workers.

During the initial period, the workers' goal was to establish trust through projecting a caring rather than punitive attitude, and they accomplished this by providing clients with concrete services or advocating for them. Workers found that these mothers needed a great deal of attention and actually resented attention given to their children by the worker. The fathers often remained aloof and mistrustful.

In the 4- to 12-month period, mothers became especially dependent on the workers for support and encouragement as well for practical help. The workers spent a good deal of time helping these mothers develop their egos. Phase three, 13 through 24 months, was characterized by a dependent relationship between the worker and client that was openly acknowledged. Clients were able to look back on their treatment and trace their growth and successes. In little ways, the mothers were beginning to develop autonomy. By 25 to 36 months, most clients were becoming independent and had little need for support. The nurturing the workers had given to the mothers seemed to be mirrored in their behavior toward their children. Their ability to cope more effectively led the workers to consider termination.

Given the variety of families who abuse and neglect and the numerous methods of treatment, how does the worker know when termination of protective services is indicated? Some generalized guidelines can be offered to answer this question.

Parents who have become aware of their needs, have found nonabusive ways to cope, and can reach for help in the future are probably ready for termination. Obstacles to future help must be minimal—in other words, parents have, or know how to obtain, access to transportation, telephone, and other methods of communication. The parents should have developed a support system—that is, a network of people to whom they can turn to share moments of joy, sorrow, and crisis. In this system, there should be someone who can recognize crises and help the family seek outside aid. Before terminating a case, the worker will want to be sure that any immediate crisis, such as poor housing, unemployment, illness, chronic alcoholism, and severe financial problems, has been resolved to alleviate stress for the client (Ragan, Salus, and Schultz, 1980; Ayoub et al., 1992; Kropenske et al., 1994).

Communication is a vital skill for maltreating parents to develop. The parents must be able to recognize their own feelings, communicate them articulately, and appreciate the feelings of others. This may be especially difficult in cultures where the norm is not to talk about feelings. It is important that they have improved self-esteem, recognize the growth they have made, and be proud of it. And finally, the way in which these parents see their children is important. They must perceive that the children are individuals with unique needs. Their expectations of their offspring should be realistic and their disciplinary methods appropriate. But most of all, it is hoped they find parenting more rewarding than they had before (Ragan, Salus, and Schultz, 1980).

Finding the type of intervention that will be most effective with a given client or family, determining how much time, effort, and financial resources can be devoted to that treatment, and deciding when termination is warranted are the challenges of working with clients who abuse and neglect their children. Treatment is not easy. There is a fundamental belief that parenting is something anyone can do. Intervening in this basic right often meets with hostility and lack of cooperation. Agencies, though well intentioned, may have different philosophies or fail to communicate effectively. Treatment efforts cannot make everything all right for the family. The protective service system can only hope to make a difference. To give a more accurate picture of the treatment efforts necessary, each type of maltreatment and the implications of each follow.

Treatment of Physically Abusive Families

The primary goal of treatment with the physically abusive family is for the battering to cease, which often happens as soon as the social service system intervenes. The future protection of the child, however, depends on the parent learning to cope differently in instances that had provoked beating in the past. Prevention includes parents recognizing what feelings or events led to the initial abuse, learning to read the warning signals that immediately precede the abusive behavior, and learning alternative coping skills to handle anger and frustration. They may also gain more pride in themselves as parents and in their child and learn to understand child development so they can adopt realistic expectations of their children.

To accomplish these goals, it is necessary to assess and remove, to the extent possible, environmental stresses—inadequate housing or unemployment, for example. Services for children and other family members can be explored. One mother was particularly frustrated by a young child who "never listened." After testing, it was discovered the child had a substantial hearing loss and in fact could often not tell she was being spoken to. Providing a hearing aid and helping the mother realize that her daughter's slow development was a result of the hearing loss alleviated much of the anxiety between parent and child.

Another family was caring for the father's mother, who had slowly deteriorated, both physically and emotionally. The young wife with two babies at home (ages 2 and 4) had never wanted the care of her husband's mother. Now she not only resented the responsibility but felt overwhelmed in her role as a mother. Her husband was frequently away from home on business and gave her no support. Once this young mother was helped to verbalize her feelings and alternative arrangements were made for the paternal grandmother, the pressure was diminished and the battering of the 2-year-old ceased. Therapy was centered on developing better skills for future periods of heightened stress.

Treatment efforts also need to be directed toward an assessment of relationships within the family and with the extended family. Does the marital relationship or do the relationships with grandparents or parents' siblings require attention to reduce the stress that results in abuse? Abusive parents are frequently involved in pathological relationships with their families of origin. These may take the form of symbiotic, overly dependent, hostile-dependent, or rejecting relationships that sap the parents' energies and make it difficult for them to parent (Daley, 1983; Peterson and Urquiza, 1993).

Since abusive parents are usually products of unsatisfying childhoods themselves, the conflicting feelings they have toward their families of origin are more understandable.

One of the most obvious aspects of abusive parents is their negative self-images. Helping professionals need to help the parent identify his or her own strengths. Many protective services' clients find it difficult to believe they do anything well. In fact, they often sabotage their own successes. Treatment may include helping parents engineer small successes so they can be convinced of their own potential for handling larger problems. Being able to praise and nurture one's self is actually a prerequisite for the healthy nurturance of others (Bronson, 1983; Peterson and Urquiza, 1993; Williams, 1998).

What of the parents who do not think their treatment of their children is a problem? Parents who respond to their children as their own parents treated them often claim there is nothing deviant about their child-rearing practices. In other instances, some parents abuse their children as part of religious or cultural beliefs or values that differ from the larger society. Some ethnic subcultures use corporal punishment. The issue here becomes a legal one. The law is interpreted by agencies who define abusive behaviors. Anyone living under these laws is expected to abide by them. Therefore, treatment in such cases may involve letting families know which laws must be respected and making them aware of appropriate disciplinary techniques. Failure to comply or adapt may mean removal of the children. However, the skillful worker will understand the cultural values of a family and endeavor to help that family to maintain their cultural integrity while still abiding by the dictates of their adopted home (Atkinson et al., 1993).

Parents who do not perceive they are harming their children may never gain insight into the effect their behavior has on them. If the family is able to maintain at least adequate child-rearing practices, the child usually remains with his or her parents. This is preferable to the trauma of separation. These families may be maintained on an agency's caseload for what is technically called *supervision* (i.e., periodic visits by a worker to monitor the situation). The agency may or may not continue its efforts to treat or stimulate change. More recently, cutbacks in funding have meant that services must be denied to these long-term supervision cases. Some agencies do not feel able to keep families when the agency workers do not perceive progress. In addition, the 1990s appear to be bringing a shift toward a more conservative view about the rights of parents who are not able to care for their children adequately. Will the move to terminate parental rights more quickly—especially those of unwed mothers—and the move toward welfare reform have a significant impact on family preservation efforts in the future?

Family-Centered Services

In years past, children who were abused or neglected were removed from their homes on a regular basis. But as increased attention was paid to how separation affects children, the philosophy of protective service agencies changed. Treatment, it is now believed, should be family based whenever possible. But how does a social worker visiting once or twice a month really help families to change? With some families it does not. The current trend is toward family-centered services. These intensive short-term, family-based services can be divided into two categories: family preservation and family support. Savage describes these as follows:

> Family preservation services are mandated, usually after a crisis of child maltreatment has entered the CPS [child protective services] directly or through a law enforcement agency. Family preservation attempts to keep families together by direct, formal intervention, usually in the home of the child and his/her family. Family support services are sought voluntarily and are generally categorized as the prevention of negative indicators of child well-being in a given family, community, or society (Savage, 1998, p. 200).

The Child Welfare League of America stresses the importance of such "intensive family-centered services" or IFPS to children (Pecora et al., 1992a). One of the oldest IFPS programs in the country is the HOMEBUILDERS, which was established in Tacoma, Washington in 1974. Described by some as a "behavior-modification program" (Sauer, 1994), models like this provide families with intensive skill building. Therapists use such techniques as values clarification, parenting training, problem solving, and other cognitive-behavioral methods. The program staff listens to their problems and model problem solving to find solutions. This may necessitate connecting with concrete services such as housing, food supplements, transportation, medical care, employment training and daycare. Throughout the process, parents are encouraged to take as much responsibility as possible in meeting their own needs. It is the intensive support of the worker which enables them to do this (Pecora et al., 1992a, 1992b; Bath and Haapala, 1993).

Families become available for IFPS services if their children are at risk for out-of-home placement. Although admitting that IFPS is "not a panacea," Pecora, Fraser, and Haapala (1992) concluded that the HOMEBUILDERS program did succeed in preventing placement and strengthening the majority of the families in their study, by providing clients with an average of 36 hours per week of intensive in-person or telephone contact. This type of model appears to be effective in maintaining families who might have been at extremely high risk in years past.

IFPS programs are not without their critics. Berliner (1993) points out that not all parents comply with treatment plans with the result that abuse can recur. Gelles (1993) recognizes that because family preservations are popular, it is difficult to argue against them. However, he points out that it is too soon to predict how the children involved in family preservation programs will fare in the future. He suggests instead a new child welfare policy which would be child centered and based, not as much on whether or not children live with their birth family, but rather on whether or not they are able to develop a nurturing relationship with an adult. The failure of adequate permanency planning robs children of the ability to bond effectively, which is the basis of all future relationships.

Shared Family Care

The search for solutions to protecting children while enabling families to care for them has been a long one. While family preservation, as just discussed, may work for some, other families find it difficult to function with the 10 to 30 hours a week for six to ten weeks which programs that are community based provide (Barth, 1994).

> *Ms. Barber was drug addicted when she came to the attention of protective services for physically abusing her five-year-old son. From an alcoholic family herself, Ms. Barber had a great many conflicts about parenting. She loved her son, but did not feel confident to care for him. Initially, Ms. Barber attended a detox program while her son was placed in foster care. When she was released, it was felt that this mother would be able to care for her son and he was subsequently released to her. Social workers provided weekly visits to support and encourage the mother. Ms. Barber responded well. For a day or so after the social worker's visit, she was able to practice the suggestions given to her and give her child adequate care. But as the week passed, she would often become lonely and depressed and was at risk for returning to her drug taking. Feeling she could benefit, the agency referred Ms. Barber to a shared family care pilot project. The residence housed drug-involved women and their children. Along with support and counseling, the staff provided modeling for child care.*

Shared family care is the provision of out-of-home care in which host caregivers and the parent(s) care for the children simultaneously. The eventual goal is independent living for the family. There are five types of shared family care currently available in some areas of the United States: (1) Drug treatment programs for mothers with their children, (2) drug treatment programs for adults which also offer treatment to the children, (3) residential programs for pregnant and parenting teens, (4) residential programs for children which also offer live-in treatment programs for the parents, and (5) foster family homes for both the parent(s) and the children (Barth, 1994, p. 515). The advantage of such programs is that instead of the few hours a week, the parents can have the advantage of the support, modeling, and guidance on a 24-hour basis. Battered women's shelters have long provided this type of care with success varying from center to center. Homes for unwed teens, too, will often be structured so that the clients can continue living there after the baby is born. This model is especially important for mothers seeking drug treatment to enable them to avoid separation from their children. The crucial element of such programs is how well they foster independence so that family and children can return to the community.

Certainly family preservation programs are sufficient for some families. But others, like the Barbers, cannot succeed on the limited services provided in the community. For these parents, shared family care and the subsequent return to a community setting, with additional skills and support, may be the difference between effectively parenting and having their children placed.

Treatment of the Child

Medical Services

When the battered-child syndrome was first discovered by physicians, the early concerns surrounded medical issues. Bruises, burns, fractures, and other results of abusive behavior were first considered. Medical treatment often focused on long-term effects of injuries such as brain damage, tumors, sensory losses, effects of improperly healed fractures, or other such problems. Sometimes examinations and tests uncovered other long-untreated conditions related to parental neglect, fear of disclosure, or inattention to other than the obvious medical needs. Lynch (1975), for example, found that abused children had a higher incidence of ear infections, respiratory diseases, and general infections than did other children. In some cases, they had not received the necessary childhood immunizations (Beezley, Martin, and Alexander, 1976).

Once the child's medical problems had been treated, the primary goal became protection within the home or removal to a safer setting. Because child abuse was a family problem, it was assumed that treatment of the parents would provide a therapeutic environment for the children. Protective agencies, taught to focus on the total family picture, saw children's problems, when not marked by blatant pathology, resulting from and influenced by parental mental health (Hollerman, 1983). A variety of services addressed the needs of children and their families.

Social Services

Crisis nurseries

For the very young, crisis nurseries protect children from injury by giving parents a respite from constant child care. Abusive parents need to allow their children to be nurtured by others (McQuiston, 1976; Fontana and Moolman, 1994). These settings give the overwrought mother time to leave the baby for several hours while she mobilizes her own coping resources. The settings also have the therapeutic value of helping abusive parents learn how to use the help of others and recognize the increasing risk of harm to their children if help is not sought. The nurseries are staffed 24 hours a day, 7 days a week, by those trained to provide consistency and care for young children, and are often located in daycare centers, foster homes, and other independent settings. Some facilities screen children to foresee the need for other types of treatment (Kempe and Helfer, 1972; Beezley, Martin, and Alexander, 1976; Fontana and Moolman, 1994). Although not as popular as they once were, crisis nurseries still exist—often under other names—to provide a valuable service for mother and child.

Daycare

Daycare provides alternative daily care for children on a more regular basis than the drop-in nature of crisis nurseries. Mothers leave their children for prescribed periods of time either so the mothers can work or have time for themselves. Here, the children socialize with others, try out their own skills, and, it is hoped, find models of positive caregiving.

Remedial Help

For children with developmental problems or delays, special remedial services may be required. For example, while a high percentage of abused children experience developmental delays or deficits, little routine screening to uncover these exists in the initial assessment done by social service agencies and medical facilities (Martin and Miller, 1976; Berns, 1985). Language delays, learning problems, perceptual handicaps, and motor coordination deficits can be addressed either by referral at the preschool level or as part of special education programs once the child becomes eligible.

Parental Aides

Sometimes called *lay therapists* (or other titles, depending on the agency), parental aides provide another useful service to children as well as their parents. Sometimes volunteers and sometimes paid, aides are chosen from students exploring the field, mothers returning to work, or foster grandparents interested in children and continuing to feel needed. The aides are selected and trained based on their ability to handle the frustrations of protective work. They go into the home, form a relationship with the parents, and provide stimulation for the children. Their positive interactions provide models of caring behavior that can be adopted by parents. Parents often describe these aides as their friends and know they will care and provide advocacy for them. These adults provide children attention and take the pressure off overwhelmed parents (Kempe and Helfer, 1972; Ragan, Salus, and Schultz, 1980).

Big Brothers and Sisters

These trained volunteers give the child special attention, a sense of consistency, and an adult on whom the child can depend. They allow the child an opportunity to feel special and to try out a healthy relationship, and also they may pick up clues to otherwise unnoticed therapeutic needs.

Psychotherapy

Until fairly recently little attention was given to individual or group psychotherapy for physically abused children, unless the child was displaying blatant pathology. Often it is difficult to determine when a child is in need of psychotherapy. Because children are characterized by ever-changing developmental stages, each with its own crisis, it is not always clear which behavior is stage appropriate and which symptoms may become fixed and cause for concern (Hollerman, 1983). Certainly prolonged regression—or the return to a previous stage and failure to continue normal development—should be addressed. Treating abusive families has usually centered on work with the parents by protective services caseworkers who see their primary roles as ensuring that the child is protected within the home or monitored in placement outside the home. Large caseloads make in-depth treatment of the child impossible, and finally, parents, who themselves have been starved of affection, may have difficulty watching "their" caseworker give special attention to the child.

Numerous experts dealing with abused children, however, assert that children's psychological needs must be considered in conjunction with treatment of the parents. Physically abused children often demonstrate, to some degree, identifiable symptoms such as flat or depressed affect, hypervigilance, problems with trusting, an inability to play, hyperactivity, and destructive or self-destructive behavior. Their self-concepts are usually extremely low and they often indicate feelings of shame and doubt (Beezley, Martin, and Kempe, 1976; Hollerman, 1983; Williams, 1998).

The treatment needs of children are variously categorized by authors and theorists, but can be condensed into three major categories: their relations with others, their expression of affect, and their self-concept.

Relations With Others

Abused children tend to approach adults with a sense of mistrust, which manifests itself in several ways. Some children are hypervigilant, quietly watching every move made by the adults in their lives. Combined with this mistrust—a remnant of the betrayal they experienced at the hands of their own parents—these children also mourn the loss of nurturance that this betrayal has caused. They desperately need nurturing from adults. To this end, some children's mistrust is overridden by their need for love and they approach adults with indiscriminate friendliness. For others, the basic mistrust is permanent and they tend to antagonize the adults around them, which serves to prove to them their own unloveability (Hollerman, 1983; Briere, 1992).

The child's therapist attempts to present the child with a consistent and caring relationship, providing the nurturance and, over time, building a trusting multidimensional relationship. This is not always an easy task. In their study of 12 abused children, Beezley, Martin, and Kempe (1976) reported that the children were unable to relate to the therapist in terms other than what the therapist was doing for them. They saw the therapist as unidimensional and were unable to relate to him or her as an individual. This behavior may be a result of a well-established system of defense that helps the child guard against being hurt but does not allow new involvements.

Expression of Affect

The child's expression of affect is addressed in therapy. Poor control, aggression, and sporadic impulse control are the most obvious dysfunctions. The assessment of these must be taken within a cultural context. Some cultures (e.g., African-Americans) are more affective in the expression of feelings than they are verbal. The therapist must therefore discern the difference between spontaneity and poor impulse control. Abused children have been surrounded by violence, which they mirror in their own lives by exhibiting aggressive behavior. Unfortunately, the expression of aggression creates for them an inescapable cycle of rejection. Unable to express their anger or aggression toward the parent from whom they learned it, the abused child finds substitutes in peers and unleashes these aggressive acts on them. Resentful of this behavior, peers resist, ignore, or retaliate against the abused child, causing the child to experience more anger, which he or she will usually attempt to diffuse again on peers (see Figure 13.1).

The children are unable to express their anger toward their parents for fear of losing them. This may translate into a fear of expressing anger toward any adult; children act out this anger toward others whom they consider equals or less powerful than themselves in a clear identification with the aggressor.

Abused children lack role models to teach them how to delay gratification, suppress anger, or channel unacceptable drives, and have little idea of how to handle their own impulses. The children may perceive some need to control impulses, but their ability is tentative at best. Often with little recognition of what is happening to them, the children's loss of control manifests itself in temper tantrums, destructive behavior, and other unpredictable displays of emotion. The therapist teaches the child how not to hurt himself or herself or others. Eventually, the child can be helped to learn to recognize the breaking point of his or her control and how to sublimate this energy into functional channels for change (Hollerman, 1983).

Sexuality and aggression are closely allied and represent impulses that most children learn to control. Foster parents, as well as inexperienced therapists, are often surprised to encounter the amount of sexual acting out expressed by children who were physically abused. Although never actually sexually abusing, many immature parents never learned to channel their own sexual needs and may be seductive with their children. The affect of these parents, as well as their failure to protect the children from witnessing parental sexual exploits, causes confusion for the children.

Self-Concept

The children's negative self-concept is a result not only of what has been told them by the parent ("You're a stupid kid who can't do anything right") but of the conflicts about the parent's abusive behavior. Children depend on and love their parents as their primary source of nurturance. When the parent does not effectively nurture, or is abusive, the child perceives that there is nowhere else to turn. It is too threatening to see one's only source of comfort as negative. Therefore children turn the blame on themselves and assume that the abuse was deserved.

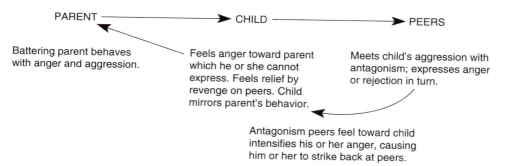

FIGURE 13.1   Abused Child's Expression of Aggression

It is difficult to convince the child who has grown up feeling "no good" that he or she is worthwhile, but it is the therapist's task to provide a caring relationship to help the child manage little successes that eventually will improve the child's self-image.

This low self-concept, combined with poor impulse control, creates in the child faulty development of the superego. What superego exists is often rigid, punitive, unyielding, and unreasonable in its demands, and since this superego has been developed at the hands of punitive, rigid parents, it could hardly be otherwise. When faced with a situation requiring the intervention of this internal conscience, the child often cannot tolerate the pressure. The result is usually a severe breach in the fragile code of ethics, a tantrum, or a total loss of control that only serves to reinforce the child's feeling that he or she is inherently bad.

The self-concept, the fear of losing control, and the rigid superego severely limit the child's capacity for pleasure. Abused children are conspicuously lacking in their ability to have fun (Beezley, Martin, and Kempe, 1976; Hollerman, 1983; Briere, 1992).

The therapist creates a relationship in which the child can observe and experience non-punitive behavior as well as enjoy warm concern. The child's negative beliefs about himself or herself and others causes a need to test—often for extended periods of time. The child wonders, "Can this adult really love the *real* me?" The intensity of the child's need to test can be taxing for the therapist, but understanding that this is a necessary stage in the therapeutic process keeps the behavior in perspective.

Play is one of the most useful types of therapy with young children. Using dolls, puppets, games, drawings, and other media, children are helped to express their fears, anxieties, and conflicts by dramatizing their lives and seeking recognition or interpretation. The classic story of play therapy, *Dibbs in Search of Self,* by Virginia Axaline, gives a clear indication of the intricacies of the therapeutic process using this technique.

Older victims who cannot tolerate just talking often respond well to board games, leisure sports, or even athletics. Much has been accomplished with adolescents during rests from shooting baskets on the court or over a pool table. Therapists who deal specifically with teens have developed a number of methods to explore conflicts and build confidence while enhancing the capacity for play.

In group therapy, children enhance their abilities to socialize, decrease their sense of isolation, and improve their relationships with peers. Knowing that others in the group have also been abused creates a bond among members that eases communication.

Therapy is not necessarily easy for abused children and can generate conflicts of its own. First, these children may never have been exposed to adults with values so different from their parents. Many school-age children have problems in understanding the difference in values expressed by their teachers and their parents. In therapy, the abused child hears that his or her parents' values (at least in the area of child rearing) are not what society expects. This is bound to create confusion. Second, a child is allowed to behave in therapy in ways that would never be tolerated at home. Instead of having to follow rigid adult rules, the child is asked to express himself or herself freely. Many children cannot believe there is no inherent danger in this freedom, and wonder if they are being led into misbehavior for which they will later be punished.

Conflict in loyalties is often a problem for children in therapy, and the abused child from a home where loyalty is a rigid requirement may be especially conflicted. This may become especially problematic with Asian/Pacific children because of the sense of family honor and devotion to and respect for parents that are so deeply embedded in the culture's value system. Not only do children feel attachments to their therapists but they are also encouraged to talk about their parents in a negative manner. This may feel unsafe. The exercise of therapy itself involves experiencing pain as issues come to the surface. Used to pain at home, the abused child may be reluctant to experience it elsewhere (Martin and Beezley, 1976b).

Parents of abused children are not always entirely supportive of therapy, although they may have initially approved the idea. Acceptance that the child has problems that need treatment validates to the parents that they have failed in their roles. Further, the parents' resentment of their children's therapy can be based on their own backgrounds. Because of their own childhoods of deprivation and desperate to have their own needs met, some parents feel jealous of the attention their children are getting as well as of the attachment that may be growing between children and therapist. In the abusive family, the children feed the parents emotionally. The narcissistic parent may feel threatened by the child's being nurtured in another adult-child relationship. And finally, therapy creates behavior changes in the child. The parents have an investment in their child's previous symptomatology. Change in the child necessitates change in them as well—a change to which they feel resistant (Martin and Beezley, 1976a).

To alleviate or reduce the obstacles parents place in the way of their children's therapy, it is necessary for the therapist to meet with the parents periodically. It is also wise for the parents to have their own therapist(s) or caseworker on whom they can depend.

Treatment of the Parents

Goals of Treatment

Whether the parents in an abusive family are seen at home by a caseworker involved in family preservation or shared family care, or are referred to therapy with another professional, the goals remain the same (see Table 13.1). The areas therapy must address are threefold: the nurturing and reparenting of the parent, therapeutic work with psychic conflicts and pathology, and amelioration of the distorted parent-child relationship (Martin and Beezley, 1976b). However, therapy with abusive parents has unique characteristics that set it apart from therapy with other types of clients. It is so important with abusive parents that they feel a part of goal setting. Rather than imposing on them the need to reach the goals outlined in Table 13.1, the effective worker joins with the family to come up with mutual goals. A written contract is often helpful in assuring that everyone understands what is expected.

The abuse of a child is a family-systems issue. The total system is dysfunctional and often exists in a delicate pathological balance. To treat one person—the abuser or the child—is to ignore that balance. If the family system is to operate in the future, all members must be treated and that treatment must be well coordinated. The common scenario in the abusing family is for one parent to abuse while the nonabusive parent supports that behavior by failure to intervene. This "silent" parent must be helped to see his or her own complicity in the abuse.

Treating abusive parents requires an abundance of patience, persistence, and outreach. Their own inability to trust creates a barrier to the formation of a therapeutic relationship. Often referred by the court, many clients do not perceive the need to change. Building a

TABLE 13.1   Treatment Goals for Physically Abusive Parents

1. Cease battering behavior.
2. Recognize the feelings or events that lead to the initial abuse.
3. Recognize the warning signals that immediately precede the abusive behavior.
4. Learn alternative coping skills to handle anger and frustration.
5. Gain pride in themselves as parents.
6. Learn to appreciate their children.
7. Begin to understand child development in order to adopt more realistic expectations of their children.
8. Minimize or reduce environmental stresses.
9. Understand their symbiotic relationships and behave more independently.
10. Improve communication with extended families or cope with the recognition that this is not possible.
11. Engineer and appreciate their own successes.
12. Recognize and reduce their isolation.
13. Learn to make their needs known to each other.
14. Meet the medical needs of their children.

relationship will be a slow, tedious process. Once engaged, parents test the therapist by a variety of acting-out behaviors and avoidance techniques; the next visit they may be so extremely dependent and needy that they sap the emotional strength of the most experienced therapist. Because of this, it is often advisable to employ more than one therapist in the treatment. For example, a caseworker goes to the home, but the client also sees a private therapist. Caseworker and therapist must keep in constant communication. Due to the depth and longevity of the issues, treatment will not be short term. Even if the initial sessions span only a few months, the clients need permission to use the relationship as a lifeline. It is not unusual for the abusive parent who has learned to trust the therapist to reach out years later—by letter, phone call, or request—for an appointment. The therapist may be the first person in their lives for whom these parents can feel trust, and thus this person is not easily dismissed.

For the therapist, abusive parents present other obstacles. It is difficult to acknowledge what has been done to a child and still provide the abuser with the nurturing and unconditional positive regard he or she needs. For this reason, some experienced therapists advise as little contact as possible between the parent's caseworker or therapist and the child. Further, the therapist or caseworker is tempted to take blaming and angry or forgiving stances. The blaming is based on what the parents have done to their children, while the forgiving says, "They had difficult childhoods themselves; they too are victims." Neither stance benefits the client. These parents must be understood but held accountable for past actions and future growth.

Within these goal areas, there will be specific issues that must be considered in treatment.

Nurturing and Reparenting

Nurturing and reparenting require consistent contact with the parents during which they are treated as individuals of worth. The void of a deprived childhood can never be totally filled, but warmth and caring will help. In time, the client may begin to feel dependence on the therapist—often the first person they perceive who has given them positive reinforcement. To prevent prolonged dependence, the parents are taught how to ask to have their needs met. Most of these clients have gone through life, expecting to be nurtured and understood without ever asking. Their disappointment when others do not magically perceive their desires can be overwhelming for them. They may develop inappropriate methods of displaying their disappointment, such as battering their child for attempting suicide. Few recognize that they can ask for what they need. Without proper intervention, couples in abusive families spend their entire lifetime hoping the partner will intuitively know what they need and being angry when the partner fails. Teaching couples to communicate helps each parent meet his or her own needs and may correct the dysfunctional marital bond. In addition, the parent can let go of the parentified child. Finding others on whom to depend, the parent can allow the child to be a child and relieve that child of the obligation of nurturing the parent (Justice and Justice, 1976; Helfer, 1978).

Families who are newly immigrated may require an additional form of nurturing. It is often helpful to them to be guided into their new culture. The worker may actually be able to help them recognize that the parenting techniques they used in their culture of origin are not the only ones. Since severe corporal punishment is illegal in the United States, for example, it is not an option. But there are other methods of ensuring the respect and obedience of children.

Acceptance by a therapist and improved communication toward having one's needs met help the parent adopt a more positive attitude toward self and others. Developing a client's more positive self-image is a long, arduous task for both client and therapist, however.

Addressing Psychic Conflicts and Pathology

The abusive parent comes to therapy with deep psychological conflicts and pathology. The client has developed life patterns that are extremely dysfunctional, and part of therapy will be to examine and hopefully change those patterns that have plagued the client. The first of these, rooted deep in childhood, is symbiosis—the neurotic smothering bond with another individual, usually someone in the parent's family of origin. Harboring a poor self-image, the client feels a need to attach to another for strength, but ironically this bond usually saps rather than supplies strength. The client frequently goes on to find such a symbiotic relationship with a spouse. Part of breaking the symbiosis is in recognizing that it exists. Many abusive families have no idea how dependent they are upon each other because the symbiotic bond has taken on hostile overtones. For example, a couple may describe their relationship as unsatisfying. They fluctuate between fighting violently for days at a time followed by periods of coldly ignoring one another. Yet they were always together and deeply dependent on this volatile relationship. These patterns can be identified in therapy and steps can be made to break this pattern. Often it requires the partners contracting with each other to change their behavior.

Abusive parents demonstrate a marked degree of isolation from others. They have no one to whom they can turn in crisis or in joy. Group therapy especially helps break this isolation. Aiding them in better communication and in identifying a support system makes them better able to handle stress in the future. Since stress often translates into abusive behavior, breaking down this isolation also provides protection for the child (Briere, 1992).

Impulse control is as much an issue for the parents in an abusive family as it is for their children. Explosive tempers in some parents contrast with the internalization, somatization (manifesting conflicts in physical ills), and eventual breakdowns in others. Identifying appropriate ways to get their needs met may be helpful (Helfer, 1978). Justice and Justice (1976) used relaxation and hypnosis techniques to help parents take charge of their outbursts.

Other dysfunctional patterns and self-destructive tendencies, such as obesity and passive-aggressive behavior, may need to be addressed.

Improving Parent-Child Relationships

The final area to stress is the improvement of the parent-child relationship. In wanting the child to be protected, therapists often focus on this area prematurely. In fact, until parents can nurture and understand themselves, they are unable to provide it for their children. When the parents feel better about themselves, they can work on the parent-child relationship. Some parents never become sufficiently stable to parent effectively, and their children are likely to be removed and their parental rights terminated. Through time, other parents are able to learn how to parent.

Abusive parents have been devoid of models of positive parenting, so an effective method of teaching is to provide them with models. Parents can watch the interaction between their child and others at daycare centers, crisis nurseries, or other programs. Homemakers, visiting nurses, or social workers help the parent in the home. In some instances, the child's therapy includes allowing the parent to observe, frequently from behind a one-way mirror. Sometimes foster mothers are asked to help the parent by teaching them to interact positively. Modeling positive interactions requires that the parents have some therapy themselves so they can view the other adult and their child without being inordinately threatened (Alexander, McQuiston, and Rodeheffer, 1976).

Parents are then encouraged to try out new ways of interacting with their children. Sometimes playing with children while the therapist watches behind a one-way mirror is effective. After the play session, the therapist praises their use of specific interactions. The way the parents now interact with the child may be the result of their observance of models, attendance at a parent awareness class, or their new knowledge of child behavior. Since many abusive parents have little idea of child development or child management, a component of therapy may be to introduce them to classes on these issues.

As therapy for the parents progresses, they can be helped to understand the child's behavior and deal with it more effectively. A prerequisite for the parents' improved communication with the child is that the parent value the child. No longer can this child be a burden to the parent. The parent must see the child as a unique individual with needs, abilities, and potential. Without this recognition, a truly positive relationship between parent and child will be impossible.

Numerous therapeutic methods are used with abusive parents. Supportive casework in the home provides some support and treatment. If the parents have insurance or are eligible for particular agencies, they may individually or as a couple be referred for psychotherapy or marital therapy. Group psychotherapy is especially effective with abusive parents. Justice and Justice (1976) saw groups of four or five couples for approximately five weeks. The objectives of these group sessions were to promote changes in the environment to ensure the child's safety, enhance the problem-solving capabilities of the parents, and promote the couples' satisfaction with life. Couples were asked to cite other problems they perceived in their lives. These issues usually fell into the categories of symbiosis, isolation, talking and sharing with the mate, impatience or temper, child development and management, and employment concerns. These therapists used a transactional analysis framework to help the couples resolve these issues.

Family therapy is sometimes used with the total family unit to enhance better communication. This type of therapy is often most effective after the members have gained insight into their own individual issues. For cultures that value family unity (e.g., Asian), this approach may actually be a starting point.

Other Family Treatment

Parent aides are especially helpful with parents. The aide or lay therapist provides nurturing of the parent and models positive interactions with the children. A homemaker is often brought in to help with housekeeping tasks and alleviate the pressures of maintaining the family.

Another effective therapeutic intervention is Parents Anonymous (PA). PA was founded in 1969 by an abusive mother, Jolly K., who felt that her needs were not being met by the social service system. Based on the Alcoholics Anonymous model, PA welcomes parents who maltreat their children and offers the support of others who have developed more healthy relationships with children and peers alike. A PA group is sponsored by an individual or an agency in the area, but functions as an autonomous self-help organization. Parents come to PA voluntarily. At the weekly (or more frequent) meetings, members discuss individual histories, coping techniques, and generally support one another (Beezley, Martin, and Alexander, 1976). PA owes its success not only to the dedication of its members but also to the fact that the meetings help abusive parents break their isolation, share with others, and feel better about themselves.

The paramount questions in the treatment of abusive parents is: When can the case safely be closed? When are these individuals able to parent effectively? Martin and Beezley contend that protective agencies frequently base these decisions on inappropriate measures:

> [A]gencies frequently expect the parents to take certain advice, such as getting a job, keeping therapy appointments, obtaining better housing and so forth. If and when these requirements are met, the agency may be inclined to return the child to the family, and conversely may advise against return of the child if these criteria have not been met. Clearly, these criteria have nothing to do with the parents' ability to provide an adequate home for the child. Meeting these criteria may only be a measure of the parents' cooperativeness with the social agency or may only be a measure of the parents' improvement in areas other than in child care. It is our position that criteria must be used which are *directly* related to positive changes in the interaction with the child. (1976b, p. 259)

What criteria then should be used? First, parents should demonstrate decreased isolation and should have developed an adequate support system. They should have people to whom they can reach out when they need help and not be afraid to do so. The parents should demonstrate better impulse control and know how to recognize and channel their anger before it becomes out of control. Through effective therapy, parents should have learned to feel better about themselves, be more realistic in their expectations of themselves, and find more pleasure in life. Stress should not be as much of a problem for these parents now that they have learned to deal with it through a variety of new coping methods.

Above all, the successful rehabilitated abusive parent has a better relationship with his or her child. The parent sees the child as a worthwhile, enjoyable individual and can tolerate the child's age-appropriate or negative behaviors. Secure in asking for and receiving gratification from others, the parent need not look to the child to satisfy his or her needs. Rather, the parent can appreciate the child as a child and participate in a loving, nurturing relationship with him or her (Martin and Beezley, 1976b).

One of the biggest frustrations of protective services work is the knowledge that these goals must be accomplished before the client flees, the court dismisses the case, or the demands of bureaucracy necessitate closing the case.

Treatment of the Siblings

If only one child within the family is abused, the siblings are often forgotten in therapy. Yet they too have therapeutic needs. Siblings who know that a brother or sister is the object of abuse harbor fear of being next. Recognizing his or her powerlessness against an adult, this child tends to identify with the abuser either by silent collusion or by verbally or physically abusive behavior toward the victim. This sibling, too, learns violence as a manner of relating to others. He or she also lacks positive parenting models to use in the future.

Though not marked by the bruises and breaks of the abused child, siblings carry another type of scar—guilt. Survivors' guilt emerges variously. These individuals feel guilty that they survived while others did not. Similarly, the siblings who watched their brother's or sister's abuse wonder how they escaped. At the same time, these children feel guilty they did not intervene on the victim's behalf—however impossible that might have been.

In situations where the victim is removed from the home, one or more siblings may become the abuser's next victim. When this happens, the sibling may demonstrate many of the feelings and behaviors of the originally abused child.

Whether in family therapy or through some type of individual therapy or program, the needs of the siblings should be addressed. They have experienced the same dysfunctional, abusive home setting as the victim and also have the potential to grow up to be unhappy needy adults.

Treatment of Neglectful Families

The treatment of neglectful families is perhaps one of the least frequently addressed issues in protective services literature. One reason is that neglect seems to permeate the lives and generational histories of the families involved and is difficult to combat, as is the depression which is so pervasive. As Kaufman comments,

> The depression is usually manifested by an impulse-ridden character disorder. These are people who have suffered the traumas of loss of parenting themselves, but who do not have a sufficiently developed ego to overcome the depression by mourning and doing the necessary grieving to resolve this. The feelings of hurt over loss become encapsulated, and because there is not sufficient ego development to face the pain of the loss, these people act out. Their acting out can take the form of antisocial behavior, stealing, promiscuity, vandalism, or reenacting the loss by deserting or abandoning their own children. (1983, p. 39)

Because of the depression, the antisocial behavior, and often the denial that there is a problem, neglectful families are difficult to engage in treatment. Polansky and his colleagues have done extensive research with such clients, and advise that

> …one's leverage for entering the neglectful family and starting to work toward diagnosis and change is going to depend on the use of authority (with some associated fear) or the mother's transferring dependent strivings onto the worker—usually both. (Polansky, DeSaix, and Sharlin, 1972, p. 218)

There are, therefore, two forms of leverage that have the potential for engaging the neglectful family in treatment: authority, based on the threat or intervention of the court, and the satisfaction of a parent's need, which is usually tangible but sometimes merely a need for attention. When a referral originates from an agency dealing with a client who is seeking the financial assistance or housing, a worker who meets these needs may more easily engage the client in additional therapeutic help.

Protective workers have discovered that one effective method of eliciting the trust of a neglectful parent is first to offer something tangible that the client wants, however small.

> *Mrs. Bates collected soda and beer cans from all over the country. Her interest in her hobby was almost childlike. The worker discovered that by bringing an occasional can that Mrs. Bates did not have, the mother was more open and willing to talk. The sessions frequently consisted of Mrs. Bates bringing out all her collected cans and explaining how she had gotten them. In between these explanations, the worker was able to talk about Mrs. Bates's care of the children and other problems in her life.*

More than any other type of leverage, neglectful parents respond to their liking of the social worker or therapist. Since these clients have such difficulty trusting, an attachment to the worker must be highly valued. Through this fondness, the neglectful parent is more likely to model and try any advice given.

The social caseworker usually undertakes treatment of neglectful parents in the home. Neglectful parents often have difficulty attending therapeutic sessions with private therapists, although some will do so after they have established a trusting relationship with the caseworker or if they perceive that they can gain something by these visits. Since both the person and the environment must be considered in the treatment of neglect, the total picture is more visible in the home setting. The neglectful mother requires insight about how her uncontrolled impulses lead to the family's lacking necessities and endangering the children, and she also needs structure to help her function with some semblance of routine in the care of the children and the maintenance of the home. Casework services may help her in all these areas (Polansky et al., 1981).

It is often necessary to call on other resources as well. For example, visiting nurses can provide the mother with help for the children's physical needs and hygiene, and can teach infant care. One mother, newly eligible for food stamps and anxious to please the caseworker with her developing skills, had little idea of how to use them to feed her family nutritionally. A homemaker came for several visits to help her shop and cook creatively. Lay therapists, or parent aides, are especially effective with neglectful families. With smaller caseloads, these lay professionals can visit the home regularly, provide guidance, support, advocacy, and, in general, give the parent a feeling that someone cares.

The social worker can provide numerous services to strengthen the family besides referral for other types of services. Table 13.2 outlines some of these supports. Two treatment models are applicable for neglectful parents: equilibrium maintenance and disequilibrium techniques.

Equilibrium Maintenance

Every family has a level at which it maintains itself most of the time. These conditions fluctuate, improve, or deteriorate. During a vacation, the family members may find that they enjoy each other's company and what they are doing together. On the other hand, when a death occurs, a parent is unemployed or ill, or one or more family members are experiencing a developmental crisis, the family functioning may be stressed. Most families have the ability to call on resources to help regain equilibrium. An extended family member comes to help the parents rally and enable them to cope with whatever crisis exists. Or the family members recognize the need to reach out to community agencies. This mobilization requires that family members have sufficient ego strength and flexibility to respond (Hally,

---

TABLE 13.2   What the Worker Can Do to Supplement the Neglectful Family

- Orchestrate the range of services the family needs to improve child care.
- Deal with the parents' emotional blocks to accepting services.
- Guide the family to needed services and facilitate the use of those services.
- Interview parents and help them improve interpersonal communication skills.
- Offer children individualized and supportive relationships.
- Reach out to family members with supportive counseling.
- Let family members know that someone is concerned about them.
- Provide parents with information and step-by-step guidelines for accomplishing tasks.
- Be a model for child-rearing techniques and for instilling family values.
- Help parents keep their fears and anxieties from growing out of proportion.
- Once mutual attachment is obtained, introduce expectations for the parents to meet.

From C. Hally, N.F. Polansky, and N.A. Polansky, *Child Neglect: Mobilizing Services* (Washington, DC: U.S. Department of Health and Human Services, 1980).

Polansky, and Polansky, 1980). These families are often good candidates for family preservation (Bath and Haapala, 1993).

Equilibrium maintenance is especially important with newly immigrated families that appear neglectful. Although the family's functioning was accepted in their original culture, it may not be in the United States. Or perhaps the family has been immobilized by the shock of being in a new and very different culture. With these families, the worker must build on their strengths to help them to once again gain a functional balance.

Neglectful families may not always have been neglectful, but in their current state they lack the resources to regain equilibrium.

> *Cheryl Levine gave adequate child care to her son Harley and daughter Jenna when they were infants. Her husband Hank was unemployed for a year and then Cheryl gave birth to twins. Her depression intensified and her housekeeping and child care deteriorated. She began sleeping a good part of the day, expecting Hank to watch the children. But Hank, too, felt overwhelmed by the situation and began staying out more and more. Eventually Harley's teacher, concerned about his listlessness and his stealing food from other children, alerted the protective agency.*
>
> *For the Levines there was a standard to return to. After several months, casework services helped the family back on its feet. In foster care herself as a child, Cheryl was determined not to lose her children. Once trust was established, she readily complied with the agencies' suggestions.*

Sometimes the care and concern shown by the social worker is enough to influence the lifestyle.

> *Bertha Sills developed a relationship with her caseworker fairly quickly because of her desperate need to be cared for. Mrs. Sills began to observe the worker's clothes admiringly. She wondered how she, too, could look "that good." It wasn't long before Mrs. Sills began to take more pride in herself and in her care of her 3-year-old daughter. She began to resent the money that her boyfriend Ralph spent on drugs—money she realized could be used for her and her child.*
>
> *Using her relationship with the worker for strength and support, Mrs. Sills was able to sever her relationship with Ralph and make appreciable efforts toward better child care. When the protective agency felt it was safe to close the case, a referral was made to a volunteer agency to provide a weekly parent aide to enable Mrs. Sills to maintain her progress.*

Like Bertha Sills, some neglectful families can be helped to change by regular visits from a caseworker or an agency volunteer. This regular contact may be the first experience they have had with a caring individual and may also provide a model on which they can base their efforts at improved child care.

Disequilibrium Techniques

Other families demonstrate an equilibrium that is inadequate to ensure even minimally acceptable child care. In these cases, it is necessary to break old patterns in an attempt to raise the family's level of functioning. This means, in essence, throwing the family off balance to improve its situation and to involve them in more acceptable life patterns. This type of treatment is referred to as *disequilibrium* (Polansky et al., 1981; Hally, Polansky, and Polansky, 1980). To create this imbalance, protective agencies use a variety of mechanisms. First, the caseworker may need to inform the parents that their child-care standards are inadequate. This is done in a firm, but caring manner. Families must recognize that failure to improve child care may have legal consequences.

> *The Long Bows, who recently moved to the northern United States from an Arizona reservation, were reported for neglect. They had been reported a month earlier but had not responded to the agency's help. The caseworker now explained to the Long Bows that it was not acceptable for the children to be dressed in lightweight, soiled clothing and holey sneakers during the coldest period of winter. Further, 1-year-old Janie must have supervision so that she did not play in the street outside the Long Bows' home. The piles of debris in the backyard were not only dangerous for the Long Bows' young children but were hiding places for rats. In addition, the two youngest children (ages 1 and 2½) could not be left alone in the care of 4-year-old Mona.*
>
> *The Long Bows were at first resentful of having their lifestyle criticized. The worker sympathetically acknowledged their feelings, but let them know that their continued lack of cooperation would necessitate court intervention.*

The ultimate dislodging mechanism for some families is to remove the children. Removal sometimes impresses on the parents the seriousness of the neglect. This may cause them to put new energy into mobilizing their resources toward establishing an environment to which the children can safely return. For still other families, removal of the children is the ultimate blow—one against which they feel unable to fight.

> *Pat Parsons had been dealing drugs and prostituting for seven or eight years prior to the report to the protective service agency that she had two small children who were suffering from her deviant lifestyle. They were severely neglected. After reluctantly establishing a relationship with the social worker, Pat made several attempts to give up drugs and prostitution. She placed her children with a neighbor while she had men in her apartment and agreed to stop selling drugs. But her ties with her lifestyle were too strong. When 4-year-old Wendy was molested by one of Pat's clients, the agency removed both children.*
>
> *Pat went into a deep depression, rousing herself only occasionally to visit her children in their foster home. Frequently she appeared high on drugs, and the foster parents complained of the effect on the children. The caseworker confronted Pat. "They'd be better off without me," the mother admitted. She dropped out of sight, and eventually the agency sought termination of parental rights through the court.*

Unfortunately all treatment efforts are not successful. In situations such as this, one can only hope to break the neglectful cycle so that the children can benefit.

One of the most overwhelming factors in the treatment of neglectful parents is dealing with their acute loneliness. Fearing intimacy, neglectful parents set up barriers between themselves and others—barriers that prevent their needs for others from being met. In a study of 156 low-income families, Polansky, Ammons, and Gaudin (1985) found that neglectful mothers were significantly lonelier and more isolated than other families in the same environment. Neighbors did not turn to these mothers when they needed assistance.

Although the social worker can help these neglectful families gain skills in developing and maintaining relationships, the task necessitates consistency and persistence. And the parents' sense of loneliness is so intense that it is often painful for the worker to empathize. Only through an adequate support system for themselves can the caseworkers resist being caught up in this permeation of loneliness and futility. For this reason, as well as the multitude of problems and the minimal progress demonstrated by some families, the neglectful family is among the most difficult to treat.

Summary

The treatment of an abusive or neglectful family does not always progress smoothly because

1. Families are difficult to engage.
2. Families do not always follow through.
3. Families are not always eligible for treatment by appropriate agencies.
4. Resources to treat may be limited.
5. Treatment methods are not sufficiently refined to ensure success.

The treatment of families may be undertaken by the protective service agency or by referrals to other appropriate agencies, in which case the worker plays a case-management role. The duration of these services is difficult to predict. Specific guidelines measure when families are ready for termination. For example, parents must

* Be more aware of their own needs and how to get them met
* Be able to reach out for help in the future
* Be able to communicate more effectively
* Have improved self-esteem
* Feel more positive toward their children

A relatively new concept in treatment is family preservation, the intensive community based treatment of families.

The primary goal with physically abusive parents is for the battering to cease. In addition, it is hoped that these parents develop coping skills for the future. Treatment for the child necessitates attention to the medical problem resulting from the abuse, providing a safer environment, and attending to the psychological scars from the abuse. Treatment of the parents necessitates patience and understanding. They must learn to trust the helper and learn to cope with the frustrations of their own lives in order to nurture their children. Such issues as symbiosis, isolation, poor self-concept, and impulse control must be addressed in treatment. The services for abusive parents may include group or individual therapy, marital therapy, the use of homemakers and parent aides, or self-help groups such as Parents Anonymous. Ideally, cases are not closed until the battering has ceased and parents have developed coping mechanisms to deal with their frustrations.

Neglectful families can also be extremely difficult to treat because of their depression, antisocial behavior, and denial that a problem exists. The threat of authority—court involvement—is often used as leverage to engage them in treatment. Treatment is usually done in the home with an emphasis on building trust. The caseworker offers tangible as well as therapeutic services. Treatment usually involves equilibrium maintenance, which attempts, through services, to return the family to a level of adequate functioning, or disequilibrium techniques, which throw the family off balance and force them to reorganize more effectively. Because of the complexity of their problems, neglectful families are often the most difficult to treat.

Exploration Questions

1. Why might maltreating families be difficult to engage and why might they not follow through?

2. What is meant by family preservation? Shared family care?

3. How does a worker know when a family is ready to terminate treatment?

4. What are some goals in treating the physically abusive family?

5. What type of services are available for abused children?

6. Why might abused children be resistant to therapy?

7. What is involved in therapy with the physically abusive parent?

8. Cite several issues in the treatment of physically abusive parents.

9. What treatment needs might siblings in an abusive family have?

10. Why is it especially difficult to treat neglectful families?

11. What types of leverage might be used with neglectful families?

12. What two treatment approaches are used with neglectful families?

Activities for Applied Learning

1. Invite a representative from the local child protective agency to speak with the class on treating abusive or neglectful parents. What family preservation efforts does this agency make?

2. Read *One Two Three: The Story of Matt, a Feral Child* by Eleanor Craig. What are the considerations in treatment of this neglectful mother? What seemed to work? What didn't?

3. Read *Dibbs In Search of Self* by Virginia Axaline. What techniques were used in the treatment of this child?

4. Is there a local Parents United or Parents Anonymous group? Invite a representative to speak to the class or interview a participant about his or her experiences in the group.

Suggested Readings

Atkinson, D. R.; Morten, G. and Sue, D. W. *Counseling American Minorities.* Dubuque, IA: Wm. C. Brown Comm., Inc., 1993.

Barth, R. P. "Shared Family Care: Child Protection and Family Preservation." *Social Work* 39 (5), (1994): 515–524.

Gelles, R. J. "Family Reunification/Family Preservation: Are Children Really Being Protected?" *Journal of Interpersonal Violence* 8 (4), (1993):556–562.

Pecora, P. J.; Fraser, M. W. and Haapala, D. A. "Intensive Home-Based Family Preservation Services: Update from the FIT Project." *Child Welfare, LXXI* 2 (1992):177–188.

Peterson, M. S. and Urquiza, A. J. *The Role of Mental Health Professionals in the Prevention and Treatment of Child Abuse and Neglect.* Washington, DC: U.S. Department of Health and Human Services, 1993.

Endnote

1. Based on an interview with Carolyn Drosier, Director of ACCESS, Leominster, Massachusetts.

References

Alexander, H. "The Social Worker and the Family." In *Helping the Battered Child and His Family,* edited by C. H. Kempe and R. E. Helfer, pp. 22–40. Philadelphia: J. B. Lippincott, 1972.

Alexander, H.; McQuiston, M.; and Rodeheffer, M. "Residential Family Therapy." In *The Abused Child,* edited by H. P. Martin, pp. 235–50. Cambridge, MA: Ballinger, 1976.

Atkinson, D. R.; Morten, G. and Sue, D. W. *Counseling American Minorities.* Dubuque, IA: Wm. C. Brown and Benchmark, 1993.

Ayoub, C. C.; Willet, J. B. and Robinson, D. S. "Families At Risk of Child Maltreatment: Entry Level Characteristics and Growth in Family Functioning During Treatment." *Child Abuse and Neglect* 16 (4), (1992):495–511.

Barth, R. P. "Shared Family Care: Child Protection and Family Preservation." *Social Work* 39 (5), (1994):515–524.

Bath, H. I. and Haapala, D. A. "Intensive Family Preservation Services with Abused and Neglected Children: An Examination of Group Differences." *Child Abuse and Neglect* 17 (2), (1993):213–225.

Beezley, P.; Martin, H.; and Alexander, H. "Comprehensive Family Oriented Therapy." In *Child Abuse and Neglect,* edited by R. E. Helfer and C. H. Kempe, pp. 169–84. Cambridge, MA: Ballinger, 1976.

Beezley, P.; Martin, H. P.; and Kempe, R. "Psychotherapy." In *The Abused Child,* edited by H. P. Martin, pp. 201–14. Cambridge, MA: Ballinger, 1976.

Berliner, L. "Is Family Preservation in the Best Interest of Children?" *Journal of Interpersonal Violence* 8 (4), (1993): 556–562.

Berns, R. M. *Child, Family, Community.* New York: Holt, Rinehart and Winston, 1985.

Briere, J. *Child Abuse Trauma.* Newbury Park, CA: Sage, 1992.

Bronson, M. "An Integration of Individual and Family Therapy." In *Child Abuse and Neglect: A Guide with Case Studies for Treating the Child and Family,* edited by N. B. Ebeling and D. A. Hill, pp. 127–42. Littleton, MA: PSG Publishing, 1983.

Chapman, S. B., and Terry, T. "Treatment of Sexually Abused Children from Minority Urban Families: A Socio-Cultural Perspective." *Clinical Proceedings of Children's Hospital National Medical Center* 40 (1984):244–59.

Daley, H. V. "Individual Treatment." In *Child Abuse and Neglect: A Guide with Case Studies for Treating the Child and Family,* edited by N. B. Ebeling and D. A. Hill, pp. 113–26. Littleton, MA: PSG Publishing, 1983.

DePanfilis, D. and Salus, M. *A Coordinated Response to Child Abuse and Neglect: A Basic Manual.* Washington, DC: U.S. Department of Health and Human Services, 1992.

Fontana, V. J. and Moolman, V. "Establish More Crisis Intervention Centers." In K. deKoster and K. L. Swisher. *Child Abuse: Opposing Viewpoints,* pp. 227–234. San Diego, CA: Greenhaven Press, 1994.

Gelles, R. J. "Family Reunification/Family Preservation: Are Children Really Being Protected?" *Journal of Interpersonal Violence* 8 (4), (1993):556–562.

Hally, C.; Polansky, N. F.; and Polansky, N. A. *Child Neglect: Mobilizing Services.* Washington: U.S. Department of Health and Human Services, 1980.

Helfer, R. E. *Childhood Comes First.* East Lansing, MI: Ray E. Helfer, 1978.

Hollerman, B. A. "Treatment of the Child." In *Child Abuse and Neglect: A Guide with Case Studies for Treating the Child and Family,* edited by N. B. Ebeling and D. A. Hill, pp. 145–81. Littleton, MA: PSG Publishing, 1983.

Jackson, H., and Nuttal, R. *Childhood Abuse: Effects on Clinicians' Personal and Professional Lives.* Thousand Oaks, CA: Sage, 1997.

James, B., and Nasjleti, M. *Treating Sexually Abused Children and Their Families.* Palo Alto, CA: Consulting Psychologists Press, 1983.

Justice, B., and Justice, R. *The Abusing Family.* New York: Human Sciences Press, 1976.

Kaufman, I. "The Professional Use of the Self: Transference and Countertransference." In *Child Abuse and Neglect: A Guide with Case Studies for Treating the Child and Family,* edited by N. B. Ebeling and D. A. Hill, pp. 27–42. Littleton, MA: PSG Publishing, 1983.

Kempe, H. C., and Helfer, R. E. *Helping the Battered Child and the Family.* Philadelphia: J. B. Lippincott, 1972.

Kropenske, V. and Howard, J. with Breitenbach, C.; Dembo, R.; Edelstein, S. B.; McTaggart, K.; Moore, A.; Sorenson, M. B.; and Weisz, V. *Protecting Chil-*

dren in Substance Abusing Families. Washington, DC: U.S. Department of Health and Human Services, 1994.

Lum, D. *Social Work and People of Color, 2nd ed.* Monterey, CA: Brooks Cole, 1992.

Lynch, M. A. "Ill Health and Child Abuse." *Lancet* 2 (1975):317–19.

Martin, H. D., and Beezley, P. "Resistances and Obstacles to Therapy for the Child." In *The Abused Child,* edited by H. P. Martin, pp. 265–73. Cambridge, MA: Ballinger, 1976a.

Martin, H. P., and Beezley, P. "Therapy for Abusive Parents: Its Effect on the Child." In *The Abused Child,* edited by H. P. Martin, pp. 189–99. Cambridge, MA: Ballinger, 1976b.

Martin, H. P., and Miller, T. "Treatment of Specific Delays and Deficits." In *The Abused Child,* edited by H. P. Martin, pp. 179–88. Cambridge, MA: Ballinger, 1976.

McQuiston, M. "Crisis Nurseries." In *The Abused Child,* edited by H. P. Martin, pp. 225–34. Cambridge, MA: Ballinger, 1976.

National Society for the Prevention of Cruelty to Children, Research Team. *At Risk.* Boston: Routledge and Kegan Paul, 1976.

Pecora, P. J.; Fraser, M. W.; and Haapala, D. A. "Intensive Home-Based Family Preservation Services: Update from the FIT Project." *Child Welfare, LXXI* 2 (1992a):177–188.

Pecora, P. J.; Whittaker, J. K.; Maluccio, A. N.; with Barth, R. P. and Plotnick, R. D. *The Child Welfare Challenge.* New York: Aldine DeGruyter, 1992b.

Peterson, M. S. and Urquiza, A. J. *The Role of Mental Health Professionals in the Prevention and Treatment of Child Abuse and Neglect.* Washington, DC: U.S. Department of Health and Human Services, 1993.

Polansky, N. A.; Ammons, P. W.; and Gaudin, J. M. "Loneliness and Isolation in Child Neglect." *Social Casework* 66 (1985):33–47.

Polansky, N. A.; Chalmers, M. A.; Buttenweiser, E.; and Williams, D. P. *Damaged Parents: An Anatomy of Child Neglect.* Chicago: University of Chicago Press, 1981.

Polansky, N. A.; DeSaix, C.; and Sharlin, S. *Child Neglect: Understanding and Reaching the Parent.* New York: Child Welfare League of America, 1972.

Ragan, C.; Salus, M. K.; and Schultz, G. L. *Child Protection: Providing Ongoing Services.* Washington: U.S. Department of Health and Human Services, 1980.

Sauer, M. "Create Family Preservation Programs." In K. deKoster and K. L. Swisher (eds.). *Child Abuse: Opposing Viewpoints.* San Diego, CA: Greenhaven Press, 1994.

Savage, J. "Family-Centered Services for Children." In C. Crosson-Tower, *Exploring Child Welfare,* pp. 195–222. Boston: Allyn and Bacon, 1998.

Williams, L. T. "Counseling for Families and Children." In C. Crosson-Tower, *Exploring Child Welfare,* pp. 160–194. Boston: Allyn and Bacon, 1998.

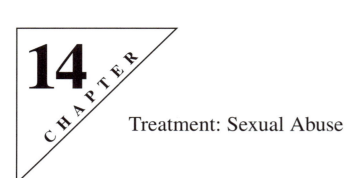

Treatment: Sexual Abuse

Even those experienced in working with physically abusive and neglectful parents are not fully prepared to deal with sexually abusive families. Although many of the problems are similar to and may be present in all types of maltreatment, sexual abuse and its treatment pose issues that other patterns of abuse do not.

Issues Surrounding Treatment

Deviant sexuality provokes reactions from society that, in turn, affect the worker engaged in treating sexually abusive families. People's desire to ignore the reality of sexual abuse often means they are uncooperative with the individual who investigates and treats it. Further, their rejection of the behavior of the client is often transferred to the worker. People wonder about the motivation of workers who specialize in sexual abuse. Is the worker obsessed with some kind of voyeurism or immoral interest? Along with the frustration of treating uncooperative clients, this suspicion from others puts a great deal of stress on workers.

Society's tendency to isolate both family and worker, combined with the family's secretiveness and will to bond in an effort to ward off intruders, makes treatment difficult. In this atmosphere, the worker, once allowed into the intimate family circle, may unintentionally collude with the clients and keep secrets from other professionals, and thus exert a negative rather than a positive influence on the family.

The helping system continues to struggle with how and who in the family to treat. Although incest is a family problem, programs are not always available to treat all members of the family. The incarcerated offender, for example, may receive treatment, but his or her family may not. Individual therapy for the child victim may not be available.

Professionals advance new theories and treatment methods, but long-term testing and evaluation are either nonexistent or just beginning. Advances make professionals optimistic, but premature optimism about the incestuous family's rehabilitation is just as harmful as undue pessimism (Mrazek, 1981b; Giardino et al., 1997).

Most types of sexual abuse are performed by family members, though children are also abused by outsiders. Although there has been progress in dealing with the incestuous family, not many community services sufficiently address the needs of the children abused outside the home, nor are their parents given attention. Although expected to support the victim, the parents themselves are dealing with their own conflicts about the extrafamilial abuse. One possible reason for this lack of support is that incest cases are handled by a social services agency, but extrafamilial abuse most often comes under the jurisdiction of the criminal justice system. Traditionally the police and the courts exert social control rather than social service. Services for extrafamilial abuse cases improve, but lack of resources remains a problem.

In cases of physical abuse or neglect, reports of maltreatment of both boys and girls are equivalent. But because boys are particularly liable to be sexually abused outside the home (Finkelhor, 1984; Hunter, 1990) and because boys are more hesitant to report the abuse (see Chapter 6), they are often not treated. Treatment of both familial and extrafamilial sexual abuse is a relatively new specialty, but there are several models and programs that have evolved.

Assumptions About the Treatment of the Sexually Abusive Family

When treating a family in which there has been sexual abuse, it is important to make several assumptions. First, *relational imbalances in the family were present before the incest occurred* (Gelinas, 1988). In fact, incest could not develop within a family if there were not significant problems in communication and the manner in which members relate to each other. Thus, the problem of sexual abuse is not simply that, but rather a symptom which results from a larger family problem. In addition, *sexual abuse is often a generational issue* which has persisted through multiple generations as families within each generation have failed to communicate in an open, functional manner. One student in a sexual abuse class created a genogram (a diagram using symbols to show family members and relationship patterns) of his family going back for four generations. If any family member had been sexually abused or was sexually abusive, his/her symbol was drawn in red. When the student shared the chart with his fellow students in class, people were shocked at how colorful the chart had become. Thus, breaking the cycle of sexual abuse is not easy when it is based upon a heritage of dysfunction.

Another consideration is that despite the dysfunction in the family, *the imbalances may have felt comfortable to the family members, on some level.* For example, the mother who emotionally absents herself in a family harboring father-daughter incest, may actually be relieved to have her daughter assume some of her tasks and roles. When treatment begins and she must re-establish her role as the disciplining parent, or the housekeeper or her husband's sexual partner, she may have difficulty. By the same token, the offender who has enjoyed the closeness with his daughter, not hampered by his wife's intervention, may now find the fact that he is allowed only supervised visits a very lonely prospect. The blurred generational boundaries may have worked for this family in some manner. Based on this fact, change may not be easy for them. All that they have known as a family unit is in upheaval and must be realigned for the benefit of all the members. In addition, the parents may have brought with them, from their own childhoods, expectations of how a family should function. Now those assumptions are being challenged.

Offenders, and sometimes their spouses, rationalize that the abuse is serving a purpose. For example, an offender may argue that he was educating his child about sexuality. At the same time, the non-abusing spouse sees that her husband and daughter are close and, sometimes even denying any suspicions she may have, is relieved that her child has a good rapport with her father. This may also leave Mom feeling freed of some of the responsibility of parenthood. Therefore it will be necessary in treatment to *discover what rationalization precipitates the behavior and find other ways to enable the parents to feel that this issue is being addressed* (Gil, 1996).

Further, *the assumption should not be made either that the family will stay together or that they will separate.* The ability of the family to remain a unit is dependent upon many factors and may not be determined until well into treatment. The main goal for clinicians in treating the family will be to build therapeutic alliances with all members of the family system, emphasizing individual and family strengths, so that the family may make its own assessments about staying together.

Since sexuality is a subject surrounded by secrecy, conflict, and embarrassment in our culture, *it will be difficult for family members to talk about sexual issues.* The need to protect the "family secret" spills over into the therapeutic relationship. Thus, trust between the family and the therapist will be essential before much real work will be done. This creates another problem in the treatment of incestuous families. While intervention usually involves case management by the child protection agency, the policy of *the agency is often to close the case once the initial steps are taken.* As one protective services worker put it

> *Our agency requires the offender to leave while we assess whether the other parent can protect the child. If she/he can protect the child, we leave the child in the home. If not, foster care or placement with relatives might be the answer. We also try to connect all the family members with concrete services. For example, if the Dad has an alcohol problem, we may make a referral for substance abuse treatment. It would be great if we could refer the whole family for treatment, but there are not too many agencies that are equipped to do that. And then, insurance becomes a problem. If the family doesn't have insurance, the options are even more limited. I hate to say it, but as long as the abuse has stopped, my agency has to close the case. That means that there are a lot of families out there who never get real treatment services.*

Fortunately, there are some innovations being made in treatment of incestuous families. It is hoped that these will increase.

Treatment Models

Of all the types of child maltreatment, sexual abuse is usually seen as foremost a criminal offense. Thus, an important part of intervention will be to determine how the offender can be held legally accountable for his offense and the impact that this will have on the whole family. Unfortunately, too often, the intervention has been to prosecute the offender and perhaps secure treatment for the victim while forgetting that this is a total family system and should be dealt with accordingly. Waterman (1986) suggests a combination of family systems treatment combined with behavior therapy to change the offender's behavior. Such combined therapies as marital treatment, family therapy, and even individual therapy are recommended by various experts in the field of sexual abuse.

Child Sexual Abuse Treatment Program

One of the first programs to treat the sexually abusive family had its incipience in the early 1970s. In 1971, Henry Giarretto was counseling victims and their families for the Juvenile

Probation Department in Santa Clara, California. Recognizing that these families needed more services than the department or he could provide, Giarretto founded the Child Sexual Abuse Treatment Program (CSATP), which, by 1978, was serving more than 600 families. Since then, CSATP has helped 2,000 families and reunited 90 percent of the children with their families. The three components of the program are the professional staff, lay volunteers, and self-help groups.

The professionals—social workers, probation officers, attorneys, and judges—orchestrate the treatment plan for the family and enlist support from the local protective agency and the court. The volunteers are student interns or others who provide transportation, one-to-one support to needy clients, and office duties. The self-help groups—Parents United, for abusive families, and Daughters and Sons United, for those molested as children—operate on the model of Alcoholics Anonymous and give support and group therapy to the members. Groups break the isolation experienced by families and help them to offer and gain from each other valuable insights (Giarretto, 1981).

Clients in CSATP undergo treatment in a particular order:

- Individual counseling for child, mother, and father
- Mother-daughter counseling
- Marital counseling (especially if the family wants to be reunited)
- Father-daughter counseling
- Family counseling
- Group counseling. (Giarretto, 1981, p. 190)

Usually, the abuser's sentence is suspended while he or she participates in CSATP. Termination of treatment occurs when the family, as a total unit, is felt to have made sufficient progress.

Numerous programs have been adapted from the CSATP efforts, probably because the threat of prosecution appears to be one of the most effective methods of engaging a perpetrator in treatment.

Sexual Trauma Treatment Program

Suzanne Sgroi's Connecticut based Sexual Trauma Treatment Program uses a multiple-modality and multi-therapist approach. Initially, each family member has a separate individual therapist. Later, mother and daughter may be seen in dyadic therapy, which may be concurrent with group therapy. Arts therapy is also used with children to help them express themselves when they are not comfortable with words (Waterman, 1986).

Treatment Methods

Issues Addressed in Family Treatment

An incestuous family is a system which is composed of subsystems and of individual members. For this reason, there are issues which involve the family system as a whole and each member individually. As a whole, the sexually abusive family has some specific tasks. First, there must be a *realignment of generational boundaries* and roles (Sgroi, 1982; Gil and

Johnson, 1993; Gil, 1996). In the hierarchy of a family where the boundaries are clear it is the adults who create a united front and have enough authority to enforce appropriate rules. But in incestuous families, the adults are split and the children may be *parentified* into assuming adult roles. Thus, it is necessary to establish a healthy hierarchy where both the marital/parental and the sibling subsystems are clear (Gil and Johnson, 1993; Gil, 1996).

Second, treatment involves *teaching the family members how to communicate effectively* so that all might get their needs met. Part of this may also be *teaching the adults parenting skills.* It is difficult for children not to have structure. Helping the children to feel safe in the future will involve helping the adults to create not only boundaries but healthy rules for the family to live by. Many families have rules that protect the family secret. For example, one family rule might be that no one talks about the fact that there are problems in the family. And yet, it is this rule that protects and continues the dysfunction. Many parents bring with them *unresolved traumas* from their own childhoods, and these may need to be addressed. And each family member has issues individually that must also be addressed (Gil and Johnson, 1993).

Phases of Treatment

Whatever the treatment method, James and Nasjleti (1983) describe the three phases that mark the incestuous family's progress from intervention through treatment: the disclosure-panic phase, the assessment-awareness phase, and the restructure phase.

Disclosure-panic

The disclosure-panic phase is the most critical period for family and social worker alike. The family's initial defenses are anger and denial. They often project blame onto others, especially the protective worker who has intervened. Workers sometimes find it difficult to be supportive while they feel under attack. Families can so skillfully intellectualize that workers may doubt the accusation.

Despite the attempt to argue away the accusation of sexual abuse, the family is in acute crisis. The perpetrator and the victim are extremely vulnerable and may have suicidal thoughts. The family members tend to overreact, sometimes violently. Underlying these intense reactions is the fear of loss and separation. For Asian families there may also be a sense of acute shame—that family honor has been lost. Loyalties vacillate. While some families blame the victim and assert that he or she is lying, others initially protect the perpetrator and accuse the social service system of unjust and unfounded allegations.

Throughout this phase, which lasts several weeks to several months, the worker uses crisis intervention techniques and empathetically supports each member. The child especially must be assured that he or she is believed by the worker and will be protected in the future. With the rest of the family, the worker firmly states that the abuse has occurred and that he or she is willing to help them face the consequences.

Each participant reacts characteristically in this initial phase. The father (usually the perpetrator) insists the allegations of abuse are false. He may express anger toward the victim and accuse the child of "wanting to send him to jail." When those around him believe the victim's story, the father may withdraw and threaten or attempt self-destruction.

The mother often denies the abuse and assumes her child is lying. There are too many painful thoughts to face if the allegation is true. Once she accepts the reality, she is hurt.

("How could he do this to me?" "Why am I not as desirable as my own daughter?") The anger she feels is directed toward the victim or the perpetrator, or she may vacillate. She is overwhelmed with shame, wondering what others will say. If she believes the child, she blames herself for not protecting her offspring. The mother also expresses concern about what will become of her. Will she lose her home and her economic support if her husband leaves?

The children who are victims blame themselves for the abuse. They are frightened by the fact that no one believes them. They may also feel they are to blame not only for the abuse but for the family disruption following disclosure. Above all, the victims protest they only wanted the abuse to stop; they never imagined the family disruption that would occur.

The siblings of the victim experience confusion—fear over what will become of the family, and anger at the victim over the disruption.

Assessment-awareness

The assessment-awareness phase occurs when the family members accept the reality of the abuse and assess what they actually have in the way of family relationships. They become dependent on the worker or therapist while each member explores what lies ahead. This is a difficult period for the helper. Consistency and patience are mandatory. The clients may cling to the worker in a manner that seems stifling. As each member begins to examine his or her role in the abusive family structure, there is a great deal of pain.

During this phase, the therapist aids the family in realigning generational boundaries. Roles of parents and children must be redefined so that members recognize their appropriate roles in the future. The marital couple receives intensive therapeutic help in communicating. The worker assists in strengthening the mother-child bond in order to provide future protection for the child. This aspect of treatment takes time because the child may feel as much if not more anger toward the nonprotecting parent as toward the perpetrator. In turn, the mother feels guilt for not protecting her child, which may cripple her ability to relate to the child now, especially if she perceives the child's anger.

As the mother-child relationship becomes more functional, the father's future role with the children is considered. It is often helpful for the father to meet with the victim and acknowledge his responsibility for the abuse. Without this apology, many victims are never able to overcome the anger they feel.

If the father has left the home, and if the family chooses not to continue in its present structure or to reunite, it is important for family members to receive therapy to help them with this separation. Loss has been a paramount fear since disclosure, so any separation will be particularly painful no matter how necessary it appears. Issues such as potential visiting between the father and the children will be an integral part of the agreement to separate.

Throughout the assessment-awareness phase, family members experience conflicting feelings. Both mother and father may continue to consciously or unconsciously blame the victim or judge that the child somehow seduced the perpetrator. The therapist will recognize and understand this kind of emotional projection. For the father, the need for projection is obvious; if the victim is also to blame, he himself does not seem so bad. The mother's feelings of worth are at stake. If her daughter, for example, is totally blameless, then the mother wonders if she is unattractive, undesirable, or unwanted by her husband. The father and mother both play the blaming game of "If you had been…" Husbands accuse their wives of not being responsive enough. Wives accuse husbands of being too demanding or under the influence of alcohol or drugs.

Bursts of insight that seem to preclude the need for further therapy are not uncommon during this phase. For example, the Moreno family began attending church regularly and felt they were now being guided by God. They wanted to terminate therapy, believing that the incest could never happen again. The therapist helped them recognize that their basic family patterns had not yet changed; although their faith might help them, the reasons for the original incest still existed.

Fear fluctuates with hope. The family fears a recurrence of the abuse, but as they begin to recognize the dysfunctional patterns and the need to make changes, the members hope that their insights will sustain them in the future.

The victim is also in conflict during this phase. Anger mingles with the need for close nurturing relationships, especially with the mother. The child may be faced with paradoxical messages. As roles become realigned, the victim is encouraged to act like a child rather than continue in a parental role. But if the child acts out in rebellion, the parents often chastise him or her. Victims begin to wonder where they fit, if they are somehow damaged or unlovable, or if they can ever trust again (Sgroi, 1982; James and Nasjleti, 1983; Hunter, 1990).

Restructure

Gradually, the sexually abusive family begins to adopt a more functional pattern of life. In the restructure phase they are reunited and have more open and honest communication. They have probably been in treatment for several years and therefore have a better understanding of when to ask for help in the future. The therapist has helped them explore coping mechanisms to keep a healthy balance. The father and mother both take responsibility for future positive parenting and admit their past mistakes. They have learned to maintain boundaries, to communicate effectively, and to give nonsexual stimulation and affection to their children. The victim feels more of a sense of power and confidence that he or she need no longer be the parent. The child recognizes that he or she has the power to resist and to ask for help if the molestation recurs.

All members of the family—parents, victim, and siblings—feel greater self-worth and can empathize with the feelings of the others.

As the family members pass through the phases of treatment, each one attempts to handle different issues.

Treatment of Specific Family Members

The Child and Adolescent

Numerous issues surface for the sexually abused child. First, the abuse itself causes elements of conflict or trauma. The family disruption following disclosure also has an impact on the victim. And if exposure to the criminal justice system is involved, the child experiences additional feelings of confusion. By receiving individual treatment—in conjunction perhaps with family treatment—it is hoped that the child will be able to deal with his or her feelings more effectively and integrate the abuse as a life occurrence in order to continue with his or her life (Mayer, 1985; Gil, 1993; Williams, 1993; Gil, 1996). Seeing the family along with the child should open communication, allowing family members to express their needs in the future and assuring the child that he or she is entitled to protection within the family unit.

The course of treatment for children depends on several variables:

- Whether and how much the family supports treatment
- Whether the child resides with the family or in a foster home
- Whether the abuse was perpetrated by a family member or nonfamily member
- Whether there is involvement with the criminal justice system

Children coming to treatment are usually grappling with 10 important issues that need to be addressed (Porter, Blick, and Sgroi, 1982; Mayer, 1985; Hunter, 1990; Gil, 1993).

1. Feeling like "damaged goods"
2. Guilt
3. Fear
4. Depression
5. Low self-esteem, leading to poor social skills
6. Repressed anger and hostility
7. Difficulty trusting
8. Blurred generational boundaries and role confusion
9. Pseudomaturity, masking the failure to have completed certain developmental tasks
10. Control and mastery over self

The first five issues tend to affect all children who have been sexually abused, while the last five are more likely to be results of abuse within the family.

The fear of being "damaged goods" is twofold. Not only do children fear physical injury or damage from the abuse but they also perceive society's message that they are changed by what has happened to them.

> When Cleo at age 11 came to treatment, she had fears about her ability to have children. The uncle who abused her had continually asked her how many children she hoped to have as he rubbed and penetrated. She became convinced that by his perversity he had ensured, in some unknown way, that she would never be able to give birth. She felt different and cheated. To further compound her feelings of isolation, the adults in her life, learning of her uncle's arrest for her abuse, began to relate to her as though she was more sexually experienced. Feeling that she was perceived as mature yet could never (in her mind) have babies, Cleo became severely depressed and withdrew, causing her worried parents to seek help for her. Cleo's therapist helped her to realize that her fears were unfounded.

In Cleo's situation, the physical damage was not as great as she perceived, but abused children face vaginal and rectal tears, scarring of tissues, and venereal disease. The therapist supports the child through whatever remedial measures are necessary for these injuries and then helps the victim come to terms with the feelings associated with the damage or loss.

Adolescents often react to their perceived damage with promiscuity, feeling, "So what, I'm damaged anyway!" Thus they embark on other sexual encounters, often with a self-destructive purpose. This behavior stems from their feelings of being damaged and from an extremely low self-concept that tells them they are worth little. Their sexual behavior then only intensifies the conviction of those around them that they are sexually wise beyond their years.

Boys carry a special burden when they are sexually abused, especially those from cultures where male dominance is the norm. The boy feels as if he is weak and should have been in control. Although male victims may also fear physical damage, the prevailing fear centers around homosexuality. The boy abused by a man wonders if the encounter has somehow made him homosexual. Since many perpetrators of this type of abuse are family men who present a picture of normalcy, the boy becomes convinced that the fault must be within himself.

The young male abused by a woman faces similar fears but for different reasons. In a society where sex between older females and younger males is viewed almost as a rite of passage, the boy wonders why he should be disturbed by such an encounter. Does his discomfort, therefore, attest to his homosexuality? Unfortunately, in both situations, society supports the boy's fears, further convincing him of the damage done (Finkelhor, 1984; Hunter, 1990).

Therapeutically, the child's fears of damage can be addressed through education, a physical examination, and by discussing the fears and misconceptions. The attitude of society is not so easily changed, but children can be helped to realize that this problem is not theirs.

Abused children feel guilt for a number of reasons. Much time in therapy is devoted to helping the child recognize that he or she did not elicit the sexual interaction. Children suffer guilt from the love they feel for the abusing parent, their delight in the attention they were given, or from the physiological pleasure they experienced. Often the perpetrator has added to this feeling by telling them how seductive or desirable they are. Taught by society to be seductive, girls become convinced that the abuse was to be expected from their behavior. Taught to be assertive, boys agonize over their inability to protect themselves and label themselves "weak" or "sissies" (Porter, Blick, Sgroi, 1982; Hunter, 1990).

Guilt also stems from the child's perception that he or she is responsible for the disclosure of the abuse and the subsequent disruption of the family. The Asian child may also see himself or herself as responsible for the loss of "family honor." Whether the victim disclosed the abuse intentionally or accidentally, he or she feels guilt at betraying the relationship with the perpetrator. The abuser has probably predicted dire consequences ("You'll be sent away" or "I'll go to jail"), and the child becomes convinced that these things will come to pass. The guilt-ridden child had no way to anticipate the intensity of the atmosphere, once disclosure is a reality and the family is thrown into crisis.

These types of guilt can only be treated by helping the child understand that he or she cannot be responsible for the actions of an adult. It is important that the child is also empowered for the future, by giving the clear message of "You are not responsible for what has happened in the past, but you can be helped to take control in the future."

Fear appears in the thinking processes of child victims in several ways. Nightmares and flashbacks attest to children's fears about the consequences of the disclosure or the fear that the perpetrator will abuse again. Children fear separation from the family and even from the perpetrator. Again, identification of these fears helps children understand them and gain insight into the likelihood of these events occurring. Setting up a mechanism to protect the child as well as providing the victim with new trust relationships helps to alleviate much of the fear. Along with the fear there will usually be some degree of depression in child victims. This depression, sometimes masked by somatic complaints, is stimulated by the child's inability to process and deal with the myriad conflicts he or she is experiencing. While the depression usually subsides as the child has an opportunity to ventilate and explore these feelings, the most immediate concern is that the depression does not precipitate a suicide attempt or self-destructive behavior (Porter, Blick, and Sgroi, 1982; Hunter, 1990).

The dysfunctional incestuous family, the fear of damage, and the guilt over participation in and disclosure of abuse lead abused children to low self-esteem. Not feeling sufficiently confident, these children are also robbed of their ability to develop adequate social skills, which in turn reinforces their low self-concept. Boys who were abused outside the home feel they are unlike their male peers—that they don't "measure up." Effective treatment gives children an opportunity to express their negative feelings about themselves. Positive feedback, often in a group setting, allows them to explore their strengths and enhances their self-esteem. With greater self-esteem comes a desire to master age-appropriate tasks with more confidence (Porter, Blick, and Sgroi, 1982; Hunter, 1990; Gil, 1996).

Anger, although it may be masked by somatic symptomatology or unexpressed fantasies, plagues most victims of sexual abuse, especially those from incestuous families and male victims. The anger is felt toward a number of people and expressed in various ways. The victims may feel anger toward the perpetrator for abusing them, toward themselves for their perceived acquiescence, and to others (especially nonabusing family members) for failing to protect them. Boys, unused to being victimized in our society, experience rage that they have been put in such a position.

Many female victims repress the rage they feel. Girls may act out—especially sexually—but the behavior only serves to mask the anger. A girl may internalize her anger and become depressed or exhibit self-destructive behavior such as suicide attempts, self-mutilation, or through eating disorders (Porter, Blick, and Sgroi, 1982; Gil, 1993). Although some boys repress their anger, they are more likely to act out their rage. Since this rage is related to their sense of powerlessness, they feel they can regain power by robbing someone else of control. It is for this reason that male victims are more likely to be aggressive toward younger children or sexually abuse other people. Through therapy, these boys can be helped to redirect their anger so that they can take power over some activity that is not abusive and will not harm others. Knowing that they have choices in regaining their sense of control is also important (Hunter, 1990; Ciottone and Madonna, 1996).

All victims can be helped to get in touch with their anger and to understand its source. Therapists can suggest ways for the child to gain control and experience mastery. As children learn to be assertive, they discover a new sense of control that will protect them in the future.

Children abused within incestuous families are faced with issues inherent in living in a dysfunctional or unprotective environment. Many of these issues relate to those dealt with in Chapters 6 and 7. These children learn that they cannot trust adults. A seemingly nurturing relationship with the perpetrator led to betrayal and exploitation, and other adults did little to stop it. Children become parents to their own parents, and this confusion in roles is imbedded in the family structure. As a result, while the victims appear to take on responsibility far beyond their years, they have actually failed to complete many developmental tasks that their peers have mastered. Such children often feel that they have little control over themselves and their own lives. They are neither children nor adults and find it difficult to discover where they fit.

Much of the treatment in these areas rests with the therapist's ability to present the child with an opportunity for a new and genuine trusting relationship. Once this is accomplished, the child can be helped to recognize what his or her role is in the family and that it is acceptable to relinquish much of the responsibility previously forced on him or her. Treatment enables the child to explore the deficiencies in development and guides him or her along the road to appropriate maturity (Porter, Blick, and Sgroi, 1982; Gil, 1993; Ciottone and Madonna, 1996). Group treatment is useful because children and adolescents join with peers who are at different levels of development.

Therapists also aid children in communicating with other family members and with peers. Education is also part of treatment. Knowledge of anatomy, normal sexuality, birth control, boy-girl relations, and parenting enhances their development. If the court system is involved, the victim will need to be carefully prepared for what is to come. Support during the court process is also a vital part of treatment.

Sexually abused children respond to different treatment techniques depending on the age of the child, the type of abuse, the cooperativeness of the family, and the skills of the therapist.

Individual therapy is useful in developing a trusting relationship on which the child can model other relationships. Such therapy often begins when the child is in crisis over disclosure. Consistency in the relationship is vital, as any breach of trust or confidentiality will convince the victim that the therapist is as untrustworthy as the other adults in his or her life. With younger children, play therapy enables them to express themselves in a manner that is less threatening (Ciottone and Madonna, 1996). Older victims enjoy games or projects over which they can talk while seeming to put their attention elsewhere.

Group therapy is especially effective with adolescent victims. Here, victims can ventilate anger in a safe environment and develop new socialization skills. Sex education is a topic that lends itself to group discussion (Mrazek, 1981a; Blick and Porter, 1982; Gil, 1993; Wherry et al., 1994). If both a male and female therapist work with the group, their relationship simulates a family situation and provides positive modeling for victims. As the therapists demonstrate their ability to communicate effectively and to protect the group members from harm, the victims learn what they have a right to expect from healthy parents.

Art therapy is useful in assessment and in treatment. Drawings portray the victims' reactions to the abuse, their self-image, confusions about role and gender, misconceptions about the abuse, and their emotional states (Kelly, 1984). Various art forms release the children's energy and free them of the constraints of talking with an adult. Music, dance, movement, mime, drama, and poetry are all methods of release for some children. Often a group or individual therapy session begins with a warm-up period. The particular type of therapy is introduced and the children or adolescents are encouraged to participate. If the session is videotaped, the discussion that follows provides both child and therapist with an integrated understanding of what has transpired (Stember, 1980; Naitove, 1982; Mayer, 1983).

Mayer (1983) suggests that poetry stimulates emotional release. Whether reading the poetry of others or creating their own, victims experience and identify emotions that enhance their treatment.

Journal and story writing are techniques that have been widely used with adult survivors and are useful in work with children—especially older victims. Keeping a diary or journal enables the child to ventilate in privacy and provides a means through which he or

TABLE 14.1 Treatment Goals with Sexually Abused Children

1. To help the victim ventilate and come to terms with feelings of anger, fear, guilt, shame, and damage
2. To help the child experience a trusting relationship with a consistent and caring adult
3. To enhance self-esteem and improve social functioning
4. To help the child reestablish appropriate communication and social or generational roles within the family to ensure the child's future protection, or to ensure protection of the child through foster placement while considering future and more permanent plans
5. To aid the child in developing assertiveness skills
6. To rechannel self-destructive behavior into more acceptable behavior
7. To diminish compulsive behavior, such as sexualizing relationships

Adapted from A. Mayer, *Sexual Abuse: Causes, Consequences and Treatment of Incestuous and Pedophilic Acts,* pp. 80–81. Holmes Beach, FL: Learning Publications, 1985. Reprinted with permission.

she and the therapist can begin to relate. Even stories written about hypothetical people allow the therapist to explore the child's fears and fantasies.

Children may be seen in therapy with other members of the incestuous family. Mother-daughter therapy, as a pair seen individually or in groups, helps to strengthen the bond, improves communication, and ensures protection for the child in the future. Later in treatment, it is also extremely beneficial for the perpetrator and child to meet and for the perpetrator to take full responsibility for his or her actions.

Whether a child is the victim of incest or an assault outside the home, therapy is extremely helpful to ensure his or her integration of the trauma and future healthy development. Tables 14.1 and 14.2 highlight the treatment goals that have been introduced in this section.

The Mother or Nonabusing Parent

The goals of treatment with the nonabusing parent are primarily to strengthen his or her role in the future protection of the child. Because of the frequency of father-daughter incest, it

TABLE 14.2 Treatment Goals with Sexually Abused Adolescents

1. To provide an opportunity to ventilate and integrate feelings of anger, fear, guilt, shame, and damage
2. To aid with the clarification of values and life goals
3. To provide training in social skills, assertiveness, and communication
4. To provide assistance in impulse control, decision making, and conflict resolution
5. To aid the adolescent in feeling in control of his or her own life
6. To help with the integration of issues associated with living in a dysfunctional family
7. To enhance self-esteem and improve social functioning
8. To ensure that the victim is not involved in self-destructive behavior such as substance abuse, attempted suicide, and eating disorders
9. To aid in the understanding of sexuality and promote healthy sexual development

From A. Mayer, *Sexual Abuse: Causes, Consequences and Treatment of Incestuous and Pedophilic Acts,* pp. 80–81. Holmes Beach, FL: Learning Publications, 1985. Reprinted with permission.

is therefore the mother who is usually the nonabusive parent. It is certainly possible for a mother to be an abuser, but in those cases the father is often absent. Because these cases are rare, there is not, as yet, a clinical outline of treatment for nonabusing fathers.

The mother has needs of her own, and until these are met, she cannot be fully available for her child. The mother in an incest triad has often been a victim of abuse or of a dysfunctional family herself. This has left her with scars that hamper her ability to parent and protect.

The therapist will recognize her acute feelings of inadequacy and strong dependency needs. Whether she appears passive and dependent or domineering and hostile, she will need unconditional acceptance and encouragement to take control of her life. This is an individual whose past history and marriage has been punctuated with messages that she is a failure. Overwhelmed by the intensity of this message, she has often lapsed into depression. Like the other members of her family, her impaired self-concept has caused her to isolate herself and has prevented her from developing adequate social skills. For this reason, group therapy is especially effective with these mothers. She often needs massive amounts of support, which can be better supplied by a group than by one therapist. In a group, she can also be encouraged to become more assertive, behavior that not only benefits her but also provides her with skills with which she can protect her child (Sgroi and Dana, 1982; Mayer, 1983; Johnson, 1992).

Communication is a major problem for incestuous families. As one member of this family system, the mother is especially unable to express herself and make her needs known. She must learn, through therapy, to recognize her own feelings and to share them with others. Many of these women have spent their lives expecting others to perceive their needs and fill them. Their disappointment when their needs remain undetected and unfulfilled does not prevent them from continuing to harbor unrealistic expectations of those around them. These mothers cannot admit that their marriages have disappointed them and that they have little communication with their children.

The mother's low self-esteem, lack of assertiveness, denial, and unrealistic expectations also prevent her from setting and enforcing limits in the family. In treatment, the mother is faced with the recognition that she failed to prevent the abusive behavior. When she comes to terms with this fact and begins to perceive herself as a responsible and autonomous person, the mother increases her ability to enforce role boundaries. If the family remains intact, she must be in a position to ensure that the incestuous father does not have the opportunity to abuse again. She must be sensitive to his behavior around the child and conscious of not leaving father and child alone. For this task, she must put aside her denial, see herself as capable and assertive, and be able to communicate her own needs and desires (Sgroi and Dana, 1982; Johnson, 1992). In working with these mothers, one must always keep their culture in mind. Although she must learn to protect her child, a mother who has also learned to be assertive and independent may become isolated in a male-dominated culture. Thus, a balance must be achieved between the needs of the child and cultural norms.

The mother's anger and her inability to trust are two underlying elements that must be addressed. Her anger may be directed toward the perpetrator or toward the victim for their perceived betrayal. She may turn this anger inward or express it openly. Mothers from dysfunctional families of origin often carry anger as a remnant from childhood. Instead of expressing it overtly, the mother may have kept this anger hidden. Anger is not an emotion that hides well, however. It is often evidenced as passive behavior toward her family or is directed inward. In the safety of therapy, the mother can admit her feelings and express her rage. She can grieve over her unmet needs and ventilate her feelings about those who have failed to meet them. Through her relationship with the therapist or with her therapy group, the mother learns how to trust. This sense of trust is important for her to carry back to her own family. Through therapy she learns that trust is based on communicating with others, being accountable, and holding others accountable for their actions.

The key word in treatment of the nonabusing mother is *support*. She may have so lacked nurturing herself that she needs to be given a great deal of support and guidance before she can give it to others.

Not all mothers opt to keep their families intact. For those who choose divorce rather than risk being betrayed again, therapy centers around supporting them through the process, enabling them to provide for and protect their children, and helping them to deal with their renewed feelings of failure, loneliness, and isolation. In addition, this mother must learn to recognize her self-abusive patterns so that the next man with whom she becomes involved does not have the same abusive tendencies as those of her husband.

Women whose husbands are incarcerated face different decisions, conflicts, and frustrations. Should she wait for his release and attempt to maintain communication across prison walls, or should she divorce him and risk being alone and perhaps feel that she has somehow betrayed him? The mother will need support in making these decisions and in helping her children adjust to whatever decision she makes. She will also need help in deciding how she will protect the child once the offender is released. Since jail/prison terms for sexual abuse are usually relatively short, this is a real concern.

Although individual therapy is effective, group therapy seems to provide more opportunities for support and growth. Sometimes concrete services such as financial assistance, child care, and transportation are also essential. If the criminal justice system is involved, the mother as well as the victim may require anticipatory guidance and backing through this process.

The Perpetrator

The type of treatment for the perpetrator of sexual abuse depends on three interrelated factors: the type of assault he or she committed; where he or she resides when treatment is undertaken; and the sex of the perpetrator.

Earlier chapters examined the differences between incestuous fathers and extrafamilial abusers. Although recent research shows that these two categories need not be mutually exclusive, the motivations of the incestuous father often differ from those of the pedophile. For this reason, treatment takes a slightly different emphasis.

At some point, the incestuous father usually has therapy sessions with the family. Although he may reside outside the home, there is usually contact with the family unit, especially when reunification is a projected goal. If the family chooses to exclude him, he may be seen alone or in group therapy to resolve his own issues. If the state in which he resides decrees automatic incarceration, or if the assault on his child was violent or included other illegal aspects (e.g., production of pornography), the incestuous father may be imprisoned. Therefore the type of treatment he receives, if any, depends on what he has done and the place of custody.

The extrafamilial abuser is more likely to be incarcerated for several reasons. First, in many states, incest is reported to protective services, but extrafamilial abuse is brought to the attention of a law enforcement agency and likely leads to prosecution. Second, extrafamilial perpetrators are more often classic pedophiles which means that they tend to abuse more frequently, begin their abusive patterns earlier in life, have more victims, and exhibit deeper pathology (Prendergast, 1991). Only occasionally is he able to be involved with treatment outside the prison setting.

Male perpetrators come to the attention of the social service agencies and judicial system more frequently, but women too practice abuse although they are not as likely to be detected. For this reason, there are very few programs that specialize in female offenders. One program, Genesis II, in Saint Paul, Minnesota, does ongoing group therapy and educational intervention with women who have committed sexual abuse. The goals of the program (Speltz, Mathews, and Mathews, 1985; Mathews et al., 1990) are to help the women to

- Take primary responsibility for their sexually abusive behavior
- Increase their understanding of and empathy for the victim
- Increase their awareness of their own emotional and psychological processes that led to the sexual abuse
- Establish a way to meet their own sexual and interpersonal needs without victimizing others

The women, some of whom reside in halfway houses and others at home, are referred to the program by child protection workers, probation officers, and private therapists.

In October 1966, Genesis II received a grant from the St. Paul Foundation to compile data on the women who had participated in the day-treatment program. The hope is that this and other such studies will shed light on the much neglected concept of the female perpetrator.

Is there a "cure" for the perpetrator? Consensus is that child sexual abuse, like alcoholism, has no cure but can be controlled. For the incestuous father whose needs are for nurturing and whose offense appears based on an imbalanced family system filled with stress, control means a combination of treating the family for its dysfunction and teaching the perpetrator other methods of coping with his response to stress. For the pedophile whose patterns are based on compulsion and on an inability to cope effectively with life issues, control necessitates additional restraints. One expert, Maureen Saylor, says the pedophile

> ...must avoid situations where kids congregate. He must not go near kids' playgrounds and parks. He must have minimal contact with kids and not get himself involved with women who have children. In some respects it raises the question about whether a child molester who marries should have any kids, period, because he can be creating his own outlet victims.
>
> While that may sound harsh and cruel, with this particular addiction the individual can fall right back into the same old patterns given the right set of circumstances. (Knopp, 1984, p. 21)

Prognoses for treatment depend on the type of perpetrator and his history (Groth, 1978; Mayer, 1983; Prendergast, 1991). At what age did he begin abusing? How long has the behavior lasted? What is the intensity or severity of the abusive behavior? How frequently do abusive episodes occur?

If the perpetrator began his abusive career early in life and has continued to abuse regularly and with more intensity, his prognosis is much more guarded than the man who began in his adulthood and had abused one or two victims and only infrequently.

Whatever the approach to therapy, there are specific goals to be met in working with both male and female perpetrators (Knopp, 1984; Mayer, 1985; Prendergast, 1991; Schwartz and Cellini, 1995). The perpetrator must

1. Accept personal responsibility for the abuse.
2. Understand the sequence of feelings, events, stimuli, and circumstances that led to the sexual offense.
3. Learn to break the pattern at the first sign leading toward abuse.
4. Learn appropriate tools and mechanisms to break the pattern and control the behavior.
5. Develop a positive self-concept.
6. Have an opportunity to test new skills in a safe environment.
7. Have posttreatment support to prevent recidivism.

At the onset of treatment, abusers must be individually assessed. Personality testing can be particularly useful. In some programs, perpetrators write in-depth autobiographies through which past experiences and thinking patterns can be analyzed. Exposing the man to groups of other offenders also provides assessment material. In behaviorally based programs, a physiological penile assessment may be administered. In this test, a small sensing device is attached to the penis to measure the individual's erection response to various stimuli. This test is used especially when some type of aversion therapy is anticipated (Knopp, 1984).

Since the primary defenses of perpetrators are denial, rationalization, and projection of blame, an important step at the onset of treatment is to help the individual take responsibility for his abusive behavior. "My daughter was too seductive" or "My wife went to work and neglected me" are not acceptable excuses for the abuse. One method of getting the offender to take responsibility is to place him in a group of offenders who are at different stages of treatment. Many of these men have already admitted their own responsibility and openly confront a man who does not.

The habitual offender probably never looked at the pattern that led to abuse. Clues may be discernible through his past history.

Ray was abused by an uncle (his mother's brother) at family reunions. The relationship between Ray's mother and her brother was not harmonious, and Ray had the courage to tell her because he felt she would be sympathetic. Instead the mother laughed derisively, "You can't even keep out of his way? He's such a wimp, but even you can't keep him away!" Ray remembers feeling shocked and betrayed, and vividly recalls his reaction of uncomfortable warmth, sweating palms, and a dry mouth. His mother taunted him about his disclosure for years.

From his adolescence, Ray remembers being rejected by a classmate whom he had asked for a date. She laughed at his awkward attempt. He remembers having the same physiological feelings and emotional hurt he had experienced with his mother. Unconsciously, he then wanted someone else to feel as weak and as helpless as he. He sought out a younger neighbor boy whom he molested. This boy was the first of many.

In treatment, Ray began to recognize that when he felt helpless or laughed at, especially by a woman, he developed the same physiological symptoms and the desire to molest.

Once the perpetrator pictures the chain of events leading to his abusive behavior, he learns methods to control his impulses. Ray learned to not set himself up for rejection, and he also developed an exhaustive program of physical activity to channel any aggressive impulses more constructively.

A variety of behavior techniques is used to help the perpetrator break his pattern. Olfactory aversion, involving an extremely unpleasant smell (such as ammonia), eventually blocks the man's arousal response to certain stimuli. For example, an abuser watching a slide presentation of a naked child is made to break a net-enmeshed capsule of spirits of ammonia and hold it under his nose. The smell inhibits his arousal and prevents an erection. Eventually he learns to associate the smell with seeing the child, and this stimulus no longer arouses him. Shocks using visual or verbal cues are other means of aversion therapy (Knopp, 1984; Prendergast, 1991; Schwartz and Cellini, 1995). (For example, the perpetrator is shown slides and a shock is administered when he sees the type of child he offended against. Or he is asked to tell of his offense in detail and is given a shock when he describes how he has victimized the child.)

A more controversial method of reducing sexual response is with Depo-Provera (medroxyprogesterone acetate), a drug that decreases the functioning of the testes and inhibits the sexual drive. Currently the drug is best known for its use at the Johns Hopkins University Hospital in Baltimore, where it is being administered weekly to a selected group of perpetrators. The concerns about this medication are based on questions of how effective it is and of its long- and short-term effects. In addition, the abuser may need continued doses after treatment. There is some question as to how these doses can be made available as the use of this type of therapy is currently experimental and somewhat controversial (Berlin, 1983; Knopp, 1984; Nagayama Hall, 1995).

Whether his behavior is controlled psychologically, behaviorally, or through the use of drugs, the offender must still be helped to improve his feelings about himself. Male offenders see themselves as inherently powerless in a society that expects men to be assertive and take command. Their choice of a significantly weaker victim—a child as opposed to a peer—is clearly indicative of these feelings. An exploration of social stereotypes, combined with an assessment of their own individual strengths, enables perpetrators to develop more positive goals for themselves. Positive reinforcement as they take steps to reach this goal allows them to feel better about themselves. This is by no means a short process. Years of abuse at home and messages from others that they were inadequate have made abusers deeply lacking in self-respect (Prendergast, 1991).

The sexual abuser has also failed to develop social skills. Despite the nature of his crime, he probably has little understanding of sexuality. Sex, to him, is often negative and dirty. He sees sex as a method of degrading or humiliating others. In treatment, the perpetrator learns about anatomy and sexuality and that sex—properly used—is not negative. He is helped to reassess his values about sex. If the abuser is in family treatment, he and his spouse may be encouraged to explore ways in which they can develop a satisfying sexual relationship.

Part of the incestuous father's early problems with healthy sexual relationships was not only his distorted understanding of sexuality but also his inability to empathize with others. This appears to be a problem for all sexual abusers. Throughout his life, the abuser has had little insight into the feelings of others—especially his victims. One method of treatment brings him face to face with survivors of sexual assault. He, too, is possibly a survivor, and helping him explore this in therapy gives him an opportunity to recognize his feelings in others. The offender who sees a child as multidimensional and recognizes the harm to that child may have a better chance to control his abusive impulses in the future.

Since a major contributor to the abuse is the perpetrator's feelings of helplessness and need to control, treatment aids perpetrators to take control over their own lives through assertiveness training and control over their substance abuse. Vocational or educational training, along with other psychosocial education, allows the men to perceive themselves as worthwhile (Groth, Hobson, and Gary, 1982; Knopp, 1984; Prendergast, 1991).

One major limitation of treatment programs for sexual abusers is that there is no built-in opportunity for the perpetrator to test his new skills in a safe environment and no insurance of follow-up services after treatment has ended. For example, incarcerated abusers who have received treatment in conjunction with a prison term often find themselves unsupported by social services following their release. In recognition of this oversight, many programs are now seeking to provide post-treatment support services. Another possible solution is for the perpetrator to become affiliated with a self-help group such as Parents United. Support services are vital to help the perpetrator center his energies on controlling his impulses. Sexual offending is usually not a one-time occurrence and commitment to treatment is a life-long necessity.

Because sexual offenders are at risk for recidivism, there is currently a great deal of emphasis on the *relapse prevention* model (Nagayama Hall, 1995; Schwartz and Cellini, 1995; Murphy and Smith, 1996). Relapse prevention involves individualized treatment that assesses the offender's own sexual fantasies, motivation, and offending cycle. It designs treatment that includes techniques for monitoring his/her ability to interrupt the impulses to abuse that could lead to recidivism. Programs using this method strive to strengthen the offenders' own self control and, while motivating them in a desire to prevent themselves from reoffending, provide them with specific behavioral techniques to achieve these goals. To date, many of these efforts have been quite successful. The Vermont Treatment Program for Sexual Aggressors (VTPSA) found that of a total population of 473 participants of their relapse prevention program, only 6 percent reoffended (Schwartz and Cellini, 1995, 20–30).

How are the treatment needs of the perpetrator addressed in various types of programs? Basically, the abuser may be treated in three structural frameworks that can, in some instances, overlap: (1) treatment in conjunction with the family unit; (2) treatment in the community, but independent of the family; and (3) treatment while incarcerated.

Treatment in the Family Unit

In family counseling, the needs of each member of the family must, at some time, be addressed. Individual counseling assesses how each one's needs can be integrated with those of other family members. Individual counseling with the incestuous father explores his willingness to take responsibility and his understanding of his own abusive patterns and helps him learn to control his desires. Skill building becomes a vital part of family therapy, and often the man is joined by his wife to explore ways to communicate better, share family roles more equitably, enjoy a better sexual relationship, and learn to manage the stresses of family life. Together, these parents may be trained in parenting skills to enable them to feel more in control. Trust between these couples is another major treatment issue.

> *Dick and Susan Hawthorne were seen in therapy shortly after it had been disclosed that Dick had been abusing 9-year-old Michelle for several years. The court agreed to allow Dick to receive treatment. At first, Dick and his wife and daughter were each seen separately by different therapists. Dick readily admitted that he had abused Michelle, but it took several months before he was ready to take full responsibility for his actions. In addition to individual counseling, Dick also participated in a group of six other men who were largely responsible for his recognition of how he had betrayed his daughter.*
>
> *After several months, Dick changed his regular individual sessions to weekly sessions with Susan. He continued to go to the fathers' group, and Susan and Michelle joined a mother-daughter group. Dick and Susan were guided in the exploration of their relationship from everyday communication and division of labor to their sexual compatibility. These weekly marital sessions lasted for several months.*
>
> *When it was suggested that Dick and Susan were ready to have family therapy, Dick objected. He realized that Michelle was well aware of what had happened, but he had convinced himself that 12-year-old Phillip and 4-year-old Tracey had not been involved. Couple therapy continued until Dick realized the necessity of bringing the family together. In family therapy, the roles and expectations of both the parents and children were explored. Phillip expressed his hurt at what he perceived was his father's rejection of him. He was jealous of Michelle despite his suspicion that something was wrong. Tracey was given an opportunity to ventilate her confusion. At her age she knew little of the reality of what had occurred but was very much aware of the tension in the household. Susan was helped to deal with her family's anger at her for abandoning them because of her frequent meetings and busy schedule. Dick was encouraged to accept his part in the abuse and to assure Michelle that he alone was to blame. The family continued in therapy for a year while Dick remained in the fathers' group.*

Fathers who receive therapy with their families may or may not be living at home. For those who live apart, rejoining the family occasionally helps them evaluate their ability to return to the home on a more permanent basis. Needless to say, this would not be possible without assurance that the children were protected and were in no real danger from renewed abuse.

Treatment in the Community
Not every incestuous father can be reunited with his family. Some seek or are compelled to seek treatment independent of their families. Pedophiles may not have a family or choose to receive treatment for their problem without involving other family members.

Treatment may be individual or in groups or a combination of the two, and the same issues described in the last section, are addressed. In some instances, treatment is a component of the man's probation or is based on the agreement that if he cooperates with treatment he will not be prosecuted. In these instances the court might also have stipulations that must be met.

> *Lex was 22 years old when he came to the attention of the court for molesting a 5-year-old girl. Although he had had numerous fantasies about children in the past, he had never had an opportunity to act upon them. Now he was unemployed, lonely, and depressed. The abuse, in his eyes, resulted from a several-month relationship with his victim.*
>
> *Because it was his first known offense, the court put him on probation with the condition that he seek therapy at a local mental health clinic. It was also stipulated that he find employment and move to an area where there were not as many small children. Part of Lex's therapy, therefore, included job-skill training, finding a job, and renting an apartment in an adult building. The prospect of being completely surrounded by adults frightened him, however, and his sessions were often devoted to helping him deal with this issue by becoming more assertive and gaining more self-esteem.*

It is uncommon for a perpetrator to seek therapy on his own. Sometimes therapists discover clients who have abusive tendencies on which they may have acted. Then the dilemma for a therapist is that he or she is mandated by law to report child abuse. Some therapists hesitate to report, despite the consequences due to their fear that reporting will destroy the delicate balance of patient-therapist relationship.

Treatment in Prison

A heated controversy is whether the perpetrator should be punished or treated. There are those who contend that child sexual abuse is a heinous crime and warrants only punishment, but experience shows that incarceration does little good. Sentences are often short and the perpetrator's life in prison is far from therapeutic. In the prison hierarchy, even below the rapist is the child molester. The sexual abuser of children is likely to be raped or beaten by his fellow inmates and usually must be kept in protective custody, away from the general population. As a result, when he is released, he is not only still a child abuser but an angry, bitter, and humiliated child abuser who is apt to further degrade his victims by using the violence he learned in prison.

Incarceration without treatment serves to keep the offender out of the community for a short time but does little toward rehabilitation. Increasingly, prisons are initiating treatment programs that differ depending on whether the sex offender is housed as part of the general population, in a separate wing, or in a separate building (Knopp, 1984; Prendergast, 1991).

Integrated programs periodically remove the prisoners from the general population and from their routines in order to attend group or individual sessions. The program is usually part of a model dealing with a variety of mental health problems, including abuse.

Programs that advocate housing offenders in a separate wing provide a more cohesive approach with more time for interaction between staff and offenders. The offenders' daily routine includes group therapy. Although this arrangement protects them from the general population, being clustered together in such a way labels and stigmatizes these inmates.

It is less common for inmates to be housed in separate buildings, largely because of financial, security, and space considerations, as well as the priorities of the particular prison. If security is ensured and a high staff-inmate ratio is maintained, such a structure can be effective (Knopp, 1984).

Although treatment within the prison is preferable to no treatment at all, it does have its drawbacks. Critics contend that the closed, protective atmosphere generates an artificial setting of security and prevents the inmates from practicing their new skills in real-life situations. Unable to practice what they have learned, will the abusers be able to stand the stresses of living outside the prison environment? In addition, participation is usually voluntary. Openly admitting sexual abuse subjects the inmate to abuse from other inmates, so perpetrators are often hesitant to join treatment programs.

To date, few prisons offer offender treatment, and those programs that do exist are often understaffed and underfunded. Since the few programs are still so recent, accurate statistics on recidivism—or chances of success—are not available.

One particularly successful in-house treatment program at Connecticut Correctional Institute at Somers offers the men choices from a series of groups (Groth, Hobson, and Gary 1982). These groups address such issues as

- Sex education
- Relationship with women
- Personal victimization
- Understanding sexual assault
- Sociodrama (roleplaying interpersonal conflicts)
- Communication skills
- Dealing with anxiety and tension
- Patterns of sexual assault and making the community aware of sexual assault (in which professionals from the community are invited to meet with offenders)

In addition, the inmate may participate in individual counseling and is given the opportunity to attend self-help groups such as Parents Anonymous or Parents United. Such an approach provides offenders with a particularly well-rounded treatment program. (For examples of other programs, see F. H. Knopp's *Retraining Adult Sexual Offenders,* 1984.)

Occasionally prison inmates are allowed to enter the community for counseling, especially when they have almost finished their sentences and attempts are being made for family reunification. Again, security is a paramount concern. Since the therapists are community based, there will be more of a chance for the abuser to maintain contact and support after his release. These therapists may be particularly influential in helping him in the transition between incarceration and freedom.

Is Treatment Effective?

There is much controversy about the way in which sexual abusers should be handled. Some advocate the solution of "slap them in prison and throw away the key," but the reality is that this does not benefit anyone. Certainly the offender does not learn patterns other than deviant ones. And further, the prison system is such that the offender *will* usually be released into the community again. The untreated offender often returns angry about the treatment he has had in prison. It is this person who will not only re-offend, but will do so with more force and anger. The alternative it would seem would be to offer effective treatment. But does treatment work? Chaffin (1994) contends that treatment of offenders who can be seen in outpatient settings does have favorable outcomes. He admits that the pathology of these abusers is often less severe in the first place. Offenders who exhibit more complex pathology have poorer treatment outcomes and more likelihood of relapse. However, Marques (1991) found, in a study of incarcerated child molesters and rapists, that treated offenders showed a decrease in deviant arousal, more internalized locus of control, fewer cognitive distortions, and an improved ability to cope with potential relapse situations. From these and other recent studies, it would seem that treatment for offenders *is* effective. Chaffin (1994) cautions against assuming that one treatment method is appropriate for all offenders, however. Each offender must be assessed individually and treatment geared specifically to him or her.

Family Preservation with Incestuous Families

Should incestuous families be kept together? Can a child be protected from further abuse? These questions are difficult to answer and are the subject of debate among social workers, therapists, police officers, attorneys, and judges (Pence, 1993; Arnold, 1993; Ewing, 1993). Sexual abuse is often woven into the fabric of a family system. Reworking that fabric can be an exceptionally difficult task. Can parental rights be respected while protection of the child is insured? When protective services intervenes in an incest situation, the preferred intervention is to remove the offender in order to stabilize the family and protect the child. This necessitates that the non-abusive parent not only believes the child but is willing to protect him or her. Mothers in incestuous families have reported that this seems like an overwhelming task.

I felt like I had to watch him every minute, reported one non-abusive mother. When my daughter first told that her father was abusing her, protective services made him leave. We got into therapy and I figured we could get things straightened out. But there was so much pressure. I couldn't trust him anymore. I couldn't leave him alone with my daughter. It was like there was always a big black cloud over our heads.

Mothers who commit themselves to monitoring their spouse's behavior may find the stress too much. The offender experiences the pressure. Karl worked at home and found that his daughter's presence worried him.

I was afraid to be around her [his stepdaughter]...afraid I would do something again. I didn't want to but I was still afraid. My wife and I had to make sure we planned things so that I never had to put her to bed or bathe her.

Intensive family intervention may help the family to achieve a balance that protects the child. But such patterns are difficult to break and many families feel the need of follow-up services to maintain themselves. It may also require a great deal of motivation on each member's part for the incestuous family to be preserved.

Parents of Children Abused Outside the Home

Parents of children who were abused by those outside the families are rarely provided treatment. One reason for this oversight is that these cases are usually reported to law enforcement rather than to child protection agencies. The goal then becomes apprehension and prosecution of the perpetrator. When the child exhibits undeniably associated symptoms, he or she receives treatment. Rarely, if ever, do the parents. Instead, they are expected to support their child and cooperate in the efforts to punish the perpetrator. Yet these parents often have conflicting feelings that make their support of the child difficult.

An overriding feeling for parents is guilt. No matter how unrealistic are their concerns, they chastise themselves for not having protected their child from harm. They agonize over "Why did I let her walk home from school alone?" or "Why did I allow him to play on that ball team?" or "Why did I choose that babysitter?"

The reaction to these feelings, in addition to self-blame, is to overprotect the child, which leads to family conflict and often augments the child's problems. In therapy the parents are helped to recognize that although adequate supervision is important, children need increasing amounts of responsibility and independence for healthy growth.

Parents also tend to project blame on each other ("Why were you late picking Sally up?" "Didn't you watch him?"). Mothers and fathers who argue over their degree of responsibility for the child create problems in their own relationships. They may also blame the child, especially if he or she was not where they expected him or her to be. For example, one boy usually walked home from school by a predominantly residential route. One day, however, he decided to walk another way, which passed a local variety store. It was on this route where he met the man who then molested him. His parents had never told him that he could not take the business route, but when they learned of his abuse, they were extremely angry with him for "disobeying." Some parents blame the child for not stopping the abuse.

They ask why the child didn't run or fight, forgetting that under their tutelage the child had learned to be in awe of and obey adults.

Parents sometimes resent the family disruption after the abuse has been disclosed. Police question family members, there may be court appearances, and the tenor of the family is usually one of anxiety and unrest. In response to a lengthy period of investigation, one father commented, "Maybe our son should never have told us about being molested; he probably would have forgotten it after a while." Despite the disruption, the parents must recognize that the child needs to feel protected. Reporting, investigation, and prosecution of the abuser gives the message to the child that the abuser is to blame and not the child.

The parents' inability to recognize and cope with the trauma of the child's abuse may be related to the parents' own past. Parents who were abused themselves as children find that residual conflicts are stimulated as they attempt to help their child through the aftermath of the experience. With therapy, parents can resolve some of their own issues.

It is natural for parents to be angry with the perpetrator. When their daughters are abused, fathers, in particular, describe wanting to retaliate by killing or maiming the abuser. They should be helped to explore their anger, recognize it as a reaction to feeling powerless, and be helped to channel their desires to act in a more appropriate way. Parents may also feel that their child is somehow permanently damaged by the abuse and express anger toward the perpetrator for this damage. Part of the child's recovery will depend on the parents' ability to lay to rest the fears about being damaged and help the child face the future. Until the parents are able to see the child as the same individual he or she was before the abuse and to love the child just as much, it will be difficult for them to be truly helpful. For these reasons, the parents of children abused by outsiders need support and insight into coping with the abuse and helping their child recover.

Summary

Workers treating sexually abused children and their families need particular skill. In treating sexual abuse, the worker discovers that society's attitude toward the clients and the workers themselves affects the treatment process. Treatment of the sexually abused and the abusers is only just evolving. To date, there are five models to treat sexual abuse: (1) the victim advocacy model, (2) the improvement model, (3) the system modification model, (4) the independent model, (5) the system alternative model, and an emerging model called (6) the "godfather offer." One of the best-known programs to treat sexual abuse is the Child Sexual Abuse Treatment Program in California. Since the late 1970s, this program has treated families and perpetrators and has become the model for numerous programs across the country.

In treatment, an incestuous family goes through specific phases: disclosure-panic, assessment-awareness, and restructure. During each of these phases, the family members experience certain conflicts that must be addressed in treatment.

Each participant or principal in sexual abuse has particular treatment needs. The child or adolescent must overcome feelings about being damaged, guilt, fear, depression, and feelings of low self-esteem. Children abused within their family have difficulty trusting again, exhibit pseudomaturity and loss of control, and feel anger toward the perpetrator and the nonprotecting parent. The goals of treatment with the nonabusing mother are to help her protect her child in the future. In order to do this, she must resolve her conflicts over her own collusion in the abuse, improve her own self-concept, learn to trust others, learn to make her needs known, communicate more effectively, and become more assertive. Underlying the mother's inability to protect is often a good deal of anger. She must learn to find the source of this anger and release it so that it can be channeled appropriately.

Treatment of the perpetrators depends on the type of assault (incestuous or extrafamilial), on their residence during treatment, and on their gender. There is little available data on treatment of female offenders, but treatment goals for perpetrators—male and female—include getting them to take responsibility for the abuse, helping them to understand their abusive patterns and how to break them, and encouraging them to develop better self-concepts. In addition to treatment, perpetrators must have opportunities to test their new skills and have support following treatment.

The treatment of sexual abusers may be done in a variety of settings. Perpetrators are treated in conjunction with the family to facilitate future healthy family interaction. Other members in the family are given individual treatment, with emphasis on their own personal functioning. If a perpetrator is incarcerated, he may or may not have treatment, but without treatment there is little hope for rehabilitation.

Treatment is rarely available to parents of children abused outside the home. Expected to support their children, these parents are often hampered by conflicts of their own. They feel guilt at having failed to protect their children and often blame their spouses or the victim for the abuse. They feel intense anger toward the perpetrator and see the child as somehow damaged. All of these feelings must be addressed before the parents can be truly supportive of their child.

Exploration Questions

1. Why is the treatment of sexual abuse different from that for neglect or abuse?

2. What are some issues to consider when treating an incestuous family?

3. What phases does an incestuous family go through in treatment?

4. What are the issues associated with each phase?

5. What are the treatment issues in working with a sexually abused child?

6. What are the special issues for male victims?

7. What types of therapy are used with children?

8. What are the goals in treatment for the nonabusing mother?

9. What are the treatment goals with a perpetrator?

10. What determines the type of treatment a perpetrator undergoes?

11. What are the conflicts experienced by parents whose children are abused outside the home?

Activities for Applied Learning

1. View the film *Something about Amelia*. What were the treatment issues for this family? What type of treatment was used? Do you feel it will be effective?

2. Invite a therapist, who works with sexually abused children, their families, or perpetrators, to discuss the issues he or she feels are involved in treatment.

3. Find out if there are self-help groups in your area (such as Parents United) that help sexually abused victims and their families. Also, is there a support group in your area for parents whose children were abused by someone outside the home? Invite people from one of these groups to address the class.

Suggested Readings

Ciottone, R. A., and Madonna, J. M. *Play Therapy with Sexually Abused Children.* Northvale, NJ: Jason Aronson, 1996.

Evert, K. and Bijkerk, I. *When You're Ready: A Woman's Healing from Childhood Physical and Sexual Abuse by her Mother.* Rockville, MD: Launch, 1987.

Faller, K. C. *Child Sexual Abuse.* New York: Columbia University Press, 1988.

Hunter, M. *The Sexually Abused Male, Vols 1 & 2.* New York: Lexington Books, 1990.

Mayer, A. *Incest: A Treatment Manual for Therapy with Victims, Spouses and Offenders.* Holmes Beach, FL: Learning Publications, 1983.

Sgroi, S. M. *Handbook for Clinical Intervention in Child Sexual Abuse.* Lexington, MA: Lexington Books, 1982.

References

Arnold, C. "Family Preservation and Reunification in Intrafamilial Sexual Abuse Cases: A CPS Attorney's Perspective." *Journal of Child Sexual Abuse* 2 (2), (1993):109–111.

Berlin, F. S. "Sex Offenders: A Biomedical Perspective and a Status Report on Biomedical Treatment." In *The Sexual Aggressor: Current Perspectives on Treatment,* edited by J. G. Greer and I. R. Stuart, pp. 83–123. New York: Van Nostrand Reinhold, 1983.

Blick, L. C., and Porter, F. S. "Group Therapy with Female Incest Victims." In *Handbook of Clinical Intervention in Child Sexual Abuse,* edited by S. M. Sgroi, pp. 147–75. Lexington, MA: Lexington Books, 1982.

Burgess, A. W.; Holmstrom, L. L.; and McCausland, M. P. "Counseling Young Victims and Their Families." in *Sexual Assault of Children and Adolescents,* edited by A. W. Burgess, A. N. Groth, pp. 181–204. Lexington, MA: Lexington Books, 1976.

Chaffin, M. "Assessment and Treatment of Child Sexual Abusers." *Journal of Interpersonal Violence* 9 (2), (1994):224–237.

Ciottone, R. A., and Madonna, J. M. *Play Therapy with Sexually Abused Children.* Northvale, NJ: Jason Aronson, 1996.

Ewing, C. P. "Family Preservation and Reunification in Intrafamilial Sexual Abuse Cases: A Justice Perspective." *Journal of Child Sexual Abuse* 2 (2), (1993):113–115.

Finkelhor, D. *Child Sexual Abuse.* New York: Free Press, 1984.

Gelinas, D. "Family Therapy: Characteristic Family Constellation and Basic Therapeutic Stance." In S. Sgroi, *Vulnerable Populations: Education and Treatment of Sexually Abused Children and Adult Survivors: Volume I.* Lexington, MA: Lexington Books, 1988.

Giardino, A. P., Christian, G. W., and Giardino, E. R. *A Practical Guide to the Evaluation of Child Abuse and Neglect.* Thousand Oaks, CA: Sage, 1997

Giarretto, H. "A Comprehensive Child Sexual Abuse Treatment Program." In *Sexually Abused Children and Their Families,* edited by P. B. Mrazek and C. H. Kempe, pp. 179–97. Elmsford, NY: Pergamon Press, 1981.

Gil, E. "Individual Therapy." In E. Gil and T. C. Johnson. *Sexualized Children,* pp. 179–210. Rockville, MD: Launch Press, 1993.

Gil, E. *Systematic Treatment of Families Who Abuse.* San Francisco, CA: Jossey-Bass, 1996.

Gil, E., and Johnson, T. C. *Sexualized Children.* Rockville, MD: Launch Press, 1993.

Groth, A. N. "Guidelines for the Assessment and Management of the Offender." In *Sexual Assault of Children and Adolescents,* edited by A. W. Burgess, A. N. Groth, L. L. Holmstrom, and S. M. Sgroi, pp. 25–42. Lexington, MA: Lexington Books, 1978.

Groth, A. N.; Hobson, W. F.; and Gary, T. S. "The Child Molester: Clinical Observations." *Social Work and Child Sexual Abuse: Journal of Social Work and Human Sexuality* 1 (1982):129–44.

Hunter, M. *The Sexually Abused Male.* New York: Lexington Books, 1990.

James, B., and Nasjleti, M. *Treating Sexually Abused Children and Their Families.* Palo Alto, CA: Consulting Psychologists Press, 1983.

Johnson, J. T. *Mothers of Incest Survivors.* Bloomington, IN: Indiana University Press, 1992.

Kelly, S. J. "The Use of Art Therapy with Sexually Abused Children." *Journal of Psychological Nursing* 22 (1984):12–18.

Knopp, F. H. *Retraining Adult Sex Offenders: Methods and Models.* Syracuse, NY: Safer Society Press, 1984.

MacFarlane, K., and Bulkley, J. "Treating Child Sexual Abuse: An Overview of Current Program Models." *Social Work and Child Sexual Abuse: Journal of Social Work and Human Sexuality* 1 (1982):69–91.

Marques, J. "Evaluating Treatment: How do we know what works?" In *Successful Interventions with Sex Offenders: Learning What Works.* Olympia, WA: Washington State Institute for Public Policy, 1991.

Mathews, R.; Mathews, J.; and Speltz, K. "Female Sexual Offenders." In Hunter, M. *The Sexually Abused Male, Vol 1,* pp. 275–293. New York: Lexington Books, 1990.

Mayer, A. *Incest: A Treatment Manual for Therapy with Victims, Spouses, and Offenders.* Holmes Beach, FL: Learning Publications, 1983.

Mayer, A. *Sexual Abuse: Causes, Consequences, and Treatment of Incestuous and Pedophilic Acts.* Holmes Beach, FL: Learning Publications, 1985.

Mrazek, P. B. "Group Psychotherapy with Sexually Abused Children." In *Sexually Abused Children and Their Families,* edited by P. B. Mrazek and C. H. Kempe, pp. 199–210. Elmsford, NY: Pergamon Press, 1981a.

Mrazek, P. B. "Special Problems in the Treatment of Child Sexual Abuse." In *Sexually Abused Children and Their Families,* edited by P. B. Mrazek and C. H. Kempe, pp. 159–166. Elmsford, NY: Pergamon Press, 1981b.

Murphy, W. D., and Smith, T. A. "Sex Offenders Against Children: Empirical and Clinical Issues." In J. Briere, L. Berliner, J. A. Bulkley, C. Jenny, & T. Reid (eds.). *APSAC Handbook on Child Maltreatment.* Thousand Oaks, CA: Sage, 1996.

Nagayama Hall, G. C. "Sexual Offender Recidivism Revisited: A Meta-analysis of Recent Treatment Studies." *Journal of Consulting and Clinical Psychology* 63(5) (1995):802–809.

Naitove, C. E. "Arts Therapy with Sexually Abused Children." In *Handbook of Clinical Intervention in Child Sexual Abuse,* edited by S. M. Sgroi, pp. 269–308. Lexington, MA: Lexington Books, 1982.

Pence, D. "Family Preservation and Reunification in Intrafamilial Sexual Abuse Cases: A Law Enforcement Perspective." *Journal of Child Sexual Abuse* 2 (2) (1993):103–108.

Porter, F. S.; Blick, L. C.; and Sgroi, S. M. "Treatment of the Sexually Abused Child." In *Handbook of Clinical Intervention in Child Sexual Abuse,* edited by S. M. Sgroi, pp. 109–45. Lexington, MA: Lexington Books, 1982.

Prendergast, W. E. *Treating Sex Offenders in Correctional Institutions and Outpatient Clinics.* New York: Haworth Press, 1991.

Schwartz, B. K., and Cellini, H. R. (eds.). *The Sexual Offender.* Kingston, NJ: Civic Research Inst., 1995.

Sgroi, S. M., ed. *Handbook of Clinical Intervention in Child Sexual Abuse.* Lexington, MA: Lexington Books, 1982.

Sgroi, S. M., and Dana, N. T. "Individual and Group Treatment of Mothers of Incest Victims." In *Handbook of Clinical Intervention in Child Sexual Abuse,* edited by S. M. Sgroi, pp. 191–214. Lexington, MA: Lexington Books, 1982.

Speltz, K.; Matthews, J.; and Matthews, R. "Genesis II: Female Sex Offender Programming." Paper read at National Conference on Child Abuse and Neglect, November, 1985, Chicago. Mimeographed.

Stember, C. J. "Art Therapy: A New Use in the Diagnosis and Treatment of Sexually Abused Children." In *Sexual Abuse of Children: Selected Readings,* edited by F. MacFarlane, pp. 59–63. Washington: U.S. Department of Health, Education and Welfare, 1980.

Waterman, J. "Overview of Treatment Issues." In K. MacFarlane and J. Waterman. *Sexual Abuse of Young Children.* New York: Guilford Press, 1986.

Wherry, J. N.; Jolly, J. B.; Aruffo, J. F.; Gillette, G.; Vaughn, L. and Metheny, R. "Family Trauma and Dysfunction in Sexually Abused Female Adolescent Psychiatric and Control Groups." *Journal of Child Sexual Abuse* 3 (1), (1994):53–65.

Williams, M. B. "Assessing the Traumatic Impact of Child Sexual Abuse: What Makes It More Severe?" *Journal of Child Sexual Abuse* 2 (2), (1993):41–59.

Foster Care as
a Therapeutic Tool

Even with treatment of the family, children may not be able to remain in the home. Out-of-home care can be foster care or some type of group or residential setting. Ideally, if substitute care becomes necessary, it should not merely be a holding environment but a part of the therapeutic process. Family foster care is usually the first choice after the child's own home but several factors can inhibit effective foster placement.

Problems with Foster Care

Often the court orders that children be placed in foster care for their protection, and the parents are forced to comply. Or, immediately after the disclosure of the abuse, the social service agency may decide that the children are in danger if left at home. Even if the placement is a voluntary agreement between the parents and the social agency, the parents may think they are pleasing the social worker and that placement will be short term. Many parents fail to recognize the implications of such a separation. If the separation is forced, the parents may well have difficulty accepting it. They may even sabotage the placement. Certainly they feel powerless and resentful. Giving up their children to other parents is a clear message of their own failure (Mnookin, 1981; Leifer et al., 1993).

Separation is traumatic for the children and causes conflicts and resistance. Sensitivity on the part of the social workers, foster parents, and natural parents is needed to support the foster child through the separation process (Conlon 1981).

There are elements of instability in foster care. Often the social worker does not know that the court has ruled that the children be returned to their own home. Also, foster parents are free to request the removal of children. Children are, therefore, unsure of where they belong.

In foster care, the child is faced with myriad adjustments. Children must first adjust to separation, to a different lifestyle, new surroundings, possibly a new school, and the new parents' own children, neighbors, and friends. Children from different cultural backgrounds often lose not only their home but their culture when they are placed in a foster home of a different culture. Even if they get used to all these things, the children are still aware of the instability of their situation.

Alternatives to Foster Care

For these and other reasons, foster placement is considered a last resort in protective work. What, then, are the alternatives to foster care? First, the social worker must be creative in examining means to protect the children in their own homes. The concept of family preservation (discussed in Chapter 13) may be one alternative to placement. Minuchin (1970) and Garbarino and Stocking (1980) advocate the use of natural support systems, such as extended family members, neighbors, the school, religious affiliations, and community groups. African-American *kinsmen* and Hispanic *compadres* often provide resources for children of their cultures. Research has shown that placement of Native American children with Native American families increases the child's stability and self-concept (Thorne, 1988). Finding these resources and contracting with them to provide support for the family is time consuming, which may account for social services not fully using these systems.

Second, the exact reason for placement must be analyzed. Is the child really in imminent danger, or does placement represent an easy solution? Working with maltreating families can be terribly frustrating, whereas coordinating services, aided by competent foster parents, may be less so. If the request for placement originates from the natural parents, their motivations must be fully explored. Do they feel compelled to place their child, or are they asking for placement in response to stresses that seem overwhelming? Often these issues can be addressed therapeutically without the removal of the children. And finally, the social service system must examine the family's potential for providing adequate child care. Would a variety of remedial and support services strengthen the family sufficiently so that placement could be avoided?

Therapeutic Potential in Foster Care

In some situations, foster placement is inevitable. In these cases, steps should be taken to ensure that foster care provides the greatest therapeutic atmosphere possible. With children from different cultures, placements in foster homes of similar cultures may enhance the therapeutic effect. There are several inherent positive aspects for the child in placement.

Foster care provides an opportunity for diagnostic screening. In a somewhat controlled atmosphere that is relatively independent of parental influence, social workers can assess delayed development and explore the children's language abilities. Infants with failure-to-thrive syndrome or who exhibit other problems related to nurturance are fed carefully and monitored. Based on these assessments, the workers can derive appropriate treatment plans.

Despite the pressures inherent in foster care, the foster home provides the child with some distance from the fears and conflicts of his or her home environment. Children learn that they need not fear abuse, that their needs are met, and that they can begin to predict the behavior of the adults around them. Admittedly, not all children respond immediately, but foster care provides an atmosphere where the healing can begin to take place (Jones, 1990).

Foster parents provide new and more positive models for their charges. Well-screened and well-matched foster parents promote positive growth and development in the children. They present reasonable expectations and consistent discipline. Ideally the marital relationship demonstrates to children that people can live together in trust and harmony.

Inherent in this assumption is that the agency effectively screened the foster parents initially and also took care to match this particular child with the household. Inadequate screening could result in foster parents responding to the pathology of the foster child, and themselves replicating the dysfunctional behavior of the natural parents.

With foster care, the agency can remedy problems in the child's developmental delays, nutritional deficits, and unmet medical needs. The family gives the child adequate stimulation, which begins to compensate for development delays. They make medical appointments and administer medication. The foster home represents a controlled environment where some degree of consistency in these remedial procedures can be ensured (Martin, 1976; Pecora et al., 1992).

A relatively new type of foster home that is much in demand is the home that is willing to accept children who are HIV infected (see Gurdin, 1990). New York State has developed a specialized program for these children. Certain qualifications are expected of these foster parents. First, there must be no other noninfected foster children and preferably no other children under age 6 in the home. Second, the foster family must be convinced that casual contact with the child in their home is not sufficient to infect them with AIDS. The family must be committed to the fact that the child will have numerous medical visits and may eventually die. They must demonstrate an ability to respond effectively to emergencies (Gurdin, 1990, pp. 111–112). Caring for this child must be of top priority, with some family member always at home or on call to meet the child's needs. Obviously, such placements put a considerable amount of stress on foster families. Due to the increased numbers of HIV-infected babies being born—largely of drug-addicted mothers—this type of foster home must be aggressively recruited in the future (Taylor-Brown, 1991).

Because of the extreme stresses associated with parenting HIV-infected children, there is an increasing recognition that agencies must provide these foster families with support. Pietrangelo (1990) describes that in the past these specialized foster families "were left feeling alone, and thinking recurrently, 'I am the only person doing this'" (p. 231). The result is a "particular form of burnout syndrome: diffuse and undirected anger, stress, frustration, anxiety, helplessness, hopelessness, a sense of impending crisis and a diminishing sense of competence and self-worth" (p. 231). Granted, not all HIV-infected children have been abused or neglected (although some states are now entertaining legislation that interprets substance abuse during pregnancy as abusive), but when the residual effects of maltreatment are compounded with the problems of parenting an HIV-infected child, the picture appears overwhelming to most potential foster parents. There promises to be an increased emphasis on services to these specialized foster parents in the future.

The responsibility rests on protective agencies to structure the placement of the child in order to ensure the greatest therapeutic success. Screening of foster parents is important. Attempts should be made in recruiting to find foster parents from all cultures represented by the children placed. Protective workers must know the backgrounds of foster parents, lest they be put in situations that, replicating their own unresolved experiences, they are unable to handle. The agency should know what type of child behavior is unacceptable to these parents. The foster parents may have their own conflicts that prevent them from parenting particular children.

If foster parents are considered part of a team effort to help the child, they will be more amenable to honesty in the screening process and cooperation with the agency (Dawson, 1989). (Unfortunately, some agencies have not yet learned to regard these individuals as team members, adding to the difficulty of the foster parents' job.) The natural parents, too, should be seen as part of the team, though traditionally this has not been practiced. The natural parents are seen as clients and although in some respect they remain so, their roles change slightly after placement of the children. The goal is to ensure what is best for the children and, in this regard, natural parents are as vital a resource as foster parents. Being encouraged to be team members may reduce the competition between these two sets of parents. It is also beneficial for the children to witness a good working relationship between their guardians. Successful placement depends on the continuation of ties between the children and their natural parents.

The Role and Importance of the Natural Parents

Despite the maltreatment the children suffered from their biological parents, the children are, nevertheless, closely tied to and involved with these individuals. The children's experience of living with their parents caused them to adopt personality traits and habits. Children identify with their parents, and cutting off this relationship is like severing a part of the child from himself or herself. Criticisms of the natural parents are felt by the child as criticisms of himself or herself. Because of these ties, children who are totally separated from their parents develop unrealistic ideas about them. They may idealize and deny, or conversely, exaggerate their maltreatment. For healthy growth, children need to learn to see their parents as multidimensional. Continued supportive contact can help them do this.

Feeling abandoned, foster children often perceive that their own weakness, inherent badness, or behavior caused their parents to leave them. Continued contact assures the child that the parents still care. The child may sincerely miss the parents he or she lived with since birth (Littner, 1981; Leifer et al., 1993; Crosson-Tower, 1998).

Instead of engendering feelings of powerlessness and defensiveness, social workers can help natural parents play an integral part in the child's adjustment to foster placement and emotional growth, and eventually facilitate the child's return home. Continued contact with the parents can actually help the child relate better to the foster parents. If children are able to process their feelings of separation and loss and take comfort that their parents care enough to visit, their energies will be freer to bond with the foster parents.

Visiting with the parents allows the child to see them more realistically. When natural parents are relieved of the burden of continuous child care, they may be able to treat the child better during visits and lay the foundation for a more positive relationship. With treatment, parents may be changing and visits will allow them brief periods when they can try out their new understanding and their skills in child management (Littner, 1981; Crosson-Tower, 1998).

The more the natural parents feel part of the team, the easier the return of the child will be. Some agencies suggest that parents—as well as the foster parents—sign a contract that outlines their responsibilities. These contracts give the parents a sense of control and purpose so that they will not need to feel in a position of having to fight about what is being done or sabotage the child's placement. Even when the outcome is the final termination of parental rights, parents can be helped to believe that they have chosen what is best for the child.

There are always cases in which parents are not willing to cooperate. These situations are especially difficult for children, social workers, and foster parents alike. If parents have been approached as part of the therapeutic team and are still unable to respond in a positive manner, other steps must be taken (e.g., permanent termination of parental rights and adoption).

The Role of Foster Parents

It is understandable that foster parents may have difficulty seeing natural parents as part of the team. The biological parents have in some way harmed the child—a fact that most concerned foster parents cannot forget. The natural parents may be difficult to deal with because their pathology often makes them uncooperative, inconsistent, and unpredictable. Their need for control and feelings of failure may result in the natural parents criticizing the foster parents. When children perceive this tension, they are apt to play one set of parents against the other. Many foster parents describe the detrimental effects parental visits have on the children. Conflicted in a variety of ways, children respond to parental visits by regression, acting-out behaviors, and general periods of unhappiness. In their desire to protect the children, foster parents find themselves blaming and growing increasingly angry at the biological parents.

The intensity of these emotional conflicts might block cooperation between foster and natural parents. But supported by the concerned social worker, foster parents can be extremely therapeutic in their approach to natural parents.

> *Anne Todd had been the foster mother to Jimmy for several months before his mother Fran began visiting. Jimmy, age 3, came into foster care because his severe neglect had caused major medical complications. When Fran requested visiting, Anne felt conflicted. Her family had grown to love Jimmy and deplored the condition in which he had come to them. But Anne also realized that the intent was to eventually return Jimmy to his mother. Not only must this mother be given an opportunity to learn to care for him, especially in light of his medical needs, but Jimmy missed his mother and talked of her often. With the support of the social worker, Anne set up regular visits with the natural mother.*
>
> *During these visits, the foster mother modeled proper care for Jimmy and encouraged Fran to emulate her. Fran began to confide in her son's foster mother and derived support from the relationship. Anne encouraged Fran to accompany her to Jimmy's frequent medical appointments and eventually suggested Fran take the responsibility for these appointments herself. Although frustrated by Fran's failure to show up on occasion and having to explain this to Jimmy, Anne realized that her continued patience could only benefit her foster child. In fact, Jimmy seemed to bask in the positive relationship between his foster mother and his natural mother. He delighted in the security of having two families.*
>
> *When an agency conference finally concluded that Fran would never be able to adequately care for Jimmy's medical needs, Anne felt a mixture of sadness and relief. Now the foster mother was able to help Fran accept the future, and Anne felt she had done all she could to facilitate the most therapeutic environment for both mother and child.*

Like Anne, foster parents can serve as models for natural parents, demonstrating appropriate child care. They can ease the transition for the child from home to placement and home again by careful explanation and by allowing the child to express feelings. The foster parent who recognizes the child's need for contact with natural parents, facilitates visiting, and helps to interpret the parents' inconsistencies so that the child sees sides of the natural parents is of great benefit to the child. Criticism of the child's parents not only puts the child on the defensive but robs him or her of the opportunity to see how adults can cooperate despite their faults (Seaberg, 1981; Ryan, McFadden, and Warren, 1981; Henry et al., 1991; Crosson-Tower, 1998).

Some foster parents act as advocates for the children and for their parents (Gil, 1982). For example, because they are in closer contact with the child than the social worker, they often recognize problems that go undetected by the social service agency. Intervening with the school or with medical facilities on the child's behalf is a common task. Since foster parents are often present during visiting between natural parents and children, they are in a position to advocate for parents who are interacting more positively with their children.

Being a foster parent is not easy. Foster parents must learn to cope not only with natural parents but with children who have a variety of behavioral and emotional problems. As one foster mother described it, "Working with foster kids means learning to anticipate their needs. Most of these kids haven't learned to tell you what they want. When they are hurt, they are more apt to withdraw or to act out than to tell you. You try to figure out what's wrong, but it's not always easy."

In reaction to their past experiences, foster children arrive with established behaviors, some of which require the foster parents' patience and creativity. Chronic masturbation, stealing, lying, eating disorders, and pyromania are just a few problems foster parents face. In addition to the behavior of the children, foster parents must deal with the social service agency and its bureaucratic requirements, red tape, and high staff turnover. Each new social worker who takes a child's case may have a different way of operating and thus cause confusion for the foster parents. With heavy caseloads, social workers are not always available when foster parents most need them. Foster parents learn to be resourceful, but the support of the agency and an occasional pat on the back are still helpful.

The competent foster parent is integral in the treatment for the child. To retain competent foster parents and prepare them to meet the myriad of crises they must handle, agencies are supplying more extensive and effective training, providing more consistent support, and making better resources available to them. When placements are well planned, and when foster parents are well screened, trained, and given adequate support, the foster care system can be a valuable resource for abused children.

Other Placement for Abused or Neglected Children

Two other types of placement—residential and adoptive—are considered as last resorts. Residential treatment usually indicates that the child's behavior has deteriorated so greatly that he or she would be too disruptive for a foster home. Adoptive placement terminates parental rights because the court or the social services system determined that the parents were unable to care for the children.

Residential Treatment

As the culmination of unsuccessful attempts at placement in foster care, the abused or neglected child goes into a residential treatment setting. As a result, children arrive there with very little trust and with the firm conviction that they are failures.

The advantages of residential treatment include providing the children with a less intensive emotional atmosphere than may occur in relationships with parental figures. Since their ability to trust has been severely hampered, the children are often unable to tolerate close emotional ties. In addition, children have a greater variety of models, one or more of whom they might feel comfortable and identify with. Behavior—especially acting out—that would not be tolerated in a foster home is more easily accepted in a residential setting.

At the same time, residential treatment provides the structure needed by some disturbed children. The daily environment is regulated to be therapeutic, and training staff oversees the children's activities and monitor their progress. The setting, the staff members, and peer-group pressure are conducive to concentrated treatment (Kadushin, 1980; Pecora et al., 1992).

The assumption in residential treatment, as in foster care, is that the child will return to his or her home or will be placed for adoption. In an institution, the emphasis is on the rehabilitation of the child, rather than helping the child await the parents' rehabilitation. The residential center staff acts as a therapeutic family rather than a substitute family (Whittaker, 1981). By the time children reach residential placement, their problems are complex and their treatment needs are more intensive. Although classwork is often part of the program, sometimes the child goes to the public school but is monitored closely. In addition, the staff offers a variety of therapies that include counseling, group counseling, and particular remedial services (e.g., special education tutoring, medical, dental, etc.).

When it seems likely that the child will go home, the staff emphasizes communication with the family and the family's caseworker. Although family involvement is encouraged, the child's parents are not always ready or able to cooperate. By the time a child reaches residential care, the parents may be less than optimistic about their child rejoining the family. In fact, because of their guilt, they may feel relief that the child is in an institution. The parents sometimes justify that residential treatment proves the child's removal from the home was his or her fault and not theirs. Some parents may want to be involved but don't know how, and many institutions are geographically distant, so transportation is difficult (Whittaker, 1981; Crosson-Tower, 1998).

To ease the child's return home, the parents must be involved. It would be unrealistic to thrust children into the same dysfunctional environment and expect them to thrive (Finkelstein, 1981). Through parental involvement in the residential setting, children can be helped to recognize the problem in their home environment and the parents can be treated in support groups and individually to help them adjust to and handle the children's issues.

When a child is expected to return home, visits that increase in length and frequency aid both family and child to make the transition. When the child was put in residential treatment, the family balance changed, and only with careful preparation will the family be able to accept the removed child and attain a new sense of balance.

Adoptive Placement

A child deserves a stable environment, and if the family will never be able to provide it, adoption may take place. The adoption process with an abused or neglected child should be undertaken slowly and with much preparation. Children must grow to trust the adoption worker whose role is to prepare them for adoption. The child needs time to grieve over the loss of the natural parents and to understand some of the reasons the parents could not keep him or her. Only after this grieving has been completed can the child bond with the new parents. A recent innovative practice is the use of *life books,* written accounts or scrapbooks depicting the child's life to date. Adoption workers encourage the child to create this book, which the child takes with him or her to the adoptive home. The adoptive parents can then talk openly with the child about his or her past and help the child see the natural parents as multidimensional human beings. Witnessing the past merging with the present enables the child to adjust more easily to adoption.

Parents who adopt abused and neglected children must be carefully screened and educated about the residual effects of maltreatment. Unlike babies, older maltreated children come with pasts that may deeply inhibit their ability to trust. Many agencies now train parents more intensively to ensure the success of the adoptive placement.

Summary

An abused or neglected child may need to be placed in foster care. Despite symbolizing failure to the parents and causing instability for the child, foster placement does have advantages. The child is provided with an opportunity to learn to trust in a more functional environment with models who, ideally, embody the more positive aspects of parenting. The agency can use this time for a more accurate diagnosis and supply remedial services when needed.

Although the tendency is for natural parents to feel powerless and, in compensation, criticize both the foster parents and the agency, those parents who are considered part of the therapeutic team are more likely to be engaged in the best interest of the child.

The foster parents must deal with difficulties presented by natural parents as well as those inherent in taking a foster child. Many natural parents are able to look to their children's substitute parents as models for positive parenting.

Abused and neglected children who cannot tolerate foster care are often placed in residential settings. The positive aspects of such a placement are that the child is spared the more intense emotional relationships of a home setting; the child has available a variety of models with whom to identify; and the child is provided with much-needed structure but the institutional setting can better deal with behavior not ordinarily tolerated in a home. If the child is expected to return home, it is important to include the parents as much as possible in the therapy and planning for the child.

When the parents do not appear to be capable of caring for the child in the future, adoptive placement is an option. Children who are placed for adoption require counseling and adequate preparation in order to ensure that this, the last resort in the treatment process, is therapeutically successful.

Exploration Questions

1. How is the effectiveness of foster care often inhibited?

2. What steps must be taken before foster care is considered?

3. What are the advantages of foster care?

4. How should foster parents be viewed?

5. What are the considerations for dealing with the natural parents of children in placement?

6. What is the role of foster parents?

7. Cite other types of placement for children besides foster care. What are the implications of each of these?

Activities for Applied Learning

1. Invite a homefinder (a social worker who studies and approves potential foster parents) to discuss how foster parents are recruited, studied, and supported.

2. Invite a foster parent to speak about his or her experiences in care of abused or neglected children.

Suggested Readings

Gil, E. *Foster Parenting Abused Children.* Chicago: National Committee for the Prevention of Child Abuse, 1982.

Gurdin, P. "Quality Care for Children: A Specialized Foster Care Program." In *Courage to Care: Responding to the Crisis of Children with AIDS,* edited by G. Anderson, pp. 107–19. Washington, DC: Child Welfare League of America, 1990.

Jones, E. P. *Where is Home?: Living Through Foster Care.* New York: Four Walls Eight Windows, 1990.

Pietrangelo, J. "Caregiver Support Groups for Foster and Adoptive Parents." In *Courage to Care: Responding to the Crisis of Children with AIDS,* edited by G. Anderson, pp. 229–45. Washington, DC: Child Welfare League of America, 1990.

Sinanoglu, P. A., and Maluccio, A. N. *Parents of Children in Placement: Perspectives and Programs.* New York: Child Welfare League of America, 1981.

References

Conlon, F. "Family Ties and Child Placement." In *Parents of Children in Placement: Perspectives and Programs,* edited by P. A. Sinanoglu and A. N. Maluccio, pp. 241–67. New York: Child Welfare League of America, 1981.

Crosson-Tower, C. *Exploring Child Welfare.* Boston: Allyn and Bacon, 1998.

Dawson, R. "Improving the Quality of Treatment Foster Care: The Concept of Certification for Providers." *Community Alternatives International Journal of Family Care* 1 (1), (1989): 11–12.

Finkelstein, N. F. "Family-Centered Group Care—The Children's Institution, from a Living Center to a Center for Change." In *The Challenge of Partnership: Working with Parents of Children in Foster Care,* edited by A. N. Maluccio and P. A. Sinanoglu, pp. 89–105. New York: Child Welfare League of America, 1981.

Garbarino, J., and Stocking, S. H. *Protecting Children from Abuse and Neglect: Developing and Maintaining Effective Support Systems for Families.* San Francisco: Jossey-Bass, 1980.

Giardino, A. P., Christian, G. W., and Giardino, E. R. *A Practical Guide to the Evaluation of Child Abuse and Neglect.* Thousand Oaks, CA: Sage, 1997.

Gil, E. *Foster Parenting Abused Children.* Chicago: National Committee for the Prevention of Child Abuse, 1982.

Gurdin, P. "Quality Care for Children: A Specialized Foster Care Program." In *Courage to Care: Responding to the Crisis of Children with AIDS,* edited by G. Anderson. Washington, DC: Child Welfare League of America, 1990.

Gustavsson, N. S. and Segal, E. A. *Critical Issues in Child Welfare.* Thousand Oaks, CA: Sage, 1994.

Henry, D.; Cossett, D.; Aulette, T. and Egan, E. "Needed Services for Foster Parents of Sexually Abused Children." *Child and Adolescent Social Work Journal* 8 (2), (1991): 127–140.

Jones, E. P. *Where is Home?: Living Through Foster Care.* New York: Four Walls Eight Windows, 1990.

Kadushin, A. *Child Welfare Services,* New York: Macmillan, 1980.

Leifer, M.; Shapiro, J. P.; and Kassem, L. "The Impact of Maternal History and Behavior upon Foster Placement and Adjustment in Sexually Abused Girls." *Child Abuse and Neglect* 17 (6), (1993): 755–766.

Littner, N. "The Importance of the Natural Parents to the Child in Placement." In *Parents of Children in Placement: Perspectives and Programs,* edited by

P. A. Sinanoglu and A. N. Maluccio, pp. 269–75. New York: Child Welfare League of America, 1981.

Martin, H. (ed.). *The Abused Child.* Cambridge, MA: Ballinger, 1976.

Minuchin, S. "The Plight of the Poverty Stricken Family in the United States." *Child Welfare* 49 (1970):124–30.

Mnookin, R. H. "Foster Care: In Whose Best Interest?" In *Parents of Children in Placement: Perspectives and Programs,* edited by P. A. Sinanoglu and A. N. Maluccio, pp. 191–233. New York: Child Welfare League of America, 1981.

Pecora, P. J.; Whittaker, J. K.; Maluccio, A. N.; with Barth, R. P. and Plotnick, R. D. *The Child Welfare Challenge: Policy, Practice, and Research.* New York: Aldine DeGruyter, 1992.

Pietrangelo, J. "Caregiver Support Groups for Foster and Adoptive Parents." In *Courage to Care: Responding to the Crisis of Children with AIDS,* edited by G. Anderson, pp. 229–45. Washington, DC: Child Welfare League of America, 1990.

Ryan, P.; McFadden, E. J.; and Warren, B. L. "Foster Families: A Resource for Helping Parents." In *The Challenge of Partnership: Working with Parents of Children in Foster Care,* edited by A. N. Maluccio and P. A. Sinanoglu, pp. 189–208. New York: Child Welfare League of America, 1981.

Seaberg, J. R. "Foster Parents as Aides to Parents." In *The Challenge of Partnership: Working with Parents of Children in Foster Care,* edited by A. N. Maluccio and P. A. Sinanoglu, pp. 209–20. New York: Child Welfare League of America, 1981.

Taylor-Brown, S. "The Impact of AIDS on Foster Care: A Family-Centered Approach to Services in the United States." *Child Welfare,* 70(2) (Mar-April 1991):193–209.

Thorne, W. "Child Abuse and N. Americans: Cultural Dimensions to Multidisciplinary Interventions." Workshop at the National Symposium on Child Victimization, Anaheim, CA, April 30, 1988.

Whittaker, J. E. "Family Involvement in Residential Treatment: A Support System for Parents." In *The Challenge of Partnership: Working with Parents of Children in Foster Care,* edited by A. N. Maluccio and P. A. Sinanoglu, pp. 67–88. New York: Child Welfare League of America, 1981.

16 CHAPTER

The Social Worker
and the System

The reality of the workings of a protective service agency and the ideal—or what should happen—sometimes diverge. An interview with a worker about a typical day illustrates both the principles and practices of protective services.

A Day in the Life of a Protective Worker

Gina Kirby has been with the agency for several years. She is a vivacious, enthusiastic, and competent worker who takes her job seriously. Gina described her most recent day:

"I got to the office at 8:45, my tea and danish in hand, with a plan for my day. My first task was to pick up a 5-year-old at his foster home and take him to a hospital 20 miles away for a psychological evaluation. Since this appointment had been difficult to arrange, I was anxious to keep it. I was scheduled to sit in on a conference at a nearby school later in the morning. The school had recently enrolled one of our adolescent clients, and the staff felt the girl had some special learning problems. The meeting was to include her teachers, the psychologist, her parent, her parent's therapist, and several other professionals involved in the case. I hoped to return to the office for lunch with several of my fellow workers—something we had been planning but never seemed to manage. In the afternoon, after getting up to date on paperwork, I would visit two foster homes I was supervising and drop in on a neglectful mother I had been monitoring. A full day to say the least.

"As I was leaving to pick up Timmy for his psychological examination, my phone rang. A call from the police alerted me to a crisis on which I had to take immediate action, including filing a petition with the court for the protection of a 7-month-old baby and appearing at the emergency hearing that afternoon. Using the form our office had developed to simplify the procedure, I took down the necessary information. As I finished on the phone, I wondered how I'd rearrange my day to include this emergency.

"'I'll file the court petition for you,' assured a sympathetic voice. Harry Sloane, my supervisor, gave me his usual cheerful smile. 'Get going,' he urged. 'Mrs. Gomez is expecting you.' He took the intake form and waved me out the door, calling, 'I'll also cover your school meeting and cancel your afternoon visits.' Harry and I, as supervisor and worker, had a good working relationship. I kept

him up to date on my activities and, as a result, he frequently covered for me when I was faced with the inevitable emergency calls.

"As I hurried out, I passed the homefinder's desk. 'I have a 7-month-old girl going to court this afternoon; could you line up a foster home in case I need it?' I asked.

" 'Sure,' she said. In our office, foster homes are found and screened by one unit of workers. When we need a home for a child, we give one of these workers the information, and they give us a listing on a foster home that seems appropriate and is available.

"Marcia Gomez, Timmy's veteran foster mother had him ready when I arrived. I was thankful for her efficiency. The drive to and from the hospital and the evaluation were uneventful. By half-past twelve, I was headed toward the office to pick up the foster home information. While Timmy was being tested, my supervisor had called me at the hospital to let me know that the hearing was at 1:00 P.M.

"With those time constraints in mind, I swung through a drive-in and got a burger and coffee for the road. So much for my lunch plans. Back at the office, no foster home had been located yet. The homefinder assured me she would have one by the time I was out of court, so I arranged to return to the office to pick up the information.

"By 1:00, I was at the courthouse, waiting and hoping my lunch would finally digest. Knowing I could wait anywhere from fifteen minutes to two hours for our case to be heard, I made some mental notes about the clients with whom I'd soon be working. A mother sat on the opposite bench; she had reportedly left her severely neglected 7-month-old baby alone overnight. The neighbors had called the police. The mother looked more like a child herself. As I introduced myself and talked with her, I noticed that she was disheveled and pale and appeared terribly frightened. She held her infant daughter on her lap and smoked one cigarette after another. I could almost feel her pain and fear. The baby sat listlessly on her mother's lap. She was small for her age, barely able to sit up, and her uncombed hair seemed lifeless and lacking the luster of that of a healthy baby. Her nose was encrusted and she coughed frequently.

"After half an hour, our case was heard. In a small room, which looked not unlike a classroom except for the elevated bench, the judge listened to police officers and neighbors who described how Melanie Merchant had continually neglected baby Kimberly until all concerned feared for her safety. Considering the facts and since Melanie was about to be evicted from her apartment, the judge ordered that Kimberly be placed in a foster home while our agency worked with her mother.

"Ms. Merchant showed little affect when I talked to her after the hearing. She seemed in shock, not believing that her child was being taken away from her. I tried to empathize with her, but found it difficult to penetrate her protective shell. 'We'll need to work on a service plan together,' I explained. 'This is a plan for helping you to visit Kim.' I further explained that the service plan would give us both guidelines and goals toward which we could work such as finding housing *for her and eventually getting her daughter back. (Mentally I added, 'if that's what you want,' remembering clients who had decided eventually that parenting was just too overwhelming for them.) We agreed that Ms. Merchant would return home, get clothes and diapers for Kimberly, and meet me at the office in an hour. At that time we could do the service plan, or if she preferred, we could just talk and complete the plan in a few days. She agreed and wordlessly handed me her daughter.*

"It always depresses me somewhat to take a child from a parent, no matter how much it seems warranted. This was no exception. The mother, who I learned was only 17, surely had her own needs too, and I hoped I could help her.

"I put Kim's dirty jacket on her, walked out, and strapped her in a car seat. She watched me closely, but made no overt response. I talked to her soothingly, explaining in soft tones what was happening. I'm not sure babies understand these words, but it always makes me feel better to tell them what's going on.

"Back at the office, another worker, after first insisting on washing Kim, played with her. I chuckled to myself; when I first started as a protective worker the condition of some of the children was difficult for me to take. Now I realized I had almost grown used to it. However, I also knew that the next time I saw this baby in her foster home, she would look different—clean and, very likely, more animated.

"My supervisor greeted me with a report on the school meeting and several other messages that had come in for me. I returned three of the calls, learning that one of my adolescent clients had run away. Tomorrow would be spent trying to track him down.

"The homefinder gave me the name of a competent foster mother whom I then called. I told her the little I knew about Kim, and she said she'd be glad to take her. She hoped I'd be able to bring her soon, however, as the dinner hour became hectic and she would like to talk with me about the baby and any visiting arrangements that had been made. I promised I'd try to get there as soon as possible.

"While I waited for Kim's mother, I filled out authorizations to place her in the foster home and forms so that the foster mother would start getting paid. I also secured a passbook that set up a system whereby Kim could receive medical treatment with a copy of the results of each visit coming to our agency for the file. In the newly opened file, I recorded what had gone on in court.

"By 4:30, it was obvious that Kim's mother was not coming. This meant my going to see her within the next few days, but in the meantime the baby had no diapers or other clothing. Hurriedly—remembering my promise to the foster mother—I put in a request for a purchase order for clothing and diapers, and with the now sleepy baby in my arms, I once again headed for my car. Juggling Kim on my hip, I bought the necessary items. By the time we reached the foster home, dinner preparations were well under way, but the foster parents greeted their new child and me warmly. I explained that visiting had not yet been established and told them what little I knew about Kim's background and needs. The baby, now safely tucked in a crib, slept as if the day had been too much for her. The foster family invited me for dinner, but I assured them that my own family would be awaiting my return.

"By 6:30 I was driving home, exhausted. I thought of the events of the day and made a note of tomorrow's plans:

- *Call Melanie Merchant and arrange to talk with her.*
- *Call Kim's foster mother to find out how the night went.*
- *Begin searching for my runaway.*
- *Record the contacts with Kim's foster family.*
- *Reschedule today's planned visits.*

"The list seemed to go on and on; I found myself thankful for the cooperation of my supervisor and fellow workers at the office. I knew how valuable their teamwork was to me. But I was especially glad for the family who was awaiting me at home."

Although it is difficult to call a day "typical," Gina's experiences are not uncommon. Amidst the crises and confusion, the worker often finds strength in his or her fellow workers and his or her own support system.

What exactly does it take to become a social worker handling a schedule such as this? (In this context, *social worker* does not mean the manner in which the person was trained but that most protective agencies call their employees social workers. Thus, someone with training in any discipline from human services—psychology, sociology, education, or even unrelated fields—could be called a social worker by virtue of the position.)

The Role of a Protective Social Worker

Qualifications and Skills

A social worker, whether protective or one who has another job function, is considered to be a professional (Deutsch, 1983; Popple and Leighninger, 1993). A professional is one who possesses

- A systematic body of knowledge
- Authority because of his or her expertise
- Sanction from the community
- A code of ethics
- A professional culture
- An obligation to professionalism or to perform competently

Knowledge

For protective services, knowledge includes understanding of the abusive or neglectful family and what can be done to help them, as well as a familiarity with interviewing techniques, case reporting, advocacy skills, and so on. Workers should also bring a sensitivity to cultural differences in clients. If there is a high population of a particular culture in the worker's agency, he or she should become knowledgeable in the values of that culture. In addition, the worker must come to the job with (or develop on the job) a sense of how to use the system—from government to community to the agency—to best help the client. Since not all workers bring with them this knowledge, they should have a commitment to acquiring it as soon as possible, whether through orientation training, on-the-job training, or additional schooling.

Authority

Clients and the community assume that protective workers have authority not only because of their knowledge and expertise but because of the authority accorded to them by the community by virtue of the agency in which they work. For example, the community recognizes that protective workers can go to a home and ask to speak with the parents about the maltreatment of their children. If the parents refuse to cooperate, the worker can gain entry with an order from the court. Again, by virtue of the legal or court system, the worker has the authority to place children in foster homes. For professionals, the possession of these three attributes—knowledge, authority, and community sanctions—are intertwined (Popple and Leighninger, 1993).

Ethics

A code of ethics, a professional culture, and an obligation to professionalism or competency are also interrelated for the protective services worker. Most social workers subscribe to the National Association of Social Workers Code of Ethics, but protective services is based on additional assumptions about clients or interpretations of the code. Most protective agencies believe the intact family benefits the child and strive to take this into consideration when making decisions about the client's future. The goal that one tries to carry out in practice is to do as little harm as possible to the child.

One aspect of any social service code of ethics that is vital to protective work is that of confidentiality. *Confidentiality* is defined as "the implicit or explicit agreement between a professional and a client to maintain the private nature of information about a client" (Zastrow, 1985, p. 40). Clients often share very personal aspects of their lives with protective workers. In turn, they expect to have this information kept between the worker and themselves. Because of the ambiguity of the nature of the information passed on to workers, it is important to have a good understanding of the issue of confidentiality. What information must be placed in the file and used for validation of abusive or neglectful behavior? This is sometimes a difficult judgment. Absolute confidentiality has other limits in addition to reporting information in the record or using it for validation in court. Certainly case conferences with supervisors or consultants must include pertinent information. Protective workers, like numerous other professionals, are mandated reporters. Any new incidences of abuse must be substantiated. Workers may also release information to other professionals, provided they have a "release of information" from the client. The important approach to confidentiality is that the client must know what can be kept between the worker and him or herself and what must be shared.

Social service professionals are trained to assume that the client has worth and that he or she has the right to self-determination. Usually self-determination is the right to govern and control one's own life—including accepting (or not accepting) treatment and focusing its content. In protective services, however, the concept is slightly altered. By law, parents who abuse or neglect children are expected to cooperate with the protective agency. If they choose not to, they may be subject to court action. However, within the relationship between worker and client, the parent is encouraged to take as much control over his or her situation as possible. In fact, rehabilitation usually entails helping the parents take control of their own lives.

Professionalism

Protective workers are part of a professional culture that shares an interest in children and families. Theoretically, this interest should reflect universal beliefs from agency to agency and provide a great deal of support for those within the profession. Some of those interested in child abuse and neglect have a network to affirm those beliefs through such forums as the National Conference on Child Abuse and Neglect. At such gatherings, the obligation professionals feel toward abused and neglected children and their families is concentrated. Organizations like the National Center on Child Abuse and Neglect, the National Committee to Prevent Child Abuse, and the C. Henry Kempe National Center for the Prevention and Treatment of Child Abuse and Neglect all provide technical assistance, information, referral, and training to strengthen the network. The American Professional Society on the Abuse of Children provides a newsletter, *The Advisor,* outlining developments in the field. This organization also strengthens the sense of identity of protective workers.

Some workers prefer to do their daily jobs without attempts to share or benefit from the work or ideas of others of their profession. The reality of a *professional culture,* therefore, is that the workers' underlying concern for families and the actions they take differ from agency to agency. In addition, social workers and administrators may hold divergent views on the needs of the clients within the context of overall agency responsibilities. Thus, there is a culture of related professionals who, despite similarities, are often quite different in their views and operations.

Ethnic Competence

As our country becomes more and more diverse in its cultural composition, protective workers must also develop what has been identified as ethnic competence. The training manual in cultural awareness produced by the School of Social Work of the University of Washington (1979) suggests the following procedures for ethnic competence (pp. 18–24):[1]

1. Clarification of the worker's personal values concerning minority persons
2. Articulation of personal and professional values and ways they may conflict with or accommodate the needs of minority clients
3. Interviewing skills reflective of the worker's understanding of the role of language in ethnically distinct communities
4. Ability to relate to minority professionals in ways that enhance their effectiveness with clients
5. Capability of using resources—agencies, persons, research—on behalf of minority communities
6. Techniques for learning the history, traditions, and values of a minority group
7. Ability to communicate information on the cultural characteristics of a given group to other professionals
8. Knowledge of the impact on minority clients of social service policies (see also Atkinson et al. 1993)

Personal Traits

Protective services require certain personal qualities in the workers. As a prerequisite, workers must exhibit warmth, sensitivity, sincerity, and a caring and nurturing attitude. These qualities are essential because so many abusive and neglectful clients need understanding and nurturance. The worker must also be sensitive to the clients' emotions and comfortable in dealing with their pain and helplessness. Yet the same childlike affect that contributes warmth and sensitivity also requires structure. The protective worker will at some time have to be authoritative, confronting, and assertive. Quick decisions are necessary, and these decisions are not always popular. Workers, therefore, must also become comfortable with hostility, especially from clients. Good problem-solving skills and flexibility are vital to success in handling the constant crises and stresses. The protective worker must communicate effectively. He or she should be open to working on a team or cooperating with other agencies on cases. Perhaps two of the most valuable assets in protective work are a sense of humor and an optimistic, but realistic, outlook. Although they cannot minimize the client's problems by unwarranted optimism, they must continue to believe in the client's ability to change. This belief stimulates workers to search for more creative ways of approaching and dealing with client issues.

Responsibilities

The duties of a protective services worker are myriad; Table 16.1 lists only a few of the most important. To accomplish these, an individual needs to have knowledge in several areas: basic helping skills, engagement skills, observation skills, communication skills, empathy skills, and cultural sensitivity.

TABLE 16.1   Basic Duties of a Protective Worker

With Clients	With Collaterals	With Colleagues in the Office
Interviewing for validation	Interviewing reporters for facts	Recording cases
Interviewing to give them emotional support	Discussing children's progress with teachers	Making calls to collaterals
Preparing children for placement	Interviewing relatives to determine best alternative plan for client	Selecting and interviewing approved foster homes
Seeing children regularly in foster homes or in clients' homes	Visiting foster homes	Setting up appointments for clients with other services, such as medical examinations or psychological testing
Visiting client regularly	Visiting schools	Completing forms
Providing transportation to medical and other appointments	Reviewing results of testing	Attending staff meetings
Arranging and orchestrating supervised visits between parents and children	Setting up treatment	Conferring with supervisor
Advocating for clients to obtain specific services	Discussing treatment progress with therapists	Presenting at and attending consultations
Appearing in court		Attending in-service training

The degree to which workers project empathy is sometimes difficult to keep in balance. Although workers become angry with clients who assault or neglect defenseless children, their desire to understand sometimes leads them to rationalize that the clients could not help it because their actions were precipitated by their own chaotic childhoods or by the pressures placed on them. But these parents are not helped by either punishing them for their actions or by overlooking them (Justice and Justice, 1976). Instead, the protective worker must be aware of clients' pressures, but nevertheless hold them accountable for their actions in a helping, nonpunitive manner.

Frustrations and Pressures

Protective services work is sometimes frustrating and filled with pressure (see Figure 16.1). For people interested in joining the profession, knowing about these frustrations and pressures is as important as knowing what qualities are useful and what duties must be performed.

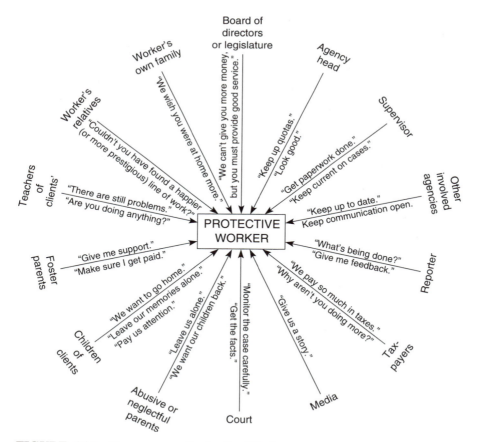

FIGURE 16.1   Pressures on Protective Workers

One basic problem for the worker is to resolve the impact of society's ambivalence toward the job it is asking him or her to do. On the one hand, society expects that children will be well cared for by their parents, but when parents fail, there is outrage. Many people feel that neglectful or abusive parents should be subject to some form of social control. Thus, society supports the protective agencies that assume this task. In fact, the existence of such agencies assures society that something is being done. However, society gives protective agencies little real support. To many people, maltreatment of children is so abhorrent that they prefer not to become involved and hope instead that the agency deals with the family quickly and relatively quietly. Therefore, the protective worker operates with a sense of isolation from the community—accepted on the one hand but mistrusted and ignored on the other. The dilemma is further intensified because the worker, acculturated by society, holds the same views as the general population and may be conflicted about his or her role. Thus, workers frequently feel stress over the conflict of values they feel and the role they must perform (Kadushin and Martin, 1988; Crosson-Tower, 1998).

Identification sometimes becomes a problem for protective workers. Some workers, especially those who experienced unsatisfactory relationships with their own parents, may overidentify with the maltreated child and create additional problems. An unbiased view—one that looks for strengths in both parents and children—is the goal for workers in each case.

Children are not always easy to work with. They lack inhibitions and are apt to react spontaneously. They may act hostile and aggressive, withdraw, or be decidedly uncooperative. Work with these small clients frequently requires shifting gears, changing plans, and being constantly sensitive to the need to explore feelings or offer explanations.

Working within a bureaucracy is also a challenge. Bureaucracies require smooth and efficient operations that are not always compatible with the ideology of protective services. Rules, red tape, and regulations may seem to impede rather than enhance the worker's ability to provide service for his or her clients. Uniform regulations measure clients' eligibility, but people's needs are quite individual. While the bureaucratic system strives to make decisions for efficiency, the worker seeks to make choices that will be of maximum benefit to the client. In addition, the worker hopes these decisions will be reviewed and implemented by those with skill and expertise in the field. But within the bureaucratic structure, decision makers and those in authority often hold their positions regardless of their skills (Zastrow, 1985). In a public agency, the rules may change each time there is a newly elected governor or other official. Because protective services work requires individuals capable of quick thinking, flexibility, and adaptability, the confines of bureaucracy can seem entirely too limiting for many workers. On the other hand, workers see clients who have very little structure in their lives, and it is often necessary for the worker to provide them with some structure.

While the bureaucratic system sometimes seems to bar effective administration of social services, this structure is, in fact, the only way these services can be provided. Bureaucracies are concerned with equity—and the equitable apportionment of limited time and resources. Agencies require rational decision making in areas of human emotions, but the policies and procedures of social agencies provide a much-needed structure. The ideal is to accept the necessity—indeed the importance—of such a structure and learn to use it to better serve clients.

The typical individual who goes into protective service sees himself or herself as tolerant, helpful, and understanding. Often a strong need to be liked conflicts with the demands to make unpopular decisions. The abundance of paperwork and frequent emergencies frustrate the organized worker who feels that it is impossible to ever finish a task. One worker's story is typical.

> *"I came in Monday morning, knowing that I had tons of paperwork from the week before. I had removed two children from their home, necessitating the completion of several forms. A foster mother had not been paid. I had to trace down an adolescent who had run away and placed herself in a friend's home. Not only did I have to check out that situation but I also had to file the appropriate forms to okay it. Several other cases needed similar authorization. I also had to write dictations on every case I had seen or acted on.*
>
> *"Braced by a strong cup of coffee, I sat down to tackle the work on my desk and bring my cases up to date. I had hardly gotten a good start when the phone rang. One of my clients was in crisis. Her husband had beaten their child, and the neighbors, hearing the child's cries, had threatened to call the police. 'Please come at once,' she begged. I felt frustrated at never seeming to get ahead of my cases, but as I put on my coat, I told myself that tomorrow was another day. Maybe tomorrow I'd be able to tackle the pile of paperwork again."*

How do workers cope with the frustrations of protective work? One answer is that despite the fact that this type of work is terribly time consuming, the worker must reserve time for himself or herself. Outside activities that provide pleasure and enable the individual to relax reduce the stresses of the job. Above all, it is important to maintain an adequate support system of people who care. A strong support system is one characteristic that distinguishes workers from their isolated clients.

These frustrations have the potential to cause burnout. Pines and Aronson (1981) define *burnout* as "a state of mind...accompanied by an array of symptoms which include a general malaise; emotional, physical and psychological fatigue; feelings of helplessness; and a lack of enthusiasm about work and even about life in general" (p. 31). The worker experiencing burnout is often short tempered, apathetic, cynical, and discouraged (Richards, 1991).

From a slightly different perspective, Cherniss (1986) speaks of burnout as a "symptom of the loss of social commitment" (p. 219). Caregivers lose their sense of commitment when they feel their work is not sufficiently valued. In protective services, workers face hostile clients who wish they had not become involved with the "helping system." Reporters and collateral agencies question whether workers are doing all they should to aid clients. And the general public, in an attempt to deny the problem of child maltreatment, often places little value on the role of the protective services worker.

A sense of commitment is born out of the workers' recognition of an explicit ideology which then dictates the way in which their roles should be carried out. Approaches to problems are rarely clear cut. There is no one way to work with abusive and neglectful families, and each case requires ingenuity and initiating to decide what will work best. This planning requires an abundance of energy. Frustration results when well-conceived treatment plans must be revised again and again because clients appear unresponsive. With no clear how-to's, workers' energies are often sapped.

To avoid losing their energy and their interest in their work, protective workers require positive leaders and adequate support from both co-workers and administrators. But much of the satisfaction in their professional roles is self-generated. A sense of humanity and adequate self-esteem are vital for the worker to aid families who lack self-esteem and to survive in a system fraught with contradictions.

Does the System Work?

Asked if protective services achieves its ends, social workers have a variety of responses.

> *"It's somewhat schizophrenic to be a worker in such a system," responded one man. "On the one hand you're asked to protect a child, and on the other, you're urged to reunite the family. The dual mandate puts the social worker in the position of knowing that there is a risk that the child will be abused or neglected again. We have the power and authority by virtue of the law to protect children and yet we can't always do it."*

Workers who see children abused or neglected again may feel that the system is not working. Yet another responded:

> *"We do the best we can. Most kids at least are given a chance to have a better life. Sure the system isn't perfect, but until someone designs a better one, it will have to do."*

When asked exactly what the problems were, a worker replied,

> *"Too high a caseload is the biggest one for me. I remember being a student. I only had 10 cases and I really felt I could do something for my clients. Now with 35, I feel I never can keep ahead of them. Good casework needs time. What's the solution? Well, there are more cases being reported than ever, so we need more staff and that's a tough one because more staff means more money and the legislature is not prepared for that."*

Another worker felt that more training would help:

> *"I learned on the job and I wasn't too efficient at first. If I'd been better trained, earlier, maybe I could have provided more services and felt more sure of myself doing it. I'd like to see really good training being done when we're hired. The procedures manual could also be written more readably so you could refer to it from time to time."*

A veteran protective worker suggested:

> *"We need more frequent consultations. I know my job pretty well by now, but there is always that case you just can't get a handle on. A good psychological consultant who came in regularly would be helpful. A lot of agencies have them, but we don't."*

Some workers express concern for their clients:

"The way in which we handle cases here must be tough for the clients. An intake worker sees the family first. Then the case is transferred to someone to investigate. If treatment is necessary, a third worker gets involved. It's difficult if the family begins to trust one worker, and then the case is transferred to someone else. Of course, there are also advantages to this system. The person who does the investigation is often seen by the family as the 'bad guy.' When the treatment worker comes along they often see that person as an ally."

Another worker commented:

"There are never enough services for minority clients. It frustrates me. We have a high Asian population in this area, but there are several nationalities represented— Cambodian, Vietnamese, Laotian, Chinese, Japanese, etc. We never have enough translators and it is impossible for us to become familiar with all these cultures."

Turnover is also a problem. Because of the frustrations, workers often leave after only a year or two, which means their cases are reassigned and their clients must establish new relationships.

"Cooperation and consistency are the important aspects of protective work," said another. "We must present our clients with consistency. Their whole lives have been chaotic and unstable. If we provide a treatment relationship that doesn't give them structure or consistency, we are perpetuating old patterns. The same is true with honesty and cooperation. We must be honest because often they feel no one else has been, and we must encourage cooperation.

"One thing we do which is detrimental is fail to communicate adequately with other agencies. If another agency is involved in the investigation or treatment of a client, we need to keep the communication between us open. If we are feuding, what kind of a model do we provide for the client? We need to show them that it is possible to work together to get things done."

Even with its flaws, the social service system works well in intervening for abused and neglected children. As long as workers provide clients with caring and nurturing, see each one as an individual, promote consistency and cooperation within the structure, and strive to improve the system, there will be hope for doing the job even better. As one worker put it:

"Sure, being a protective worker has its low points, when you wonder what you are doing in this bureaucracy trying to help people who don't seem to want help. But it has its high points, too. I watched a client grow so that the court case was dropped because they felt she really was able to be a good mother. It made me feel great. The teenager, from a neglectful and alcoholic family, who managed to keep herself straight, saw me regularly, and eventually got a scholarship to go to col-

lege to become a social worker made me feel I'd really done something worth-while. I knew I'd had a special impact on her life. For every difficult client there is one who, at some time or in some way, lets you know that you've helped. That's what this work is all about."

Looking Toward the Future

The role of a protective services worker has not become any easier over the years. Granted, there has been a move toward reducing caseloads, but many workers report that the issues have become more complex and the pathology of families greater. Some agencies try to compensate for the difficulty of the job in a variety of ways, but it often falls to individual workers to handle their own mounting stress. For this reason, it is important that the new worker approaches the role in protective services with certain expectations and a degree of preparedness.

Surviving in an Imperfect System

There are some specific tips that may help the protective services worker to cope more effectively.

Know what knowledge you will need and be sure that you are prepared. There are specific areas that are necessary to work with people, especially abusive families. These include such areas as human development, interviewing and counseling skills, psychopathology, case report writing, and sometimes budgeting or grant writing. Most social work, human services, or counseling programs include these areas. But if they do not, or if you have gotten a degree in a subject other than a helping field, you may want to do your own research. Libraries, especially those connected with colleges and universities, offer a variety of titles that could prepare you in these areas. Although you may receive training from the agency, it will be expected that you already have the basics.

Expect formal training when you begin working for an agency. Increasingly agencies are abandoning the old "throw them into the trenches for training" approach and offering formal training periods of several days to several weeks. This is extremely important for your preparation. As more workers expect and/or request such training, it is hoped that more agencies will provide it. Some agencies argue that they do not have the funds to have workers hired who are not out in the field from day one. The reality is that one major lawsuit caused by someone who was untrained and unprepared for the work will cost much more than the resources needed for formalized training.

Expect good supervision. The experienced supervisor is one of the best resources a protective services worker can have. The best supervisors should be given the newer workers, but this is not always the case. The word "expect" used in this context does not mean that you can anticipate good supervision, but rather that you must require it. If your supervisor is not giving you time on a regular basis or does not appear to have the answers you need, it is important that you discuss this either with the person and/or his/her supervisor. Supervision is an excellent way to learn. If you are not learning more about your role through this process, something is wrong.

Develop a personal support system. The worker involved in protective services will be confronted with stress on a daily basis. One of the best ways to cope with this is to have a safe haven to which to return after work. This safe haven may be peopled with family, friends, and a variety of activities you enjoy. Without them, the work will seem much more overwhelming.

Cultivate an at-work support system. The most effective offices are made up of people who support each other and encourage one another's growth. Many offices not only work together but also "play" together. One social worker recounts

> *A group of us from the office planned a hot air balloon trip. Not only was it really fun, but I learned a lot about my co-workers, especially how they handled risk. I found that after that trip we worked with each other better and appreciated each other more.*

Strive to find the best way to serve clients within an imperfect bureaucracy. Agencies run by bureaucracy are not perfect and working within them adds frustration to an already stressful job. But it is also important to learn to serve clients in a manner that does not pit them against the system but rather seeks creative ways to make the system work for the clients. Those who are interested in social services are often those who see change as a positive step. But sometimes we need to learn when change is appropriate and when better things can be accomplished by using the existing structure creatively.

Learn when change is appropriate and work for it. There are sometimes when clients would be better served if the system did change. It behooves the protective services worker to know when proposals for change, organizing toward change, or political lobbying are necessary. It is often those on the "front line" seeing clients who have little or no power, such as children, who must speak out and advocate for them. This is an important part of intervention.

Developing Cultural Awareness and Competence

Another vital aspect of becoming a protective services worker is the development of one's own cultural awareness and competence. Because, in our currently diverse society, this is so important, it will be dealt with in this separate section.

Most protective services case loads today are made up of a variety of people from different races, cultures, and with different values. Fontes (1995) comments that "[L]ack of understanding of oppression issues can [also] impede protective work, in that families are often termed pathological for issues that stem from discrimination or poverty, which results in double victimization" (p. 265). For these reasons, culturally educated workers are of great importance.

Some argue that it is better to hire those from backgrounds that mirror the cultural variations of the clientele. Fontes (1995) argues that this is not always possible, and therefore workers must learn about other cultures in order to be effective in their work. Granted, it should be the role of the protective agency to identify the diverse populations served and provide training for workers on cultural differences, but the reality is that this does not always happen. Therefore, it may fall to individual workers to make themselves into culturally competent practitioners.

Leigh (1998) suggests that, to be culturally competent, a worker must recognize that culture shapes values and behavior and that the family as defined by each culture is the place where one should intervene. One must recognize that there is also diversity within each culture and accept that although individuals may be in tune with their culture, they may also be motivated by subgroups or by their own subjective needs. It is also vital to acknowledge that, because the process is often as important as the product for people, the manner in which they are treated, and especially how that fits with their cultural expectations, is important.

How does one learn about other cultures? Leigh (1998) encourages the worker to *listen to those of other cultures as they tell their stories,* with an open mind, trying not to have the blinders of one's own cultural background. Having someone in the workplace or outside who is willing to explain the values of a particular culture can be helpful. But what if there is no one to do this? *Many colleges offer courses in the culture* of some larger groups. For example, Hispanic culture is taught at some institutions. Many look at the culture of geographic regions such as Caribbean culture or the culture of the Middle East. Taking a course in a language such as Spanish will often help one gain some insight into cultural values or rituals. *Community groups may have workshops* in cultural issues. For example, one church, finding they had a large population of Hmongs (a Laotian subgroup), invited a speaker to acquaint community leaders, educators, and others who were interested in learning more about the diverse customs of these people. Certainly *travel* can offer valuable insights but this may not always be possible. And libraries provide a few excellent books on various cultures. For example, Fontes' (1995) *Sexual Abuse in Nine North American Cultures* is one place to begin.

The question arises, what should one learn about cultures? Leigh (1998) suggests that one look for cultural variations in the areas of work, time, space, language, and roles. Further, he contends that differences may also be sought when considering how people see the individual versus the group, the rituals and superstitions present in cultures, class, and status issues, and what people value (pp. 25–28).

However one goes about becoming culturally competent, it is an important task for the protective social worker facing the next century.

Summary

Protective workers are considered to be professionals who possess a systematic body of knowledge, authority, sanction by the community, a code of ethics, a professional culture, an obligation to competence, and ethnic competence.

The duties of such a professional require specific knowledge, the most important of which are skills in basic helping, engagement, observation, and communication. Empathy is a primary personal trait required for the job.

Protective services work entails frustrations. Workers must first resolve any conflict about their role and how society views that role. Workers sometimes have difficulty overidentifying with clients—especially children. On the other hand, children are challenging clients; their spontaneity sometimes makes their behavior unpredictable and difficult to handle.

Bureaucracies present some difficulties to protective services workers. Rules and regulations can be frustrating when the worker is concerned with the needs of clients and must be flexible in order to meet them. This same structure, however, provides a framework for equity and a model of consistency.

The stresses of protective work can result in burnout. For this reason, it is important that workers develop methods of reducing this stress, especially through outside recreation and the maintenance of a healthy support system.

In spite of the frustrations of protective services, workers allude to the benefits brought about by the success stories. In addition to the client, who does make one feel needed, there is usually good support among co-workers. As one worker put it, "We work very hard at this job, so we play hard too." And it is good to know that through the efforts of the worker, children may be spared further abuse. It is these benefits that make work with abused and neglected children an extremely rewarding profession. To face the future, workers must learn to anticipate the pitfalls of the work and develop their own cultural competence.

Exploration Questions

1. List the frustrations experienced by Gina Kirby in her "typical" day. How was she helped to deal with them?

2. What constitutes a professional?

3. What are some of the elements of a protective worker's code of ethics?

4. What are the confines of confidentiality in protective services?

5. What are some of the qualifications necessary for a protective worker?

6. The duties of a worker require knowledge in specific areas. What are they?

7. What are some of the frustrations of protective work?

8. How can one combat burnout?

9. What problems do protective workers see with the system?

10. How does one develop cultural competence?

Activities for Applied Learning

1. Interview a protective worker about his or her "typical" day, or ask him or her to speak to the class.

2. What qualities do you feel you have that would be helpful in protective services? In what areas might you have difficulty?

3. What concerns would you have about going into protective work? Is there a way to prepare yourself to overcome these concerns?

4. Can you remember a time when you felt burnout? Write down how you felt and how you pulled yourself out of this slump.

5. What do you do to relieve stress? Assess your methods of stress reduction. How effective are they?

6. Read *Tender Mercies*, by Keith Richards. How would you react to some of the situations described?

Suggested Readings

Deutsch, F. "Professionals: No Promise of a Rose Garden." In *Child Services: On Behalf of Children,* edited by F. Deutsch, pp. 208–23. Monterey, CA: Brooks/Cole Publishing, 1983.

Jackson, H., and Nuttall, R. *Childhood Abuse: Effects on Clinicians' Personal and Professional Lives.* Thousand Oaks, CA: Sage, 1997.

Kadushin, A. "The Sociology of the Child Welfare Worker." In *Child Welfare Services,* edited by A. Kadushin, pp. 673–700. New York: Macmillan, 1980.

Leigh, J. W. *Communicating for Cultural Competence.* Boston: Allyn and Bacon, 1998.

Pines, A., and Aronson, E. *Burnout: From Tedium to Personal Growth.* New York: Free Press, 1981.

Richards, K. *Tender Mercies: Inside the World of a Child Abuse Investigator.* Chicago: Noble Press, 1992.

Endnote

1. Excerpt from Cultural Awareness in the Human Services: A Training Manual, Center for Social Welfare Research, School of Social Work, University of Washington, Seattle, Washington, 1979, pp. 18–24.

References

Atkinson, D. R.; Morten, G. and Sue, D. W. *Counseling American Minorities.* Dubuque, IA: Wm. C. Brown and Benchmark, 1993.

Cherniss, C. "Different Ways of Thinking About Burnout." In *Redefining Social Problems,* edited by E. Seidman and J. Rappaport, pp. 217–28. New York: Plenum, 1986.

Crosson-Tower, C. *Exploring Child Welfare.* Boston: Allyn and Bacon, 1998.

Deutsch, F., ed. *Child Services: On Behalf of Children.* Monterey, CA: Brooks/Cole Publishing, 1983.

Fontes, L. A. *Sexual Abuse in Nine North American Cultures.* Thousand Oaks, CA: Sage, 1995.

Justice, B., and Justice, R. *The Abusing Family.* New York: Human Services Press, 1976.

Kadushin, A. and Martin, J., eds. *Child Welfare Services,* 2nd ed. New York: Macmillan, 1988.

Leigh, J. W. *Communicating for Cultural Competence.* Boston: Allyn and Bacon, 1998.

Pines, A., and Aronson, E. *Burnout: From Tedium to Personal Growth.* New York: Free Press, 1981.

Popple, P. R. and Leighninger, L. *Social Work, Social Welfare, and American Society.* Boston: Allyn and Bacon, 1993.

Richards, K. *Tender Mercies: Inside the World of a Child Abuse Investigator.* Chicago: Noble Press and Washington, DC: The Child Welfare League of America, 1991.

University of Washington. *Cultural Awareness in Human Services: A Training Manual.* Center for Social Welfare Research, School of Social Work, University of Washington, Seattle, Washington, 1979.

Zastrow, C. *The Practice of Social Work.* Chicago: Dorsey Press, 1985.

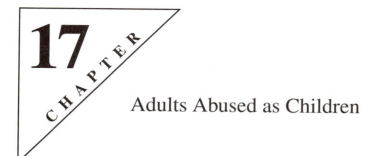

Adults Abused as Children

The last few chapters have explored intervention and treatment of child abuse and neglect as a way of alleviating the child's suffering. When society intervenes, it does so with the hope that the children will at least be able to understand the abuse and neglect and thus allow them to face adulthood with the freedom to make appropriate choices. Although social service intervention is not always successful, past victims of abuse who had not disclosed are now coming forward and elaborating on how their isolation from any kind of help intensified their suffering.

Society's Misconceptions

Society has accepted as truth several myths regarding adults who were abused as children. There are, however, other perspectives to consider.

Myth #1

The individual who was abused or neglected will abuse or neglect his or her own children.

This myth is actually the misinterpretation of a much-used statistic gleaned from studies, by several researchers, that showed that of those parents who physically and sexually abuse their children, a large percentage had themselves been abused as children. This does not mean, however, that individuals who have been abused will necessarily become abusers. Healing the hurt and changing the pattern of abuse is possible. Sometimes insight, understanding, and thought are sufficient to turn the abused from repeating the mistakes of their childhood.

On the other hand, neglect, statistically, tends toward a multigenerational pattern. Parents who neglect fail not only to meet their children's needs but to provide adequate parenting models. But, once again, adults who recognize the dysfunctional patterns of their families of origin may be better able to work toward overcoming them in their nuclear families.

Myth #2

Abused and neglected children become deviant adults, involved in crime, drugs, or prostitution.

Of those involved in crime, drugs, and prostitution, many were abused or neglected, but not all past victims lean toward a deviant lifestyle in adulthood. For every inmate of a correctional facility who was abused as a child, there may be 50 or more who were abused but have not turned toward deviant behavior. Abuse can create anger and bitterness, but each victim directs or channels this anger differently.

Myth #3

The effects of abuse or neglect are irreparable and render the future adult incapable of leading a fulfilling and happy life.

Once again, the myth distorts the whole picture. The abuse or neglect is irreparable only in that it is history: It happened and that fact cannot be undone. The child is left with scars, but these scars need not prevent the emerging adult from leading a fulfilling life.

Successful survivors of child abuse say they have learned not to live in the past. The past—with its memories of abuse—represents pain and a sense of helplessness and powerlessness. Control of the individual's life was seen as "outside" himself or herself. To survive and succeed, the victim must recognize that

1. The abuse or neglect did happen and exists as part of one's childhood history.
2. At that time, the victim had little control (by virtue of being a child) over what was happening.
3. Although the victim cannot change the past, he or she can affect the future.
4. By taking control of one's own life, one can have a fulfilling life in spite of the residual scars of childhood.

Many past victims have learned to regain control of their own lives and have overcome what were the burdens of childhood. Whether or not they have complete control of their lives, the reality is that adults abused as children *survived* the abuse. For this reason, many authors and therapists refer to these individuals as abuse *survivors*. Some survivors point out that survival is not a destination but rather, surviving the after-effects of childhood maltreatment is an ongoing process.

Reasons for Adults' Disclosure

If the survivor's history of abuse or neglect is not made obvious through some form of deviant behavior, how is it recognized? Some past victims never disclose that they suffered maltreatment. Although some do attempt to tell a therapist or friends, they are often not heard. They may not know the words to use, or more likely the therapist or friend is not able to be receptive, possibly because of his or her own conflicts. One survivor's story emphasizes this problem.

> *"I was in therapy for almost nine years. I had problems in my marriage, an array of affairs, and an overwhelming fear of failure. I had pushed what had happened to me—the fact that my father sexually and physically abused me—out of my mind. But I began having nightmares—remembering only bits. I kept trying to describe the dreams to my therapist. Finally I was able to piece it together. I remembered exactly what my father had done. It was as if my therapist couldn't believe it. But who could make up the horrible, bizarre details of what happened!*

> *"Soon after I told him, my therapist suggested we end our sessions. I was dev-astated. I vowed then to never again share my horrible secret. That was 12 years ago—and I haven't told anyone again—until now."*

Fortunately, therapists are now becoming better trained in the area of abuse—espe-cially sexual abuse. Part of this training should aim to make them aware of why they are reluctant to hear about child maltreatment.

Survivors disclose their sexual or physical abuse in later life for a variety of reasons.

Relationships

Relationships often determine the decision to talk about what had previously been a well-guarded secret. Some survivors want to be completely honest with their partners. There may be an element of need—the need to be accepted and loved by this intimate in spite of any event or relationship in the past. Low self-esteem may also push the survivor to disclose sexual abuse. These individuals, consciously or unconsciously, feel they have been tainted by the abuse and will, therefore, be rejected by their loved ones. Their ability to trust is often so limited that they are sure that husbands, wives, or lovers could never accept the "evil" they feel is theirs. The survivors often disbelieve accepting, sympathetic mates, but reject-ing mates reinforce their damaged trust.

Sexual dysfunction in the present affects relationships. Past victims often avoid sexual intimacy and isolate themselves from relationships that lead to sex. Conversely, they some-times behave promiscuously, which excludes closeness or deep feelings of attachment. When a relationship does have meaning, however, the survivor often finds it difficult to feel comfortable.

> *Lisa was a college senior who sought counseling because she was deeply involved with a fellow student, but could not tolerate his sexual advances. The two had dated for six months with no sexual contact. When Ed initiated sex with affection and tenderness, Lisa began having anxiety attacks. Subsequent counseling revealed that Lisa had been sexually abused by a brother for several years. She had felt close to this brother, but when the sexual abuse began she felt betrayed and used. Now she saw Ed's sexual advances in the same light.*

Sex therapists seeing couples who complain of sexual dysfunction often discover that one or both partners were victims of sexual abuse. There is some evidence that physical abuse also creates a mistrust of sexual involvement.

Pressures of Adulthood

Developmental issues also precipitate disclosure in late teens and early adulthood. The first deeply intimate relationship is one such issue. However, stress and fears related to career or financial success may cause the survivor to feel undeserving or unprepared and thus precip-itate disclosure. Past victims frequently do not relate these present issues with the abuse and usually only discover the connection while in therapy. The birth and growth of the survivor's own children stimulates memories of the individual's own dysfunctional childhood.

> *"When Robbie was born I kept wondering—no, more than wondering, I was obsessed with what kind of a mother I'd be. My mother was an alcoholic and my father beat my brother and me. To make up for the way my mother neglected me, I was probably overprotective. But the worse part was that whenever Bill touched Robbie, I'd get really tense. 'Don't hurt him,' I'd say, as if my husband would. It got so bad that I'd hardly let Bill touch our son. I knew I had to get some help. I told my friend about the abuse. I'd never told anyone. Ours was such a perfect family. My mother hid her drinking well and no one would have ever suspected that Dad beat us. But I began to realize that I was seeing all fathers as hurting their kids."*

As children grow, parents see themselves in their offspring and consequently fear for their children's safety. Often this fear leads the adults to talk about their abuse.

> *Jane began having severe headaches and muscle pains when April was 8 years old. Concerned about her mother, April often came directly home from school to be with her. Jane's mother insisted that Jane seek medical advice. No organic reason could be found, and the physician suggested that Jane seek therapy. Jane refused. Several months later, April's teacher expressed her concern about April's preoccupation and inattention in school. When Jane realized that April's fears were of her dying, she sought help. Intensive therapy disclosed that at age 8, Jane had been repeatedly sexually abused by a neighbor. She began to understand her fears about April's walking to school or going out in the neighborhood as an intense need to protect her daughter from what had happened to her.*

Loss, Depression, or Trauma

Loss is often a problem for those who have survived dysfunctional families. Losses in adulthood may precipitate a need to face the original loss—the deprivation of a loving, protecting, or nonabusive family. Thus, disclosure can be associated with death of a loved one, death of the perpetrator, the nonprotecting parent, children leaving home, loss of a job, and a variety of other normal changes in life.

And finally, some past victims begin to explore their childhoods to overcome persistent, nonspecific, and often nondebilitating depression, usually caused by low self-esteem.

> *"I just never thought much of myself," said Bruce. "I don't know why, but I just figured I wasn't worth much." Bruce had been raised by two alcoholic parents who were severely neglectful. He had learned early how to survive and as a result had made a success of his life. It was not until he considered the pain of his childhood, though, that he could even begin to appreciate his own successes.*

It is rare that a flash of insight prompts disclosure of abusive or neglectful family backgrounds. Often the perception and understanding of past dysfunctional family life is clouded by present life stresses. The pieces of memory emerge slowly and must be fitted together in an understandable pattern so that the victim can face them. Some individuals struggle for a lifetime to gain this understanding. Others prefer not to risk reexperiencing the pain and they never discuss what happened to them. Some sexual abuse survivors are jolted into reexperiencing and remembering childhood abuse by trauma in adult life. For example, many adult rape victims are reminded of issues they have repressed as they attempt to put the current rape in perspective.

For most survivors, the symptoms of the residual effects of the abuse precede the recognition of their origin. Therefore, it is important to consider the residual effects in some depth.

Residual Effects of Child Abuse and Neglect

In the 1970s, Ray E. Helfer, pediatrician, therapist, and expert in the area of child abuse, coined the acronym WAR, for the World of Abnormal Rearing (Helfer, 1978), to refer to the experiences of children who were exposed to dysfunctional families. Victims of WAR, Helfer says, have not learned some basic lessons. Mentioned in Chapter 5, these unlearned skills include

1. How to get their needs met appropriately
2. How to delay gratification
3. How to make decisions
4. How to take responsibility for their own actions
5. How to separate feelings from actions

Because symptoms may mask the real problem, therapists often do not recognize that their clients did not learn these tasks. The residual effects of neglect, abuse, and sexual abuse are quite similar (see Table 17.1). However, there is value in considering the way in which these emotional scars manifest themselves depending on the type of maltreating family.

TABLE 17.1   Residual Effects of Familial Maltreatment

Physical Abuse	Neglect	Sexual Abuse
Difficulty trusting others	Difficulty trusting others	Difficulty trusting others
Low self-esteem	Low self-esteem	Low self-esteem
Anxiety and fears	Anger	Anxiety and fears
Physical problems	Impaired object relations	Shame and guilt
Anger	Impaired parenting abilities	Physical problems
Internalization of aggression	Lowered intelligence	Anger
Depression	Impaired development	Self-abusive tendencies
Difficulty with touching	Verbal inaccessibility	Depression
Inability to play	Inability to play	Difficulty with touching
Difficulty with relationships	Difficulty with relationships	Inability to play
Abuse of alcohol and drugs	Abuse of alcohol and drugs	Distorted view of body
Perception of powerlessness	Perception of powerlessness	Difficulty with relationships
		Abuse of alcohol and drugs
		Perception of powerlessness
		Sexual problems

Effects from the Neglecting Family

Trust

The personalities of all types of maltreatment survivors exhibit difficulty with trust. Trust is a basic aspect of socialization, and the development of our ability to trust begins in the first years of life. Society expects babies to be nurtured by a loving parent or parents who allow them to develop free from harm. A child who does not receive these entitlements may not recognize it initially, but as an adult the individual begins to realize that his or her parents were emotionally unavailable.

In adulthood, the betrayal is reflected by

- An inability to trust others
- An inability to trust self
- An inability to trust the environment

Parents of neglected children provided little—or at least inconsistent—nurturing and support. Indifference characterizes the parents' relationship with their children, which becomes a pattern on which the children model their own behavior. Their expectations of support, attention, and stimulation become a distant memory (Briere, 1992). As adults, they no longer expect that their needs will be met, but these individuals desperately desire nurturance. The result is that many past victims of neglect demonstrate dependency with little underlying trust. History has taught them that people are not trustworthy. Polansky, Borgman, and DeSaix (1972) described neglectful mothers, most of whom had been themselves neglected as children, as demonstrating an "absence of intense personal relationships beyond forlorn clinging, even to [their] children" (p. 54). So pervasive is this lack of hope and trust that it often infects the helpers who deal with neglectful families.

Required to provide for themselves at an early age, survivors of neglect might be expected to develop some degree of proficiency. Although past victims demonstrate an ability to survive despite incredible odds, they lack a true sense of trust in themselves. Not only have they lacked encouragement and stimulation to develop a healthy self-image but they have modeled themselves on parents who thought little of themselves also. Comprehending that one was not loved can be so devastating that the survivor turns inward and assumes he or she must have deserved being treated with such indifference (Polansky et al., 1981; Briere, 1992). Lack of trust in one's self is manifested by an inability to make decisions, extremely low self-esteem, an inability to accept one's own accomplishments, as well as other types of self-defeating behavior.

Often neglected children were exposed to deviant subcultures, the members of which see themselves as different from the greater society. The school and the community frequently accentuate these differences. In addition, many of these children have learning disabilities.

"I kept hearing from day one that nobody understood where we was comin' from," said Chico, the past victim of neglect in a largely rundown neighborhood. "The bunch of us in our block stuck together. We smoked grass and just did our thing. Our parents didn't care and no one else did. But we got a reputation, see. They

*said we was tough, and we maybe tried to prove how tough we really was. I got so
as I knew that if you wasn't from Broad Street, you wasn't worth trusting."*

Chico's inability to trust permeated his life. He had difficulty in school and was frequently suspended, thus reinforcing his feelings that he could trust no one.

Anger

Anger often creates problems for the survivor. Feeling robbed of childhood, betrayed, and
powerless, the adult reacts to the injustice with anger, which can become an intense rage.
The past victim may turn the anger inward or act out the anger toward others.

Anger turned inward results in depression and self-abusive tendencies. Adele, severely
neglected as a child, had difficulty parenting her own children. She demonstrated an emotional numbness and a stubbornly negative attitude that social workers confused with
chronic depression.

For some neglected children, anger is expressed through aggressive or delinquent
behavior. Polansky, Borgman, and DeSaix (1972) refer to the process that leads to delinquency or acting out of anger as the *deprivation-aggression sequence.* Failure to meet a
child's basic needs results in frustration. Frustration translates into aggression. Bender
(1948) also attributes aggressive behavior to unmet needs: "Since the child is under the
impression that adults can satisfy his needs, he considers any deprivation an act of aggression and reacts accordingly.... A failure in this regard is a deprivation and leads to frustration and reactive-aggressive response" (p. 360).

Fontana (1973) and Chase (1975) cite the life histories of famous killers Lee Harvey
Oswald, James Earl Ray, Sirhan Sirhan, Jack Ruby, and Charles Manson as examples of
maltreated children. This type of guilt-free expression of aggression Polansky, Borgman,
and DeSaix (1972) categorize as part of the deprivation-detachment sequence.

> The massive inhibition of feeling that derives from indifferent and unempathetic moth-
> ering amounts, we think, to a kind of splitting in the ego. Since the person is unable to
> be aware of his own hurts and suffering, he is certainly unable to empathize with those
> of others. Such a person can inflict suffering on other people then, with coldness and
> calculation of which more normal persons would be quite incapable. (Polansky et al.,
> 1981, p. 7)

Relational Imbalances

A failure to trust and low self-esteem, in addition to repressed or aggressively expressed
anger, hamper the survivor's abilities to form satisfying relationships. Experience with an
inconsistent, withholding family of origin limits the later adult's ability to give. The expectation of being unfulfilled and unnurtured is reinforced by merging with a similarly emotionally needy individual (Polansky et al., 1981; Briere, 1992).

> *Joan was severely neglected as a child. Her mother had little time or energy for
> her five children. The care of them was left largely to Joan and her older brother,
> Rick. Joan left school at age 16 and worked in a fast-food restaurant. She was*

quiet and timid and found meeting customers difficult. She eventually got a job in the kitchen where she did well. Harry was a fellow cook, and although they talked little, she realized that Harry's background was not unlike her own.

When Joan was 18 and pregnant, they were married. In the years that followed, Joan returned from work to care for the young children but she fought with Harry over his sexual pursuits of other women. Her dreams of being loved, protected, and cared for soon became illusions.

Past victims of neglect may never have learned how to negotiate, compromise, or problem solve—skills that are vital for the endurance of relationships (Gil, 1983). Instead, their storytale thinking, combined with no models for appropriate relationships and a severely limited ability to trust, greatly reduces the chance of healthy relationships. Often by recognizing these problems, survivors increase their chances of having satisfying relationships.

Low Self-Esteem

The neglected child feels at fault for the indifference of his or her parents, but the caregivers may have directly contributed to the feelings of blame or worthlessness.

"If it weren't for you, your father would not have left."
"You kids drive me nuts; that's why I drink."
"Can't you do anything right, you stupid kid?"

These and other such statements echo through the memories of many past victims. Sanford and Donovan (1984), in their assessment of the origin of women's self-esteem, comment that

As children, we could not distinguish unfair expectations (which had nothing to do with us) from realistic assessments of who we were. And because we were absolutely dependent on our parents for our survival, we looked up to them. Hence, when they said, we are "plain," "stupid," or "lazy," we did not question their credentials, much less the fairness of their expectations. Their judgment became reality to us. We were not likely to pick and choose among the labels they applied to us. We integrated them all, to some degree, even when they were overwhelmingly negative. (p. 58)

Although these authors refer to only women's self-esteem, the integration of negative descriptors certainly describes the experiences of men as well.

As children exemplify these negatives in their behavior, parents respond with increased rejection. School personnel, neighbors, and other children react to the symptoms of the child's distress rather than the causes. Attention-seeking behavior is met with criticism, suspension, or expulsion from school. The culmination of these experiences is the individual's view of himself or herself as fundamentally at fault, unworthy, and a "bad" person.

Impaired Social Skills

Children of neglect, feeling negative about themselves and perhaps about others, often demonstrate impaired social skills. Limited stimulation has impeded development and possibly lowered their intellectual abilities. Increased responsibilities and the need to fight for existence hamper the adults' ability to play or enjoy the simple pleasures of life. Past victims often describe their recreational activities as ways of escaping unfulfilled lives rather than as enjoyments to be savored. The impulsivity that characterizes the neglectful family often creates adults who have difficulty with responsibility and who opt for escape when they feel stressed (Polansky et al., 1981).

Polansky and colleagues (1981) describe *verbal inaccessibility*—or the inability to effectively communicate—as a problem in dealing with neglectful families. A poor command of language and the inability to conceptualize and verbalize feelings stem largely from a lack of experience in talking with people other than on a superficial level. This verbal inaccessibility is often a contributor to, as well as a byproduct of, impaired intellectual development. Until they develop proficiency in communication, survivors of neglect continue to feel isolated and misunderstood.

Substance Abuse

The use of drugs and alcohol is decidedly a cultural issue, but its prevalence as a form of escape or to ease social interaction is common in individuals with impaired social skills. The influence of addictive substances in the neglected child's life may have been significant, and the use of these substances as an adult may be a result of modeling, peer pressure, identification, or a variety of other issues. Even those who are not practicing alcoholics exhibit the symptoms of alcoholic behavior and there ceases to be a personality distinction between the active alcoholic and those who suffer the effects of parental alcoholism.

Physical Problems

Insufficient care promotes health problems in later years. Nutrition alone has been tied to impeded growth, lower intelligence, poor teeth, and a variety of other problems (Chase and Martin, 1970; Martin, 1976; Polansky et al., 1981). Some children suffer throughout life from the effects of neglect.

> At age 2, after he swallowed a product designed to unclog kitchen drains, Simon's mouth and throat had to be reconstructed. It was unclear whether Simon's swallowing the substance was accidental or intentional because his mother had been both neglectful and abusive in the past. Even after treatment, Simon had difficulty swallowing, and throughout his adulthood he complained of feeling that he was choking.

The body responds to emotional as well as physical care. Past victims of neglect often complain of physical problems that originated in their physiological and emotional history. Physical symptoms require attention, but often the complaints are ill-defined remnants of a lifetime of poor care as well as chronic stress (Polansky, Borgman, and DeSaix, 1972). Although often very real, victims' somatized problems require that they pamper themselves and ask for attention from others—a right they may have been denied in childhood.

Although the physical and emotional problems of adults, for whom neglect was a byproduct of alcoholism or abuse, have been documented, little attention has been directed to the scars of neglect itself. Studies (Oliver and Taylor, 1971; Polansky et al., 1981) attest to the continuation of the neglectful cycle from generation to generation. But the experience of the individual who breaks the pattern is not as well documented. "The adult's remembrance of childhood deprivation is masked by the merciful process of repression, which is part of the adaptability of the human ego" (Polansky et al., 1981, p. 6).

Effects from the Physically Abusing Family

Many of the problems of the survivors of neglectful families are duplicated in the adults who were physically abused as children. The difference is that neglect is an omission, whereas abuse more often represents a commission. The neglected child may be chronically uncared for or unattended to, whereas the abused child may only suffer intermittently. However, the nonabusive periods, filled with parental stimulation, attention, and contrition, confuse the developing child.

Trust

Difficulty with trust becomes a manifestation of the recognition that life—and those who represent that life—is unpredictable. Life's unpredictability is a given, but the past victim of abuse has learned that the unpredictable event is usually hurtful. In an instant, a loving mother or father would instead scream, hit, or threaten. Therefore, to trust was to become even more vulnerable. To be cautious and anticipate the abuse, the child would hide and try to avoid the situation that seemed to stimulate the abuse.

Many adult survivors become particularly adept at anticipating and avoiding conflict, while others flee from intimacy in the fear that closeness is synonymous with vulnerability to pain.

Isolation, based largely on their inability to trust others, is a significant problem for both abusive parents and for past victims of physical abuse (Briere, 1992). As adults, survivors feel that by not risking trust, they will not be betrayed or hurt. In fact, they often lack trust in their own ability to find others who will not hurt them. The result is a cautious, ever-vigilant individual who isolates himself or herself and often builds up a protective barrier.

> *"Anyone would have said I was the model of mental health," laughed Nancy, with a tinge of irony. "I was president of everything—from women's groups to PTA to Toastmistress to the historical society. You name it and I was in a leadership role. And was I busy! I had little time for much else. I was probably a good leader in that I got things done, but my biggest problem was that I couldn't delegate. Once I tried, but the woman didn't do the task the way I thought it should be done. That clinched it. I knew that no one would follow through as I could.*
>
> *"I guess that's what happened to my marriage too. I just had trouble with closeness. Ned told me that I never trusted him. I really didn't, I guess. I was sure he'd find someone more interesting and more desirable. When he did, I wasn't at all surprised. It took me a while before I found out though. I was so busy I didn't realize what was happening. When I did learn of his affair, I looked around for someone to commiserate with but there was no one there. I realized that my*

hyperactivity was my way of shielding myself from trusting anyone enough to let them get to know me well. I had acquaintances from my committees, but no real friends."

Anger

For survivors of abuse, anger is a familiar emotion but one that has been so integral to their upbringing that they often have difficulty recognizing it. The anger they feel over being abused and unprotected is turned inward or projected outward.

Turning anger inward usually results in depression or self-abusive behavior. The display of anger through aggression results not only from frustration but also from the child victim's identification with the aggressor. The physically abused child learned from observation that anger is synonymous with physical aggression. The child perceived that the abuser had power by virtue of his or her violent behavior. As the child grew into adulthood, he or she felt that the only way to have power was to take it. This individual did not learn that the feeling of anger need not be followed by physical action (Warner, 1981; Briere, 1992). Frustrated, overwhelmed, and needy, the past victims, now parents, may lash out at their own children. By learning to identify this anger as their own and learning to channel it, these parents can, however, avoid the abuse of their own children.

Relational Imbalances

Crippled by the inability to fully trust and therefore to achieve true intimacy, the survivors of abuse seek out the familiar—people who behave similarly to the abuser or the nonprotecting parent of the past. By so doing, these individuals unconsciously predispose themselves to abusive treatment, such as battering, emotional abuse, or alcoholism (Helfer, 1978; Briere, 1992). Or past victims join together in symbiotic relationships with others who experienced the same types of emotional problems. Symbiosis may occur with a shift from an enmeshed family of origin into a marital relationship. Feeling dependent on parents but often resenting that dependence, the survivor often marries young, in the hope that this new husband or wife will provide a conflict-free and nurturing relationship. Justice and Justice (1976) comment that in physically abusive families "there is constant competition over who will be taken care of" (p. 31). But spouses' dependency on one another is not rewarded, partially because the individuals cannot fully trust each other and because both have deeply unmet needs and unrealistic expectations. The result is anger and disillusionment. Anger further alienates the couple but increases their need to cling to each other, in hostile dependency, in the hope that their needs may somehow be met (Justice and Justice, 1976). Frustrated, the couple often turn to their children for nurturance. These children then carry the burdens of their parents' unfinished business into their own adulthoods.

Bowen (1966) terms this fusion and inability to break with the family of origin as *undifferentiation.* Undifferentiated individuals have great difficulty developing relationships with any but those who harbor similar needs.

Fear of physical contact often creates problems in intimate relationships. Touch may have been only hurtful in childhood, and beatings the only physical contact the child experienced.

Low Self-Esteem

Children who are physically abused, like those who are neglected, attribute the cause of their parents' behavior to themselves. Abused children assume that the punishment inflicted on them resulted from their misdeeds, regardless of the fact that the misdeeds were not specified. The feeling of being inherently wrong or at fault follows children into adulthood and colors their behavior. This thinking also creates distinct splits in how these adults view other people or issues. They often view the world in black-and-white or good-and-bad terms. They see their parents as good; otherwise they would have to admit and grieve over their loss of nurturing. It follows, then, that the victims are all "bad," and that others in their lives surely are better than they are. Therefore, survivors of abuse continue to see themselves as unable to live up to the actions or the expectations of those around them.

For some, protection is the only recourse. They may assume an aggressive or even hostile demeanor. Some past victims use humor to justify their existence and protect themselves against the depression of never being good enough. The underlying drive for these individuals, whether they manifest it in their behavior or protect themselves against feeling inferior, derives from their inability to believe that anyone could find them worthwhile since their parents did not (Briere, 1992).

Coping Skills

Like the neglected child, in adulthood the physically abused battle feelings of powerlessness, somatic symptoms, escape through substance abuse, and are unable to play or enjoy themselves. Unlike past victims of neglect, who may never accumulated enough psychic energy, survivors of abuse often compensate through overachievement.

Some achievement-driven past victims precipitate stress with which they have not learned to deal. Life at home was often controlled and regimented. Parents made decisions, and children's input was discouraged or discounted. As a result, survivors never learned to solve problems in a logical manner. As adults, their making even the smallest decision often causes a major crisis. Partialization may truly be out of their grasp. Many past victims find themselves easily overwhelmed, which leads to acute anxiety, physical symptoms, loss of control over temper, substance abuse, or a total inability to function. Learning to consciously separate problems into their various components and proceeding to function in a step-by-step fashion are necessary for the survivor to begin to feel in control (Helfer, 1978).

Long-Term Effects of Domestic Violence

The attention given to the long-term effects of domestic violence is a relatively new phenomenon. In fact, it is only within the last decade that protective services agencies have developed units devoted to intervention with families where children witness the battering of one parent by another. For this reason, the life-long trauma to the individual has been discussed more in antidotal form than as the subject of research findings. Increasingly, however, there is consideration being given to the adults who witnessed violence as children.

Henning et al. (1996) studied 617 adults to determine the impact on adults of having been child witnesses to violence between their parents. One hundred and twenty three (20 percent) remembered seeing physical conflict in the home. Of this sample, women reported a higher level of psychological distress than their male counterparts. It was difficult, however, to separate the effects of the violence from the residual influence of the other family dysfunction.

Certainly many of the issues reported by children in other types of abusive families are present in some survivors of witnessed violence. As Margarita put it

> *I still abhor violence! I flinch whenever anyone yells, expecting that the blows will come next. I have trouble trusting men, especially those who have loud voices or who are big. And I don't trust anyone to protect me...either man or woman. Neither my mother or father did when I was little. I cannot believe that anyone can now!*

Much research needs to be done on the adult who witnessed violence as a child (Groves, 1996). The current interest in domestic violence may well lead to this additional research.

Effects from a Sexually Abusing Family

Because of the attention given by survivors and by the women's movement, sexually abusing families are widely researched. Adult past victims of incest demonstrate many of the same symptoms as those from other dysfunctional families, but the taboo associated with sexual abuse—and especially incest—stimulates additional problems that plague adult past victims. The necessity of keeping the secret often augments adults' feelings of anger and guilt. Being beaten does not carry the same degree of censure in our society as being sexually abused within one's own family. Society, therefore, intensifies the symptoms and feelings of the adult who was a victim of child sexual abuse.

Finkelhor and Browne (1985) cite four major categories of trauma resulting from child sexual abuse: betrayal, traumatic sexualization, stigmatization, and powerlessness. These categories can be most useful in understanding the effects of this type of maltreatment.

Betrayal

Trust is as fundamental an issue for the sexual abuse survivor as it is for past victims of other maltreatment. Betrayal of this trust is often devastating. As a child, the individual trusted the parents and often felt that this trust was respected and understood. Recognition that the victim was used for the abuser's pleasure is confusing and hurtful.

> *Donna describes the sexual abuse by her father as not fitting the picture. "He was the most loving, giving individual I ever met. He had infinite patience with me, unlike my mother who could be abrupt and demanding. I just assumed that when he started touching me and telling me it was okay, he was right. I had a feeling that it was strange, but in those days, I believed my father implicitly. When a friend*

*and I read a book about an unhealthy relationship between a father and daughter,
I was really hurt by the disgust my friend registered. I was so confused. Now I'm
just angry. How could he do that when I trusted him so?"*

Not only did one parent abuse the child but the other failed to protect. The result for
the adult past victim is a sense of mistrust (especially of members of the sex of the perpetrator), anger, grief, and often depression. The adult feels not only unable to trust but inadequate to judge who is trustworthy. This, in turn, makes past victims more vulnerable to
further victimization (Finkelhor and Browne, 1985; Russell, 1986; Tower, 1988). Chapman
and Terry (1984) point out that minorities—especially African-Americans—also experience betrayal at the hands of the system designed to help them. When racially imbalanced
attitudes and policies further victimize the victim, her or his sense of betrayal is intensified.

Traumatic Sexualization

Traumatic sexualization refers to the child's premature indoctrination into adult sexuality
and the confusion this process involves. During the years when children should be learning
gradually about sexuality, the perpetrator equates sex with affection and rewards the child
for sexual behavior. The result for adult victims is not only the confusion between sex and
affection but also a distorted perception of sexual norms. Often they compensate in promiscuity or prostitution.

Promiscuity seems a consequence of self-destructive tendencies that may originate in
repetition compulsion; that is, individuals attempt to alleviate their anxiety and perhaps
recapture the pleasure experienced with the abusing parent. The original relationship's pain
and pleasure and betrayal and intimacy become paradoxically entwined in the performance
of sexual acts for recognition and attention (Maltz, 1991).

The motivation for prostitution seems similar. Although only a small percentage of
incest victims (Meiselman, 1978; deYoung, 1982; Russell, 1986) actually become prostitutes, a high percentage of prostitutes studied reported incest in their childhood (Silbert and
Pines, 1983). As a child, the individual learned from the perpetrator that sexual favors could
be traded for rewards. As an adult, more sophisticated barter ensured a relatively lucrative,
albeit dangerous, lifestyle.

Some theorists (Finkelhor, 1984; Faria and Belohlovek, 1984; Maltz, 1991) contend
that promiscuity and prostitution are a combination of anger, mind-body split, feelings of
worthlessness, and the attitude of "My body has been used already, so why not?" Or some
feel that the promiscuous individual seeks acceptance and affection which she/he confuses
with sexuality (Downs, 1993).

Some past victims experience an aversion to sex, demonstrating such problems as
arousal dysfunction, desire dysfunction, or difficulty in achieving orgasm (Courtois, 1988;
Maltz, 1991). Meiselman (1978) reported that 74 percent of his sample of women over age
18 had experienced orgasmic dysfunction at least once (p. 234). Some victims avoid or feel
phobic about intimate encounters. Often sexual contacts stimulate flashbacks.

*"Whenever I let anyone touch me," explained Helen, "I think of my father. My
partner's hands become my father's hands in my mind, and the guilt and pain I
feel over the incest turns off any positive feelings I have about having sex now."*

Russell (1986) found that women who had been abused were more likely to reject sexual advances and, as a consequence, suffer more sexual violence, especially rape in marriage.

Confusion over sexual identity often plagues survivors. Finkelhor (1984) found that "boys victimized by older men were *four times* more likely to be currently engaged in homosexual activity than were nonvictims" (p. 195). He also noted, however, that it is difficult to discern whether the abuse was a precipitating factor in homosexual activity or whether boys with a predisposition toward a homosexual lifestyle were more vulnerable to abusers. Both Nasjleti (1980) and Finkelhor suggest that having been abused may increase a boy's chance of becoming homosexual. One explanation for this could be related to stigma. A boy who has been involved with an older man may see himself as homosexual not only because he has had the sexual experience with a man but also because his male abuser apparently found him sexually stimulating. The boy attaches authority and power to the adult and assumes that if the abuser sees him as homosexual, he must be. Thus, the boy chooses a homosexual lifestyle to be consistent with his image of himself and his perception of how others see him (Finkelhor, 1984; Parker, 1990; Maltz, 1991).

Finkelhor (1984) attributes the choice of female partners as stemming from the conclusion that men are not to be trusted. Forward and Buck (1978) suggest that a woman who was abused by her mother may adopt the same pathological symptomatology and choose women as sexual partners. (Evert and Bijkerk, 1987). Meiselman (1978) notes that only a minority of lesbians cite incest as a significant factor in their sexual orientation.

Stigmatization and Self-Esteem

The child who was sexually abused incorporates deep feelings of guilt, shame, and "badness" in his or her self-image. As an adult, the individual has harbored the secret for some time. This need to guard the secret at all costs, compounded by the isolation necessary to feel safe in keeping it, makes the adult feel negatively toward himself or herself (Russell, 1986; Kinzl and Biebl, 1992). Victims experience a sense of being damaged and in this tainted stance see themselves as different from others. Some past victims think their bodies are marred and detestable. They may also feel anger toward their bodies, feeling that the flesh somehow acquiesced to the abuse while the spirit or the essence of the person did not. Some individuals describe feeling angry at their bodies for experiencing physical pleasure during the abuse. The image of the body becomes distorted; it is seen as deformed, too fat, too thin, or ugly (Sgroi, 1982; Goodwin, 1982; Maltz, 1991). Survivors may somatize their conflicts, presenting anorexia nervosa, bulimia, headaches, nausea, menstrual or vaginal problems, colitis, and so on. These symptoms are based on both the impaired picture of self and on internalized anger and guilt. Some past victims describe seeing their bodies as so plagued by problems that they can focus on these and therefore not have to consider the psychological memories of the abuse (Sgroi, 1982; Goodwin, 1982; Gelinas, 1983; Blume, 1990; Briere, 1992).

Increasing attention has been given to the concept of dissociation in survivors, and its relationship to self-esteem. *Dissociation* has been defined as:

> …a defensive disruption in the normally occurring connections among feeling, thoughts, behavior, and memories, consciously or unconsciously invoked in order to reduce psychological distress (Briere, 1992, p. 36).

People dissociate to escape from the reality which is too painful or traumatic to face. Dissociation is a type of anesthesia which allows the personality to cope. Briere (1992) suggests three forms of dissociation which are common to survivors. These are disengagement, detachment/numbing, and observation. *Disengagement* involves moments of "spacing-out" where one is oblivious to external events. These moments may be conscious or unconscious and rarely last more than a few seconds to several minutes. When a survivor has extreme difficulty with negative events *detachment* or *numbing* may occur. The individual psychologically removes her/himself (not always consciously) so that he/she is unaware of the negative feelings triggered by certain memories, thoughts and events. In its more extreme form, this type of dissociation may create someone who is totally unaware of feelings. The detached person can look at situations in an intellectualized nonemotional manner (Briere, 1992).

Observation occurs when individuals watch themselves involved in certain distressing activities. For example, some survivors speak of the mind and body as almost separate entities. Researchers and clinicians see the origin of this mind-body split in the victim experiencing so much emotional or physical pain during the actual abuse that the mind temporarily separates from the body.

> *Tessa describes feeling this mind-body split whenever she and her lover have sex. "When my father used to sexually abuse me, I would leave my body almost. Sometimes I'd take my mind into a wall or the couch. I thought that he could abuse my body but not my mind. But that defense became so much a part of sex that now I can't stop doing it when I am making love. My therapist and I are working on helping me to 'stay' during lovemaking."*

This phenomenon should not be confused with more serious psychosis unless it continues for extended periods and the thought processes become grossly distorted. The splitting of the mind and body has been referred to by some as self-hypnotic anesthesia (Gelinas, 1983; Courtois, 1988).

Some past victims, often those subjected to bizarre, ritualistic, or serious abuse, experience more severe forms of dissociation; amnesia or multiple personality disorder (MPD). Psychogenic *amnesia* is a way of avoiding deep-seated psychological conflicts. The individual has totally blocked out and cannot remember personal events or behaviors—a state which goes beyond normal forgetfulness. Past victims with *multiple personality disorder* exhibit two or more separate personalities which may or may not be aware of each other's existence (Courtois, 1988; Briere, 1992; DiTomasso and Routh, 1993). (See Courtois, 1988, pp. 153–159, for more complete treatment of dissociative disorders.)

Self mutilation is another residual symptom of an abused past. Past victims report using substances such as drugs and alcohol to either punish the body, dull the senses, or escape the memories of abuse (Gelinas, 1983; Kinzl and Biebl, 1992). Some past victims also cut or burn themselves. Nora describes her hospitalization and self-abuse as a result of being sexually abused:

> *"I had been hospitalized for severe depression. I was 19 years old and my father had gone to jail because he'd molested me. But the trial had taken two years, and by then I was pretty upset. I remember my mother calling me, saying my father had been beaten up by the other inmates. She berated me for almost an hour on the*

phone—about how it was my fault and all. I went back to my room really shaken. I don't even remember doing it, but the next thing I knew I was running down the hall on fire. I'd set the leg of my jeans on fire—I didn't even know it."

The ultimate destruction is suicide. Suicide, the last escape, may be attempted once, or more frequently. At the root of these attempts are deep depression, self-blame, and a feeling of being so different that one cannot hope to be with others (Herman and Schatzow, 1984; Sgroi, 1982; Goodwin, 1982; Faria and Belohlovek, 1984; Courtois, 1988).

While some survivors see the body as the offending part of the self, others see the damage as more intrinsic. Both men and women feel shame and guilt not only about the incest, which they often feel they engendered or contributed to, but also about all that was wrong with the family. "If I could have been better" is often heard from guilt-ridden past victims. A fundamental part of the parentification process, guilt aided the abuser and now it continues to plague the past victim.

Another element of feeling different is the "Why me?" question.

Gert was one of seven children. At the age of 7, she was raped by her father. He continued to sexually abuse her for several years. Although she believes that at least one brother knew of the incest, no one ever mentioned it. Gert has no idea why her three sisters were never abused. Today she has told two of them. They advise her to "put it behind you and live a happy life." Their attitudes infuriate Gert, who grapples daily with the anger and guilt over being her father's chosen victim.

Survivors often fantasize about what made them so different from their siblings who were not abused. If they discern a difference, they translate it into something negative, and thus feel even more guilty and despicable.

Survivors' guilt is often an issue for past victims of incest. Here, the individuals realize that they have survived either emotionally or physically but that others close to them who also experienced the abuse did not. Incest survivors describe being plagued with guilt when they see brothers and sisters react with greater pathology to the abuse (Sgroi, 1982).

The guilt and shame compound the survivors' sense of hopelessness and the feeling that they have neither the right nor the power to take control of their own lives.

Powerlessness

Feeling out of control or powerless becomes a major problem for the past victim of sexual abuse. Fears permeate his or her life. Nightmares, phobias, and attacks of anxiety keep the individual ever-mindful of the abuse and of the terror or pain associated with it. Decisions become difficult. Survivors describe feeling vulnerable. There is, in fact, a high risk of future victimization for those who feel powerless to avoid or protect themselves from it (Finkelhor and Browne, 1985).

Male survivors suffer significantly from feelings of incompetence. Although females also feel powerless, society accepts this in a woman. Men, on the other hand, feel stigmatized for their inability to take control, and their guilt compounds the problem. For some, this is translated into withdrawal and even sexual impotence. Other males overcompensate and become overly aggressive and sometimes abusive (Groth, 1979; Hunter, 1990). Mike repressed the sadistic sexual abuse by his father until it surfaced in a recurring dream that attested to his sense of powerlessness.

> *"I see my father coming at me with a pipe. He is dressed in black and looks very sinister. He smiles as he brings the pipe crashing down on me—again and again. I want to run or protect myself, but I can't. I can't scream. I can't cry out. I feel hot and wet and then I see it—a river of my own blood running past me. Then I envision the street and I see the blood running down the gutter and into the sewer. I want to cry, 'Come back,' because it feels like with that stream all the strength— the life, in fact—has gone out of me."*

Barbara, too, remembers her mother's sexual abuse of her. These flashbacks left her feeling anxious and perspiring profusely. Every detail of the abuse flashed before her and she felt powerless to control the incidents. The events were so vivid in her mind that she worried that she was becoming seriously ill.

Ellenson (1986) and Courtois (1988) describe these involuntary disturbances in perception among female incest survivors. The phenomenon results from an inability to control flashbacks and compounds the past victim's feelings of vulnerability and lack of control. Some individuals, like Barbara, report an array of hallucinations or perceptions for "which there is no external stimulus" (Ellenson, 1986, p. 150).

Ellenson interviewed more than 60 adult female incest victims and discovered that they described unusually similar recurring hallucinations. Past victims described visual hallucinations, such as shadowy figures reminiscent of traumatic elements of the incest experience; movement in the peripheral vision, which disappeared when confronted directly; and elaborate recreations of incestual events (p. 152). Women reported hearing intruder sounds (e.g., scrapes, footsteps, or breathing) as well as childlike cries for help. Inner voices were either comforting and helpful or directed the past victim toward maltreatment of themselves or others. Touch and smell also played a part in the hallucinatory experiences of some of the women. Ellenson suggested that not only must the reality of sensations not be denied by patients and therapists but that recognition of their content provides the therapeutic process with a wealth of beneficial material.

The feeling of powerlessness also results in an overall sense of impaired efficacy. Survivors feel they are less capable and less effective in their work. Some past victims somatize this feeling and develop physical ailments to excuse their failures. Conversely, others become compulsive overachievers and excel with an intensity and drive (Finkelhor and Browne, 1985; Briere, 1992). One woman described her experience:

> *"I knew I was a good bookkeeper, but that's all I believed I could do. So I was determined to become the best bookkeeper the company ever had. I worked at it constantly. In retrospect, I'm sure I drove everyone nuts. Their paperwork had to be just so. But I made myself nuts, too—or figuratively at least. I ended up in the hospital with exhaustion, severe depression, and a pretty lousy outlook on the world."*

Anger

Survivors may feel powerless because of their inability to protect themselves, to perceive reality accurately, or to demonstrate competence. But they may also feel powerless to control their anger. The anger stems from being used or victimized, being out of control or vulnerable, and being unprotected. Some individuals feel anger over being robbed of childhood. Anger can be turned inward; the past victim may feel anger at himself or herself for what he or she perceives as ineffectual behavior or contributing to the abuse. Survivors may feel anger at their own helplessness or powerlessness. "Why wasn't I able to say no?" they agonize. In these situations, it is necessary to help the person recognize the variety of reasons why children are not able to say no.

Anger is often directed toward the nonprotecting parent as well as the perpetrator. But often it is difficult to recognize, admit, or express this anger.

> *"My father came to me when he realized he was terribly ill. I was already angry with him and had been for years. But his reaching out to me infuriated me even more. How could he, after what he'd done to me! But then I felt guilty; he was sick. How could I turn him away. After all, he was my father. So I took care of him."*

In the end, this past victim turned her anger inward because she was unable to direct it toward the appropriate person. She became depressed and ill until she was eventually helped to understand the origin of these symptoms.

A common technique used with survivors is to have the individual write a letter to the perpetrator or to the unprotecting parent, expressing this rage. For some, the pain and sadness resulting from the writing is sufficient to exorcise much of the anger. For others, confronting the person—advisedly with the support of a trusted therapist or intimate—is the best way to direct the anger appropriately.

Anger is not always directed inward or appropriately. Anger may be diffused throughout the individual's life or directed toward loved ones, intimates, children, or other substitutes. Perhaps the past victim does not even recognize what he or she feels is anger. Sometimes the anger is expressed through actions, and the differentiation between the feeling and action is impossible for the survivor to make. Parents who were victims find themselves struggling to control their annoyance over their children's behavior. The spouse of a past victim may find that his or her mate acts illogically in disagreements. The degree of anger expressed can be mild, moderate, or even dangerously pathological.

Groth (1979), in his studies of rapists, found that some of the men expressed their anger through sexual violence.

> In some cases of sexual assault, it is very apparent that sexuality becomes a means of discharging feelings of pent up anger and rage. The assault is characterized by physical brutality.... The rape experience for this type of offender is one of conscious anger and rage, and he expresses his fury both physically and verbally. His aim is to hurt and debase his victim. (pp. 13–14)

Many rapists experienced childhoods fraught with conflicts. Anger toward significant others is displaced on their victims.

In some cases, the victim of the anger rapist is the actual person toward whom the offender harbors such anger, but in other cases, she is simply a substitute person; a symbolic and available "object" against whom the assailant discharges his wrath and fury. (Groth 1979, pp. 16–17)

The inability to cope with anger intensifies the survivor's feelings of powerlessness and further undermines his or her self-esteem. Since some people find the expression of or even the admission of anger is difficult to accept, past victims who recognize their feelings as anger wonder if they are unique in the intensity of this anger. "Why am I so angry?" "Does anyone else feel this way?"

Because anger is so deeply felt but so difficult for past victims to label or express appropriately, its existence often impedes the forming of healthy relationships.

Relational Imbalances

Relational problems are based on numerous factors, several of which relate to the survivor's

- Need to repeat the past or gravitate toward the family of origin
- Difficulty trusting
- Inability to label and express feelings appropriately and thereby have meaningful communication with intimates
- Strong need to have others meet their needs
- Low self-esteem

For past victims, childhood did not provide security. But people find security in the familiar and are often frightened by the unknown. Victims of past familial injustices are particularly threatened by the insecurity of the unknown, and although they may vehemently protest their intentions to have a different homelife from that of their family of origin, they often marry individuals much like their parents or themselves.

Gelinas (1983) describes the dysfunctional relationships in the formation of an incestuous family:

In families where incest develops, the mothers have usually been parentified children. Continuing their caretaking relational style in young adulthood, these women are drawn to, and tend to attract, men for whom caretaking is important. Many of these men have experienced early emotional deprivation because of maternal death, depression or illness. They tend to be relatively dependent, immature and insecure with strong narcissistic features. They tend to respond to the caretaking of the parentified women they marry.

Each partner thus carries the relational imbalances of their families of origin into the new relationship. Usually things go smoothly until the arrival of the first child. Their individual responses also exacerbate the maladaptive responses of the other, systemically spiraling them into progressively more severe mutual estrangement. (p. 320)

Gelinas further characterizes the wife's ambivalence toward the birth of the child, which she somehow recognizes will augment her already myriad emotional responsibilities. At the same time, the husband, perceiving the impending loss of his wife's total attention, responds by intensifying his demands. The result is that two needy individuals grow more emotionally distant, each feeling overwhelmed and undernurtured. Isolated from one another, they turn to their child (often a female child), usually casting her in the role of the parent. By so doing, she will, as an adult, probably seek to compensate for the nurturance she has been denied, paradoxically choosing another immature and needy individual whom she will nurture and resent.

Adult men who were abused, or witnessed the abuse of a sister, often seek the all-loving mother who will give them the unconditional love their mothers did not. Feeling understood only by partners with similar backgrounds or feeling they deserve nothing more, these men also perpetuate the cycle of the dysfunctional family. In a society that prescribes action in males, these men are more likely to practice some type of abuse—emotional, physical, or sexual—on their wives and children (Hunter, 1990).

Another issue for past victims of sexual abuse is that they may have grown up believing that the abuse they suffered was synonymous with being loved (Downs, 1993). Many have never learned to separate sex and affection and, combined with their fear of trust to achieve true intimacy, they form superficial sexual attachments. But along with the sexual relationship comes the remembrance of being used or violated. Without even knowing why, victims find their relationships empty, unsatisfying, and even abusive. Some continue these dysfunctional liaisons because they are convinced they deserve no better or are panic-stricken at the idea of being alone. Others fear risking and prefer to live with the familiar.

Incest survivors have trouble both with spousal relationships and with their children. The past victims' own helplessness, low self-esteem, and difficulty handling anger impede their abilities to provide organizational structure, consistency, and an appropriate balance between affection and discipline. Gelinas (1983) comments that, as mothers, past victims

> tend to be easily overwhelmed by their children, and if they eventually attempt to muffle that effect by withdrawal or alcohol, our experience has shown that they tend to be pursued by their children, often through mischievousness or misbehavior (serious squabbling or fighting, property damage, accident proneness or frank self destructiveness) unconsciously calculated to induce the mother to intervene and pay attention (p. 323)

These mothers demonstrate difficulties in setting limits, so that children quickly learn that because of her guilt, the mother can be cajoled, prodded, or often disobeyed beyond what she claims are her limits. Unfortunately, children then often blame their mother for her weakness much as she blamed her own mother (Gelinas, 1983).

Families of origin frequently impinge on the lives of survivors and their new families and create a resurgence of old issues that confuse current roles. The perpetrator may attempt to molest the former victim's children, or the victim's mother may require care and plead with her daughter for help.

> *"My mother actually had the nerve to complain to me about my father. She'd sit at my kitchen table for hours saying what a horrible man he was. I don't know what she expected from me. All I could think of was 'Where were you when I needed protection from him?'"*

Siblings often blame the survivor for his or her problems. If the siblings knew of the abuse, their guilt may prevent them from recognizing the past victim's feelings in light of their own complicity. Siblings who did not know of the abuse often cannot or will not believe it.

"Two of my sisters knew that my father had raped me, and one brother must have known. But my other brothers didn't know, I'm sure. But it didn't help for them to know. All my brothers and sisters kept telling me that I had to forget what happened. My father was dead and I had to put it in the past. I think they blamed me for upsetting my mother by telling her. They also blamed me for my anxiety attacks when I'd call them and beg to talk. It was as if they couldn't hear what my father had done to me. It was easier to assume I was nuts!"

Multiple Victimization

Research shows that individuals, especially women, who were victims of incest have a higher incidence of repeat victimization. Russell (1986) reported that of the 940 women she studied, 82 percent of incest victims again suffered some type of serious sexual assault, compared to only 48 percent of women who were not incest victims (p. 158). In addition, 46 percent of the incest victims reported physical or sexual violence in marriage, compared to 19 percent who had not been incest victims. And 53 percent were subjected to sexual harassment from an authority figure (p. 158).

Undoubtedly, at least for the women in Russell's sample, repeated victimization is a reality. Because women have been conditioned to be victims, they are more likely than men to be victimized again (Finkelhor, 1984; Briere, 1992). However, even some men again experience exploitation, which creates feelings reminiscent of the abuse.

Chapter 6 described the damaged-goods syndrome (Sgroi, 1982). The perception of damage is twofold. Not only do abused children feel inherently tainted but society sees them as different from other children. Because the child was previously violated, another perpetrator, aware of the past abuse does not feel inhibited. Perpetrators often rationalize that the child, or later the adult, is more knowledgeable—and even seductive (Russell, 1986). Some husbands of past victims need to abuse or violate them as a form of exorcism. Perpetrators sometimes find excitement from the knowledge that the victim had been part of an illicit activity. And finally, society often sees victims as responsible for their fate—a rationalization used frequently by those prone to violent physical and sexual behavior (Russell, 1986).

In addition to others' views of them, the survivors' views of themselves are manifested in an internalized powerlessness. The individuals often see themselves as vulnerable and do not perceive they have the right to resist effectively. Reactivated fears paralyze the past victim.

"The worst thing that my father's abuse did was rob me of my ability to scream—literally. After I escaped the abuse at home, I was raped twice. The first time, I was 19, and I called my mother, crying. She told me it was my own fault if I went out at night. The second time, I was married and my husband and I were swimming with two other couples at night. A bunch of motorcycle guys came up. They dragged me

off and raped me. I couldn't even scream. Afterwards, my husband and the others were upset with me. They said I must have wanted to be raped. That really hurt. They just couldn't understand that I couldn't cry out. I was paralyzed."

Being robbed of anger or the ability to react can follow a survivor throughout life.

The propensity of former victims to repeat the past or gravitate toward the familiar often predisposes them to revictimization. Tower (1988) describes a victim of incest who married three times in an attempt to break the pattern of returning to the familiar.

I got married when I was nineteen. I married a guy I realize now who came from the same kind of family I did. He had a sister who was a heroin addict and a prostitute, and I think his father had molested her. He used to constantly put me down.... My father was always putting me down, and I'd had it. So I left my first husband. My second husband was like my father, too. He was suffering from post-Vietnam stress and did some crazy [abusive] things to me, just like my father. I was only married to him for ten months and then I left. My third husband was quiet and passive.... You know I married my father twice and then I married my mother.... My mother always ignored me. I was always looking for her love, but I never felt like I got it. (p. 113)

Another aspect of the survivor's sense of self is the impaired ability to avoid danger. Most children project tentative antennae and take risks, and if the world proves too much, they can run home for comfort. But if the hurt is at home as well as outside, the individual's sense of reality of what is safe or unsafe becomes distorted. Thus, as adults, these past victims are not always able to discern what situations are potentially harmful. Janoff-Bulman and Frieze (1983) explain that the psychological impact of victimization includes the shattering of some basic beliefs about the world. Most of us assume that the world is comprehensible and meaningful and that we are personally invulnerable. Once these perceptions become distorted, it is difficult for individuals to test and avoid danger. Often they become victims again.

Survivors of dysfunctional families, whether neglectful or physically or sexually abusive, pay for their vulnerability. In time, the residual effects of family pathology can be reduced through greater self-knowledge.

Effects from Extrafamilial Abuse

Since physical abuse and neglect are, by definition, at the hands of a caregiver, the only type of abuse possible outside the home is sexual assault or molestation. Chapter 8 discussed the range of abuse from molestation by an acquaintance or a stranger to involvement in pornography and prostitution rings or satanic cults. Children molested or exploited outside their homes demonstrate similar problems to those who were victims of incest. Feeling damaged appears to be a universal, residual effect of sexual exploitation. The inner sense of damage and society's perception of damage intensifies the blame of self. Depression, self-destructive behavior, and low self-esteem result from the blame and guilt the victim carries (Finkelhor et al., 1986; Ryder, 1992). Many past victims describe fears that plague them in flashbacks, in nightmares, or in anxiety over future victimization. In the words of one survivor,

> *"I'm still frightened when a strange man passes me on the street after dark. Even when I'm with someone, I cling to that companion. I feel so vulnerable. I'm afraid that if anyone approached me again, I'd just freeze and let it happen."*

The particular fears the victim has often relate to the type of assault or the amount of force used. Sandra's abuse and her later reactions characterize a victim who was initially cajoled by the perpetrator.

> *Sandra had seen the perpetrator at the playground on several occasions. He frequently talked to the children or took their pictures. One day he engaged several children, including Sandra, in a game of hide-and-seek. Sandra "found" him in the utility shed, and they began talking. He offered her money to remove her clothes. When she refused, the perpetrator drew a knife, threatened her into compliance, and molested her.*
>
> *Following the episode, Sandra ran home in tears, but was afraid to tell anyone. She was sure she had led the man on and would be blamed for what happened. She withdrew from her friends, threw herself into schoolwork, and returned home immediately after school. Sandra remembers recurring nightmares, some about being victimized again and others that centered around her image of herself as tainted and "evil." She placed herself, unconsciously, in situations where she was again and again taken advantage of by boys she dated.*
>
> *When Sandra was 19 and in college, she was raped by an acquaintance at a party. Her reaction to the rape was to become completely hysterical—confusing in her uncontrollable sobbing the events of this rape with her experience as a child. In therapy, she was eventually able to separate the two events and to understand her feelings of being exploited and her sense of guilt, blame, and shame.*

While women feel a continued sense of powerlessness, male victims often describe intense fears about being out of control both at the time of the assault and in later adulthood. In order to gain control, some male victims become perpetrators. Although both males and females experience sexual fears and problems, males are more likely to express confusion about their sexual identity. Women, on the other hand, report increased sexual inhibitions and decreased sexual desire. It is not unusual for past victims of extrafamilial abuse to also be vulnerable for further victimization.

More and more survivors of abuse by cults have spoken up in the last few years. These survivors describe similar symptoms as other abuse survivors, but also exhibit fears and behaviors peculiar to this type of abuse. Ryder (1992) points out that issues like extreme fear of circles, fear of being the center of attention, overreaction to supernatural films, fear of abandonment, and phobias about blood, robed figures, candles, demons and snakes may be present in those who experienced ritualistic cult abuse. Because this type of abuse can be so bizarre and so out of one's frame of reference, it is often difficult for past victims to remember and make sense of what they have experienced.

Current statistics project that one out of three girls and one out of five boys will be sexually abused prior to the age of 18. Of this number, 40 to 60 percent will be victims of incest. This means that approximately half the victims experience exploitation outside the family unit. Yet very little has been written about these individuals as adults, so knowledge in this area is limited.

Comparison of the Sexual Victimization of Males and Females

What are the differences in residual effects of sexual abuse in men and in women? Fritz, Stoll, and Wagner (1981), in their study of 952 college students, reported that females are significantly more traumatized by sexual abuse than are males. Of the 410 males in their study, only 10 percent of the 4.8 percent who reported being molested complained of problems in adult adjustment. Of the 7.7 percent molested females, however, 23 percent reported residual difficulties in current functioning (p. 56). Finkelhor (1984) also attests that the number of men reporting abuse and resulting aftereffects is significantly lower than that of women. He points out, however, that two factors may account for this: (1) boys are less likely to *interpret* sexual encounters with adults as assaultive and (2) boys are less likely to report the abuse. Few studies have been done on males and females beyond the college-age population, so it is difficult to assess accurately the residual effects of abuse in males. Recently research on male victimization, however, attests to the fact that emotional scars for males are also significant (Hunter, 1990).

Treatment of Adults Who Were Abused as Children

Chapters 13 and 14 discussed the treatment of abused and neglected children and their families. In recent years, there has been an emphasis on therapeutic services for adults who did not disclose the abuse in childhood. Many of these past victims carried the abuse hidden deep in their memories for years.

Repressed Memories

"For years I had a vague feeling that something had happened to me as a child. In fact, I couldn't remember much of my childhood. Following my divorce, I sought out a therapist mainly because I was feeling like such a failure. And then the dreams started coming. I would dream that there was a shadow in my bedroom. I was petrified to have that dream. It took several years before the memories returned...the memories of my father coming to my room at night and sexually abusing me. Throughout those years I remembered things in bits and pieces...in smells and images."

It is not uncommon for people who have been traumatized to repress the memories of this experience or relegate them to the darkest part of one's mind. When this happens, these feelings and the recall of these experiences may lie dormant for years. Remembering them may be triggered by certain events. The occurrence of a similar situation (e.g., a mother's child is abused at about the same age she had been abused), the death of the perpetrator, the birth of one's child, becoming free of an addiction, feeling safe, or experiencing a new trauma (e.g., being raped as an adult when one had repressed the memory of childhood sex abuse) are all examples of "triggers" which could bring up old memories (Fredrickson, 1992). The term *repressed memory syndrome* was developed to describe those who have no memory of the abuse they suffered. Some survivors, unlike the one quoted above, not only have no memory but no sense that anything happened to them. Only after the memories are triggered do they begin to emerge (Sheiman, 1993).

Currently there is much controversy over the concept of repressed memories. Some critics have blamed therapists for leading their clients into "remembering" experiences that never happened and then falsely accusing others of abusing them. The fact that memories return in vague images which may require some interpretation compounds the argument. It is the wise therapist who helps the client make connections and interpretations rather than making them for him/her. As one therapist put it:

> *Bev described memories and dreams she was having which sounded much like those recounted by my sexually abused clients. I felt fairly sure that eventually she would remember that she was abused. But when she asked me "Do you think I was sexually abused?", my response had to be: "Bev, that is for you to tell me, not for me to tell you." And eventually she did remember and told me about her experiences.*

Research tells us that survivors do repress memories of abuse...memories which are too painful to keep in their conscious mind (Fredrickson, 1992; Sheiman, 1993). When adults abused as children seek therapy, there are several methods which might help them.

Individual Therapy

Traditional therapies can be helpful to the past victim, provided the therapist is educated and skilled in working with survivors—especially those of sexual abuse. Since sexual abuse is a painful issue, not all therapists are comfortable dealing with it.

> *"I finally told my therapist of 10 years that I'd been sexually abused by my father. He nodded and started asking me about something unrelated. I couldn't believe it. Here I'd gotten up the courage to mention it, and he wasn't even hearing me."*

Tower (1988) states that in order to work with sexual abuse victims a therapist must

1. Be comfortable, informed, and skilled in discussing sexual issues
2. Be comfortable, informed, and clear about his or her own sexuality
3. Have achieved an awareness and comfortable relationship with his or her own family of origin
4. Have developed a sense of autonomy
5. Be comfortable with his or her own vulnerability

There are variations to individual therapy. Through *psychotherapy,* victims come to terms with the trauma that occurred and their guilt surrounding their perceived complicity.

The individual is encouraged to develop connections between past and present and to enhance present coping capabilities (Forward and Buck, 1978).

Gestalt therapy focuses on the present, with less emphasis on the past or the future. The goal is to help the individual recognize the current feelings and to take responsibility for behavior. Gestalt therapists have patients conduct dialogues between parts of themselves (e.g., body parts, wishes, and feelings) to help victims accept themselves as whole people (Forward and Buck, 1978; Tower, 1988).

Critics of *behavior therapy* suggest that the symptom rather than the cause is addressed. During therapy, the survivor learns to identify current dysfunctional behavior and works to find and substitute more acceptable or functional behavior. This approach does help the individual take control of various aspects of life and teaches him or her how to act rather than to react (Corey, 1983; Tower, 1988).

Crisis intervention is often necessary with survivors for whom the past stimulates acute anxiety attacks or exaggerates other problems. This therapy is designed to help the individual mobilize internal resources to face the immediate crisis (Forward and Buck, 1978). The past is not dealt with in any depth. Some past victims continue to seek help in crisis after crisis because they do not want to recognize that there may be a pattern that can be traced to the abuse. For others, the benefit from crisis intervention gives them confidence in the therapeutic system and they seek additional therapy.

Justice and Justice (1976, 1979) have been successful in treating physically and sexually abusive families and past victims with *transactional analysis*. Transactional analysis identifies three ego states: the *child,* who seeks gratification, the *parent,* who expresses himself or herself by being either critical or nurturing, and the *adult* (sometimes called *the computer*), who processes facts. The way that these ego states transact or interact through life is referred to as a *life script.* Through script analysis, victims are helped to recognize how they think, feel, and behave, and they discover the roots of these feelings, thoughts, and actions. The therapist helps clients discard outdated scripts in favor of those that are more functional. The remnants of an abusive family are often a part of the life script that the past victim is helped to discard (Forward and Buck, 1978).

Adult survivors also benefit from a variety of new therapeutic approaches, influenced by or espousing humanistic psychology. The basis of these approaches is for the victim to take control of his or her life, by recognizing that daily living presents many choices and that by making these choices the individual actively takes charge of his or her own life. The therapist encourages clients to exercise their own wills and tap their inner potential in order to once again care, trust, and feel more spontaneously.

Therapists draw from a variety of approaches through interviews and recommendations. Victims should seek the therapist who meets his or her own particular needs.

Group Therapy

Many therapists prefer to use group treatment because past victims feel very isolated from others and unique in their circumstances. Meeting other individuals with similar issues dispels these fears and reduces feelings of loneliness. By interacting with other group members, survivors practice building or rebuilding their social skills. Group members also have an opportunity to reduce the pain they feel through ventilating their feelings. In sharing, members gain different perspectives on their experiences, which enables them to begin to recognize their feelings and understand their trauma (Herman and Schatzow, 1984).

Survivor groups are most often either all male or all female, but occasionally groups are mixed. Such programs are sponsored by feminist organizations, mental health clinics, family service agencies, or other organizations.

Herman and Schatzow (1984) conduct their practice with groups of five to seven women and two therapists.

> Three conditions are required for inclusion in a group: (1) that prospective members express generally positive feelings about participating in a group with other incest victims; (2) that prospective members be functioning reasonably well in day-to-day life; and (3) that group members have an appropriate ongoing relationship with an individual therapist.
>
> The co-leader then screens potential members to ensure that they conform to the criteria, were not in current acute crisis, and were well established in their individual therapy. Since groups can be an unsettling experience, it is necessary for individuals to have therapists to monitor their stress, help them deal with particularly intense feelings and integrate their learnings once the group has terminated. (pp. 606–07)

The groups last for 10 sessions of 90 minutes each. Goals of members were found to fall into four categories: "recovery of memories, improved relationships, improved self-esteem and sharing the incest secret with a close acquaintance or family member" (p. 610). A follow-up study six months after the Herman-Schatzow groups indicated that of the 71 percent of the women who responded, all felt that they had been positively influenced by the experience.

Other groups provide similar positive experiences. One past victim relates,

> *"Our group combined everything. At first we just shared our stories. In the beginning, we were asked to keep diaries or journals on our reactions to the group, on what we did well, and on how we didn't cope so well between group meetings. After a time, we read these journals aloud. It was scary at first, but we got used to it. Reading them aloud really helped. Occasionally we had homework, such as having to answer questions or assess certain ideas or attitudes we had. Sometimes we would agree to work on some particular behavior for a week. We also did role-playing where we had to face an empty chair. When I did it, the chair was supposed to hold my father, and I could say whatever I chose. It really helped me realize how angry I was."*

Role playing, keeping journals, and writing—but not sending—letters help sexual abuse survivors. Journal writing encourages the identification of positive and negative feelings about the abuse, the perpetrator, and the nonprotecting parent. In writing down these emotions, survivors are helped to understand more clearly who they are. By keeping a journal over a period of time, the writer can also trace his or her progress. And finally, by placing the journal on a shelf, the survivor symbolically puts aside the memories, when the therapy is over or the victim temporarily feels the need to separate from the hurt.

Through roleplaying past victims practice telling others of the abuse and their feelings or prepare to confront significant individuals. Confronting the perpetrator, for example, may at first be altogether too threatening, but in these exercises victims rehearse what they will say and also anticipate possible reactions from the perpetrator.

Writing to someone with whom the past victim has unresolved issues helps to express his or her feelings. Such a letter aids the person to prepare to talk or to revise and deliver the letter.

Jane describes the use of her letter:

> *"I had never intended to send my mother the letter. Writing it had really helped me. I was able to express feelings I'd never admitted to. But I finally decided I would give it to her. I went over to her house, handed it to her, and left the room while she read it. I couldn't be there. When I got the courage to return, she just sat there with tears in her eyes. 'I'm sorry,' she cried. 'I'm sorry I wasn't there for you, but I was so afraid of him myself.' At first it seemed like her usual denial of my father's abuse of me, but then I realized how vulnerable we both were. That letter opened up real communication between us."*

Some groups, more issue-oriented than those described above, deal with topics such as sex education, coping with anger, communication skills, assertiveness, and building new skills. Group therapy, used extensively with past victims of sexual abuse, has also been effective with survivors of other childhood abuses. Whatever the focus of the group, victims can be helped to build and rebuild social skills and learn that they are not alone.

Self-Help Groups

Self-help groups, often modeled on Alcoholics Anonymous, have a history of effectiveness with individuals who feel isolated by their problems.

Parents Anonymous
Although originally designed for parents who physically abused their children, this group now attracts parents who are former victims of all types of maltreatment. The members build support systems while they learn to cease their abusive or potentially abusive behavior.

Adults Molested as Children
This group evolved from the Child Sexual Abuse Treatment Program in California (see Chapter 14) and was designed for past victims of incest who felt the need of support.

Commonly a group member is in her late twenties. The incestuous situation has not been reported to the authorities and she has not been able to resolve the experience either with her mother or offending father to her satisfaction. Both parents avoid or frustrate her attempts to confront them. Ever since her adolescence, the victim has abused herself unmercifully—by promiscuity, by substance abuse, and/or by sabotaging or not fulfilling the potential of intimate relationships. She comes to the group angry, guilty, self-pitying, fearful of authority figures, and apprehensive over her sexuality and sexual identity. (Giarretto, 1982, p. 28)

In the group, women express their anger, shame, and guilt. They learn that others feel as they do. After at least two eight-week sessions, the participants join a Recontact Group, composed of unrelated nonoffending and offending parents. The former victims—through contact with these parents—begin to complete unfinished emotional business. Eventually, past victims find themselves bonding with these other parents and, in this way, reestablish trust and open communication. Survivors are then asked to transfer the confrontation to and to open communication with their own parents. Even when their parents are not available, past victims appear to gain a significant amount from the group experience and are able to use their experiences in other relationships (Giarretto, 1982).

Writers' Groups

In these groups, members express their feelings and their experiences through various literary forms. Two books, *I Never Told Anyone: Writings by Women Survivors of Child Sexual Abuse* (Bass and Thornton, 1983) and *Voices in the Night: Women Speaking about Incest* (McNaron and Morgan, 1982) resulted from such groups. One past victim recounted how she started a writers' group.

> *"I was affiliated with a woman's center, and they knew I wrote quite a bit. They invited me to lead a literary group. When I suggested a group for incest survivors, I think they were a bit taken aback, but they agreed. Initially five women came. We met once a week and would write on a particular topic. For example, 'Was there any one person that you can point to who helped you to survive?' or 'What survival skills have you developed?' Rather than becoming immersed in the details of the abuse, we tried to focus on the survival aspect. I guess we were almost congratulating ourselves for surviving. You can't exactly run out and tell everyone you survived, but with special people or through writing, it's nice to celebrate your victories."*

A variety of self-help groups are emerging. Gay and lesbian groups and those specifically for men are gaining prominence. For the adult who was abused or neglected as a child, the support of peers is comforting and leads to understanding and recovery.

Legal Actions

Recently, there has been a move for survivors to take legal action against their perpetrators, often in the form of suit for money for therapy. Advocates of these actions describe them as not only just retribution but therapeutic and validating as well (Friess, 1993). Other survivors report that the act of suing one's father alienates them from the rest of the family, making the past victim feel as alone and isolated as he or she did in childhood (Penelope, 1992). Friess, in her autobiographical book *Cry the Darkness* (1993), describes her suit of her father and the emotional toll it took on her and her family.

Certainly any survivor contemplating legal action against a perpetrator should have the support of those around her or him. In addition it is helpful for a therapist to review with the survivor her or his feelings and the impact that this action will have on the survivor and those close to her or him.

Summary

As society becomes more conscious of the existence of child maltreatment, an increasing number of former victims are coming forward to tell their stories. They disclose for a number of reasons. They may be troubled by symptoms seemingly unrelated to the abuse, by relational or sexual dysfunction, with problems of loss, or by issues related to the normal progress of their lives.

All types of child maltreatment leave scars. Often these scars are similar, but the symptoms specifically related to neglect, abuse, or sexual abuse are somewhat different in their degree or expression.

Individuals who were neglected as children have difficulty trusting. The inconsistency and lack of nurturance in their childhoods make it difficult for them to expect support from others or even to depend on themselves. These survivors feel anger over their parents' lack of care—an anger that may lead to depression, delinquency, or aggressive behavior. They may have trouble relating to others in any but a superficial manner. Their low self-esteem, combined with poor social skills, can promote difficulty in communication as well as in everyday functioning. Physical problems result from early malnutrition and poor emotional health.

Physically abusing families leave scars that hamper the victims' ability to trust, express and identify anger, and form and maintain relationships. Low self-esteem in these victims interferes with their coping skills and inhibits their ability to parent. There is a need for research into the effects of domestic violence on the lives of the adults who experienced it as children.

Victims of past sexual abuse experience wounds from feeling betrayed, traumatic sexualization, powerlessness, and stigmatization. They have difficulty trusting and often feel powerless to control their own lives. This powerlessness often results in sexual problems, revictimization, problems with relationships, confused sexuality, and impaired self-esteem. Because of their need to repeat the past, survivors may reconstruct the patterns of their childhoods if they do not seek help. Some past victims repress memories that are too difficult to handle.

Treatment of adult former victims can be given individually or in groups. Individual therapies include traditional psychotherapy, gestalt, behavior, crisis intervention, and transactional analysis. Groups, however, are also considered to be very effective. Therapy groups use techniques such as journal writing, unsent letters, and roleplaying to enable past victims to understand and deal with their trauma. Self-help groups also contribute to the therapeutic efforts. With therapy, survivors can be helped to take control of their own lives and live more effectively despite the traumas of dysfunctional childhoods.

Exploration Questions

1. What are the myths commonly held about adults who were maltreated as children?

2. What might cause former victims to disclose their abusive childhoods during adulthood?

3. Why does the victim of neglect in childhood have difficulty trusting? The abused victim?

4. How might anger result from particular kinds of maltreatment? How might it be expressed?

5. What is meant by *verbal inaccessibility?* Why is it a problem?

6. What types of physical symptoms plague neglect survivors and what are their origins?

7. Why do past victims of abuse experience relational imbalances? How are these manifested?

8. Why do past victims of abuse have difficulty coping?

9. What do Finkelhor and Browne cite as the primary residual effects of child sexual abuse?

10. Why might there be a correlation between homosexuality and past sexual abuse?

11. What is meant by *mind-body split,* and how does it affect victims of sexual abuse? How do many former victims feel about their bodies?

12. Why do past victims of sexual abuse feel guilt? How is it manifested?

13. Why might survivors of child sexual abuse again become victims in adult life?

14. Is there a difference between those sexually abused outside the home and those who are survivors of incest?

15. What differences do males and females who suffered abuse demonstrate?

16. What types of therapies are available for former victims of maltreatment?

17. Why are groups especially effective with former victims?

18. What self-help groups are available for former victims?

Activities for Applied Learning

1. Read *Mommie Dearest* by Christina Crawford, *Daddy's Girl* by Charlotte V. Allen, or *My Father's House* by Sylvia Fraser and discuss the residual effects for these past victims.

2. Search out biographies of or biographical information on individuals such as James Earl Ray, Charles Manson, Sirhan Sirhan, Albert deSalvo, and Lee Harvey Oswald and consider how their backgrounds affected their behavior.

3. Investigate the services that are specifically for former victims of abuse and neglect offered in your community. Invite a speaker to address the class.

Suggested Readings

Blume, E. S. *Secret Survivors: Incest and Its Aftereffects in Women.* New York: Wiley, 1990.

Cleveland, D. *Incest: The Story of Three Women.* Lexington, MA: Lexington Books, 1986.

Courtois, C. *Healing the Incest Wound: Adult Survivors in Therapy.* New York: Norton, 1988.

Evert, K. and Bijkerk, I. *When You're Ready: A Woman's Healing From Childhood Physical and Sexual Abuse by her Mother.* Rockville, MD: Launch, 1987.

Fraser, S. *My Father's House: A Memoir of Incest and Healing.* New York: Harper and Row, 1987.

Friess, D. *Cry the Darkness.* Deerfield Beach, CA: Health Communications, 1993.

Lew, M. *Victims No Longer: Men Recovering from Incest.* New York: Harper and Row, 1990.

Oliver, B. and Utain, M. *The Healing Relationship.* Deerfield Beach, CA: Health Communications, 1991.

Tower, C. C. *Secret Scars: A Guide for Survivors of Child Sexual Abuse.* New York: Viking Penguin, 1988.

References

Becker, J. "Incidence and Types of Sexual Dysfunction in Rape and Incest Victims." *Journal of Sex and Marriage Family* 8:65–74.

Bender, L. "Psychopathic Behavior Disorders in Children." In *Handbook of Correctional Psychology,* edited by R. Lindner and R. Seliger. New York: Philosophical Library, 1948.

Blume, E. S. *Secret Survivors: Incest and Its Aftereffects in Women.* New York: Wiley, 1990.

Bowen, M. "The Use of Family Theory in Clinical Practice." *Comprehensive Psychiatry* 7 (1966):345–74.

Briere, J. N. *Child Abuse Trauma,* Newbury Park, CA: Sage, 1992.

Chapman, S. B., and Terry, T. "Treatment of Sexually Abused Children from Minority Urban Families: A Socio-Cultural Perspective." *Clinical Proceedings: Children's Hospital National Medical Center* 40 (1984):244–59.

Chase, H., and Martin, H. "Undernutrition and Child Development." *New England Journal of Medicine* 282 (1970):933–39.

Chase, N. A. *A Child Is Being Beaten.* New York: McGraw-Hill, 1975.

Corey, G. *I Never Knew I Had a Choice.* Monterey, CA: Brooks/Cole Publishing, 1983.

Courtois, C. A. *Healing the Incest Wound: Adult Survivors in Therapy.* New York: Norton, 1988.

deYoung, M. *The Sexual Victimization of Children.* Jefferson, NC: McFarland, 1982.

DiTomasso, M. J. and Routh, D. K. "Recall of Abuse in Childhood and Three Measures of Dissociation." *Child Abuse and Neglect* 17 (4), (1993):477–485.

Downs, W. R. "Developmental Considerations for the Effects of Childhood Sexual Abuse." *Journal of Interpersonal Violence* 8 (3) (1993):331–342.

Ellenson, G. "Disturbances of Perception in Adult Female Incest Survivors." *Social Casework: The Journal of Contemporary Social Work.* March (1986):149–59.

Evert, K. and Bijkerk, I. *When You're Ready: A woman's healing from childhood physical and sexual abuse by her mother.* Rockville, MD: Launch Press, 1987.

Faria, G., and Belohlovek, N. "Treating Female Adult Survivors of Childhood Incest." *Social Casework* 65 (1984):465–71.

Finkelhor, D. *Child Sexual Abuse.* New York: Free Press, 1984.

Finkelhor, D., and Browne, A. "The Traumatic Impact of Child Sexual Abuse: A Conceptualization." *American Journal of Orthopsychiatry* 55 (1985):530–41.

Finkelhor, D.; with Araji, S.; Baron, L.; Browne, A.; Peters, S. D.; and Wyatt, G. E. *A Sourcebook on Child Sexual Abuse.* Beverly Hills, CA: Sage, 1986.

Fontana, V. *Somewhere a Child Is Crying.* New York: Macmillan, 1973.

Forward, S., and Buck, C. *Betrayal of Innocence: Incest and Its Devastation.* New York: Viking Penguin, 1978.

Fraser, S. *My Father's House: A Memoir of Incest and of Healing.* New York: Harper and Row, 1987.

Fredrickson, R. *Repressed Memories.* New York: Simon & Schuster, 1992.

Friess, D. *Cry the Darkness.* Deerfield Beach, CA: Health Communications, 1993.

Fritz, G.; Stoll, K.; and Wagner, N. "A Comparison of Males and Females Who Were Sexually Molested as Children." *Journal of Sex and Marital Therapy* 7 (1981):54–9.

Gelinas, D. "The Persisting Negative Effects of Incest." *Psychiatry* 46 (1983):312–32.

Giarretto, H. *Integrated Treatment of Child Sexual Abuse.* Palo Alto, CA: Science and Behavior Books, 1982.

Goodwin, J. *Sexual Abuse: Incest Victims and Their Families.* Littleton, MA: PSG Publishing, 1982.

Grosso, E. "The Persephone Complex: Understanding and Treating Lesbians after Father-Daughter Incest." Unpublished paper, 1984.

Groth, N. *Men Who Rape.* New York: Plenum Publishing, 1979.

Groves, B. M. "Growing Up in a Violent World: The Impact of Family and Community Violence on Young Children and Their Families." In E. J. Erwin (ed.). *Putting Children First.* Baltimore, MD: Paul H. Brooks, 1996.

Helfer, R. E. *Childhood Comes First: A Crash Course in Childhood for Adults.* East Lansing, MI: Ray E. Helfer, 1978.

Henning, K., Leitenberg, H., Coffey, P., Turner, T., and Bennett, R. T. "Long-Term Psychological and

Social Impact of Witnessing Physical Conflict Between Parents." *Journal of Interpersonal Violence.* 11(1) (1996):35–51.

Herman, J., and Schatzow, E. "Time Limited Group Therapy for Women with a History of Incest." *International Journal of Group Psychotherapy* 34 (1984):605–16.

Hunter, M. *The Sexually Abused Male.* Newbury Park, CA: Sage, 1990.

Janoff-Bulman, R., and Frieze, I. "A Theoretical Perspective for Understanding Reactions to Victimization." *Journal of Social Issues* 39 (1983):1–17.

Justice, B., and Justice, R. *The Abusing Family.* New York: Human Services Press, 1976.

Justice, B., and Justice, R. *The Broken Taboo: Sex in the Family.* New York: Human Services Press, 1979.

Kinzl, J. and Biebl, W. "Long-Term Effects of Incest: Life Events Triggering Mental Disorders in Female Patients with Sexual Abuse in Childhood." *Child Abuse and Neglect* 16 (4) (1992):567–573.

Maltz, W. *The Sexual Healing Journey: A Guide for Survivors of Sexual Abuse.* New York: HarperCollins, 1991.

Martin, H. *The Abused Child.* Cambridge, MA: Ballinger, 1976.

Nasjleti, M. "Suffering in Silence: The Male Victim." *Child Welfare* 59 (1980):269–75.

Oliver, J., and Taylor, A. "Five Generations of Ill-Treated Children in One Family Pedigree." *British Journal of Psychiatry* 119 (1971):472–80.

Parker, S. "Healing Abuse in Gay Men: The Group Component." In Hunter, M. *The Sexually Abused Male, Vol. 2,* pp. 177–198. New York: Lexington Books, 1990.

Penelope. "Suing My Perpetrator: A Survivor's Story." *Journal of Child Sexual Abuse* 1 (2) (1992):119–124.

Polansky, N.; Borgman, R. D.; and DeSaix, C. *Roots of Futility.* San Francisco: Jossey-Bass, 1972.

Polansky, N.; Chalmers, M. A.; Buttenwieser, E.; and Williams, D. *Damaged Parents: An Anatomy of Child Neglect.* Chicago: University of Chicago Press, 1981.

Roth, S. and Newman, E. "The Process of Coping with Incest for Adult Survivors." *Journal of Interpersonal Violence* 8 (3), (1993):363–377.

Russell, D. *Secret Trauma.* New York: Basic Books, 1986.

Ryder, D. *Breaking the Circle of Satanic Ritual Abuse.* Minneapolis, MN: CompCare, 1992.

Sanford, L., and Donovan, M. E. *Women and Self-Esteem.* Garden City, NY: Doubleday Anchor Press, 1984.

Sgroi, S. *Handbook for Clinical Intervention in Child Sexual Abuse.* Lexington, MA: Lexington Books, 1982.

Sheiman, J. A. "I've Always Wondered if Something Happened to Me: Assessment of Child Sexual Abuse Survivors with Amnesia." *Journal of Child Sexual Abuse* 2 (2), (1993):13–21.

Silbert, M., and Pines, A. "Early Sexual Exploitation as an Influence in Prostitution." *Social Work* July–Aug. (1983):285–89.

Tower, C. C. *Secret Scars: A Guide for Survivors of Child Sexual Abuse.* New York: Viking Penguin, 1988.

Warner, C. G. *Conflict and Intervention in Social and Domestic Violence.* Bowie, MD: Robert J. Brady, 1981.

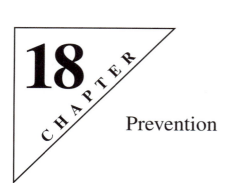

18 CHAPTER

Prevention

There are no easy remedies for the problem of child abuse and neglect. Despite treatment of the families and of adult survivors of child maltreatment, much more must be done to correct this national problem. Prevention is one way to combat all forms of child abuse and neglect.

Of the three types of prevention, primary prevention is the effort to educate the general population to prevent maltreatment; secondary prevention consists of efforts directed toward high-risk populations; and tertiary prevention is intervention to prevent abuse or neglect from continuing. So far, this book has discussed intervention, but primary and secondary prevention deserve closer consideration.

Agencies across the nation are committed to efforts that further child abuse prevention. The National Committee for Prevention of Child Abuse, founded in 1972 by Donna Stone, set as its goal to reduce child abuse by at least 20 percent by 1990. The committee continues to work toward this goal through public awareness and education, specific prevention programs, advocacy, research, and evaluation. Although funding is always a problem, over the last few years money has come from a variety of sources, one of which is the Children's Trust Fund.

In the late 1970s, Dr. Ray Helfer founded the Children's Trust Fund to support states' prevention efforts. Currently the Children's Trust Fund is employed in 40 states, raising monies for prevention through surcharges on marriage licenses, birth certificates, and divorce decrees or through specifically earmarked tax refunds. State advisory committees set up guidelines to govern the distribution of available monies. More recently, states have been encouraged to develop Children's Trust Funds by the Child Abuse Prevention Federal Challenge Grant, which matches one-fourth of the money a state makes available for prevention funds (Daro, 1988; Scott and Birch, 1986; Donnelly, 1991). Trust Funds use these funds for a variety of prevention programs. For example, the Massachusetts Children's Trust Fund recently developed a booklet to help educators establish a child abuse reporting protocol in their schools. In addition to state and federal resources, private industry, individual agencies, and communities are using more innovative methods to raise needed funds.

Prevention has been successful in four areas: in schools, with families, with professionals, and within the community.

Prevention Efforts in Schools

Prevention efforts should begin in the schools where the parents of tomorrow learn what will be expected of them. The hope is that if children are taught what abusive parents have never learned, they will have a better chance of becoming healthy adults and concerned parents. The school can aid in child abuse prevention by providing

- Life skills training
- Preparation for parenthood
- Self-protection training
- Educational services for the community
- Help for at-risk families

Life Skills Training

To cope with our complex society, children need more—or at least different—skills than those of generations ago. This is especially true for newly immigrated children. Children today may not need to learn how to milk a cow or till a field; the skills they require are more subtle. The same learning that prepares them for the complexities of our society helps them become better parents as well. Several basic and appropriate skills can be taught to children.

Coping with Stress
Schools can teach children to assign priorities in order to enable them to choose between myriad tasks. In developing problem-solving skills, children learn perspective. Some schools even teach relaxation techniques to help minimize physical and mental stress.

Coping with Crisis
Another life skill children need is the ability to cope with crisis. Some schools teach their students the appropriate people to approach when a crisis occurs. Officers from fire and police departments and representatives from other community organizations give talks to promote safety. More recently children are also being educated on what to do during the crisis of being abused (e.g., say no, run away and tell someone). By knowing the multitude of resources available to them, children are less likely to become isolated adults who do not know how to seek help.

Making Decisions
Helfer (1978) suggests that important skills that abusive parents failed to develop be taught to children to prevent their becoming abusive parents. Children need to learn to make decisions. To make choices is, in fact, fairly easy to impart, but the assumption must be that children have the right to choose. Increasingly schools are creating more flexible curricula to encourage choices and develop this skill.

Learning Socialization
Children must also be encouraged to learn appropriate ways to get their needs met. When adults actively listen to children, they encourage children to express their needs. When children know that they have been heard, they are then more likely to be patient in waiting to have these needs met and to delay gratification. Teachers are learning to allow children to express their feelings more openly, and in this way children find how to separate feelings from actions. In a society filled with violence, children must learn that violence need not

follow feelings of anger. In whatever they do, children must learn to take responsibility for their own actions.

Building Positive Self-image

School personnel know the importance of building a positive self-image for healthy adulthood. Books, such as *100 Ways to Enhance Self-Concepts in the Classroom* (Wells and Canfield, 1994), and *Unlocking Doors to Self-Esteem* (Fox and Weaver, 1990), address this issue and suggest exercises for teachers to use in helping children feel better about themselves. Building self-image is being more fully integrated into the curriculum, and teachers are helping children create and enjoy successes in order to feel better about themselves.

These are just a few of the life skills that children can be taught. In addition, vocational training, budgeting instruction, and time-management practices are useful to prepare for adulthood. Teaching life skills should help children become healthy adults who feel capable of controlling their own lives and more comfortable in caring for and guiding their own children in the future.

Preparation for Parenthood

To prepare today's children to be tomorrow's healthy parents, they must be provided with knowledge about normal sexuality, child development, and parenting skills.

Normal Sexuality

Since most members of sexually abusive families know little about healthy sexual relationships, teaching children more about their bodies and the sexual functions might actually protect them from being abused and abusing. Normal sexuality should be part of the regular curriculum. As children mature, the amount of knowledge they require will increase, therefore high schools need to help them integrate this knowledge. Teaching basic material should be addressed more fully than can be done in one high school health or biology course. Giving children age-appropriate material beginning in elementary school will increase their comfort with and broaden their understanding of their own sexuality. When children learn about sexuality and that information becomes a normal, natural part of their education, they are better prepared to enter into healthy sexual relationships as adults. The ability to communicate sexual needs removes one of the many stresses in marriage. Poor communication between spouses greatly hampers each individual's ability to parent effectively.

Child Development

Adolescents who babysit should be acquainted with the developmental stages of children. If these teens become parents, some knowledge on the subject will save them a great deal of worry and frustration. If adolescents are taught what to expect from children, child rearing might be viewed more realistically and less idealistically.

Parenting Skills

Along with learning what to expect from children, students must learn parenting skills. Parenting skills involve the roles and responsibilities expected by society. In one particularly useful exercise, students pair up as couples and care for an egg. The egg—representing their baby—must be kept warm and given proper care. The egg must not be left alone and must be protected from harm. At the end of the exercise, the participants discuss what they have learned about the joys and burdens of parenting. The exercise must not become a game, and the seriousness of the task must be emphasized. Some classes hold mock child abuse proceedings or court hearings when a "parent" has damaged the egg. Students may also be helped to grieve over their egg if it "dies." The students find the experience enlightening.

Discussions on a variety of parenting issues, both in this culture and in others, are also helpful. Debates on discipline, the assignment of chores, the question of allowances and budgeting, and the facts about nutrition may even help children recognize how their own parents are feeling about and handling these issues. Children who learn what parenting entails may be less eager to become parents too early, but are more prepared to be effective when, and if, they do.

Self-Protection Training

Teachers

Schools have become increasingly involved in helping children protect themselves, especially in the area of sexual abuse. A prerequisite to classroom prevention programs, however, is the training of teachers to become involved with and committed to this aspect of child abuse prevention education. The National Education Association's Child Abuse and Neglect Training Program (Tower, 1984a, 1984b) exemplifies a national effort to train teachers so that they will feel more comfortable bringing prevention into the classroom. School systems now offer this and other forms of in-service training to teachers and other school personnel, and invite teachers to write proposals for grants to bring in experts to train the school staff.

Children

Once teachers become comfortable with the material, they can plan prevention programs for children. Such programs are becoming more prevalent. A recent survey by the National Committee to Prevent Child Abuse found that 25 percent of public schools, nationwide, had instituted some type of prevention training for at least one grade level (Daro, 1988). In 1982, California passed a law that children be introduced to child abuse prevention training at least three times during their educational career. Basically, the numerous programs now available strive to (1) educate children about what sexual abuse is, (2) make children more aware of who potential abusers are, and (3) teach children what action to take when someone tries to abuse them (Finkelhor, 1986; Daro, 1988). Program material addresses all ages of children, and total programs provide age-appropriate information from kindergarten through sixth grade (Tutty, 1994). The Personal Safety Curriculum (Crisci, 1983), designed for teachers to train children to protect themselves against sexual abuse, offers segments for each grade level. Another, called the Child Assault Prevention Project, brings in experts to help children of all grades recognize sexual abuse and how to combat it (Cooper, Lutter, and Phelps, 1983). Books, such as *Red Flag-Green Flag* (Williams 1980), *Come Tell Me Right Away* (Sanford, 1982), *He Told Me Not to Tell* (Fay, 1979), and *Top Secret* (Fay and Flerchinger, 1982), and tapes, such as "A Dragon in My Closet" (Tower, 1984a) and "Deborah Wore Designer Jeans" (Tower, 1984b), are used in classrooms either alone or to supplement other programs. When these teaching aids are used in school prevention programs, the values of various cultures must be addressed.

Prevention efforts in classrooms emphasize that children have the right not to be hurt, and that if they are being abused, they should tell a trusted adult. One reason teachers must be comfortable with this material is that with the programs' emphasis on seeking help, children are led to confide in an adult—especially teachers. Teachers must be receptive to children's attempts to tell them and must know where to go with the information (Olson, 1985; Plummer 1986).

How successful have these classroom efforts been? Beginning in 1984, attempts to look critically at the training began. Finkelhor (1988) considered twenty-five of these evaluative studies to ascertain the usefulness of the child empowerment efforts. Of the twenty-five studies, twenty-three trained children in classroom settings, one was homebased and the other was sponsored by the Campfire Girls organization. The children were between three and twelve years old, with the highest number in the third, fourth, and fifth grades. Paper and pencil tests, questionnaires, role plays, skits, viewing and discussing films or by actual simulation were the methods of assessment (Finkelhor, 1988).

Finkelhor's conclusion was that children did learn prevention concepts. The most easily learned were what abuse is, parts of the body, and types of touching. The children found most difficult to comprehend that abuse can be perpetrated by known—and sometimes loved—adults. Concepts were more easily grasped than was behavior changed. This conclusion has been supported by more recent studies (Wurtele et al., 1992; Tutty, 1994).

The evaluators also explored commonly expressed concerns about in-school prevention programs. For example, despite the warnings of some critics, researchers found that children who received training did not appear unusually fearful or alienated from adults (Finkelhor, 1988; Wurtele et al., 1992). Another benefit of prevention programs, besides

teaching children concepts that will protect them from possible sexual abuse, is that training stimulates disclosure. Children who have been abused tend to come forward to report once they have taken part in school training. Through these efforts, children communicate more openly both in the classroom and at home with their parents.

Three aspects of these programs, however, are debatable. School districts that are hesitant to teach sex education are unlikely to institute sex abuse prevention training. Does sex abuse prevention training distort the picture of sexuality when deviance is taught before the normal role of sexual development? What happens to children who are later abused when programs suggest that saying no prevents abuse?

Evaluation of existing training programs is fairly recent. Originally, most studies evaluated only one approach with no control group. Most researchers studied children between 8 and 12 years of age, so it was unknown at what age prevention education would be most successful (Wolfe et al., 1986; Daro, 1988). More recently, Tutty (1994) compared the reactions of children of various developmental ages to school prevention programs. This researcher concluded that younger children (grade 1) had difficulty with such concepts as defying an adult's request, and that someone in the family could touch them inappropriately. They were also more likely to see themselves to blame if abuse did occur. As children got older, they were better able to integrate these ideas. The author concluded that while children do learn the concepts and benefit from school prevention programs, the model should include a repetition of the material through the school years to allow for maximum absorption of ideas. Wurtele et al. (1992) wondered whether teachers or parents were more effective in helping preschoolers learn sexual abuse prevention concepts. They concluded that pre-schoolers gained higher levels of personal safety from both parents and teachers with little or no distinction. In addition, fears that children would be frightened by prevention materials were unfounded (Wurtele et al., 1992; Elrod and Rubin, 1993). Franzem (1993) suggested that games be further integrated into prevention curricula. Games are within a child's frame of reference and offer predictability. This may enable them to learn more effectively.

Hopefully, there will continue to be evaluation and revision of school-based prevention programs, so that children can be adequately prepared to protect themselves.

Educational Services for the Community

Prescriptions for prevention include community awareness. Schools can further these efforts through workshops, opening their facilities to self-help groups, and through adult education.

Many school prevention programs expand the curriculum to include at least one workshop for the community. The National Education Association's Child Abuse and Neglect Program, for example, suggests five workshops for teachers and a sixth for the community. This last session acquaints the participants with the problems facing abusive parents, educates them as to resources available to combat child abuse or neglect, and engages them in a discussion of how to prevent child maltreatment in the future (Tower, 1984a, 1984b).

In addition to providing training for the community, schools offer support to other prevention programs by allowing the use of their facilities and resources. Self-help groups such as Parents Anonymous or Parents United appreciate the use of meeting rooms. Schools' films or books could also be made available for interested groups or individuals (Darmstadt, 1990).

And finally, schools could provide adult education programs for parents. Along with the usual offerings designed to improve skills or introduce new interests, schools might include evening courses in child development, parenting skills, budgeting, stress reduction, and problem-solving skills to help parents expand their capabilities, feel more in control at home, and perhaps be less likely to abuse. At one innovative school, a course entitled "Understanding Child Abuse and Neglect for Parents" attracted a number of people, including several potential parents and one or two who admitted, well into the course, that they feared they were abusive. The instructor worked with these concerned individuals to improve their coping skills and to help them become more relaxed parents.

Help for At-Risk Families

In every community, there are families who are potentially abusive or neglectful. Families need to minimize their stresses and strengthen their coping abilities. Schools could offer evening programs for parents who work or for those who need extra relief from child care responsibilities. Late afternoon recreation programs for adolescents might alleviate the stress that is commonly felt before the dinner hour.

Underutilized schools sometimes donate space to crisis nurseries. When parents feel the need of support or temporary relief from child care, they can stop in or leave their children for a while. As part of their course structure, high school students assist in these nurseries.

Prevention Efforts with Families

It is important to educate the parents of tomorrow so that they will not be abusive, but what of the families of today? There are many ways to help families cope with stress as a prevention for maltreatment. Some parenting enhancement programs are offered to those who are specifically designated as at high risk of abusive or neglectful behavior. Others are designed for parents who are interested or feel the need to take such courses.

The most effective programs for parents focus on improving their coping skills, educating them about child development, facilitating bonding and communication with their children, and increasing their ability to approach helping resources (Daro, 1988, Daro, 1993).

Education need not stop with adolescents' anticipating future parenthood. Those who are currently parents wonder at the effectiveness of their techniques. An extremely useful program, called Responsive Parenting (Lerman, 1983), has been adopted by community groups and social service agencies in an effort to promote positive parenting. The program is designed to be used with issue-oriented discussion groups, with topics such as children's developmental stages, children's fears and feelings, family relationships, positive discipline, children's independence, cooperation and responsibility, and children's self-esteem. Originally used with high-risk families, this program (once called Parent Awareness Training) now attracts many parents who want to develop better child-management abilities. Spinoffs from Gordon's Parent Effectiveness Training (1970) make the demanding job of parenting a little easier. Such programs are offered by parenting centers, family life centers, and YMCAs.

A particularly effective program, the Minnesota Early Learning Demonstration (MELD), provides mothers with intensive training and support through two three-hour weekly meetings for two years. In MELD, the mothers discuss such topics as child development, family management, and personal growth. While the women listen to speakers, watch demonstrations, view films, prepare specifically designed homework, and share experiences, their children are cared for (Daro, 1988).

Another such program, Good Start, sponsored by the Massachusetts Society for the Prevention of Cruelty to Children, is also designed to teach new families how to cope with parenting. Good Start, a voluntary, home-based program provides counseling, family life, medical and nutritional education, parent support groups, infant play groups, and child care/development training. The program targets families of newborns, providing them not only with the above services but also, in some instances, with volunteer parent-aides who give support, child care assistance, and community information. In the four years of its operation, Good Start has served over 320 families who were at risk for abuse and neglect (Meade, 1991). Kowal and colleagues (1989) found that the Good Start program has demonstrated positive changes in the abilities of these families.

Based on the success of programs such as these, the National Committee to Prevent Child Abuse (NCPCA) in partnership with Ronald McDonald's Children's Charities (RMCC) and collaborating with the Hawaii Family Stress Center and the Hawaii Health Department, in January of 1992, instituted a national initiative called Healthy Families America (HFA). This home visiting program targets first-time parents in their homes with the goal of giving children a healthy start and preventing child maltreatment. Central to this program is the help that families receive in making connections with other programs and organizations in the community to insure the continuation of a support system once HFA is no longer involved. Statewide task forces oversee the operation of the program in each state. Workers carried caseloads of not more than 15 families and receive intensive training. Services are designed to be more intensive at first and then taper off as the families are helped to gain more independence. Only through such intensive services can some families gain independence and be able to parent effectively (Mitchell and Donnelly, 1993).

Although fathers contribute to child maltreatment, they receive far less instruction in how to parent effectively than do mothers. Biller and Meredith's *Father Power* (1974) attempted to stimulate programs to educate men to interact with their wives and children. Many fathers are unaware of the issues related to child development, pregnancy, or childbirth itself until they find themselves faced with them. Understanding children may endow fathers with more realistic expectations of their offspring. In addition, researchers (see especially Finkelhor, 1984) postulate that mothers are less likely to sexually abuse because of their involvement in the total functioning of the child—from feeding and bathing to toilet training. Fathers, on the other hand, have traditionally been less involved in these daily tasks and therefore not as emotionally involved on a multidimensional level. Perhaps the training of fathers in other areas would enable them to become more appropriately involved with their children and less likely to see them in a sexual context.

Training fathers and mothers is vital. Parenting is one of the most important jobs many individuals will ever undertake, but it is also the one for which they are the most inadequately trained. This is especially true if their models in childhood were distorted or ineffective.

Medical staff or social service personnel may be able to recognize high-risk parents during pregnancy. High-risk parents are those who demonstrate a variety of characteristics that have been associated with later abuse or neglect (Kennell, Voos, and Klaus, 1976; Helfer, 1976). (See Chapter 3.) By identifying these parents, social workers can make them aware of additional resources to help prevent their possibly maltreating their children.

The ethics of screening must be considered. Who, and by what standards, has the right to screen for future child abuse or neglect? Helfer (1976) likens this type of screening to those for other medical prevention, such as testing a pregnant woman for tuberculosis, high blood pressure, or venereal disease—all of which would affect the baby. Why, then, not screen for future physical care and protection for the child?

One answer might be to do a routine screening of all potential parents to determine what type of services could be made available for their particular potential deficiency. Who would do the screening and from what type of facility remain unanswered. Some critics say screening violates basic human rights. Yet many hospitals and social agencies are instituting programs to screen either routinely or those parents who previously demonstrated that they are high risk.

The word *screening* implies distinguishing between those who can and cannot parent effectively. For proponents, screening is not intended to pass judgment on potential parents but to serve merely as a way to determine what services might be necessary to aid parents in the best care for their children. But arguments arise from this proposition. For example, who determines what adequate parenting entails? Other than the legal definition of adequate parenting—meeting minimal basic needs—this subject will need sensitive interpretation.

When screening of high-risk parents does occur, it begins in the early prenatal period. An assessment of family circumstances sheds some light on the environment into which the baby will arrive. Does the marriage appear stable? Do the parents support each other? What type of support system does the mother have? Do the parents describe their own upbringings as positive? Was the baby planned and wanted? Does the family or mother have stable employment or an adequate source of income? Since pregnancy can be a period during which parents are especially vulnerable, it is helpful to aid the future parents in creating as stable an environment as possible.

A great deal can be learned about the mother's support system by whom she brings to prenatal visits and how she relates to these individuals. If she consistently comes alone, is this by choice or because she has no one to whom she can turn for support? How involved does the father seem in the pregnancy?

Numerous hospitals have begun screenings. For example, in 1981, Sacred Heart Hospital in Pensacola, Florida, received a federal grant to undertake such a project, which had been piloted at the University of Virginia Medical Center in its Perinatal Support Services Project. The main activity under the grant was to train hospital personnel to recognize mothers who might be at risk for later abusive behavior (Moulder, 1985). Knowing the correlation between complications in labor and delivery and in faulty mother-child bonding and their later relation to incidence of abuse, the staff was encouraged to anticipate maternal complications and to prepare for maximum support if these conditions appeared. The hospital social worker investigated finances, housing, and other environmental stresses—all of which place the expectant mother at risk. After the high-risk mother delivered, the social worker continued to see her and help her make provisions for the future. Follow-up after hospital discharge ensured continuity of care, reduced isolation, and helped parents feel as though someone cared (Moulder, 1985).

Once high-risk parents have been screened and identified, a variety of agencies across the nation offer in-home service to support and train families in order to prevent maltreatment of children. This approach seems especially useful with teenage parents. In this type of home service, a trained volunteer, professional, or team of professionals provide assistance to the mother or both parents on a regular basis. The home visitor may teach parenting skills, furnish transportation, assume an advocacy role, or perform other services. (These services are similar to those described in Chapters 13 and 14, but the difference here is that these parents have not yet abused or neglected their children.) Daro (1988) included among the many benefits of in-home service an increase in parental ability to recognize and respond to the child's emotional, physical, and developmental needs; a decrease in subsequent pregnancies; an increase in seeking out and using health care and job training resources; a decrease in the use of welfare; and an increase in the rates of employment and in the number of high school completions.

Helfer (1976) states that there are three times when there is a natural opportunity to screen and subsequently educate future and present parents: at the high school level; when they seek services for pregnancy and the impending birth of their children; and when these children enter the school system.

Screening children for problems when they enter the school system is, and should be, routine in most, if not all, schools. The school needs to know the special needs of this child, his or her developmental level, possible barriers to future learning, and the general health of the child. Through interviewing the parent and talking with the child, there is an opportunity to assess the home environment. How does the child see himself or herself in the family system? Does he or she feel loved and protected, or isolated? In discussion with the parents, many school personnel ask for a developmental history and not only listen for problems and delays but observe how the parents describe the child. If the child is viewed as different, are there negative connotations? The parent-child interaction shows much about the relationship, and the teacher or counselor may detect the child's ability to trust and learn from another adult.

The question is what happens with this information? The family's right to privacy cannot be ignored. How can this information aid the child in his or her school career? Information that helps remove barriers to the child's learning ability is valuable. The child may need remedial work, aid with self-esteem, or extra attention in his or her transition into the school setting. These needs may call for immediate referral or may simply be noted in the teacher's records.

Parent-child problems are slightly more difficult. Some parents just need support. Entrance into school, especially with the first child, is when parents' child-raising practices come under scrutiny. Parents may feel unsure of themselves and nervous about public exposure. Reassurance is helpful. Some parents perceive that there is a problem and ask for help. Other parents deny problems. If these parents are not receptive to offers of help, the school personnel will want to keep close track of this child and his or her progress, unless the child is in immediate danger.

Parent support groups address a variety of problems. Unfortunately, support groups are frequently considered to be for parents with problems, while the average parents are expected to be more or less self-sufficient. Yet many parents describe moments when they question the effectiveness of their child-management skills and would appreciate the support and advice of other parents. Schools often become involved in parent support groups. One innovative school had a program, sponsored by the Parent-Teachers Association, that provided a series of groups focusing on children's specific developmental milestones. For example, the first of these was entitled "When Your Child Goes to School" and included sessions on the problems children encounter in the early grades, helping the child make the transition from home to school, parents' use of free time, sibling rivalry, and children and television. Each session took up a different topic, and parents came together to discuss their views. Another group dealt with "The Transition Year." Many educators think third grade marks the transition between socializing and more demanding learning skills, and this grade presents problems for some children. "When Your Child Reaches Puberty" and "Your Values, the Schools', and Your Child's," along with the younger age problems encountered, encouraged parents to reach out for help or gave them confidence in their own parenting abilities.

Information for immigrants is not easily imparted. In the late 1800s and early 1900s, immigrants were attracted to settlement houses like Hull-House in Chicago (for more information, see Addams, 1910) where they were helped to assimilate our culture and child-rearing practices. Now, however, immigrants get little support, and practices that are well accepted in their culture may be considered abusive in ours—yet no one tells these parents this until society intervenes.

Many communities sponsor English as a second language programs. Why not incorporate (especially for parents) information on the United States as a second culture? But do we have the right to dictate to those from other cultures how they should raise their children? When their practices violate federal or state laws, they are informed, but it seems only fair to communicate this information early after their arrival rather than subject these parents to notification by the protective service system.

As society becomes more aware of the incidence of child sexual abuse and increasingly committed to prevention, parents are being encouraged to train their children to protect themselves. Books such as Sanford's *The Silent Children: A Parent's Guide to the Prevention of Sexual Abuse* (1980) and Adams and Fay's *No More Secrets: Protecting Your Child from Sexual Assault* (1981) paved the way for parental involvement in the education and protection of children from sexual abuse. Although parents have always sought to protect their children, they are now learning that the warnings of the 1950s and 1960s ("Don't get in a car with strangers" or "Don't take candy from strangers") were inadequate. Research proves that the danger from strangers is not as significant as abuse administered by parents or acquaintances.

Finkelhor (1984, 1986) discovered that of 521 parents of children aged 6 to 14, only 29 percent had discussed sexual abuse specifically with their children. Of this 29 percent, only 53 percent mentioned abuse by an adult acquaintance and 22 percent by a family member. Often, too, the discussion between parents and their children occurred around the age of 9—too late since a good proportion of children are sexually abused before then.

Some parents do not feel the need or cannot talk to their children about sexual abuse. Some feel they supervise their children sufficiently and therefore preparation for the possibility of abuse is unnecessary. Others feel that they do not want to frighten their children needlessly. Yet these parents often alert their children to the possibility of kidnapping—a much more frightening concept for children.

Parents often do not feel they have the appropriate vocabulary to talk about sexual abuse. They may be unsure of their own values about sexuality and fear that a discussion of sexual abuse will uncover their ambiguity. For some parents, talking about molestation brings back painful memories of their own abuse or of other sexual conflicts (Finkelhor, 1986). For whatever reasons, many parents are hesitant to educate their children on the subject.

Prevention educators want to train parents to talk with their children. Although women tend to be the primary attendees of such educational programs (and also the primary source of sexual education information for children), men should also be encouraged to participate, if for no other reason than to decrease the likelihood of becoming abusers themselves (Finkelhor, 1986).

Some parents educate themselves in the interest of preventing their children from being abused. Elrod and Rubin (1993) studied fifty-one mothers and fifty fathers of preschool children to get a picture of the parents who desire to be primary educators in their children's sexual abuse prevention training. These researchers learned that only 40 percent of these parents had sufficient or entirely correct information. Ninety-nine percent of the parents obtained their information from the media or a small percentage (27 percent) from pamphlets in physician's offices (p. 530). While parents had good intentions about talking with their children about sexual abuse, over half planned to discuss only less threatening aspects. For example the topic "why abuse happens" was rated unacceptable by 69 percent of parents and "abuse could happen to you" by 80 percent of the sample (p. 532). A large majority preferred that educators be the ones to talk to children about sexual abuse (p. 530). This is an interesting finding given the reluctance of some daycare centers and schools to teach prevention materials for fear of parental disapproval.

The findings of this study imply a greater need, not only for formal parent education, but also for the collaboration of schools and parents in sexual abuse prevention efforts.

In addition to educating their children, parents have an obligation to create a home atmosphere that discourages keeping harmful secrets, encourages open communication, and creates healthy sexuality (Sanford, 1980). Sanford thinks the most important element of prevention is parents teaching their children to be nonvictims. Children are less likely to be victims when they feel good about themselves, when they are not hampered by sexual stereotypes, when they have learned to master their environment, and when they know that they have parents who will listen and take their fears seriously.

The importance of parents educating their children about sexual abuse cannot be understated. Perhaps one of the most convincing testimonies to this concept comes from an inmate incarcerated for the sexual abuse of children.

> *"I look for the kid who looks vulnerable—you know—the one who doesn't have much confidence, who's probably been taught to obey adults no matter what. And I really know that I have it made if no one's explained anything about sex to the kid. Then I can tell him or her anything I want and he or she will believe me. When parents don't talk to kids about sex or abuse and when the kid knows he or she can't ask questions, that's when I have no trouble getting a child to go along with me. Maybe parents should know that. If they want to protect their kids against someone like me, they should talk to them—tell them honestly what could happen."*

Prevention Efforts by Professionals

Although much has been done over the last few years to train teachers, physicians, nurses, police, and mental health professionals to recognize and report child abuse, the work is far from completed. Much of the training has focused on intervention rather than prevention. Physicians can notice potential for abuse as well as educate parents about child care issues. Police frequently participate in school safety programs and sometimes include information about abuse. Mental health professionals are crucial in uncovering, preventing, and treating abuse.

Professionals need to be more aware of the prevalence—and prevention—of child pornography. Education should center on the statistics, the victims, perpetrator profiles, perpetrator methods of engagement, and the long-term effects on children used in pornography (O'Brien, 1983). With greater awareness, professionals can better combat child pornography and other abuse.

Prevention Efforts Within the Community

Children should have the opportunity to grow up in safe communities—at least in communities where the incidence of child abuse and neglect is understood, and where sincere efforts are made to provide successful intervention, comprehensive treatment, and communitywide prevention.

Communities must first be dedicated to educating residents about child maltreatment. This can be accomplished in part by the sponsorship of awareness programs' outlining the symptoms of abuse and what can be done about it. Numerous public affairs pamphlets discuss the different types of abuse and neglect. Libraries stock books on the subject for all age groups and, at various times, feature displays to encourage readership. Support given to school-sponsored programs for the community stimulates more community resources.

How effective are such community education programs? The National Committee to Prevent Child Abuse has collected data to determine if the prevention efforts made in the last few years have had an impact on the general public (Daro and Gelles, 1992). The results of the last few surveys demonstrate changes in several areas of public attitudes. First, there has been a decline in physical punishment during the last few years. Parents now seem to recognize the harmful effects of yelling, and swearing at children on a long term basis (p. 518). African Americans, Hispanic Americans, and blue collar workers are most likely to report spanking children, but the rate has declined (p. 519). The surveys also indicated that parents are more likely to stop and think before hitting. Daro and Gelles (1992) concluded that the educational programs about child abuse have been effective in decreasing the maltreatment of children. To enhance future educational efforts, these authors divided families into three types: consumer families, dependent families and resistant families. *Consumer families* are those who recognize their limitations in knowledge and voluntarily sign up for educational groups and parent groups. These families call hotlines and generally seek to keep from abusing their children. *Dependent families* need more help and need to know how to access education and services. They need outreach and follow-up. But it is the *resistant families,* those who are dysfunctional, abuse alcohol and drugs, have deficient parenting skills, and are resistant to efforts to change that require the most attention. Daro and Gelles feel that by categorizing families, prevention efforts can be tailored to the needs of specific populations.

The understanding of and support for agencies involved in the intervention and treatment of abuse is also vital. There is also an opportunity for all types of community groups to be involved in prevention programs. For example, the Campfire Girls undertook a popular prevention project in child sexual abuse whereby children were trained to recognize and react to abusive situations. A community men's service group purchased prevention packages and sponsored training for teachers, parents, and interested citizens. A council of family service agencies hosted a series of parenting courses. The possibilities for involvement and the ideas for prevention activities are limitless.

The prevention of child abuse and neglect must be given increased priority in the future. Although efforts in intervention and treatment have had some success, they have only addressed a part of the problem. Effective prevention should mean that fewer children need ever be exposed to the hurt of being abused or neglected. Only a combined and coordinated effort can accomplish this goal.

Summary

Earlier in this book, intervention and treatment of child abuse and neglect have been discussed, but new programs must concentrate on prevention. The target populations for prevention efforts are schools, families, professionals, and communities.

Schools are becoming increasingly aware of the need to integrate prevention materials into the curriculum. Children who are given training in basic life and parenting skills become healthy adults and better parents. Self-protection information enables children to be better prepared to resist abusive individuals or helps them recognize the importance of telling trusted adults when they are being abused or have been approached. Schools can lead community awareness programs on the problems of abuse and neglect and how to prevent them, donate space for support groups and prevention programs, and expand adult education to benefit parents. Schools can also sponsor or provide space for services to high-risk families.

Prevention efforts must also be directed toward families. Parenting education enables parents to perform their roles more effectively and can alleviate some of the stresses unsure parents feel. High-risk parents can be identified by medical, social services, or school personnel, and can be offered additional resources. Parent support groups promote more positive parenting. Such support, as well as culturally specific information, should be given to immigrant parents to help them understand appropriate and inappropriate child-management practices.

Parents who educate their children about potential sexual abuse make them less vulnerable to the advances of an abuser.

Allied professionals are becoming more aware of the need for prevention, but they need to concentrate on combating child pornography. Engaging teams of professionals and laypeople in prevention efforts should begin to make our communities safer places in which children can grow. But this commitment must be communitywide in order to make a significant impact.

Exploration Questions

1. What are three prevention measures?

2. In what areas should prevention efforts concentrate?

3. How can schools help in the prevention of child abuse and neglect?

4. What three goals do most school-based prevention programs espouse?

5. How can schools further prevention efforts within the community?

6. In what way can families be involved in prevention?

7. Why are some parents hesitant to talk to their children about sexual abuse?

8. How can various professionals become involved in prevention efforts?

9. What should communities be doing in the interest of prevention?

Activities for Applied Learning

1. Research how the schools in your community are involved in child abuse or neglect prevention. Have they integrated materials into the curriculum? Do they teach life skills? Parenting skills?

2. To what extent does your newspaper cover child abuse and neglect? Are the articles based on sensationalism or do they outline suggestions for intervention or prevention? Research articles printed over the last five years. Has the emphasis changed?

3. Search out books published for all age levels that deal with child abuse and neglect. Are any of these books in your local library? Consider giving a copy of your list to the library.

4. Have there been any prevention efforts or programs in your community lately (e.g., community awareness lectures or self-protection seminars for children and parents)? If you are not sure, go to a local agency that deals with child abuse and neglect. What recent efforts can they tell you about? If nothing has been done, help the class plan a community awareness seminar or other type of prevention program.

References

Adams, C., and Fay, J. J. *No More Secrets: Protecting Your Child from Sexual Assault.* San Luis Obispo, CA: Impact Publishing, 1981.

Addams, J. *Twenty Years at Hull-House.* New York: Signet, 1910.

Biller, H. B., and Meredith, D. L. *Father Power.* New York: David McKay, 1974.

Cooper, S.; Lutter, Y.; and Phelps, C. *Strategies for Free Children.* Columbus, OH: Child Assault Prevention Project, 1983.

Crisci, G. *Personal Safety Curriculum.* Hadley, MA: Crisci, G., 1983.

Darmstadt, G. L. "Community-Based Child Abuse Prevention." *Social Work* 35 (6), (1990):487–489.

Daro, D. *Confronting Child Abuse: Research for Effective Program Design.* New York: Free Press, 1988.

Daro, D. "Home Visitation and Preventing Child Abuse." *The APSAC Advisor* 6 (4), (1993):1–4.

Daro, D. and Gelles, R. J. "Public Attitudes and Behaviors with Respect to Child Abuse Prevention." *Journal of Interpersonal Violence* 7 (4), (1992):517–531.

Donnelly, A. H. C. "What Have We Learned About Prevention: What Should We Do About It?" *Child Abuse and Neglect* 15 (1), (1991):99–106.

Elrod, J. M. and Rubin, R. H. "Parental Involvement in Sexual Abuse Prevention Education." *Child Abuse and Neglect* 17 (4), (1993):527–538.

Fay, J. *He Told Me Not to Tell.* Renton, WA: King County Rape Relief, 1979.

Fay, J., and Flerchinger, B. J. *Top Secret.* Renton, WA: King County Rape Relief, 1982.

Finkelhor, D. *Child Sexual Abuse.* New York: Free Press, 1984.

Finkelhor, D. *A Sourcebook on Child Sexual Abuse.* Beverly Hills, CA: Sage, 1986.

Fox, C. L. and Weaver, F. L. *Unlocking Doors to Self-Esteem.* Rolling Hills Estates, CA: Jalmar Press, 1990.

Franzem, R. T. "Prevention: Using Games to Teach Children About Sexual Abuse." *Journal of Child Sexual Abuse* 2 (2), (1993):75–84.

Gordon, T. *Parent Effectiveness Training.* New York: Peter Wyden, 1970.

Helfer, R. E. "Basic Issues Concerning Prediction." In *Child Abuse and Neglect: The Family and the Community,* edited by R. E. Helfer and C. H. Kempe, pp. 363–75. Cambridge, MA: Ballinger, 1976.

Helfer, R. E. *Childhood Comes First.* East Lansing, MI: Ray E. Helfer, 1978.

Kennell, J.; Voos, D.; and Klaus, M. "Parent-Infant Bonding." In *Child Abuse and Neglect: The Family and the Community,* edited by R. E. Helfer and C. H. Kempe, pp. 25–53. Cambridge, MA: Ballinger, 1976.

Kowal, L. W.; Kottmeier, C. P.; Ayoub, C. C.; Komives, J. A.; Robinson, D. S.; and Allen, J. P. "Characteristics of Families at Risk of Problems in Parenting: Findings From a Home-Based Secondary Prevention Program." *Child Welfare* 68(5) (Sept-Oct 1989):529–38.

Lerman, S. *Responsive Parenting.* Circle Pines, MN: American Guidance Service, 1983.

Meade, D. M. Massachusetts Society for the Prevention of Cruelty to Children. Personal communication, Oct. 9, 1991.

Mitchell, L. and Donnelly, A. C. "Healthy Families America: Building a National System." *The APSAC Advisor* 6 (4), (1993):9–27.

Moulder, P. "Child Abuse Prevention Starts Before Birth." In National Center on Child Abuse and Neglect, *Perspectives on Child Maltreatment in the Mid 80s.* Washington: U.S. Department of Health and Human Services, 1985.

O'Brien, S. *Child Pornography.* Dubuque, IA: Kendall/ Hunt, 1983.

Olson, M. "A Collaborative Approach to Prevention of Child Sexual Abuse." *Victimology* 10 (1985):131–39.

Plummer, C. A. "Prevention Education in Perspective." In *Preventing Child Sexual Abuse,* edited by M. Nelson and K. Clark, pp. 1–5. Santa Cruz, CA: Network Publishing, 1986.

Sanford, L. T. *The Silent Children: A Parent's Guide to the Prevention of Sexual Abuse.* Garden City, NY: Doubleday, 1980.

Sanford, L. T. *Come Tell Me Right Away.* Fayetteville, NY: Ed-U Press, 1982.

Scott, J., and Birch, T. *Summary of Children's Trust Funds.* Working Paper, No. 20. Chicago: National Committee for Prevention of Child Abuse, 1986.

Tower, C. C. "A Dragon in My Closet." Audiotape from *National Education Association Child Abuse and Neglect Training Program.* Washington: National Education Association, 1984a.

Tower, C. C. "Deborah Wore Designer Jeans." Audiotape from *National Education Association Child Abuse and Neglect Training Program.* Washington: National Education Association, 1984b.

Tutty, L. M. "Developmental Issues in Young Children's Learning of Sexual Abuse Prevention Concepts." *Child Abuse and Neglect* 18 (2), (1994):179–192.

Wells, H., and Canfield, J. *100 Ways to Enhance Self-Concepts in the Classroom.* Englewood Cliffs, NJ: Prentice-Hall, 1994.

Williams, J. *Red Flag-Green Flag.* Fargo, ND: Rape and Abuse Crisis Center, 1980.

Wolfe, D.; MacPherson, T.; Blount, R.; and Wolfe, V. "Evaluation of a Brief Intervention for Educating School Children in Awareness of Physical and Sexual Abuse." *Child Abuse and Neglect* 10 (1986):85–92.

Wurtele, S. K.; Gillispie, E. I.; Currier, L. L.; and Franklin, C. F. "A Comparison of Teachers vs. Parents as Instructors of a Personal Safety Program for Preschoolers." *Child Abuse and Neglect* 16 (1), (1992):127–137.

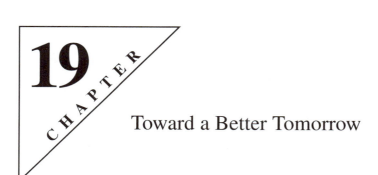

Toward a Better Tomorrow

Prevention efforts are alerting people to the problem of child abuse and neglect and the need for intervention, but additional efforts must focus on three areas: changes in the helping system, changes in society, and additional research. Each area connects closely with the others and all are vital to reduce the cases of child abuse and neglect.

Changes in the Helping System

Although the social service system has some inadequacies in its intervention with abusive and neglectful families, these problems are related to some basic premises surrounding that system.

Redefining the Framework of Helping

In our culture, individuals have specific rights. There are entitlements that people can claim by virtue of their citizenship, but as funds continue to be cut and services redefined, these entitlements include less and less. In a culture full of stress, people are expected to function relatively autonomously, with few supports. Parents are given few supports in their role until they fail to parent adequately. Then society intervenes. Provided parents can pay the price of stigma, they will get financial aid, counseling, or protective services.

The concept of government or state services as a safety net for parental failure is outmoded. Back when closely knit communities and neighborhoods compensated for individual inadequacies, the social service system was used only as a form of crisis intervention. Today, however, with increased mobility, broken families, and eroded neighborhoods, more services are vital. Instead of making services difficult because of stigma and stringent eligibility requirements, there should be available—no matter what their parenting capabilities—the tools to more effectively perform their roles. Parenting education and the teaching of family problem solving along with a variety of tangible services would contribute greatly to the prevention of maltreatment.

In addition to recognizing supports to parenting as a human right, based on the investment in children as our future, there must also be more methods to answer early cries for help from overwhelmed parents. Currently, our legal system allows response to maltreatment only after the fact. Anticipating their own weaknesses, even parents who reach out for help may not be eligible for supportive services. Once the abuse occurs, however, the services are available.

Wilma Fitz had had two children removed by the court and eventually placed for adoption. When she became pregnant again seven years later, she was determined to be a good parent to this child. But when the baby was several months old, Wilma found the baby's constant crying and need for attention aggravated her to the point where she was afraid she would again be abusive. She approached a local agency and requested daycare for several hours each day and support if she needed it. This protection agency informed her that there were no openings for daycare available and referred her to another agency, which suggested she go into counseling. After several referrals that led nowhere, Wilma gave up. She attempted to cope in the same state of isolation that had characterized her previous parenting experience. When the baby was 9 months old, the protective agency received a call from a local hospital saying that the baby had been admitted with multiple breaks and bruises, the cause of which appeared to be abuse by the mother.

Granted, some communities might have found resources to help Wilma before she battered once again, but the ability to help before the fact depends more on worker or agency creativity than on any formal or national structure. Communities must also become increasingly aware of the needs of minorities and newly immigrated populations. Services tailored to the majority often do not meet the needs of certain subcultures.

Surveys of community needs and concerns could more effectively anticipate children's needs as well as the needs of their parents. Some agencies survey providers and community members and ask what they perceive as the major gaps in services provided for children. For example, the Office of Children in Massachusetts frequently distributes general issues-oriented surveys to assess community needs. These questionnaires are compiled into a final report that becomes a public document. This office invites interested citizens to provide input at open meetings. The finished reports are sent to legislators to encourage their backing or their proposal of bills to meet the needs of children. Based on the reports, agencies may create new programs or apply for grant funds. In short, such a procedure affords community proaction rather than reaction to children's needs.

Money is always an issue in the provision of services. Needs assessments must document the reality of children's needs. Since much of public funding is provided through legislation, having a voice in the legislature is important. But children cannot vote for those services. Instead, they depend on interested advocates to further their causes. Needs assessments give advocates tools to make the point and substantiate it, based on the record of community concern.

How else can the community become acquainted with the needs of children and their families and begin to advocate for more money to provide for these necessities? Reid states, "I know of one community where the churches held a series of dinners, the menus consisting of food that could be purchased with the money that was available to relieve families in the community" (1979, p. 11). Such creative programs heighten public awareness.

Removing the stigma attached to the intervention process with troubled families, promoting positive parenting, and making more people within the community aware of children's needs will provide better alternatives to maltreatment.

Creating a Unified Response

Despite the enactment of a federal child abuse and neglect prevention and treatment act, states have, for the most part, freedom to interpret the act as they choose and form their own policies. Initially states adopted reporting laws in an attempt to demonstrate concern for children. Early laws reflected no cost figures but proved the legislators' desire to protect their weakest constituents. It soon became obvious that money had to be designated to augment protective agencies and expand treatment facilities (Nelson, 1984). Some states appropriated more resources and financial backing to these services than others, and as a result, states differ significantly in the specificity of their reporting laws and in their commitment to helping the maltreated child. For example, the penalty for not reporting abuse and neglect varies, from state to state, from a large fine or time in jail to a small fine or no penalty at all. In some states, incarceration of the convicted perpetrator is automatic; others mandate little for the treatment or punishment of sexual abusers. An abusive or neglectful parent may find numerous services available in one state, but few in another. Depending on the court and the community interpretation of penalties, treatment plans for offenders and abusive parents vary considerably.

To adequately address the problem of abuse and neglect, several steps should be taken. First, laws must be written more succinctly to be more specific and less subject to individual interpretation. National standards would enable agencies to have guidelines that standardize services. Communication among state agencies would ensure a more unified approach.

As efforts to encourage reporting from professionals on a national level increase, the type of followup offered must also improve.

One particular school district received intensive training in the detection and reporting of child abuse. As a result, the number of reported cases of abuse within the school system doubled. But the community had an understaffed protective service agency that was overwhelmed by the number of these new reports. Much to the frustration of the teachers and other reporting professionals, the cases were not handled immediately. After a short period of time, mandated reporters began overlooking reportable cases because they realized little would be done if the report was made.

The solution to such an issue may be for the protective services agency to look for ways to bolster services. One method is to document the need versus the availability of personnel and request additional funding to hire more staff. Given the workings of government, this process can be extremely slow. In the preceding example, the agency had not used all its appropriated contract funds, so the protective workers were primarily assigned intake responsibilities while private personnel were contracted to provide investigative services. Treatment was already a contracted service, but the worker who undertook treatment was from the same agency doing the investigation.

Whatever the plan, followup services must keep pace with the reporting to be truly effective.

Looking Within, Between, and Beyond Agencies

One of the biggest complaints among workers, especially new protective workers, is the lack of sufficient training. Although some agencies do give their workers initial and periodic training, many agencies think on-the-job training is best.

When Sara Craft was hired by a large protective agency, she received only brief training on how to fill out appropriate forms. Directly out of college, with a major in English, Sara knew little about multiproblem families, nor was she familiar with the Hispanic culture, a strongly represented population in the area. After her two-day instruction on forms, she was assigned 10 cases, all of which had been uncovered for quite some time. Of these 10 cases, 4 were severely neglectful families who had proved a challenge to previous workers. On her fifth day of work, Sara was sent out alone to deal with these families, three of whom were Mexicans who spoke little or no English. Her inexperience and acute frustration soon became apparent.

Although her supervisor met with her before and after she visited the families, this neophyte worker lacked the knowledge of basic skills. When this same agency later instituted a two-week training period, in which basic skills, knowledge of abusive and neglectful families, information about the Hispanic culture, and information about forms was imparted, the effectiveness of new workers was greatly increased. In addition, workers tended to demonstrate higher satisfaction with the job and stayed in their positions longer.

Periodic training is also necessary for social workers. Protective services is a rapidly developing field requiring new ideas and skills. Workers must be informed of such advances. In addition, training makes many protective workers feel revitalized and helps them to aid clients in new ways. The individual seeking employment in protective services is wise to look for an agency that devotes time and provides funds for staff development and training.

In addition, colleges and universities must take a more active role in providing ongoing educational opportunities for those professionals who intervene in child maltreatment. For example, Fitchburg State College in Massachusetts offers a two-year graduate-level certificate in child protection as part of the newly created Child Protection Institute. Professionals from all disciplines working with abuse and neglect cases (social workers, educators, attorneys, court system, law enforcement, etc.) take courses in areas such as understanding victimization, the psychology of offending behavior, and abusive family systems, culminating in a field based practicum. Students are helped to tailor their learning experiences to their own particular disciplines. As they enhance their skills, these professionals develop community networks which should eventually help to create multidimensional support and treatment systems for victims and families as well as promote new prevention strategies.

Part of any social service training should focus on the needs of minorities. It is not enough to have one or two Spanish-speaking workers on a protective service staff; every member of the agency staff should be trained to recognize cultural problems and differences. In areas where there are Native American, Hispanic, and Asian populations, workers should have a knowledge of differing values in order to adapt their impressions and methods of dealing with these cases. Some agencies now train or encourage workers to seek training in oppression issues. The more staff members are able to examine their own values, the more effective they will be with clients.

Other competencies may not currently be given sufficient attention in training protective workers. Drake (1994) elicited responses from both consumers (parents) and child welfare workers about what competencies were necessary to be a successful practitioner in child welfare. Both consumers and workers identified *relationship competencies* as the most crucial. Consumers pointed to the need for workers to show respect for others, have effective communication skills, be comfortable with relationships, be nonjudgmental and nondefensive, and be calm in the face of crisis or client anger. Workers felt that they and their colleagues should demonstrate appropriate attitudes (e.g., nonjudgmental, nonaggressive, respect for clients' values, etc.), be able to communicate well, not prejudge, empower the client to participate, and recognize the impact that protective services can have on the lives of clients. Despite these observations, it is often the interpersonal skills which are not adequately addressed in worker training. Agencies must become more aware that beyond training their staff to complete the necessary forms, relationship skills must be highlighted for both new and experienced staff (Drake, 1994).

Another important consideration is the support given to protective workers. Work with abusive and neglectful families is extremely demanding and can be quite draining. Workers need to know not only that they are supported in their decisions but that they are encouraged to form strong support systems with fellow workers. Like private industry, which is now sponsoring recreational activities for its employees, social service agencies must recognize that playing as well as working together improves staff morale.

Many agencies, in addition to increased staff training and support, could benefit from consumer representation on boards and committees. The low-income client or the formerly abusive parent could help restructure services to ensure maximum efficiency. From the days of Jane Addams and her contemporaries, large numbers of social workers have been recruited from middle-class and upper-middle-class backgrounds. These individuals have had little contact with the social system from a consumer perspective. Their values may be quite different from those of clients. Therefore, inviting those who have recently been, or currently are, using social services to participate in planning and decision making is extremely beneficial in making the workers more sensitive to the clients' needs and values. Some agencies have citizen advocacy teams review cases periodically. These teams consist of professionals and consumers, and all members have input on how cases should be handled. The team recommendation is used by the protective agency for decision making.

The team approach has its problems. The instability that brought these clients to the attention of the system often makes interaction difficult. In addition, confidentiality must be strictly guarded. Consumers who participate in decision making must be aware of the importance of keeping what they learn about other clients confidential. Screening may be necessary to ensure that individuals are not reviewing their friends' cases.

In order to better serve clients, communication between and within agencies must improve, particularly in the area of duplication of services. In states' interpretation of mandatory reporting, laws designate one agency to receive and, usually, investigate abuse reports, thus eliminating competition. But there is still considerable overlap in treatment services, and, paradoxically, one client can find several agencies willing to treat him or her yet another finds himself or herself ineligible for any agency service.

Many communities have excellent working relationships between agencies. In others, the competition and duplication of services continues. Reid (1979) contends that the problem is especially prevalent between public and private agencies. Private agencies, he feels, often have a superior attitude toward public agencies. Admittedly, many private agencies, able to maintain a higher percentage of trained personnel and lower caseloads, see themselves as providing higher-quality service than their public counterparts. Rarely do public and private agencies support each other. For example, staff from the public agency are as unlikely to recommend to a United Way or Community Chest that more money be allocated to a certain private agency as that agency is to testify at a public budget hearing in favor of the public agency's increased funding. Yet in a time when protective services are so much needed and funds are so limited, these agencies would find strength in mutual support.

Advocacy for children's needs is a next step in providing better protective services (Costin, Bell, and Downs, 1991; Paul, 1977; Donnelly, 1991). Children and their families sometimes become caught in the maze of bureaucracy or between agencies and their requirements. Children's advocates, either as employees of a separate advocacy agency or in the role of case managers, must see that children receive all the services to which they are entitled. With new programs being instituted and existing programs closing due to insufficient funding or resources, there is the need to explore the field thoroughly before making the decision as to what services can be provided.

The child advocate plays an important role in ensuring that the child and the family are adequately served. Sometimes advocacy necessitates mediating between agencies and encouraging agencies to use flexibility in their interpretation of eligibility standards. Despite agency constraints, the client must come first, and advocacy often means finding the best way to provide service to a given client when agencies argue that it cannot be done.

The final change necessary is to train and prepare potential social workers to learn the processes that affect protective services agencies. Many colleges and universities have majors that prepare students to work with child abuse. Training should not only help the student to recognize and treat abused/neglected children but also help him or her become familiar with the context in which that treatment occurs. Some social work, human service, and other preparatory programs fail to train their students to understand the influence of federal, state, and local tax structures; to be knowledgeable of the ability of communities to provide services; or to be aware of the relationship between tax-supported agencies and private agencies. Private agencies increasingly seek public tax funds to buttress a financial structure weakened by ineffective solicitation of private funds (Reid, 1979; Costin, Bell, and Downs, 1991).

More attention should be paid to the importance of community structures and working through community leaders. To be proactive in the field of social services, one must recognize the importance of intervention in the power structure. Knowing how and when to intervene can provide maximum help to clients.

In addition to understanding how to create changes in both clients and in the community, potential protective workers must be helped to recognize that this field can be a frustrating one. Changes are slow and laborious. Success stories may seem to be few. Educational programs must provide the student with not only an understanding of this reality but also with ways to combat the frustrations. Training in methods of stress reduction, avoiding burnout, and building an adequate support system are as vital to the protective worker as a knowledge of human development. By recognizing the frustrations of the job as well as developing the professional skills, the new worker will be infinitely better prepared to make the system work for the client.

Changes in Society

The helping system alone cannot solve the problems of child abuse and neglect. Society too must make some important changes.

Reversing the Trend toward
Socially Impoverished Families

If society truly cares for and wants to protect children, then an investment must be made in the families that nurture them. Unfortunately, our culture has come to value things over people. But money and goods alone—as witnessed by the insufficiency of welfare allotments—are not the only answer. We must also protect that which perpetuates and strengthens the family. Poverty, the erosion of neighborhoods, and geographic mobility are all destructive forces to the family. Poverty, for example, subjects children to

> damaging stresses by placing them in threatening situations and by undermining the ability of their parents to give what children rightfully deserve—a finely tuned and affectionate responsiveness. Severe economic deprivation robs families of the social necessities of life, leading to social impoverishment. The pervasive presence of social impoverishment often interferes with nonmaterial factors related to the quality of life such as social needs. Thus, social impoverishment is the most direct threat to human development. (Deutsch, 1983, p. 44)

Whether the family can triumph over poverty and numerous stresses has been found to be influenced by the neighborhood in which it lives. (See Garbarino and Crouter, 1978; Garbarino and Sherman, 1980; Garbarino and Stocking, 1980). Garbarino and Sherman (1980) studied two neighborhoods—one that had a high rate of child maltreatment and one that had an extremely low rate. The high-risk neighborhood was inhabited by isolated families who described high levels of stress, in relief from which they expected no help from neighbors. There was little interaction, and this suspicion and mistrust transferred to the relationships between parents and children as well. In the low-risk neighborhood, there was a spirit of cooperation and the feeling that this was a healthy place to raise children.

How does a community create and maintain a healthy neighborhood? Healthy neighborhoods are much like small towns where small business supports community needs. Re-zoning is one way such neighborhoods are being destroyed. Urban renewal entails demolishing old homes, often of lower socioeconomic groups, and building new apartments and condominiums, which are well beyond the financial reach of former residents. Not until there is a commitment to refurbish existing neighborhoods in a manner that will still make them accessible to old neighbors will society maintain or regain the healthy neighborhood (Costin, Bell, and Downs, 1991; Popple and Leighninger, 1993).

The low-income individual is not the only one whose support system suffers in today's society. Geographic mobility, frequently employment related, has caused families to separate from their relatives and friends. Those with good interpersonal skills may readjust, whereas others remain isolated and feel unsupported in new communities. Still others, tired of frequent moves and making new friends who too will soon be left, isolate themselves through their job or other interests. As generation after generation experiences this trend, there will be an increasing breakdown of interpersonal relationships and an inhibited ability to trust and develop adequate support systems. Greater efforts on the part of communities to include citizens in planning and recreational projects may alleviate this problem somewhat. Businesses that move employees frequently must also take some responsibility for integrating workers and their families into new social environments.

Supporting Parenting

Until very recently parenting was more highly valued than it is today. Women were expected to care for and nurture while men supported their efforts monetarily. Today, with more mothers in the workforce and more fathers wanting to be involved in parenting, modern technology often asks parents to choose between their children and their jobs. Long hours, the need for daycare, and the inability to stay home with sick children put added stress on working parents. What can businesses do to support parenting? Some companies support flex-time, in which employees put in the required amount of hours but begin work anytime between 7:30 and 10:00 A.M. This enables parents to tailor their days to their children's school hours. Still other businesses have job sharing—an arrangement whereby two employees share a full-time job. Thus, each works part time for pro-rated benefits (Berns, 1985). Increasingly there is also more support for equal parenting. It is important that the father who wants to share responsibilities with the new family be granted paternity leave and flex-time as well.

More recently, some industries have adopted the custom in the People's Republic of China of instituting on-site daycare facilities for their employees. This way, even very young children can be visited by the parent throughout the working day. Parent centers are an innovation. Such centers offer literature, books, and classes, and even loan large items of baby equipment such as car seats. Even more important than these benefits is the attitude that employees can be effective parents too. Perhaps another service that will come in time is employee-sponsored parent support or parent training groups. Here, employees could come during free hours to meet with and gain support from other working parents, to learn new skills to help them parent more effectively, and to handle parenting and employment with greater ease.

Today, when half the families in the nation have dealt with divorce (Hess et al., 1993), children have often become the victims of this emotional turmoil. Children's ability to cope with divorce is directly related to how their parents have handled it. The Children of Separation and Divorce (COSD) Center, in Maryland, is designed to help children adjust to separation and divorce. After working with over 4,000 families, the COSD staff believe that if parents understand what their children are experiencing, they can help their children to cope. Thus the COSD offers parenting seminars where parents can learn how to reduce the stress divorce places on children. Parents involved in these seminars are less likely to inflict the emotional abuse on children which has often been a by-product of divorcing families (Frieman et al., 1994).

Realigning Societal Values

Our society holds several values that directly support the high incidence of child abuse and neglect. The assumption is made, for example, that anyone can parent and should be encouraged to have children. Typically, young couples are asked when they expect to begin their family. There is little question in most people's minds that it is only a matter of time before they will. The response that they do not intend to have children is met by parents, relatives, and even friends with surprise and disbelief and then with disappointment and often pressure to reconsider. Yet many of these couples have made this decision only after much thought. They may or may not change their minds, but for now they have made their choice—one that should be respected by those around them.

Society should support parents in their roles rather than perpetuate a romanticized idea of parenting. Parenting is hard work and should not be minimized by society's assumption that having children is not just a right but a duty. For no role in our lives do we receive less formal training than for that of being a parent.

One young woman, who had become pregnant during adolescence, related her feelings about giving up the baby for adoption.

"It's not that I don't think it was right for him," she relates, "His adoptive parents were great and I'm sure he's really happy. It's the grief people gave me afterwards. So many people said, 'How could you?' that I felt awful about it. In almost every conversation about adoption someone will say, 'How could a parent ever give up a child?' I began to feel like some kind of monster for doing something I felt was best for my baby."

Pressure on individuals to become parents greatly contributes to their potential to be abusive or neglectful. When society recognizes the individual's right not to parent but offers support and education to those who choose to, it will be doing much to prevent child maltreatment.

Another contribution to child abuse is our culture's affinity for violence. Saturday morning cartoons feature violent encounters between animated characters. Children then graduate to TV shows where people are killed savagely and with predictable regularity. The most popular movies feature power and vengeance. At sports events, fights between players are applauded more vehemently than the actual game plays. Children learn patterns from their environment, so as adults they may use violence not only for recreational escape but to get their needs met.

Along with violence, our society also worships sex, and, through advertising, communicates that sexuality can be used as a form of barter. Sex sells everything from jeans, hairspray, and cars, to books on the best-seller list. When the sexually abusive father convinces his daughter that sex will buy her his attention and special favors, we should not be surprised that she accepts this.

Sanford and others (Butler, 1978; Herman, 1981) argue that until we change sexual stereotypes, we will continue to predispose children to abuse.

Little girls are supposed to be ladylike, polite, accommodating, nurturing, entertaining and helpful. It is an unfortunate coincidence that these are the very traits the offender seeks in a girl victim…. Little boys are supposed to be brave, adventurous, curious, able to handle any situation. When confronted with a potential abuser, his first reflex may be to run away, but his 'voice from within' may rule, "I don't want to run away and look like a sissy." (Sanford, 1980, p. 22)

Sanford suggests that children who are given a variety of models to emulate—assertive, self-sufficient, nonvictim women and men who can express fear, sadness, and other deep emotions—will be more likely to act in their own best interests when confronted with potentially abusive situations. Unfortunately, the prevention of sex-role stereotyping goes beyond parents—although it must start with them. Clothes manufacturers still use pinks and pastels for girls and vibrant colors for boys. Rarely, if ever, does a commercial feature a boy playing with a doll.

Facing a New Era?

There is much speculation over the form and substance of the social welfare system as we approach the twenty-first century. The recent changes in majority congressional control and increases in conservative approaches to government, presage major policy and programmatic changes. Newt Gingrich, Speaker of the House, promised new reform in the first 100 days of the Republican-controlled Congress. He proposed major cuts in welfare costs, and term limits for welfare benefits such as "…deterring out-of-wedlock births by stopping benefits for recipients after two years" (Tumulty, 1995). His suggestion that out-of-home care might well be served by reinstituting "orphanages" has also caused much debate.

What effect might these changes have on children and families? Will more rigid expectations create additional stressors for the already stressed family? Will out-of-home care continue to exist as we know it? How will the re-emphasis on the "Puritan ethic" change society's concern for the welfare of others? These and other such questions will present challenges for the remainder of this century and beyond.

Research Needs

The last area of importance in reducing the incidence of child abuse and neglect is related to the research needed to explore patterns, programs, and modes of treatment.

Finkelhor (1986) suggests that sexual abuse needs extensive future research. Abusive relationships must be more universally defined. Studies are necessary on abuse by nonfamily members, by older children, and by peers—especially adolescent abusers. Studies, using control or comparison groups as further validation of findings, should explore the short-term and long-term effects of child sexual abuse. More knowledge about personalities and motivations of offenders would also be beneficial in treatment as well as in prevention efforts.

Garbarino and Stocking (1980) have found valuable information in the neighborhoods in which maltreating parents reside. Additional research on environmental contributors to abusive or neglectful behavior would provide insight into the stresses that push the parent to become abusive. Studies continue to be proposed on the societal influences that promote child abuse and neglect. These must continue if we are ever to gain insight about how we can change in order to prevent it.

Gray and DiLeonardi (1982) stress the importance of evaluating existing programs for their effectiveness, especially prevention programs. How do we know if these efforts are working? Are children more empowered by learning assertive behavior? Are they equipped through our prevention efforts to secure help when it is needed?

Another area for research might include more extensive study on the nonabusive family. What skills do parents need to adequately fill their roles? What means do they use to more effectively cope with the stresses of child rearing? Perhaps through isolating factors that contribute to a positive family atmosphere, we can offer more in the way of treatment to abusive families.

We also need more crosscultural research. How do other societies define and deal with problems such as child abuse and neglect? What can these other cultures offer us in our attempts to combat child maltreatment?

And finally, people can learn a great deal from talking with survivors of abuse and neglect. When we encounter those who have experienced abuse and neglect but who go on to lead productive, uninhibited lives, we wonder what has made the difference for them. How can these survivors' experiences help us to help others?

Opportunities for research on child abuse and neglect abound, and it is this research that will enable us to better understand and intervene for our maltreated children.

Summary

Despite our prevention efforts, much more must be done to decrease the incidences of child abuse and neglect. Our efforts should be directed to changes in the helping system, changes in society, and additional research.

A fundamental change must take place in the way in which we regard services to families. Instead of waiting until parents fail and intervention is necessary, we should anticipate needs through needs assessments and heed the cues of parents who reach out for help before the abuse occurs. Perhaps these actions would help remove some of the stigma surrounding social services and their clients.

We must also promote a unified response to abuse reports from state to state and insist on prompt and adequate followup. To ensure better services within the protective agency, workers should be adequately trained and given ongoing support in their jobs. Some training in minority needs and issues would further improve worker effectiveness.

Consumers are important contributors to decision making and planning in protective services. The use of consumers requires more attention to confidentiality issues, but should in the long run promote more efficiency in service provisions.

Communication between agencies is necessary to maximize the services that can be provided. Agencies often duplicate each other's efforts counterproductively. Sometimes advocacy is used to ensure that client interests are paramount.

Society as well as the helping system must make changes in order to reduce the rate of child abuse. Foremost, families must be supported in the nurturing of their children. Poverty, eroded neighborhoods, and geographic mobility endanger interpersonal relationships and pose a threat to healthy family life. Businesses must recognize and provide services to enhance the parents' ability to be both competent workers and effective parents. As a culture, our propensity for assuming anyone can and must parent, our fascination with violence, and our tendency to socialize children in sex-role stereotypes actively contribute to child maltreatment. This must end.

Perhaps one of our hopes for the future lies in research—not only to further define and understand abuse but also to evaluate existing programs. Only through our commitment to change and our willingness to research what will create a better future will we combat the growing problem of child abuse and neglect.

Exploration Questions

1. In what areas must we direct our efforts in order to reduce the rate of child maltreatment?

2. How must we reframe our current concept of helping?

3. Although federal reporting laws mandate the provision of protective services, why might problems exist from state to state?

4. What is the importance of adequate training?

5. What causes family impoverishment? How can the trend be reversed?

6. How can business support parenting?

7. What values espoused by our culture must be changed in order for us to address the problem of maltreatment?

8. What specific areas should be considered in future research?

Activities for Applied Learning

1. Make a list of changes you believe are necessary to reduce the incidences of abuse. Do you have a plan to accomplish these changes?

2. Contact a business or several businesses in your area. What type of support, if any, do they provide for working parents? How could they provide more?

3. Do you feel that our society is enamored of violence? What evidence do you have to support your view? Conduct a panel discussion on violence in society and how it affects child abuse.

Suggested Readings

Garfinkel, I. *Assuring Child Support.* New York: Russell Sage, 1992.

Gray, E., and DiLeonardi, J. *Evaluating Child Abuse Prevention Programs.* Chicago: National Committee for Prevention of Child Abuse, 1982.

Nelson, B. J. *Making an Issue of Child Abuse.* Chicago: University of Chicago Press, 1984.

Wollons, R. *Children at Risk in America.* Albany: State University of New York Press, 1993.

References

Berns, R. M. *Child, Family, Community.* New York: Holt, Rinehart, and Winston, 1985.

Butler, S. *Conspiracy of Silence.* San Francisco: Volcano Press, 1978.

Costin, L. B., Bell, C. J., and Downs, S. W. *Child Welfare: Policies and Practice.* New York: Longman, 1991.

Deutsch, F. *Child Services: On Behalf of Children.* Monterey, CA: Brooks/Cole Publishing, 1983.

Donnelly, A. C. "What We Have Learned About Prevention: What We Should Do About It." *Child Abuse and Neglect* 15 (1), (1991): 99–106.

Drake, B. "Relationship Competencies in Child Welfare Services." *Social Work* 39 (5), (1994): 595–605.

Finkelhor, D. *A Sourcebook on Child Sexual Abuse.* Beverly Hills, CA: Sage, 1986.

Frieman, B. B.; Garon, R. and Mandell, B. "Parenting Seminars for Divorcing Parents." *Social Work* 39 (5), (1994): 607–610.

Garbarino, J., and Crouter, A. "Defining the Community Context of Parent-Child Relations: The Correlates of Child Maltreatment." *Child Development* 49 (1978):604–6.

Garbarino, J., and Sherman, D. "High-Risk Families and High-Risk Neighborhoods." *Child Development* 51 (1980): 188–98.

Garbarino, J., and Stocking, S. H. *Protecting Children from Abuse and Neglect.* San Francisco: Jossey-Bass, 1980.

Gray, E., and DiLeonardi, J. *Evaluating Child Abuse Prevention Programs.* Chicago: National Committee for Prevention of Child Abuse, 1982.

Herman, J. *Father-Daughter Incest.* Cambridge, MA: Harvard University Press, 1981.

Hess, B. B.; Markson, E. W.; and Stein, P. J. *Sociology.* New York: Macmillan, 1993.

Nelson, B. J. *Making an Issue of Child Abuse.* Chicago: University of Chicago Press, 1984.

Paul, J. L. "The Need for Advocacy." In *Child Advocacy Within the System,* edited by J. L. Paul, G. R. Newfield, and J. W. Pelosi. Syracuse, NY: Syracuse University Press, 1977.

Popple, P. R. and Leighninger, L. *Social Work, Social Welfare, and American Society.* Boston: Allyn and Bacon, 1993.

Reid, J. *Child Welfare Perspectives.* New York: Child Welfare League of America, 1979.

Sanford, L. T. *The Silent Children.* Garden City, NY: Doubleday, 1980.

Tumulty, K. "Man with a Vision." *Time* 145 (2), (1995): 22–32.

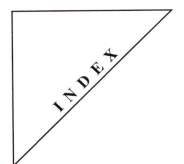

Abused children as adults, 364–394
  anger of, 93, 370, 374, 382–383
  coping skills of, 375
  developmental issues, 105–107,
    366–367
  disclosure of abuse, 365–368
  domestic violence and, 375–376
  and extrafamilial abuse, 386–388
  gender differences, 387–388
  myths related to, 364–365
  from neglecting family, 369–373
  from physically abusive family,
    367–368, 373–375
  problems of, 368–388
  relationships of, 366, 370–372,
    374, 383–385
  repeat victimization, 385–386
  sense of loss, 367–368
  from sexually abusing family,
    376–386
  somatic symptoms of,
    372–373, 381
  treatment of, 388–394
  trust of, 369–370, 373–374,
    376–377
Abusive parents
  and adolescents, 108–110
  control and, 44, 57, 106
  feelings of, 105
  isolation of, 105, 298–299, 306
  parenting styles of, 42–43, 92–94
  unlearned childhood tasks of,
    105–107
  See also Fathers; Mothers
Abusive siblings, 111–112
Achievement orientation, minority
    family, 28
Acting out, of abused adolescents,
    103, 209–210
Addams, Jane, 5, 408, 418

Administrators, school, 255
Adolescents
  and abusive parents, 108–110
  acting out of, 103, 209–210
  delinquent behavior of, 102–104
  dysfunctional development
    and abuse, 55–57, 102–104,
    209–210
  and neglect, 74
  as sexual abuse offenders, 133–134
  as sexual abuse victims, 316–321
  in treatment of sexual abuse,
    316–321
Adoption, 343–344
Adults, abused children as. See
    Abused children as adults
Advocacy
  in court, 268–269, 274
  need for, 419
Affect of child, and psychotherapy,
    293–294
African-American family, 2, 3, 5, 21,
    27–28, 76, 207
Agencies
  attorneys and court process, 270
  child protection, 14–15, 89–90,
    118, 123, 312–313, 330, 352
  needs and requirements of,
    416–419
Aggression, of abused children, 101,
    209–210, 293–294
Aid to Families with Dependent
    Children, 36, 69
Alcoholism
  of adults abused as children, 372
  and emotional abuse, 211
  and families, 83–85
  fetal alcohol syndrome, 48, 83–84
  and incest, 127, 130
  See also Substance abuse

American Civil Liberties Union, 193
American Humane Association, 11,
    12, 14, 89
American Professional Society on the
    Abuse of Children, 352
Amnesia, 379
Ancient Society (Morgan), 8
Anger
  of abused children, 101
  of adults abused as children, 93,
    370, 374, 382–383
  expression of, 51, 293–294
  of nonabusing parent, 322–323
  of parents of sexually abused,
    322–323, 333
  of pedophiles, 178–179
  of sexual abuse victims, 316, 319
Anorexia nervosa, 56
Anticipatory guidance, 237
Appeal of legal case, 267–268
Art therapy, 320
Asian/Pacific Island family, 3, 24, 25,
    30–32, 64, 207, 208
Assessment-awareness phase, in
    treatment of sexual abuse,
    315–316
At-risk families
  prevention efforts, 404–409
  screening of, 405–407
Attentional problems, 102
Attorneys. See Lawyers
Autonomy, development of, 50–53
Aversion therapy, 325–326

Battered-baby syndrome, 12, 13
Battered child syndrome, 12, 89
Behavior problems, and abuse,
    102–104
Behavior therapy, nature of, 390
Bergh, Henry, 10–11

Betrayal, 56–57

Beyond the Best Interests of the Child
    (Goldstein, Freud, and Solnit),
    35, 36

Bible, 8

Big Brothers and Sisters, 292

Blame, 106

Bordellos, 197–198

Boundaries, family, 23–24

Boys, sexual exploitation of, 6, 117,
    123, 125–128, 130, 311, 318,
    319, 378, 387–388

Broken Chord, The (Dorris), 84

Bruises, in physical abuse, 98–99

Burnout, social worker, 356–357,
    359–360

Burns, in physical abuse, 100

C. Henry Kempe National Center for
    the Prevention and Treatment of
    Child Abuse and Neglect, 352

Calvin, John, 3

Carroll, Lewis, 6

CASA (Court Appointed Special
    Advocate), 269

Case of Lucy Bending, The (Sanders),
    7

Chance events, and abuse, 94–95

Character-trait model of physical
    abuse, 92–94

Charity Organization Societies, 5

Child abuse
    defined, 118
    use of term, 89–90

Child Abuse and Neglect Training
    Program (NEA), 401, 403

Child Abuse Prevention and
    Treatment Act (1974), 12–13,
    118, 193

Child Abuse Prevention Bill, 12

Child Abuse Prevention Federal
    Challenge Grant, 398

Child labor, 4–5

Child Neglect Index, 65–68

Child pornography, 6–7, 188–192
    collectors of, 188–189
    cycle of, 191–192
    defined, 188
    effect on victims, 192
    incidence of, 123–124
    pornographers, profile of, 189–190
    production of, 190
    scope of, 120
    uses by pedophiles, 188–190

victims, profile of, 190

Child prostitution, 6–7, 192–199
    bordellos, 197–198
    and children's rights movement,
        193
    female prostitutes, 193–195,
        197–199
    incidence of, 123–124, 192–193
    lifestyles of prostitutes, 196–199
    male prostitutes, 195–197
    pimps for, 197, 198–199
    profile of prostitute, 193–199
    rise in problem of, 192–193

Child protection
    agencies, 14–15, 89–90, 118, 123,
        312–313, 330, 352
    approach to, 246–257
    current status, 13–16
    and feminist movement, 117–118
    historical view, 6–7, 10–13
    philosophy of, 117, 118
    rights of children, 35–38
    See also Intervention

Children's Bureau, 11

Children's Trust Fund, 398

Child Sexual Abuse Treatment
    Program (CSATP), 312–313

Child Welfare League of America
    (CWLA), 11, 289

Child Well-Being Scale, 65

Clergy, sexual abuse by, 182–184

Collectivism, 26–27

Communication
    among professionals, 14
    family, 24–25, 28, 30, 32, 33, 287
    in incestuous families, 322
    minority families, 24–25, 28, 30,
        32, 33

Community
    prevention efforts, 403–404,
        410–411, 414–416
    resources of, 284–285

Confidentiality, 281, 351

Conflict-avoiding families, 146–147

Conflict-regulating families, 147

Control
    and abused child, 57, 101, 103
    and abusing parent, 44, 57, 106

Counselors, school, 255–256

Countertransference, 281

Courts, 253, 261–278
    civil courts, 263
    criminal court, 263, 273–276
    guardianship, 263, 272

impact on children, 276
    juvenile court, 263, 264–273
    legal rights of parents and children,
        262–263
    and media, 277
    situations for involvement of, 261
    See also Criminal court; Juvenile
        court

Cousins, incestuous, 168

Criminal court, 263, 273–276
    disadvantages of, 274–276
    and district attorney, 274–276
    plea bargaining, 274
    process of, 274–276
    and victim-witness advocates, 274

Crisis intervention, nature of, 390

Crisis nurseries, 291–292

Cry, of abused infant, 101

Cry the Darkness (Friess), 393

Cults, 387

Cultural differences. *See* Minority
    families

Custody of child
    adoption, 343–344
    foster care, 337–344
    intervention and, 244–246
    placement of children and
        investigation, 265–267, 271–272
    residential treatment, 342–343

Damaged-goods syndrome, 385

Daycare centers
    sexual abuse in, 184–185
    as treatment setting, 292

Decision making, and abused
    child, 106

Declaration of the Rights of
    the Child, 37–38

Delayed gratification, 106–107

Delinquent behavior, 102–104

Dependence
    of abusive parents, 93, 105
    of children, 2–3
    in symbiotic families, 95, 96–97,
        105, 298

Dependent-dependent families,
    146, 148

Dependent-domineering families,
    146, 148

Depo-Provera, 326

Depression
    of adults abused as children,
        367–368
    and emotional abuse, 209

of neglectful mothers, 80–82,
302–303
of sexually abused, 318–319
Deprivation-aggression sequence, 370
Deprivation-detachment sequence,
370
Detachment, 379
Development
adolescent, 55–57, 102–104,
209–210
and adults abused as children,
105–107, 366–367
birth to one year, 45–50
developmental milestones, 46–47
dysfunctional development and
abuse, 42–43, 48–51, 55–57,
102–104, 209–210
eight to twelve years, 54–55
four to eight years, 53–54
and maltreatment, 42–43, 57–58
normal, 34, 46–47, 400
one to four years, 50–53
pregnancy and birth, 43–45, 83–84
psychological requirements for, 42
sexual, 42–43
unlearned childhood tasks of
abusive parents, 105–107
Dibbs in Search of Self (Axaline), 295
Dickens, Charles, 4, 10
Discipline, historical view, 3
Disclosure-panic phase, in treatment
of sexual abuse, 314–315
Disclosure phase
abused children as adults, 365–368
sexual abuse, 122
Disengagement, 379
Disequilibrium techniques, treatment
methods, 304–306
Dissociation, 378–379
District attorney, 274–276
Divorce
as an area for abuse, 211
in sexually abusive families, 323
stress on children, 421
Domestic violence, 110–111,
375–376
Drugs. *See* Substance abuse
Drug therapy, for sexual
offenders, 326
Dwarfism, and abuse, 71–72

Early childhood
dysfunctional development and
abuse, 50–53

and neglect, 73–74
Ecological causes, of child neglect,
68–69
Economic factors, in child neglect, 68
Educational team, 253–256
administrators, 255
pupil personnel services, 255–256
teachers, 253–255, 401
See also Schools
Eglinton, J. Z., 7
Elizabethan Poor Law, 2, 10
Emergencies, intervention for, 227,
291–292, 390
Emotional abuse, 205–213
characteristics of, 209–210
cultural factors, 207, 208
defined, 205–208
intervention problems, 212
parental factors, 210–212
patterns of destructive
behavior, 207
roots of, 208–209
See also Treatment of physical
abuse and neglect
Engagement phase, of sexual
abuse, 121
Enjoyment of life, and abuse, 101
Enuresis and encapresis, 71, 101, 154
Environmental stress model, of
physical abuse, 95
Equilibrium maintenance, treatment
method, 303–304
Ethical code, social worker, 351–352
Expectations, of child by abusive
parents, 106–107
Expert witnesses, 266–267
Extended families, 29

Failure, fear of, 102
Failure-to-thrive syndrome, 49
Fallen Angel (film), 176, 189
False allegations movement, 125
False Memory Syndrome Foundation,
125
Family
alcoholism and, 83–85
boundaries in, 23–24
communication patterns, 24–25,
28, 30, 32, 33, 287
definition and function of, 21–23
and maltreatment, 35–38
multiproblem, 33–35, 285
normal, aspects of, 143
patriarchal, 117–118, 145–146

preservation services, 289–291
reactions to exposure of abuse,
242–244
and rights of parents and children,
35–38
roles in, 24
shared family care, 290–291
subsystems of, 23–24
See also Fathers; Minority families;
Mothers
Family rehabilitation, 11
Family-systems model, 95
Family ties, minority family, 29–30,
31–32, 33
Family treatment
addressing pathology, 298–299
closing case, 301
cultural issues, 215–216
difficulties of, 296–297
improvement of parent-child
relationship, 299–300
nurturing and reparenting, 297–298
parental aides, 292, 300, 303
Parents Anonymous, 13, 285, 300,
330, 392, 403
for physical abuse and neglect,
296–306
prevention programs, 404–409
for sexual abuse, 311–333
siblings, treatment of, 301
treatment goals for parents,
296–297
Fatalism, minority family, 32
Fathers
absent, 52, 75, 126
father-daughter incest, 7, 55, 127,
128, 129–130, 145–155
father-son incest, 53, 55–56, 127,
155–157, 378
in pregnancy, 44
prevention programs, 405
sexual development of child and,
52–53
stepfathers, 126
Father's Day (Brady), 169
Fear, of sexually abused, 318–319
Feminist movement, and child
protection, 117–118
Fetal alcohol syndrome, 48, 83–84
Folkhealers, 30
For Money or Love (Lloyd), 193
Foster care, 337–344
alternatives to, 337–338, 342–344
for HIV positive children, 339

Foster care *(continued)*
problems of, 337
role of foster parents in, 341–342
role of natural parents in, 340
therapeutic potential of, 338–340
Fox, J. K., 8–9
Fractures
in physical abuse, 99
types of, 99
Freud, Sigmund, 7, 9
Frozen watchfulness, and abuse, 50, 101

Gault, Gerald, 193
Genesis II program, 324
Genograms, 311
Gestalt therapy, 390
Gil, David, 15
Good Start, 405
Grandfathers, incestuous, 167–168
Greek Love (Eglinton), 7
Group therapy, 295, 298–300
for adults abused as children, 390–392
for sexual abuse, 320, 322, 323
Guardian ad litem, 269
Guardianship, 263, 272
Guilt
of parents of sexually abused, 332–333
of sexually abused, 318, 380

Harmony, minority family, 32
Head injuries, in physical abuse, 99
Health, Education, and Welfare, U.S. Department of, 12–13, 14, 227
Health and Human Services, U.S. Department of, 70
Health problems. *See* Somatic symptoms
Hispanic family, 3, 21, 29–30, 51, 161
HIV positive children
foster care for, 339
prognosis for, 84
HOMEBUILDERS, 289–290
Home visit, 221–223
cultural factors, 221–223
information gained from, 221–223
and resistant client, 223
Homosexuality, 53, 155, 156, 195–196
of adults abused as children, 378
and father-son abuse, 55–56
and sibling abuse, 165–166

Hull House, 5, 408
Hypervigilance, 50, 53, 58, 101, 102, 293

IFPS (Intensive Family Preservation Services), 289–290
Impulsive behavior
and abused child, 74, 78–79, 293, 295
in abusive families, 299
of neglectful mothers, 78–79
parental, 78–79, 299
of perpetrators, 136
Incest, 143–170
and adolescent, 55–56
alcoholism and, 127, 130
ceasing of relationships, 169–170
cousin, 168
daughter, profile of, 153–154, 157–159
effects of, 55–56, 156–157, 159, 161, 164–165, 376–386
family dynamics in, 55, 143–145, 155–156, 157–158, 160–161, 163–164
father-daughter, 7, 55, 127, 128, 129–130, 145–155
fathers, profile of, 147–150
father-son, 53, 55–56, 127, 155–157, 378
grandfather-granddaughter, 167–168
mother-daughter, 53, 129, 130, 138, 157–159, 378
mother-son, 53, 127, 128, 130, 138, 159–161
and parental relationship, 55, 145–147, 151–153, 155–156
perpetrators, 129–131, 147–150
predetermined factors, 55
risk to child, 224
secrecy of, 121, 143–144, 154
sibling, 128, 131, 162–166
siblings in incestuous families, 154–155
taboo, 8–10
types of activities, 119–120
uncle-niece, 166–167
wife in incestuous family, profile of, 145–147, 151–153, 155–156
See also Sexual abuse; Treatment of sexual abuse
Incest (Meiselman), 9
Indenture, 4

Indian Child Welfare Act (1978), 262–263
Individualism, 26–27
I Never Told Anyone (Bass and Thornton), 393
Infancy
cry of abused infant, 101
dysfunctional development and abuse, 48–51
and neglect, 71, 72–73
special circumstances and abuse, 97–98
Infanticide, 1–2
Infantile personality, 76
Institute for the Community as Extended Family (ICEF), 126
Intermarriage, historical view of, 9–10
Internal injuries, in physical abuse, 99–100
International Society for the Prevention and Treatment of Child Abuse and Neglect, 13
Intervention
assessment of cause of abuse, 226–227
assessment of client, 243–244
assessment of risk to child, 223–226
basic orientations, 16, 17
cultural sensitivity, 215–216, 352, 360–361
custody of children, 244–246
and developing child, 58
educational team in, 253–256, 401
emergency situations, 227, 291–292, 390
home visit, 221–223
interviewing adults, 227–231
interviewing children, 231–238
investigation, 220–221
legal team in, 251–253, 261–278, 409
medical team in, 246–251, 256, 409
mental health team in, 256–257
problem in child neglect, 70, 75, 85
problems in emotional abuse, 212
reactions of family to exposed abuse, 242–244
and reporting of abuse, 217–220
team approach, 246–257, 418–419
validation of abuse, 220–221, 235–237, 238, 247–248

See also entries beginning with "Treatment"
Interviewing adults, 227–231
  areas for information gathering, 230–231
  cultural factors, 229
  questioning technique, 227–231
  use of language, 227–229, 233–234
Interviewing children, 231–238
  anticipatory guidance in, 237
  engaging the child, 234
  questioning techniques, 234–235
  setting for interview, 234
  special factors in, 231–234
  validation of event, 235–237, 238
  videotaping of, 238
Investigation of abuse, 220–221.
  See also Intervention
Isolation
  of abused child, 103–104, 130, 206
  and abusive parents, 105, 298–299, 306
  of sexual abuser, 130

Journal writing, 320–321, 391
Judge, role in court process, 268
Jung, Carl, 9
Juvenile court, 263, 264–273
  advantages and disadvantages of, 272–273
  agency attorneys, 270
  child advocate, 268–269
  judge's role, 268
  parents' attorney, 269–270
  process in, 264–268
  settlements, 271–272
  social workers, 270–271
  witnesses, 265–267, 271

Kinship bonds, minority family, 27

Language development
  and abuse, 49, 53, 102
  and neglect, 74
Lawyers
  agency attorneys, 270
  child advocate, 268–269
  district attorney, 274–276
  parents' attorney, 269–270
Lay therapists, 292, 303
Lead Us Not Into Temptation (Berry), 182–183
Learning
  and abuse, 53–54

methods of, 43
Legal action
  against perpetrator, 393–394
  See also Courts; Lawyers
Legal rights
  intervention ideology based on, 17
  of parents and children, 262–263
Legal team, 251–253
  courts, 253, 261–278
  police, 251–253, 409
Life books, 344
Life script, 390
Life skills training, in prevention, 399–400
Logistical factors, treatment, 285–286
Lolita (Nabokov), 7

Machismo, 29
Maltreatment
  dysfunctional development and, 33–35, 42–43, 48–51
  and family system, 35–38
  history of, 1–7
  See also specific types of abuse
Masturbation, 52, 137, 157–158, 181, 188
Meat Rack investigation, 123–124
Media
  and abuse cases, 277
  and courts, 277
  impact on abuse and treatment, 15–16
Medical examination, and validation of abuse, 238, 247–248
Medical team, 246–251
  medical social worker, 250–251
  nurses, 248–250, 256
  physicians, 238, 247–248, 409
Medical treatment, of physically abused, 291
Meiselman, K., 9
Mental health team, 256–257
  and child protection, 256–257
  and disclosure of abuse, 256
Mental-illness model
  of emotional abuse, 211–212
  of physical abuse, 92
Mental retardation, of neglectful mothers, 79–80
Minnesota Early Learning Demonstration, 404–405
Minority families
  African-American family, 21, 27–28, 76, 207

Asian/Pacific Island family, 24, 25, 30–32, 64, 207, 208
  communication patterns, 24–25, 28, 30, 32, 33
  cultural sensitivity and intervention, 215–216, 352, 360–361
  and detection of abuse, 64–65, 76, 104, 109–110, 207, 208
  family ties, 29–30, 31–32, 33
  Hispanic family, 3, 21, 29–30, 51, 161
  and home visits, 221–223
  and interviewing, 229
  Native American family, 3, 21–22, 32–33, 207, 262–263
  social worker skills with, 215–216, 352, 360–361
  and treatment, 284
  variables in family functioning, 26–33
Missing children, 188–189, 199–200
  prevention, 200
  reasons for, 199
Model Child Protection Act, 227
Morgan, L. H., 8
Mothers
  and autonomy, 50–53
  mother-daughter incest, 53, 129, 130, 138, 157–159, 378
  mother-son incest, 53, 127, 128, 130, 138, 159–161
  and Munchausen by Proxy, 107–108
  neglectful, 74–85, 302–303
  of sexually abused, 145–147, 151–153, 155–156
  wife in incestuous family, profile of, 145–147, 151–153, 155–156
Multiple personality disorder (MPD), 379
Munchausen by Proxy, 107–108

Nabokov, Vladimir, 7
National Center for Missing and Exploited Children (NECMEC), 188–189, 199
National Center for the Prevention of Child Abuse and Neglect, 12
National Center on Child Abuse and Neglect (NCCAN), 12–13, 14–15, 70, 89, 118, 123, 193, 352

National Center on Child Abuse
Prevention Research, 90, 123
National Child Abuse and Neglect
Data System (NCANDS), 90
National Committee for Prevention of
Child Abuse (NCPCA), 14,
89–90, 123, 352, 398, 405, 410
National Committee to Prevent Child
Abuse, 401
National Conference on Child Abuse
and Neglect, 352
National Education Association
(NEA), 14, 217–218, 401, 403
National Society for the Prevention of
Cruelty to Children, 286
Native American family, 3, 21–22,
32–33, 207, 262–263
Negativity, and emotional abuse,
209–210
Neglectful parents
apathetic-futile mother, 77–78
areas of limited abilities, 75–76
characteristics of, 74–85, 302–303
impulsive mother, 78–79
lifestyles of, 75
mentally retarded mother, 79–80
psychotic mother, 82–83
reactive-depressive mother, 80–82,
302–303
treatment methods, 301–306
Neglect of children, 63–86
and adolescents, 74
causes of, 68–70
Childhood Level of Living Scale,
64–65
conditions related to, 73–74
and cultural factors, 64–65, 76,
109–110
defined, 63–64
and early childhood, 73–74
ecological causes of, 68–69
economic causes of, 68
effects in adulthood, 369–373
infants, 71, 72–73
parent characteristics, 74–85
problems in intervention, 70,
75, 85
signs of neglect, 71–72
societal causes of, 69–70
See also Neglectful parents;
Treatment of physical abuse
and neglect
Neonatal assessment scale, 58
New York Foundling Hospital, 70–71

New York State Youth Commission,
36–37
Nonorganic failure to thrive
syndrome (NFTT), 71
North American Man Boy Love
Association (NAMBLA), 181,
186
Numbing, 379
Nurseries, crisis, 291–292
Nurses, 248–250
information gathering by, 249–250
school nurse, 256
Nurturing, as treatment method,
297–298

Observation, 379
Oliver Twist (Dickens), 10

Parental aides, 292, 300, 303
Parent Effectiveness Training, 404
Parentified child, 24, 27–28, 55, 92,
95, 314
Parenting styles
abusive, 42–43, 92–94
incestuous, 145–147
See also Abused children as adults
Parsons, Talcott, 9
Passivity
and abuse, 53, 101
apathetic-futile syndrome, 77–78
parental, 77–78, 93
Patriarchal family, 117–118, 145–146
Pederasty, 6, 179–182
behavioral types for, 180–181
defined, 120, 179
incidence of, 179
issues related to, 181–182
organizations for, 181, 182
profile of boy involved with, 181
profile of pederast, 179–181
Pediculosis, 73
Pedophilia, 130, 176–179, 328–329
characteristics of pedophile,
132–133, 176–178
defined, 120, 176
fixated and regressed pedophiles,
132, 176–178
methods of pedophile, 178–179
uses of child pornography,
188–190
Personality testing, 325
Physical abuse, 89–112
behavioral signs of, 100–104
causes of, 90–97

characteristics of abused child,
97–98
character-trait model, 92–94
controllable and uncontrollable,
92–94
domestic violence, 110–111,
375–376
effects in adulthood, 367–368,
373–375
environmental stress model, 95
interactional components of, 94–95
laws preventing, 12–13, 38, 118,
227
mental-illness model of, 92
parent characteristics, 105–110
physical damage from, 57–58,
98–100
psychodynamic model of, 90,
91–92
psychosocial systems model of,
96–97
by siblings, 111–112
social-learning model of, 95–96
social-psychological model of, 96
See also Abusive parents;
Treatment of physical abuse and
neglect
Physicians
fear of reporting abuse, 247–248
prevention efforts, 409
treatment by, 247–248
and validation of abuse, 238,
247–248
Pimps, 197, 198–199
Play therapy, 295
Plea bargaining, 274
Poe, Edgar Allan, 6
Police, 251–253
importance in abuse cases,
252–253
issues related to abuse, 252–253
prevention efforts, 409
and reports of abuse, 252–253
Pornography. *See* Child pornography
Possessive-passive families,
145–146, 147–148
Powerlessness
of abused child, 57, 154
of abusing fathers, 147
of adults abused as children,
380–381, 386
of mothers in abusing families,
152
sexual abuse and, 136, 154, 326

Pregnancy
  birth as dysfunctional event, 97–98, 250
  as developmental stage, 43–45
  fetal alcohol syndrome, 48, 83–84
  prenatal abuse, 48, 83–84
Prevention, 414–424
  aid to at-risk families, 404–409
  books on, 401–402, 408
  community based, 403–404, 410–411, 414–416
  family-based prevention, 404–409
  laws regarding, 12–13, 38, 118, 227
  life skills training, 399–400
  preparation for parenthood, 400–401
  and professionals, 409–410
  redefining helping framework in, 414–415
  research needs, 423–424
  in schools, 14, 217–219, 253–256, 398–404
  scope of effort needed for, 415–416
  self-protection training, 401–403
  societal changes needed, 419–423
  and training of professionals, 416–419
Priests, sexual abuse by, 182–184
Prison
  sexual offenders in, 323
  and treatment of sexual offenders, 329–330
Promiscuity
  of adults abused as children, 377–378
  of incest victim, 127, 165
Property, children as, 1–3, 5–6
Prostitution, 377. *See also* Child prostitution
Psychodynamic model, of physical abuse, 90, 91–92
Psychological abuse. *See* Emotional abuse
Psychosis, of neglectful mothers, 82–83
Psychosocial dwarfism, 71–72
Psychosocial systems model, of physical abuse, 96–97
Psychotherapy, 292–296
  addressing expression of affect, 293–294
  for adults abused as children, 389–390

art therapy, 320
building self-concept, 294–296
forms of, 389–390
group therapy, 295, 298–300, 320, 322, 323, 390–392
parental resentment of, 296
play therapy, 295
for sexual abuse, 320, 323, 327–328
trusting relationship in, 293
Pupil personnel services, 255–256

Questioning techniques, in interviewing, 227–231, 234–235

Rape
  child rape, 6, 118–119
  defined, 118–119
  See also Incest
Regression, 102
Relapse prevention model, 327
Relationships, of adults abused as children, 366, 370–372, 374, 383–385
Religion, minority families, 28, 30, 32, 33
Remedial services, 292
René Guyon Society, 181
Reparenting, as treatment method, 297–298
Repeated victimization, of adults abused as children, 385–386
Reporting of abuse, 217–220
  anonymous reports, 219–220
  events in, 218
  mandated reports, 217–220, 247–248, 253–254
  police and, 252–253
  state guidelines, 217–219
  underreporting in, 124, 311
Repressed memories, 388–389
Residential treatment, 342–343
Resistance
  to home visit, 223
  to treatment, 282–283, 296
Responsive Parenting program, 404
Restructure phase, in treatment of sexual abuse, 316
Retraining Adult Sexual Offenders (Knopp), 330
Rights of children, 35–38
Risk to child
  aid to families, 404–409
  assessment of, 223–226

investigation of, 223–226
  of sexual abuse, 126–127
Rituals, 25–26
Role reversal. *See* Parentified child
Roles
  dysfunctional, 27–28
  family, 24, 27–28, 95
  parental perception of child, 93
  parentified child, 24, 27–28, 55, 92, 95, 314
  scapegoat, 24, 95
Rousseau, Jean Jacques, 3
Rules, 25
Runaways (Ambrosino), 192
Runaway Youth Act (1974), 192–193

Sanders, Lawrence, 7
Scapegoat role, 24, 95
School problems, 74, 103
Schools
  preventive efforts, 14, 217–219, 253–256, 398–404
  screening at-risk children, 407–408
  See also Educational team
Secrecy
  disclosure issues, 365–368
  and sexual abuse, 121, 143–144, 154
Self-abuse, of adults abused as children, 379–380
Self-esteem
  of adults abused as children, 369, 371, 375, 379–380
  building in therapy, 294–296
  low, 52, 53, 55–56, 57, 101, 103, 105, 209–210, 319, 322, 369, 371, 375
  minority family, 27, 32
  of nonabusing parent, 322
  sibling incest, 165
Self-help, minority family, 27
Self-help groups, 407–408
  Adults Molested as Children, 392–393
  Alcoholics Anonymous, 313
  Daughters and Sons United, 313
  Parents Anonymous, 13, 285, 300, 330, 392, 403
  Parents United, 313, 327, 330, 403
  writers' groups, 393
Self-hypnotic anesthesia, 379
Self-protection training, 401–403
Separation anxiety, 49
Settlement houses, 5, 408

Settlements, juvenile court, 271–272
Sex play, normal stages of, 233
Sex rings, 185–188, 189–190
  characteristics of, 186
  effects on children, 187
  means of involvement in, 186–187
  parental reactions to, 187–188
  types of, 185–186
Sexual abuse, 13–14, 116–139
  adolescent offenders, 133–134
  adolescent victims, 316–321
  at-risk children, 126–127
  of boys, 6, 117, 123, 125–128, 130,
    311, 318, 319, 378, 387–388
  categories of, 119–120
  child pornography, 6–7, 120,
    123–124, 188–192
  child prostitution, 6–7, 123–124,
    192–199
  and child protection movement,
    117
  by clergy, 182–184
  criminal proceedings for, 263,
    274–276
  daycare settings, 184–185
  defined, 118–119
  degree of trauma in, 128–129
  disclosure phase of, 122, 365–368
  effects in adulthood, 376–386
  engagement phase of, 121
  extrafamilial abuse, 120, 126,
    131–134, 174–201, 323–324,
    332–333, 386–388
  false allegations movement, 125
  familial. *See* Incest
  and feminist movement, 117–118
  forced sex contacts, 121
  guilt of victim, 318, 380
  incidence of, 123–125, 127
  interviewing children about,
    231–238
  lack of parental supervision in,
    175–176
  male perpetrator model of,
    137–138
  and missing children, 199
  parenting styles in, 42–43,
    145–147
  pederasty, 6, 120, 179–182
  pedophilia, 130, 132–133,
    176–179, 328–329
  preconditions for, 134–136
  pressured sex contacts, 121
  by priests, 182–184

profile of abused child, 125–128
profile of perpetrator, 129–138
progression of events in, 120–122
and secrecy, 121, 143–144, 154
and sex rings, 185–188, 189–190
and sexual addicts, 131
sexual interaction phase of, 121
suppression phase of, 122
terms related to, 118–119
trauma, influencing factors,
  174–175
underreporting of, 124, 311
See also Abused children as adults;
  Incest; Treatment of sexual
  abuse
Sexual addicts, and sexual abuse, 131
Sexual assault, defined, 119
Sexual development
  and abuse, 53
  process of, 52–53
Sexual dysfunction, of adults abused
  as children, 366
Sexual exploitation
  of boys, 6, 117, 123, 125–128, 130,
    311, 318, 319, 378, 387–388
  defined, 118
  historical view, 5–7
  protection against, 6–7
Sexual identity problems, of adults
  abused as children, 378
Sexuality
  distorted understanding of, 327
  normal, 400
  societal attitudes to, 144–145
Sexual misuse, 119
Sexual molestation, defined, 119
Sexual stereotypes, 422–423
Sexual Trauma Treatment Program,
  313
Shared family care, 290–291
Siblings
  abuse by, 111–112
  incestuous, 128, 131, 162–166
  in incestuous family, 154–155
  role in family, 24
  treatment of, 301
Slavery, 2
Social development
  and abuse, 103
  of adults abused as children,
    371–372
  and neglect, 74
Social-learning model, of physical
  abuse, 95–96

Social-psychological model, of
  physical abuse, 96
Social Security Act, 11
Social workers, 347–362
  agenda for typical day of, 347–350
  basic duties of, 353–354, 360–361
  burnout, 356–357, 359–360
  ethical code, 351–352
  ethnic competence of, 215–216,
    352, 360–362
  frustrations and pressures of,
    354–357
  future of, 359–361
  medical social worker, role of,
    250–251
  neglectful parents and, 85
  personal qualities of, 353
  prevention efforts, 409
  responses to protective service
    system, 357–359
  role in court hearing, 270–271
  skills requirements of, 350–352
  training needs, 416–419
  See also Intervention
Society
  factors in child neglect, 69–70
  needs and requirements for
    prevention, 419–423
Society for the Prevention of Cruelty
  to Animals (SPCA), 10–11
Society for the Prevention of Cruelty
  to Children (SPCC), 11
Somatic symptoms
  of adults abused as children,
    372–373, 381
  and emotional abuse, 209–210
  and Munchausen by Proxy,
    107–108
  and neglect, 372–373
  of sexual abuse, 378
Stepfathers, and sexual abuse, 126
Stigmatization, and abused child, 57
Story writing, 320–321
Stranger anxiety, 49
Substance abuse, 83–85
  of adults abused as children, 372
  and emotional abuse, 211
  and incest, 127, 130
  precipitating abuse, 83–85
  during pregnancy, 48, 83–84
  See also Alcoholism
Suicide, of adults abused as children,
  380
Superego and abuse, 54, 103, 295

Suppression phase, of sexual abuse, 122
Symbiosis
  in family, 95, 96–97, 105, 298
  of incestuous fathers, 130

Teachers, 253–255
  fears in reporting abuse, 253–254
  observations about abuse, 254–255
  self-protective training, 401
Team approach, 246–257
  educational team, 253–256, 401
  legal team, 251–253, 261–278, 409
  medical team, 246–251, 256, 409
  mental health team, 256–257
  problems of, 418–419
Television. *See* Media
Time factors
  court delays, 276
  hours of reports of abuse, 253
Toynbee, Arnold, 4–5
Toynbee Hall, 4–5
Training
  life skills, 399–400
  of professionals, 401, 416–419
  self-protection, 401–403
Transactional analysis, nature of, 390
Transference neurosis, of abusive parents, 92
Traumatic sexualization
  of adults abused as children, 377–378
  process of, 56
Treatment of adults abused as children, 388–394
  group therapy, 390–392
  psychotherapy, 389–390
  self-help groups, 392–393
Treatment of physical abuse and neglect, 281–306
  barriers to treatment, 282–285
  Big Brothers and Sisters, 292
  and community resources, 284–285
  crisis nurseries, 291–292
  daycare, 292
  difficulties of, 282–285, 301–303

disequilibrium techniques, 304–306
eligibility for treatment, 284
equilibrium maintenance in, 303–304
family preservation services, 289–291
family treatment, 296–306
length of treatment, 286–287
logistical factors, 285–286
medical treatment, 291
neglectful families, 301–306
parental aides, 292, 300, 303
psychotherapy, 292–296
remedial services, 292
resistance to, 282–283
supplementation of family, 292, 303
treatment goals, 287–289, 296–297
Treatment of sexual abuse, 310–334
  adolescent victim, 316–321
  assumptions about, 311–312
  child victim, 316–321
  extrafamilial abuse, 332–333
  family preservation in, 323, 331–332
  family treatment, 311–333
  group therapy, 320, 322, 323
  individual therapy, 320
  issues addressed, 313–314
  issues related to, 310–311
  mother (nonabusing), 321–323
  nonabusing parent, 321–323
  parents of children abused outside home, 332–333
  perpetrator, 323–331
  phases of treatment, 314–316
  shared family care, 290–291
  trauma model, 313
  treatment goals, 321
  treatment models, 312–313
  victim advocacy model, 312–313
Trust
  of adults abused as children, 369–370, 373–374, 376–377
  assessment of ability to trust, 243–244

building in therapy, 293
mistrust and abuse, 49, 53, 293
and nonabusing parent, 322–323
and sexual abuse victims, 319–320

Uncles, incestuous, 166–167
United Nations Declaration of the Rights of the Child, 37–38

Validation of abuse, 220–221
  aspects of, 235–237, 238
  in interviewing process, 235–237, 238
  medical, 238, 247–248
Values, minority family, 29–30, 31–32, 33
Vermont Treatment Program for Sexual Aggressors (VTPSA), 327
Victim advocacy model, in treatment, 312–313
Victim-witness advocates, 274
Victorian era, sexuality during, 6–7
Videotaping, interviews with child, 238
Violence
  cultural affinity for, 422
  domestic, 110–111, 375–376
Violence Against Children (Gil), 15
Voices in the Night (McNaron and Morgan), 393

Wadsworth, William, 6
Westermarck, E., 8–9
White House Conference on Dependent Children (1909), 11
Wilson, Mary Ellen, 10–11, 13, 15
Withdrawal, and abused child, 101, 103–104
Witnesses
  expert witness, 266–267
  role in court hearing, 265–267, 271
Work orientation, minority family, 28
Writers' groups, for adults abused as children, 393

Young People's Bill of Rights, 36–37, 38